WAR OF 1812: VIRGINIA
BOUNTY LAND & PENSION APPLICANTS

A quick reference guide to ancestors
having War of 1812 service
who served, lived, died, or married in
Virginia or West Virginia.

By Patrick G. Wardell

HERITAGE BOOKS, INC.

Other Titles By Patrick G. Wardell:

Virginians & West Virginians, 1607-1870, Vol. 1

Alexandria City & County, Virginia
Wills, Administrations, & Guardian Bonds, 1800-1870

Published 1987 By

HERITAGE BOOKS, INC.
3602 Maureen Lane, Bowie, Maryland 20715

ISBN 1-55613-055-4

FOREWORD

This volume contains data extracted from the National Archives microfilms of the file jacket covers of the files of War of 1812 pension and bounty land warrant receivers who served, lived, married, or died in Virginia or West Virginia. In many cases, the data includes date and place of death, spouse's name(s), date and place of marriage, date and place of spouse's death, as well as last noted residence of husband or surviving spouse.

Unfortunately, the file jacket covers for soldiers with names beginning with I through Z were not filled out as completely as those with names beginning with A through H. However, this volume does contain all of the names on the jackets where any connection with Virginia or West Virginia is indicated. Thus this volume provides a quick reference for those people seeking clues to the files of possible ancestors. Those who wish to obtain copies of the records contained in the file jackets must visit the National Archives, or one of its branches, or write to the main office in Washington, D. C., for the copies. Any known variations of the spelling of the names should be provided to the National Archives officials, since many of the veterans were known by variously spelled names, both first and last, or even aliases. Examples of name variations are ACHOR vs. ACHRE and RUNNELS vs REYNOLDS.

Abbreviations used are as follows:

P	pension
BLW	bounty land warrant(s)
LNR	last noted residence
md	married
c	about
nr	near
USA	US Army regular troops, as opposed to VA militia
USN	US Navy

Military service was in the Virginia state militia, unless otherwise noted, such as other states militia, or U.S. regular forces.

Not all of the War of 1812 veterans or their widows applied for bounty land warrants or pensions. Those who did apply were not always awarded a warrant or pension, due to many reasons, such as insufficient proof of service or of marriage, or failure to submit the required forms of documents to the National Pension Office. In some cases, the veteran or his spouse died before the pension or warrant could be approved. The mails at the time being slow and government bureaucracy even slower, considerable time passed between applications and approval. Many of the applicants had to solicit the aid of their congressmen to speed up the process. Proof of marriage was often difficult because of the loss of public records, especially in Virginia where fires destroyed courthouses in a number of the counties. Affadavits from witnesses to the marriages were often hard to find, especially when the widows were of advanced age, or had moved out of state.

ROLL NO. 1

AARONHELT, ADAM (BLW), died 19 Sep 1842, Coshotocton Co, OH; md 25 Feb 1819 Sarah McCaully (P), Hampshire Co, VA

ABBOTT, JEREMIAH (BLW), died 11 Aug 1854, Jeffersonville, Clark Co, IN; md 2 Oct 1814 Mary A Berry (P), Frankfort Twp, Mineral Co, VA. Her LNR Jeffersonville, Clark Co, IN, 1873

ABBOTT, THOMAS P. (BLW), died 18 Dec 1871, Halifax Co, VA; md 28 Dec 1830 Nancy Edmonson (P), Halifax Co, VA. Her LNR Omega, Halifax Co, VA, 1878

ABBOTT, WILLIAM (BLW), died 19 Nov 1859, Pittsylvania Co, VA; md 22 Dec 1816 Temperance Owen (P), Pittsylvania Co, VA. She died c1882, Haystack, Surry Co, NC

ABELL, THOMAS (BLW), died 1837/38, Warrenton, Fauquier Co, VA; md 28 Dec 1816 Frances/Fanny Thomas (P), Dumfries, Prince William Co, VA. She died c 1883, LNR Bristow Station, Fauquier Co, VA

ABERNETHY, RALEIGH H. (BLW), died 30 Jun 1858, Brunswick Co, VA; md (1) Martha T. Avery, (2) 22 Jun 1843 Susan Peterson (P), Brunswick Co, VA. She died 4 Jun 1880, LNR Sturgeonville, Brunswick Co, VA

ABERNATHY, THOMAS whose

ABERNATHY (continued) widow applied for a pension

ABINGTON, WILLIAM S. (BLW), md Frances S. (__) Shelton, widow of James Shelton, also a War of 1812 veteran. See below.

ABSHIRE, JOHN whose widow Margaret applied for a pension

ABSTON, WILLIAM (BLW), died 22 Oct 1857, Clinton Co, KY; md 10 May 1826 Sarah Dove (P), Pittsylvania Co, VA. She died 20 Feb 1883, LNR Charleston, Coles Co, IL

ABY, JONAS (BLW), died 25 Feb 1849, Middletown, VA; md 28 Jul 1808 Barbara Hulett (P), Winchester, VA. Her LNR P. O. Middletown, Frederick Co, VA, 1871

ACHOR/ACHRE, ABRAHAM (P, BLW), died 7 Feb 1876; md Feb 1815 Nancy Ellis, Owen Co, KY. Her LNR Clark's Prairie, Daviess Co, IN, 1879

ACORS, WILLIAM (P, BLW), LNR Spotsylvania Co, VA, 1871

ACREE, AMBROSE (BLW), died 7 Nov 1867, King & Queen Co, VA; md 1 Nov 1853 Hannah Broaddus (P), Smyrna Church, King & Queen Co, VA. She died 7 Oct 1899, LNR Bruington, King & Queen Co, VA, 1879

ACREE, LEONARD (BLW), died 8 Apr 1872, King William Co, VA; md 5 Jan 1821 Eliza Fisher (P), LNR Old Church, Hanover Co, VA, 1878

ADAMS, JOHN (P, BLW), died

1

ADAMS (continued)
17 Oct 1880, Guyandotte, WV; md (1) Jane ---, (2) 5 Jan 1854 Sarah Ann (---) Elkins (P), Cabell Co, VA. Her LNR Huntington, Cabell Co, WV, 1881

ADAMS, JOHN (BLW), died 17 Dec 1856, Greenville, IL; md (1) ?, (2) 16 Jun 1842 Mary Jane (Sparks) Culberson (P), Paris, Edgar Co, IL. She died c1889, LNR Altamont, Effingham Co, IL, 1888

ADAMS, JOHN L. whose widow Martha applied for a pension

ADAMS, JOHN (BLW), died 5 Nov 1850, Sussex Co, VA; md 22 Apr 1829 Jackey P. Magee (P), Sussex Co, VA. She died c1879, LNR Sussex Co, VA, 1878

ADAMS, JOHN (P, BLW), died 27 Apr 1888; md 16 Oct 1846 Mary Cundiff (P), Botetourt Co, VA. She died c1890, LNR DuQuoin, IL, 1888

ADAMS, MABERY (P, BLW), LNR Adairsville, Logan Co, KY, 1871; md 1820 Martha ---, Logan Co, KY

ADAMS, SAMUEL (BLW), MD militia, died 27 Jul 1848, Somerset Co, MD; md Jun 1825 Mary Ann Wilson (P), Somerset Co, MD. She died c1883, LNR Frankton, Northampton Co, VA, 1881

ADAMS, THOMAS (P, BLW), died 8 Sep 1878, Rollins Fork, King George Co, VA

ADAMS, THOMAS F. (P,BLW), died 15 Feb 1875, Milton Co, GA; md (1) Ritter Crawford, (2) 20 Jan 1846 Elizabeth Jenkins (P), Elbert Co, GA. Her LNR Big Creek District, GA, 1878

ADAMS, WARREN (BLW), died 15 Mar 1835 or 1838, King William Co, VA; md 8 May 1815 Mary Huxter (P), King William Co, VA. Her LNR

ADAMS (continued)
Enfield, King William Co, VA, 1878

ADAMS, WYATT (P,BLW), died 4 Jul 1876, Mecklenburg Co, VA; md (1) Mary Chambliss, died 1855, (2) 6 Jul 1857 Mary B. Vaughan (P), Mecklenburg Co, VA. Her LNR Cabbage Farm, Mecklenburg Co, VA, 1878

ADAMSON, FREDERICK (BLW) whose widow Martha applied for a pension

ADCOCK, JOEL J. (P,BLW), died 23 Dec 1884, Millersburg, MO; md 19 Jul 1820 Elizabeth ---, Maysville, VA

ADCOCK, LAWSON (BLW), died 12 Sep 1855, Carroll Co, KY; md 17 Dec 1817 Nancy Gurden/Jivordand, Buckingham Co, VA. Her LNR Carroll Co, KY, 1878

ADDISON, KENDALL (P, BLW), died 1 Jul 1826, Northampton Co, VA; md 16 Sep 1819 Jane O. Coward (who later md Thomas M. Bayly). Her LNR Richmond, VA, 1856

ADDISON, WILLIAM (BLW), died 1 Nov 1859, Northampton Co, VA; md 23 Jul 1844 Caroline I. Bayly (P), Pungoteague, Accomac Co, VA. Her LNR Hadlock, Northampton Co, VA, 1878

ADIE, HUGH (P, BLW), alleged not to be md, LNR Garrisonville, Stafford Co, VA, 1871

ADKERSON, JAMES whose widow Priscilla applied for a pension

ADKERSON, THOMAS (BLW), died 9 Nov 1859, Bedford Co, VA; md 5 Sep 1808 Sally Hogans (P), Bedford Co, VA. She died 25 Jun 1878, Liberty, Bedford Co, VA.

ADKINS, PARKER (BLW), died 10 May 1857, Raleigh Co, VA; md (1) Jane ----, (2) 5 May 1851 Mary Ann Willis (P),

2

ADKINS (continued)
Raleigh Co, VA. She died 14 Jan 1887, Union District, Lincoln Co, WV. Mary Ann was previously married.

ADKISSON, JAMES (P,BLW), LNR Buckeye Cove, Pocahontas Co, WV, 1871; md May 1815 Matilda Dorson, Madison Co, VA

AERY, JOHN (BLW), died 12 Nov 1869, Greene Co, OH; md 18 Aug 1817 Margaret Turner (P), Clinton Co, OH. She died c1880, LNR Xenia, Greene Co, OH, 1878

AGEE, SAMUEL (BLW), died 13 Jul 1869, Cumberland, Cumberland Co, VA; md (1) --- Anderson, died c1846, (2) 8 Jul 1848 Mary M. Anderson (P), Cumberland Co, Va. She died 29 Apr 1881, LNR Cumberland Co, Va, 1878

AGEE, THOMAS (BLW), died 24 May 1853, Buckingham Co, VA; md 31 Oct 1811 Elizabeth Wooldridge (P), Buckingham Co, VA. Her LNR Cumberland Co, VA, 1871

AKERS, ROBERT (BLW), died 15 Mar 1854, Lawrence Co, OH; md 18 Dec 1813 or 25 Mar 1815 Rebecca Hollingsworth (P), Patrick Co, VA. She died c1880, LNR Ironton, Lawrence Co, OH, 1871

ALBAUGH/ALBROUGH, WILLIAM H. (P, BLW), MD militia, died 28 Aug 1873, Frederick Co, MD; md (1) --- Holliday, (2) 8 Oct 1863 Susan ---, Frederick Co, MD. She died 12 Nov 1887, Kearneysville, WV

ALBERT, FELIX (P, BLW), not married, LNR Georgetown, Lewis Co, WV, 1871

ALBRIGHT, DAVID whose widow Susanna applied for a pension

ALBRIGHT, JOHN (P, BLW), md 1 Oct 1839 Christian Lin-

ALBRIGHT (continued)
damood, Shenandoah Co, VA

ALDERSON, JOHN (BLW), died 16 Sep 1855, Monroe Co, VA; md 8 Jul 1826 Nancy Johnson (P), Monroe Co, VA. She died 27 June 1878, LNR Summers Co, WV, 1878

ALDERSON, THOMAS whose widow Martha applied for a pension

ALESHIRE, HENRY (P, BLW), died 11 May 1868, Greenup, Cumberland Co, IL; md (1) Dec 1827 Rebecca R. Mauck (P),Shenandoah (now Page) Co, VA. She died c1885, LNR Muscatine, Muscatine Co, IA

ALESHIRE, JACOB (P, BLW), died 31 Dec 1877, LNR Mackerville, Mason Co, WV; md Jan 1825 Sarah Vansickles, Mason Co, VA

ALESHITE, GEORGE (BLW), died Apr 1862, Page Co, VA; md Jan 1838 Whitha Turner (P), page Co, VA. She died 30 Dec 1894. LNR Honeyville, Page Co, VA, 1878

ALEXANDER, JAMES (BLW), died 11 Dec 1854, Monroe Co, VA; md 22 Oct 1817 Ingabo B. Ruddell/Ruddle (P), Augusta Co, VA. Her LNR Union, Monroe Co, WV, 1878

ALEXANDER, JOHN (P, BLW), LNR Stuart's Draft, Augusta Co, VA, 1871; md 1829 Catharine T. Long, South River, Augusta Co, VA

ALEXANDER, William (BLW), died 9 Jun 1854, Port Republic, VA: md 5 Jan 1803 Ann/Anna Bibbins (P), Albemarle Co, VA. Her LNR Waynesboro, Augusta Co, VA

ALEXANDER, William (BLW), died 10 Apr 1839, Hanover Co, VA; md 27 Jul 1825 Mary Parsley (P), Hanover Co, VA. Her LNR Old Church, Hanover

ALEXANDER (continued)
Co, VA 1878

ALGER, SETH (BLW), died 1868-1871; md (1)Sally Coonrod, (2) Apr 1845 Rosana Fifer (P), Rockingham Co, VA. Her LNR Middletown, IN 1878

ALIFF, JAMES (BLW)), died 17 Dec 1870, Marion Township, Harrison Co, MO; md 9 Sep 1813 Nancy White (P), Bedford Co, VA. She died Feb 1882, Eagleville, MO

ALKIRE/ALICAR, DAVID (BLW) whose widow Rachell applied for a pension

ALLBRIGHT, FREDERICK (BLW), died 18 Aug 1854 Waveland, IN; md 26 Mar 1812 Elizabeth Ornbaum (P), Rockbridge Co, VA. Her LNR Crawfordsville, IN, 1855

ALLCOCK, IRA (P, BLW), died 20 Jul 1882, Charlemont, VA; md (1) Phoebe Johnson, (2) 24 Jun 1841 Frances J. Whittington (P), Amherst, Amherst Co, VA. She died 10 Jul 1893, LNR Big Island, VA, 1883

ROLL NO. 2

ALLEN, ARCHIBALD (P, BLW), died 19 Mar 1875, Calloway Co, MO; md (1) Ann Calbreath, (2) Nancy Hamilton (3) 5 Mar 1875 Margaret (---) Brown (P), Calloway Co, MO. She died 15 Feb 1890, Calloway Co, MO

ALLEN, DAVIS (BLW), died 24 Mar 1859, Nottoway Co, VA; md (1) Nancy Fliffin, (2) Sarah Paine, (3) 10 Feb 1848 Lucy Foster (P), Prince Edward Co, VA. Her LNR Green Bay, Prince Edward Co, VA, 1882

ALLEN, EDWARD C. (BLW), died 5 Aug 1829, Granville Co, SC; md 19 Dec 1807 Julia Brent (P), Charlotte Co, VA

ALLEN, GEORGE (BLW), died 27 Jun 1862, Caroline Co, VA;

ALLEN (continued)
md 26 Sep 1817 Marie E Bowlware (P), Caroline Co, VA

ALLEN, ISAAC (P, BLW), LNR Murphysboro, Jackson Co, IL, 1871; md 26 Jul 1819 Patsey W. Mayberry, Logan Co, KY. She died 16 Feb 1841

ALLEN, ISAAC (P, BLW), LNR Powhatan Courthouse, Powhatan Co, VA 1871; md 16 May 1811 Susan Mosby, Powhatan Co, VA

ALLEN, ISAM (BLW), died 23 Feb 1862, Pleasant Grove Township, Mahaska Co, IA, md 22 Oct 1816 Martha Montgomery (P), Scott Co, VA. She died c1886, LNR Union Township, Poweshiek Co, IA, 1882

ALLEN, JAMES (BLW), died Apr 1857, Williamson Co, TN; md 31 Dec 1811, Mary/Polly Denton (P), Lunenburg Co, VA. She died 3 Feb 1883, South Harper, Williamson Co, TN

ALLEN, JAMES C. (BLW), died 24 Jul 1856, Pittsylvania Co, VA; md (1) Mary Bradley, (2) 3 Feb 1831 Lavicy F Vaden (P), Pittsylvania Co, VA. Her LNR P.O. Chatham, Pittsylvania Co, VA 1878

ALLEN, JOHN (P), died Spring 1883, St. Albans, WV; md 1802 Sarah Austin, Carter Co, TN. She died 27 Jul 1849

ALLEN, JOHN and widow Nancy both applied for a pension

ALLEN, JOHN (BLW), died 13 Jan 1870, Nelson Co, VA; md May 1834 Phoebe Ann Kelly (P), Nelson Co, VA. She died 2 Jan 1889, LNR Lovingston, Nelson Co, VA, 1878

ALLEN, JOHN W. (BLW), died 5 Mar 1843, Amherst Co, VA; md 3 Sep 1829 Polly J. Clements/Clemens (P), Amherst Co, VA. Her LNR Allwood, Amherst Co, Va 1878

ALLEN, JOSEPH (BLW), died 27

4

ALLEN (continued)

Apr 1858, Augusta Co, VA; md 6 Feb 1845 Jane Walters (P), Augusta Co, VA, LNR P.O. Meyers Cave, Augusta Co, VA, 1878

ALLEN, Joseph whose widow Lydia applied for a pension

ALLEN, LAWSON (BLW), died May 1861, Williamson Co, TN; md (1) Nancy Clark, (2) 11 Feb 1851 Martha A. (---) Whitfield (P), Davidson Co, TN. Her LNR Springville, Henry Co, TN, 1878

ALLEN, MEREDITH (P, BLW), died 15 Oct 1877, Wayne Co, WV; md 3 June 1834 Jane Coffee/Coffey (P), Amherst Co, VA. Her LNR Ceredo, Wayne Co, WV 1871

ALLEN, REUBEN (P, BLW), not married, LNR Mt. Jackson, Shenandoah Co, VA, 1871

ALLEN, RICHARD (P, BLW), LNR P.O. Painesville, Amelia Co, VA, 1874; md 27 Jan 1822 Martha Rogers, Amelia Co, VA

ALLEN, THOMAS (BLW), died 7 Jul 1841, Jackson Township, Fountain Co, IN; md 1 Feb 1809 Elizabeth Summers (P), Russell Co, VA. Her LNR Covington, Fountain Co, IN, 1873

ALLEN, THOMAS M. (P, BLW), died 10 Oct 1871, Boone Co, MO; md 18 Mar 1818 Rebecca W. Russell, Fayette Co, KY

ALLEN, WILLIAM (BLW), died 2 Feb 1871, Shadwell, VA; md 109 Sep 1814 Elizabeth Morris (P), Louisa Co, VA. Her LNR Shadwell, Albemarle Co, VA, 1871

ALLEN, WILLIAM (P, BLW), died 17 Oct 1876, Long Branch, VA; md (1) Susan Smith, (2) 15 Dec 1872 Martha (---) Boyd (P), Franklin Co, VA. She died 1 Oct 1910 LNR P.O. Long Branch, Franklin

ALLEN (continued)

Co, VA, 1878

ALLEN, WILLIAM D. (P, BLW), LNR Wilkinson Co, MS, 1876; md (1) Martha Scutt Landrum, (2) 12 Nov 1846 Eliza Landrum, Woodville, MS. Her LNR Jackson, LA, 1879

ALLEY, DAVID (BLW), died 16 Jun 1871, Lead Mines, Wythe Co, VA; md 24 Dec 1811 Sarah Hammond (P), Lead Mines, VA. Sarah's mother remarried a man named Norris, by which Sarah was afterward known. Sarah's LNR Lead Mines, Wythe Co, VA, 1881

ALLIMONG, CASPER (P, BLW), died 11 Jan 1872, White Hall, Frederick Co, VA; md 27 Jan 1818 Christina Dick, Frederick Co, VA

ALLISON, BALEY (P, BLW), LNR Salem, Fauquier Co, VA, 1871; md 17 Dec 1817 Ellen Skinner, Fauquier Co, VA

ALLISON, BURGES (P, BLW), LNR P.O. Fairview, Hancock Co, WV, 1878

ALLISON/ELLISON, ELSEY (P, BLW), died 14 May 1888, Madisonville, Ralls Co, MO; md 1821 Lucinda Poe, Warrenton, Fauquier Co, VA

ALLISON, HENRY (BLW), died 27 Dec 1872, Smithton, Pettis Co, MO; md (1) 1818 Jane Campbell Voss, who died 1819 Madison, VA, (2) 8 Oct 1826 Mary Selena Swift (P), Petersburg, Dinwiddie Co, VA. She died 31 Mar 1885, Sedalia, MO

ALLISON, RICHARD D. (BLW), died 7 Aug 1857, Graves Co, KY; md (1) Elizabeth Crafton, (2) Feb 1830/1 Mary Mullins (P), Rutherford Co, TN. She died 9 Jan 1902, LNR P.O. Water Valley, Graves Co, KY, 1878

ALLISON, DENNIS (P, BLW),

ALLISON (continued)
LNR Fairfax Co, VA, 1871; md
18 Dec 1827 Sarah Smith, Fair-
fax Co, VA
ALLMAN, JACOB (BLW), LNR
Salisbury Township, P.O. Mid-
dleport, Meigs Co, OH, 1871
ALLTON/AULTON, SAMUEL (P,
BLW), LNR Union Township,
P.O. Murphy's Mill, Wood Co,
WV, 1871; md 16 Oct 1816
Nancy H. Santee, Greene Co,
PA
ALMAN, SAMUEL (BLW), died 4
Oct 1855,Harrisonburg, Rock-
ingham Co, VA; md 13 Aug
1850 Nancy (---) McDorman
(P), Rockingham Co, VA. Her
LNR Harrisonburg, Rockin-
gham Co, VA, 1878
ALMOND, HENRY whose widow
Joica applied for a pension
ALPINE, JACOB (P, BLW), died
2 Feb 1881, Jalapa, Monroe
Co, TN; md Oct 1848 Mahala
Farmer (---) Duff (P), McMinn
Co, TN. She died 16 Mar 1894,
Lamontville, TN, her LNR
Jalapa, TN, 1881
ALSOP, BEN (P, BLW), died 31
Jan 1883, Owensboro, Daviess
Co, KY, served as a substitute
for his father, Robert Alsop;
md 1 Jan 1821 Lucy M Taylor,
Jefferson Co, KY
ALTICK, SOLOMON (P, BLW),
LNR Walker Township, P.O.
Volcano, Wood Co, VA, 1871;
md Mar 1805 Elizabeth Mit-
chell, Franklin Co, VA
ALVERSON, BECKNULL (BLW),
died 5 May 1859, Cole Co,
MO; md 20 Nov 1818 Lucy
Powell (P), Frederick Co, VA.
She died c1882, LNR Ver-
sailles, Morgan Co, MO, 1878
ALVIS, WILLIAM E. (BLW),
died 21 June 1863, Goochland
Co, VA; md 3 Jan 1834 Mary
S. Harris (P), Goochland Co,
VA. She died 11 Aug 1905,
LNR Dover Mines, Goochland

ALVIS (continued)
Co, VA, 1878
AMBLER, THOMAS M (BLW),
died 4 Sep 1875, Fauquier Co,
Va; md 15 Apr 1819 Lucy H
Johnson/Johnston (P), Camp-
bell Co, VA. She died 10 Nov
1888, LNR Markham, Fauquier
Co, VA, 1878
AMICK, JACOB (P, BLW), died
22 Sep 1892, LNR Back Creek,
Frederick Co,VA 1871; md 19
Dec 1850 Jane McKee, Capon
Springs, VA
AMICK, JACOB (BLW), died 6
Sep 1859, Nicholas Co, VA;
md 5 Jun 1814 Rachael Stroyer
(P), Pendleton Co, VA. She
died c1894, LNR Pool,
Nicholas Co, WV, 1885
AMISS, JOHN S. (P, BLW), LNR
Howardsville, Albemarle Co,
VA, 1871; md 1 Aug 1816 Mary
T (---) Shiffett (P), Albemarle
co, VA. Her LNR Woodbridge,
Albemarle Co, VA 1885/6
AMMONS, WILLIAM (BLW),
died 11 May 1858, Charles
City Co, VA; md (1) Sarah Hil-
liard, (2) 7 Jan 1820 Elizabeth
H. Hughes (P), Charles City
Co, VA. Her LNR Wilsons
Landing, Charles City Co, Va
1878
AMONETT, ANDREW (BLW),
died 11 Feb 1871, Florence,
AL; md 20 Nov 1816 Juliet
Shepard (P), Steam Chastain,
AL. She died 14 Mar 1885,
Florence, AL
AMOS, ASA (P, BLW), died 31
May 1880,Patriot, Gallia Co,
OH; md 25 Dec 1816 Nancy
Hunter, Stokes Co, NC
AMSPOKER, JOHN (BLW), died
23 Feb 1852, Washington Co,
PA; md 11 Oct 1804 Mary Ann
Ramsey (P), Washington Co,
PA. She died 26 Jul 1880,
LNR New Concord, Muskingum
Co, OH, 1871
ANCELL, JAMES (P, BLW), died

6

ANCELL (continued) 27 Nov 1876, LNR Myers, Howard Co, MD; md 2 Jan 1816 Frances Estis, Orange Co, VA

ANDERSON, EDMUND M. (P, BLW), died c1886, LNR P.O. Verdon, Hanover Co, VA, 1871; md 5 Nov 1835 Emily H. Day, Hanover Co, VA

ANDERSON, EDWARD WATKINS (P, BLW), LNR P.O. Russellville, Logan Co, KY, 1875; md Mr 1819 Obedience Branch, Chesterfield Co, VA

ANDERSON, GARLAND (BLW), died 15 Apr 1855, Louisa Co, VA; md (1) Maria Pleasants, (2) 29 Dec 1825 Mary C. Shelton (P), Louisa Co, Va. Her LNR Hopeful, Louisa Co, VA, 1878

ANDERSON, GENET whose widow Maria D. applied for a pension

ANDERSON, ISAAC (P, BLW), LNR Golconda, Pope Co, IL, 1870

ANDERSON, JAMES (BLW), died 9 Mar 1870, Middletown, Frederick Co, VA; md 11 Nov 1808 Leah Senseney (P), Winchester, Frederick Co, VA. Her LNR Winchester, VA, 1871

ANDERSON, JAMES (BLW), died 16 June 1860, Buckingham Co, VA; md (1) Elizabeth Flood, (2) 1 Feb 1829 Martha M. Flood (P), NC. She died Dec 1902, Andersonville, VA

ANDERSON, JESSE (BLW), died 2 Sep 1862, Pittwylvania Co, VA; md 20 Jul 1812 Catharine B. Irby (P), Halifax Co, VA. Her LNR Peytonsburg, Pittsylvania Co, Va, 1871

ANDERSON, JOHN (P, BLW), KY militia, died c1880, LNR Quincy, IL, 1871; md 3 Jan 1819 Elizabeth Guerant, Canton, Buckingham Co, VA. She died before 13 Apr 1871

ANDERSON, JOHN whose widow Margery applied for a pension

ANDERSON, JOHN (P), died 22 Jun 1877, Urbana, OH; md 28 Dec 1815 Nancy Lower (P), Orange Co, VA. She died c1881, her LNR Urnana, OH, 1878

ANDERSON, JOHN (BLW), died 23 Jan 1862, Louisa Co, VA; md (1) Nancy ---, (2) 25 Mar 1855 Mildred A. (---) Johnson (P), Loudoun Co, VA. Her LNR P.O. Cobham, Louisa Co, VA, 1879

ANDERSON, JOHN whose widow Nancy applied for a pension

ANDERSON, JOHN (BLW), died 14 Sep 1861, Halifax Co, Va; md (1) Elizabeth Ferguson, (2) 22 Apr 1830 Tabitha Whitworth (P). She died c1887, her LNR P.O. Vernon Hill, Halifax Co, 1878

ANDERSON, JOHN B. (BLW), died 27 Nov 1836, Cynthiana, Harrison Co, KY; md 13 Jul 1814 Ann P. Peebles (P), Greenbrier Co, VA. She died c1883. (Ann was erroneously pensioned as wife of another John B. Anderson who served in Hubbard, Smith, and Anderson Companies. Ann's husband served in Capt Taylor's Company). Ann's LNR, Cynthiana, Harrison Co, KY, 1871

ANDERSON, JOHN C. (BLW), died 27 Aug 1856, Washington Co, VA; md 21 Oct 1819 Jane Willoughby (P), Washington Co, VA. Her LNR Sullivan Co, TN, 1878

ANDERSON, JOHN C. (BLW), died 24 Apr 1869, Monroe Co, GA; md 1 Mar 1821 Nancy Maddox (P), Eatonton, Putnam Co, GA. She died 11 Jun 1885, Paran, GA, LNR New Market, Monore Co, GA, 1878

ANDERSON, JOHN J. whose widow Permelia applied for a

ANDERSON (continued)
pension
ANDERSON, JOHN N. (BLW),
died 9 Aug 1865, Bedford Co,
VA; md 5 Feb 1818 Ann/Nancy
W. Camm (P), Bethel, Am-
herst Co, VA. She died Nov
1883, Liberty, Bedford Co, VA
ANDERSON, JOHN R. (BLW),
died 8 May 1826, Jefferson Co,
VA; md 4 Jan 1821 Abigail
Thomas (P), Leesburg, Ludoun
Co, VA. Her LNR Rochester,
Cedar Co, IA, 1879
ANDERSON, JOSEPH (BLW),
died c12 Nov 1846, Ross Co,
OH; md 14 Jun 1811 Catharine
Brown (P), Botetourt Co, VA.
She died c1875, LNR Waverly,
Pike Co, OH, 1871
ANDERSON, JOSEPH whose
widow Mary applied for a pen-
sion
ANDERSON, JOSEPH B. (BLW),
died 3 Apr 1873, Amelia Co,
VA; md (1) Sally Merriwether,
(2) 5 May 1852 Jane S. Archer
(P), Cumberland Co, VA. She
died 20 Oct 1885, Richmond,
VA
ANDERSON, LOUIS (P, BLW),
died 11 Feb 1876, Nelson Co,
VA, LNR Rockfish Depot, Nel-
son Co, VA; md 12 Nov 1819
Sophia A. Pettit (P), Albe-
marle Co, Va. Her LNR P.O.
Orlando, Nelson Co, VA, 1878
ANDERSON, MELCON/CARROL,
whose widow Unetta applied
for a pension
ANDERSON, PETER L. (BLW),
died 29 Jan 1861, Greenbrier
Co, VA; md c1815-16 Rebecca
Flack (P), Greenbrier Co, VA.
She died 1 Sep 1883, Lewis-
burg, Greenbrier Co, WV
ANDERSON, RICHARD (BLW),
died 3 Aug 1870, Bedford Co,
VA; md 6 Jun 1811 Elizabeth
Bowles (P), Bedford Co, VA.
Her LNR Chamblissburg, Bed-
ford Co, VA, 1871

ANDERSON, ROBERT whose wi-
dow Margaret applied for a
pension
ANDERSON, ROBERT (BLW),
died 26 Jul 1853, Hanover Co,
VA; md (1) Nancy Caster, (2)
24 Sep 1844 Mary F. Jordan
(P), Hanover Co, VA. She died
24 Nov 1887, LNR P.O. Old
Church, Hanover Co, VA, 1878
ANDERSON, THOMAS (P, BLW),
LNR Clarksburg, Harrison Co,
WV, 1871; md 18 Jun 1835
Elizabeth Davis, Clarksburg,
VA
ANDERSON, WILLIAM (P,
BLW), died 16 Dec 1871, St.
Genevieve Co, MO; md Eliza-
beth Downing (P), Port
Tobacco, Charles Co, MD.
She died c1881, LNR P.O.
Punjab, MO 1871
ANDERSON, WILLIAM L. (P,
BLW), LNR Buckhannon, Up-
shur Co, WV, 1871
ANDERTON, THOMAS (P, BLW),
died 25 Sep 1877, Morgan Co,
IL; md 26 Dec 1829 Lucy
Briggs (P), Person Co, NC.
She died 26 Oct 1885, LNR
Franklin, Morgan Co, IL, 1878
ANDRESS, ANDREW (BLW),
died 15 or 16 Dec 1825 or
1828, Washington Co, IN; md
24 Mar 1814 Mary Shutters (P),
Washington Co, VA. Her LNR
P.O. Kecks Church, Martin Co,
IN 1874
ANDREWS, ABRAHAM, (P,
BLW), died 10 Aug 1875,
Fayette Co, KY; md (1) ?, (2)
28 Oct 1869 Cassandra (---)
Sageser (P), Lexington, KY.
Her LNR Campbellsburg, Hen-
ry Co, KY, 1878
ANDREWS, BURWELL G.
(BLW), died 8 Mar 1843,
Limestone Co, AL; md 17 Oct
1817 Mary A. Ogburn/Augbourn
(P), Halifax Co, NC. She died
4 Jan 1892, LNR P.O. Athens,
Limestone Co, AL, 1878

ANDREWS, DANIEL H. (BLW), died 13 Jan 1852, Goochland Co, VA; md (1) Sophia Ann Parrott, (2) 25 Feb 1839 Margaret T. Whitlock (P), Goochland Co, VA. Her LNR Charlottesville, Albemarle Co, VA, 1878

ANDREWS, ERASMUS G. (P, BLW), died 7 Jun 1875, Chesterfield Co, VA; md (1) Mason Andrews, (2) 20 Aug 1845 Rebecca B. Scott (P), Dinwiddie Co, VA. Her LNR Chesterfield Co, VA, 1879

ANDREWS, RICHARD J. (P, BLW), died 6 Jun 1887, Rodgersville, VA; md 16 Oct 1816 Martha G. Coleman, Lunenburg Co, VA

ANDREWS, VARNEY (BLW), died 13 Mar 1879, Grayson Co, TX; md 10 Sep 1826 Mary W. Maxey (P), Monroe Co, KY. Her LNR Grayson Co, TX, 1879

ROLL NO. 3

ANGLEA, ALLEN C. (P, BLW), died 22 May 1880, Prince Edward Co, VA; md 7 Dec 1825 Mary E. Richie (P), Prince Edward Co, Va. She died Jan 1899, Farmville, VA

ANGLEA, HARTWELL (BLW), died Sep 1846-7, Sumner Co, TN; md 1832-4 Eliza Ferguson (P), Charlotte Co, Va. Her LNR P.O. Pondville, Sumner Co, TN, 1878

ANGUS, WILLIAM (BLW), died 4 Jun 1865, Amherst Co, VA; md 31 May 1810 Elizabeth/Betsey Fulcher (P), Lowesville, VA. She died Feb 1882, Amherst Co, VA

ANKERS, JOHN (BLW), 23 Jan 1867, Loudoun Co, VA; md 5 Apr 1825 Harriet A. Hess (P), on banks of Potomac Co, MD. Her LNR Gilford, Loudoun Co,

ANKERS (continued) VA, 1879

ANNETT, SAMUEL (P, BLW), died 5 Jul 1875, Clover Depot, VA, LNR Halifax Co, VA, 1871; md c27 Dec 1819 Catharine Hughes (P), Halifax Co, VA

ANTHONY, CHARLES applied for a pension

ANTHONY, MARK (BLW), died 17 Jul 1859, Campbell Co, VA, md 13 Dec 1799 Emelia Leftwich (P), Bedford Co, VA. Her LNR Staunton Township, Bedford Co, VA, 1871

APPELBERRY, JOHN P. (BLW), died 7 Apr 1868, Valles Mines, MO; md 30 Jun 1831 Eliza Stephens (P), Jefferson Co, MO. She died c1891, LNR Avoca, Jefferson Co, MO, 1887

APPERSON/EPPERSON, JOHN (P, BLW), died 6 Jun 1877, Paradise, Coles Co, IL; md 2 Aug 1821 Sidney Hanson (P), Lebanon, Russell Co, VA. She died c1888, LNR Windsor, Shelby Co, IL, 1887

APPERSON/EPPERSON, MAJOR D. (P, BLW), LNR New Kent Co, VA, 87; md 30 Nov 1816 Martha Jones, New Kent Co, VA

APPERSON, REUBEN (P, BLW), LNR Culpeper, Culpeper Co, VA, 1871; md 20 Mar 1828 Jane Keeling, Russell Co, VA

APPERSON, THOMAS (BLW), died 31 Jan or 1 Feb, 1866, Barboursville, VA; md Dec 1813 Evelina Palmer (P), Orange Co, VA. Her LNR Stevensburg, Culpeper Co, VA, 1873

APPERSON/EPPERSON, WILLIAM applied for a pension

APPLEWHITE, THOMAS (BLW) whose wife was Mary Ann

ARBAUGH, GEORGE (BLW)

ARBOGAST, JOSEPH whose widow Sarah applied for a pen-

9

ARBOGAST (continued)
sion
ARBOGAST, WILLIAM (BLW), died 26 Feb 1847, Green Bank, Pocahontas Co, VA; md 25 Oct 1826 Jane G. Tallman (P), Greene Co, PA. She died 17 Jul 1884, LNR Green Bank, Pocahontas Co, WV, 1878

ARCHER, AMOS (P, BLW), died 20 Mar 1875, Monroeville, Monroe Co, AL; md 3 Jul 1828 Elizabeth Hendrix (P), Lexington Co, SC. She died 19 Oct 1900, LNR Monroeville, AL, 1885

ARCHER, RICHARD F. (BLW), died 1 Jun 1861, Fayette Co, GA; md (1) Elizabeth Brown, (2) 11 Dec 1828 Prudence Ann Vinson (P), Hall Co, GA. Her LNR Dallas, Paulding Co, GA, 1878

ARCHER, WILLIAM (BLW), died 15 May 1852, Jersey Co, IL; md 27 Nov 1812 Priscilla Merrill (P), Frederick Co, VA. She died 5 Nov 1874, LNR Monterey, Calhoun Co, IL, 1871

ARGABRITE, MARTIN (BLW), died 5 Mar 1869, Reedy Creek, WV; md May 1822 Catharine Burditt (P), Monroe Co, VA. She died 6 Aug 1894, Peniel, WV

ARGENBRIGHT, JOHN (BLW), died 3 Nov 1870, Macomb, IL; md 15 Mar 1818 Christina "Tiny" Baker (P), Harrison Co, TN. She died Sep 1883, Blandinsville, IL, LNR Macomb, McDonough Co, IL, 1879

ARIE, JOSEPH (BLW), died 26 Aug 1869, Peoria, Peoria Co, IL; md 17 Nov 1832 Nancy Humphreys (P), Greenbrier Co, VA. She died 21 Sep 1887, LNR Galesburg, Knox Co, IL, 1879

ARISMAN, JACON (BLW), died 25 Nov 1878, Morgan Co, MO;

ARISMAN (continued)
md 17 Dec 1823 Malinda Hall (P), Augusta Co, Va. She died 11 Oct 1886 Morgan Co, MO

ARISON/ORISON, JOHN (BLW), died 2 Mar 1870, Fayette Co, PA; md 16 Sep 1812 Catherine Day (P), Leesburg, VA. Her LNR Flatwood, Fayette Co, PA, 1878

ARMENTROUT, ABRAHAM (P, BLW), died 7 Jan 1889, LNR Hayesville, Ashland Co, OH, 1873; md 22 Feb 1821 Priscilla Wade, Newville, Richland Co, OH

ARMENTROUT, CHRISTOPHER (BLW), died 23 Feb 1839, Augusta Co, Va; md 14 Feb 1822 Amy Deeds (P), Rockingham Co, VA. She died c1889, LNR Keezletown, Rockingham Co, VA, 1878

ARMENTROUT, DAVID (P, BLW), LNR Knox Co, OH 1871; md Oct 1808 Barbara Lahman, Rockingham Co, VA

ARMENTROUT, PHILIP (BLW), died 10 FEb 1869, Whitley's Point, Moultrie Co, IL; md 13 Jan 1824 Mary Greenwood (P), Xenia, Greene Co, OH. She died 9 Oct 1889, Gays, Moultrie Co, IL

ARMENTROUT, PHILIP (BLW), LNR Knox Co, OH, 1855

ARMENTROUT, PHILLIP (BLW), LNR Page Co, VA, 1855

ARMISTEAD, JAMES (P, BLW), LNR Farmville, Prince Edward Co, VA, 1871; md 15 Mar 1821 Elizabeth D. Howard, Prince Edward Co, VA

ARMISTEAD, RALPH (BLW), died 9 Aug 1864, Matthews Co, Va; md cMay 1813/14 Sarah Grinnel (P), Mathews Co, VA. She died 24 Apr 1882, Mathews Court House, Mathews Co, VA, LNR Port Haywood, Mathews Co, VA, 1878

ARMISTEAD, THOMAS (P, BLW), died 2 Sep 1889, Mathews Co, VA; md (1) Eliza Rutherford, (2) 28 Aug 1845 Harriet J. Miller (P), Mathews Co, VA. She died c1892, LNR Port Haywood, Mathews Co, VA

ARMSTRONG, JAMES (BLW), 25 Apr 1870, Parkersburg, Wood Co, WV; md Dec 1836 Sarah Smith (P), Franklin, Pendleton Co, VA. She died 1898, LNR Maroa, Macon Co, IL, 1878

ARMSTRONG, JOHN (BLW), died 23 May 1831, Culpeper Co, VA; md 23 Jun 1808 Cynthia D. Spilman (P), Culpeper Co, VA. She died 19 Mar 1874, LNR Jefferson Township, Culpeper Co, VA, 1871

ARMSTRONG, JOHN (BLW), died 3 Feb 1868, Wilmington Co, OH; md 10 Oct 1821 Mary Standforth (P), Staunton, Augusta Co, Va. She died c1880, LNR Berryville, Highland Co, OH, 1880

ARMSTRONG, NEHEMIAH whose widow Achsah applied for a pension

ARMSTRONG, PHARES (P, BLW), died 7 Apr 1883, Cave Spring, VA, LNR P.O. Big Lick, Roanoke Co, VA, 1871; md 28 Sep 1819 Jane Harris, Botetourt Co, VA.

ARMSTRONG, THOMAS (BLW), died 1855-1858, Rockbridge Co, VA; md (1) Peggy Harris, (2) 16 Apr 1856 Patsy Ann Standoff (P), Rockbridge Co, VA. She died 29 Apr 1897, LNR Collerstown, Rockbridge Co, VA, 1878

ARMSTRONG, WILLIAM (BLW), died 23 Nov 1862, Louisa Co, VA; md 21 Dec 1850 Frances A. Smith (P), Louisa Co, VA. She died 1 Sep 1888, LNR Tollersville, Louisa Co, VA, 1878

ARNALL/ARNOLD, WILLIAM

ARNALL/ARNOLD (continued) applied for a pension

ARNETT, ARCHIBALD (P, BLW), died 12 Dec 1872, Louisa, Louisa Co, VA; md 5 Jun 1828 Frances L. Trice (P), Louisa Co, VA. She died c1897, LNR Louisa Co,VA, 1878.

ARNETT, NATHANIEL (BLW), died 9 Aug 1819, Snickersville, VA; md 1806/7 Ann Burke (P), Castleman's Ferry, Clark Co, Va, or Frederick Co, VA. Her LNR Hamilton, Loudoun Co, VA, 1871

ARNOLD, HENRY (BLW), died Sep 1856, Hanover Co, VA; md 17 Jul 1823 Sarah W. Harris (P), Hanover Co, VA. Her LNR Richmond, VA, 1878

ARNOLD, JOHN (BLW), died 7 Apr 1863, King George Co, VA; md (1) Fanny Price, (2) 15 Jan 1852 Jane Went (P), King George Co, VA. She died 24 Oct 1883, Passapatanzy, King George Co, VA

ARNOLD, JOHN G. (BLW), LNR Owensboro, Daviess Co, KY; md 23 Dec 1819 Elizabeth Yager, Shelby Co, KY. She died c1859

ARNOLD, MOSES whose widow applied for a pension

ARNOLD, NOEL (BLW), died after 22 Feb 1856, Trenton, Gibson Co, TN; md Nov 1814 America Nowell (P), Springfield, TN. Her LNR Dyer Station, Gibson Co, TN 1878

ARNOLD/ARNALL, RICHARD (P, BLW), LNR Chilesburgh, Caroline Co, VA; md 27 Dec 1821 Catharine S. Butler, Hanover Co, VA

ARNOLD, WILLIAM applied for a pension

ARRASMITH, CHARLES (P, BLW), died c1877. LNR Tranquility, Adams Co, OH, 1871; md Sarah Groves, Fau-

11

ARRASMITH (continued)
quier Co, VA
ARRINGTON, ARTHUR applied for a pension
ARRINGTON, CHARLES (BLW), died 21 Oct 1848, Appomattox Co, Va; md 10 Dec 1810 Sarah/Sally M. Rosser, Campbell Co, Va. Her LNR Spout Spring, VA, 1871
ARRINGTON, EDWARD (BLW), died 15 Dec 1865, Peaksville, Bedford Co, Va; md Oct 1802 Sallie Wade (P), Granville Co, NC. Her LNR Peaksville, Va, 1874
ARRINGTON, RICHARD (BLW), died 16 Feb 1837, Halifax Co, VA; md 10 Dec 1816 Martha Wall (P), Halifax Co, VA. She died 21 Oct 1880, LNR Red Bank, Halifax Co, VA
ARRINGTON, THOMAS (P, BLW), LNR Mason Co, WV, 1871; md 16 Mar 1821 Esther A. Gould, Buckingham Co, VA
ARTHUR, CARY (BLW), died Apr 1837 or 1840, Norfolk, VA; md 5 or 6 Apr 1815 Lucy West (P), Franklin, Franklin Co, VA. Her LNR Flat Rock, Mason Co, WV, 1882
ARTHUR/ANTON, HUGH whose widow Jane applied for a pension
ARTHUR, JOHN (BLW), died 21 Aug 1844, Franklin Co, VA; md 7 Sep 1818 Charlotte Smith (P), Franklin Co, VA. Her LNR Naffs, Franklin Co, VA, 1878
ARTHUR, JONAS (BLW), died 11 Sep 1860, Cartersville, VA; md (1) Catharine M. Fulcher, (2) 19 Oct 1851 Narcissa P. (---) Watkins (P), Cartersville, VA. Her LNR Cartersville, Cumberland Co, VA, 1878
ARTHUR, LARKIN (P, BLW), LNR P.O. Monticello, Wayne Co, KY; md Jane Dixon, Liberty Court House, VA

ARTHUR, LEWIS (P, BLW), died 4 Apr 1878, Guyandotte, Cabell Co, WV; md Jul 1819 Lucy Dillion (P), Franklin Co, VA. She died 18 Jun 1887, LNR Guyandotte, WV, 1878
ARTHUR, WILLIE (BLW), died 25 Jul 1856, Clark Co, OH; md 20 Jun 1821 Millie Freeman (P), Bedford Co, VA. She died c1880, LNR South Point, Lawrence Co, OH, 1878
ARTHUR, ZEBULON (P) whose widow Sarah B applied for a pension
ARTZ, JOHN (P, BLW), LNR Aledo, Mercer Co, IL, 1871; md 18 Nov 1819 Sarah Lambert, Woodstock, Shenandoah Co, VA
ASBURY, WILLIAM (P, BLW), LNR Champaign Co, IL, 1871; md 28 Oct 1842 Janetta Woods, Lewisburg, Greenbrier Co, VA
ASH, JACOB (BLW), died 25 Jun 1849, Shelby Co, IN; md 16 Mar 1815 Isabella Marsh (P), Harrison Co, VA. She died 4 May 1885, Eri, NE, LNR Shelby Co, IN, 1878
ASH, MOSES applied for a pension
ASBY, JAMES (BLW), died 9 May 1865, Pittsylvania Co, VA; md 20 Dec 1826 Lucinda Sykes (P), Pittsylvania Co, VA. She died 27 May 1879, Pittsylvania Co, VA
ASHBY, JOHN (BLW); md Mary McNish, widow of William Pickett
ASHBY, NATHAN (BLW), whose widow Mary applied for a pension
ASHBY, THOMPSON (BLW), died 14 Jul 1850, Paris, Fauquier Co, VA; md 20 Oct 1809 Ann S. Menifee (P), Culpeper Co, VA. Her LNR Alexandria, VA, 1873
ASHBY, WILLIAM R. (BLW),

ASHBY (continued)
died 21 May 1843, Bel Air, VA;
md 3 Apr 1817 Rebecca R.
Buck (P), Bel Air, VA. She
died 5 Aug 1878, Bel Air, Warren Co, VA

ASHENHURST, JOHN (BLW),
died 6 May 1856 Dalton,
Wayne Co, OH; md 31 Jan
1805 Mary Young (P), Brooke
Co, VA. Her LNR Christ-
ianville, Mecklenburg Co, VA,
1872

ASHENHURST, OLIVER (BLW),
died 13 May 1859 or 23 May
1860, Greene Township, Mercer Co, IL; md 7 Aug 1828
Euphemia Bishop (P), Brown
Co, OH. She died c1884, LNR
Aledo, Mercer Co, IL, 1878

ASHER, NEROWAY whose widow
Rosanna applied for a pension

ASHER, WALLER R. (BLW),
died Nov 1862, Culpeper Co,
VA; md 26 Dec 1805 Elizabeth
Shannon (P), Culpeper Co, VA.
Her LNR Culpeper Co, VA,
1871

ASHINGHURST, JOHN whose
widow Lucy A. applied for a
pension

ASHON, SAMUEL applied for a
pension

ASHTON, HENRY W. applied for
a pension

ASHTON, RICHARD W. whose
widow Mary Devereux applied
for a pension

ASKEW, ANTHONY (BLW), died
4 Jun 1858, Campbell Co, VA;
md 20 Apr 1811 Jane Perdue
(P), Campbell Co, VA. She
died 30 Mar 1876, LNR P.O.
Concord Depot, Campbell Co,
VA, 1871

ASKEW, CHILDRESS (BLW),
died 11 Aug 1849, Butler Co,
KY; md 5 Jan 1817 Paulina
Mormon (P), Campbell Co,
VA. She died 5 Feb 1883, Ar-
mour, TX, LNR P.O. Chil-
howee, Johnson Co, MO 1878

ATHEY, BURGESS (P, BLW),
LNR Pleasant Mount, Miller
Co, MO, 1871; md 28 Oct 1824
Hannah Owens, Parkersburg,
VA

ATHEY, SAMUEL (P, BLW),
living Wood Co, VA, 1855,
LNR P.O. Rocky Mount, Miller
Co, MO, 1871. Not married.

ATHEY, WILLIS (BLW), LNR
Orlean, Fauquier Co, VA,
1871; md 11 Aug 1831 Roxey
Ann Barten

ATKINS, JOHN (P, BLW), died
13 Apr 1876, Rappahannock
Co, VA; md 16 Mar 1837 Frances L. Campbell (P), Rap-
pahannock Co, Va. She died
12 Dec 1892, LNR Sperryville,
Rappahannock Co, Va, 1878

ATKINS, JOHN (P, BLW), died
14 May 1859, King and Queen
Co, VA; md 19 Dec 1812 Nan-
cy Taylor (P), King and Queen
Co, VA. She died 3 Dec 11876,
King and Queen Co, VA

ATKINSON, ARCHIBALD applied
for a pension

ATKINSON, JOHNSON (BLW),
died 26 Jan 1851, Glascow,
KY; md (1) Tildy White, (2) 6
Mar 1833 Elizabeth L. Johns
(P), Glascow, Barren Co, KY.
Her LNR Freeding, Barren Co,
KY, 1879

ATKINSON, WILLIAM (P, BLW),
LNR Steubenville, Jefferson
Co, OH; md 25 May 1813
Amelia Owens, Brooke Co, VA

ATKINSON, WILLIAM (P, BLW),
LNR Yanceyville, Caswell Co,
NC, 1871; md 23 Nov 1809
Mary Holt, Nottoway Co, VA

ATKINSON, WILLIAM A. (BLW),
died 20 Jan 1860, New Kent
Co, VA; md 14 Mar 1821 Eliz-
abeth Moore (P), New Kent Co,
VA. She died 16 Jan 1886,
Richmond, Va

ATKINSON, CHARLES (P, BLW),
died 1 Dec 1880, McKinney,
TX, LNR Otterville, Cooper

13

ATKINSON (continued)
Co, MO, 1871; md 19 Dec 1816
Lucy M. Field, Albemarle Co,
VA

ATKISSON/ATKINSON, John (P,
BLW), LNR Warsaw, Benton
Co, MO, 1871

ATWELL, WILLIAM applied for
a pension

ATWOOD, ENOCH (P, BLW),
died 5 Mar 1879 Cedar Point,
Page Co, VA; md 15 Sep 1833
Margaret Ann Walker (P),
Rileyville, Shenandoah (now
Page) Co, VA. She died
c1884, LNR Cedar Point, Page
Co, VA, 1879

AUGUSTIN, AMARIA whose
widow Alcy applied for a pension

AULICK, FREDERICK (P, BLW),
died 28 Feb 1872, LNR Winchester, Frederick Co, VA,
1871; md 13 Jun 1817 Elizabeth Smith, Winchester, VA

AULTZ, ADAM (BLW), died 15
Mar 1868, Kanawha Co, WV;
md 6 Apr 1818 Patsey Samuels
(P), Kanawha Co, VA. She
died 9 Mar 1892, Kanawha Co,
WV. LNR P.O. Ripley Land-
ing, Kanawha Co, WV, 1879

AUSTIN, ALEXANDER (P,
BLW), died Mar 1874, New
London, Campbell Co, VA; md
c6 Jan 1812 Elizabeth Burgess, Halifax Co, NC

AUSTIN, BENNETT applied for a
pension

AUSTIN, JOSEPH (P, BLW), died
10 Mar 1888, LNR Morgan-
town, Monongalia Co, WV,
1871; md Dec 1813 Camilla
Martin, Monongalia Co, VA

AUSTIN, PETER (BLW), died 5
Oct 1835, Bedford Co, VA; md
7 Jul 1819 Sarah/Sally Leftwick (P), Bedford Co, VA. She
died 18 Jul 1882, Carrollton,
Carroll Co, MO

AUSTIN, THOMAS (BLW), died
Dec 1840 or 1848; md 29 Jan

AUSTIN (continued)
1825 Sarah C. Faucett, Hanover
Co, VA. Her LNR Richmond,
VA, 1878

AUSTIN, THOMAS (P, BLW),
died c1878-9; LNR Monticello,
IN; md 24 Mar 1826 Sally Halbert, Athens Co, OH

AUSTIN, WILLIAM (BLW), died
cJun 1850, Richmond VA; md
(1) Susan Wade, (2) c14 Sep
1837 Ann ---, Hanover Co,
VA. Her 1st husband was Edmund Quarles. Her LNR
Richmond, VA, 1878

AUSTON, JOHN whose widow
Morning applied for a pension

ROLL NO. 4

AVERETT, THOMAS H. (BLW),
died 30 Jun 1855; md 3 Jan
1822 Martha Coleman (P),
Prince Edward Co, VA. Her
LNR Danville, VA, 1878

AVERY, JAMES applied for a
pension

AVIS/ALVIS, ZEPHANIAH whose
widow Lucy applied for a pension

AYERS, DANIEL (P, BLW), LNR
P.O. Bales Mills, Lee Co, VA,
1871; md Sep 1808 Polly
Crucy, Washington Co, VA

AYERS, LEONARD (P, BLW),
LNR Spencers Store, Henry Co,
VA, 1881; md 18 Dec 1818
Elizabeth Harris, Patrick Co,
VA

AYERS, WILLIAM P. (BLW),
died 6 Nov 1836, Niles Co,
VA; md 10 Aug 1814 Catharine
Yates (P), Patrick Co, VA.
She died 28 Dec 1881, Fancy
Gap, Carroll Co, VA

AYRES/EYRES, JOHN (P, BLW),
died 1 Sep 1876, Rockbridge
Co, VA; md 16 Sep 1817 Rachel Entsminger (P), Rockbridge Co, VA. Her LNR P.O.
Lexington, Rockbridge Co, VA,
1878

AYRES, LITTLETON (BLW), died 12 Jul 1861, Masonville, Accomac Co, VA; md (1) Rachel ---, (2) 4 Jun 1846 Elizabeth Russell (P), Masonville, VA. She died 16 May 1885, Masonville, VA

AYRES, MATTHIAS (BLW), died 8 May 1851, Saline Co, MO; md 19 Jan 1814 Nancy G. Howell (P), Buckingham Co, VA. Her LNR Cambridge, Saline Co, MO, 1878

AYRES, NATHAN (BLW), whose widow Martha L. applied for a pension

BABB, PETER (BLW), OH militia, died 1 Oct 1851, Marysville, Jackson Co, VA; md 18 Jul 1816 Sarah Galaher/Gallager (P), Beaver Co, PA. She died 10 Jan 1879, East Liverpool, Columbiana Co, OH

BABCOCK, SIMEON (BLW), OH militia died 14 Jan 1870, Salem, Shelby Co, OH; md 16 Mar 1837 Elizabeth O. Stout (P), Harrison Co, VA. She died 20 Dec 1894, Walworth, WI

BABER, AMBROSE/EDWARD whose widow Mary applied for a pension

BABER, EDWARD whose widow Jane S. applied for a pension

BABER, PETER (BLW), died 19 Sep 1858, Robertson Co, TN; md 4 Feb 1829 Frances Correll (P), Botetourt Co, VA. She died c1883, LNR P.O. Russellville, Logan Co, KY, 1880

BACKUS, GURDEN B. (BLW), died 16 Sep 1829, Hinesburg, Chittenden Co, VT; md 1 Oct 1813 Lucy Nichols (P), Burlington, VT. She died 10 Aug 1888, LNR Sacramento, CA, 1879

BACON, JOHN (BLW), died 6 Apr 1864; md 6 Apr 1837 Amy Wells (P), LNR Petersburg,

BACON (continued) Dinwiddie Co, VA, 1878

BACON, WILLIAM SAVAGE (BLW), died 3 Dec 1856, James City Co, VA; md 7 Dec 1830 Maria A. Marston (P), James City Co, Va. She died c1886, her LNR James City Co, VA, 1878

BACUM/BECKOM, MATHIAS whose widow Elizabeth applied for a pension

BADGLEY/BADSLEY/BAGELY, ABRAHAM (P, BLW), LNR Wood Co, WV, 1871; md 15 Feb 1821 Mary Grogan, Lee Creek, Wood Co, VA

BAGBY, BENNET M. (P, BLW), died 30 Nov 1884, Powhatan Co, VA; md (1) Rebecca ---, (2) --- Montague, (3) --- Davis, (4) 11 Dec 1860 Louisa B. Flippin (P), Prince Edward Co, VA. She died c1 Jul 1903, LNR Powhatan Courthouse, Powhatan Co, VA, 1885

BAGBY, FREDERICK (BLW), died Dec 1863, LNR Logan Co, KY; md Sep 1810 Nancy Sears (P), Buckingham Co, VA

BAGBY, HENRY (BLW), died 10 Feb 1868, Cumberland Co, VA; md 10 Jan 1921 Susan Hudgens (P), Buckingham Co, VA. She died 9 Jan 1888, LNR Flanagan Mills, Cumberland Co, VA

BAGBY, JOHN (P, BLW), LNR King and Queen Co, VA, 1878; md Elizabeth Motley, King and Queen Co, VA

BAGBY, LANDON (P, BLW), died 3 Sep 1874, LNR P.O. St. Joseph, Buchanan Co, MO; md 24 Dec 1818 Nancy Field (P), Barren Co, KY. Her LNR Buchanan Co, MO, 1878

BAGBY, ROBERT (P, BLW), LNR P.O. Olmstead, Logan Co, KY, 1871; md Apr 1817 Frances ---, Buckingham Co, VA. Widower.

BAGGS, JOHN (BLW), died 20 Oct 1863, Morrow Co, OH; md 23 Oct 1825 Isabell Kilgore (P), Richland Co, OH. She died c20 Sep 1891, Corsica, OH, LNR P.O. Corsica, Morrow Co, OH, 1879

BAGNALL, HENRY (BLW), died 25 Mar 1869, Isle of Wight Co, VA; md (1) --- Addison, (2) --- Riggan, (3) --- Bloxum, (4) 22 Feb 1864 Julia Ann --- (P), Isle of Wight Co, VA. Her LNR P.O. Smithfield, Isle of Wight Co, VA, 1878

BAGWELL, HELEY (P, BLW), MD militia, LNR Bell Haven, Accomac Co, VA, 1871; md 23 Dec 1819 Elizabeth Bloxsom, Locustville, VA

BAILES, JOSEPH (BLW), died 25 Oct 1864, Moultrie Co, IL; md 19 Sep 1822 Elizabeth Devins (P), Ross Co, OH. She died c1896, LNR Sullivan, Moultrie Co, OH, 1887

BAILES, WILSON (P, BLW), died c1876, LNR Jackson Co, OH, 1871; md 17 Mar 1868 Sarah Mackinson, Jackson Co, OH

BAILEY, ANDREW (BLW), KY militia, died 24 Aug 1851, Leonard, KY; md 18 Apr 1814 Anna Kelly (P), Lee Co, VA. She died 17 Jan 1896, Leonard, Harlan Co, KY

BAILEY, ELISHA (BLW), died 6 Dec 1860, Chesterfield Co, Va; md 16 Nov 1841 China W. Chalkley (P), Chesterfield Co, VA. She died c1891, LNR Ettricks, Chesterfield Co, VA, 1879

BAILEY, GEORGE whose widow Frances applied for a pension

BAILEY, JAMES (P, BLW), LNR Millville, King George Co, VA, 1871

BAILEY, JAMES (P, BLW), died 4 Jul 1882, Campbell Co, TN; md (1)Susan Clark, (2) 23 Feb

BAILEY (continued) 1873 Sophia (---) Heninger (P), Campbell Co, TN. Her LNR P.O. Wellspring, Campbell Co, TN, 1882

BAILEY, JEREMIAH whose widow Mary H. applied for a pension

BAILEY, JOHN (BLW), OH militia, died Norfolk, VA; md 31 Dec 1806 Nancy Shephard (P), Fluvanna Co, VA. Her LNR Lattaville, Ross Co, OH, 1872

BAILEY, JOHN (BLW), died 5 Nov 1829, Campbell Co, VA; md 14 Feb 1811 Mary Callaham (P), Campbell Co, VA. Her LNR P.O. Mt. Zion, Campbell Co, VA, 1878

BAILEY, JOHN (BLW), died 24 Apr 1856, Urbana, VA; md 7 May 1827 Eliza Hughes (P), New York, NY. She died 24 Apr 1896, LNR Urbana, Middlesex Co, VA, 1878

BAILEY, JOHN (BLW), died 30 Apr 1862, Darbyville, OH; md 20 Feb 1817 Jane Stufflebeam (P), Pickaway Co, OH. She died 28 Apr 1887, Five Points, Pickaway Co, OH

BAILEY, JOHN H. (BLW), died 3 Apr 1858,Hardin Co, KY; md c9 Dec 1809, Mary/Polly Gooden/Goodwin (P), Albemarle Co, VA. Her LNR P.O. Elizabethtown, Hardin Co, KY, 1871

BAILEY, JOSEPH (BLW), died 11 Dec 1875, Harrison Co, WV; md (1) Peggy Hickman, (2) 7 Jul 1827 Delila Davison/Johnson (P), Harrison Co, VA. She died 11 Nov 1898, LNR Clarksburg, Harrison Co, WV, 1878

BAILEY, LEWIS M. (BLW application rejected), died 17 Oct 1817, Madison Co, Va; md 10 Oct 1816 Phebe Howson Clark (P), Halifax Co, VA. Her LNR

BAILEY (continued)
P.O. Scottsburg, Halifax Co, VA, 1878

BAILEY, NUNNERY (BLW), died 1852/3 Equality, IL, LNR Gallatin Co, IL, 1852; md Oct 1808 Margaret Stephens (P), New London, Campbell Co, VA. She died 21 or 22 Apr 1885, LNR Lynchburg, Campbell Co, VA

BAILEY, ROBERT (P, BLW), LNR Millstadt, St. Clair Co, IL, 1871; md 1817 Nancy Jarrard, Wellesville, Hancock Co, VA. She died Oct 1820

BAILEY, SAMUEL (P, BLW), LNR P.O. Mulloys, Robertson Co, TN, 1871

BAILEY, TARLTON (P, BLW), died 31 Oct 1874, Plattsburg, Clinton Co, MO; md (1) Malinda Wheeler, (2) 18 Apr 1841 Elizabeth Hudson (P), Tazewell, Claiborne Co, TN. She died 12 Jan 1889, LNR P.O. Lazette, Cowley Co, MO, 1878

BAILEY, WILLIAM whose widow Frances applied for a pension

BAILEY, WILLIAM B. (P, BLW), died Jul 1871, not married. His LNR Burhamsville, New Kent Co, VA, 1871

BAILEY, WILSON (BLW), died 27 Apr 1863, Lincoln Co, TN; md 10 Nov 1821 Nancy Moore (P), Albemarle Co, VA. She died c1894, LNR Lincoln Co, TN

BAILEY, ZACHARIAH (P, BLW), died 7 Apr 1884, McDowell Co, WV; md (1) Ester Amburn, (2) 14 Jun 1832 Rachel Gladon (P), Crooked Creek, Grayson Co, VA. She died 29 Aug 1902, Mayhenry, WV, LNR P.O. Pocahontas, McDowell Co, WV, 1886

BAILIE, ROBERT (BLW), died 2 Feb 1854, Scott Co, VA; md 1803 Eleanor Carnahan (P),

BAILIE (continued)
County Down, Ireland. Her LNR Estillville, Scott Co, VA, 1871

BAILY, WALTER (BLW), died 21 Mar 1864, Selma, IL; md Jun 1812 Orpha Wilson (P), Leesburg, Loudoun Co, VA. She died c1879, LNR Pleasant Hill, McLean Co, IL, 1872

BAIN, HOPE (P, BLW), MD militia, died 5 Oct 1876, Goldsboro, NC; md (1) Mariah Roach, (2) 23 Dec 1847 Joanna E. Ogden (P), Portsmouth, Norfolk Co, VA. Her LNR Goldsboro, NC, 1878

BAINES, BRAY (P, BLW), LNR P.O. Suffolk, Nansemond Co, VA; md 1840 Lavinia Harrell, Nansemond Co, VA

BAIRD, PETER (P, BLW), LNR Surry Co, VA; md 1817 Eliza M. Bingham, Prince George Co, VA

BAKER, ABRAHAM applied for a pension

BAKER, ABRAM (BLW), died 4 Mar 1846, Dubois Co, IN; md 1817 Jane Stewart (P), Bath Co, VA. Her LNR Mt. Prospect, Crawford Co, IN, 1878

BAKER, DANIEL (P, BLW), substitute for brother John, died 11 Aug 1887, LNR Appleton, Licking Co, OH, 1871; md 5 Jan 1820 Rebecca Fravel, Hardy Co, VA

BAKER, DICKERSON (BLW), died 20 Mar 1870, Martin Co, NC; md 22 Jun 1825 Nancy Jordan (P), Martin Co, NC. Her LNR Palmyra, Halifax Co, VA, 1878

BAKER, HILLARIUS applied for a pension

BAKER, ISAAC whose widow Savilla applied for a pension

BAKER, JACOB (P, BLW), LNR Winchester, Frederick Co, VA, 1871; md 6 Jan 1814 Catherine F. Street, Winchester, VA

BAKER, JAMES whose widow Catharine applied for a pension

BAKER, JAMES whose widow Harriet A. applied for a pension

BAKER, JOHN (P, BLW), LNR P.O. Blue Grass, Scott Co, IA; md 6 May c1817 Rhoda Simkins, Stonelick, Clermont Co, OH

BAKER, JOHN (BLW), died 2 Apr 1849, Mt. Crawford, VA; md 1 Nov 1810 Mary Spader (P), Mt. Crawford, VA. She died 3 Jun 1879, Rockingham Co, VA

BAKER, JOHN (BLW), died 29 Mar 1853, Adams Co, IN; md 10 Dec 1812 Sarah Turner (P), Rockingham Co, VA. She died c1876, LNR Ganges, Richland Co, OH, 1874

BAKER, MESHACK whose widow Eleanor applied for a pension

BAKER, PETER (BLW), Ohio Militia, died c3 Oct 1838 or 1840, Miami Co, OH; md c1809 Anna Leseney (P), Franklin Co, VA. She died c1876, LNR Montra, Shelby Co, OH, 1871

BAKER, PHILIP (BLW), died 19 Aug 1851, Rockingham Co, VA; md (1) Elizabeth Fulk, (2) 3 Sep 1838 Matilda (---) Zirkle (P), Shenandoah Co, VA. She died 2 Dec 1880, LNR P.O. New Market, Shenandoah Co, VA, 1878

BAKER, SIMON (P, BLW), died 17 Nov 1882, LNR P.O. Terre Haute, Champaign Co, OH; md (1) Nov 1823 Catherine Darnall, Champaign Co, OH, (2) 16 Nov 1867 Sarah Julien, Addison, Champaign Co, OH

BAKER, WILLIAM (BLW), died 8 Aug 1861, Overton Co, TN; md 10 Feb 1825 Permelia Ganmar (P), Washington Co, VA. She died 1892, LNR Hull, Pickett Co, TN

BALDEN, ALLEN (BLW), died 17 Oct 1861, near Winfield, WV; md 27 Jun 1831 Malinda Wilson (P), Culpeper Court House, Culpeper Co, VA. She died 8 Apr 1901, Charleston, Kanawha Co, WV

BALDERSON, GILBERT H. (BLW), died 9 Feb 1847, Richmond Co, VA; md (1) Rebecca Leycock, (2) 10 Apr 1831 Elizabeth Pope (P), Richmond Co, VA. She died 1 Apr 1889, LNR P.O Newland, Richmond Co, VA, 1878

BALDWIN, BENJAMIN (BLW), died 17 Feb 1865, White Hall, Greene Co, IL; md 9 Apr 1816 Martha Varner (P), Lebanon Co, OH. She died 10 Oct 1888, Roodhouse, IL

BALDWIN, ROBERT T. (BLW), died 11 Sep 1863, Winchester, VA; md (1) Sally Macky, (2) 22 Feb 1830 Portia Lee Hopkins (P), Winchester, Frederick Co, VA. Her LNR Winchester, 1878

BALDWIN, WILLIAM (P, BLW), died 3 Oct 1873, Campbell Co, KY; md (1) ? (2) 1841 Mary (---) Cheek (P), Adams Co, OH. Her LNR P.O. Alexandria, Campbell Co, KY, 1871

BALDWIN, WILLIAM (BLW), died 1 Mar 1858, Morgantown, VA; md 8 Oct 1807 Nancy Burris (P), Morgantown, VA. Here LNR Morgantown, Monongalia Co, WV, 1871

BALES, VINCENT whose widow Joanah applied for a pension

BALL, CURTIS (BLW), died 20 Sep 1851, King and Queen Co, VA; md 24 Dec 1814 Martha Burnett (P), Essex Co, VA. She died c1887, LNR P.O. Old Church, Hanover Co, VA, 1879

BALL, FANTLEY (BLW)

BALL, GEORGE L. (P, BLW),

18

BALL (continued)
LNR Warrenton, Fauquier Co, VA, 1871; md c17 Nov 1816 Catharine Kerfoot, Clarke Co, VA

BALL, HORATIO applied for a pension

BALL, JOHN (BLW), died 7 Jan 1871, Culpeper Co, VA; md (1) Ann Carver, (2) 7 Sep 1837 Athaline Pilcher (P), Fauquier Co, VA. She died c1885, LNR P.O. Fauquier Springs, Fauquier Co, VA, 1878

BALL, THOMAS (BLW), died 15 Apr 1814, Northumberland Co, VA; md 24 Apr 1800 Louisa Edwards (P). She later md --- Spiller, her LNR Northumberland Co, VA, 1859

BALLARD, AARON (P, BLW), died 1 Oct 1877, Henry Co, IN; md (1) --- De Witt, (2) 5 Jan 1832 Nancy Pearson (P), Franklin Co, Va. Her LNR Henry Co, IN, 1878

BALLARD, ASA (BLW), died 20 Oct 1846, Perry Co, IN; md 22 Oct 1820 Sarah Webb (P), Smith, Stokes Co, NC. She died Apr 1881, LNR P.O. Reno, Perry Co, IN, 1879

BALLARD, CHARLES whose widow Ursula applied for a pension

BALLARD, CHRISTOPHER A. (BLW), died c1886; md 25 Oct 1838 Louisa S. --- (P), Carthage, Hancock Co, IL. Her LNR P.O. Pleasanton, Atascosa Co, TX, 1881

BALLARD, JAMES (BLW), died Sep 1848, Spotsylvania Co, VA; md 10 Apr 1843 Mary Ann Pusey (P), Spotsylvania Co, VA. She died 27 Apr 1881, LNR P.O. Fredericksburg, Spotsylvania Co, VA, 1879

BALLARD, PHILIP (BLW), died 6 Oct 1864, LNR West Kinderhook, Tipton Co, IN, 1856; md (1) --- Smock (2) 29 Nov 1938

BALLARD (continued)
Ruth --- (P), Marion co, IN. She died 13 Jun 1888, IN, LNR Tipton Co, IN, 1878

BALLARD, THOMAS (BLW)

BALLARD, WILLIAM (P, BLW), LNR P.O. Mechum's River, Albemarle Co, VA, 1871

BALLARD, WILLIAM (P, BLW), died 4 Jan 1877, Marion Co, IA; md (1) Lucy ---, (1) 31 Mar 1864 Phebe --- Strots (P), Marion Co, IA. Her LNR Pleasantville, Marion Co, IA, 1878

BALLENTINE, CASTOR F. (BLW), died 5 Apr 1856, Feliciana, Fulton Co, KY; md 1 Dec 1828 Nancy Taylor (P), Wilson Co, TN. She died 20 Dec 1886, LNR Gadsden, Crockett Co, TN, 1879

BALLINGER, RICHARD (BLW), died 10 Jul 1859, Floyd Co, VA; md (1) Sally Wade, (2) 9 Mar 1857 Martha Lovel (P), Jacksonville, Floyd Co, VA. She died 3 Jun 1892, LNR P.O. Floyd Court House, Floyd Co, VA, 1888

BALLOW, CHARLES A./ANDERSON (BLW), died 4 July 1865, Halifax Co, VA; md 10 Jun 1823 Rebecca A. Medley (P), Halifax Co, VA. Her LNR News Ferry, Halifax Co, VA, 1878

BALLOW, THOMAS H. (BLW) whose widow Parmelia J. applied for a pension

BALSAR/BOLSER, BENJAMIN (P, BLW), died 18 Feb 1873, LNR P.O. Brownsburg, Rockbridge Co, VA, 1871

BALSLEY, JACOB (BLW), died 28 Mar 1862, Augusta Co, VA; md (1) Nancy Rippeteo (2) 27 Dec 1855 Martha Ann Claytor (P), Staunton, Augusta Co, VA. She died 3 Oct 1906, LNR Sherando, Augusta Co, VA, 1879

BALTHIS, GEORGE W. (BLW),

BALTHIS (continued)
died Spring 1865, Culpeper Court House, Culpeper Co, VA; md 3 Feb 1825 Sarah Ann Day (P), Charlottesville, VA. Her LNR Charlottesville, Albemarle Co, VA, 1878

BANDAY, THOMAS (BLW), died 15 Sep 1844, Bedford Co, VA; md Mary/Polly West (P), Bedford Co, VA. She died 16 May 1889, Christiansburg, Montgomery Co, VA

BANDY, SAMUEL whose widow Nancy applied for a pension

BANDY/BRADY, WILLIAM (P, BLW), LNR Sanford, Vigo Co, IN; md 1811 Elizabeth Jordan, Botetourt Co, VA

BANE, HUGH (BLW), died 16 Oct 1858, Pleasantville, Marion Co, IA; md (1) ?, (2) 9 Feb 1829 Louisa Kanson/Crusen (P). She died c Feb 1895 Carbondale, CO

BANKHEAD/BANKET, CHARLES L. (BLW), died 19 Jun 1833, Charlottesville, VA; md (1) ?, (2) 1 Dec 1829 Mary Ann Carthrae (P), Port Republic, VA. Her LNR Orange Courthouse, Orange Co, VA, 1878

BANKHEAD, WILLIAM applied for a pension

BANKS, JOHN applied for a pension

BANKS, JOHN F. (P, BLW), died 6 Aug 1883, LNR Decatur, Morgan Co, AL, 1878; md 2 Aug 1822 Frances Elizabeth Roberts, Culpeper Co, VA

BANTON, WASHINGTON (BLW), died 25 Apr 1842, Monroe Co, MO; md 27 May 1818 Elizabeth Maxey (P), Buckingham Co, VA. She died c1883, LNR Bethany, Harrison co, MO

BARBEE, JOHN S. (BLW), died 3 Sep 1856, Vigo Co, IN; md 1 Dec 1825 Margaret Thurman (P), Spencer Co, KY. Her LNR

BARBEE (continued)
P.O. Pimento, Vigo Co, IN, 1878

BARBEE, JOHN F. applied for a pension

BARBEE, JOSEPH A. applied for a pension

BARBEE, OWEN F. applied for a pension

BARBEE, SAMPSON, Sr. (P, BLW), LNR Indianapolis, Marion Co, IN, 1871; md 17 Jan 1809 Lucy Payne, Stafford Co, VA

BARBEE, WILLIAM W. (BLW), died 12 or 13 Nov 1857/8, Columbia, KY; md 14 Nov 1816 Sallie Foley (P), Fauquier Co, VA. She died c1887, LNR Columbia, Adair co, KY, 1878

BARBER, CALEB (P, BLW), died 5 Jun 1877, Pittsylvania Co, VA; md (1) Elizabeth Custer, (2) 21 Sep 1843 Tabitha A. Robertson (P), Chatham, Pittsylvania Co, VA. She died 21 May 1901, LNR P.O. Bergers Store, Pittsylvania Co, VA, 1878

BARBER, JOHN (P-rejected, BLW), died 1 Jun 1875, Pittsylvania Co, VA; md (1) Mourning Robertson, (2) 20 Apr 1864 Eliza Carter (P), Pittsylvania Co, VA. She died 10 Jan 1902, LNR P.O. Chatham, Pittsylvania Co, VA

BARBER, LAWSON (P-rejected, BLW), died 20 Oct 1876, Winchester, VA; md Aug 1826 Elizabeth Tooms (P), nr Port Royal, Essex Co, VA. She died 15 Feb 1885, Winchester, Frederick Co, VA

BARBOUR, THOMAS (P, BLW), died 14 Mar 1874, Amherst Co, VA; md 1 Mar 1821 Elizabeth I. M. Yancy (P), Bedford Co, VA. Her LNR P.O. Cool Well, Amherst Co, VA, 1879

BARCLAY, ROBERT (BLW),

BARCLAY (continued)
died 8 or 19 Oct 1847,
Portsmouth, VA; md (1) ---
Dickson, (2) 25 Dec 1833
Selina White (P), Portsmouth,
VA. She died 1 Jul 1887,
Portsmouth, Norfolk Co, VA
BARDIN, JOHN K. (P, BLW)
LNR Morven, Amelia Co, VA;
md Dec 1815 Catharine Sadler
BARE/BEAR, VALENTINE/
FELTY (BLW), died 15 Jun
1855, Rockingham Co, VA; md
2 Oct 1808 Christina Ritchie
(P), Rockingham Co, VA. Her
LNR Brocks Gap, Rockingham
Co, VA, 1873
BARGAHISER, JACOB (P,
BLW), died Aug 1871, Shelby,
Richland Co, OH
BARGDOLL/BARTHALL, SOLO-
MON (P, BLW), died 8 Oct
1874, Chillicothe, Livingston
Co, MO; md (1) Christina
Peters, (2) --- Smith, (3) 12
Dec 1870 Elizabeth (---)
Brown, (P-rejected). She died
28 Jan 1880, Livingston Co,
MO, LNR Chillicothe, MO
BARGER, FREDERICK (BLW)
BARGER, PETER (BLW), died
11 Apr 1855, Rockbridge Co,
VA; md (1) Ann Pettigrew, (2)
22 Feb 1849 Mary Keffer (P),
Rockbridge Co, VA. She died
4 July 1893, LNR P.O. Lexi-
ngton, Rockbridge Co, VA,
1879
BARKER, ALEXANDER (BLW),
died 26 Jun 1859, Sussex Co,
VA; md 24 Dec 1839 Annie
Jane Tatum (P), Prince George
Co, VA. She died 28 Oct 1905,
Waverley, VA, LNR Waverly
Station, Sussex Co, VA, 1878
BARKER, ANDERSON whose wi-
dow Susan applied for a pen-
sion
BARKER, BROOKEY (BLW),
died 10 Jul 1866, Henryville,
IN; md (1) Margaret B. Barker
(2) 11 Jul 1840 Elizabeth (---)

BARKER (continued)
Chappell (P), Shepherdville,
Bullitt Co, KY. She died 4
Mar 1881, Louisville, Jeffer-
son Co, KY
BARKER, GEORGE (P, BLW),
died 14 Jul 1873, Hanover Co,
VA; md (1) Mildred Lipscord,
(2) 12 Nov 1840 Mary Wade
(P), Hanover Co, VA. She died
26 Mar 1898, LNR Old Church,
Hanover Co, VA
BARKER, HENRY (BLW), died
Jul 1863, Hamilton Coi, OH;
md Mar 1853 Mary Spencer
(P), Lee Co, VA. She died 2
Jan 1905, Stickleyville, Lee
Co, VA
BARKER, JAMES whose widow
Nancy applied for a pension
BARKER, JOHN whose widow
Mary S. applied for a pension
BARKER, WILLIAM (BLW), died
27 Dec 1863, Herndon, Fairfax
Co, VA; md Aug 1856/7 Milly
Williams (P), Herndon, VA.
Her LNR Herndon, VA, 1878
BARKER, WILLIAM A. (BLW),
died 14 Feb 1837, Giles Co,
VA; md 22 Oct 1817 Sarah
Hobbs (P), Franklin Co, VA.
Her LNR Wyandott, Wyandott
Co, KS, 1878
BARKSDALE, ELISHA (BLW),
died 16 June 1850, Halifax Co,
VA; md (1) Elizabeth Logan,
(2) 22 Dec 1819 Rebecca F. L.
Spragins (P), Halifax Co, VA.
She died 19 Apr 1883, Barks-
dale, Halifax Co, VA
BARKSDALE, JOHN (BLW), died
8 Aug 1825, Pickens Co, AL;
md 12 Jul 1805 Ann P, Green
(P), Halifax Co, VA. Her LNR
P.O. DeKalb, Kemper Co, MS,
1874
BARKSDALE, JOHN (P, BLW),
died 30 Nov 1871, LNR P.O.
Stony Point, Albemarle Co,
VA, 1871
BARLEY, JACOB (P, BLW),
LNR Smith's Creek, Rocking-

21

BARLEY (continued)
ham Co, VA; md 10 Mar 1820 Phoebe Hurton, Smith's Creek, VA

• BARNER, WILLIAM (BLW), died 1 Jul 1871, Brunswick Co, VA; md 11 Feb 1817 Catharine C. Steed (P), Warren Co, NC. She died 5 Jan 1892, LNR P.O. White Plains, Brunswick Co, VA, 1878

BARNES, ABRAHAM applied for a pension

BARNES, CHARLES (BLW)

BARNES, CHARLES (BLW)

BARNES, EDWARD D. whose widow Mary applied for a pension

BARNES, ENOS (BLW), died 9 Jan 1862, Watkins, Schuyler Co, NY; md (1) Rebecca Weeks, (2) 21 Jun 1832 Eliza Kilpatrick (P), Starkey, Yates Co, NY. She died c1888, LNR Wellsville, Allegany Co, NY, 1878

BARNES, HENRY (BLW), died 5 Jul 1840, Madison Co, VA; md (1) --- Gibbs, (2) 21 Sep 1833 Letitia Ann Rapley (P), Madison Court House, Madison Co, VA. She died 7 May 1889, LNR P.O. State Mills, Rappahannock Co, VA, 1879

BARNES, JAMES (P, BLW), died c1876, LNR P.O. Olympus, Overton Co, TN, 1871; md 12 May 1819 Nancy Mullins, Overton Co, TN

BARNES, JAMES, died 11 or 15 Feb 1872, Nansemond Co, VA; md (1) Elizabeth ---, (2) 26 Apr 1863 Martha A. (---) Beaman (P), Isle of Wight Co, VA. She died 16 Jan 1893, LNR Isle of Wight Co, VA

BARNES, JONATHAN (BLW), died 26 Oct 1860 at sea; md 27 Mar 1815 Charlotte Moore (P), Craney Island, VA. She died c1882, LNR Orrington, Penobscot Co, ME

BARNES, JOSEPH P. (P, BLW),

BARNES (continued)
died 25 May 1881, Richmond, VA

BARNES, RICHARD (BLW), whose widow was Lucy A.

BARNES, WILLIAM whose widow Elizabeth J. applied for a pension

BARNES, WILLIAM J. (BLW), died 8 Feb 1867, Lawrence Co, AL; md 9 Jul 1824 Sarah Gray (P), Lawrence Co, AL. She died c1896, LNR P.O. Oakville, Lawrence Co, AL, 1880

BARNETT, AMOS (BLW), died 29 Jun 1869, Clark Co, MO; md 26 May 1815 Sarah Gibbons (P), Wood Co, VA. She died 20 Apr 1890, Athens, Clark Co, MO

BARNETT, ISAAC whose widow Susannah applied for a pension

BARNETT, JOSEPH (BLW), died Nov 1832, Clarksburg, Harrison Co, VA; md 23 Feb 1827 Rebecca Barker (P), Smithtown, Monongalia Co, VA. She died 1 Jul 1892, LNR P.O. Randall, Monongalia Co, WV, 1879

BARNETT, ROBERT (BLW), died 1 Jul 1871, Montgomery Co, VA; md (1) Nancy Willis, (2) 19 May 1834 Elizabeth Jewell (P), Montgomery Co, VA. She died 25 Dec 1898, LNR P.O. McDonald's Mill, Montgomery Co, VA, 1878

BARNETT, WILLIAM (P, BLW), LNR Hickory, Newton Co, MS, 1872; md 24 Dec 1816 Lucy Barnett, Leaksville, Rockingham Co, NC

BARNHART, PETER whose widow Nancy applied for a pension

BARNS, JOHN (BLW), died 6 Dec 1846, Sanes Mills, Hardin Co, KY; md 4 Jan 1809 Frances H. Burch (P), Pittsylvania Co, VA. Her LNR P.O. Hows Valley, Hardin Co, KY, 1871

BARNS, STEPHEN (BLW)

BARR, JOHN D. (P, BLW), died 16 Jun 1868, Upperville, Fauquier Co, VA; md 1818 Lydia Shipman (P), Pauquier Co, VA. She died 28 Oct 1886, Upperville, VA

BARR, WILLIAM (P, BLW), LNR P.O. Centerville, Delaware Co, OH; md 24 Dec 1818 Elizabeth Yoe, Frederick Co, VA

BARRATT, JAMES (P, BLW), LNR P.O. Emory Mines, Roane Co, TN

BARRETT, CHARLES (BLW), NY militia, died 15 Sep 1838, Hamilton Co, OH; md 13 Jun 1826 Mildred Gentry (P), Albemarle Co, VA. She died 8 Mar 1904, LNR P.O. Forest Hill, Decatur Co, IN

BARRETT, FREDERICK (P, BLW), died 11 Oct 1879, Hell Grove, VA; md 1815 Martha Lawson, Charlotte Co, VA

BARRETT, SAMUEL (BLW), died 2 Oct 1863, Knightstown, Henry Co, IN; md 27 May 1819 Clarissa B. McComas (P), Cabell Co, VA. Her LNR Knightstown, IN, 1878

BARRETT, WILLIS (BLW)

BARRICK, ISAAC and widow Mary both applied for a pension

BARRON, JAMES whose widow Mary B applied for a pension

BARROT/BARRETT, JOHN (BLW), died 20 Jan 1844 or 1845, Hawkins Co, TN; md 12 Aug 1828 Elizabeth (---) Kelly (P), Hawkins Co, TN. Her LNR P.O. Estellville, Scott Co, VA, 1878

BARROTT, JOHN whose widow Mary applied for a pension

BARROW, LOUIS (BLW), died 9 Aug 1857, Brunswick Co, VA; md (1) ?, (2) 26 Jun 1839 Mary J. Browder (P), Brunswick Co,

BARROW (continued) VA. She died 8 Apr 1898, LNR P.O. Barrows Store, Brunswick Co, VA

BARTEE, JOHN (BLW), died 21 May 1857, Norfolk, VA; md (1) Mary Widgeon, (2) 10 Apr 1845 Ellen (---) Hodges (P), Norfolk, VA. She died c1894, LNR Baltimore, MD, 1878

BARTLETT, JAMES (BLW), died 10 Feb 1866, Columbia, VA; md 30 Jan 1808 Sarah Troop (P), Westmoreland Co, VA. Her LNR Columbia, Fluvanna Co, VA, 1871

BARTLEY, MERRIWEATHER whose widow Sally M. applied for a pension

BARTON, NICHOLAS (BLW), died 21 Jan 1858, Rockbridge Co, VA; md (1) Magdalene Harvey, (2) 24 Apr 1854 Sallie C. McClelland (P), Nelson Co, Va. She died 19 Apr 1908, LNR P.O. Centreville, Queen Anne Co, MD, 1880

BARTON, THOMAS (P, BLW), LNR P.O. Shinnston, Harrison Co, WV, 1871; md 28 Feb 1808 Sally Drummond. She died 20 Oct 1853, Fayette Co, PA

BARTON, WILLIAM died 18 Dec 1862, Mt Crawford, VA; md 11 Oct 1842 Nancy M. Hill (P), Rockingham Co, VA. She died 4 Apr 1904, Hagerstown, MD, LNR Martinsburg, Berkeley Co, WV, 1887

BARTRUM, JAMES P. (P, BLW), died 23 Sep 1875, Boyd Co, KY; md 28 Feb 1870 Rebecca Sexton (P-rejected), Boyd Co, KY. Her LNR Foutouma, Carter Co, KY, 1890

BASCUE, CHARLES (P, BLW), LNR Hillsborough, Loudoun Co, VA, 1871; md 16 Jan 1816 Rachel Buckles, Shepherdstown, VA. (Served under name of Charles Pascue)

BASETT/BASSETT, ALEXANDER H. (P, BLW), died 8 Oct 1880, Henry Co, VA; md (1) Mary Kroger, (2) 3 Dec 1872 Ann R. Hardy (P), Henry Co, Va. She died c1890, LNR P.O. Spencer's Store, Henry Co, VA, 1880

BASHAM, NATHAN (BLW), died 6 Nov 1869, Floyd Co, Va; md 27 Jan 1810 Ellen/Ellender Ross (P), Bedford Co, VA. Her LNR Floyd Court House, Floyd Co, VA, 1871

BASHAW, HOLMAN (BLW), died 17 Jul 1864, Fluvanna Co, VA; md (1) Polly Snead, (2) 13 Dec 1840 Elizabeth H. (---) Bramham (P). She died c1889, LNR Fork Union, Fluvanna Co, Va, 1878

BASHAW, PETER (P, BLW), died c1872, LNR P.O. Central Plains, Fluvanna Co, VA, 1871

BASKET, REUBEN (BLW), died 6 Apr 1857, md (1) ?, (2) 15 Jul 1852 Mary W. Brown (P), King and Queen Co, VA. Her LNR Walkerton, King and Queen Co, VA, 1879

BASKETT, JAMES (BLW), died 28 Mar 1863, Shelby Co, KY; md 9 Feb 1813 Mildred Shepherd (P), Fluvanna Co, VA. Her LNR P.O. Badgad, Shelby Co, KY, 1871

BASKETT/BASKET, JESSE (BLW), died 21 Dec 1836, Fluvanna Co, Va; md (1) Sallie T. Kent, (2) 9 Mar 1824 Susan C. Perkins (P), Louisa Co, VA. Her LNR P.O. Hunter Lodge, Fluvanna Co, VA, 1878

BASKETT, ROBERT (P, BLW), died 20 Mar 1880, Howard Co, MO; md (1) Lucy Cruidson, (2) Sarah ---, (3) 10 May 1877 Mary (---) Kingsberry (P), Macon City, Macon Co, MO. She died 20 May 1901, LNR Callao, Macon Co, MO, 1885

BASS, ROBERT (BLW), died 12

BASS (continued) Oct 1870, Powhatan Co, VA; md (1) Ann Ellett, (2) Martha Gates, (3) 22 Dec 1853 Mary A. Atkinson (P), Powhatan Co, VA. She died 30 Jun 1898, LNR P.O. Powhatan Court House, Powhatan Co, VA, 1878

BASYE, JOSEPH (BLW), died 2 Jan 1850, Heatsville, Northumberland Co, VA; md (1) Hannah Martin, (2) 22 Sep 1844 Sallie E. C. (McNamara) Lawson (P), Northumberland Co, VA. Her LNR Whitestone, Lancaster Co, VA, 1879

BATEMAN, SMITH (BLW), died 23 Jul 1860, Augusta Co, VA; md 23 Oct 1816 Susan Lohr (P), NC. She died 1 Jul 1886, Fishersville, Augusta Co, VA

BATEMAN, WILLIAM (BLW), died 22 Jan 1855, Port Republic, Va; md 2 Jun 1813 Elizabeth Allen (P), Augusta Co, VA. Her LNR Port Republic, Rockingham Co, VA, 1872

BATES, JAMES W. (BLW), died 3 Sep 1864, Taylor Co, KY; md 15 Mar 1837 Nancy Terrell (P), Campbell Co, VA. She died 1 Oct 1895, LNR P.O. Greensburg, Green Co, KY

BATES, ROWLAND H. (BLW), died 3 Oct 1871, Albemarle Co, VA; md (1) Ann Boyd, (2) 30 Oct 1849 Susan G. Woods (P), Albemarle Co, VA. She died 31 May 1880, Batesville, Albemarle Co, VA

BATES, WILLIAM P. (P, BLW), LNR Spencer, Roane Co, WV; md 2 Jan 1824 Catharine Crist, Greenbrier Co, VA

BATES, WILLIAM H. (BLW), USA, died 5 Dec 1833, Norfolk, VA; md 28 Aug 1815 Eliza Boyle (P), Baltimore, MD. She died 17 Feb 1881, San Francisco, VA, LNR Salinas, Monterey Co, CA, 1878

BATEY/BEATIE, THOMAS applied for a pension
BATIS, CHARLES (P, BLW), LNR New Hope, Augusta Co, VA, 1871. Widower.
BATTIN, WILEY (BLW), died 31 Jan 1865, Isle of Wight Co, VA; md 24 Feb 1825 Anna Holding (P), Isle of Wight Co, VA. Her LNR P.O. Isle of Wight Court House, Isle of Wight Co, VA, 1878
BAUGH, RICHARD (P, BLW), died 16 Aug 1878, Campbell Co, Va; md 31 Dec 1816 Elizabeth H. Lewellin (P), Campbell Co, VA. Her LNR P.O. Campbell Courthouse, Campbell Co, VA, 1878
BAUGHAN, MOSES whose widow Sarah applied for a pension
BAUGHAN, WILLIAM (BLW), died 16 May 1861, Hanover Co, Va; md (1) Sidner Terrill, (2) 3 Feb 1850 Elizabeth P. Sledd (P), Hanover Co, VA. She died c1886, LNR Richmond, Henrico Co, VA, 1878
BAUGHER, JOHN (BLW), died Aug 1859, Wabash Co, IN; md Jun 1811 Rachel Hall (P), Rockingham Co, VA. She died 5 Mar 1883, LNR P.O. Liberty Mills, Wabash Co, IN, 1872
BAUGHMAN, DAVID whose widow Ann applied for a pension
BAUGHMAN, JOHN (BLW), TN militia, died 1857, Carroll Co, AR; md 22 Jan 1805 Dorothy Moier (P), Botetourt Co, VA. Her LNR Marble Creek, Iron Co, MO
BAXTER, JAMES whose widow Sarah applied for a pension
BAXTER, WILLIAM (BLW), died 4 Nov 1864, Fauquier Co, VA; md (1) Rebecca ---, (2) 21 Jan 1856 Elizabeth Green (P), Stafford Co, VA. Her LNR P.O. Bristersburg, Fauquier Co, VA, 1879
BAYES, ISHAM (P, BLW), died

BAYES (continued) 22 Jul 1874, LNR P.O. Salyersville, Magoffin Co, KY; md 9 Jul 1818 Polly Taylor, Patrick Co, VA
BAYLES, JESSE (BLW), whose widow Elizabeth also received BLW
BAYLIS, JOHN E. (P, BLW), LNR Winchester, Frederick Co, VA, 1871; md Catherine Davis, Frederick Co, VA
BAYLIS, THOMAS B. (BLW), died 13 Sep 1869, Frederick Co, VA; md 3 Jan 1825 Mary K. Wilson (P), Frederick Co, VA. Her LNR Winchester, VA, 1878
BAYLOR, GEORGE (BLW), died 1 Jan 1866, Georgetown, IN; md c26 Apr 1813 Eva Argenbright (P), Augusta Co, VA. Her LNR P.O. Georgetown, Floyd Co, IN, 1871
BAYLY/BAGLY, ALBERT (P, BLW), died 12 Dec 1876, Delaplane Station, VA; md 8 Nov 1817 Sallie Hobson (P), Washington, DC. Her LNR P.O. Delaplane, Fauquier Co, VA, 1878. Albert was erroneously pensioned as BAGLEY
BAYLY, THOMAS M. (BLW), died 7 Jan 1834, Accomac Co, VA; md (1) Margaret Cropper, (2) 21 Dec 1826 Jane O. (Coward) Addison (P), Northampton Co, VA. She died c1888, LNR Richmond, Va, 1878. Her first husband was Col. Kendal Addison
BAYS, JAMES (BLW), NC Militia, died 4 May 1870, Choctaw Co, MS; md Jul 1816 Nancy Cannon (P), Patrick Co, VA. Her LNR P.O. Greensboro, Sumner Co, MS
BEACH, JAMES (BLW), died 8 Jul 1856, Northampton Co, VA; md (1) Ester Hall, (2) 17 Dec 1844 Elizabeth (---) Robins

BEACH (continued)
(P). She died c1887, LNR Hadlock, Northampton Co, VA, 1878

BEACH, JOHN S. whose widow Elizabeth B. applied for a pension

BEADLE, WILLIAM (BLW), TN militia, died 2 Feb 1863, Wilson Co, TN; md 11 May 1800 Sarah Owens (P), Halifax Co, VA. Her LNR P.O. Lebanon, Wilson Co, TN, 1871

BEAHM/BEEM, MARTIN R. (P, BLW), LNR P.O. Green Mount, Rockingham Co, VA; md 9 Jun 1823 Christina Neff, New Market, VA

BEAL, DRURY (BLW), died Sep 1870, Northampton Co, NC; md (1) Temperance ---, (2) Sally Flythe, (3) Dec 1866 Susan (Johnson) Blythe (P), Northampton Co, NC. Her LNR P.O. Murfreesboro, Northampton Co, TN, 1886

BEAL/BEALE/BEEL/BELL, RICHARD (P, BLW)

BEAL, WILLIAM (BLW), died 7 Feb 1844, Henry Co, VA; md 22 Dec 1814 Nancy Lea (P), Pittsylvania Co, VA. She died 9 Jul 1878, Ridgeway, Henry Co, VA

BEALE, CHARLES, died 17 Apr 1853, Gordonsville, Va; md 18 Feb 1820 Mary H. Gordon (P), Gordonsville, Orange Co, VA. Her LNR Gordonsville, 1878

BEALE, JOHN W. (P, BLW), died 5 Dec 1881, LNR Eureka, St. Louis Co, MO, 1872; md 10 Dec 1815 Ann M. Beale, Mason Co, VA

BEALE, RICHARD (BLW), died 29 Mar 1833, Natchez, MS; md (1) Hannah Wilson, (2) 26 Nov 1829 Margaret (---) Clark (P), Breckenridge Co, KY. She died 31 Dec 1884, LNR Cynthiana, Harrison Co, KY

BEALE, SAMUEL whose widow

BEALE (continued)
Rebecca applied for a pension

BEALE, WILLIAM C. (BLW), died 22 or 25 Apr 1850, Fredericksburg, VA; md (1) Susan Vowles (2) 20 Feb 1834 Jane B. Howison (P), Fredericksburg, VA. Her LNR Fredericksburg, Spotsylvania Co, VA, 1878

BEALL, BENJAMIN (BLW), died 24 Mar 1853, Princeton, OH; md Oct 1814 Mary Gosney (P), Ohio Co, VA. She died 23 Apr 1879, West Chester, Butler Co, OH

BEALE, GEORGE H. (BLW), died 20 Jun 1867, Gilmer Co, WV; md 24 Sep 1812 Mary Parsons (P), Randolph Co, VA. Her LNR P.O. Glenville, Gilmer Co, WV, 1871

BEALL, TOWNSEND H. (P, BLW), LNR P.O. DeKalb, Gilmer Co, WV, 1871; md Catharine Parsons, Randolph Co, VA

BEALS, EZRA whose widow Margaret applied for a pension

BEAN, ISAAC (P, BLW), died c1880, LNR Pickaway Co, OH, 1871. Widower.

BEAN, JOHN (P, BLW), LNR P.O. Knoxville, TN, 1871; md Sarah Camp, Wythe Co, VA

BEAN, THOMAS (P, BLW), LNR Pleasanton, Athens Co, OH, 1872; md Sarah Hill, Hardy Co, VA

BEAR, VALENTINE see BARE, VALENTINE

BEARD, ADAM (P, BLW), died 30 Mar 1873, LNR P.O. Harmony, Mason Co, WV, 1871; md 8 Mar 1814 Margaret E. Crouch, Bedford Co, VA

BEAR, JOHN whose widow Elizabeth applied for a pension

BEARD, THOMAS (BLW), died Sep 1837, Natchez, MS; md c20 Oct 1808 Elizabeth Kessler (P), Rockingham Co, VA.

26

BEARD (continued)
Her LNR White Oak, OH, 1871
BEARD, THOMAS (BLW), died
31 Mar 1867, Henry Co, TN;
md Feb 1818 cousin Mary
Beard (P), Augusta Co, Va.
She died 26 Mar 1883, Henry
Co, TN, LNR P.O. Paris,
Henry Co, TN

ROLL NO. 7

BEASLEY, CORNELIUS (BLW),
died 20 Apr 1871, Herndon,
MO; md 5 Oct 1808 Martha
Carr (P), Albemarle Co, VA.
She died c1886, LNR Herndon,
Saline Co, MO, 1879
BEASLEY, JOHN (BLW), died 4
Aug 1864; md (1) T. U. Taylor,
(2) 30 Nov 1852 Mary T. (---)
Baugh (P), Chesterfield Co,
VA. Her LNR P.O. Clover
Hill, Chesterfield Co, VA,
1878
BEASLEY/BEAZLEY, VALEN-
TINE (BLW), died 31 Aug
1845, Greene Co, VA; md 30
Jun 1803 Frances Powell (P),
Orange (now Greene) Co, VA.
Her LNR Stanardsville, Greene
Co, VA, 1871
BEASLEY, YOUNG (BLW), died
19 Jul 1850, Chesterfield Co,
VA; md 11 Sep 1839 Martha
Crostick (P), Chesterfield Co,
VA. Her LNR Matoaca, Ches-
terfield Co, VA, 1889
BEATLEY, WILLIAM (P, BLW),
LNR Winchester, Frederick
Co, Va, 1871; md 1817 Eliz-
abeth Loyer, nr Winchester,
VA
BEATON, ROBERT (BLW), died
15 Feb 1845, Middle River,
VA; md 1 Aug 1811 Hannah
Rush (P), Augusta Co, VA.
Her LNR Staunton, Augusta
Co, VA, 1871
BEATTY, JAMES (P, BLW), died
c1877, LNR P.O. Washington
Courthouse, Fayette Co, OH,

BEATTY (continued)
1871; md 15 Oct 1829 Elizabeth
Evans, Highland Co, OH
BEATTY, JAMES S. (P, BLW),
LNR Pickaway Co, OH, 1871;
md Elizabeth Stump, Franklin
Co, OH
BEATTY, THOMAS (BLW), died
13 Jan 1871, Harlem Springs,
OH; md 15 Feb 1816 Rachel
Cummings (P), Loudoun Co,
VA. She died 6 May 1886,
LNR Harlem Springs, Carroll
Co, OH
BEATY, JAMES (BLW), died 26
May 1847, Washington Co,
VA; md 14 Oct 1830 Elizabeth
McQuown (P), Washington Co,
VA. Her LNR P.O. Lodi,
Washington Co, VA, 1878
BEAVER, MICHAEL (P, BLW),
died 3 May 1881, LNR P.O.
Clarinda, Page Co, OH; md
----. She died 28 Feb 1868
BEAVERS, JOHN (P, BLW), died
c1878, LNR P.O. South Perry,
Hocking Co, OH; md 21 Apr
1821 Uphamy Updike, Culpeper
Co, VA
BEAZLEY, THOMAS (P, BLW),
LNR P.O. Columbia, Boone
Co, MO, 1871; md 16 Mar 1833
Elizabeth Woolfold, Christian
Co, KY
BEAZLEY, WILLIAM whose wi-
dow Susannah applied for a
pension
BEAZLY, JOHN (BLW), died 8
Apr 1864, Middlesex Co, VA;
md (1) Laura L. Montague, (2)
28 Aug 1858 Lucy B. Palmer
(P), New Hope, King and
Queen Co, VA. She died 27
Jun 1889, LNR Urbanna, VA,
1878
BECHTOL, JACOB whose widow
Mary Ann applied for a pension
BECK, JESSE (BLW), died 19
Aug 1858, Dickson Co, TN; md
9 Nov 1815 Judith T. Thumond
(P), Amherst Co, VA. Her
LNR P.O. Charlotte, Dickson

BECK (continued)
Co, TN, 1878
BECK, JOHN W. (BLW), died 19 Mar 1872, Ohio Co, WV; md 15 Dec 1814 Elizabeth Cox (P), Ohio Co, VA. She died 10 Sep 1884, LNR P.O. West Liberty, Ohio Co, WV
BECK, PRESTON (P, BLW), died 20 Jun 1886, Darlington, IN, LNR Darlington, Montgomery Co, IN, 1878; md 6 May 1828 Isabel Galbreath, Henry Co, IN
BECK, WILLIAM (P, BLW), LNR Castleton, Marion Co, IN, 1871; md 24 Feb 1824 Margaret Keene, Fairfax Co, VA. She died 4 Sep 1868 Hamilton Co, IN
BECKETT, SAMUEL (P, BLW), died 27 Jun 1880, Nine Mile, OH; md 12 Jul 1818 Amy Fitzpatrick (P), Clermont Co, OH. She died 17 Sep 1893, Brazier, Clermont Co, OH
BECKNER, JOHN (BLW), died 18 Feb 1860, Flora, Carroll Co, IN; md (1) Margaret Lowry, (2) 19 May 1836 Nancy Allan (P), Carroll Co, IN. Her LNR Flora, Carroll Co, IN, 1896
BECKNER, SAMUEL (P, BLW), died c1884, LNR P.O. Retreat, Franklin Co, VA, 1871; md 15 Mar 1812 Margaret Raupe, Franklin Co, VA
BECKWITH, RICHARD B. (BLW), died Dec 1826, St. Louis, MO; md 23 Sep 1813 Sally Eleanor Hite (P), Charlestown, Jefferson Co, VA. She died 26 Jan 1879, LNR Jefferson Co, WV
BEDDO/BEDDOW, NATHANIEL (BLW), died 26 Dec 1860 or 1864, Albemarle Co, VA; md (1) Ellen McClary, (2) 2 Sep 1847 Sarah Ann Marshall (P), Albemarle Co, VA. She died 28 Jun 1900, Albemarle Co, VA, LNR Rivanna, Albemarle Co, VA, 1887

BEEDLE, BENJAMIN (BLW), died 30 Nov 1839, St. Louis, MO; md Feb 18-- Letitia Smith (P), Shenandoah Co, VA. Her LNR P.O. Madison, Yolo Co, CA, 1889
BEEDLE, EPHRAIM (P, BLW), LNR P.O. Vienna, Fairfax Co, VA, 1871; md 28 Mar 1830 Nancy Peacock, Georgetown, DC
BEELER, CHARLES H. (BLW), died 11 Mar 1862, Andrew Co, MO; md (1)?, (2) ?, (3) 1 Sep 1857 Martha (---) Arbgass (P), Andrew Co, MO. She died c1892, LNR P.O. Avenue City, Andrew Co, MO, 1881
BEHEN, LANCELOT (BLW), died 30 Aug 1862, Pruntytown, VA; md Feb 1809 Emenetia Sulivan (P), Harrison Co, VA. Her LNR Pruntytown, Taylor Co, WV, 1871
BEHER, SAMUEL (BLW), died 2 Oct 1860, Rush CO, IN; md (1) --- Ellis, (2) 25 Oct 1835 Eliza --- (P), Cincinnati, OH. She died c1887, LNR P.O. Rushville, IN, 1880
BEIDLEMAN, VALENTINE applied for a pension
BELCHER, BURWELL B. (P, BLW), LNR Clarksville, Mecklenburg Co, VA, 1871; md 19 Dec 1835 Amy Murray, Brandons Hill, VA
BELCHER, EDMUND B. (BLW), died 6 Jul 0r Oct 1842, Chesterfield Co, VA; md 20 Feb 1811 Sally Andrews (P), Chesterfield Co, VA. Her LNR Chester, Chesterfield Co, VA, 1871
BELCHER, ISAAC (BLW), died 30 Apr 1864, Butler Co, Ky; md 1 Jun 1805 Tabitha Webster (P), Amelia Courthouse, VA. Her LNR P.O. Morgantown, Butler Co, KY, 1871
BELCHER, JOHN (BLW), died 24 Jan 1864, Monroe Co, KY;

BELCHER (continued)
md 3 Sep 1812 Permelia Biggers (P), Franklin Co, VA. Her LNR P.O. Tompkinsville, Monroe Co, KY, 1872
BELCHER, OBADIAH (P, BLW), LNR P.O. Princeton, Mercer Co, WV, 1871; md 15 Feb 18-- Martha Prince, Giles Co, VA
BELCHER, SUTTON E. (BLW), died 29 Aug 1866, Wilson Co, TN; md 25 Sep 1817 Abigail Hicks Ellis (P), Wilson Co, TN. She died 9 Sep 1882, Tucher Cross Roads, Wilson Co, TN
BELFIELD, JOHN W. (BLW), died 2 May 1863, Belplains, VA; md 26 May 1814 Mary B. Dangerfield (P), Richhill, Fremont Co, VA. She died 30 Jan 1873, Belplains, Richmond Co, VA
BELFIELD, THOMAS W. (P,BLW), died 25 Feb 1873, Westmoreland Co, VA; md 24 Nov 1821 Fanny F. Sanford (P), Westmoreland Co, VA. Her LNR P.O. Montross, Westmoreland Co, VA, 1871
BELILES/BELISLE, JESSE (P, BLW), LNR Butler Co, KY, 1871; md Peggy Russ
BELKNAP, THOMAS (P, BLW), died 30 Nov 1883, Braxton Co, WV; md (1) Mary ---, (2) 26 Jul 1850 Emsey Fisher (P), Braxton Co, VA. She died 2 Mar 1907, LNR Lloydsville, Braxton Co, WV, 1902
BELL, BOYLE B. (BLW), died 8 Sep 1851, Amelia Co, Va; md 5 Oct 1826 Elizabeth N. Morris (P), Amelia Co, VA. She died c1884, LNR P.O. Painesville, Amelia Co, VA, 1855
BELL, BUCHANAN (P, BLW), TN militia, LNR Sommonsville, Craig Co, VA, 1872
BELL, GEORGE (P, BLW), died c1877, LNR P.O. Marshall,

BELL (continued)
Highland Co, OH, 1871; md (1) Sarah Bennett, (2) May 1820/22 Mary Trump, Brushcreek, Highland Co, OH
BELL, ISAAC (P, BLW), died 7 May 1882, Pocahontas Co, WV; md (1) Roda Slater, (2) Elizabeth Pines, (3) 21 Sep 1825 Nancy Shrader (P), Mercer Co, VA. Her LNR Barkers Ridge, Wyoming Co, WV
BELL, JACOB whose widow Nancy B. Kelley applied for a pension
BELL, JAMES (BLW), died c1836/7, Amelia Co, VA; md Oct 1818 Mason Wingo (P), Amelia Co, VA. Her LNR P.O. Amelia Courthouse, Amelia Co, VA
BELL, JAMES (BLW), died 17 Mar 1840, Augusta Co, VA; md 19 Feb 1818 Rebecca Crawford (P). Her LNR Augusta Co, VA, 1878
BELL, JOHN (BLW), died 15 Nov 1856, Sussex Co, DE; md 10 Aug 1836 Elizabeth Stevens (P), Berlin, Worcester Co, MD. She died 13 Jun 1892, LNR P.O. Frankford, Sussex Co, DE, 1890
BELL, MICHAEL (BLW), died 15 Jan 1855, Campbell Co, VA; md 7 Feb 1812 Nancy Bybee (P), Campbell Co, VA. She died 7 Nov 1879, LNR Campbell Co, VA, 1871
BELL, STEPHEN (BLW), died 10 Apr 1845, White Hall, VA; md 3 Jun 1821 Martha Lynn/Linn (P), White Hall, VA. She died 1 Feb 1885, LNR White Hall, Frederick Co, VA
BELL, WILLIAM (P, BLW), died 24 May 1873, Harrison Co, WV; md 3 Jun 1824 Elizabeth Bond (P), Harrison Co, VA. Her LNR P.O. Quiet Dell, Harrison Co, WV, 1871
BELL, WILLIAM (BLW), died 28

BELL (continued)
Jun 1828, Southampton Co, VA; md 28 Mar 1812 Grizzia J. Arrington (P), Southampton Co, VA. Her LNR Assamoosick, Southampton Co, VA, 1871

BELL, WILLIAM (P, BLW), died 28 Mar 1871, Portland, OH; md (1) Mary Bell, (2) 20 May 1842 Jane (Atwood) Burch (P), Meigs Co, OH. She died 1883, Fairbury, Jefferson Co, NE

BELL, WILLIAM (P, BLW), LNR Dallas, TX, 1873; md 24 Dec 1821 Frances M. Newman, Orange Co, VA

BENDER, ADAM whose widow Elizabeth applied for a pension

BENDER, ISAAC (BLW), PA militia, died 18 Mar 1863, Webster Co, WV; md 7 Nov 1824 Rebecca Williams (P), Lewis Co, VA. She died 7 Oct 1889, LNR Knawles Creek, Braxton Co, WV

BENEDUM, JOHN (BLW), died 5 Jul 1876 Leesville, OH; md 10 Dec 1816 Mary Carr (P), Loudoun Co, VA. She died c1881, LNR P.O. Leesville, Carroll Co, OH

BENN, THOMAS (BLW), died 11 Feb 1844, Nansemond Co, VA; md (1) Sarah Colly, (2) 8 Apr 11835 Nancy Tartt (P), Norfolk Co, VA. She died 22 Feb 1889, LNR Norfolk Co, VA, 1888

BENNETT, ALLEN (P, BLW), died 9 Jan 1879, LNR Turner Station, Clinton Co, MO, 1871; md 25 Mar 1819 Sarah H. Archer, Brunswick Co, VA

BENNETT, BARTLETT (BLW), died 28 Mar 1859, Patrick Co, VA; md 3 Jun 1817 Mary Brown (P), Pittsylvania Co, VA. She died c1883, LNR P.O. Buffalo Ridge, Patrick Co, VA, 1878

BENNETT, COVINGTON (BLW), died 18 Apr 1857, Hacks Neck,

BENNETT (continued)
Accomac Co, VA; md (1) Sally Parks, (2) 31 Aug 1826 Margaret Caruthers (P), Accomac Co, VA. She died 12 Jul 1880, Hacks Neck, VA

BENNETT, GEORGE (P, BLW), OH militia, died 10 Oct 1880, LNR P.O. Scioto, Scioto Co, OH; md 15 Oct 1815 Mary Williams, Monongalia Co, VA

BENNETT, GEORGE applied for a pension

BENNETT, JACOB (BLW), died Mar 1862, Ritchie Co, VA; md Oct 1810 Rachel Davis (P), Pendleton Co, VA. She died 27 Apr 1878, Salt Lick Bridge, Braxton Co, WV, LNR DeKalb, Gilmer Co, WV, 1873

BENNETT, JAMES (BLW), died 6 Mar 1868, Lockport, KY; md 22 Jan 1811 Frances Brackett (P), Lunenburg, Lunenburg Co, VA. Her LNR Lockport, Henry Co, KY, 1871

BENNETT, JESSE (BLW) whose wife was Lucy

BENNETT, JOHN (BLW), died cSep 1833, Dearborn Co, IN; md 1816 or Apr 1824 Catherine Michael (P), Monongalia Co, VA. She died 13 Oct 1878, Jewell Co, KS, LNR Burr Oak, Jewell Co, KS, 1878

BENNETT, JOHN whose widow Lydia applied for a pension

BENNETT, JOSEPH (P, BLW), died 27 Sep 1880, Gilmer Co, WV; md (1) Mary Phillips, (2) ?, (3) 20 Jan 1858 Jane (---) Clelland (P-rejected), Calhoun Co, VA. She died 12 Jan 1883, LNR P.O. Grantsville, Calhoun Co, WV, 1871

BENNETT, REUBEN (P, BLW), LNR P.O. Pruntytown, Taylor Co, WV; md Nov/Dec 1824 Martha Plummer, Taylor Co, VA

BENNETT, THOMAS (BLW), died 23 May 1853, Jefferson

BENNETT (continued)
Co, VA; md 30 Aug 1811 Malinda Crow (P), Sharpsburg, MD, LNR Jefferson Co, WV, 1871

BENNETT, THOMAS whose widow Elizabeth M. A. applied for a pension

BENNETT, WALKER (P), TN militia, LNR P.O. Sparta, White Co, TN, 1871; md 2 Apr 1808 Charity Hughs, Lee Co, VA

BENSON, JAMES applied for a pension

BENSON, JOHN (BLW), died Jan 1861, Rockbridge Co, VA; md 27 May 1813 Lusander Hite (P), Staunton, VA. Her LNR P.O. Moffett's Creek, Rockbridge Co, VA, 1872

BENSON, ROBERT A. (P, BLW), died c1882, LNR Buckhannon, Upshur Co, WV;md 15 Sep 1815 Sarah L. Donaghe, Naked Creek, VA

BENT, CHARLES (P, BLW), died 18 Jan 1881, LNR P.O. New Richmond, Clermont Co, OH, 1877; md Apr 1816 Margaret Caines, Fauquier Co, VA

BENT/BROADBENT/BROADBELT/BROAD, JAMES (BLW), died 11 Oct 1851, Lewis Co, VA; md 25 Dec 1832 Mary Sims (P), Lewis Co, VA. She died 3 Apr 1887, Lewis Co, WV, LNR P.O. Jacksonville, Lewis Co, WV, 1878

BENTHALL, AZEL (BLW), died 30 Mar 1861, Nansemond Co, VA; md 15 Jan 1852 Martha Draper (P), Nansemond Co, VA. She died 27 Jul 1899, LNR Windsor, Isle of Wight Co, VA, 1879

BENTLEY, ROBERT applied for a pension

BENTLY, WILLIAM applied for a pension

BENTON, WILLIAM (P, BLW),

BENTON (continued)
LNR Middleburg, Loudoun Co, VA, 1871

BERKELEY, REUBEN, died 13 Jan 1840, Warren Co, MS; md 28 Jul 1818 Nancy D. Hancock (P), Frederick Co, VA. She died c1891, LNR P.O. Marlboro, Frederick Co, VA

BERKLEY, THOMAS L. who applied for a pension

BERLIN, PHILIP (BLW), died 4 Mar 1870, Clarke Co, VA; md (1) ?, (2) 13 Jan 1859 Sarah Jane Hooe (P), Clarke Co, VA. She died 11 Aug 1901, Clarke Co, VA, LNR P.O. Berryville, Clarke Co, VA, 1878

BERREY, REUBEN (P, BLW), died 14 May 1876, Belleville, IL; md (1) Mildred Reasson (2) Elizabeth Davis, (3) 30 Jan 1869 Drucilla (---) (Taylor) Davis (P), Belleville, IL. She died c1886, LNR Belleville, St Clair Co, IL, 1881

BERRY, DAVID (BLW), died 1 Mar 1871, Rockingham Co, VA; md (1) Elizabeth Foster, (2) 29 Mar 1849 Elizabeth (----) Weller (P), Rockingham Co, VA. Her LNR Mt Clinton, Rockingham Co,VA, 1879

BERRY, FIELDING (BLW), died Oct 1862, Braxton Co, VA; md 19 Feb 1818 Elizabeth McPherson (P), Loudoun Co, VA. She died 16 Jun 1884, LNR P.O. Braxton Courthouse, Braxton Co, WV, 1878. Fielding Berry was a substitute for James Berry in the War.

BERRY, GEORGE, (P-rejected), died 6 June 1873, Bentonville, Clinton Co, OH; md 15 Apr 1815 Sally Floyd (P), Romney, Hampshire Co, VA. She died 14 Apr 1880, Clinton Co, OH, LNR Wilmington Co, OH,

BERRY (continued)
1880
BERRY, HENRY (BLW), died 29 Aug 1864, Augusta Co, VA; md 25 Jul 1825 Catherine Wise (P), Rockingham Co, VA. Her LNR McNelly's Ford, Nelson Co, VA, 1878
BERRY, ISAAC (P, BLW), died 23 Nov 1881, LNR Williamsburg, Clermont Co, OH, 1871; md 7 Oct 1819 Elisabeth Dunkel, Romney, Hampshire Co, VA
BERRY, JAMES (P, BLW), died 8 Jan 1875, Oldham Co, KY; md 17 Apr 1817 Frances Finks (P), Madison Co, Va. She died c1886, LNR P.O. La Grange, Oldham Co, KY, 1878
BERRY, JOHN (P, BLW), LNR Keezletown, Rockingham Co, VA, 1871; md 1825 Harriet Bolton, Mt Clinton, Rockingham Co, VA
BERRY, JOHN (P, BLW), died 18 May 1872, LNR Augusta, Woodruff Co, AR, 1871; md 2 Aug 1826 Soreno Turner, Jackson Co, AL
BERRY, JOHN and widow Kitty both applied for a pension
BERRY, JOHN (BLW), MD militia, died 10 Apr 1862, Prince George Co, MD; md 5 Sep 1811 RachelW. Harper (P), Alexandria, VA. Her LNR Washington, DC, 1878
BEST, JOHN H. (BLW), died 2 Jan 1852, Prince George Co, VA; md 26 Jul 1821 Elizabeth D. Simmons (P), Prince George Co, VA. Her LNR P.O. Disputant, Prince George Co, VA, 1878
BETTIS, WILLIAM (P, BLW), died 22 Nov 1875, LNR P.O. Hartwood, Stafford Co, VA, 1851
BETTS, CHARLES (P, BLW), LNR Rural Dale, Muskingum Co, OH, 1871. Widower.

BETTS, ELISHA (BLW), died 5 Oct 1872, Halifax Co, VA; md (1) Fanny H. Marable, (2) Elizabeth A. Averett, (3) 28 Jun 1855 Parthenia C. Johnson (P), Halifax Co, VA. She died 17 Mar 1891, LNR P.O. Halifax Courthouse, Halifax Co, VA, 1878
BETTS, WILLIAM M. (BLW), died 24 Sep 1851, Norfolk, VA or on Chesapeake Bay; md 12 Apr 1831 Ann Fitnam (P), Norfolk, VA. She died c1892, LNR Baltimore, MD, 1887
BETS, ABRAHAM (P, BLW), died 10 Oct 1875, Franklin Co, Va; md (1) --- Ramsey, (2) 1 Mar 1817 Sally Stewart (P), Franklin Co, VA. She died 23 Aug 1881, Franklin Co, VA, LNR P.O. Hales Ford, Franklin Co, VA
BIBB, JOHN (P, BLW), died 10 Aug 1877, Louisa Courthouse, Louisa Co, VA
BIBB, THOMAS (BLW), died 11 Jan 1868, Muhlenburg Co, KY; md 15 Aug 1831 Cynthia Ann Shaver (P), Butler Co, KY. She died 25 Aug 1884, LNR P.O. South Carrollton, Muhlenburg Co, KY, 1878
BIBLE, JOHN (P, BLW), LNR Franklin, Pendleton Co, WV, 1871; md Oct 1814 Mary Skidmore, Reeds Creek, Pendleton Co, WV
BIBLE, JOHN (P), died Feb 1875, LNR Cherry Grove, Rockingham Co, VA; md Aug 1829 Polly Tafflinger, Rockingham Co, VA
BICKLE/BUKLE, ANTHONY (BLW), whose widow Dinah applied for a pension
BICKEL/BICKLE, GEORGE (P, BLW), died 29 Dec 1879, Roann, IN; md 4 Feb 1830 Elizabeth Michael (P), Easton, Preble Co, OH. She died 18 Jan 1885, LNR Roann, Wabash

BICKEL/BICKLE (continued) Co, IN

BICKERS, ALEXANDER (P, BLW), LNR Culpeper Co, VA; md 14 Apr 1831 Mary Jones, Orange Co, VA

BICKERTON, WILLIAM (BLW), died 23 Dec 1859, Rockingham Co, VA; md 9 Apr 1840 Polly Hiser (P), Mt Crawford, VA. She died c1893, LNR P.O. Bridgewater, Rockingham Co, VA, 1878

BIDWELL, CHARLES D. applied for a pension

BIGBIE, WILLIAM (BLW), died 21 Apr 1866, Bedford Co, VA; md (1) Frances W. Sharp, (2) 25 Oct 1837 Lucy G. Wingfield (P), Bedford Co, VA. She died 2 Sep 1907, LNR Lynchburg, Campbell Co, VA, 1888

BIGGER, THOMAS B. (P, BLW), LNR Richmond, VA, 1879

BIGGS, WILLIAM (BLW), died cDec 1849, Black Rock, VA; md 4 Feb 1819 Mary Coppage (P), Amissville, Culpeper Co, VA. Her LNR P.O. Milldale, Warren Co, VA, 1878

BILLER, CHRISTIAN (P, BLW), LNR P.O. Mt Clifton, Shenandoah Co, VA, 1871; md 28 Nov 1815 Hannah Price, Rockingham Co, VA

BILLINGS, NEWMAN (BLW), died 27 Dec 1827 or 1828, Mansfield, OH; md 2 Oct 1801 Jane Roberts (P), Berkeley Co, VA. Her LNR Mansfield, Richland Co, OH

BILLINGS, PIERCE (BLW), died 30 Jun 1849, Pittsylvania Co, VA; md 9 Aug 1827 Calva Gray (P), Pittsylvania Co, VA. She died 22 Jun 1895, LNR Henry Co, VA, 1878

BILLINGSLEY, CLEMENTS T. (BLW) applied for a pension

BILLS/BAILES/BALES, PRESLEY applied for a pension

BILLS, WILLIAM died 11 Oct

BILLS (continued) 1850, Pleasants Co, VA; md 7 May 1812 Martha Alley (P), Green Co, PA. Her LNR St Marys, Pleasants Co, WV, 1871

BILLUPS, MANN (BLW), died 28 Apr 1839, Mathews Co, VA; md 31 Dec 1828 Lucy (---) Thomas (P), Mathews Co, VA. She died 16 Aug 1886, LNR Baltimore, MD, 1878

BILLUPS, ROBERT (BLW), MD militia, died 23 Dec 1833 Norfolk, VA; md 29 Jul 1810 Louisa Wynn (P), Baltimore, MD. Her LNR Baltimore, MD, 1871

BILLUPS, ROBERT (P, BLW), LNR P.O. Mathews Courthouse, Mathews Co, VA, 1871

BILLUPS, THOMAS (BLW), died 22 Nov 1849, Franklin Co, MO; md 3 Apr 1815 Ann Cleaveland (P), Albemarle Co, VA. She died 1881, Union, Franklin Co, MO, LNR Gray's Summit, Franklin Co, MO, 1871

BILLUPS, WILLIAM (BLW), died 4 Dec 1865, Mathews Co, VA; md 20 Jun 1812 Lusy Ransom (P), Mathews Co, VA. Her LNR Mathews Co, VA, 1855

BINGHAM, FREDERICK (BLW), died 10 Mar 1859, Greene Co, IN; md 1810 Obedience A. Farmer (P), Halifax Co, VA. Her LNR Solsberry, Greene Co, IN, 1872

BIRAM, WILLIAM (BLW), died 14 Aug 1845, Long Bottom, OH; md 15 Jul 1823 Hannah Vermilye (P), Long Bottom, OH. She died 21 Dec 1889, Long Bottom, Meigs Co, OH

BIRCH/BURCH, JOHN (BLW), died 28 Jan 1855, Alexandria, VA; md (1) Mary ---, (2) Sarah Glover, (3) 1843 Susan Glover (P), Alexandria, VA. She died 4 Dec 1899, LNR Georgetown,

BIRCH/BURCH (continued)
DC, 1884
BIRCH, SAMUEL (P, BLW), died
30 Nov 1873, Alexandria, VA;
md 27 Sep 1821 Ann Cleveland
(P), Alexandria, VA. She died
c1885, LNR P.O. Falls
Church, Alexandria Co, VA,
1878
BIRD, BEMJAMIN (BLW), died
19 Dec 1837, Floyd Co, VA;
md 6 Dec 1829 Lucy Grady
(P), Patrick Co, VA. She died
3 Oct 1893, LNR P.O. Hills-
ville, Carroll Co, VA, 1878
BIRD, MASON and widow Hannah
M. James both applied for a
pension
BIRD, THOMAS (BLW), died 2
Oct 1859, Lincolnton, NC; md
5 Jan 1805 Elizabeth/Betsy
Norris (P), Bedford Co, VA.
She died 30 Nov 1872, LNR
Lincolnton, Lincoln Co, NC,
1872
BIRDSONG, JAMES (BLW), died
24 Jan 1878, California, MO;
md (1) Peggy Hill, (2) 1 Nov
1855 Mary (Foster) Saling (P),
Cooper Co, MO. She died
c1892, LNR P.O. California,
Moniteau Co, MO, 1878
BIRDSONG, JAMES applied for a
pension
BIRDSONG, WILLIAM (BLW),
died 13 Sep 1863, Moniteau
Co, MO; md 3 May 1816 Win-
aford Allee (P), Barren Co,
KY. She died 25 Jul 1886,
LNR P.O. California, Moniteau
Co, MO, 1878
BISHOP, ABRAHAM (P, BLW),
LNR P.O. Bluff Creek,
Johnson Co, IN; md Martha
Rush, Johnson Co, IN
BISHOP, ELIJAH (BLW), TN
militia, died 13 Apr 1862, Lee
Co, VA; md 3 Oct 1811 Levina
Clark (P), Lee Co, VA. Her
LNR P.O. Jonesville, Lee Co,
VA, 1873
BISHOP, JAMES M. (P, BLW),

BISHOP (continued)
LNR Palmyra, Fluvanna Co,
VA; md 18 Jun 1818 Mary C.
Shacklefort, Lovinston, VA
BISHOP, JOHN T. (BLW), died
31 Jul 1837, St Louis Co, MO;
md 11 Feb 1820 Mary Ann Jef-
fries (P), Albemarle Co, VA.
She died 10 Apr 1878, La-
fayette Co, MO, LNR P.O.
Odessa, Lafayette Co, MO,
1878
BISHOP, JOSHUA W. (P, BLW),
LNR Georgetown, DC, 1871;
md 27 Dec 1818 Mary Randall,
Fauquier Co, VA
BISHOP, RICHARD (P, BLW),
LNR Prince George Co, VA,
1873; md 15 Mar 1831 Mary
----, Surry Co, VA
BISHOP, WILLIAM (BLW), died
10 Oct 1855, McLean Co, IL;
md 2 Nov 1820 Margaret Lake
(P), Middleburg, Loudoun Co,
VA. She died 9 Apr 1891
Bloomington, IL, LNR Bloom-
ington, McLean Co, IL, 1887.
William served as a sub-
stitutefor Aquila Bishop in the
War
BIXLER, PETER applied for a
pension
BLACK, DANIEL B. (BLW), died
22 Aug 1856, Mercer Co, KY;
md 24 Mar 1821 Mary Clouch
(P), Pulaski Co, KY. Her LNR
Harrodsburg, Mercer Co, KY,
1887
BLACK, DANIEL (P, BLW), LNR
Lynchburg, Campbell Co, VA,
1871; md 24 Sep 1818 Mildred
A. Roper, Green Hill, Camp-
bell Co, VA
BLACK, GEORGE see George
Schwartz
BLACK, GREENVILLE (BLW),
disappeared 1818; md Mar
1812 Mary Hall (P), Campbell
Co, VA. Her LNR Castle
Craig, Campbell Co, VA, 1871
BLACK, HENRY (BLW), died 7
Jul 1867, Fremont Co, IA; md

34

BLACK (continued)
13 May 1819 Elizabeth Mennich (P), Washington Co, VA. She died c1888, LNR P.O. Riverton, Fremont Co, IA, 1887
BLACK, JACOB (P, BLW), TN militia, LNR P.O. Frazier's Bottom, Putnam Co, WV, 1871; md 6 Sep 1803 Johanna Lamb, Pocahontas Co, VA
BLACK, JAMES (P, BLW), whose widow Rosanna applied for a pension
BLACK, JOEL/JOSEPH (P, BLW), died 6 Aug 1883, Twelve Mile, IN; md (1) Elizabeth ---, (2) 24 Jun 1855 Elizabeth Cowell (P), Twelve Mile, IN. Her LNR Twelve Mile, Cass Co, IN, 1883
BLACK, JOHN (BLW), died Mar 1868, Tenth Legion, VA; md (1) Lucy Rama, (2) 25 Oct 1852 Elizabeth Hottinger (P), Rockingham Co, VA. Her LNR P.O. Oakwood, Rockingham Co, VA, 1880
BLACK, JOHN (BLW), died 6 Jun 1820, Albemarle Co, VA; md 9 Jun 1814 Martha P. Perkins (P), Hanover Co, PA. Her LNR P.O. Centerville, Saline Co, MO, 1876
BLACK, WILLIAM (BLW), died 30 May 1831, Oldham Co, KY; md 26 Dec 1809 Matilda Rowe (P), Albemarle Co, VA. Her LNR P.O. West Port, Oldham Co, KY, 1871
BLACKBURN, JAMES (BLW), born in VA
BLACKBURN, ROBERT whose widow Jane applied for a pension
BLACKBURN, THOMAS R. (BLW), died 28 Aug 1867, Staunton, VA; md 6 Apr 1817 Mary Ann H. Wright (P), Fredericksburg, Spotsylvania Co, VA. Her LNR Staunton, Augusta Co, VA, 1878
BLACKBURN, WILLIAM whose

BLACKBURN (continued)
widow Nancy applied for a pension
BLACKEMORE/BLAKEMORE, JOSEPH whose widow Polly applied for a pension
BLACKFORD, THOMAS T. (BLW), died 27 Feb 1863, Lynchburg, VA; md 24 Oct 1820 Caroline Steenberger (P), Shenandoah Co, VA. She died c1888, LNR Baltimore, MD
BLACKMORE/BLACKMAN, OWEN W. (P, BLW), LNR P.O. Greensburg, Decatur Co, IN, 1871; md 1816 Eliza Fulton. She died 1844
BLACKSTOCK, JAMES (P, BLW), died c1874, Vernon Hill, VA, LNR News Ferry, Halifax Co, VA, 1871. Not married
BLACKSTOCK, JOHN (P, BLW), died c1877, LNR Pittsylvania Co, VA; md 1818 Permelia Hill
BLACKWELL, JOHN (BLW), whose widow was Mary A.
BLACKWELL, JOSEPH (P, BLW), died 1 Dec 1835, LNR P.O. Saltville, Washington Co, VA; md Elizabeth ---, Abingdon, VA
BLACKWELL, MOSES whose widow Rebecca applied for a pension
BLACKWELL, WILLIAM (BLW), died 3 Feb 1868, Harrison Co, OH; md 31 Dec 1811 Catharine Spencer (P), Fauquier Co, VA. Her LNR P.O. Deerville, Harrison Co, OH, 1872
BLACKWOOD, JAMES (P, BLW), LNR Milton, Rutherford Co, TN, 1871. Not married
BLACKWOOD, LEVI applied for a pension
BLADEN, JOHN B. (BLW), died 5 Feb 1857, Alexandria, Va; md 16 Dec 1811 Millie Maussee (P), Fairfax Courthouse,

BLADEN (continued)
Fairfax Co, VA. Her LNR
Alexandria, VA, 1874
BLAIN, CHARLES (BLW), died 6
Jul 1846, Sharonville, OH; md
(1) ?, (2) 14 Jul 1837 Hannah
Chandler (P), Lancaster, Fair-
field Co, OH. She died 29 Mov
1904, LNR Sharonville, Pike
Co, OH
BLAINE, JOHN (P, BLW), died 1
Jun 1873, Dry River, Rockin-
gham Co, VA; md (1) Eliz-
abeth Phillips, (2) 1 Mar 1849
Eliza A. Long (P), Rockin-
gham Co, VA. She died 7 Apr
1894, LNR P.O. Ottobine,
Rockingham Co, VA
BLAIR, SAMUEL (BLW), died
22 Mar 1870, Pittsylvania Co,
Va; md (1) Polly Reynolds, (2)
22 Feb 1824 Clarissa W. Ful-
ler (P), Pittsylvania Co, VA.
She died c1890, LNR P.O. Cal-
lards, Pittsylvania Co, VA
BLAIR, THOMAS (BLW), died 3
Sep 1843, Fayette Co, OH; md
15 Jun 1815 Dianah Wood (P),
Culpeper Co, VA. She died 21
Dec 1884, LNR Fayette Co,
OH, 1878
BLAIR, WILLIAM (BLW), died
15 Aug 1866, Perry Co, OH;
md 14 Jan 1810 Mary/Polly
McQueen (P), Culpeper Co,
VA. Her LNR P.O. New Lexi-
ngton, Perry Co, OH, 1871

ROLL NO. 9

BLAKE, CHARLES (BLW),
whose wife was Margaret
BLAKE, JOHN P. (P, BLW), died
20 Jul 1878, LNR Wyanet,
Bureau Co, IL, 1871; md 24
Feb 1816 Helen Newton,
Greenbrier Co, VA
BLAKE, LEWIS (P, BLW), LNR
Columbia, Fayette Co, IN,
1871; md 19 Dec 1833 Anna R.
Elliot, Gloucester Co, VA
BLAKE, THOMAS (BLW), died

BLAKE (continued)
1839/41, Gloucester Co, VA;
md Jul 1810 Mary P. Drisgal
(P), Gloucester Co, VA. She
died 9 Feb 1875, LNR Glou-
cester, Gloucester Co, VA,
1873
BLAKE, WARNER C. (BLW)
BLAKE, WILLIAM (P, BLW),
whose widow Elizabeth re-
ceived a pension
BLAKE, WILLIAM (BLW) whose
widow Sarah applied for a pen-
sion
BLAKELY, JOHN (P, BLW),
LNR Redkey, Delaware Co, IN,
1871; md 1824 Dicy A. Taylor,
VA. She died 10 Apr 1870
BLAKEMORE, JOSEPH (BLW),
died 27 or 28 Jul 1868, Front
Royal, Warren Co, VA; md 18
May 1814 Polly Connell (P),
Augusta Co, VA. Her LNR
Linden, Warren Co, VA, 1871
BLAKEMORE, THOMAS (BLW),
died 22 Jun 1838, Cedar Grove,
Frederick Co, VA; md 30 Aug
1825 Elizabeth W. Brooke (P),
Frederick Co, VA. She died c
1889, LNR Staunton, Augusta
Co, VA, 1888
BLALOCK, AUSTIN (BLW), NC
militia, died 28 Jan 1861,
Scott Co, VA; md (1) ---
Monce, (2) 30 Mar 1843 Mary
C. Green (P), Sullivan Co, TN.
She died 8 Mar 1881, Scott Co,
VA, LNR P.O. Estillville,
Scott Co, VA, 1879
BLANCH, G. F. W. applied for a
pension
BLANCHETT, WILLIAM (P,
BLW), NC militia, died 11 Jan
1881, Patrick Co, VA; md (1)
Susan Beasley, (2) Stacy Fitz-
gerald, (3) 27 May 1878 Mary
Fulcher (P), Patrick Co, VA.
She died 11 Oct 1898, Patrick
Co, VA, LNR P.O. Patrick
Courthouse, Patrick Co, VA,
1879
BLAND, AMBROSE (P, BLW),

BLAND (continued)
LNR Hanover Junction, Hanover Co, VA, 1871

BLAND, JOHN (BLW), died 24 Feb 1850, Centreville, Nottoway Co, VA; md 18 Sep 1814 Mary B. Perkinson (P), Amelia Co, VA. Her LNR Petersburg, Dinwiddie Co, VA, 1871

BLAND, JOHN (BLW), died 25 Nov 1864, Upper Sandusky, OH; md (1) --- Pancoast, (2) 8 Feb 1855 Mary --- (P), Upper Sandusky, Wyandot Co, OH. She died 11 Apr 1897, LNR Republic, Seneca Co, OH, 1887

BLAND, RICHARD (BLW), died 29 Jun 1864, Chesterfield, VA; md (1) Adeline Manton, (2) 13 Aug 1829 Martha Elizabeth Ledbetter (P), Prince George Co, VA. She died 25 Jan 1889, LNR Baltimore, MD, 1878

BLAND, THOMAS (BLW), PA militia, died 11 Jul 1867, Janelew, Lewis Co, WV; md 10 Dec 1815 Mary Newlon (P), Pruntytown, VA. She died 31 Dec 1879, LNR P.O. Weston, Lewis Co, WV

BLAND, THOMAS (BLW), died 6 Oct 1865 Wyandot Co, OH; md 1 Oct 1820 Martha Cunningham (P), Pendleton Co, VA. She died 5 Oct 1893, LNR P.O. McCutchenville, Wyandot Co, OH

BLAND, THOMAS (P, BLW), died 24 Feb 1774 Greene Co, PA; md (1) Elizabeth McCullough, (2) 15 Mr 1849 Sarah (Dowell) Carrel (P), Greene Co, PA. Her LNR Greene Co, PA

BLAND, THOMAS (BLW), died 1863, Caroline Co, VA; md 10 Nov 1847 Martha Bowler (P), Caroline Co, VA. She died 16 May 1906, LNR P.O. Rappahannock Academy, Caroline Co, VA, 1879

BLANFORD, FRANCIS D whose widow Sarah aplied for a pension

BLANKENBECKLER, AARON whose widow Amanda applied for a pension

BLANKENSHIP, GEORGE (BLW), died 1 Jul 1862, Chesterfield Co, VA; md 1 Sep 1808 Polly Charlton (P), Chesterfield Co, VA. She died 26 Oct 1872, LNR Chesterfield Co, VA, 1871

BLANKENSHIP, JESSE M. (BLW), died 11 Oct 1870, Randolph Co, MO; md 15 Oct 1839 Susan Law (P), Sumner Co, TN. She died 23 Sep 1886, Hubbard, Randolph Co, MO, LNR P.O. Clifton Hill, Rahdolph Co, MO, 1878

BLANKENSHIP, JOEL (BLW), died 30 May 1870, Campbell Co, VA; md 21 Jul 1814 Nancy Trent (P), Campbell Co, VA. She died 22 Feb, Campbell Co, VA, LNR Hat Creek, Campbell Co, VA, 1871

BLANKENSHIP, WILLIAM whose widow Sally applied for a pension

BLANKINSHIP, BENJAMIN applied for a pension

BLANKINSHIP, BERRY (P, BLW), died c1888, LNR P.O. Narrows, Giles Co, VA, 1878; md 24 Feb 1859 Sarah Crawford, Mercer Co, VA

BLANKINSHIP, CHASTAIN (BLW), died 20 Jun 1849 or 16 Jun 1851, Chesterfield Co, VA; md 25 Sep 1823 Sarah Wyatt (P), Chesterfield Co, VA. She died c1884, LNR Rickmond, Henrico Co, VA, 1878

BLANKINSHIP, LEVI (BLW), died 9 Nov 1860, Wayne Co, VA; md 19 Nov 1837 Permelia Blankenship (P), Wayne Co, VA. She died 15 Mar 1886, Wayne Co, WV. LNR P.O. Huntington, Wayne Co, WV,

BLANKINSHIP (continued)
1878

BLANKS, ROBERT B. (BLW),
died 13 Dec 1841, Campbell
Co, VA; md 28 Apr 1825
Amanda M. F. Smithson (P),
Amherst Co, VA. She died
c1879, LNR Lynchburg,
Campbell Co, VA, 1878

BLANN, SAMUEL (BLW), died 3
Jun 1868, Isle of Wight Co,
VA; md (1) Elizabeth Hines,
(2) 21 Feb 1846 Elizabeth
Busby (P), Isle of Wight Co,
VA. She died 23 Nov 1894,
LNR Isle of Wight Co, VA,
1878

BLANTON, GREEN (BLW), died
4 Dec 1861, Mecklenburg Co,
VA; md (1) Nancy Overbey, (2)
28 Dec 1852 Elizabeth Lambert (P), Warren Co, NC. She
died 29 Apr 1906, LNR P.O. St
Tammany, Mecklenberg Co,
VA, 1904

BLANTON, LAWRENCE (BLW),
died 2 Aug 1871, Cumberland
Co, VA; md 29 Mar 1809 Gilly
Colby (P), Cumberland Co,
VA. She died 6 May 1879,
Cumberland Co, VA

BLANTON, MEREDITH (P,
BLW), died 5 Jul 1879, Union-
ville, TN; md 7 Apr 1814 Nan-
cy Crisp (P), Cumberland Co,
VA. She died c1879, LNR
Uninville, Bedford Co, TN

BLANTON, VINCENT applied for
a pension

BLAUCET, WILLIAM, TN and
VA militia, and widow Sally
both applied for a pension

BLEDSOE, HOWARD (BLW),
died 11 Jan 1851, Madison
Courthouse, VA; md 23 Apr
1810 Julia Yager (P), Madison
Co, VA. Her LNR Madison
Courthouse, Madison Co, VA,
1871

BLEDSOE, ISAAC (P, BLW),
died c19 Aug 1880 near Fair-
fiew P.O., Scott Co, VA, LNR

BLEDSOE (continued)
Spurs Ferry, Scott Co, VA, 1878

BLEDSOE, MOSES (BLW), died 3
Sep 1850 Orange Co, VA; md
10 or 14 Dec 1831 Sidney
Wright (P), Orange Co, VA.
She died c1889, LNR Orange
Co, VA

BLESS/BLISS, HENRY/CHRIS-
TIAN HENRY, (P, BLW), died
3 Nov 1870, St Francis Co,
AR; md (1) Priscilla Bless, (2)
1 Mar 1860 Caroline Fowler
(P), Geneva, Shelby Co, IN.
She died c1900, LNR P.O.
Smithfield, Fulton Co, IL

BLESS/BLISS, STEPHEN (P,
BLW), died c1875, LNR P.O.
Bernadotte, Fulton Co, IL,
1871; md 25 1820 or 1821 Ann
McKenzie, Lewis Co, KY

BLESS, WILLIAM (P, BLW),
LNR P.O. Shelbyville, Shelby
Co, IN, 1872; md 26 Aug 1859
Elizabeth Womack, Shelby-
ville, IN

BLIZZARD, JAMES (BLW), died
24 or 25 Dec 1847, Grundy Co,
MO; md 20 Sep 1809 Mary/
Margaret W. Wagoner (P),
Pendleton Co, VA. Her LNR
Blue Mound, Livingston Co,
OH, 1873

BLOCK, JOHN (BLW), PA
militia; md (1) Margaret
Gumph, (2) 17 Mar 1856 Mary
Lions (P), Lancaster Co, PA.
She died 6 Jun 1907 Norfolk,
VA

BLUE, JOHN (BLW) applied for a
pension

BLUFORD, JOHN (BLW), died
Jan 1857, Currituck Co, NC;
md 10 Feb 1816 Elizabeth
Cnsalvo (P), Norfolk, VA. She
died 13 Jan 1888, Norfolk, VA

BLUME, PHILIP (P, BLW), LNR
P.O. Mountain Cove, Fayette
Co, WV, 1871; md 1819 Eliz-
abeth Smith, Berkeley Co, VA

BLUNDEN, THOMAS (BLW)

BLUNKALL/BLANKHALL, RO-

BLUNKALL (cont.)
BERT (BLW), died 18 Jun 1870, Davidson Co, TN; md 9 Aug 1817 Martha M. Ladd (P), Goochland Co, VA. Her LNR P.O. Nashville, Davidson Co, TN, 1878

BOARD, CHRISTOPHER (P, BLW), LNR Hammonville, Hart Co, KY, 1871

BOARD, GEORGE (P, BLW), LNR P.O. Bunceton, Cooper Co, MO, 1871; md 17 Nov 1816 Mary Swann, Fauquier Co, VA

BOARD, HENRY (P, BLW), died 17 Jul 1880; md 25 Dec 1823 Nancy Majors (P), Franklin Co, VA. She died c1887, LNR Taylors Store, Franklin Co, VA

BOARD, JOHN (P, BLW), died 29 Jan 1877, Bedford Co, VA; md (1) Elizabeth McCabe, (2) 23 Sep 1834 Cleopatra A. Mc-Daniel (P), Bedford Co, VA. She died Summer 1884, Davis Mills, VA

BOARD, STEPHEN (P, BLW), died 18 Jul 1878, Cheraw, SC; md (1) Sally Utley, (2) 21 Aug 1860 Mary A. (Wallace) Williams (P), Chesterfield Co, SC. She died 13 Sep 1915, LNR Cheraw, Chesterfield Co, SC, 1903

BOATWRIGHT, BENJAMIN (P, BLW), died 20 Jun 1873, Carmel, Highland Co, OH; md 1816 Mary Johnson, Prince Edward Co, VA. She died c1857. Benjamin was a substitute for his brother Richard in the War

BOATWRIGHT, LITTLEBERRY (BLW), died 6 Mar 1860 or 1861, Powhatan Co, Va; md 11 Dec 1817 Judith Sublett (P), Powhatan Co, VA. She died 1 Jun 1881, LNR P.O. Powhatan Courthouse, Powhatan Co, VA, 1878

BOATWRIGHT, MEADOR (P, BLW), died 24 Dec 1876, Scott

BOATWRIGHT (continued)
Co, VA; md 17 Sep 1828 Mary Pendleton (P), Scott Co, VA. She died 26 Feb 1903, Ft Blackmore, Scott Co, VA

BOATWRIGHT, POWHATAN (P), LNR P.O. Farmersville, Union Parish, LA, 1873; md 24 Jul 1826 Nancy Buck, Claiborne Parish, LA

BOAZ, ROBERT (P, BLW), LNR P.O. Ridgeway, Henry Co, VA, 1871; md 17 Feb 1818 Martha W. Sandifer, Patrick, Co, VA

BOBBITT, CALEB (BLW), died 1 Jun 1830 Flat Lick, Pulaski Co, KY; md 3 Mar 1795 Nancy Blair (P), Grayson Co, VA. Her LNR Lisbon, Howard Co, MO, 1873

BOBBITT, RANDOLPH (P, BLW), died 1 Jul 1876 Linn Co, MO; md 5 Feb 1852 Jemimah Lambert (P), Linn Co, MO. She died 21 Aug 1896, LNR P.O. St Catherine, Linn Co, MO, 1878

BOBBITT, ROBERT; md Dicey ---- (P). She died c1884, LNR P.O. Cairo, Randolph Co, OH, 1893. Her papers were lost while they were in care of the Senate Committee on Pensions

BOBBITT, THOMAS (BLW), died 8 Apr 1859, Clinton Co, OH; md 20 Dec 1815 Mildred Dalton (P), Pittsylvania Co, VA. She died 3 Sep 1884, LNR New Vienna, Clinton Co, OH, 1878

BOBLETT, PETER (P, BLW), LNR Panora, Guthrie Co, IA, 1871; md 21 Oct 1824 Elizabeth Ann Evans, Bedford Co, VA

BODINE, HENRY (BLW)

BODINE, JAMES (BLW), died 15 Jul 1876, Marshall Co, AL; md 27 Jan 1815 Catherine Butler (P), Fairfax Co, VA. She died c26 Nov 1880, LNR Guntersville, Marshall Co, AL, 1871

BOGARD, ABRAHAM (P, BLW),
USA, LNR Moundsville, Mar-
shall Co, WV, 1871
BOGGS, THOMAS (P, BLW),
LNR P.O. Kingston, Ross Co,
OH, 1871; md 13 or 14 Sep
1811 Nancy Stillwell, Berkeley
Co, VA
BOHANNON, AMBROSE (BLW),
died 20 or 22 Mar 1868, Marion
Co, KY; md 4 or 9 Jul 1810
Elizabeth Marrible (P), Milton,
NC. She died 1 Apr 1876, LNR
P.O. Lebanon, Marion Co, KY,
1871
BOHANNON, JOHN (BLW), died
Dec 1857; md (1) Polly Bur-
ges, (2) 6 Sep 1846 Franky
(----) Arnold (P), Stokes Co,
NC. Her LNR P.O. Danburt,
Stokes Co, NC, 1883
BOHANNON, JOSEPH (BLW),
died 21 Aug 1862, Pittsylvania
Co, VA; md Fall 1803 Eliz-
abeth Baynes (P), Halifax Co,
VA. Her LNR P.O. Ringgold,
Pittsylvania Co, VA, 1871
BOHANNON, THOMAS (BLW),
died 18 Sep 1828, Richmond,
VA; md 1 Sep 1808 Maria Fox
(P), King William Co, VA.
Her LNR Richmond, VA, 1871
BOHON, WILLIAM (BLW), died
20 Apr 1870, WV; md 25 Apr
1830 Eliza/Athaliah Goff (P),
VA. Her LNR St George, Tuc-
ker Co, WV, 1878
BOICE, JOHN (BLW), died 14 Jul
1855, Rushville, IL; md (1) ?,
(2) ?, (3) 10 Jan 1833 Rebecca
Snyder (P), Washington Co,
MD. She died 12 Mar 1894,
Rushville, IL
BOLEN/BOLIN, SAMUEL
(BLW), died 1 Dec 1860,
Athens Co, OH; md Apr 1808
Mary Hudnall (P), VA. Her
LNR Athens Co, OH, 1871
BOLES/BOYLE/BOWLES,
CALEB (BLW), died 9 or 15
Apr 1855 or 1856, Greenbrier
Co, VA; md 9 Dec 1813 Peggy

BOLES (continued)
Taylor (P), Monroe Co, VA.
Her LNR Greenbrier Co, WV,
1876
BOLEY/BOWLEY, JOHN (P,
BLW), LNR Paris, Fauquier
Co, VA, 1878
BOLIN, DANIEL (P, BLW), died
22 Sep 1881, Uniontown, PA;
md 1827 Mary T. King (P),
Culpeper Co, VA. Her LNR
Uniontown, Fayette Co, PA,
1883
BOLIN, MICHAEL applied for a
pension
BOLING, BENJAMIN (BLW),
died 14 Aug 1870, Tazewell
Co, VA; md 24 Feb 1813 Nan-
cy McFarland (P), Washington
Co, VA. Her LNR P.O. Jeffer-
sonville, Tazewell Co, VA,
1871
BOLING, JOHN whose widow
Sarah applied for a pension
BOLING, LEWIS (P), LNR
Freedom, Owen Co, IN, 1871;
md 5 Jan 1816 Margaret Hef-
lin, Stafford Co, VA
BOLINGER, WILLIAM (P,
BLW), LNR Union, Monroe
Co, WV, 1871; md Sep 1802
Rebecca Shearer, Winchester,
Frederick Co, VA
BOLLING, JOHN P. (BLW), died
16 Jun 1861, Petersburg, VA;
md 16 Nov 1820 Nancy Gilliam
(P), Petersburg, VA. Her LNR
Petersburg, Dinwiddie Co, VA,
1878
BOLLY/BOWLEY, JOHN (BLW)
BOLT, ISAAC (BLW), died 23 Jul
1860, Bolts Fork, Boyd Co,
KY; md 27 May 1813 Elizabeth
Booten (P), Beech Fork, Ca-
bell Co, VA. Her LNR Bolts
Fork, Boyd Co, KY, 1871
BOLTON, JACOB Sr. (P, BLW),
died 2 Jul 1871, Pendleton Co,
WV; md 15 Jul 1807 Margaret
Hartman (P), Franklin, VA.
She died 6 Apr 1883, LNR
Franklin, Pendleton Co, WV,

40

BOLTON (continued)
1871
BOLTON, MATTHEW whose widow Frances applied for a pension
BOLTON, RICHARD S. whose widow Elizabeth W. applied for a pension
BOLTON, ROBERT H. (BLW), died Feb or Mar 1862, Hart Co, KY; md 20 Apr 1819 Hannah M. Lang (P), Fincastle, Botetourt Co, VA. Her LNR P.O. Munfordville Courthouse, Hart Co, KY, 1879
BOMAN/BOWMAN, ISAAC applied for a pension
BOMBACK/BOMBAUGH, ANDREW (P, BLW), LNR P.O. Zanesville, Muskingum Co, OH, 1871; md 3 Aug 1820 Mary Ann Sweeny, Muskingum Co, OH
BOND, HUGH (P, BLW), PA militia, died 9 Feb 1880, Cabell Co, WV, LNR P.O. Middleport, Meigs Co, OH, 1871; md 18 Apr 1818 Jane Crawford, Trumbull Co, OH
BOND, ISAAC (BLW), died 18 Nov 1857, Floyd Co, VA; md 1811 or 1812 Nancy Goard/Goad (P), Patrick Co, VA. She died c1879, LNR P.O. Indian Valley, Floyd Co, VA, 1872
BOND, ISRAEL (BLW), died 1 May 1849, Randolph Co, IN; md 20 Dec 1821 Emily Swain (P), Bedford Co, VA. She died c1885, LNR Cerro Gordo, Piatt Co, IL, 1878
BOND, JAMES (BLW), died 13 Jun 1854, Norfolk, VA; md 10 Jan 1818 Mary Tucker (P), Norfolk, VA. She died 7 Apr 1888, Deep Creek, Norfolk Co, VA
BOND, JOHN (BLW), died 11 Mar 1841, Tyler Co, VA; md 30 May 1824 Margaret Turbee (P), Tyler Co, VA. She died 19 Oct 1889, LNR P.O. Ripley, Tyler

BOND (continued)
Co, WV, 1878
BOND, NATHAN applied for a pension
BOND, REUBEN (P, BLW), died 15 Nov 1880, Harrison Co, WV; md (1) ?, (2) 3 May 1841 Edith McCullough (P), Harrison Co, VA. She died 22 Jun 1883, Harrison Co, WV, LNR P.O. Quiet Dell, Harrison Co, WV
BOND, RICHARD (BLW), died 13 Sep 1865, Monticello, IL; md Dec 1813 Prudence Powers (P), Harrison Co, VA. She died c1886, LNR Champaign, Champaign Co, IL, 1871
BOND, THOMAS (P, BLW), LNR P.O. Unionville, Orange Co, VA, 1871; md Jun 1812 Mary Henehie, Louisa Co, VA
BONDURANT, THOMAS M. (BLW), died 8 May 1862, Buckingham Co, Va; md 18 Nov 1823 Marcia L. Moseley (P), Buckingham Co, VA. Her LNR P.O. Buckingham Courthouse, Buckingham Co, VA, 1878
BONHAM, JOHN whose widow Anna applied for a pension
BONNELL, WILLIAM (BLW), died 28 or 30 Dec 1848, Cambridge, OH; md 15 Sep 1850 Hannah Dixon (P), Guernsey Co, OH. She died c1891, LNR New Concord, Muskingum Co, OH, 1887
BONNER, SAMUEL (BLW), whose widow Sarah applied for a pension
BONNER, WILLIAM (BLW), died 23 Jan 1871, Petersburg, VA; md (1) Mary Williams, (2) Sarah Williams, (3) 17 Sep 1840 Elizabeth Bunchett (P), Petersburg, VA. Her LNR Petersburg, Dinwiddie Co, VA, 1879
BONNETT, PHILIP (BLW), died 26 Mar 1860, Jefferson Co, IA;

BONNETT (continued)
md 25 Feb 1812 Sarah Linger
(P), Harrison Co, VA. Her
LNR Centerville, Appanoose
Co, IA, 1875
BOOK, JOHN who applied for a
pension
BOOKER, BERRYMAN (P,
BLW), died 24 May 1872,
Surry Co, NC; md 12 Jan 1817,
Claramond Callahan (P), Rock-
ingham Co, NC. She died 17
Feb 1879, Surry Co, NC, LNR
Mt Airy, Surry Co, NC, 1879
BOOKER, EDWARD (P, BLW),
died 8 Mar 1882, Ridgeway,
VA; md 6 Feb 1820 Elizabeth
Anglin (P), Patrick Co, VA.
She died c1887, LNR Ridge-
way, Patrick Co, VA, 1878
BOOKER, GERMAN (BLW), died
6 Nov 1854, Cumberland Co,
VA; md (1) Martha Ballew, (2)
3 Apr 1822 Ann F. Woodson
(P), Cumberland Co, VA. She
died 7 Jan 1896, Cumberland
Co, VA
BOOKER, ISAAC (BLW), TN
militia, died 6 Apr 1863,
Washington Co, VA; md 9 Jul
1815 Catherine Miller (P), Sul-
livan Co, TN. Her LNR
Washington Co, VA, 1879
BOOKER, JOHN (BLW), TN mi-
litia, died 19 Feb 1873,
Montgomery Co, IN; md 298
Jun 1813 Margaret Zim-
merly/Zimmerlie (P), Wash-
ington Co, VA. Her LNR P.O.
Darlington, Montgomery Co,
IN, 1878
BOOKER, PURKETHOM D./
PINKETHMAN D. (BLW), TN
militia, died 1 May 1871,
Miami, Mo; md 26 Mar 1822
Martha A. Posell (P), Not-
toway Co, VA. She died
c1896, LNR P.O. Miami, Sa-
line Co, MO, 1880
BOOKER, RICHARD (BLW), died
26 Jan 1853, Powhatan Co,
VA; md 4 Aug 1825 Selena

BOOKER (continued)
Turpin (P), Manchester, Ches-
terfield Co, VA. She died 9
Jun 1885, LNR Powhatan
Courthouse, Powhatan Co, VA,
1878
BOOKER, WILLIAM (P, BLW),
died 8 Jun 1876, Nicholas Co,
WV; md 26 Aug 1823 Matilda
Horne (P), Rockbridge Co, VA.
Her LNR P.O. Fowlers Knob,
Nicholas Co, WV, 1881
BOOKER, WILLIAM (BLW), died
15 Apr 1851, Amelia Co, VA;
md (1) Sarah ---, (2) 30 Mar
1826 Mary Crittenton (P),
Amelia Co, VA. Her LNR
P.O. Chula, Amelia Co, VA,
1878
BOOTH, JOHN (P, BLW), died
17 Mar 1876, Elk Garden, Rus-
sell Co, VA; md (1) Alley ---,
(2) 27 Nov 1868 Mary W. Son-
ders (P), Lyons Gap, Smyth
Co, VA. Her LNR Elk Garden,
Russell Co, VA, 1878
BOOTH, RICHARD (BLW), died
5 Nov 1871, Surry Co, VA; md
(1) Elizabeth Baven, (2) (Jul
1863 Mary D. Pond (P), Sussex
Co, VA. Her LNR Surry Co,
Va, 1871
BOOTH, SAMUEL (BLW), died
20 Jan 1876, Sussex Co, VA;
md (1) ?, (2) 22 Dec 1859 Mary
E. (Tatum) Owen (P), Sussex
Co, VA. She died 5 Jul 1891,
LNR P.O. Wakefield, Sussex
Co, VA, 1879
BOOTH, SAMUEL M. (BLW),
died Dec 1860, Lincoln Co,
WV; md 19 Mar 1812 Rachel
Hays (P), Pittsylvania Co, VA.
Her LNR Falls Mills, Lincoln
Co, WV, 1871
BOOTH, WILLIAM (BLW), died
6 Dec 1854, Newton, White-
side Co, IL; md 20 Apr 1803
Deborah Hart (P), Beverly,
Randolph Co, VA. Her LNR
Kingsbury, Whiteside Co, IL,
1871

BOOTH, WILLIAM (BLW), died
Jun 1857, Franklin Co, VA; md
9 Feb 1820 Keziah Burnett(P),
Bedford Co, VA. She died 10
Jan 1882, Hales Ford, VA
BOOTHE, JOHN (BLW), died 23
Jan 1843, Pulaski Co, VA; md
19 May 1815 or 1818 Mary F.
O'Neal (P), Pittsylvania Co,
VA. She died 5 May 1881,
Pulaski Co, VA
BOOTHE, WILLIAM (BLW),
died 5 Jun 1874, Md 21 Feb
1814 Dorothy/Dolly Wingfield
(P), Albemarle Co, VA. Her
LNR Charlottesville, Albe-
marle Co, VA, 1871
BOOZ, HENRY (P, BLW), died
23 Sep 1875, LNR P.O. Har-
risonburg, Rockingham Co,
VA, 1871; md 2 Aug 1820
Matilda Hite, Milton, Caswell
Co, NC

ROLL NO. 10

BORAKER/BURACHER, HENRY
(P, BLW), died 1876, LNR
P.O. Crawfordsville, Mont-
gomery Co, IN, 1871; md 10
Jan 1813 Mary Ann Bartas,
Woodstock, VA
BORDEN, BEMJAMIN (BLW),
died 12 Mar 1862, Brown Co,
OH; md 26 Dec 1813 Mary
Martin (P), Highland Co, OH.
She died 3 Sep 1879, Shelby
Co, IN, LNR P.O. Sugartree
Ridge, Highland Co, OH, 1873
BORDEN, PHILIP (BLW), died 5
Jun 1868, Shenandoah Co, VA;
md 18 Mar 1819 Mary Funk-
houser (P), Shenandoah Co,
VA. Her LNR Capon Road,
Shenandoah Co, VA, 1884
BOROUGH/BORRER/BORER,
JACOB (P, BLW), LNR P.O.
Beverly, Randolph Co, WV,
1872; md 5 Jun 1809 Sarah
Helmich, Randolph Co, VA
BORUM, RICHARD B. (BLW),
died 26 Apr 1840, Halifax Co,

BORUM (continued)
VA; md (1) --- Ragland, (2) 2
Jul 1829 Eliza A. Chastain
(P), Halifax Co, VA. She died
7 Nov 1896, LNR P.O. Scot-
tsburg Depot, Halifax Co, VA,
1878
BOSHER, JOHN (BLW), died 16
Dec 1840, Cumberland Co, VA;
md 6 Jun 1810 Unity/Verity
Wheeler (P), Buckingham or
Cumberland Co, VA. Her LNR
P.O. Kanawha Courthouse,
Kanawha Co, WV, 1871
BOSHER, WILLIAM (P, BLW),
died 1 Jul 1884, Manquin, VA,
LNR P.O. Manquin, King Wil-
liam Co, VA; md 24 Dec 1811
Gabrilla H. Lipscomb, King
William Co, VA
BOSLEY, GEORGE, VA or MD
militia, applied for a pension
BOSMAN/BOZMAN, EDWARD
(BLW), died 1 Oct 1872,
McConnellsville, OH; md (1)
?, (2) ?, (3) 17 Nov 1853 Nancy
(---) Murphy (P), McCon-
nellsville, Morgan Co, OH.
She died 14 Jul 1899, Bristol,
Morgan Co, OH
BOSSERMAN, FREDERICK (P,
BLW) LNR P.O. Mint Springs,
Augusta Co, VA; md 1811
Margaret Burbeck, Augusta Co,
BOSSERMAN/BOSSLEMAN,
GEORGE (P, BLW), died 26
Nov 1875, Augusta Co, VA; md
1 Oct 1816 Catharine Brubeck
(P), Augusta Co, VA. Her
LNR P.O. Middlebrook, Au-
gusta Co, VA, 1878
BOSTIC, ARCHIBALD whose wi-
dow Sarah applied for a pen-
sion
BOSWELL, JOHN (P, BLW),
died c1876, LNR P.O. Green-
castle, Putnam Co, IN; md
after 1812 Katie Pheffley, Fin-
castle, VA
BOSWELL, JOHN I. (BLW), died
15 Dec 1846, Lunenburg, Co,
VA; md (1) Nancy Coleman,

BOSWELL (continued)

(2) 18 Dec 1838 Ellen J. Somerville (P), Petersburg, Dinwiddie Co, VA. Her LNR Wattsborough, Lunenburg Co, 1878

BOTKIN, JOHN whose widow Elizabeth applied for a pension

BOTKIN, WILLIAM (P, BLW), died 7 May 1872, Auglaize Co, OH; md (1) Malinda Shepherd, (2) 31 Jan 1855 Sarah (Green) Copsey/Cropsey (P), Auglaize Co, OH. She died c1882, LNR P.O. St Marys, Auglaize Co, OH, 1878

BOTTOM, ARMISTEAD (P, BLW), died 3 Aug 1872, McMinnville, TN, LNR McMinnville, Warren Co, TN, 1871; md Jane Robinson. She died 15 Oct 1862 McMinnville, TN

BOTTS, CHARLES (P, BLW), LNR P.O. Salem, Washington Co, IN, 1878

BOTTS, JOSHUA (BLW), died 23 Aug 1838, Boone Co, KY; md 9 Jun 1807 Emily Hutchinson (P), Georgetown, DC. Her LNR P.O. Burlington, Boone Co, KY, 1871

BOUGHTON, REUBEN B. (P, BLW), LNR Tappahannock, Essex Co, VA, 1871; md 21 Dec 1815 Susan Brooks

BOULDIN, JOHN (P, BLW), died 20 Oct 1877, Camp Springs, NC; md (1) --- Connally, (2) Catharine Garner, (3) 18 Sep 1845 Celia McCollum (P), Mishah, Rockingham Co, NC. She died 19 Aug 1902, LNR Caswell Co, NC, 1878

BOULDIN, LOUIS C. (BLW), died 20 Oct 1860, Nottoway Co, VA; md 16 Feb 1842 Catharine C. Ward (P), Nottoway Co, VA. Her LNR P.O. Jennings Ordinary, Nottoway Co, VA, 1879. Her pension dropped 14 Nov 1882 because of remarriage

BOULDIN, ROBERT E. (P,

BOULDIN (continued)

BLW), died 25 Mar 1881, Charlotte Co, VA; md 20 Jan 1820 Sarah B. Britton (P), Halifax Co, VA. She died c1884, LNR Charlotte Co, VA.

BOULDIN, WILLIAM GRAVES (BLW)

BOULTON, JOEL (P-rejected, BLW), died 29 Jun 1873, Owen Co, KY; md 20 Oct 1819 Margaret Russell (P), Gallatin Co, KY. Her LNR P.O. West Union, Owen Co, KY, 1884

BOULWARE, TURNER (P, BLW), died 3 Oct 1873 Caroline Co, VA; md 28 May 1829 Mary Ann Creel (P), Wood Co, VA. She died 10 Oct 1892, Wirt Co, WV, LNR California House, Wirt Co, WV, 1878

BOURN, STEPHEN (P, BLW), LNR P.O. Elk Creek, Grayson Co, VA, 1871; md 20 Jan 1820 Milla Martin, Grayson Co, VA

BOURN, WILLIAM (P, BLW), died 15 Oct 1882, Independence, VA, LNR Independence, Grayson Co, VA, 1878; md 10 Jul 1817 Polly Johnston, Wilkes Co, NC

BOURNE, JOHN (BLW), died 18 Sep 1815, Buffalo Springs, VA; md 27 Dec 1808 Nancy Sandidge (P), Buffalo Springs, Amherst Co, VA. Her LNR Lynchburg, Campbell Co, VA, 1871

BOURNE, WILLIAM (P, BLW), died 29 Oct 1879, Fluvanna Co, VA; md 11 Aug 1821 Mary Moss (P), Goochland Co, VA. She died 24 Mar 1893, LNR P.O. Cobham, Albemarle Co, VA, 1887

BOUSE, ADAM (P, BLW), died 31 Dec 1876, Tipton Co, IN; md 12 Oct 1819 Annis Dolly (P), Pendleton Co, VA. She died Sep 1884, Tipton Co, IN, LNR P.O. Goldsmith, Tipton

BOUSE (continued)
Co, IN, 1878
BOUTZ, GEORGE (P, BLW),
LNR Alexandria, VA, 1871; md
(1) c1820 Mary Benter, Alex-
andria, VA, (2) c1840 Margaret
Baker, West End, Fairfax Co,
VA
BOWDEN, WILLIAM (BLW),
died 13 Jun 1823, Wil-
liamsburg, VA; md 10 Dec
1808 Mildred Davis (P),
Yorktown, VA. Her LNR Wil-
liamsburg, James City, Co,
VA, 1871
BOWEN/BOAN, DAVID whose
widow Elizabeth applied for a
pension
BOWEN, FRANCIS (BLW), died
20 Aug 1867, Boone Co, IN;
md Aug 1806 Sarah J. Turley
(P), Frederick, MD. Her LNR
P.O. Thorntown, Boone Co, IN,
1871
BOWEN, JAMES M. (P, BLW),
died 31 Mar 1880; md 1820
Frances S. Stark (P), Culpeper
Co, VA. She died c1891, LNR
Greenwood Depot, Albemarle
Co, VA, 1879
BOWEN, JOHN (BLW), died 5
Jul 1862, DeKalb, MO; md 25
Oct 1836 Jeanette J. Newman
(P), Farifax Co, VA. She died
17 Jul 1879, DeKalb, MO, LNR
DeKalb, Buchanan Co, IN,
1878
BOWEN, JOHN (P), LNR P.O.
Williamsboro, Granville Co,
NC, 1871; md 11 Jan 1818
Nancy Murry
BOWEN, JOHN whose widow Re-
becca applied for a pension
BOWEN, JOHN whose widow Sa-
rah applied for a pension
BOWEN, MAYBERRY (P, BLW),
died 18 Apr 1877, LNR Shelby,
Cleveland Co, NC, 1871; md
---- Sparkes
BOWERS, JACOB whose widow
Mary applied for a pension
BOWERS, JAMES (BLW), died 2

BOWERS (continued)
Jun 1855, Portsmouth, VA; md
(1) Rachel Lockwood, (2) 11 or
18 Dec 1835 Lydia Mathews
(P), Norfolk, VA. She died 29
Nov 1897, Portsmouth, VA
BOWERS, JOSEPH (BLW), died
18 Oct 1861, Straight Creek,
VA; md 24 Dec 1814 Barbara
Vanderender (P), South Fork,
Pendleton Co, VA. Her LNR
Straight Creek, Highland Co,
VA, 1878
BOWERS, LEONARD whose wi-
dow Martha T. applied for a
pension
BOWERS, PETER (BLW), died 2
May 1859; md 16 Aug 1824
Mary Williams (P), Shenan-
doah Co, VA. She died 20 Mar
1885, LNR Kingston, Urbana
Co, OH, 1879
BOWERS, SAMUEL (P, BLW),
died 5 Dec 1875, Punx-
sutawney, PA; md 24 Mar 1824
or 1827 Catharine Weaver (P),
Jefferson Co, PA. Her LNR
Punxsutawney, Jefferson Co,
PA, 1879
BOWIE, JOHN C. (BLW), died 9
Jan 1850, Caroline Co, VA; md
11 Jul 1836 Sarah A. Cox (P),
Westmoreland Co, VA. She
died 23 Oct 1887, Port Royal,
Caroline Co, VA
BOWLEN, ABIJA (BLW), died
Mar 1858, Stafford Co, VA; md
1819 Fannie ---- (P). She
died 17 Aug 1879, Stafford Co,
VA. Her LNR P.O. Catlett
Station, Fauquier Co, VA, 1878
BOWLEN, NELSON applied for a
pension
BOWLER, ROBERT (BLW), died
22 Dec 1862, Orange Co, VA;
md (1) Frances T. Donahoe,
(2) 12 Mar 1835 Caroline V.
Bowling (P), Spotsylvania Co,
VA. She died c1890, LNR
P.O. Unionville, Orange Co,
VA
BOWLES/BOALES, JACOB (P,

45

BOWLES/BOALES (continued)
BLW), died c1881, LNR Law-
rence Furnace, Lawrence Co,
OH, 1871; md 16 Sep 1825
Susan Cordow
BOWLES, PLEASANT (P, BLW),
died 18 Aug 1873, Chesterfield
Co, VA; md 22 Nov 1814 Mary
Page Farmer (P), Chesterfield
Co, VA. Her LNR, Genito,
Powhatan Co, VA, 1881
BOWLES, ZACHARIAH (P,
BLW) died 4 Apr 1873, Am-
herst Co, VA; md 16 Jun 1812
Judith/Judy Scott (P), Amherst
Co, VA. Her LNR P.O. Am-
herst Courthouse, Amherst Co,
VA, 1873
BOWLIN, GEORGE (BLW), died
1 Feb 1865, Holden, MO; md
1820-23 Nancy Kirby (P),
Sumner Co, TN. She died
c1890, LNR P.O. Lake City,
Jackson Co, MO
BOWLIN, LEWIS applied for a
pension
BOWLIN/BOLING, THOMAS
(BLW), died 6 Jan 1831, Ho-
wards Ferry, Wythe Co, VA;
md 6 Apr 1817 Polly Smith
(P), Patrick Co, VA. Her LNR
P.O. Patrick Courthouse, Pat-
rick Co, VA, 1879
BOWMAN, ARCHELAUS (P,
BLW), LNR San River, Patrick
Co, VA, 1878. He was a sub-
stitute for Gilbert Bowman in
the War
BOWMAN, DANIEL whose widow
Mary applied for a pension
BOWMAN, GEORGE (BLW),
died 2 Dec 1863, Huntington
Township, Gallia Co, OH; md
16 Apr 1808 Eva Catharine
Aumiller (P), Woodstock,
Shenandoah Co, VA. Her LNR
Vinton, Gallia Co, OH, 1871
BOWMAN, GEORGE W. (P,
BLW), LNR Petersburg,
Menard Co, IL, 1871
BOWMAN, HAWKINS (BLW),
TN militia, died 13 Apr 1870,

BOWMAN (continued)
Harlan Co, KY; md 1838 Nancy
Barbour (P), Estillville, Scott
Co, VA. She died 11 Aug
1887, LNR P.O. Harlan Court-
house, Harlan Co, KY, 1879
BOWMAN, ISAAC applied for a
pension
BOWMAN, JOHN (BLW), died 24
Dec 1859, Lee Co, IA; md 14
Jan 1824 Sally Zahn (P),
Augusta Co, VA. She died
1882, LNR P.O. Luray, Clark
Co, MO, 1878
BOWMAN, JOHN (BLW), died 15
Sep 1858, Miami Co, IN; md
25 May 1820 Polly Cromer (P),
Montgomery Co, VA. Her LNR
P.O. New Waverley, Cass Co,
IN, 1879
BOWMAN, JOHN (BLW), died 15
Aug 1866, Gallia Co, OH; md
(1) Sarah A. Boop, (2) 9 Feb
1857 Polly S. (----) Holcomb
(P), Vinton, Gallia Co, OH.
Her LNR Kendallville, IN,
1887
BOWMAN, JOHN (P, BLW),
LNR Burksville, Cumberland
Co, Ky, 1871; md 15 Dec 1833
Mickey Motley, Cumberland
Co, KY. Widower.
BOWMAN, WILIAM (P, BLW),
LNR P.O. Independence,
Montgomery Co, KS, 1873; md
23 Dec 1816 Mary A. Becon,
Buckingham Co, VA
BOWRY, HENRY whose widow
Eliza W. Durfey applied for a
pension
BOWRY, THOMAS (BLW), died
19 Feb 1863, Charles City Co,
VA; md 28 Feb 1833 Sarah Ann
Bagwell (P), Charles City Co,
VA. She died c1888, LNR
Richmond VA, 1888
BOWSEL/BOWSELL, MAT-
THEW (BLW), died 3 Sep
1861, Georgetown, DC; md 24
Sep 1818 Jane K. Calvert (P),
Fairfax Co, VA. Her LNR
Richmond, VA, 1878

BOWYER, GEORGE (BLW), died 8 Jul 1851, Rappahannock co, VA; md 3 Jan 1828 Elizabeth F. Kinsey (P), Culpeper Co, VA. She died 22 Jul 1893, LNR P.O. Culpeper, Culpeper Co, VA, 1878

BOWYER, ISAAC whose widow Rebecca applied for a pension

BOWYER, JOHN (P, BLW), died 17 Dec 1878, Winfield, VA; md (1) Purmelia Crawford, (2) 17 Jan 1871 Elizabeth A. (Elmore) Smith (P), Putnam Co, WV. She died 19 Mar 1909 Winfield, Putnam Co, WV

BOYD, JAMES (BLW), died 12 Nov 1849, Albemarle Co, VA; md 5 Sep 1811 Jane M. Rice (P), Albemarle Co, VA. She died 5 Sep 1871, Mechums River, Albemarle Co, VA

BOYD, JOHN (P, BLW), LNR P.O. Louisa Courthouse, Louisa Co, VA, 1871; md 13 Feb 1821 Mary L. Cobbs, Albemarle Co, VA

BOYD, JOHN whose widow Elizabeth applied for a pension

BOYD, JOHN H. (P, BLW), LNR Richmond, VA, 1871; md 8 Aug 1866 Sarah E. Hobson, Richmond, VA

BOYER/BYER, JOHN (BLW), died 8 Aug 1849, McGaheysville, Rockingham Co, VA; md 28 Mar 1809 Margaret Weaver (P), Port Republic, Rockingham Co, VA. Her LNR Trotwood, Montgomery Co, OH, 1871

BOYER, PETER (P, BLW), LNR McGaheysville, Rockingham Co, VA, 1872; md Aug 1810 Rachel Hudlow, Rockingham Co, VA

BOYER, SAMUEL (P, BLW), LNR P.O. Elk Creek, Grayson Co, VA, 1871. Not married

BOYERS, JOSEPH (BLW), died 22 Jan 1870, Cedar Co, Mo; md 30 Jul 1818 Elizabeth

BOYERS (continued) Ewen (P), Cow Pasture, Augusta Co, VA. She died c1880, LNR Redman, Edgar Co, IL, 1878

BOYLES, PRICE (P, BLW), died 1 May 1877, Barbour Co, WV, LNR Philippi, Barbour Co, WV; md 1841 Margaret Stemple, Preston Co, VA. She died 23 Feb 1876, Weston, WV.

BRADBURY, JAMES applied for a pension

BRADFIELD, JOHN (BLW), died 27 Sep 1840, Hamilton Co, TN; md 17 Mar 1825 Susannah Thurman (P), Bledsoe Co, TN. Her LNR P.O. Falling Water, Hamilton Co, TN, 1878

BRADFIELD, WILLIAM (BLW), died 4 Dec 1862, Snickersville, Loudoun Co, VA; md 4 Apr 1816 Elizabeth L. Alder (P), Loudoun Co, VA. She died 22 May 1881, LNR Purcellville, Loudoun Co, VA, 1878

BRADFIELD, WILLIAM W. whose widow Maria applied for a pension

BRADFORD, JOHN (BLW), MD militia, died 21 Jan 1853, Madison or Orange Co, VA; md (1) Ann Stricker, (2) 10 Jun 1845 Mary Armistead (P), Baltimore, MD. She died c1884, LNR Big Lake, Sherburne Co, MN

BRADFORD, JOHN B. (BLW), died 21 Oct 1842, Accomac Co, VA; md 1 Jan 1811 Margaret/Peggy Addison (P), Northampton Co, VA. Her LNR Northampton Co, VA, 1855

BRADFORD, LABAN (BLW), died 4 Oct 1841, Accomac Co, VA; md 30 Sep 1835 Leah Teagnier (P), Accomac Co, VA. Her LNR P.O. Locust Mount, Accomac Co, VA, 1878

BRADFORD, THOMAS H. whose widow Elizabeth applied for a pension

BRADLEY, AUGUSTINE (BLW), died 23 Jun 1849, Madison Co, VA; md 26 Feb 1805 Mary/ Polly Lillard (P), Culpeper Co, VA. Her LNR P.O. Luray, Page Co, VA, 1871

BRADLEY, DAVID (P, BLW), LNR P.O. Flanagans Mills, Cumberland Co, VA, 1881

BRADLEY, JESSE (BLW), died 9 Apr 1871, Bedford Co, VA; md 26 Nov 1822 Sally Richards (P), Bedford Co, VA. She died c1879, LNR P.O. Goodview, Bedford Co, VA, 1878

BRADLEY, PHILIP (BLW), died 21 or 22 Nov 1826, Franklin Co, VA; md 18 Oct 1817 Elizabeth Forbes (P), Franklin Co, VA. She died 5 Jul 1884 LNR Haleford, Franklin Co, VA, 1879

BRADLEY, THOMAS applied for a pension

BRADLEY, WILLIAM P. (BLW), died 26 Mar 1861, Valley Bend, VA; md 26 Aug 1819 Mary C. Burr (P), Middle Fork, Randolph Co, VA. She died 3 Jan 1888, LNR Valley Bend, Randolph Co, WV, 1878

BRADSHAW, BENJAMIN (P, BLW), died 5 Jul 1872, Lovingston, VA; md 14 Sep 1826 Rhoda Ann Griffin (P), Nelson Co, VA. She died 25 Jan 1903, LNR Montrail, Nelson co, VA, 1871

BRADSHAW, HENRY (BLW), died 15 Dec 1862, Gleason Station, TN; md (1) Mary Leath, (2) Amy Fodge, (3) 27 Apr 1846 Mary Facen (P), Weakley Co, TN. She died c1895, LNR Gleason Station, Weakley Co, TN, 1880

BRADSHAW, HEZEKIAH (P, BLW), died 27 May 1878, LNR P.O. Berlin, Southampton Co, VA, 1871

BRADSHAW, JAMES (BLW), died 28 Feb 1849, Manchester,

BRADSHAW (continued) VA; md 6 Mar 1818 Mancy A. Hudson (P), Prince Edward Co, VA. She died 25 Dec 1886, Manchester, VA, LNR Manchester, Chesterfield Co, VA, 1878

BRADSHAW, JAMES (BLW), died 14 Jul 1871, Southampton Co, VA; md (1) Sarah Barnes, (2) 14 Feb 1855 Permelia Mumford (P), Isle of Wight Co, VA. She died c1895, LNR P.O. Vicksville, Southampton Co, VA, 1884

BRADSHAW, THOMAS (P, BLW), died 3 Jan 1878; md Jan 1815 Frances S. Eperson (P). She died c1882, LNR P.O. New Canton, Hawkins Co, TN

BRADSHAW, WILLIAM (BLW), died 16 Jun 1863, Prince Edward Co, VA; md 16 Jun 1834 Lucy Ann Marshall (P), Prince Edward Co, VA. Her LNR P.O. Rice's Depot, Prince Edward Co, VA, 1878

BRADSHAW, WILLIAM (BLW), died 18 Mar 1860, Indianapolis, IN; md 19 Oct 1820 Margaret Coyner (P), Augusta Co, VA. She died 8 Jan 1887, Indianapolis, IN, LNR Indianapolis, Marion Co, IN, 1878

BRADY, JOHN (P, BLW), died 20 Oct 1882, Lincoln Co, TN; md (1) Susanna Gunn, (2) 27 Nov 1856 Lucinda (----) Williams (P), Lincoln Co, TN. She died 22 Dec 1905, LNR P.O. Fayetteville, Lincoln Co, TN, 1871

BRADY, RICHARD whose widow Nancy applied for a pension

BRAGG, JAMES (P, BLW), LNR Bartramsville, Lawrence Co, OH, 1871; md 15 Nov 1811 Susannah Pusey, Fluvanna Co, VA

BRAGG, JOHN (BLW), died 24 Sep 1858, Petersburg, VA; md

BRAGG (continued)
24 Apr 1839 Maria A. Hill (P), Raleigh, NC. Her LNR Raleigh, Wake Co, NC, 1878

BRAGG, JOSEPH (BLW), died 11 Mar 1836, Greenbrier Co (now Summers Co), VA; md 11 Dec 1803 Judith/Judy Adkins (P), Lick Creek, Greenbrier Co, VA. Her LNR Hinton, Summers Co, WV, 1873

BRAGG, TALBOT (P, BLW), LNR Troy, Lincoln Co, MO, 1871; md 5 Aug 1830 Eliza S. Ragland, Charlottesville, VA

BRAGG, THOMAS (P, BLW), died 1 Feb 1879d, Fluvanna Co, VA, LNR Chapel Hill, Fluvanna Co, VA; md 15 Dec 1809 Nancy Johnson, Fluvanna Co, VA

BRAGG, WYATT (BLW), died 31 May 1847, Louisa Co, VA; md 5 Dec 1826 Sallie H. Desper (P), Louisa Co, VA. Her LNR P.O. Poindexters Store, Louisa Co, VA, 1878

BRAITHWAITE/BRATHWAIT, BENJAMIN (P, BLW), died 11 Sep 1871, LNR P.O. Acorn Hill, Frederick Co, VA, 1871; md 7 Nov 1823 Maria Huff, Frederick Co, VA

BRAITHWAITE, JOHN (BLW), died 19 Jan 1864, Frederick Co, VA; md 8 May 1828 Susan Farmer (P), Frederick Co, VA. She died c1889, LNR P.O. Cross Junction, Frederick Co, VA, 1878

ROLL NO. 11

BRAMMELL/BRAMEL, JOHN (BLW), died 8 Apr 1875, Prince William Co, VA; md Aug 1817 Sarah Upton (P), Prince William Co, VA. Her LNR P.O. Occoquan, Prince William Co, VA, 1878

BRAMMER, JAMES applied for a pension

BRAMMER, JOSEPH H. (P, BLW), died 14 Nov 1878, Owen Co, IN; md 24 Aug 1836 Frances Hartsof (P), Columbus, Bartholomew Co, IN. She died 12 Jun 1896, Owen Co, IN, LNR P.O. Patricksburgh, Owen Co, IN, 1871

BRAMMER, WILLIAM whose widow Mary applied for a pension

BRANAMAN, ABRAHAM (BLW), died 15 Mar 1874, Lexington, KY; md (1) Elizabeth Heneem, (2) 12 Jan 1835 Mary A. Carpenter (P), Mt. Vernon, KY. She died c1892, LNR Mt. Vernon, KY, 1878

BRANCH, BENJAMIN whose widow Emma applied for a pension

BRANCH, BRITTEN, died 20 Dec 1845, Monroe Co, KY; md 20 Jun 1811 Mary Branch (P), Buckingham Co, VA. She married (2) Moses Campbell. Her LNR P.O. Mud Lick, Monroe Co, KY, 1875. Her pension was suspended on 16 Apr 1880 for fraud -- widow being remarried.

BRANCH, EDWARD (P, BLW), died 28 Oct 1874, Attala Co, MS; md 24 Mar 1830 Winiford Ragland (P), Hinds Co, MS. Her LNR P.O. Kosciusko, Attala Co, MS, 1878

BRANCH, LeROY (P, BLW), LNR P.O. Manchester, Chesterfield Co, VA, 1871; md 1 Dec 1823 Matilda Archer Bruse, Chesterfield Co, VA

BRANCH, ROBERT F. (BLW), died 9 Nov 1858, Dinwiddie Co, VA; md 12 Mar 1857 Harriet T. (----) Johnson (P), Dinwiddie Co, VA. Her LNR San Marino, Dinwiddie Co, VA, 1878. Her 1st husband was Benjamin Johnson.

BRAND, JAMES (P, BLW), died 27 Jul 1882, LNR P.O. Little

BRAND (continued)

Osage, Vernon Co, MO, 1871, md 11 Mayu 1815 Sarah Burrows, Morgantown, VA

BRAND, SAMUEL (P, BLW), LNR West Point, Lee Co, VA, 1871. Not married

BRANDON/BRANDOM, FRANCIS applied for a pension

BRANDON, ROBERT (P, BLW), LNR P.O. New Bloomfield, Calloway Co, MO, 1871; md 17 Jan 1811 Jane Holt, Halifax Co, VA. She died 2 Apr 1858

BRANDON, WILLIAM applied for a pension

BRANHAM, AARON (BLW), died 26 Feb 1840, Greenbrier Co, VA; md 24 Nov 1831 Sarah Gregory (P), Greenbrier Co, VA. She died 19 Feb 1883, LNR P.O. Lewisburg, Greenbrier Co, WV

BRANHAM, NATHANIEL (BLW), died 1861; md c1810 Jemima ---- (P), Louisa Co, VA. Her LNR P.O. Harrisonburg, Rockingham Co, VA, 1872

BRANIGAN/BRANIJIN, JOHN whose widow Lucy F. applied for a pension

BRANNON, THOMAS (BLW), died 17 Jan 1860, Bartholomew Co, IN; md (1) Sally Parks, (2) 5 Apr 1837 Elizabeth Fulwider (P), Newborn, Bartholomew Co, IN. She died 2 Jan 1905, LNR Indianapolis, Marion Co, IN, 1892

BRANNON, LEVI (P, BLW), died 10 Feb 1876, Berkeley Co, WV; md 7 Jun 1827 Ruth Gray (P), Edwardtown, Berkeley Co, VA. Her LNR Glengary, Berkeley Co, WV, 1871

BRANSCOM, BENJAMIN (BLW), died 7 Feb 1862, Jackson Co, OH; md 7 Dec 1815 Tabitha Seward (P), Brunswick Co, VA. She died 1891, LNR P.O. Jackson Courthouse, Jackson

BRANSCOM (continued)

Co, OH

BRANSCOMB, JAMES (P, BLW), died 10 Mar 1881, Carroll Co, VA; md 5 Mar 1815 Francis Jones (P), Grayson Co, VA. She died c1887, LNR Pipers Gap, Carroll Co, VA

BRANSCOMB, REUBEN (BLW), died 12 Feb 1870, Carroll Co, VA; md 28 Sep 1811 Hannah O'Neal (P), Grayson Co, VA. She died 13 Sep 1880, LNR P.O. Hilleville, Carroll Co, VA, 1878

BRANTLEY, ETHELRED applied for a pension

BRASFIELD, GEORGE W./ THOMAS J. (BLW), died 21 Sep 1837, Shelby Co, KY; md 10 Jul 1821 Sophia Cotton (P), Fayette Co, KY. She died 12 Mar 1887, Crawfordsville, IN, LNR Crawfordsville, Montgomery Co, IN, 1879. She alleged her husband served as a substitute for his brother in the War

BRATTON, ROBERT (P, BLW), LNR Callaghan, Alleghany Co, VA, 1871; md 25 Jul 1825 Hannah Otey, Rockbridge Co, VA

BRATTON, THOMAS (BLW), died 14 Feb 1833/34, Montgomery Co, VA; md 1807/9 Mary Jordan (P), Botetourt Co, VA. Her LNR P.O. Princeton, Mercer Co, WV, 1874

BRATTON, THOMAS whose widow Sarah applied for a pension

BRAWLEY, WILLIAM S. (BLW), died Jul 1831 or 12 Jul 1833, Kanawha Co, VA; md 4 Apr 1811, Frances Keeney (P), Greenbrier Co, VA. Her LNR P.O. Kanawha Court House, Kanawha Co, WV, 1871

BRAWNER, HENRY (P, BLW), LNR Trousdale Co, TN, 1871; md Mar 1817 Mary Gammon,

BRAWNER (continued)
South Co, TN
BRAY, JAMES (BLW), died 12
Mar 1871, Richmond, VA; md
13 Jan 1814 Mary S. Staples
(P), Richmond, VA. Her LNR
Stuarts Draft, Augusta Co, VA,
1878
BREARDY, JOHN (BLW), died 7
Jul 1866, Mt. Olivet, Belmont
Co, OH; md 29 Dec 1813
Nancy Moore (P), Loudoun Co,
VA. Her LNR Barnesville,
Belmont Co, OH, 1871
BREEDLOVE, MARTIN D.
(BLW), died Jun 1867 Bote-
tourt Co, VA; md 12 Mar 1833
Eleanor Brads (P), Lexington,
Rockbridge Co, VA. She died
12 Jan 1855, Charleston,
Kanawha Co, WV
BRELSFORD, JESSE (BLW),
died 29 Nov 1845, Hampshire
Co, VA; md 14 Jan 1814 Mary
E. Jacobs (P), Hampshire Co,
VA. She died c1900, LNR
Frederick Co, VA, 1878
BRENNON/BRINNON, SHEL-
TON/CHILTON (BLW), died
17 Jul 1866, Champaign Co,
OH; md 12 Nov 1829 Elizabeth
Sanford (P), Westmoreland Co,
VA. She died c1880, LNR Me-
chanicsburg, Champaign Co,
OH
BRENT, JOHN H. (P, BLW), died
20 Aug 1882, Mount Hope,
Fauquier Co, VA; md 6 Mar
1833 Lucy Page Baylor (P),
Warrenton, Fauquier Co, VA.
She died 15 Jul 1898,
Alexandria, VA
BRENT, KENNER (P, BLW),
died 27 Nov 1878, Ellison, IL;
md (1) Elizabeth ---, (2) 31
Jul 1867 Ann N. (Hubbard)
Leland (P), Lancaster, VA.
She died 24 May 1911, LNR
Ellison, IL
BRESSIE, WILLIAM (BLW), died
13 Mar 1867, Norfolk, VA; md
1 Feb 1840 Elizabeth Ann

BRESSIE (continued)
Sykes (P), Norfolk Co, VA. She
died 14 Oct 1883, Deep Creek,
Norfolk Co, VA
BREWBAKER, ABRAHAM (P,
BLW), died c1888, LNR Fin-
castle, Botetourt Co, Va; md 5
Sep 1816 Anne Dil, Botetourt
Co, VA
BREWER, AARON (P, BLW),
died c1876, LNR P.O. Marco,
Green Co, IN, 1871. Not
married
BREWER, HOPKINS (BLW), died
17 Nov 1865, Franklin Co, VA;
md 9 Mar 1835 Susan A. Mit-
chell (P), Franklin Co, VA.
She died cMar 1884, LNR
Shady Grove, Franklin Co, VA,
1878
BREWER, ISAAC whose widow
Elizabeth applied for a pension
BREWER, SAMUEL/BENJAMIN
applied for a pension
BREWER, WILLIE/WILEY/
WILLIAM (BLW), died Jul
1867, Brunswick Co, VA; md
Jan 1817 Tabitha W. Pearson
(P), Brunswick Co, VA. She
died c1888, LNR Powelton,
Brunswick Co, VA
BREWER, WILLIAM (BLW),
died 11 Aug 1862, Halifax Co,
VA; md 14 Aug 1828 Anna Ed-
wards (P), Halifax Co, VA.
Her LNR P.O. South Boston,
Halifax Co, VA
BREWER, WILLIAM (P, BLW),
died 28 Sep 1873, Campbell
Co, VA; md 18 Sep 1817 Litha
(Hurt) Johnson (P), Charlotte
Co, VA. She died 24 or 30 Apr
1888, Hat Creek, Campbell Co,
VA
BRIANT, CHARLES E. (BLW),
died 4 Nov 1857, Wil-
liamstown, Wood Co, VA; md
20 Nov 1817 Sarah King (P),
Elizabeth, Wood Co, VA. Her
LNR Parkersburg, Wood Co,
WV, 1878
BRICKHEAD, NEHEMIAH

BRICKHEAD (continued)
(BLW), died 4 Jul 1862, Albemarle Co, VA; md (1) Mary Jemerson, (2) 16 Aug 1855 Mary Prichett (P), Albemarle Co, VA. She died c1889, LNR P.O. Earleysville, Albemarle Co, VA, 1878

BRICKHOUSE, GEORGE (P, BLW), died 2 Apr 1878, Eastville, VA, LNR Franktown, Northampton Co, VA, 1878; md 21 Dec 1815 Ann J. Sanford, Northampton Co, VA. His pension claim was rejected 20 Aug 1872 and reopened but rejected again 10 May 1878. Claim was admitted 16 May 1878, but rejected 6 Jan 1880. Certificate for pension never issued

BRIDGES, ALEXANDER (BLW), died 15 Nov 1865, Wilson Co, TN; md 18 Aug 1829 Elizabeth Rolls (P), Wilson Co, TN. She died 27 Apr 1902, LNR P.O. Gladeville, Wilson Co, TN, 1878

BRIDGES, BENJAMIN (P, BLW), LNR P.O. Guilford, Loudoun Co, VA, 1878

BRIDGES, ROBERT whose widow Ann R. applied for a pension

BRIDWELL, ISAAC whose widow Mary applied for a pension

BRIGGS, ALEXANDER (BLW), died 17 Jul 1843, Southampton, VA; md (1) Nancy Jones, (2) 7 Mar 1827 Rebecca Williams (P), Southampton Co, VA. She died 18 Oct 1887 LNR Jerusalem, Southampton Co, VA, 1878

BRIGHAM, CHARLES J. (BLW), died 11 Mar 1864, Johnston Co, NC; md (1) Mary Creech, (2) 26 Oct 1846 Cassandra Langdon (P), Johnston Co, NC. Her LNR P.O. Elevation, Johnston co, NC, 1879

BRIGHT, ADAM (BLW), died 28 Mar 1852, Mason Co, VA; md

BRIGHT (continued)
24 Nov 1814 Sarah Headley (P), Staunton, Augusta Co, VA. Her LNR P.O. Leon, Decatur Co, IA, 1872

BRIGHT, ELIJAH (BLW), TN militia, died 13 Apr 1849, Scott Co, VA; md 26 Oct 1808 Dorcas Trimble (P), Arcadia, Sullivan Co, TN. Her LNR Scott Co, VA, 1871

BRIGHTWELL, BARNET (BLW), died 1840, Henrico Co, VA; md 17 Feb 1821 Sally Crittenden (P), Henrico Co, VA. She died 4 Feb 1893, LNR P.O. Richmond, Henrico Co, VA, 1878

BRIGHTWELL, BARNETT U. (BLW), died 13 Jul 1855, Prince Edward Co, VA; md 10 Dc 1812 Judith W. Boatwright (P), Buchingham Co, VA. Her LNR Prospect Depot, Prince Edward Co, VA, 1871

BRILL, ISAAC (P, BLW), died 13 May 1883, Shenandoah Co, VA; md (1) Mary/Polly Conner, (2) 10 Apr 1870 Sarah Elizabeth Keckley (P), Shenandoah Co, VA. Her LNR P.O. Woodstock, Shenandoah Co, VA, 1871. She was dropped from the pension roll on 29 Oct 1884

BRILL, JOSEPH (P, BLW), died 28 Jun 1877, Frederick Co, VA; md (1) Rebecca Orndorff, (2) 14 Nov 1861 Mary Catharine Orndorff (P), Frederick Co, VA. She died Nov/Dec 1904, LNR Wheatfield, Shenandoah Co, VA, 1904

BRIMER/BRIMMER, ZACHARIAH (P, BLW), LNR P.O. Spotsylvania Courthouse, Spotsylvania Co, VA, 1871; md 29 Sep 1833 Lucy Brimer, Spotsylvania Co, VA

BRISCOE, JOHN (BLW),

BRISCOE, THOMAS whose widow Juliet Wood applied for a pension

BRISCOE, WILLIAM H. (BLW), died 1838, St. Louis, MO; md 3 Oct 1816 Eliza H. Harris (P), Leesburg, VA. She died 12 Aug 1887, LNR Leesburg, Loudoun Co, VA, 1878

BRISTOR/BRISTER, GEORGE (BLW), died 30 May 1826, Baltimore, MD; md 27 Jul 1826 Susan Lusby (P), Baltimore, MD. Her LNR Baltimore, MD, 1878

BRITT, BOLLING (BLW), died 1 Jun 1856, Hittle, IL; md (1) Polly Sotler, (2) 30 Jan 1855 Lois O. (----) Morse (P), Hittle, IL. She died c1892, LNR P.O. Hittle, Tazewell Co, IL, 1886

BRITT, JONATHAN T. (BLW), died 21 or 22 Jun 1866, Southampton Co, VA; md 28 Dec 1813 Margaret Ward (P), Hertford Co, NC. Her LNR Hertford Co, NC, 1880

BRITT, ROBERT (BLW), MD militia, died 7 Aug 1866, near Wellsburg, WV; md 10 Nov 1818 Jemimah Linton (P), near Wellsburg, VA. Her LNR P.O. Wellsburg, Brooke Co, WV, 1878

BRITT, TANDY H. (BLW), died 9 Jan 1852, Montgomery Co, MO; md (1) Mary Hughes, (2) 11 Sep 1838 Martha J. (----) Harvey (P). She died 14 Sep 1887, LNR P.O. Montgomery City, Montgomery Co, MO, 1887

BRITT, WILLIAM (P, BLW), died 28 Nov 1873, Albemarle Co, VA; md (1) Anna Barnett, (2) Polly Bruffy, (3) 6 Jun 1864 Moaning Bishop (P), Albemarle Co, VA. She died 30 Jan 1908, LNR P.O. Charlottesville, Albemarle Co, VA, 1878

BRITTON, GEORGE (BLW), died 23 Jun 1865, Hope Mills/Springfield, Page Co, VA; md

BRITTON (continued) 4 Feb 1818 Rebecca Brewer (P), Washington DC. Her LNR Luray, Page Co, VA, 1879

BRITTON, JOHN (P, BLW), LNR P.O. Troy, Lincoln Co, MO, 1871. Wife's name not given

BRITTON, JOHNAH (BLW), died 22 May 1865 Highland Co, OH; md 30 Dec 1820 Martha J./Patty Lock (P), Frederick Co, VA. She died c1897, LNR Willettsville, Highland Co, OH, 1878

BRITTON, NATHAN (BLW), died 3 Mar 1871, Bedington, Berkeley Co, WV; md Mar 1823 Nancy Meracle (P), Berkeley Co, VA. She died 12 May 1892, LNR P.O. Martinsburg, Berkeley Co, WV, 1887

BROADIE/BRODY/BROADY, WILLIAMSON (BLW), died 14 Apr 1868, Franklin Co, VA; md 10 Oct 1822 Nancy Bobbett (P), Franklin Co, VA. She died 21 Apr 1885, LNR P.O. Shady Grove, Franklin Co, VA, 1878

BROADWATER, WILLIAM E. (BLW), died Jul 1835, Loudoun Co, VA; md 24 Nov 1817 Margaret Daine (P), Fairfax Co, VA. Her LNR P.O. Martinsburg, Audrain Co, MO, 1879

BROADY, RICHARD whose widow Ellen applied for a pension

BROCKETT, ROBERT (BLW), died 22 Jun 1867, Alexandria, VA; md 14 Dec 1815 Elizabeth Longden (P), Alexandria, VA. Her LNR Alexandria, VA, 1878

BROCKMAN, ASA (BLW), died cMar 1861, Orange Co, VA; md 21 Jan 1819 Lucy E. Quisenberry (P), Orange Co, VA. Her LNR P.O. Madison Run, Orange Co, VA, 1878. Erroneously pensioned as Lucy A. Brockman

BROMLEY, ROBERT (BLW), died 8 Jan 1859, King William Co, VA; md 20 Dec 1832 Mildred M. Bagby (P), King and Queen Co, VA. She died c1890, LNR P.O. Lanesville, King William Co, Va, 1878

BRONAUGH, THOMAS (BLW), died 5 Jul 1866, Oak Grove, VA; md 25 Feb 1813 Judith Hart (P), Locust Grove, Louisa Co, VA. Her LNR Oak Grove, Louisa Co, VA, 1871

BRONAUGH, WILLIAM J. (P, BLW), died 19 Feb 1879, Prince William Co, VA; md 25 Jan 1817 Mary C. Mitchell (P), Georgetown, DC. She died c1889, LNR P.O. Waterfall, Prince William Co, VA, 1879

BROOKES, JOHN (BLW), USA, died 13 Jul 1858, Prince Goerge Co, MD; md (1) Sarah Taliaferro Daingerfield, (2) Ellen H. Waring, (3) 23 Apr 1846 Esther Jane Fowle (P), Alexandria, VA. Her LNR Alexandria, VA, 1878

BROOKOVER, JACOB (P, BLW) LNR P.O. Statler's Run, Monongalia Co, WV, 1871; md 28 Feb 1816 June Scott, Green Co, PA

BROOKS, ALEXANDER (BLW), died 22 Dec 1862, Richmond, VA; md 26 Aug 1830 Mary McRae (P), Manchester, Chesterfield Co, VA. She died Oct 1899, Richmond, VA, LNR Richmond, VA, 1878. Alexander served as a substitute for Zachariah Brooks in the War

BROOKS, DABNEY (BLW), died 23 Sep 1858, Spotsylvania Co, VA; md 4 Jun 1832 Elizabeth Wren (P), Spotsylvania, VA. She died c1889, LNR P.O. Andrews, Spotsylvania Co, VA, 1878

BROOKS, DAVID and his widow Stacey A. both applied for a

BROOKS (continued) pension

BROOKS, ELKANAH (P, BLW), LNR P.O. Hopeful, Louisa Co, VA, 1878

BROOKS, EMANUEL (BLW), died 8 May 1843, Jackson Co, OH; md (1) Caroline Baldwin, (2) Ann Richardson, (3) 23 Feb 1842 Phebe Shepard (P), Jackson Co, OH. She died 30 Jun 1880, LNR Wellston, Jackson Co, OH, 1878

BROOKS, GEORGE K. (BLW), died 4 Mar 1849, Mathews Co, VA; md 7 Jan 1813 Elizabeth Miller (P), Mathews Co, VA. She died 13 Nov 1872, LNR P.O. Mathews Courthouse, Mathews Co, VA, 1871

BROOKS, JAMES (BLW), died 4 Mar 1868, Campbell Co, VA; md 6 Oct 1814 Rhoda Brooks (P), Campbell Co, VA. Her LNR P.O. Concord Depot Campbell Co, VA, 1871

BROOKS, JAMES (BLW), died 9 Apr 1847, Goochland Co, VA; md 24 Dec 1823 Eliza Poor (P), Brooks Cross Roads, VA. She died 29 Aug 1880, Goochland Co, VA, LNR Bula, Goochland Co, VA, 1878

BROOKS, JOHN (BLW), died 17 Jan 1854, Charlotte Co, VA; md 21 Dec 1820 Elizabeth M. Rawlins (P), Charlotte Co, VA. She died 28 May 1888, Drakes Branch, Charlotte Co, VA

BROOKS, LAWSON applied for a pension

BROOKS, LEWIS D. A. (P, BLW), died 3 Nov 1876, Essex Co,VA; md (1) Maria Alexander, (2) Fanny Greggs, (3) 8 Nov 1827 Sarah Roy (P), Essex Co, VA. She died 3 Jul 1885, LNR P.O. Millers Tavern, Essex Co, VA, 1878

BROOKS, THOMAS (BLW),

BROOKS, THOMAS (P, BLW), died 11 Jan 1872, Stafford Co,

BROOKS (continued)
VA; md (1) Milly Bridwell, (2)
Mar 1840/41 Elizabeth Bussell
(P). She died 18 Jan 1892,
LNR P.O. Stafford Courthouse,
Stafford Co, VA, 1888
BROOKS, THOMAS (BLW) whose
widow was Mary
BROOKS, TUNIS (P, BLW), LNR
P.O. Ettieville, Gentry Co,
MO, 1871; md Jan 1816 Sarah
Hartman, Botetourt Co, VA
BROOKS, WILLIAM (P, BLW),
died 25 Feb 1879, Campbell
Co, VA, LNR P.O. Concord
Depot, Campbell Co, VA, 1871
BROOKS, WILLIAM (BLW), died
14 Nov 1857, Augusta Co, VA;
md 29 Apr 1824 Elvira A. Dodd
(P), LNR Staunton, Augusta
Co, VA, 1878
BROOKS, ZACHARIAH whose wi-
dow Martha applied for a pen-
sion

ROLL NO. 12

BROTHERS, JACOB (BLW), died
Jul 1865, Nansemond Co, Va;
md 5 Feb 1812 Emily Duke
(P), Gates Co, NC. She died
15 Mar 1873, LNR P.O. Suf-
folk, Nansemond Co, VA, 1871
BROUGHMAN, JOHN (BLW),
died 3 May 1864, Rockbridge
Co, VA; md 1820 Elizabeth
Cox (P), Botetourt Co, VA.
She died c1888, LNR P.O.
Lexington, Rockbridge Co, VA,
1879
BROUNLEE, WALTER (P,
BLW), LNR Oregon, Holt Co,
MO, 1871. Living Brooke Co,
VA, 1850
BROWDER, JOSEPH (BLW),
died 7 Mar 1857, Brunswick
Co, VA; md 24 Dec 1811
Fanny Johnson (P), Brunswick
Co, VA. Her LNR P.O. Burnt-
ville, Brunswick Co, VA, 1871
BROWN, ABRAM (BLW), OH
militia, died 31 Jul 1866,

BROWN (continued)
Noble Co, IN; md 10 Feb 1820
Mary Fergus, Montgomery Co,
VA. Her LNR Legonier, Noble
Co, IN, 1878
BROWN, ABRAM applied for a
pension
BROWN, ANDREW A. (BLW),
died 4 Jun 1850, Amherst Co,
VA; md 25 Dec 1821 Polly R.
Duncan (P), Amherst Co, VA.
Her LNR Paynesville, Pike
Co, MO, 1878
BROWN, ARCHIBALD (BLW),
died 11 Aug 1835, Leesburg,
OH; md 28 Jan 1819 Nancy
Wise (P), Hillsborough, OH.
She died c1888, LNR Hills-
borough, Highland Co, OH,
1878
BROWN, ARCHIBALD (P, BLW),
died c1876, LNR Waverley,
Pike Co, OH, 1871
BROWN, ASA (P, BLW), died 20
Mar 1872, Waterford, Loudoun
Co, VA; md 7 Jan 1819 Jane
Arena Crook (P), Frederick Co,
MD. She died c1855, LNR
Kansas, Edgar Co, IL, 1878
BROWN, BENJAMIN applied for
a pension
BROWN, BURELL (BLW), died
24 May 1867, Rutherford Co,
TN; md 16 Jan 1813 Jane
Haley (P), Charlotte Co, VA.
Her LNR P.O. Murfreesboro,
Rutherford Co, TN, 1871
BROWN, CHESLEY (P, BLW),
died 25 Jun 1872, LNR Spring
Hiill, Cumberland Co, VA,
1871; md 12 Dec 1817 Mary
Bradley, Spring Hill, VA
BROWN, ELISHA (BLW), died 22
Apr 1857, Webster Co, MO;
md Jun 1805 Martha Stanley
(P), Halifax Co, VA. She died
10 May 1874, Webster Co,
MO, LNR Mornington, Webster
Co, MO, 1871
BROWN, ELLIS (BLW), died 22
Jul 1870, Richmond, VA; md
(1) ---- Bosher, (2) 17 Jan

BROWN (continued)
1833 Virginia Hughes (P), Richmond, VA. Her LNR Richmond, VA, 1878

BROWN, EVAN (P, BLW), died 21 Feb 1872, Culpeper, VA. He was a substitute for William Brown in the War

BROWN, FELIX whose widow Agnes applied for a pension

BROWN, FRIEND whose widow Amelia applied for a pension

BROWN, GARLAND (P, BLW), LNR P.O. Afton, Nelson Co, VA, 1871. Widower.

BROWN, GEORGE (BLW), died 27 Aug 1852, Albemarle Co, VA; md 2 Jan 1819 Susanna Meddings (P), Fluvanna Co, VA. Her LNR P.O. Scottsville, Albemarle Co, VA, 1878

BROWN, HENRY (P, BLW), died 26 Feb 1874, Brown Co, IL; md 11 Mar 1824 Edith Davis (P), Pickaway Co, OH. She died c1885, LNR P.O. Mt. Sterling, Brown Co, IL, 1878

BROWN, HEZEKIAH (P, BLW), died 8 Jan 1875, New Holland, OH; md 27 Apr 1823 Mary Williams (P), Fayette Co, OH. She died 10 Aug 1883, New Holland, OH, LNR New Holland, Pickaway Co, OH, 1878

BROWN, JAMES (P, BLW), TN militia, died 13 Mar 1879, Gladeville, Wise Co, VA; md (1) Mary Lowe, (2) 17 Oct 1874 Mary (----) Vance (P), Wise Co, VA. She died c1892, LNR P.O. Gladeville, Wise Co, VA, 1879

BROWN, JAMES applied for a pension

BROWN, JAMES (BLW), died 5 Jun 1859, Logan Co, VA; md 10 Aug 1815 Polly Vance (P), Russell Co, VA. She died 6 Feb 1888, LNR P.O. Rich Creek, Logan Co, WV, 1878

BROWN, JAMES whose widow Malinda applied for a pension

BROWN, JAMES P. (P, BLW), died 27 May 1873, Ross Co, OH; md (1) Elizabeth Miller, (2) 24 Feb 1848 Mary A. Black (P), Union Township, Ross Co, OH. She died 26 Feb 1894, Bourneville, OH, LNR Twin Township, Ross Co, OH, 1878

BROWN, JOHN (BLW), TN militia, died 11 May 1846, Tazewell Co, VA; md 22 Mar 1810 Sally Ayres (P), Rockbridge Co, VA. Her LNR Tazewell Co, VA, 1871

BROWN, JOHN (P, BLW), died 23 May 1872, Culpeper Co, VA, LNR Rappahannock Co, VA, 1871; md 29 Jun 1820 ----, Fauquier Co, VA. She died 1850

BROWN, JOHN (P, BLW), died 3 Aug 1881, LNR Orange, Orange Co, VA, 1871; md Oct 1811 Sallie Hinchey, Hanover Co, VA

BROWN, JOHN (BLW), died Jun 1861, Edinburg, VA; md (1) Elizabeth Bushong, (2) 13 Dec 1836 Catharine Cremore (P), Woodstock, Shenandoah Co, VA. She died c1890, LNR Edinburg, Shenandoah Co, VA, 1878

BROWN, JOHN (BLW), died 2 Sep 1861, Saline Co, MO; md (1) Adelaide Kyle, (2) 16 May 1850 Julia A. (----) Carthrae (P), Miami, Saline Co, MO. Her LNR Fairville, Saline Co, MO, 1888

BROWN, JOHN (BLW), died 18 Aug 1861, Lewis Co, VA; md 20 Mar 1820 Mercy Woofter (P), Lewis Co, VA. She died 4 Apr 1889, LNR Cold Water, Doddridge Co, WV, 1878

BROWN, JOHN (BLW), died 8 Sep 1838, Wayne Co, OH; md (1) Sarah Core, (2) 2 Aug 1829 Sarah Carr (P), Wayne Co, OH. She died 3 Apr 1881, LNR P.O. Orrville, Wayne Co, OH, 1879

BROWN, JOHN (BLW), died 16 Jul 1850, Westmoreland Co, VA; md (1) ?, (2) 31 Jan 1838 Susan Seef (P), Westmoreland Co, VA. She died c1882, LNR Oldhams Crossroads, Westmoreland Co, VA, 1878

BROWN, JOHN Jr. (P, BLW), died c1882, LNR P.O. Earleysville, Albemarle Co, VA. His wife died Sep 1858

BROWN, JOHN D. applied for a pension

BROWN, JOHN D. G. (BLW), died 24 Jan 1867, Hanover Co, VA; md 14 Oct 1824 Harriet I. Sheppard (P), Scotchtown, Hanover Co, VA. She died 29 Nov 1880, LNR P.O. Negrofoot, Hanover Co, VA, 1878

BROWN, LEWIS S. (BLW), died 13 Nov 1856, Lewis Co, MO; md 26 Mar 1832 Ann Maria Toler (P), Washington, DC. She died c1895, LNR Durham, Lewis Co, MO, 1879

BROWN, LITTLEBERRY G. (P, BLW), LNR P.O. Prospect Depot, Prince Edward Co, VA, 1871

BROWN, MOSES (P, BLW), LNR Hamlin, Lincoln Co, WV, 1872; md 9 Dec 18-- Lettie Gillespie, Kanawha Co, VA

BROWN, NELSON (P, BLW), died 27 Apr 1880, Amherst Co, VA; md 9 Nov 1833 Malinda U. Wheat (P), Albemarle Co, VA. She died 19 Sep 1898, LNR Amherst Co, VA, 1872

BROWN, NOAH (BLW), died 14 Mar 1864, Pulaski Co, KY; md 16 Nov 1815 Mary M. Marable (P), Lunenburg Courthouse, Lunenburg Co, VA. Her LNR Pulaski Co, KY, 1878

BROWN, PETER whose widow Hannah applied for a pension

BROWN, PETER (BLW), died 1 Jan 1858, Rockingham Co, VA; md 16 Aug 1821 Elizabeth Huffman (P), Rockingham Co, VA.

BROWN (continued) She died 1880, LNR P.O. Harrisonburg, Rockingham Co, VA, 1878

BROWN, ROBERT (BLW), died 7 Jun 1851, Logan Co, OH; md (1) Winnafred Glasscock, (2) 5 Dec 1832 Elizabeth Mathis (P), Urbana, Champaign Co, OH. She died 27 Mar 1892, LNR P.O. Degraff, Logan Co, OH, 1887

BROWN, ROBERT applied for a pension

BROWN, SAMUEL (BLW), died 12 Jul 1821, Kanawha Co, VA; md 19 Apr 1804 Martha H. Thompson (P). Her LNR Rocky Mount, VA, 1874

BROWN, SAMUEL and widow Gracie both applied for a pension

BROWN, SAMUEL A., alias BROWNE, ALFORD (BLW), died Sep or 12 Dec 1850, Portsmouth, VA; md 23 Oct 1823 Mary Ann Poulson (P), Portsmouth, VA. She died 28 Sep 1885, Portsmouth, Norfolk Co, VA

BROWN, SAMUEL B. (BLW), died 18 Mar 1859, Preston Co, VA; md 20 May 1821 Permelia Brown (P), Preston Co, VA. Her LNR P.O. Clinton Furnace, Monongalia Co, WV, 1878

BROWN, SOLOMON applied for a pension

BROWN, THOMAS (BLW), died 15 Mar 1858, Pine View, VA; md 11 Feb 1821 Nancy A. Brooks (P), Morrisville, Fauquier Co, VA. She died 7 Jan 1879, Pine View, Fauquier Co, VA

BROWN, THOMAS (BLW), died 26 Aug 1862, Frederick Co, VA; md 25 Jul 1809 Sarah H. Williams (P). Her LNR Winchester, Frederick Co, VA, 1871

BROWN, WALTER (P, BLW), NY militia, LNR Tazewell, Claiborne Co, TN, 1871; md 1819 Sally Quicksall, Richmond, VA

BROWN, WALTER (P, BLW), LNR P.O. Gallatin, Sumner Co, TN, 1871; md Effie Wallace, Buckingham Co, VA

BROWN, WILLIAM (P, BLW), died 28 Oct 1873, LNR P.O. Manchester, Chesterfield Co, VA, 1871

BROWN, WILLIAM (P, BLW), died 13 Feb 1873, LNR Chapel Hil, Fluvanna Co, VA, 1872; md 15 Aug 1815 Elizabeth Eades, Louisa Co, VA

BROWN, WILLIAM applied for a pension

BROWN, WILLIAM applied for a pension

BROWN, WILIAM (P, BLW), LNR Waynesboro, Augusta Co, VA, 1871; md 25 Apr 1811 Martha Hillhouse, Waynesboro, VA. Widower.

BROWN, WILLIAM (BLW)

BROWN, WILLIAM (BLW), died 11 Feb 1868, Linn Co, IA; md Jun 1819 Elizabeth H. Britton (P), Augusta Co, VA. She died c1889, LNR Jefferson, Greene Co, IA, 1878

BROWN, WILLIAM LILLY (BLW), died 17 Feb 1859, Bledsoe Co, TN; md 14 Sep 1816 Nancy Humphrey (P), Fluvanna Co, VA. Her LNR P.O. Pikeville, Bledsoe Co, TN, 1878

BROWN, WILLIAMSON/WILLIAM (BLW), died 1 Nov 1859, Scottsville, IL; md (1) ?, (2) ?, (3) 22 Nov 1835 Casandra Cherry (P), Scottsville, Macoupin Co, IL. She died 8 Mar 1887, LNR Waverly, Morgan Co, IL, 1878

BROWN, ZEDEKIAH (BLW), died 17 Aug 1848-1850, Buckingham Co, VA; md 5 Nov

BROWN (continued)
1812 Judith Duncan (P), Buckingham Co, VA. Her LNR Hickory Plains, Prairie Co, AR, 1886

BROWNING, ELIAS WESLEY (P, BLW), died 9 Oct 1874, Portland, OH; md 10 Apr 1866 Samantha Cowdery (P), Pomeroy, OH. She died 28 Nov 1909, Portland, Meigs Co, OH

BROWNING, JACOB (BLW), died 17 May 1861, Harlan Co, KY; md Apr 1813 Sarah Clem (P), Abingdon, Washington Co, VA. Her LNR P.O. Harlan Courthouse, Harlan Co, KY, 1878

BROWNING, WILLIAM W. (BLW), died 13 Nov 1864, Springfield, IL; md 26 Oct 1820 Sarah Smith Farrow (P), Fauquier Co, VA. She died 17 Oct 1883, LNR P.O. San Jose, Santa Clara Co, CA, 1880

BROWNLEE, JOHN (P, BLW), died 10 Mar 1877, Augusta Co, VA; md 28 Oct 1819 Nancy Bell (P), Augusta Co, VA. She died 7 Dec 1886, Augusta Co, VA, LNR P.O. Greenville, Augusta Co, VA, 1878

BROWNLEY, JAMES (BLW), died 7 Aug 1870, Princeton, IN; md (1) Jane Edwards, (2) 29 Oct 1829 Jane Bigham (P), Gibson Co, IN. Her LNR Princeton, Gibson Co, IN, 1878

BROWNLEY, THOMAS whose widow Sarah applied for a pension

BROWNLOW, TIPPO S. (P, BLW), died 27 Jan 1879, Warrenton, NC; md 31 May 1817 Martha Maria Robert Crittenden (P), Southampton Co, VA. Her LNR Warrenton, Warren Co, NC, 1879

BROYLES, LARKIN applied for a pension

ROLL NO. 13

BRUCE, BAILEY (BLW), USA, died 17 Mar 1831, Fauquier Co, VA; md 20 Jun 1815 Sally Newhouse (P), Fauquier Co, VA. Her LNR Sperryville, Rappahannock Co, VA, 1889. Sally md (2) John O. Lawrence in 1842, and he died in 1844

BRUCE, CHARLES (P, BLW), LNR P.O. Lebanon, Wilson Co, TN, 1871; md Dec 1846 Sally Hankins, Wilson Co, TN

BRUCE, GEORGE (P, BLW), died 20 Oct 1877, Cumberland Co, IL; md 4 Oct 1873 Sophronia Roberts (P), Cumberland Co, IL. She died Sep 1884, Union Centre, Cumberland Co, IL

BRUCE, GEORGE (BLW), died 28 Feb 1839, Wilmington, OH; md 30 Sep 1813 Jane B. McPherson (P), Frederick Co, VA. She died 2 Dec 1884, LNR Cincinnati, Hamilton Co, OH, 1871

BRUCE, JAMES (BLW), applied for a pension

BRUCE, REUBEN (P, BLW), died 25 Dec 1871, Sperryville, VA; md 1816 Maria Whalan (P), Culpeper Co, VA. She died c1879, LNR P.O. Sperryville, Rappahannock Co, VA, 1871

BRUE/BRUGH, ABRAHAM (BLW), died 27 Jan 1860, Greene Co, GA; md 18 Jul 1852 Ridley Coley (P), Greene Co, VA. She died 29 May 1813, Greensboro, GA. Abraham served as a substitute for brother Harman Brugh in the War

BRUFFLER, MARK (P, BLW), died c1872, Brazil, IN, LNR Brazil, Clay Co, IN, 1871; md 29 Aug 1839 Susan Bullock, Clay Co, IN

BRUGH, JOHN (BLW)

BRUMFIELD, ISAAC (BLW), died 11 Jan 1849, Pittsylvania

BRUMFIELD (continued) Co, VA; md Sep/Dec 1818 Letitia Mayhue (P), Pittsylvania Co, VA. Her LNR P.O. Chatham, Pittsylvania Co, VA

BRUMFIELD, WILLIAM B. (P, BLW), died 18 Jan 1875, McMinn Co, TN; md (1) Susanna Oaks, (2) 10 Oct 1877 Jane (----) Barnett (P), McMinn Co, TN. She md Nathan Green 17 Sep1878, LNR McMinn Co, TN, 1878

BRUMLEY, LARKIN whose widow Sarah applied for a pension

BRUNER/PRUDEN/PRUNER, HENRY (BLW), died 6 Mar 1861, Hawkins Co, TN; md 1829 Sarah Mefford (P), Sullivan Co, TN. Her LNR P.O. Estillville, Scott Co, VA, 1878

BRUNNEMER, ANTHONY (BLW), died 29 Jan 1857, Clark Co, MO; md 12 Feb 1839 Martha E. Brenton (P), Indianapolis, Marion Co, IN. She died c1894, LNR Omio, Jewel Co, KS, 1880

BRUNNEMER, CONRAD (BLW), whose widow Catharine applied for a pension

BRUNTY, BARNABAS (P, BLW), died 26 Apr 1874, Pike Co, MO; md (1) Elizabeth Linry, (2) 7 Feb 1865 Mary E. Nesbit (P), West Ely, Marion Co, MO. She died 7 Apr 1903, LNR P.O. Spencerburg, Pike Co, MO, 1878

BRYAN, FREDERICK (BLW), died 18 Sep 1856, Fairfield Co, OH; md 23 Dec 1817 Martha W. Lee (P), James City Co, VA. She died c1890, LNR Middleport, Meigs Co, OH, 1878

BRYAN, JOHN L. (BLW), died 11 May 1866, Granville, OH; md 20 Nov 1832 Calista Griswold (P), Windsor, Ashtabula Co, OH. She died 27 Oct 1892,

BRYAN (continued)
LNR Granville, Licking Co, OH, 1878

BRYAN, JOSEPH whose widow Percia applied for a pension

BRYAN, RICHARD (BLW), died 1 Jul 1885, Wilson Co, TN; md 10 Dec 1817 Mary Brown (P), Halifax Co, VA. Her LNR Wilson Co, TN. Richard was a substitute for Nelson Bryan in the War

BRYAN, ROBERT who applied for a pension

BRYANT, BENJAMIN whose widow Cynthia Ann applied for a pension

BRYANT, FINNEY (BLW), died 18 Mar 1842/3, Franklin Co, KY; md 6 Mar 1812 Nancy Rucker (P), Amherst Co, VA. Her LNR Owenton, Owen Co, KY, 1871

BRYANT, HENRY (P, BLW), LNR Columbus, Bartholomew Co, IN, 1871; md 13 Jul 1867 Ann M. Hickey

BRYANT, REUBEN (BLW), died 20 Dec 1818, Buckingham Co, VA; md May 1810 Sarah/Sally Amos (P), Buckingham Co, VA. She died 28 Aug 1879, Glenmore, VA, LNr Buckingham Co, VA, 1854

BRYANT, THOMAS W. (BLW), whose widow Frances applied for a pension

BRYANT, WILLIAM S. (P, BLW), died 28 Dec 1877, Nelson Co, VA; md 24 Dec 1817 Martha Bryant (P), Fluvanna Co, VA. She died c1889 LNR P.O. Arrington Depot, Nelson Co, VA, 1878

BRYARLY, TATE (BLW), died 30 Oct 1852, Clarksville, TN; md 30 Jul 1829 Mary Smith Gray (P), Clarksville, TN. Her LNR Clarksville, Montgomery Co, TN, 1878

BRYTE/BRIGHT, JOHN (BLW), died 12 Sep 1839, Preston Co,

BRYTE/BRIGHT (continued)
VA; md 27 Dec 1806 Esther/ Ester Gibson (P), Monongalia Co (now Preston Co), VA. Her LNR Preston Co, WV, 1871

BUCHANAN, EBENEZER applied for a pension

BUCHANAN, EDWARD J. (BLW), died 17 Apr 1864, Pulaski Co, KY; md (1) Frances Mayfield, (2) 5 Dec 1855 Rachel (----) Yates (P), Somerset, Pulaski Co, KY. Her LNR P.O. Science Hill, Pulaski Co, KY, 1829

BUCHANAN, JOHN (P, BLW), died 10 Dec 1877, Sharpe Co, AR; md (1) Peggy Brightwell, (2) c1848 Nancy Clapton (P), Lauderdale Co, TN. She died c1895, LNR P.O. Evening Shade, Sharpe Co, AR, 1878

BUCHANAN, ROBERT applied for a pension

BUCHER/BUCKER, ABRAHAM (P, BLW), LNR Noblesville, Noble Co, OH, 1871

BUCK, HENRY (BLW), MD militia, died 31 Oct 1864/5, Greene Co, OH; md 21 Nov 1816 Hannah Fiser (P), Shepherdstown, VA. She died c1878, LNR DeGraff, Logan Co, OH, 1872

BUCK, ISAIAH (P, BLW), died 8 Mar 1892, Morgan Co, WV; md (1) ---- Waugh, (2) 30 Oct 1873 Mary C. Culp (P), Bath, Morgan Co, WV. She died Jan 1907, LNR P.O. Berkeley Springs, Morgan Co, WV, 1892

BUCK, JOHN S. (P, BLW), KY militia, LNR Louisa Courthouse, Louisa Co, VA; md 15 Jan 1846 Eliza T. Wilson (P), Spotsylvania Co, VA. She died 9 Aug 1858, Louisa Co, VA

BUCKHANAN/BUCKHANON, JAMES (P, BLW), died 18 Oct 1880, Senecaville, OH; md 1 Nov 1819 Lucretia Taylor (P), Morgantown, Monongalia Co,

BUCKHANAN (continued)
VA. She died 23 Jul 1885, Caldwell, Noble Co, OH. LNR Sarahsville, Noble Co, OH, 1881

BUCKLEY, JAMES (P, BLW), LNR Clifton, Fairfax Co, VA, 1878

BUCKLEY, SAMUEL G. (BLW), died 20 Oct 1823, Wood Co, VA; md 10 Sep 1815 Nancy Reeves (P), Fairfax Co, VA. She died 31 Aug 1881, LNR Bellefille, Wood Co, WV, 1871

BUCKLEY, WILLIAM (BLW), died Aug 1823/4, Prince William Co, VA; md Mar 1815 Fannie Gossum (P), Fairfax Co, VA. She died c1881, LNR Fairfax Courthouse, Fairfax Co, VA, 1879

BUCKNER, BAILEY (BLW), died 15 Jan 1832, Fredericksburg, VA; md 19 May 1814 Mildred Strother (P), Wayfield, VA. Her LNR, wayfield, Rappahannock Co, VA, 1872

BUCKNER, CHARLES (P, BLW), died 20 Apr 1873, Coosa Co, AL; md (1) ?, (2) 27 Jan 1850 Mary Suttle (P), Coosa Co, AL. Her LNR Sykes Mills, AL, 1880

BUCKNER, RICHARD M. (BLW), died 6 Apr 1874, Hopkins Co, KY; md 8 Sep 1829 Adeline M. Grace (P), Montgomery Co, TN. She died 18 Jul 1901, Hopkins Co, KY, 1878

BUFFINGTON, WILIAM (P, BLW), LNR Purcellville, Loudoun Co, VA, 1871

BUFKIN, DAVID (P, BLW), died 2 Jun 1879, Spencer Co, IN; md (1) ?, (2) 10 Dec 1868 Mary (----) Oskins (P), Spencer Co, IN. She died 1 Sep 1892, LNR P.O. Buffaloville, Spencer Co, IN, 1887

BUFORD, PASCHAL (BLW), applied for pension, died 23 Jul

BUFORD (continued)
1875, Bedford Co, VA; md 31 Aug 1820 Frances A. Otey (P), Bedford Co, VA. Her LNR Bufordsville, Bedford Co, VA, 1878

BUGG, TARLTON (BLW), died 15 Dec 1861; Mason Co, VA; md 3 Feb 1818 Frances Melton (P), Fluvanna Co, VA. Her LNR Point Pleasant, Mason Co, WV, 1878

BUGG, WILLIAM H. whose widow Martha applied for a pension

BUKEY, WILIAM (P, BLW), died 1 Nov 1883, Riegel, OH, LNR P.O. Galloway, Franklin Co, OH, 1878

BULGER, REUBEN (P-rejected, BLW), died 9 Apr 1877, Barnesville, OH; md 20 Apr 1820 Sarah Tilman (P), Winchester, VA. She died 30 Aug 1887, LNR Bethesda, Belmont Co, OH, 1878

BULGER, THOMAS B. (P, BLW), died 8 Mar 1879 Preble Co, OH, LNR P.O. Eaton, Preble Co, OH, 1871; md 18 Oct 1814 Sarah Keppler, Woodstock, Shenandoah Co, VA

BULL, JESSE (P, BLW), TN militia, died 7 Jan 1874, Bell Co, KY; md cJan/Feb 1818 Jane Daniel (P), Harlan Co, KY. She died 15-18 Nov 1883, Harlan Co, KY, LNR P.O. Balls Mills, Lee co, VA, 1878

BULL, JOHN (P-rejected, BLW), died 30 Aug 1872, Cooper Co, MO; md 10 Aug 1814 Jane Phillips (P), Drummondtown, Accomac Co, VA. She died 11 Feb 1902, LNR New Palestine, Cooper Co, MO, 1884

BULLARD, REUBEN D. (P, BLW), LNR Passapatanzy, King George Co, VA, 1872; md 8 Sep 1816 Lucy A. F. Cross, King George Co, VA

BULLINGTON, JAMES (BLW),

61

BULLINGTON (continued)
died 24 Mar 1856, Busville, VA; md 24 Aug 1824 Ann Hundon (P), Pittsylvania Co, VA. She died c1886, LNR Martinsville, Henry Co, VA, 1882

BULLMAN, JOHN (BLW), died 19 Jul 1858, Tyler Co, VA; md 20 Feb 1811 Clarissa Ankrom (P), Ohio Co, VA. She died 30 Sep 1878, LNR P.O. Wick, Tyler Co, WV, 1871

BULLOCK, JOHN T. (BLW), died 18 Jun 1872, Caroling Co, VA; md 8 Aug 1821 Eliza Holloway (P), Caroline Co, VA. She died 6 Mar 1888, Caroline Co, VA, LNR Rappahannock Academy, Carolina Co, VA, 1878

BUMGARNER, SAMUEL (BLW), died 29 Sep 1850, Mason Co, VA; md 8 Feb 1816 Rebecca Oliver (P), Ten Mile Creek, Mason Co, VA. Her LNR Hartford City, Mason Co, WV, 1878

BUNCH, BENJAMIN whose widow Elizabeth applied for a pension

BUNCH, JESSE whose widow Sarah applied for a pension

BUNCH, POUNCY/PORENCY (BLW), died 24 Jan 1865, Albemarle Co, VA; md 28 Dec 1813 Sarah Flanagan (P), Fluvanna Co, VA. She died c1883, LNR Batesvile, Albemarle Co, VA, 1879

BUNDRANT, JOHN (BLW), died 30 Jun 1850, Lawrence Co, TN; md (1) Tabitha Bays, (2) 21 Apr 1816 Lucy Gilley (P), Henry Co, VA. She died 9 Sep 1882, LNR Warren Co, TN, 1878

BUNNELL, JOHN (P, BLW), LNR Narrow Shore, Currituck, Co, NC, 1873

BUNNER, JOSEPH (BLW), died 18 Aug 1863, Marion Co, WV; md Fall 1813 Nancy Springer (P), Monongalia Co, VA. Her

BUNNER (continued)
LNR Winfield Township, Marion Co, WV, 1871

BUNTIN, JOHN (P, BLW), died 5 Jan 1872, Halifax Co, VA; md 29 Aug 1821 Susan Miller (P), Halifax Co, VA. She died 23 Aug 1900, LNR Halifax Courthouse, Halifax Co, VA, 1878

BUNTING, SMITH (BLW), died 4 Feb 1845, York Co, VA; md (1) Ann Maria ----, (2) 14 Jul 1829 Ann/Nancy Topping (P), York Co, VA. Her LNR Grafton, York Co, VA, 1879

BURCH, HENRY W./WODDELL (P, BLW), LNR Greenville, Augusta Co, VA, 1871; md 1817 Harriet Edsall, Middlebrook, Augusta Co, VA

BURCH, JOHN (BLW), died 29 Sep 1849, Warren, MO; md 15 Jul 1824 Cynthia Cobbs (P), Charleston, Kanawha Co, VA. She died c1897, LNR Warren, Marion Co, MO, 1883

BURCH, NICODEMUS (BLW), died 22 Mar 1837, Waterloo, Monroe Co, IL; md 14 Jul 1804 Mary Homan (P), Amherst Co, VA. Her LNR Quincy, Adams Co, IA, 1871

BURCH, SAMUEL (P, BLW), LNR Lynchburg, Campbell Co, VA, 1871; md 23 Nov 1823/4 Mary Puryear, Lynchburg, VA

BURCH, SIMEON A. (BLW), died 7 Dec 1870, Amherst Co, VA; md Oct 1840 Louisa Dempsey (P), Amherst Co, VA. She died 22 Jan 1888, LNR Allwood, Amherst Co, VA, 1878

BURCH, WILLIAM Sr. (BLW), applied for a pension

BURCHETT, JOHAH/JONAS (P), died c1877, LNR Watertown, Washington Co, OH, 1877; md Margaret Skipton, Wood Co, VA. She died Mar 1868

BURDETT, JAMES (P, BLW), died 4 or 5 Aug 1874, Henry

BURDETT (continued)
Co, TN; md (1) Sarah Broadus,
(2) 19 Oct 1843 Matilda Gaines
(P), Culpeper Courthouse, Culpeper Co, VA. Her LNR
McKenzie, Carroll Co, TN,
1878

BURDETT, WILLIAM (P, BLW),
LNR Pittsylvania Co, VA,
1872

BURDETT, WILLIS whose widow
Nancy applied for a pension

BURDITT/BERDICK/BURDICK,
JOHN (P, BLW), died 1 Oct
1885, Callaway Co, MO; md
(1) Lucinda Robinson, (2) 6
Mar 1845 Elizabeth Wood (P),
Callaway Co, MO. Her LNR
P.O. Fulton, Callaway Co, Mo,
1879

BURGE, FRANCIS A. (P, BLW),
died 5 Aug 1872, Warren Co,
KY, LNR P.O. Bowling Green,
Warren Co, KY, 1871; md 7
Oct 1819 Frances E. Smith,
Brunswick Co, VA. At one
period in War, Francis furnished Bradford Burge as a
substitute

BURGE, JAMES WILLIAM
(BLW), died 18 Feb 1866,
Elizabeth City Co, VA; md
1817 Keziah Evans (P),
Hampton, Elizabeth City Co,
VA. Her LNR P.O. Hampton,
Elizabeth City Co, VA, 1878

BURGE, LARKIN (P, BLW), died
1 Jun 1879, Stokes Co, NC,
LNR P.O. Patrick Courthouse,
Patrick Co, VA, 1871; md 1861
Nancy Durham, NC

BURGE, PETERSON (BLW), died
9 Feb 1870, Muhlenberg Co,
KY; md 7 Feb 1815 Eliza N.
Palmer (P), Wilson Co, TN.
She died c1889, LNR McKin-
ney, Collins Co, TX, 1880

BURGESS, JAMES (BLW), died
10 Dec 1852 or 13 Dec 1852,
Loudon Bridge, VA; md 6 Jan
1821 Mary McCall (P), Loudon
Bridge, VA. Her LNR P.O.

BURGESS (continued)
Loudon Bridge, Princess Anne
Co, VA, 1879

BURGESS, MEREDITH (BLW),
died 4 Oct 1870, Logan Co,
WV; md 27 Nov 1820, Matilda
Farley (P), New River, Monroe
Co, VA. Her LNR P.O. Logan
Courthouse, Logan Co, WV,
1879

BURGIN, JOHN whose widow
Susannah applied for a pension

BURK, DAVID whose widow Mary
applied for a pension

BURK, HENRY F. (P, BLW),
died 5 Apr 1879, Floyd Co,
VA; md 3 Dec 1842 Lucy/
Lucinda (----) Phillips (P).
She died 14 Jun 1885, Floyd
Co, VA, LNR P.O. Indian Val-
ley, Floyd Co, VA, 1879

BURK, JAMES (P, BLW), died 8
Dec 1879, Covington, VA; md
(1) Sophia Landrum, (2) 10 Mar
1852 Jane C. (----) Clark (P),
Washington Co, VA. Her LNR
Covington, Alleghany Co, VA,
1879

BURKE, ASAHEL whose widow
Zeviah applied for a pension

BURKE, ROWLAND P. (P,
BLW), LNR Richfountain,
Osage Co, MO, 1871; md Aug
1817 Nancy Tinsefley, Am-
herst Co, VA

BURKE, WILLIAM (BLW), died
23 Nov 1858, Lincoln, Loudoun
Co, VA; md (1) Rebecca Dilon,
(2) 1840 Mahala (----) Wright
(P), Philomont, Loudoun Co,
VA. She died 21 Mar 1891,
LNR Waterford, Loudoun Co,
VA, 1878

BURKHART, HENRY (BLW),
died 25 Sep 1870, Albion, Mar-
shall Co, IA; md 29 Mar 1814
Elizabeth Mercer (P), Wythe
Co, VA. She died 23 May
1884, Maryville, Nodaway Co,
MO, LNR Oscola, Clarke Co,
IA, 1879

BURKS, ARTHUR L. (P, BLW),

BURKS (continued)
died 17 Jun 1878, Botetourt Co,
VA; md 3 Nov 1825 Demaris
Wilson (P), Botetourt Co, VA.
Her LNR P.O. Salt Petre Cave,
Botetourt Co, VA, 1878

BURKS, GEORGE F. (P, BLW),
died 19 Jun 1872, Shelby Co,
TN; md 5 Apr 1817 Harriet B.
Key (P), Charlotte Co, VA.
She died Feb/Mar 1884,
Searcy, AR, LNR P.O. Searcy,
White Co, Ar, 1879

BURKS, SAMUEL C. (P, BLW),
LNR Gilmores Mill, Rock-
bridge Co, VA 1871; md 8 Sep
1811 Remelia Anna Hunter,
Rockbridge Co, VA

BURLEY, THOMAS (BLW), died
25 Dec 1825, Amherst Co, VA;
md 18 Aug 1809 Elizabeth
Grant (P), Amherst Co, VA.
Her LNR Amherst, Amherst
Co, VA, 1871

BURLEY, TILMAN (BLW), died
11 Jan 1863, Henrico Co, VA;
md 8 Jan 1828 Sarah Bond (P),
King William Co, VA. Her
LNR P.O. Richmond, Henrico
Co, VA, 1879

ROLL NO. 14

BURNER, JOHN R. (BLW), died
Oct 1860, Page Co, VA; md 19
Mar 1838 Susannah (----)
Hershberger (P), Page Co, VA.
Her LNR P.O. Luray, Page Co,
VA, 1878

BURNETT, ALEXANDER S. (P,
BLW), died 9 Dec 1884,
Hayward, CA; md (1) Eliza
Gamble, (2) Elizabeth Batche,
(2) 21 Jan 1841 Margaret Sul-
livan (P), Madison, Jefferson
Co, IN. She died 4 Jan 1900,
LNR San Francisco, CA, 1885

BURNETT, JOHN N. (BLW), died
3 Jun 1855, Nelson Co, VA;
md 25 Feb 1842 Mary Ann
Wood (P), Nelson Co, VA.
Her LNR P.O. Lovingston,

BURNETT (continued)
Nelson Co, VA. 1878

BURNETT, THOMAS (BLW),
died 4 May 1860, Bedford Co,
VA; md 17 Dec 1816 Frances
Timberlake (P), Campbell Co,
VA. Her LNR Columbia, Maury
Co, TN, 1878

BURNHAM, CHARLES C. (P,
BLW), VA and PA militia,
died 1 Mar 1873, Brookville,
PA; md 5 Feb 1831 Sophia
Kreitzer (P), Washington Co,
MD. She died 25 Jan 1902,
LNR Brookville, Jefferson Co,
PA, 1887

BURNHAM, LYMAN (BLW),
died 5 Jan 1866, Lindsay
Depot, VA; md 18 Jul 1839
Mary E. Clarkson (P), Al-
bemarle Co, VA. She died 31
Jan 1894, LNR Bentivogle,
Albemarle Co, VA, 1887

BURNS, GEORGE W. applied for
a pension

BURNS, JACOB (P, BLW), MD
militia, died 13 Sep 1881, LNR
Lewisburg, Preble Co, OH,
1871; md 23 May 1823 Elizabeth Marker, Martinsburg, VA

BURNS, JAMES (P, BLW), died
28 Jan 1879, Limerick, OH;
md (1) Elizabeth Knight, (2) 6
Jul 1836 Peachy E. Patyon
(P), Orange Co, VA. She died
30 Apr 1911, Richmond Dale,
Ross Co, OH, LNR Limerick,
Jackson Co, OH, 1887

BURNS, JOHN (P, BLW), died 18
Feb 1883, Polk, MO, LNR Sen-
tinel Prairie, Polk Co, MO,
1871; md 25 Jan 1816 Elender
Jordan, Cabell Co, VA. She
died c1877

BURR/BUR/BOAR, JOHN H.
(BLW), died 15 Sep 1860, Jay
Co, IN; md 29 Apr 1830 Susan-
nah Stover (P), Preble Co, OH.
Her LNR P.O. Jordan, Jay Co,
IN, 1879

BURRIS, WILLIAM (BLW), died
19 Apr 1850, Mt. Morris, PA;

BURRIS (continued)
md 25 Dec 1823 Sarah Donley
(P), Greene Co, PA. She died
2 Jan 1902, LNR Mt. Morris,
Greene Co, PA, 1878
BURRIS/BURROUGHS, ZACH-
ARIAH applied for a pension
BURROUGHS, JAMES (BLW),
died 24 Jul 1861, Franklin Co,
VA; md 5 Aug 1818 Elizabeth
W. Robertson (P), Bedford Co,
VA. She died c1895, LNR
P.O. Davis Mills, Bedford Co,
VA, 1878
BURROUGHS, JOHN (P, BLW),
died 26 Oct 1872, Bedford Co,
VA; md 4 Jan 1827 Leanna M.
Pullen (P), Bedford Co, VA.
She died 19 Nov 191, Bedford
Co, Va. LNR P.O. Fancy
Grove, Bedford Co, VA, 1878
BURROUGHS, THOMAS whose
widow Katherine G. applied for
a pension
BURROW, BARDON alias BAR-
DON, CLOYD (P, BLW), died
2 Jun 1879, Norfolk, VA; md
31 Dec 1832 Ann Elizabeth
Henry (P), Norfolk, VA. She
died 2 Jan 1895, Norfolk, VA,
LNR Norfolk, VA, 1888
BURRUS/BURREYS, GEORGE S.
(P, BLW), LNR P.O. Orange
Courthouse, Orange Co, VA,
1871
BURSON, LABAN (BLW), died
cMay 1851/2, Union, Loudoun
Co, VA; md 19 Oct 1809 Sarah
McFarlin (P), Columbiana Co,
OH. She died 22 May 1882,
Cardington, OH, LNR Car-
dington, Morrow Co, OH, 1872
BURTON, BENJAMIN (BLW),
died 10 Oct 1867, Chesterfield,
VA; md 1 Oct 1863 Elizabeth
(----) May (P), Chesterfield
Co, VA. She died c1886, LNR
P.O. Crow Springs, Chester-
field Co, VA, 1878. Eliz-
abeth's 1st husband was John
May
BURTON, DAVID (BLW), died 8

BURTON (continued)
May 1872, Stokes Co, NC; md
16 Aug 1819 Winney Lawson
(P), Stokes Co, NC. Her LNR
P.O. Danbury, Stokes Co, NC,
1878
BURTON, EDMON (P, BLW),
died 11 May 1872 Larue Co,
KY; md (1) ?, (2) ?, (3) 17 May
1826 Susanna Perman (P),
Danville, Pittsylvania Co, VA.
She died 17 Feb 1880, Larue
Co, KY, LNR P.O. Hod-
gensville, Larue Co, KY, 1878
BURTON, ELIAS whose widow
Catharine applied for a pension
BURTON, GARRISON whose
widow Sally T. applied for a
pension
BURTON, IRA E. (BLW), died 12
Mar 1867, Cresaptown, MD;
md (1) Nany Green, (2) 15 Feb
1849 Maria (----) McKenzie
(P), Cresaptown, Allegany Co,
MD. She died 21 Oct 1891,
LNR P.O. Frostburg, Allegany
Co, MD, 1879
BURTON, MATHEW and his
widow Thena both applied for a
pension
BURTON, SAMUEL A. (BLW),
died 22 Jun 1845, Amelia Co,
VA; md 22 May 1817 Elizabeth
C. Wingo (P), Amelia Co, VA.
She died c1885, LNR P.O.
Morven, Amelia Co, VA, 1878
BURUCKER/BURACKER, JOHN
applied for a pension
BURWELL, BLAIR applied for a
pension
BURWELL, LEWIS (BLW), died
15 Apr 1847, Mecklenburg Co,
VA; md 13 Oct 1803 Sally E.
Green (P), Amelia Co, VA.
Her LNR Mecklenburg Co, VA,
1871
BURWELL, NICHOLAS (P,
BLW), died 11 Jun 1879, West
Union, OH; md 9 Apr 1820
Sally Fenton (P), Adams Co,
OH. She died 14 Jan 1885,
LNR West Union, OH, 1879

BURWELL, PEYTON R. (P), USA, LNR Boydton, Mecklenburg Co, VA, 1872. Not married

BURWELL, THOMAS M. (BLW)

BUSBY, WILLIAM (BLW), NC militia, died 16 Jan 1862, Putnam Co, MO; md 5 Oct 1834 Mary Johnson (P), Kanawha Co, VA. She died 7 Jan 1886, LNR Putnam Co, MO

BUSFORD, WILLIAM J. applied for a pension

BUSH, DAVID (BLW), USA

BUSH, JOHN (BLW), died 7 Sep 1870, near Deerfield, Augusta Co, VA; md (1) Sarah Steele, (2) Elizabeth D. Martin, (3) 4 Sep 1850 Mary A. Harris (P), Staunton, VA. She died c1884, LNR Staunton, Augusta Co, VA, 1878

BUSSABARGER, JOHN (P, BLW), LNR Corydon, Harrison Co, IN, 1871; md 15 Sep 1822 Elizabeth Gable, Woodstock, Shenandoah Co, VA

BUSSEAR, MARTIN (BLW), died 15 Jul 1834, Butler, OH; md 18 May 1815 Sarah Callahan (P), Jefferson Co, VA. Her LNR P.O. Trenton, Randolph Co, IN, 1878

BUSSELL, CHARLES (BLW), USA, died 16 Nov 1875, Mountain View, VA; md (1) Mary Black, (2) 18 Jan 1867 Lucy Ann Wine (P), Mountain View, VA. She died 8 Nov 1908, Staunton, Augusta Co, VA, LNR Mountain View, Stafford Co, VA, 1878

BUSSEY, WILLIAM W. (P, BLW), died 29 May 1873, LNR P.O. Gogginsville, Franklin Co, VA; md 1 Sep 1840 Julia A. Dodd, Fauquier Co, VA

BUTCHER, JOHN (BLW), died 5 Oct 1868, Lewis Co, WV; md 25 Mar 1804 Christina Alkire (P), Harrison Co, VA. Her LNR Willey Township, Wes-

BUTCHER (continued) ton, Lewis Co, WV, 1871

BUTCHER, PETER (BLW), died 15 Mar 1852, Delaware Co, OH; md 6 Nov 1847 Elenor Anderson (P), Delaware Co, OH. She died 8 Dec 1881, LNR Farmersville, Livingston Co, MO, 1880

BUTLER, ALLEN (BLW), died 15 Dec 1837, Isle of Wight Co, VA; md 1800 Sally Daughtry (P), Isle of Wight Co, VA. Her LNR Suffolk, Nansemond Co, VA, 1871

BUTLER, BAYLES (P, BLW), died 23 Feb 1879, LNR P.O. Washington, Rappahanock Co, VA, 1871; md 19 Jan 1818 Lucy Elkins

BUTLER, CHARLES applied for a pension

BUTLER, FIELDING (BLW), died 7 Feb 1836, Barren Co, KY; md 9 Mar 1809 Elizabeth Huffman (P), Culpeper Co, VA. Her LNR P.O. Glasgow, Barren Co, KY, 1871

BUTLER, FLEMING (BLW), died 5 Jul 1862, Gallia Co, OH; md 25 Aug 1816 Elizabeth Eagle (P), Greenbrier Co, VA. She died c1881, Gallia Co, OH, LNR P.O. Vinton, Gallia Co, OH, 1878

BUTLER, HEZEKIAH (BLW), died Mar 1858, Louisa Co, VA; md 12 Mar 1829 Susan H. Harlow (P), Louisa Co, VA. She died 3 Feb 1890, LNR Louisa Courthouse (Bells Crossroads), LouisaCo, VA, 1878

BUTLER, ISAAC (P, BLW), died c1877, LNR P.O. Hewletts, Hanover Co, VA, 1871; md 24 Dec 1816 Nancy Childs, Caroline Co, VA

BUTLER, JAMES (P, BLW), OH militia, died c1878, LNR P.O. Walhonding, Coshocta Co, OH; md 14 Jun 1820 E. Rod Heaver, Preston Co, VA

BUTLER, JETHRO H.(BLW), died 8 Dec 1851, Nansemond Co, Va; md (1) Sally Butler, (2) Margaret Doughtrey, (3) 1 Apr 1830 Nancy (Pinner) Russell (P), Nansemond Co, VA. She died c1889, LNR Berlin, Southampton Co, VA, 1879

BUTLER, JOHN (P, BLW), died 6 Jun 1880, Fairfax Co, VA; md 7 Apr 1815 Catharine Taylor (P), Fairfax Co, VA. Her LNR P.O. Herndon, Fairfax Co, VA, 1880

BUTLER, JOSEPH applied for a pension

BUTLER, JOSEPH whose widow Susan Ann applied for a pension

BUTLER, PASCHAL (P, BLW), died c1875, LNR P.O. Oxford, Lafayette Co, MS, 1871; md 28 Aug 1819 Mary Nobb/Noble, Bedford Co, VA

BUTLER, PATRICK (BLW), died 16 Dec 1848, Louisa Co, VA; md 6 Apr 1815, Mildred White (P), Louisa Co, VA. She died 20 Mar 1880, Louisa Co, VA, LNR Louisa Co, VA, 1878

BUTLER, WILLIAM (P, BLW), LNR P.O. Herndon, Fairfax Co, VA, 1871; md 1 Feb 1827 Linney Ambrose, Washington, DC

BUTLER, WILLIAM H. (BLW), died 9 Apr 1867, Fairfax Co, VA; md Dec 1822 Frances Jenkins (P), Fairfax Co, VA. Her LNR Clifton Station, Fairfax Co, VA, 1878

BUTRAM, ELIJAH applied for a pension

BUTT, BASIL (BLW), died 16 Nov 1854, Licking Co, OH; md 25 May 1826, Mahala Green (P), Licking Co, OH. She died 2 Dec 1884, Johnston, OH

BUTT, MICHAEL (P, BLW), died 28 Feb 1873, LaFayette, Montgomery Co, VA; md 3 Feb 1814 Elizabeth Arnold (P),

BUTT (continued) Rockingham Co, VA. Her LNR LaFayette, Montgomery Co, VA, 1874

BUTT, ROBERT B. (BLW), died 9 May 1846, Portsmouth, VA; md (1) Mary P. Harding, (2) 20 May 1830 Mary M. Wilson (P), Portsmouth, VA. Her LNR Portsmouth, Norfolk Co, VA, 1878

BUTTERWORTH, BUCKLEY (BLW), died 11 Jun or Jul 1854, Campbell Co, VA; md 26 Dec 1823 Sally Callihom/Callihan (P), Campbell Co, VA. She died c1883, LNR P.O. Coney Branch, Green Co, TN, 1878

BUTTERWORTH, JOHN (P, BLW), LNR P.O. Goodletsville, Davidson Co, TN, 1871; md 1 Apr 1818 Lucy Lally

BUTTS, DANIEL C. (BLW), USA, died 4 Jan 1850, Petersburg, VA; md 24 Oct 1837 Mary Ann Parsons (P). Her LNR Petersburg, Dinwiddie Co, VA, 1878

BUTTS, WILLIAM (P, BLW), died 1 Dec 1871, Hillsborough, VA, LNR Hillsborough, Loudoun Co, VA, 1871; md Apr 1816 Margaret Houseworth

BUXTON, HARVEY (BLW), CT miitia, died 16 Nov 1867, Blakesburg, IA; md 11 Apr 1824 Sagey G. Brown (P), Kanawha Co, VA. She died 10 Dec 1883, Blakesburg, Wapello Co, IA

BUXTON, JOHN (P, BLW), died 14 Feb 1874, Benton Co, AR; md (1) Sary ----, (2) Mar 1823 Frances Jenno (P), Sparta, White Co, TN. Her LNR P.O. Bentonville, Benton Co, AR, 1878

BYAS/BIAS/BIUS, JAMES (P, BLW), died 22 Apr 1872, LNR Amherst Courthouse, Amherst Co, VA, 1871; md 22 Nov 1802

BYAS/BIAS/BIUS (continued)
Elizabeth Whitten
BYER/BOYER, JOHN see John
Boyer
BYRAM, BAILEY (P, BLW),
LNR P.O. Pine Village, War-
ren Co, IN, 1871; md Ellen
Cooper. She died c1859
BYRD, ANDREW H. (BLW), died
16 Sep 1862, Highland Co, VA;
md 5 Jan 1818 Elizabeth
Capito (P), Franklin, Pen-
dleton Co, VA. She died 13
Feb 1888, LNR Highland Co,
VA, 1880
BYRD, JAMES (BLW), died
c1843, Nansemond Co, VA; md
25 May 1817 Nancy Gardner
(P), Nansemond Co, VA. Her
LNR P.O. Suffolk, Nansemond
Co, VA, 1878
BYRD, JOHN (BLW), died 24 Dec
1848, Nansemond Co, VA; md
9 Jun 1812 Esther Hamil-
ton/Hamlington (P), Nan-
semond Co, VA. Her LNR
P.O. Suffolk, Nansemond Co,
VA, 1871
BYRD, THOMPSON C. (BLW),
died 30 Apr 1866, Wood Co,
WV; md 26 Sep 1822 Lavinia
Rose (P), Fairfax Co, VA. Her
LNR P.O. Kanawha Station,
Wood Co, WV, 1878
BYRD, WILLIAM (BLW), died 9
Nov 1865, Grayson Co, VA; md
(1) Sarah Martin, (2) 27 Jan
1844 Ann Anderson (P), Gray-
son Co, VA. Her LNR Spring
Valley, Grayson Co, VA, 1878
BYRNE, SAMUEL (BLW), died
1 Jun 1846, Braxton Co, VA;
md 21 Jan 1825 Elizabeth
Lough (P), Lewis, Braxton Co,
VA. She died c1879, LNR
Clay Co, IL
BYRNS, JOHN (P, BLW), LNR
Brownsboro, Madison Co, AL,
1871; md 17 Mar 1826 Martha
Johnson, Maysville, AL. She
died 24 Feb 1866, Madison Co,
AL. John served as a sub-

BYRNS (continued)
stitute for his father William
Byrns in the War
BYWATERS, ZACHARIAH and
his widow Sarah G. Hudson
both applied for a pension

ROLL NO. 15

CACKLEY, BENJAMIN whose
widow Francie applied for a
pension
CACKLEY, WILLIAM (BLW),
died 20 Mar 1860, Clinton, IL;
md 28 Feb 1815 Jane Gay (P),
Bath Co, VA. She died c1880,
LNR Clinton, DeWitt Co, IL,
1878
CAIN, CHARLES (BLW), died 11
Jan 1867/68, Prince George
Co, VA; md 26 Feb 1818 Su-
sanna Ambrose (P), Sussex
Co, VA. Her LNR P.O. Tem-
pleton, Prince George Co, VA,
1878
CAIN, JAMES (P, BLW), LNR
Sycamore Dale, Harrison Co,
WV, 1871
CAIN, JOHN (P, BLW), died 4
Jan 1872, Wirt Co, WV; md 14
Feb 1804 Nancy Hickman (P),
Harrison Co, VA. She died 27
Jan 1879, Newark, WV, LNR
P.O. Newark, Wirt Co, WV,
1872
CAIN, WALTER (BLW), died 28
Jun 1831, Jefferson Co, OH;
md 10 Jun 1813 Anna N. Nay-
lor (P), Steubenville, Jefferson
Co, OH. Her LNR Moravia,
Appanoose Co, IA, 1871
CAKELY/KEGLEY, GEORGE
(BLW), died 5 Oct 1871,
Greenwood, Vernon Co, WI;
md 6 Jan 1820 Catherine Sluss
(P), Wythe Co, VA. She died
c1882, LNR Debello, Vernon
Co, WI, 1878
CALDWELL, JOHN (P, BLW),
died 14 Mar 1876, Craig Co,
VA; md (1) Ann Hively, (2) 31
Dec 1830 Ruth Reynolds (P),

CALDWELL (continued)
Botetourt Co, VA. She died Apr 1885, Sinking Creek, VA, LNR P.O. Simmonsville, Craig Co, VA, 1879

CALDWELL, JOSEPH F. applied for a pension

CALDWELL, ROBERT (BLW), died 3 Jul 1836 John's Creek, Craig Co, VA; md 21 Sep 1813 Mary Magdaline Smith (P), Sinking Creek, Botetourt Co, VA. Her LNR P.O. New Castle, Craig Co, VA, 1871

CALE/KALE, DAVID (P, BLW), died 13 Aug 1876, Randolph Co, IN, LNR P.O. Winchester, Randolph Co, IN, 1871

CALE, JACOB (P, BLW), died 4 Feb 1885, Pleasant Hill, WV, LNR P.O. Pleasant Hill, Preston Co, WV, 1871; md Apr 1819 Rachel Jenkins, Preston Co, VA

CALE, JOHN (P, BLW), died 2 Mar 1882, LNR P.O. Pleasant Hill, Preston Co, WV, 1871

CALES/KALE, JOHN (P, BLW), LNR Mackinaw, Tazewell Co, IL, 1871; md Apr 1816 Elizabeth Ott, Augusta Co, VA

CALHOUN, WILLIAM (P, BLW), died 2 Feb 1873, Pendleton Co, WV; md (1) Elizabeth Mallet, (2) 6 Mar 1840 Sarah (Simmons) Sigafoose (P), Dry Run, VA. She died c1896, LNR Dry Run, Pendleton Co, WV

CALLAHAN, BESTON/SEBESTON/SEBASTIAN (BLW), died 6 Feb 1862, Benton Co, AR; md (1) Hannah Sharp/Dorchester, (2) Cynthia Stevenson, (3) 16 Feb 1854 Jane S. (----) Daniels (P), Benton Co, AR. She died 1 Jan 1899, LNR Benton Co, AR

CALLAHAN, ELISHA (P, BLW), died 22 Jan 1879, Campbell Co, VA, LNR Campbell Courthouse, Campbell Co, VA, 1871

CALLAWAY, JAMES (BLW)

CALLAWAY, JAMES (BLW), whose widow was Margaret

CALLIS, ROBERT (P, BLW), died 9 Nov 1872, LNR P.O. Mathews Courthouse, Mathews Co, VA; md 13 Mar 1816 Lucy Weston, Mathews Co, VA

CAMERON, DANIEL (P, BLW), died 23 Feb 1875, Shepherdstown, WV; md 25 Oct 1818 Mary Nisley (P), Hagerstown, Washington Co, MD. Her LNR Shepherdstown, Jefferson Co, WV, 1878

CAMERON, DUNCAN (P, BLW), died 18 or 19 Dec 1886, Bland Co, VA; md (1) Margaret Spangler, (2) 2 Jul 1835 Margaret Fox (P), Burkes Garden Tazewell Co, VA. She died c1892, LNR P.O. Hicksville, Bland Co, VA, 1887

CAMERON, HUGH (BLW), died 26 Jun 1866, Dunbar, PA; md 20 Mar 1821 Jane White (P), Uniontown, Fayette Co, PA. She died 6 Jun 1884 LNR Dunbar, Fayette Co, PA, 1879

CAMERON, JOHN (P, BLW), died c1882, LNR Keep Tryst, Washington Co, IN, 1878

CAMERON, WILLIAM (BLW), died 7 Apr 1862, Lincoln Co, MO; md 15 Aug 1832 Elvina Coil (P), Montgomery Co, MO. She died c1882, LNR Warrenton, Warren Co, MO, 1879

CAMERY, CHRISTOPHER (P, BLW), died 3 Mar 1874, Marshall Co, IL; md 16 Apr 1821 Nancy Messick (P), Harrisonburg, VA. She died before 14 Aug 1886, LNR Saratoga, Marshall Co, IL, 1878

CAMMERON/CAMRON, DANIEL (BLW), died 13 Sep 1835 Jessamine Co, KY; md 24 Jul 1810 Ruthie Rowland (P), Pittsylvania Co, VA. She died 23 May 1877, LNR Lexington, KY, 1874

CAMP, GEORGE (BLW), died 1840, Benton Co, TN; md (1) ?, (2) 5 Nov 1836 Thursea Burns (P), Benton Co, TN. She died Sep 1884, LNR Kingston, Madison Co, AR, 1878

CAMP, GEORGE W. (BLW), died 10 Aug 1860, Todd Co, KY; md (1) ?, (2) 4 Nov 1829 Maria Adams (P), Todd Co, KY. Her LNR Elkton, Todd Co, KY, 1880

CAMPBELL, AMBROSE (BLW), died 16 Jul 1857, Cove Pasture Bridge, Allegany Co, VA; md Jun 1811 Dorcas Etzel (P), South Bottom, Rockbridge Co, VA. She died Aug 1885, LNR P.O. Lexington, Rockbridge Co, VA, 1872

CAMPBELL, ARCHIBALD (BLW), died 26 May 1869, Yellow Creek, Bell Co, KY; md 12 Apr 1815 Sarah Gibson (P), Christiansburg, Montgomery Co, VA. Her LNR P.O. Flat Lick, Knox Co, KY, 1878

CAMPBELL, DANIEL (BLW), died 15 Aug 1856, Amherst Co, VA; md (1) Orphia Mays, (2) 5 Oct 1825 Sophia Mays (P), Amherst Co, VA. Her LNR P.O. Lowesville, Amherst co, VA, 1878

CAMPBELL, DAVID (BLW), died 13 Sep 1854, Washington Co, VA; md 25 Jun 1816 Ann Ryburn (P), Washington Co, VA. She died 3 Jan 1883, Abingdon, VA

CAMPBELL, DAVID (BLW), died 10 Jul 1855, Henry Co, VA; md (1) Milly Dempsy, (2) 5 Jul 1831 Mary C. Dillon (P), Henry Co, VA. She died c1891, LNR P.O. Traylorsville, Henry Co, VA, 1878

CAMPBELL, DOUGAL (BLW), died 23 Dec 1844, Tuscarora, Berkeley Co, VA; md 21 Feb

CAMPBELL (continued) 1805 Sarah Wallace Lyle (P), Berkeley Co, VA. Her LNR Gerrardstown, Berkeley Co, WV, 1871

CAMPBELL, HEDGEMAN (BLW), died 1858, Rappahannock Co, VA; md c1810 Jemima Hoffman. Her LNR P. O. Woodville, Rappahannock Co, VA, 1872

CAMPBELL, HENRY whose widow Sarah applieed for a pension

CAMPBELL, JAMES (P, BLW), TN militia, died 20 Aug 1885, North Salem, Hendricks Co, IN; md 27 May 1832 Eleanor Simms, Lee Co, VA

CAMPBELL, JAMES (BLW), died 30 Oct 1863/4, Kanawha Co, WV; md 14 Nov 1812 Cena/Sency Jane Wingo (P), Charlotte Co, VA. Her LNR P.O. Kanawha Courthouse, Kanawha Co, WV, 1871

CAMPBELL, JAMES (P, BLW), LNR P.O. O'Fallon, St. Charles Co, MO; md 8 Feb 1808 Lucinda G. Watkins, Bedford Co, VA

CAMPBELL, JAMES D. whose widow Ellen applied for a pension

CAMPBELL, JEREMIAH whose widow Malinda applied for a pension

CAMPBELL, JOHN (BLW), died 4 Aug 1854, Summit Point, VA; md (1) Polly Barton, (2) 8 Jul 1832 Nancy Kerns (P), Fauquier Co, VA. She died 24 Jul 1884, LNR Brownsville, Washington Co, IN, 1879

CAMPBELL, JOHN B. (BLW), died 6 Jul 1867, Haywood Co, TN; md 17 Aug 1820 Demartha Wood (P), Bedford Co, VA. Her LNR Brownsville, Haywood Co, TN, 1878

CAMPBELL, JOHN W. (BLW), died 23 Feb 1849, DeKalb Co,

CAMPBELL (continued)
GA; md 11 Mar 1818/9 Belinda Cash (P), Amherst Co, VA. Her LNR P.O. Cross Keys, DeKalb Co, GA, 1879

CAMPBELL, LAND ANGUISH/ ANGUISH (BLW), died 30 Sep 1866, Palestine, IL; md (1) Nancy Squire, (2) 21 Mar 1823 Sarah Ann Bailey (P), Fauquier Co, VA. She died 17 Feb 1879, Palestine, Crawford Co, IL

CAMPBELL, ROBERT (BLW), whose widow was Jane

CAMPBELL, ROBERT L. (BLW), died 1 Aug 1855, P.O. Lees Creek, Clinton Co, OH; md 7 May 1818 Anna M. Atkins (P), Orange Courthouse, Orange Co, VA. She died 21 Dec 1885, LNR New Vienna, Clinton Co, OH, 1883

CAMPBELL, ROBERT MORRIS whose widow Sallie Ann applied for a pension

CAMPBELL, THOMAS (P, BLW), died 26 May 1879, Decatur Co, IN; md 11 Aug 1825 Rebecca Clutter (P), near Maysville, Mason Co, KY. She died before 1 Sep 1883, LNR Zenas, Jennings Co, IN, 1879

CAMPBELL, WILLIAM (BLW), died 5 or 6 May 1842, Wood (now Wirt) Co, VA; md 24 Dec 1812 Mary Eyres/Ayres/Ayers (P), Rockbridge Co, VA. Her LNR Indian Creek, Ritchie Co, WV, 1871

CAMPBELL, WILLIAM (P, BWL), LNR P.O. Frankford, Greenbrier Co, WV, 1872; md 22 Mar 1836/39 Rebecca Brown, Greenbrier Co, VA

CAMPBELL, WILLIAM whose widow Nancy applied for a pension

CAMPBELL, WILSON (P, BLW), LNR P.O. Raymond, Union Co, OH, 1871. Widower

CAMPER, PETER (BLW) and widow Fannie both received a pension

CAMRON/CAMON/CAMERON, MARTIN (P, BLW), LNR P.O. Hunters Lodge, Fluvanna Co, VA, 1871; md 24 Dec 1820 Sarah Stargel, Fluvanna Co, VA

CANADA, MARTIN (P, BLW), died c1873, Halifax Co, VA, LNR Providence, Halifax Co, VA, 1871. Martin was a substitute for John Canada in the War

CANADA, WILLIS (BLW), died 29 May 1851, Halifax Co, VA; md (1) Annie Wilke, (2) 2 Dec 1843 Maria Canada (P), Halifax Co, VA. She died 10 Mar 1889, LNR Cross Roads, Halifax Co, VA, 1878

CANDLER, WILLIAM A. (P, BLW), died 9 Feb 1892, LNR Rustburg, Campbell Co, VA, 1871

CANNON, WILLIAM applied for a pension

CANTLEY, ALEXANDER (P, BLW), died 2 Mar 1884, Raleigh Co, WV; md (1) Mary Scott, (2) 24 Aug 1876 Tempey (Ball) Hopkins (P), Dry Creek, Raleigh Co, WV. She died 8 Dec 1903, Lewiston, Kanawha Co, WV

CAPLINGER, JOHN (BLW), died 20 Jul 1825, Wood Co, VA; md 2 Apr 1807 Catharine Culp/ Colp (P), Wood Co, VA. Her LNR near Mineral Wells, Wood Co, WV, 1871

CAPPER, GABRIEL (P-rejected, BLW), died 21 Mar 1873, Deersville, OH; md 13 Oct 1818/20 Malinda E. Chamberlin (P), Hampshire Co, VA. She died 9 Mar 1886, LNR Deersville, Harrison Co, OH, 1885

CARAWY, WILLIAM whose widow Amy Sykes applied for a

CARAWY (continued)
pension

CARBIERE, WILLIAM (P, BLW), NY militia, died 30 Jun 1877, Southern Branch Soldiers Home, Hampton, VA; md 12 May 1814 Harriet Davis (P), New York, NY. She died 19 Nov 1884, Binghamton, Broome Co, NY

CARDEN, ANSELM (P, BLW), died 30 Mar 1875, LNR P.O. Lloyds Crossroads, Union Co, TN, 1871; md 25 Jan 1816 Nancy Merritt, Stokes Co, NC. She died 8 May 1866, Union Co, TN

CARDEN, DAVID M. (P, BLW), died 9 Aug 1878, Hart Co, KY; md 10 Feb 1824 Judith Richardson (P), Hart Co, KY. Her LNR P.O. Rowletts, Hart Co, KY, 1878

CARDER, JOHN (BLW)

CARDER, JOHN G. (P, BLW), died 30 Jun 1876, Harrison Co, WV; md 17 Jan 1822 Frances Spicer (P), Culpeper Co, VA. She died Apr 1883, LNR Kinchelow, WV, 1878

CARDER, WILLIAM whose widow Priscilla C. applied for a pension

CARDER, WILLIAM J. applied for a pension

CARDIN, JAMES (BLW), died 13 Aug 1857, Barren Co, KY; md (1) Frances E. Foster, (2) 22 Jan 1834 Marandy S. (Foster) Smith (P), Glasgow, KY. Her LNR P.O. Glasgow, Barren Co, KY, 1885

CARDOZO, ISAAC (BLW), died 27 Aug 1850, Powhatan Co, VA; md 2 Nov 1819 Mahala A. Baugh (P), Powhatan Co, VA. She died 19 Jun 1885, Richmond, VA, LNR Richmond, Henrico Co, VA, 1878

CARDWELL, GEORGE whose widow Mary L. P. applied for a pension

CARDWELL, RICHARD L. (BLW), died 14 Nov 1833, Richmond, VA; md 19 Mar 1804 Lucy Adams (P), Dinwiddie Co, VA. She died 23 Jan 1874, LNR Richmond, VA, 1871

CARDWELL, RICHARD M. (BLW), died 28 Jan 1850, Rockingham Co, NC; md 20 May 1816 Sarah Crowder (P), Caswell Co, NC. She died c1892, LNR P.O. Clear Spring, Grainger Co, TN, 1878

CARDWELL, WILTSHIRE (BLW), died 23 Aug 1862, Charlotte Co, VA; md 23 May 1848 Jane M. Spencer (P), Charlotte Co, VA. She died c19 Jan 1894, LNR P.O. County Line Crossroads, Charlotte Co, VA, 1878

CARICO, WILLIAM Jr. whose widow Louisa applied for a pension

CARLISLE/CARLYLE, ROBERT (BLW), died 22 Mar 1871, Snickersville, VA; md 4 Nov 1806 Catharine Brown (P), Loudoun Co, VA. Her LNR P.O. Snickersville, Loudoun Co, VA, 1878

CARLISLE, SAMUEL (BLW), died Dec 1856, Monroe Co, VA; md 12 Oct 1820 Jane Reed (P), Monroe Co, VA. She died before 26 Sep 1882, LNR P.O. Union, Monroe Co, VA, 1878

CARLTON, CHRISTOPHER (BLW), whose widow was Rachel

CARLTON, VINCENT (P), LNR Dresden, Weakley Co, TN, 1872; md Sep 1825 Nancy Younger

CARLTON, WASHINGTON (P, BLW), died 28 Oct 1873, Hawesville, KY; md 1 Jul 1817 Eliza Stewart (P), Richmond, VA. She died 27 May 1880, Hawesville, Hancock Co, KY

72

CARMICHIEL/CARMICLE, JOHN whose widow Nancy applied for a pension

CARNAL, ELISHA (P, BLW), LNR P.O. Palestine, Pickaway Co, OH, 1871; md 7 Mar 1815 Nancy D. Price, Albemarle Co, VA

CARNALL, JOHN (BLW), died 28 Feb 1871, Fauquier Co, VA; md (1) ?, (2) 21 Feb 1854 Hannah Norris (P), Fauquier Co, VA. She died 25 Jun 1887, Fauquier Co, VA, LNR P.O. New Baltimore, Fauquier Co, VA, 1878

CARNECLE/CARNICLE, JACOB applied for a pension

CARNELL, DANIEL (BLW), died 21 May 1863, Arrowsmith, IL; md 13 Oct 1815 Elizabeth Parker (P), Cumberland, Alleghany Co, MD. She died c1881, LNR Arrowsmith, McClean Co, IL, 1879. She was erroneously pensioned under the name of Elizabeth Cornell.

CARNEY, CHARLES (BLW), died 18 Jul 1853, Roanoke Co, VA; md 28 Mar 1816 Susan Gish (P), Botetourt Co, VA. She died 26 Jul 1888, Roanoke Co, VA, LNR Bonsacks Depot, Roanoke Co, VA, 1878

CARNEY, WILLIAM (P, BLW), died 17 Apr 1873, Fishers Point, Kanawha Co, WV; md 10 Apr 1815 Margaret Bonnet (P), Mason Co, VA. She died c1887, LNR Kanawha Co, WV, 1878

CARNEY, WILLIAM (BLW), died 9 Mar 1861, Prince William Co, VA; md 1818 Nancy F. Carney (P), Prince William Co, VA. She died before 27 Oct 1885, LNR P.O. Independent Hill, Prince William Co, VA, 1878

CARNOL/CARNEAL, JAMES CARNOL/CARNEAL (continued) (BLW)

CARNOL/CARNEAL/CARNAL, JAMES (BLW) whose widow Mary M. applied for a pension.

CARPENTER, JESSE (BLW), died Jun 1850 or 1843, Braxton Co, VA; md 1814 Margaret Cottell/Cottrell (P). She died 24 Nov 1880, LNR Clay Co, WV

CARPENTER, JONATHAN/JOHN and his widow Ann both applied for a pension

CARPENTER, SAMUEL (P, BLW), died 3 Aug 1875, near Opdyke, Jefferson Co, IL; md 8 Jan 1822 Malinda Spurling (P), Westmoreland Co, VA. She died c1889, LNR Lynchburgh, Jefferson Co, IL, 1871

CARPENTER, THOMAS (P, BLW), died 4 Feb 1883, LNR P.O. Veto, Washington Co, OH; md 24 Jul 1823 Polly Pugh, Wood Co, VA

CARPENTER, WILSON (P, BLW), died 5 Jan 1882, LNR Holden, Johnson Co, MO, 1871; md 4 Aug 1824 Elizabeth M. Riggin, White Co, IL. She died 3 Jul 1874

CARPER, ABRAHAM (P, BLW), died 8 Jul 1877, Beverly, WV; md 21 Sep 1817 Margaret Stewart (P), Buckhannon, Upshur Co, VA. Her LNR Beverly, Randolph Co, WV, 1878

CARPER, JOSEPH (BLW), died 28 Aug 1867, Perry Co, OH; md 16 Aug 1823 Jane Maria Harper (P), Athens Co, OH. She died 31 Jul 1888, Delaware Co, OH, 1887

CARPER, WILLIAM (P, BLW), LNR Winchester, Frederick Co, VA, 1871; md 1 Jul 1815 Kitty Drake, Hagerstown, MD

CARR, BURTON W. (P, BLW), died 9 May 1881, Metcalf Co, KY, LNR P.O. Edmondton,

CARR (continued)
Metcalf Co, KY, 1871
CARR, DABNEY who applied for
a pension
CARR, DAVID (P, BLW), died 9
Mar 1884, Hamilton, VA, LNR
Hamilton, Loudoun Co, VA,
1878; md 1819 Susanna Brown,
Frederick Co, MD
CARR, ISAIAH (P, BLW), died 1
Apr 1883, Muskingum Co, OH;
md (1) Tamar Lacey, (2) 13
Dec 1882 Penelope Shrigley
(P), Zanesville, OH. She died
27 Nov 1890, LNR Norwich,
Muskingum Co, OH, 1871
CARR, JAMES (P, BLW), P.O.
Braxton Courthouse, Braxton
Co, WV, 1871; md Jan 1825
Rebecca Boggs, Braxton Co,
VA
CARR, JAMES M. see James M.
Kerr
CARR, ROBERT W. (P, BLW),
died before 23 Mar 1886, LNR
Shieldsboro, Hancock Co, MS;
md 1 Oct 1821 Deborah W.
Cox, Montgomery, Montgomery
Co, AL
CARR, THOMAS T. whose widow
Sally applied for a pension
CARR, WILLIAM H. (P, BLW),
died before 16 Mar 1882, LNR
P.O. Hammondville, Hart Co,
KY
CARRINGTON, JOHN B. (BLW),
died 24 Apr 1864, Halifax Co,
VA; md 11 Sep 1828 Judith A.
Wimbish (P). She died 31 Aug
11878, LNR P.O. Wolftrap,
Halifax Co, VA, 1878
CARROL, JOSHUA whose widow
Catharine H. applied for a pen-
sion
CARROLL, CHARLES (P, BLW),
died 17 Jan 1874, Springvale,
VA; md (1) Susan Vermillion,
(2) 25 Nov 1856 Ann (Follin)
Pearson (P), Vienna, Fairfax
Co, VA. She died 5 May 1886,
Great Falls, Fairfax Co, VA,
LNR Springvale, Fairfax Co,

CARROLL (continued)
VA, 1878
CARROLL, DEMPEY/DEMPSON
(BLW)
CARROLL, LUKE whose widow
Elizabeth applied for a pension
CARROLL, PLEASANT P. (P,
BLW), USA, died 14 Jan 1878,
Rockingham Co, VA; md 1854
Lydia Nighten (P), Rockin-
gham Co, VA. Her LNR P.O.
Rawley Springs, Rockingham
Co, VA, 1878
CARROLL, SAMUEL whose
widow Juliet applied for a pen-
sion
CARROLL, THOMAS R. (P,
BLW), died 17 Aug 1888, LNR
P.O. Canfield, Mahoning Co,
OH, 1878; md 28 Dec 1820
Nancy Stacy, Isle of Wight Co,
VA
CARSON, ALEXANDER (BLW),
USA, died 22 Nov 1861,
Monroe Co, VA; md 4 Oct 1821
Nancy Adams (P), Botetourt
Co, VA. She died 19 Dec
1893, LNR Buck, Summers Co,
WV, 1885
CARSON, ELIJAH (BLW), died
26 Mar 1860, Augusta Co, VA;
md (1) Polly Haupe, (2) Jan
1841 Margaret Rowan (P),
Augusta Co, VA. Her LNR P.
O. Middlebrook, Augusta Co,
VA, 1878
CARSON, JOHN (BLW), died 24
Oct 1852, Rockbridge Co, VA;
md 10 Sep 1818 Margaret K.
McKee (P), Moffatts Creek,
Augusta Co, VA. She died 6
Nov 1882, LNR Ruther Glen,
Caroline Co, VA, 1878
CARSON, WILLIAM (BLW), TN
militia, died 23 Aug 1870,
Caledonia, MO; md (1) Jane
Rutledge, (2) 19 Oct 1826
Rosannah Allison (P), Mont-
gomery Co, VA. She died 8
Jan 1885, Florissant, St. Louis
Co, MO, LNR Caledonia,
Washington Co, MO, 1879

CARTER, ABNER (P, BLW), died before 3 Nov 1884, LNR Hillsdale, Warren Co, VA, 1871. His 3rd wife died c1868

CARTER, BANES/BAINS (BLW), died Nov 1865, Patrick Co, VA; md 26 Apr 1817 Julia Philpott (P), Patrick Co, VA. She died 9 Jul 1884, LNR Patrick Co, VA

CARTER, CARY (P, BLW), died 27 Oct 1877, LNR Horsepasture, Henry Co, VA, 1871; md 15 Jan 1812 Mahala Lewis, Henry Co, VA

CARTER, CHARLES W. (BLW), died 7 Nov 1867, Charlottesville, Albemarle Co, VA; md 16 Apr 1816 Mary Cocke (P), Scottsville, Albemarle Co, VA. She died 5 Mar 1888, LNR University of VA, Albemarle Co, VA, 1887

CARTER, CURTIS (BLW), died 2 Aug 1850, Mechanicsville, Henrico Co, VA; md (1) ---- Taliaferro, (2) 21 Mar 1848 Fanny A. ---- (P), Essex Co, VA. She died 12 Jan 1879, Essex Co, VA, LNR P.O. Dunnsville, Essex Co, VA, 1878

CARTER, DAVID N. (P, BLW), LNR Boydton, Mecklenburg Co, VA, 1872; md 13 Jan 1824 Cary Happy Brame

CARTER, EDWARD M. (P, BLW), died before 19 Jun 1886, LNR P.O. Spotsylvania Courthouse, Spotsylvania Co, VA, 1871; md 26 Nov 1830 Mary A. ----, Caroline Co, VA

CARTER, ELISHA (BLW), died 17 Jul 1834, Monroe Co, OH; md (1) ?, (2) 20 Dec 1818 Elizabeth Price (P), Amherst Co, VA. She died 26 Feb 1884, Paris, Monroe Co, MO

CARTER, ENIS and his widow Margaret both applied for a pension

CARTER, FIELDING (BLW), died 4 Apr 1864, Clay Co, IN;

CARTER (continued) md 17 Aug 1826 Phebe Murphy (P), Warren Co, OH. Her LNR Staunton, Clay Co, IN, 1878

CARTER, FRANCIS (BLW), died 26 Jul 1875, Prince Edward Co, VA; md (1) Martha K. Farmer, (2) Amelia Hatchett, (3) 11 May 1842 Sarah Jane Leigh (P), Prince Edward Co, VA. She died 29 Oct 1898, Rice Depot, Prince Edward Co, VA, LNR Green Bay, Prince Edward Co, VA, 1879

CARTER, GEORGE whose widow Hellen applied for a pension

CARTER, GEORGE (P, BLW), died before 5 Jul 1883, LNR P.O. Prospect Depot, Prince Edward Co, VA, 1871

CARTER, GEORGE (BLW), died 21 Feb 1826, Caroline Co, VA; md 8 Dec 1818 Ann Shackleford (P), Caroline Co, VA. She died 16 Mar 1881, Spotsulvania Co, VA, LNR P.O. Spotsylvania Courthouse, Spotsylvania Co, VA, 1878

CARTER, HENRY (BLW), died 26 Jun 1866, Fauquier Co, VA; md 22 Dec 1819 Susan Redmond (P), Fauquier Co, VA. She died c1886, LNR Poolesville, Montgomery Co, MD, 1880

CARTER, JAMES (BLW), died 7 Nov 1860, Albemarle Co, VA; md 14 May 1822 Jane Newcomb (P) Orange Co, VA. Her LNR Charlottesville, Albemarle Co, VA, 1878

CARTER, JAMES B. (BLW), died Oct 1848, Caroline Co, VA; md 1820 Eliza Carter (P), Caroline Co, VA. She died 21 Nov 1880, LNR P.O. Bowling Green, Caroline Co, VA, 1878

CARTER, JOHN (P, BLW), died c1878, LNR Greenfield, Greene Co, IL, 1871; md 25 Dec 1818 Alsa Butler, Frederick Co, VA

CARTER, JOHN (P, BLW), LNR

CARTER (continued)
P.O. Brentsville, Prince William Co, VA, 1871; md 4 May 1811 Jane Thomas, Fairfax Co, VA

CARTER, JOHN (P, BLW), died 31 Dec 1873, Monroe Co, IN; md (1) Nancy ----, (2) 18 Mar 1851 Amelia C. Thompson (P), Monroe Co, IN. Her LNR Bloomington, IN, 1887

CARTER, JOHN T. (BLW), died 11 Apr 1874, Williamson Co, IL; md 29 Jun 1820 Jane Gregory, Mecklenburg Co, VA. She died c1881, LNR P.O. New Burnside, Johnson Co, IL, 1879

CARTER, JOHATHAN (P, BLW), died 6 Apr 1882, Monroe Co, WV; md 8 Sep 1814 Mary Ann Hunter (P), Monroe Co, VA. She died before 31 Oct 1890, LNR Union, WV, 1882

CARTER, LEVI (P, BLW), LNR P.O. Marion, Grant Co, IN, 1871; md 15 Apr 1814 Elizabeth Judd, Braxton Co, KY

CARTER, LITTLE BERRY/ LITTLEBERRY applied for a pension

CARTER, LITTLE BERRY (BLW), died 4 Jun 1870, Bedford Co, VA; md (1) Nancy Stinnett, (2) 15 Aug 1848 Elizabeth F. Parker (P), Bedford Co, VA. She died 3 Mar 1897, Reba, VA, LNR P.O. Liberty, Bedford Co, VA, 1878

CARTER, MILLER (BLW), died 10 Oct 1869, Union Landing, Tangipahoa Co, LA; md (1) ---- Miles, (2) Sep 1825 Winney Maria Reeves (P), Perry Co, MS. Her LNR Tangipahoa, Tangipahoa Co, LA, 1878

CARTER, NATHAN (BLW), died 3 Jul 1857, Pittsylvania Co, VA; md 25 Aug 1803 Elizabeth Adkins (P), Pittsylvania Co, VA. Her LNR Pittsylvania Courthouse, Pittsylvania Co,

CARTER (continued)
VA, 1871

CARTER, PHILIP (BLW), died 10 Nov 1871, Prince William Co, VA; md 10 Apr 1820 Sally Tansville (P), Prince William Co, VA. She died 26 Mar 1888, LNR Prince William Co, VA

CARTER, ROBERT H. (P, BLW), LNR Buffalo Springs, Amherst Co, VA, 1871

CARTER, SAMUEL applied for a pension

CARTER, SANFORD (P, BLW), LNR P.O. Stafford Courthouse, Stafford Co, VA, 1871

CARTER, SILAS (P, BLW), LNR P.O. Patrick Courthouse, Patrick Co, VA, 1871

CARTER, THEODORE/ THEODORICK / THEODORIC (P, BLW), died 29 Jun 1873, Prince Edward Co, VA; md (1) Martha Badwin, (2) Elizabeth Baker, (3) 15 Jul 1838 Julia A. Morgan (P), Prince Edward Co, VA. She died 17 Aug 1898, LNR Pamplin, Appomattox Co, VA, 1871

CARTER, THOMAS (BLW), died 25 May 1871, Snake Run, Halifax Co, VA; md 30 Jun 1807 Catharine McCannon (P), Halifax Co, VA. Her LNR Snake Run, Allegany Co, VA, 1872

CARTER, THOMAS Jr. (BLW), died 16 Jun 1863, Nelson Co, VA; md (1) Pollie Scruggs, (2) 20 Apr 1838 Eliza A. Moore (P), Nelson Co, VA. She died 17 Feb 1895, Norwood, Nelson Co, VA, LNR P.O. Tye River Station, Nelson Co, VA, 1878

CARTER, WILLIAM (P, BLW), died c1879, LNR P.O. Russellville, Crown Co, OH, 1872; md Mar 1819 Nancy Davidson, Adams Co, OH

CARTER, WILLIAM (P, BLW), died c1880, LNR P.O. Summum, Fulton Co, IL; md Sep

CARTER (continued)
1819 Judy Curtley, Barren Co, KY

CARTER, WILLIAM (P, BLW), LNR Santa Fe, Maury Co, TN, 1879

CARTER, WILSON (BLW), died 30 Jul 1858, Prince Edward Co, VA; md 11 Sep 1851 Mary S. Taylor (P), Prince Edward Co, VA. She died c1887, LNR Prince Edward Co, VA, 1882

CARTY, JOHN D. (BLW), died 3 Jul 1864, Johnson Co, TN; md (1) Catherine Kelly, (2) 27 Aug 1846 Parthana Able (P), Johnson Co, TN. She died 16 Mar 1883, Taylorsville, Johnson Co, TN

CARUTHERS, JOHN (P, BLW), died 11 Dec 1880, Columbia, MO, LNR Columbia, Boone Co, MO, 1871; md Dec 1828 Ann R. Martin, Albemarle Co, VA

CARVER, HENRY (BLW), USA, died 18 Jan 1856, Rosebury, VA; md 17 Oct 1804 Catharine Crosser (P), Laughlintown, Westmoreland Co, PA. Her LNR Moundsville, Marshall Co, WV, 1871

CARVER, JOHN C/JOHN, Jr. (P, BLW), LNR P.O. Hopkinsville, Christian Co, KY, 1872; md c1822 Nancy Carver. She died c1857

CARY, GILL A. (BLW), died 18 Mar 1843, Hampton, VA; md 18 Nov 1818 Sarah E. S. Baytop (P), Gloucester Co, VA. She died 15 Apr 1879, Richmond, VA

CARY, RICHARD (BLW), died 30 May 1860, Campbell Co, VA; md 5 Jan 1809 Rebecca Johnson (P), Charlotte Co, VA. She died 22 Nov 1880, LNR Hat Creek, Campbell Co, VA, 1871

CARY, SAMUEL (BLW), died 11 Feb 1864, Nottoway Co, VA;

CARY (continued)
md 8 Jul 1819 Mary Ann Farley (P), Nottoway Co, VA. Her LNR Burkeville, Nottoway Co, VA, 1878

CASSADAY, THOMAS P. (P, BLW), died 1872, LNR P.O. Dayton, Rockingham Co, VA, 1871

CASE, JACOB (BLW), died 11 Apr 1880; md 28 Sep 1820 Penelope West (P), MD. Her LNR Cardington, Morrow Co, OH, 1879

CASEBOLT, THOMAS (P, BLW), died 24 Jul 1872, Pocahonta Co, WV; md 11 Oct 1811 Mary Swope (P), Ohio Co, KY. Her LNR near Mt. Murphy, Pocahontas Co, WV, 1878

CASEY, JOSHUA W. (P, BLW), died 14 May 1880, Amherst Co, VA; md 2 Aug 1837 Mary A. Hensey, Amherst Co, VA

CASEY, THOMAS (P, BLW), died 2 Jan 1883, Falmouth, KY; md (1) Jane Newman, (2) 10 Nov 1864 Sarah W. (----) Abernathy (P), Falmouth, KY. She died before 11 Dec 1895, LNR Falmouth, KY, 1888. Thomas served as a substitute for his father, William Casey, in the War

CASEY, THOMAS C. applied for a pension

CASH, JESSE (BLW), died 7 Mar 1859, Nelson Co, VA; md 28 Nov 1816 Cynthia Mays (P), Amherst Co, VA. She died c1891, LNR Nelson Co, VA, 1878

CASH, JOHN (P, BLW), died 29 May 1877, Shenandoah Co, VA, LNR Woodstock, Shenandoah Co, VA, 1872

CASH, PEACHEY applied for a pension

CASHWELL, FLEMING (P, BLW), died 4 Jul 1875, LNR P.O. Nebraska, Appomattox Co, VA, 1871; md 2 Jul 1815

77

CASHWELL (continued)
(?) Sophia Pendleton
CASKEY, THOMAS A. (BLW),
died 1 Jan 1868, Centerville,
OH; md (1) ?, (2) 21 Apr 1853
Ann (Ardinger) Lathers (P),
Centerville, OH. She died 23
May 1879, LNR Centerville,
Montgomery Co, OH, 1879
CASON, GEORGE (P, BLW), died
23 Dec 1877, Howard Co, MO;
md 7 Jan 1820 Maria E. Part-
low (P), Spotsylvania Co, VA.
She died c1895, LNR P.O.
Glasgow, Howard Co, MO,
1879
CASON, JAMES (P, BLW), died
11 Oct 1873, LNR El Dorado
Co, CA; md (1) Adaline
Owens, (2) 1837 Adrine Owen,
Buckingham Co, VA
CASON, JOHN M. (BLW), died 7
Aug 1845, Howard Co, MO; md
17 Jun 1818 Rebecca L. Cropp
(P), Stafford Co, VA. She died
27 Jul 1879, Howard Co, MO,
LNR P.O. Glasgow, Howard
Co, MO, 1878
CASSADAY, JESSE (BLW), died
6 Aug 1864, Howard Co, MO;
md 9 Jan 1842 Mary Ann (---)
Franklin (P), St. Clair, MO.
She died 7 Oct 1894, Hillsboro,
Washington Co, OR, LNR
Trenton, Henry Co, IA, 1880
CASSELL, JOHN (BLW), died 13
Jun 1871, Franklin Co, VA; md
7 Jan 1813 Lucy Dent (P),
Franklin Co, VA. Her LNR P.
O. Rocky Mount, Franklin Co,
VA, 1882
CASTELOW/CASTLOW, JOHN
(P, BLW), LNR P.O. Ellen-
boro, Ritchie Co, WV, 1871;
md Jan 1817 U. Reed, Harrison
Co, VA
CASTLE, ELIJAH (P, BLW), MD
militia, LNR P.O. Tunnelton,
Preston Co, WV, 1871; md Sep
1830 Sarah A. Smart, Mar-
tinsburg, VA. Widower.
CASTLEMAN, ALFRED (P,

CASTLEMAN (continued)
BLW) LNR Clark Co, VA, 1878
CASTLEN, JOHN whose widow
Eliza applied for a pension
CASTLIN, ANDREW (BLW), died
19 Feb 1857, New Albany, IN;
md (1) Nancy Leet, (2) 21 Oct
1833 Eveline Ort (P), New
Richmond, Clermont Co, OH.
She died c1887, LNR New Al-
bany, Floyd Co, IN, 1887
CASTO, DANIEL (BLW), died 22
Aug 1847, Jackson Co, VA; md
10 Mar 1817 Mary Chamblin
(P), Pt. Pleasant, Jackson Co,
VA. She died c1882, LNR P.
O. Pekin, Tazewell Co, IL,
1878
CASTO, DAVID D. (P, BLW),
LNR Buckhannon, Upshur Co,
WV, 1871
CASTO, JAMES (BLW), died 22
Dec 1866, Jackson Co, WV;
md 27 Aug 1817 Sidney Kessel
(P), Harrison Co, VA. Her
LNR P.O. Jackson Courthouse,
Jackson Co, WV, 1878
CASTO, JONATHAN (BLW), died
22 Oct 1851, Jackson Co, VA;
md 10 Jun 1816 Magdalena
Wetherholt (P), Randolph Co,
VA. She died before 25 Aug
1886, LNR Jackson Court-
house, Jackson Co, WV, 1878
CASTOR, HEZEKIAH (P, BLW),
died c1875, LNR Meigs Co,
OH, 1871; md 12 Jan 1813 Su-
san Graham, Gallia Co, OH

ROLL NO. 17

CATLETT, JOHN (BLW), died 9
Jan 1860, Knox Co, KY; md
Feb 1842 Pheraby (----) Crab-
tree (P), Claiborne Co, TN.
She died before Jun 1895, LNR
P.O. Flat Lick, Knox Co, KY,
1879
CATLETT, WILLIAM (BLW),
died 26 Apr 1845, Fork Union,
VA; md 19 Jun 1817 Mary W.
Seay (P), Fluvanna Co, VA.

78

CATLETT (continued)
She died c1885, LNR P.O. Fork Union, Fluvanna Co, VA, 1878

CATLING/CATLIN, THOMAS (BLW), died 12 Mar 1850, Nelson Co, VA; md 18 Mar 1850 Elizabeth/Betsey McCue (P), Nelson Co, VA. She died c1886, LNR New Hope, Augusta Co, VA, 1871

CATTERTON, FRANCIS (BLW), died Jan 1834, Orange Co, VA; md 12 Oct 1815 Nancy Clarkson (P), Albemarle Co, VA. She died 16 Mar 1880, LNR P.O. Nortonsville, Albemarle Co, VA, 1878

CAUDY, DAVID (P, BLW), died c1881, LNR P.O. Rainsboro, Highland Co, OH, 1871

CAVE, JAMES (BLW)

CAVE, JOHN ST. CLAIR whose widow Sarah applied for a pension

CAVE, JONAS (BLW), LNR P.O. Stony Man, Page Co, VA, 1871; md 1828 Elizabeth Parks, Shenandoah Co, VA

CAVE, WILLIAM (BLW), whose widow Elizabeth Roach applied for a pension

CAVENDISH, ANDREW (BLW), died 16 Jan 1846, Fayette Co, VA; md 27 Apr 1809 Jenette McClung (P), Greenbrier Co, VA. She died 31 Mar 1872, Mountain Cove, Fayette Co, WV

CAW, ISAAC (BLW), died 8 Mar 1870, Cass Co, IN; md Fall 1815 Marthey Michael (P), Berkeley Co, VA. Her LNR P. O. Logansport, Cass Co, IN, 1879

CAWOOD, DANIEL (BLW), died 12 Feb 1872, Alexandria, VA; md 18 Mar 1816 Mary McFee (P), Alexandria, VA. She died Mar 1888, LNR Alexandria, VA, 1887

CAWOOD, GRAFTON (BLW), died 4 Oct 1831, Fairfax Co,

CAWOOD (continued)
VA; md 24 Feb 1824 Sally R. Madden (P), Alexandria, VA. She died 9 Mar 1879, Alexandria, VA

CAWTHON, CHRISTOPHER whose widow Elizabeth applied for a pension

CAYTON, CORNELIUS (BLW), died 10 Oct 1852, Henry Co, VA; md Oct 1809 Nancy Davis (P), Rockingham Co, NC. Her LNR P.O. Martinsville, Clark Co, IL, 1871

CECIL, WILLIAM H. (P, BLW), PA militia, LNR Moundsville, Marshall Co, WV, 1878

CERTAIN, ASA (BLW), died 29 Mar 1861 or Jan 1863, DeKalb Co, TN; md (1) Susan Holmes, (2) 17 May 1827 Rebecca Hooper (P), White Co, TN. Her LNR P.O. Smithville, DeKalb Co, TN, 1878

CHADDUCK, PRESLEY (BLW), died 16 Mar 1860, Rappahannock Co, VA; md 9 Nov 1827 Mary Murphy (P), Rappahannock Co, VA. She died 2 Mar 1901, LNR P.O. Waterloo, Culpeper Co, VA, 1888

CHAFFIN, JOHN (BLW), died 25 Dec 1814, Halifax co, VA; md 6 Dec 1802 Tabitha Chaffin (P), Charlotte Co, VA. She died c1872, LNR P.O. Mount Laurel, Halifax Co, VA, 1872

CHAFFIN, THOMAS (BLW), died 8 Jan 1848, Dupress Store, Charlotte Co, VA; md 17 Mar 1803 Nancy Mayse (P), Charlotte Co, VA. She died 5 Feb 1876, LNR P.O. Drakes Branch, Charlotte Co, VA, 1871

CHALKLEY, SPENCER (BLW), died 30 Sep 1833, Chesterfield Co, VA; md 22 Dec 1818 Rebecca Hatcher (P), Chesterfield Co, VA. Her LNR P.O. Drewry's Bluff, Chesterfield Co, VA, 1878

CHAMBERLAIN, PAUL (P, BLW), LNR Brownville, Nemana Co, NE, 1871; md Jun 1815 Catherine Peterfish, Rockingham Co, VA

CHAMBERLAYNE, LEWIS W. (BLW), died 28 Jan 1854, Montrose, Henrico Co, VA; md 11 Apr 1820 Martha B. Dabney (P), Mount Prospect, New Kent Co, VA. Her LRN Richmond, Henrico Co, VA, 1878

CHAMBERS, HARDEN applied for a pension

CHAMBERS, JOHN (BLW), USA, died 14 May 1850, Harpers Ferry, VA; md (1) Ann Jeffries, (2) 4 Jun 1829 Ellen Maria O'Boyle (P), Fredericktown, Frederick Co, MD. She died before 23 Jan 1885, LRN Harpers Ferry, WV, 1878

CHAMBERS, MUSTOE (BLW), died 30 Aug 1865, Tipton, IA; md 7 Nov 1816 Mary Ann Lewis (P), Rockingham Co, VA. She died 26 Dec 1884, Tipton, Cedar Co, IA

CHAMBERS, WILLIAM (BLW), MD militia, died 11 Dec 1857, Bolivar, Jefferson Co, VA; md 1 Sep 1839 Amelia D. Binns (P), Baltimore, MD. She died 8 Jul 1888, LNR Harpers Ferry, Jefferson Co, WV, 1879

CHAMBLIN, NELSON (P, BLW), died 17 Jun 1874, Montgomery, Wood Co, OH; md 28 Mar 1813 Sarah Koonce (P), Hillsboro, Loudoun Co, VA. She died c1879, LNR P.O. Freeport, Wood Co, OH, 1874

CHAMBLISS, JAMES (BLW), whose wife was Lucy

CHAMBLISS, THOMAS A. (P, BLW), died 25 Apr 1878, Oak Grove, Brunswick Co, VA; md 21 Oct or Dec 1824 Evelena B. Smith, Woodville, Brunswick Co, VA. Widower.

CHAMPION, JOHN whose widow Rebecca applied for a pension

CHAMPLIN, FRANCIS R. (P, BLW), OH militia, died 12 Apr 1880, Vinton Co, OH; md 16 Jul 1822 Rachel Gibbons (P), Wood Co, VA. She died 19 Jul 1888, LNR Hamden, Vinton Co, OH, 1880

CHANCE, SAMUEL applied for a pension

CHANCELLOR, SANFORD (BLW), died 25 Feb 1860, Spotsylvania Co, VA; md 7 Jan 1823 Fannie L. Pound (P), Spotsylvania Co, VA. She died c1892, LNR P.O. Fredericksburg, Spotsylvania Co, VA, 1878

CHANDLER, ALLEN (BLW), died 5 Feb 1834, Pittsylvania Co, VA; md Nov 1815 Sarah Huddleston (P), Halifax Co, VA. She died Spring 1885, Sneedville, TN, LNR P.O. Blackwater, Lee Co, VA, 1878

CHANDLER, CHARLES applied for a pension

CHANDLER, GEORGE (BLW) whose widow was Julia Ann

CHANDLER, HARVEY/HERVEY (P, BLW), LNR P.O. Hope, Bartholomew Co, IN, 1871; md 1 Aug 1816 Mary Jones, Spotsylvania Co, VA

CHANDLER, JAMES (BLW)

CHANDLER, JOEL (P, BLW), died 30 Jan 1876, Halifax Co, VA; md (1) Hannah Davis, (2) 4 Apr 1852 Lucy H Moore (P), Halifax Co, VA. She died cJan 1876, LNR P.O. Roxboro, Person Co, NC, 1879

CHANDLER, SPENCER (BLW), died 4 May 1870, Logan Co, KY; md 13 Aug 1812 Keziah Belcher (P), nr Amelia Courthouse, Amelia Co, VA. She died c1870 LNR P.O. Russellville, Logan Co, KY, 1872

CHANDLER, WILLIAM C. (BLW), died 3 Apr 1834, Alenbury, Westmoreland Co, VA; md (1) ---- Crabbe, (2) 11 Jan

CHANDLER (continued)
1821 Susanna (Critcher) Mongat (P), Water View, Westmoreland Co, VA. Her LNR P.O. Hague, Westmoreland Co, VA, 1878

CHANDOIN, JOHN P. (BLW), died 25 May 1869, Greene Co, KY; md 23 Nov 1809 Eliza Scout (P), Buckingham Co, VA. She died before 1884, LNR P.O. Greensburgh, Greene Co, KY, 1878

CHANEY, JACOB (BLW), died 15 Apr 1846, Owen Co, IN; md 25 Dec 1815/16 Mary Mills (P), Halifax Co, VA. She died c1888, LNR P.O. Atkinsonville, Owen Co, IN, 1878

CHANEY, JAMES whose widow Frances applied for a pension

CHANEY, JESSE (P, BLW), LNR P.O. Patrick Courthouse, Patrick Co, VA, 1871; md 12 Sep 1861 Serena A. Nelson, Patrick Co, VA

CHANEY, JONAS (P, BLW), died 13 Dec 1880, Cedar Co, MO; md (1) Nancy Hitts, (2) 3 Jul 1828 Sarah/Sally Harding (P), Lansingburg, Lunenburg Co, VA. She died 14 Mar 1885, Filley, MO, LNR P.O. Stockton, Cedar Co, MO, 1880

CHANEY, WILLIAM (BLW), died 1843 Pittsylvania Co, VA; md 6 Jan 1806 Dicey Dodson (P), Pittsylvania Co, VA. Her LNR P.O. Ringold, Pittsylvania Co, VA, 1871. Dicey was erroneously pensioned as the widow of another William Chaney (next listed)

CHANEY, WILLIAM (P, BLW), died 29 Feb 1876; md (1) Nancy Polly, (2) 30 Apr 1822 Elizabeth Bradley (P), Pittsylvania Co, VA. She died 28 Aug 1883, LNR Laurel Grove, Pittsylvania Co, VA, 1878

CHAPMAN, GREENBERRY whose widow Susannah applied

CHAPMAN (continued)
for a pension

CHAPMAN, JACOB (P-rejected, BLW), died 25 Jan 1892, Colburn, IN; md 8 Mar 1827 Elizabeth Brugh (P), Botetourt Co, VA. She died 17 Sep 1885, LNR P.O. Parsons, Labette Co, KS, 1881

CHAPMAN, JASON/CHASON (P, BLW), died 18 Nov 1880; md (1) ?, (20 10 Dec 1856 Susanna (----) Stout (P), Union Co, OH. She died 19 Aug 1882, LNR P.O. Rush Creek, Union Co, OH, 1881

CHAPMAN, JESSE M. (P, BLW), LNR Chandlerville, Cass Co, IL, 1871

CHAPMAN, JOHN applied for a pension

CHAPMAN, JOHN (P, BLW), died 1 Nov 1881, Milton, WV; md 13 Apr 1816 Lucy Hutson (P), Cabell Co, VA. Her LNR P.O. Milton, Cabell Co, WV, 1882. John Was a substitute for William Chapman in the War

CHAPMAN, JOHN (BLW), died 17 Jun 1855, Selma, Green Co, OH; md 14 Sep 1829 Mary Carper (P), Winchester, VA. She died c1884, LNR Bellflower, McLean Co, IL, 1878

CHAPMAN, JOSEPH (P, BLW), TN militia, died 17 Oct 1875, Russell Co, VA; md 25 Apr 1815 Reity Lovens (P), Hawkins Co, TN. She died cJan 1880, LNR P.O. Hansonville, Russell Co, VA, 1878

CHAPMAN, PHILIP (BLW), died 10 Jun 1870, Williamson Co, TN; md 11 Feb 1819 Elizabeth Steele (P), Campbell Co, VA. She died c1885, LNR Williamson Co, TN

CHAPMAN/CHATMAN, THOMAS (P, BLW), died c1887, LNR P.O. Jacksboro, Campbell Co, TN, 1871; md

CHAPMAN (continued)
Winey Witt, Hawkins Co, TN

CHAPPALEAR, GEORGE (BLW), died 2 Jul 1857 New Lexington, OH; md 1 Feb 1814 Susan Jones (P), Gains Crossroads, Culpeper Co, VA. She died c1880, LNR New Lexington, Perry Co, OH, 1871

CHAPPEL, ISAIAH (P, BLW), LNR Warrenton, Warren Co, MO, 1878; md 14 Jan 1819 Lucinda Hawley, Fairfax Courthouse, Fairfax Co, VA

CHAPPLEAR/CHAPELAER/ CHAPELIER, WILIAM A. (BLW), died 19 Jul 1859, Union, Morgan Co, OH; md (1) Nancy Bradfield, (2) 11 Sep 1836 Nancy Jones (P), Somerset, Perry Co, OH. She died 27 Mar 1887, New Lexington, Perry Co, OH, LNR Union, Morgan Co, OH, 1878

CHARLTON, ABRAHAM (BLW), died 1 Sep 1869, Hickory Co, MO; md (1) Rebecca ----, (2) 5 Jan 1855 Jane (----) Moore (P), Osceola, St. Clair Co, MO. Her LNR Union, Cass Co, NE, 1890

CHARLTON, JOHN R. (P, BLW), died 1 Aug 1859, LNR P.O. Christiansburg, Montgomery Co, VA, 1878

CHARLTON, JOHN W. (BLW), died 26 Mar 1865, Patterson, Wayne Co, MO; md 30 Jun 1831 Araminta Akers (P), Christiansburg, Montgomery Co, VA. She died c1891, LNR Wayne Co, MO, 1879

CHARLTON, WILLIAM B. (BLW), died 14 Feb 1867, Montgomery Co, VA; md 20 Dec 1826 Malinda Jane Ingles (P), Montgomery Co, VA. She died 3 Feb 1999, Montgomery Co, VA, LNR Christiansburg, Montgomery Co, VA, 1878

CHASTAIN/CHASTEEN, JACOB (P, BLW), died 17 Oct 1873,

CHASTAIN/CHASTEEN (cont.) Henry Co, MO; md 21 Dec 1818 Eleanor Britt (P), Logan Co, KY. She died c1891, LNR Henry Co, MO, 1878

CHEATHAM, FRANCIS (BLW), died 17 Feb 1840, Chesterfield Co, VA; md 22 Feb 1821 Martha Ball (P), Chesterfield Co, VA. Her LNR Winterpock, Chesterfield Co, VA, 1878

CHEATHAM, JOSEPH whose widow Mary Ann applied for a pension

CHEATHAM, THOMAS L. (BLW), died c17 Nov 1871, Spring Mill, VA; md c16 Dec 1830 Nancy Cheatham (P), Lunenburg Co, VA. She died 19 Jan 1892, LNR P.O. Spring Mill, Appomattox Co, VA, 1878

CHELF/JELPH, FIELDING (P, BLW), LNR P.O. Greensburg, Green Co, KY, 1871; md 6 Oct 1831 Virenda Newman, Culpeper Co, VA

CHENAULT, HENRY (BLW), died 3 Nov 1863, Manchester, VA, md (1) Ann Wheeler, (2) 24 Apr 1825 Elizabeth Bosher (P), Buckingham Co, VA. Her LNR Manchester, Chesterfield Co, VA, 1878

CHENNAULT, WILLIAM whose widow Sarah applied for a pension

CHERRY, JAMES (BLW), died 24 Dec 1851, Xenia, OH; md 12 Apr 1815 Elizabeth Greenwood (P), Botetourt Co, VA. She died c1883, LNR Xenia, Greene Co, OH, 1878

CHESER/CHEESER, SAMUEL (BLW), died 1 Jun 1848 or 10 Jun 1849 on Mississippi River; md (1) ?, (2) 15 Feb 1816 Sarah Godlove (P), Hampshire Co, VA. She died c1887, LNR Haydenville, Hocking Co, OH, 1878

CHEUVRRONT/CHEVERONT, AMOS (P, BLW), died 12 Jan 1873, Meigs Co, OH; md 12 Sep 1819 Sarah Joseph (P), Harrison Co, VA. She died 29 Jan 1892, LNR Portland, Meigs Co, OH, 1878

CHEWNING, GEORGE (BLW), died 15 May 1853, Spotsylvania Co, VA; md (1) Susan Oliver, (2) 5 Jun 1839 Delilah Hilman (P), Orange Co, VA. She died c1891, LNR Spotsylvania Co, VA, 1878

CHEWNING, JOSEPH (P-rejected, BLW), died 8 Jul 1873, Spotsylvania Co, VA; md Dec 1808 Elizabeth Massey (P), Spotsylvania Co, VA. Her LNR P.O. Fredericksburg, Spotsylvania Co, VA, 1878

CHEWNING/TUNING, WALTER (P, BLW), died 14 Apr 1881, Franklin Co, VA; md (1) Lucy Turner, (2) 6 Feb 1849 Nancy Spradlin (P), Franklin Co, VA. She died c1885, LNR Hules Ford, Franklin Co, VA, 1881

ROLL NO. 18

CHICK, WILLIAM (BLW)

CHILCOTT/CHILCOT, JOHN (BLW), died 19 Mar 1849, Brownstown, IN; md (1) Rachel Robinson, who died 1832, (2) 8 Aug 1839 Rachel Smith (P), Brownstown, Jackson Co, IN. She died 29 Dec 1880, LNR Maryville, Nodaway Co, MO, 1879

CHILDERS, JOSEPH (BLW), died 4 Feb 1858, Westport, IN; md 19 Jan 1815 Mary Hix/Hicks (P), Greenbrier Co, VA. She died 18 Jul 1881, Unionville, MO, LNR Westport, Decatur Co, IN, 1878

CHILDERS, WILLIAM JR. (BLW)

CHILDERS, WILLIAM F (BLW)

CHILDRESS, ABRAM (BLW), died 1 Mar 1866, Franklin Co, VA; md 17 Jul 1851 Jane (---) Turner (P), Franklin Co, VA. Her LNR P.O. Halesford, Franklin Co, VA, 1878

CHILDRESS, ANDREW (BLW), died 24 Mar 1851, Rockbridge Co, VA; md 8 Jan 1835 Sophia McManamy (P), Brownsburg, Rockbridge Co, VA. She died c1888, LNR P.O. Buffalo Forge, Rockbridge Co, VA, 1878

CHILDRESS, CHARLES (P, BLW), died 30 Mar 1872, Hanover Co, VA; md 16 Jan 1832 Sarah H. Apperson (P), Hanover Co, VA. She died 12 Apr 1881, Auburn Mills, Hanover Co, VA

CHILDRESS, PENDLETON R. (P, BLW), LNR P.O. Johnsons Springs, Goochland Co, VA, 1871; md 18 Dec 1817 Nancy Faudree, Goochland Co, VA

CHILDRESS, THOMAS (BLW), died 25 Dec 1870/75, Goochland Co, VA; md 28 Nov 1821 Jane M. Birch (P), Goochland Co, VA. She died c1890, LNR P.O. Columbia, Fluvanna Co, VA, 1878

CHILDRESS, WILLIAM (BLW), died 17 Nov 1866, Wolf Co, KY; md 13 Nov 1810 Winney Bruden (P), Russell Co, VA. Her LNR Wolf Co, KY, 1871

CHILES, THOMAS (P, BLW), LNR P.O. Hazelhurst, Copiah Co, MS, 1871; md Dec 1815 Lucy F. Hargraves, Chesterfield, Chesterfield Co, VA, SC

CHITTUM, STEPHEN G. (P, BLW), died before 18 Aug 1888, LNR P.O. Buffalo Springs, Amherst Co, VA, 1871; md 1818 Betsy Green, Rockbridge Co, VA

CHITTURN, JOHN A. whose widow Sarah Ann applied for a pension. Her LNR P.O. Deer

CHITTURN (continued)
Creek, OH, 1878
CHOWNING, JOHN (BLW),
whose widow was Cordelia
CHRISMAN, GEORGE P. (P,
BLW), died 15 Jul 1871; md
(1) Dorothy Saunders, (2) 5 Sep
1837 Thirza Ann E. (----)
Henshaw (P), Highland Co,
OH. Her LNR Harlan, Shelby
Co, IA, 1878
CHRISMOND/CHISMOND, JOHN
B. (P), died before 30 Aug
1883, LNR P.O. Greensboro,
Choctaw Co, MS, 1872; md
1821 Sarah Motherhead, West-
moreland Co, VA
CHRISP, WILLIAM (BLW), died
19 Feb 1863, nr Trenton, Gib-
son Co, TN; md 12 Apr 1821
Mary Jeffers Elder (P), Ruther-
ford Co, TN. She died 7 Oct
1881, LNR P.O. Higginson,
White Co, AR, 1880
CHRISTIAN, JAMES H. (BLW),
died 1 Mar 1873, Charles City
Co, VA; md (1) Susan Hill, (2)
15 Jun 1859 Bettie (----)
Bowry (P), Charles City Co,
VA. Her LNR c/o Wilcox's
Wharf, Charles City Co, VA,
1878
CHRISTIAN, JOHN applied for a
pension
CHRISTIAN, JONES R. whose
widow Caroline M. applied for
a pension
CHUMBLY, JAMES (P, BWL),
LNR P.O. Spring Hill, Maury
Co, TN, 1871; md Oct 1810
Patsy Adams. She died 27
May 1880
CHUMNEY, EDWARD (P,
BLW), LNR Prince Edward
Co, VA, 1871; md 13 Aug 1815
Nancy Larkin Waddell, Green-
ville, Pitt Co, NC
CHURN, JOHN applied for a pen-
sion
CIRCLE, JOHN L. (P, BLW),
LNR Botetourt Co, VA, 1882;
md Martha L. Hook

CLAIBORNE, DEVEREUX J.
(BLW), died 17 Oct 1871,
Brunswick Co, VA; md (1)
Martha Lewis, (2) 27 Jun 1849
Sallie a. (----) Taylor (P),
Brunswick Co, VA. She died
29 Apr 1889, LNR P.O. Wall-
thall's Store, Brunswick Co,
VA, 1878
CLARE, ROBERT (BLW), died 6
Mar 1857, Pine Top, VA; md
(1) Eliza Humphreys, (2) 4 Jul
1855 Virginia J. Major (P),
Middlesex Co, VA. She died 2
May 1906, LNR Pine Top,
Middlesex Co, VA, 1887
CLARK, ALEXANDER (P, BLW),
LNR P.O. Pendleton, Madison
Co, IN, 1871; md 3 Jun 1819
Catharine Riffe, Monroe Co, IN
CLARK, ANDREW (BLW), TN
militia and USA, died Feb
1859, Jackson Co, TN; md 3
Aug 1810 Polly McFall (P),
Botetourt Co, VA. Her LNR
P.O. Granville, Jackson Co,
TN, 1871
CLARK, BENJAMIN (BLW), died
2 Oct 1847, Farmers Station,
OH; md (1) Polly Miller, (2) 24
Dec 1841 Lettice Hamrick (P),
Clinton Co, OH. She died 1
Dec 1891, LNR New Vienna
Station, Clinton Co, OH, 1887
CLARK, BENJAMIN whose widow
Eliza J. applied for a pension
CLARK, CHRISTOPHER whose
widow Sarah applied for a pen-
sion
CLARK, ELIAS (BLW), died Jul
1856/57, Belmont Co, OH; md
22 Dec 1815 Rachel A. Childs
(P), Frederick Co, VA. She
died 24 Mar 1885, Barnesville,
Belmont Co, OH
CLARK, ELLISON whose widow
Ann C. applied for a pension
CLARK, GEORGE (BLW), died
24 Apr 1864, Norfolk, VA; md
27 Jun 1807 Ann Murphy (P),
Norfolk, VA. Her LNR Nor-
folk, VA, 1871

CLARK, GEORGE W. (P, BLW), died c1892, LNR Winchester, Scott Co, IL, 1887; md 10 Oct 1819 Jane R. Shelton, Brunswick Co, VA

CLARK, HATCHER (P, BLW), died 12 Sep 1875, Lunenburg Co, VA; md (1) Phebe F. Newby, (2) 1823 Elizabeth Furgussen (P), Chesterfield Co, VA. Her LNR Pleasant Grove, Lunenburg Co, VA, 1878

CLARK, HENRY (BLW), died 13 May 1854, White Hall, Greene Co, IL; md (1) Mary Clark, (2) 21 Mar 1853 Mary (----) Jackson (P), Carrollton, Greene Co, IL. She died c1880, LNR Berdan, Greene Co, IL, 1880

CLARK, HENRY J. (P, BLW), died 21 Mar 1874, Eureka, IL; md (1) Mary Mansfield, (2) 22 Jul 1860 Mary J. Bell (P), Danvers, McLean Co, IL. She died 2 May 1914, Patoka, IL, LNR Eureka, Woodford Co, IL, 1878

CLARK, JAMES (BLW), whose former widow was Elizabeth J. Keen

CLARK, JAMES (BLW) died 30 Dec 1842, Simpson Co, KY; md (1) ?, (2) 7 Oct 1819 Selina Bavington (P), Glasgow, Barren Co, KY. She died c1891, LNR Sedalia, Pettis Co, MO, 1880

CLARK, JAMES H. whose widow Cindarilla applied for a pension

CLARK, JOHN (P, BLW), LNR P.O. New Vienna, Clinton Co, OH, 1872; md 18 Oct 1817 Rhoda C. Hamrick, Pittsylvania Co, VA

CLARK, JOHN (P, BLW), died 15 or 18 Oct 1882, LNR P.O. Ohio, Marshall Co, KY, 1878; md 15 Aug 1819 Sally Blanton, Dover, Stewart Co, TN

CLARK, JOHN whose widow Catharine applied for a pension

CLARK, JOHN whose widow Rebecca applied for a pension

CLARK, JOHN C. (P, BLW), died 30 Jul 1876, Franklin, Simpson Co, KY; md 10 Feb 1820 Benete Hughes (P), Sumner Co, TN. Her LNR P.O. Elkton, Todd Co, KY, 1878

CLARK, JOHN C. (BLW), died 3 Jun 1856, Vincennes, IN; md (1) Nancy McCutchen, (2) 4 Jan 1852 Eliza C. (----) Vanderburg (P). Her LNR Vincennes, Knox Co, IN, 1884

CLARK, JONATHAN (BLW), died 11 Jul 1862, Metcalfe Co, KY; md 3 Jan 1813 Patsey Hensley (P), Henry Co, VA. Her LNR P.O. Edmonton, Metcalfe Co, KY, 1871

CLARK, NELSON H. (P, BLW), died 19 Sep 1871, LNR Lexington, Rockbridge Co, VA, 1871

CLARK, PETER (BLW), died 29 Mar 1855, Dinwiddie, VA; md 7 Dec 1812 Nancy Clarke (P), Nottoway, Nottoway Co, VA. Her LNR P.O. Burkville, Nottoway Co, VA, 1871

CLARK, ROBERT (P, BLW), died 20 May 1877, Lewis Co, WV; md (1) Anna Bogarth, (2) 14 May 1837 Elizabeth (----) Stone (P), Lewis Co, VA. Her LNR P.O. Walkersville, Lewis Co, WV, 1878

CLARK, ROBERT (P, BLW), died 6 Aug 1874, Rockbridge Co, Va; md 14 Apr 1825 Jane Wilson (P), Rockbridge Co, VA. Her LNR P.O. Buffalo Forge, Rockbridge Co, VA, 1878

CLARK, ROBINSON whose widow Ann J. applied for a pension

CLARK, SAMUEL (BLW), died 5 Jun 1864; md 3 Nov 1807 Nancy Holloway (P), Bedford Co, VA. Her LNR P.O. Madison Crossroads, Madison Co, AL, 1873

CLARK, SOLOMON (P, BLW), died c14 Apr 1883, Dawson Co, GA; md 24 Dec 1816 Susanna Wilkerson (P), Bedford, Bedford Co, VA. She died before 9 Aug 1887, LNR Amicalola, Dawson Co, GA, 1883

CLARK, THOMAS (P, BLW), LNR P.O. Hill Grove, Pittsylvania Co, VA, 1871; md 28 Jan 1841 Mildred H. Hart

CLARK, THOMAS (P, BLW), died c1877, LNR P.O. Republican Grove, Halifax Co, VA, 1871; md 8 Dec 1808 Peggy Henderson. Widower.

CLARK, THOMAS (BLW), died 3 Feb 1857, Petersburg, VA; md 16 Oct 1814 Mary Ann F. Pegram (P), Petersburg, VA. Her LNR Carrollton, Carroll Co, MS, 1764

CLARK, THOMAS whose widow Mary applied for a pension

CLARK, THOMAS whose widow Elizabeth applied for a pension

CLARK, WARREN (BLW), died 10 Jan 1864/65, Trigg Co, KY; md (1) Rebecca Frizzell, (2) 5 Jan 1843 Rebecca S. Faughan (P), Trigg Co, KY. She died c1896, LNR P.O. Marion, Crittenden Co, KY, 1880

CLARK, WILLIAM (P, BLW), LNR P.O. Paris, Lamar Co, TX, 1877; md 15 Jan 1818 ?, Orange Co, VA

CLARK, WILLIAM applied for a pension

CLARK/CLARKE, WILLIAM (BLW), died 14 Feb 1822, Richmond, VA; md 10 Nov 1818 Elizabeth H. Winston (P), Richmond, Henrico Co, VA. Her LNR Maysville, Blount Co, TN, 1878

CLARK, WILLIAM (BLW), died 27 Jun 1870, Lincoln Co, TN; md (1) Barbara Talbott, (2) 12 Oct 1826 Harriet Shugart (P). Her LNR Renfro's Station, Lincoln Co, TN, 1878

CLARK/CLARKE, WILLIAM (P, BLW), LNR Trafalgar, Johnson Co, IN, 1871; md 8 Jan 1811 Margaret M. Cook, VA

CLARKE, HENRY (BLW), died 3 Feb 1854, Surry Co, VA; md (1) Mary E. Harrison, (2) 14 Oct 1852 Minerva J. Atkinson (P), Surry Co, VA. Her LNR P.O. Wakefield, Sussex Co, VA, 1879

CLARKE, SAMUEL (BLW), died 20 Oct 1866, Waynesboro, VA; md 27 Jan 1820 Matilda Johnson (P), Waynesboro, VA. She died 8 Feb 1887, LNR Charlottesville, Albemarle Co, VA, 1882

CLARKE/CLARK, THOMAS (P, BLW), LNR Louisville, Jefferson Co, KY 1872; md 4 Mar 1819, Sarah Stiffle, Dumfries, VA

CLARKE/CLARK, WILLIAM (P, BLW), died 9 Dec 1875, LNR P.O. Horn Lake, DeSoto Co, MS, 1874

CLARKE, WILLIAM (BLW), died 15 Aug 1865, Urbana, OH; md 1 Nov 1821 Sarah Harnsbarger (P), Augusta Co, VA. She died 10 Feb 1892, LNR Urbana, Champaign Co, OH, 1878

CLARY, HEROD (P, BLW), LNR P.O. White Plains, Brunswick Co, VA, 1871

CLAY, HENRY (BLW), died 12 Jan 1866, Oceana, Wyoming Co, WV; md (1) ?, (2) 9 Jan 1838 Marthy Miller (P), Her LNR Pineville, Wyoming Co, WV, 1880

CLAY, JORDAN/JORDON (BLW)

CLAY, THOMAS (P, BLW), LNR P.O. Ellettsville, Monroe Co, IN, 1871; md Nov 1812 Susan Smart, Halifax Co, VA

CLAY, WALTER applied for a pension

CLAY, WILLIAM (P, BLW), died 28 Nov 1875, Union Co, TN;

CLAY (continued)
md 14 Sep 1821 Permelia
Stone (P), Meadsville, Halifax
co, VA. Her LNR P.O.
Tazewell, Claiborne Co, TN,
1878
CLAYBROOK, EDWARE (BLW),
died 27 Jan 1855, Mason Co,
KY; md (1) Daisy Bailey, (2)
11 Mar 1838 Missaniah Ander-
son (P), Mason Co, KY. Her
LNR Germantown, Mason Co,
KY, 1878
CLAYPOOL, LEVI (BLW), died 2
Feb 1867, Menard Co, IL; md
7 Dec 1819 Melinda Rawlings
(P), Champaign Co, OH. She
died c1892, LNR Athens,
Menard Co, IL, 1887
CLAYTON, JOHN (BLW), died 8
Mar 1857, Marion Co, VA; md
22 Mar 1821 Susanna Jones
(P), Monongalia Co, VA. She
died 6 Oct 1884, LNR P.O.
Gray's Flat, Marion Co, WV,
1880
CLAYTON, WILLIAM W.
(BLW), died 2 Mar 1853,
McDonough Co, IL; md 24 Dec
1812 Martha/Patsy Vest (P),
Washington Co, VA. She died
13 Mar 1883, LNR Colches-
ter, McDonough Co, IL, 1871
CLAYTOR/CLATOR, COLEMAN
(BLW), died 25 Jan 1871,
Alma, IL; md (1) Elizabeth
Watkins, (2) 11 Oct 1825
Phebe Buchanan (P), Lexi-
ngton, Rockbridge Co, VA.
She died c1885, Alma, Marion
Co, IL
CLAYTOR, JOEL (BLW), USA,
died 4 Jan 1862, Caroline Co,
VA; md 24 Dec 1850 Amanda
Beazley (P), Caroline Co, VA.
Her LNR P.O. Upper Zion,
Caroline Co, VA, 1889
CLAYTOR, ROBERT M. (BLW),
died 3 Jul 1865, Bedford Co,
VA; md 30 Jan 1817 Julia
Graham (P), Bedford Co, VA.
Her LNR Liberty, Bedford Co,

CLAYTOR (continued)
VA, 1878

CLEATON, CHARLES D. (BLW),
died 30 Nov 1855, Mecklenburg
Co, VA; md 4 Dec 1816
Frances Walker (P). She died
17 Aug 1885, Marengo, Meck-
lenburg Co, VA
CLEGHORN, JAMES (P, BLW),
died 27 Jan 1875, Smyth Co,
VA; md Oct 1816 Rachel
James (P), Washington Co,
VA. She died before Mar 1883,
LNR P.O. Town House, Smyth
Co, VA, 1878
CLEMENS, WILLIAM applied for
a pension
CLEMENTS, HARRIS (P, BLW),
died 10 Mar 1872, Lynchburg,
VA; md (1) Sally Snead, (2) 17
Sep 1852 Martha J. Davis (P),
Palmyra, Fluvanna Co, VA.
She died 9 Mar 1880, Lynch-
burg, Campbell Co, VA
CLEMENTS/CLEMENT, ISHAM
(BLW), died 22 Nov 1840,
Goochland Co, VA; md 21 Mar
1823 Cary Hicks (P), Gooch-
land Co, VA. She died 25 Mar
1883, LNR Derkinsville,
Goochland Co, Va, 1878
CLEMENTS, MOSES (BLW)
whose widow was Elizabeth
CLEMENTS, REUBEN (P,
BLW), LNR Petersburg, VA,
1871; md 31 Dec 1829 Virginia
Minitree, Petersburg, VA. She
died 17 Feb 1849
CLEMENTS, ROBERT A. (P,
BLW), LNR P.O. Danielle,
Montgomery Co, MO, 1871.
Wife's name not given
CLEMINGS, ALFRED (P, BLW),
died c1877, LNR P.O. Newark,
Licking Co, OH, 1874; md 1
Jan 1820 Matilda Payne,
Loudoun Co, VA
CLEMONS, PETER (P, BLW),
LNR P.O. Marysville, Blount

CLEMONS (continued) Co, TN. Not married.

CLENDENING, ROBERT Y. applied for a pension

CLERENGER, GEORGE P. whose widow Elizabeth applied for a pension

CLICE, HENRY (P, BLW), died c1878, LNR P.O. Stockport, Morgan Co, OH, 1871; md 6 Apr 1817 Sarah Triplett, Loudoun Co, VA

CLIENTINCK/CLINEDINST, ISAAC (BLW), died 9 Nov 1855, Shenandoah Co, VA; md 9 Mar 1925 Lydia Holler (P), Shenandoah Co, VA. Her LNR Edinburgh, Shenandoah Co, VA, 1878

CLIFT/CLEFT, GEORGE W. (BLW), died 15 Jul 1833, Cumberland Co, VA; md 4 Mar 1824 Delila Martin (P), Powhatan Co, VA. She died 20 Sep 1893, LNR P.O. Cartersville, Cumberland Co, VA, 1878

CLIFT, THORNTON applied for a pension

CLIFTON, JOHN (P, BLW), died 1 Mar 1877, WV; md 20 Jun 1815 Sarah Miller (P), Randolph Co, VA. She died c1883, LNR P.O. Webster Courthouse, Webster Co, WV, 1878

CLINE, ABRAHAM (P, BLW), died 10 Feb 1879, Delaware Co, IA; md 27 Jul 1853 Sarah (----) McPeak (P), Delaware Co, IA. She died 14 Jan 1895 Hopkinton, Delaware Co, IA

CLINE, DAVID (BLW), died 25 Jan 1861, Memphis, Scotland Co, MO; md 28 Oct 1855 Mary Baker (P), Scotland Co, MO. She died 17 Jan 1895, Watsonville, WI, LNR Lost Creek, Deer Lodge Co, MT, 1878

CLINE, GEORGE whose widow Elizabeth applied for a pension

CLINE/CLEIN/KLINE, GEORGE (P, BLW), LNR P.O. War

CLINE (continued) densville, Hardy Co, WV, 1871; md 18 Jul 1816 Susan Didowick, Shenandoah Co, VA

CLINE, LEWIS (P, BLW), died 10 Jul 1873, Shelby Co, IN; md (1) Lane Pugh, (2) 17 Oct 1850 Julia H. Chambers (P), Shelby Co, IN. Her LNR P.O. Sulphur Hill, Shelby Co, IN, 1878

CLINE, WILLIAM (BLW), died 10 Dec 1867, Logan Co, OH; md 27 Sep 1812 Elizabeth Coffee (P), Chillicothe, Ross Co, OH. Her LNR Logan Co, OH, 1872

CLIPPARD, JOHN (P, BLW), died 3 Apr 1882, LNR P.O. Morrow, Warren Co, OH, 1871; md 25 Feb 1813 Nancy Henry, Shenandoah Co, VA

CLISER/CLYZER/CLYSER, MARTIN (BLW), died 10 Aug 1849, Page Co, VA; md 28 Dec 1826 Sarah Fletcher (P), Shenandoah Co, VA. Her LNR Luray, Page Co, VA, 1878

CLOPTON, NATHANIEL V. (BLW), died 6 Oct 1855, Grassdale, Fauquier Co, VA; md 17 Oct 1821 Sarah S. G. Skinker (P), Spring Farm, Fauquier Co, VA. Her LNR Grassdale, Fauquier Co, VA, 1878

CLOPTON, THOMAS (P, BLW), died 7 Dec 1874, Sumter Co, GA; md (1) ?, (2) ?, (3) 11 Mar 1858 Cornelia H. Palmer (P), Putnam Co, GA. Her LNR Americus, Sumter Co, GA, 1920

CLOUD, JEREMIAH (BLW)

CLOUD, WILLIAM (P, BLW), died 8 May 1876, LNR P.O. Winchester, Frederick Co, VA, 1811; md Nancy Butterfield, Winchester, VA

CLOWE/CLOE, CHARLES B. (BLW), died 12 Aug 1858, Prince William Co, VA; md 1 Jan 1812 Harriet Wyatt (P),

CLOWE (continued)
Gainesville, Prince William Co, VA. She died 23 Mar 1879, Prince William Co, VA, LNR P.O. Catharpin, Prince William Co, VA, 1878

CLOWER, SAMUEL whose widow Mary applied for a pension

CLUTTER, JOHN J. whose widow Catherine applied for a pension

CLYBORN, CHARLES A. (BLW), died 28 Sep 1864, Ross Co, OH; md 7 Oct 1812 Mahala Pettis (P), Fluvanna Co, VA. She died 15 Oct 1879, Highland Co, OH, LNR P.O. Rainsborough, Highland Co, OH, 1871

COALTER, ROBERT whose widow Mary applied for a pension

COATES/COATS, JAMES (BLW), died 11 Apr 1863, Culpeper Co, VA; md 27 Jan 1820 Mary R. Smith (P), Culpeper Co, VA. Her LNR P.O. Boston, Culpeper Co, VA, 1878

COATES, WILLIAM (BLW), died Aug 1842, Halifax Co, VA; md c1 May 1824 Nancy Shipp (P), Halifax Co, VA. She died 29 Jul 1893, Halifax Co, VA, LNR P.O. Rabat, Halifax Co, VA, 1884

COATS, JAMES (BLW), died 1862, Madison Co, VA; md 27 Dec 1810 Nancy Howell (P), Madison Co, VA. She died 20 May 1871, Madison Co, VA, LNR Madison Courthouse, Madiaon Co, VA

COBB, HENRY whose widow Martha R. applied for a pension

COBB, EDMUND M. (P, BLW), died 3 Mar 1882, Lookout, MO, LNR Boonville, Cooper Co, MO, 1871. Wife's name not given

COBBS, HIRAM (P, BLW), died 29 Apr 1871, Kanawha, WV; md (1) Nancy Woods, (2) 25 Sep or 22 Nov 1825 Ann Parthena Carter (P), Charleston,

COBBS (continued)
VA. She died 27 Jul 1896, LNR Spring Hill, Kanawha Co, WV, 1886

COCHRAN, ELIJAH (BLW), died 23 Sep 1844, Knox Co, OH; md 27 Nov 1817 Susannah Richardson (P), Loudoun Co, VA. She died 12 Aug 1883, West Carlisle, Coshocton Co, OH

COCK/COOK, JOHN (BLW), died 18 Mar 1871, Bland Co, VA; md (1) Jane Philips, (2) 30 Jan 1852 Louisa J. Day (P), Carroll Co, VA. She died c1890, LNR P.O. Dug Spur, Carroll Co, VA, 1888

COCKE, GEORGE R. applied for a pension

COCKE, JOHN F. (BLW), died 20 Apr 1857, Goochland Co, VA; md 9 Dec 1830 Harriet W. Holland (P), Goochland Co, VA. Her LNR P.O. Hadensville, Goochland Co, VA, 1878

COCKE, THOMAS H. (P, BLW), USA, LNR P.O. Newsoms Depot, Southampton Co, VA, 1871; md 2 Jan 1820 Rebecca Richards, Surry Co, VA

COCKE, WILSON C. (P, BLW), LNR P.O. Lawrenceburg, Anderson Co, KY, 1871; md 7 Jan 1819 Cecelia Ann Russell, Shelby Co, OH. Wilson was a substitute for James Cocke to serve the balance of his time in the War.

COCKERELL, THOMAS (BLW)

COCKERELL, WILLIAM S. (P, BLW), died c1879, LNR Greenfield, Highland Co, OH, 1871; md Mar 1810 Anna Leetman, Hampshire Co, VA

COCKRAN, JOHN M. and widow Mariah R. both applied for a pension

COCKERLL, THOMAS (BLW)

COCKRHAN/COCKRAM, ALLEN (P, BLW), died 18 Feb 1876, Nottoway Co, VA; md 1820 or 1823 Nancy L. Waller (P),

COCRHAN (continued)
Nottoway Co, VA. Her LNR
P.O. Jeffress Store, Nottoway
Co, VA, 1878

COCKRILL, PETER (BLW), died
5 Jul 1870; md 21 Oct 1816
Catharine Riley (P), Wood Co,
VA. She died 28 Mar 1886,
LNR P.O. Waller, Ross Co,
OH, 1878

COE, AMZI (BLW), NY militia,
died 1 Jun 1866, Falls Church,
Fairfax Co, VA; md 23 Dec
1829 Anna Sherwood (P),
Hempstead, Rockland Co, NY.
She died 26 Jun 1884, Gil-
bertsville, Otsego Co, NY

COE, GEORGE H. (P, BLW),
LNR Marshall Co, MS, 1871;
md 3 Jun 1818 Margaret
Wright, Huntsville, Madison
Co, AL

COEN, EDWARD (P, BLW), MD
militia, LNR Wheeling, Ohio
Co, WV, 1871; md 28 Oct 1827
Grace McCully, Steubenville,
OH

COEN, ISAAC whose widow Susanna applied for a pension

COEN/COAN, WILLIAM (P,
BLW), LNR Wheeling, Ohio
Co, WV, 1872; md 30 Sep 1817
Patient Ann Jones, Ohio Co,
VA

COFFELT, GEORGE (P, BLW),
LNR Stony Creek, Sussex Co,
VA, 1871

COFFLAND, JAMES (BLW), died
Nov 1859, Belmont Co, OH;
marriage bond 8 Jul 1801 with
Eleanor Potts (P), Berkeley
Co, VA. Her LNR P.O. East
Richland, Belmont Co, OH,
1871

COFFMAN/KOFFMAN, DANIEL
(P, BLW), LNR Stoney Creek,
Shenandoah Co, VA, 1871

COFFMAN, HENRY (P, BLW),
LNR Hardin Co, KY, 1872; md
18 Dec 1819 Hester Buley

COFFMAN, JACOB (P, BLW),
died 21 May 1886, Gold Hill,

COFFMAN (continued)
Grant Co, WV; md Mar 1834
Emily R. Porter (P), Hardy Co,
VA. She died 27 Feb 1896,
Gold Hill, Grant Co, WV, 1886

COFFMAN, JOHN (P, BLW),
LNR Woodstock, Shenandoah
Co, VA, 1872

COFFMAN, MATHIAS (BLW),
died 18 Jun 1844, Mt. Clifton,
VA; md 8 Mar 1813 Elizabeth
Fadeley (P), Shenandoah Co,
VA. Her LNR P.O. Mt. Clif-
ton, Shenandoah Co, VA, 1871

COGAR, THOMAS (P, BLW),
died c1873, LNR P.O. Webster
Courthouse, Webster Co, WV,
1871; md 1819 Eve Spillman,
Union Mills, Fluvanna Co, VA

COGBILL, EDWARD H (P,
BLW), died 20 Apr 1863,
Chesterfield Co, Va; md 13
Nov 1838 Elizabeth Cole (P),
Chesterfield Co, VA. Her LNR
Chesterfield Co, VA, 1871

COGER, JACOB (P, BLW), died
before 28 Sep 1882, LNR P.O.
Holly River, Braxton Co, WV,
1871; md 1820 Margaret Mollohan, Holly River, VA

COGER/KOGER, WILLIAM (P,
BLW), LNR P.O. Middleport,
Webster Co, WV, 1871; md
1799 Elizabeth Kingery,
Franklin Co, VA. Widower

COGHILL, WILLIAM G. (BLW),
died May 1834/35; md 4 Mar
1816 Mary/Polly Samuel (P),
Caroline Co, VA. Her LNR
P.O. Milford, Carolina Co, VA,
1878

COHAGAN, THOMAS (BLW),
died 5 Aug 1844, Perry Co,
OH; md Jun 1810/12 Catharine
Fling (P), Loudoun Co, VA.
She died 9 Aug 1872, Hocking
Co, OH, LNR P.O. Logan,
Hocking Co, OH, 1871

COHEN, THOMAS (BLW), died
26 Feb 1863, St. Louis, MO;
md 30 Nov 1809 Mary W.
Heath (P), Lynchburg, VA. She

COHEN (continued)
died 1 Dec 1876, LNR St.
Louis, MO, 1873
COIL, JOHN whose widow Dolly
applied for a pension
COLBERT, JOEL/JOSEPH (P,
BLW), LNR P.O. Dalton,
Whitfield Co, GA, 1871

ROLL NO. 20

COLE, CHARLES (BLW), died 7
Jun 1854, Tazewell Co, VA;
md 8 Mar 1804 Anna Freeman
(P), Patrick Co, VA. She died
7 Mar 1873, LNR P.O. Taze-
well Courthouse, Tazewell Co,
VA, 1871
COLE, DANIEL (P, BLW), MD
militia, died 16 Jan 1879; md
(1) Hannah ----, (2) 17 Apr
1831 Ruth Bumgardner (P),
Hampshire Co, VA. She died
before 27 May 1887, LNR
Capon Springs, VA, 1880
COLE, EDWARD T. (BLW), died
22 Nov 1855, Mecklenburg Co,
VA; md 19 Nov 1823 Ann E.
Beal (P), Mecklenburg Co, VA.
Her LNR P.O. North View,
Mecklenburg Co, VA, 1878
COLE, JACKSON whose widow
Eliza/Liza applied for a pen-
sion
COLE, JOHN (BLW), died 9 Apr
1863, Madison Co, VA; md 23
Dec 1807 Nancy Wharton (P),
She died 26 Apr 1878, LNR
P.O. Madison Courthouse,
Madison Co, VA, 1871
COLE, JOHN R. and widow
Catharine both applied for a
pension
COLE, JOHN T. (BLW), died 13
Dec 1860, Mecklenburg Co,
VA; md (1) Patsey Cheatham,
(2) 20 Apr 1845 Rebecca
(Thompson) Lambert, Meck-
lenburg Co, VA. She died 12
Sep 1884, LNR P.O. Smith
Crossroads, Mecklenburg Co,
VA, 1880

COLE, PELEG (BLW), died 15
Aug 1858, Washingtoh Co, VA;
md (1) Polly Todd, (2) 27 Sep
18323 Martha Ketchum (P),
Washington Co, VA. Her LNR
P.O. Loves Mills, Washington
Co, VA, 1878
COLE, RICHARD (BLW), died 5
Apr 1859, Greenbrier Co, VA;
md 22 Nov 1808 Lydia Perry
(P), Bath Co, VA, LNR White
Sulphur Springs, Greenbrier Co,
WV, 1871
COLE, SAMUEL (BLW)
COLE, SAMUEL (BLW)
COLE, WILLIAM (BLW), OH
militia, died 27 Jan 1827
Loudoun Co, VA; md (1) Han-
nah Rogor, (2) 19 Oct 1823
Priscilla Roler (P), Loudoun
Co, VA. She died c1882, LNR
Adamsville, Muskingum Co,
OH, 1878
COLE, WILLIAM (BLW)
COLEMAN, AUGUSTINE B.
(BLW), died 18 Jun 1851,
Dinwiddie, Dinwiddie Co, VA;
md 5 May 1842 Mary C.
Branch (P), Cumberland Co,
VA. Her LNR P.O. San
Marino, Dinwiddie Co, VA,
1878
COLEMAN, JAMES (P, BLW),
LNR P.O. Spotsylvania Court-
house, Spotsylvania Co, VA,
1871; md 20 Feb 1820 Lucy
Stewart, Spotsylvania Co, VA
COLEMAN, JAMES (BLW), died
11 Mar 1863, Appomattox Co,
VA; md (1) Polly Watkins, (2)
8 Jul 1847 Judida Duncan (P),
She died 5 Apr 1895, LNR P.O.
Jordan Springs, Montgomery
Co, TN, 1876
COLEMAN, JAMES B. (P,
BLW), died Dec 1883, Erin,
TN, LNR P.O. Jordan Springs,
Montgomery co, TN, 1876
COLEMAN, JOHN served as a
substitute for Joel Boulton in
the War.
COLEMAN, ROBERT (P, BLW),

COLEMAN (continued)
died 9 Mar 1879, Patrick Co,
VA; md (1) Mary King, (2)
Sally Mills, (3) Sarah Cruise,
(4) 3 Dec 1863 Mary Headen
(P), Patrick Co, VA. Her LNR
Bateman, Patrick Co, VA,
1899

COLEMAN, ROBERT S. (BLW),
died 29 Dec 1858, Gibson Co,
TN; md 16 Sep 1818 Sarah
Dunnavant (P), Amelia Co,
VA. Her LNR P.O. Humboldt,
Gibson Co, TN, 1879

COLEMAN, SAMUEL A. applied
for a pension

COLEMAN, WILLIAM serves as
a substitute for James Blanton
in the War

COLEMAN, WINSTON L. and
widow Nancy both applied for a
pension

COLEY, WILLIAM (P, BLW),
died 5 Aug 1875, Martinsburg,
IL; md 1 Apr 1823 Elizabeth
McClain (P-rejected), Germantown, Bracken Co, KY. She
died c1879, LNR P.O. Pi-
ttsfield, Pike Co, IL, 1878

COLLETT, JEREMIAH (BLW),
died 9 or 18 May 1852, Wood
Co, VA; md 16 Jan 1812 Eliz-
abeth Davis (P), Loudoun Co,
VA. She died 2 Feb 1889,
Wheeling, WV

COLLEY, GEORGE (BLW), died
7 Nov 1869, Ironton, OH; md
(1) Polly Brown, (2) 14 Aug
1841 Margaret (Stridlen) Stratton (P), Scoioto Co, OH. She
died cJun 1897. LNR Ironton,
Lawrence Co, OH, 1887

COLLEY, OBADIAH (BLW), died
15 Sep 1860, Tarryall, South
Park, CO; md 1817 Sallie Wil-
lis (P), Pittsylvania Co, VA.
She died 22 Jul 1881, LNR
Canton, Lewis Co, MO, 1881.
Obadiah also served in the
Black Hawk Indian War in MO
in 1832.

COLLEY, WILLIAM (P, BLW),

COLLEY (continued)
died 26 Jun 1875, Halifax Co,
VA; md (1) Martha Carter, (2)
12 Jun 1849 Sarah A. Burks
(P), Halifax Co, VA. She died
c1896, LNR P.O. Laurel
Grove, Pittsylvania Co, VA,
1878

COLLIER, CHARLES M. (BLW)

COLLIER, SHADRACH (P,
BLW), died 15 Feb 1872, LNR
Hillsville, Carroll Co, VA,
1871; md 8 Feb 1803 Lucy
Bobbit, Grayson Co, VA. Wi-
dower.

COLLIER, WILLIAM (BLW),
whose widow was Frances

COLLINS, CHARLES (BLW),
died 18 Jun 1853, Mount View,
VA; md 21 Feb 1832 Catherine
Jesse (P), Caroline Co, VA.
She died 4 May 1887, Milford,
Caroline Co, VA

COLLINS, DILLARD W. whose
widow Mary A. applied for a
pension

COLLINS, ISAAC whose widow
Catherine applied for a pension

COLLINS, JACOB (BLW), died
21 Apr 1859, Delaware Co, IN;
md 7 Feb 1825 Elizabeth
Fisher (P), Miami Co, OH.
Her LNR P.O. New Burlington,
Delaware Co, OH, 1879

COLLINS, JAMES (P, BLW),
LNR P.O. Bentonville, Warren
Co, VA, 1871; md 4 May 1820
Nancy Hancock, Shenandoah
Co (now Warren Co), VA

COLLINS, JAMES R. (P, BLW),
LNR P.O. Paris, Henry Co,
TN, 1871. Never married.

COLLINS, JOHN whose widow
Abie applied for a pension

COLLINS, JOHN applied for a
pension

COLLINS, JOHN whose widow
Christina Wilson applied for a
pension

COLLINS, ROBERT (P, BLW),
LNR P.O. Lubeck, Wood Co,
WV, 1871; md 20 Feb 1827

COLLINS (continued)
Elizabeth Selock, Fauquier Co, VA
COLLINS, SAMUEL (BLW), died 13 Aug 1834, Russell Co, KY; md 23 Dec 1814 Agnes Maxwell (P), Washington Co, VA. Her LNR P.O. Jamestown, Russell Co, KY, 1871
COLLINS, THOMAS (P, BLW), LNR P.O. Arbor Hill, Augusta Co, VA, 1871
COLLINS, WILLIAM (P, BLW), died 20 Mar 1876, Cabell Co, WV; md (1) ?, (2) 10 Jan 1837 Zilpha Cornel (P), Cabell Co, VA. She died 6 Aug 1881, LNR P.O. Cabell Courthouse, Cabell Co, WV, 1878
COLLISON, ISAAC (P, BLW), LNR Clay Co, WV, 1871; md 1816 Cynthia Robinson, Nicholas Co, VA
COLLY, WILLIAM W. (P, BLW), LNR P.O. Hallsboro, Chesterfield Co, VA, 1871; md 6 Apr 1816 S. Liggin, Powhatan Co, VA
COLMAN/COLEMAN, ROBERT (BLW), NH militia, died 30 Mar 1852, Portsmouth, VA; md (1) ?, (2) 5 Jul 1837 Catharine (----) Smith (P), Portsmouth, VA. She died 27 Feb 1890, LNR Portsmouth, Norfolk, Co, VA, 1887
COLSTON, EDWARD (BLW), died 21 Apr 1851, Berkeley Co, VA; md (1) Jane Marshall, (2) 28 May 1825 Sarah Jane Brockenbrough (P), Richmond, VA. She died before 5 Nov 1890, LNR Martinsburg, Berkeley Co, VA, 1878
COLVERT, WILLIAM P. (BLW), died Sep 1859, Nashville, TN; md 24 Aug 1820 Harriet Weedon (P), Culpeper Co, VA. Her LNR Smithville, DeKalb Co, TN, 1878
COLVILLE, JAMES (P, BLW), died 7 Nov 1878, md 25 Jul

COLVILLE (continued)
1827 Leah Baker (P), Licking Co, OH. She died c1886, LNR P.O. Long Run, Licking Co, OH, 1879
COLVIN, AMBROSE (P, BLW), LNR Carrollton, Carroll Co, MO, 1873; md 1840 Louisa Plemmons, Cole Co, MO
COLVIN, BENJAMIN (P, BLW), LNR State Mills, Rappahannock Co, VA, 1871
COLVIN, GEORGE (P, BLW), died 2 Jul 1881, Belmont Co, OH; md 11 May 1820 Melevy Broiles (P), Madison Co, VA. She died 28 Jun 1888, LNR Colerain, Belmont Co, OH, 1881
COLVIN, JOHN (BLW), died 21 or 23 Jul 1871, Fayette Co, OH; md 27 Feb 1817 Margaret Youill (P), Culpeper Co, VA. She died c1887, LNR Washington Courthouse, Fayette Co, OH, 1881
COLVIN, WILLIAM (P, BLW), LNR P.O. Spencerburg, Pike Co, OH, 1871; md 18 Jan 1816 Frances Burton, Albemarle Co, VA
COLWELL/CALDWELL, JAMES (P, BLW), died 19 Jul 1876, Scioto Co, OH; md 9 Jun 1819 Betsy Saxton (P), Gallia Co, OH. She died 11 Oct 1886, Vinton Co, OH, LNR P.O. Hales Creek, Scioto Co, OH, 1878
COMBS, BENJAMIN (BLW), died 19 Apr 1870, Loudoun Co, VA; md (1) ?, (2) 30 Jan 1851 Margaret A. Pritchett (P), Stafford Co, VA. She died 4 Sep 1805, Baltimore, MD, LNR Baltimore, MD, 1887
COMBS, DAVID (P, BLW), died 29 Oct 1871, Elizabeth, IN; md 22 Feb 1808 Jane Rogers (P), Hampshire Co, VA. She died c1876, LNR Elizabeth, Harrison Co, IN, 1872

COMBS, JOHN (BLW), died 4 Oct 1857, Carroll Co, OH; md 11 Apr 1816 Anna M. Milner (P), New Lisbon, Columbiana Co, OH. She died cDec 1881, LNR Leon, Decatur Co, IN, 1878

COMBS, JOHN (BLW), died 1 Jun 1861, Chaplin, KY; md 1 Aug 1818 Fanny Harrison (P), Nelson Co, KY. Her LNR Chaplin, Nelson Co, KY, 1878

COMER, NATHANIEL (P, BLW), died 27 Jul 1873, Davie Co, NC; md (1) Catharine Godber, (2) 24 Jun 1852 Rachel Jones (P), Davie Co, NC. Her LNR P.O. Calahan, Davie Co, NC, 1878

COMER, SAMUEL (BLW), died 6 Jan 1870, Page Co, VA; md (1) Elizabeth Smith, (2) 2 Nov 1828 Elizabeth Strole/Strob (P), Page Co, VA. She died 13 Jan 1885, LNR Luray, Page Co, VA, 1878

COMER, THOMAS B. (BLW), died 1 Jan 1863, Halifax Co, VA; md 19 Dec 1827 Susan T. Dunkley (P), Halifax Co, VA. She died 5 Jan 1880, Omega, Halifax Co, VA, LNR Halifax Courthouse, Halifax Co, VA, 1878

COMPHER, PETER (P, BLW), LNR P.O. Lovettsville, Loudoun Co, VA, 1878

COMPTON, JORDAN (BLW), GA militia, died 30 Mar 1864, Jasper Co, GA; md 7 May 1807 Susan Chappell (P), Halifax Co, VA. Her LNR P.O. Monticello, Jasper Co, GA, 1871

COMPTON/CRUMPTON, THOMAS (BLW), died 22 Sep 1855, Pike Co, KY; md (1) ?, (2) 2 Feb 1850 Anna (----) Johnson (P), Russell Co, VA. She died 3 Oct 1900, LNR P.O. Piketon, Pike Co, KY, 1878. Anna's first husband was Peyton Johnson.

CONANT, LOT (BLW), MA militia, died 14 Oct 1868, Brooke Co, WV; md 19 Mar 1815 Mary McClallan (P), Oakham, Worcester Co, MA. Her LNR Wheeling, Ohio Co, WV, 1878

CONAWAY/CONWAY, DANIEL (P, BLW), LNR Harrison Co, WV, 1871

CONAWAY, ISAAC (P, BLW), died c1876, LNR Spencerville, Allen Co, OH, 1871; md 4 Mr 1813 Nancy Bodine, Berkeley Co, VA

CONDREY, YOUNG, died 24 Oct 1852, Chesterfield Co, VA; md (1) Judith W. Goode, (2) 10 Feb 1842 Catharine Ford (P), Chesterfield Co, VA. She died before 12 Jul 1883, LNR P.O. Skin Quarter, Chesterfield Co, VA, 1879

CONE, LITTLETON/SAMUEL or COAN/LITTLETON A. (BLW), died May 1851, Portsmouth, VA; md 21 Dec 1831 Nancy Culpeper (P), Norfolk Co, VA. She died 9 Sep 1889, LNR Portsmouth, Norfolk Co, VA, 1855

CONNELLY/CONNELLEE/CONELY, ROBERT (BLW), died Feb 1867, Richmond, VA; md (1) Lucy Hazard, (2) 19 Aug 1856 Fanny B. (----) Balderson (P), Richmond, VA. Her LNR Essex Co, VA, 1878. Fanny's first husband was Henry Balderson.

CONGROVE, ELIJAH, died 1 Jan 1846, Meigs Co, OH; md 2 Feb 1838 Elizabeth Taylor (P), Racine, Meigs Co, OH. She died c1895, LNR Murrayville, Jackson Co, WV, 1880

CONLEY, JAMES (BLW), died 29 Jun 1859, Hastings Run, VA; md (1) Asona Romine, (2) 13 Oct 1825 Nancy Middleton (P), Hastings Run, VA. Her LNR Hastings Run, Harrison Co, WV, 1878

CONLEY/CONNELLY, JESSE (BLW), died 14 Jul 1852, Goochland Co, VA; md 17 Dec 1812 Martha Ann Sheppard (P), Goochland Co, VA. She died 22 May 1876, P.O. Richmond, Henrico Co, VA, 1871

ROLL NO. 21

CONNELLY, ROBERT (BLW), died 14 Apr 1853, Brunswick Co, VA; md 4 Feb 1836 Mary A. Bottom (P), Brunswick Co, VA. She died 29 Nov 1879, Brunswick Co, VA, LNR P.O. Charlie Hope, Brunswick Co, VA, 1878

CONNER, JAMES (BLW), died 7 Apr 1857, Tuscumbia, AL; md 11 Jul 1825 Martha T. Scales (P), Courtland, Lawrence Co, AL. Her LNR Brownsville, Haywood Co, TN, 1878

CONNER, JOHN whose widow Martha Ann applied for a pension

CONNER, JOHN (BLW), died 23 Nov 1856, Halifax Co, VA; md 19 Mar 1823 Rebecca Powell (P), Halifax Co, VA. She died 8 Dec 1880, LNR Knoxville, Knox Co, TN, 1878

CONNER, THOMAS (BLW), died 2 Apr 1834, Halifax Co, VA; md (1) Lucy Carlton, (2) 1 May 1822 Susanna P. Cardwell (P), Halifax Co, VA. She died c1882, LNR Como, Henry Co, TN, 1878

CONNER, WILLIAM (P, BLW), died 23 Jan 1879, Perry Co, OH; md (1) Rachel More, (2) 18 Dec 1838 Anna (----) Crook (P), Somerset, Perry Co, OH. She died 31 Dec 1884, LNR P.O. Bremen, Perry Co, OH, 1879

CONRAD, CHARLES (BLW), died 17 Dec 1837, Winchester, VA; md 10 Aug 1811 Elizabeth Copenhaver (P), Hagerstown,

CONRAD (continued) MD. Her LNR Winchester, VA, 1871

CONRAD, DANIEL PEYTON (BLW), died 22 Dec 1843, Piqua, Miami Co, OH; md 22 Jan 1818 Mary Ann Richards (P), Leesburg, Loudoun Co, VA. She died c4 Nov 1882, LNR Piqua, Miami Co, OH, 1878

CONRAD, ISAAC (P, BLW), died c1876, LNR Newark, Licking Co, OH, 1871

CONRAD, JACOB (P, BLW), died 22 or 23 Sep 1872, Gilmer Co, WV; md 22 Sep 1815 Eunice Mace (P), Little Kanawha River, Harrison Co, VA. She died 2 Mar 1895, LNR P.O. Glenville, Gilmer Co, WV, 1878

CONRAD/CONROD, PETER (BLW), died 10 Dec 1868, Wirt Co, WV; md 21 Apr 1842 Jane Blesser (P), Jackson Co, VA. She died 19 Jul 1888, LNR Wirt Co, WV, 1878

CONRAD/CONROD, SOLOMON (BLW), died 6 Mar 1862, Green Bank, VA; md 6 Dec 1862 Mary H. Brown (P), Montgomery Co, VA. Her LNR Green Bank, Pocahontas Co, WV, 1878

CONWAY, JAMES (BLW), died 24 Dec 1871, Muhlenburg Co, KY; md 15 Apr 1817 Martha E. Stanfield (P), Dinwiddie Co, VA. She died before 27 Jan 1892, LNR P.O. Gordonsville, Logan Co, KY, 1886

CONWAY, JOHN (BLW), died 22 Mar 1865, Caroline Co, VA; md 16 Mar 1815 Harriet E. Thornton (P), Caroline Co, VA. She died 17 Nov 1879, Caroline Co, VA

COOK, CALEB applied for a pension

COOK, CHARLES B. (BLW), died 30 May 1861, Oldham City,

COOK (continued)
KY; md 27 Nov 1828 Sarah/
Salley (----) Harvey (P), Bed-
ford, KY. Her LNR Bedford,
Trumble Co, KY, 1880

COOK, DAVID (P, BLW), LNR
P.O. Staunton, Augusta Co,
VA, 1871

COOK, GILES (BLW), died Sep
1873, King and Queen Co, VA;
md (1) Polly Broach, (2) Dec
1845 Parthena Wilson (P),
King and Queen Co, VA. She
died 6 Apr 1893, LNR P.O.
Stephens Church, King and
Queen Co, VA, 1878

COOK, JOHN (BLW), died 4 May
1864, Mecklenburg Co, VA; md
23 Dec 1812 Sallie Pennington
(P), Mecklenburg Co, VA. Her
LNR P.O. Lombardy Grove,
Mecklenburg Co, VA, 1871

COOK, JOHN (BLW), died 15 Jul
1859, Pioneer, OH; md 21 May
1818 Elizabeth Mayers (P),
Covington, Alleghany Co, VA.
She died 10 Feb 1883, LNR
Pioneer Station, Lawrence Co,
OH, 1878

COOK, JOHN (BLW), died 3 Nov
1871, Neosho Co, KS, md 25
Sep 1821 Nancy Martin (P),
Greenbrier Co, VA. She died
c1881, LNR Cove, Jackson co,
OH, 1880

COOK, JOHN L. (BLW), MD
militia, died 22 Apr 1836,
Richmond, VA; md 16 Nov
1806 Elizabeth O. Darrows (P),
Richmond, VA. Her LNR Richmond, Henrico Co, VA, 1871

COOK, JOHN R. (BLW), USA,
died 18 Aug 1866, Jay Co, IN;
md 25 Oct 1815 Mary Harford
(P), Culpeper Co, VA. Her
LNR Randolph, Randolph Co,
IN, 1878

COOK, RICHARD (P, BLW), died
c1876, md ?, LNR Richwood,
Union Co, OH, 1871

COOK, SAMUEL (BLW), died 17
Jun 1872, Cicero, IN; md 15

COOK (continued)
Mar 1846 Hannah Neff (P),
Washington, Wayne Co, IN.
She died 13 Dec 1893, LNR
Cicero, Madison Co, IN, 1880

COOK, SOLOMON (BLW), died 1
Oct 1841, Cabell Co, VA; mar-
riage bond 4 Oct 1810 Sarah
Cook (P), Madison Courthouse,
Madison Co, VA. Her LNR
P.O. Cabell Courthouse,
Cabell Co, WV, 1872

COOK, THEODORE, VA or DC
militia, applied for a pension

COOK, VALENTINE (BLW), died
3 Nov 1859, Waynesboro, VA;
md 18 Oct 1804 Catharine A.
Croft (P), Rockingham Co, VA.
Her LNR P.O. Waynesboro,
Augusta Co, VA, 1873

COOK, WILSON (BLW), died 7
Jul 1853, Madison Co, AL; md
24 Dec 1826 Elizabeth Clarke
(P), Madison Co, AL. She
died 18 May 1887 Cluttsville,
AL, LNR P.O. Cluttsville,
Madison Co, AL, 1878

COOKE, EDWARD E. (P, BLW),
died 20 Aug 1873, Charlestown, WV; md (1) Ann Norris,
(2) 15 Feb 1831 Margaret L.
Harrison (P), Loudoun Co, VA.
Her LNR Paris, Bourbon Co,
KY, 1878

COOKE, JOHN (BLW), died Oct
1866, King and Queen Co, VA;
md Feb 1824 Lucy Harper (P),
King and Queen Co, VA. She
died c1892, LNR P.O. Newton,
King and Queen Co, VA, 1878

COOKSEY, BENJAMIN (BLW),
died 2 Nov 1865, Dent Co, MO;
md 25 Mar 1826 Sarah D. Watson (P), Prince Georges Co,
MD. She died 6 Mar 1881,
LNR Dent Co, MO

COOLEY, ELIJAH (BLW), died
27 Mar 1868, Roane Co, TN;
md (1) Jemima Walden, (2) 2
May 1836 Elizabeth/Betsy
Ford (P), Roane Co, TN. She
died c1890, LNR P.O. Erin,

COOLEY (continued)
Houston Co, TN, 1878

COONS, JOHN (P, BLW), died c1881, LNR P.O. South Plymouth, Fayette Co, OH, 1871; md Sep 1821 Hannah Jones, Morgan Co, VA

COOPER, ARTHUR (P, BLW), LNR Georgetown, DC, 1871; md 22 Oct 1807 Elizabeth Suggs, Norfolk, VA

COOPER, EZEKIEL (P, BLW), LNR Dublin Wayne Co, IN; md 26 Oct 1826 Margaret M. Lenord, Augusta Co, VA

COOPER, FRANCIS whose widow Elizabeth applied for a pension

COOPER, GEORGE (BLW), died 29 Nov 1856, Franklin Co, VA; md 23 Sep 1824 Mary H. Wingfield (P), Franklin Co, VA. She died c1897, LNR P.O. Snow Creek, Franklin Co, VA, 1878

COOPER, HENRY (P, BLW), LNR P.O. Chamblissburg, Bedford Co, VA, 1871

COOPER, ISAAC (BLW), died 9 Mar 1870, Marklesville, IN; md (1) ---- Pullin, (2) 6 Jul 1842 Cynthia A. (----) Blake (P), Madison Co, IN. Her LNR Marklesville, Madison Co, IN, 1880

COOPER, ISAAC (BLW), died 12 Nov 1879, Monongalia Co, WV; md 11 Dec 1814 Sarah Chalfant (P), Fayette Co, PA. She died 13 Apr 1885, Bridgeport, WV, LNR Morgantown, Monongalia Co, VA, 1871

COOPER, JEREMIAH (P, BLW), died 19 Jul 1878, Huttonsville, Randolph Co, WV; md 10 Jan 1824 Mary S. Atwell, Charlestown, VA

COOPER, JOHN (BLW) whose widow was Hester

COOPER, JOHN JR. (BLW)

COOPER, JOHN (P, BLW), LNR P.O. Christiansburg, Mont-

COOPER (continued)
gomery Co, VA, 1871; md 2 Oct 1821 Polly Thompson, Montgomery Co, VA. Widower.

COOPER, JOHN (P, BLW), LNR Bellbrook, Greene Co, OH, 1871. Wife died 6 Sep 1864.

COOPER, JOHN SR. (BLW), died 6 Jan 1863, Carroll Co, VA; md (1) Elizabeth Lavanard, (2) 1 Aug 1858 Elizabeth (----) Wilson (P), Carroll Co, VA. She died 31 Jul 1896, LNR Hillsville, Carroll Co, VA, 1893

COOPER, LEONARD whose widow Elizabeth applied for a pension

COOPER, WILLIAM (P, BLW), LNR Eldorado, Saline Co, IL, 1872; md Elizabeth Quales, Wythe Co, VA. Wife died c1854.

COOPER, WILLIAM N. (P, BLW), LNR Vincennes, Knox Co, IN, 1871; md Oct 1818 Elenor Daley, Leesburg, VA

COOTES/COUTTS, SAMUEL (P, BLW), LNR P.O. Coots Store, Rockingham Co, VA, 1878; md ? 7 Jan 18--

COPELAND, ANDREW (BLW), died 2 Jan 1855, Loudoun Co, VA; md 17 May 1825 Jane Copeland (P). She died 25 Mar 1888, LNR P.O. Hillsborough, Loudoun Co, VA, 1887

COPELAND, HEZEKIAH B. (BLW)

COPENHAVER, HENRY (BLW), died 20 Jul 1869, Smyth Co, Va; md 8 Oct 1818 Barbara Philipy (P), Wythe Co, VA. Her LNR Smyth Co, VA, 1878

COPIN, CHAPMAN (P, BLW), died 8 May 1880, Prince William Co, VA; md 19 Dec 1820 Annie Copin (P), Prince William Co, VA. Her LNR P.O. Independent Hill, Prince William Co, VA, 1880

COPPEDGE, CHARLES D. and

COPPEDGE (continued)
widow Rebecca both applied
for a pension
COPPEDGE/COPPAGE, JOHN H.
(BLW), died 27 Feb 1860,
Rappahannock Co, VA; md 22
Nov 1838 Sarah Vaughn (P),
Culpeper Co, VA. She died 4
Aug 1887, Rappahannock Co,
VA, LNR Flint Hill, Rap-
pahannock Co, VA, 1878
CORATHERS, JOHN (P, BLW),
LNR P,O. Georgetown, Lewis
Co, WV, 1871
CORBAN, LEVI whose widow
Catherine Smoot applied for a
pension
CORBIN, BUFORD (BLW), died 1
Mar 1861, Madison Co, VA;
md 1 Aug 1814 Rebecca J.
Nicholson (P), Madison Co,
VA. She died before 12 Apr
1877, LNR P.O. Culpeper,
Culpeper Co, VA, 1872
CORBIN, DENNIS (P, BLW),
LNR P.O. Fairfax, Highland
Co, OH, 1871; md 19 or 22 Jun
1865 ---- (----) Lemons/
Timings, Highland Co, OH
CORBIN, JAMES (P, BLW), died
before 7 Mar 1886, LNR P.O.
Pleasanton, Decatur Co, IA.
1871; md 5 Sep 1823 Jane
Corbin, Culpeper Co, VA
CORBIN, JAMESON (P, BLW),
LNR P.O. Pittsylvania Court-
house, Pittsylvania Co, VA,
1871; md 9 Oct 1818 Sarah
Davis, Pittsylvania Co, VA
CORBIN, JOHN (P, BLW), died
24 Jul 1878, Ritchie Co, WV;
md 14 Jan 1819 Rebecca Wil-
liams (P), Monongalia Co, VA.
She died 10 or 21 Apr 1885,
LNR P.O. Ellenboro, Ritchie
Co, WV, 1878
CORBIN, WILLIAM (BLW), died
25 Mar 1856, Rappahannock
Co, VA; md 23 Dec 1817 Nan-
cy Scott (P), Corbins Cross-
roads, Rappahannock Co, VA.
She died 14 Feb 1879, Gains

CORBIN (continued)
Crossroads, Rappahannock Co,
VA
CORBITT/CORBETT, MATHEW
(P, BLW), LNR Cold Springs,
Campbell Co, KY, 1873; md 1
Aug 1830 Martha Guy, Camp-
bell Co, KY
CORDELL, SAMUEL (P, BLW),
died c1879,LNR Ashland, Ash-
land Co, OH, 1878; md 15 Sep
18-- Catharine Carnes, Lou-
doun Co, VA
CORDER, JESSE whose widow
Frances applied for a pension
CORDER, JOSEPH whose widow
Jane applied for a pension
CORDER, SIMEON (BLW), USA,
died Jul 1855, or Jun 1857,
Fauquier Co, VA; md Jan 1819
Susan Gorden (P), Shenandoah
Co, VA. Her LNR Front
Royal, Warren Co, VA, 1880
CORE, CHRISTIAN applied for a
pension
CORE, JOHN (BLW), PA militia,
died 7 Dec 1870, Clarksburg,
WV; md (1) ---- McClellan, ()
14 Jan 1841 Jane Johns (P),
Sutton, Braxton Co, VA. She
died c1898, LNR Clarksburg,
Harrison Co, WV, 1887
CORKER, DANIEL (BLW), died 4
Feb 1851,Hanover Co, VA; md
(1) Nancy Olns, (2) 27 Jan
1820 Nancy Martin (P), Han-
over Co, VA. She died 29 Jan
1879, Nolls, Hanover Co, VA
CORLEW, DANIEL applied for a
pension
CORLEY, JAMES (BLW) whose
widow was Elizabeth
CORLEY, JAMES (P, BLW),
CORLEY (continued)
LNR P.O. Peterstown, Monroe
Co, WV, 1871; md Polly As-
berry
CORLEY, THOMAS (P, BLW),
LNR P.O. Amissville, Rap-
pahannock Co, VA, 1871; md
16 Nov 1835 Christine Wince

CORMANY/KORMANY, GEORGE whose widow Elizabeth applied for a pension

ROLL NO. 22

CORNELISON, JOHN applied for a pension

CORNELL, DAVID BALDWIN (BLW), died 2 Apr 1865, Doddridge Co, WV; md Aug 1827 Elcy Spencer (P), PA. She died c1891, LNR New Salem, Harrison Co, WV, 1878

CORNUTT, JESSE (BLW), died 10 Sep 1860, Grayson Co, VA; md (1) ?, (2) 1 Jan 1850 Elizabeth S. (----) Roberts (P), Grayson Co, VA. She died before 17 Sep 1884. Jesse was a substitute in the War for John Cornutt.

CORNUTT/CORNETT, REUBEN (P, BLW), LNR P.O. Bridle Creek, Grayson Co, VA, 1871; md 19 Oct 1816 Celia Penington, Grayson Co, VA

CORNWELL, ISHAM (BLW), died 17 Mar 1862, Rappahannock Co, VA; md (1) Clarissa Postlaw, (2) Lucy A. Pullin, (3) 25 Jun 1857 Mary E. Guant (P), Rappahannock Co, VA. Her LNR P.O. Sherryville, Rappahannock Co, VA, 1878

CORNWELL, JOHN (BLW)

CORNWELL, THOMPSON/THOMAS applied for a pension

CORNWELL, WILLIAM (BLW), died 20 Nov 1860, Prince William Co, VA; md 20 Sep 1831 Nancy Posey (P), Weams, Prince William Co, VA. Her LNR P.O. Independent Hill, Prince William Co, VA, 1878

CORNWELL, WILLIAM G. (P, BLW), died 2 Apr 1877, Difficult, TN; md (1) Betsy Yeaman, (2) Letitia Dodd, (3) 1857 Judy Reese (P), Smith Co, TN. She died c1890, LNR P.O. Difficult, TN, 1879

CORRICK, FREDERICK (BLW), died 17 Sep 1867, Davis Co, IA; md 10 May 1813 Parmelia Chicoate (P), Randolph Co, VA. Her LNR Schuyler Co, MO, 1872

CORRON, JAMES (BLW), died 12 Oct 1863, Blue Ridge, VA; md (1) Elizabeth McDade, (2) 20 mar 1838 Ailcy Connor (P), Blue Ridge, Rappahannock Co, VA. She died 25 Jan 1889, LNR Waynesville, Warren Co, OH, 1878

CORRON/CARRON, JOSEPH (P, BLW), died 9 Dec 1871, LNR P.O. Nicholas Courthouse, Nicholas Co, WV, 1871; md 15 Mar 1808 Nancy Wall, Greenbrier Co, VA

COSNER, DAVID (BLW), died 30 Apr 1863, Hardy Co, VA; md 1 May 1817 Catharine Henline (P), Hardy Co, VA. She died 1 Apr 1885, P.O. Grant Courthouse, Grant Co, WV, 1878

COTHRON/CAWTHARN, THOMAS (P, BLW), died 16 Sep 1882, LNR Upper Sandusky, Wyandot Co, OH; md Aug 18-- Mary Hickle, Fluvanna Co, VA

COTTERILL, THOMAS (P-rejected, BLW), died 28 Feb 1872, Hardy Co, WV; md (1) Polly Mathas, (2) 25 Mar 1855 Lea (Bollinger) Wilson (P), Lost River, VA. She died 30 May 1892, LNR Lost River, VA, 1878

COTTRELL, DAVID C. whose widow Mary applied for a pension

COTTRILL/COTTRELL, SAMUEL (P, BLW), LNR P.O. Clarksburg, Harrison Co, WV, 1871

COTTRILL, WATSON (P, BLW), LNR Crown Point, Lake Co, IN, 1871; md Aug 1813 Sarah A. Gratehouse, Clarksburg, VA. She died c1853

COUCH, JOHN (BLW), died 1 Aug 1854, Monroe Co, MO; md 18 Apr 1844 Elizabeth Harrison (P), Monroe Co, MO. She died 14 Oct 1886, Shelby Co, MO, LNR P.O. Paris, Monroe Co, MO, 1879

COUCH, WILLIAM whose widow Rachel applied for a pension

COUNCIL, HARDY (BLW), whose wife was Elizabeth

COUNCIL, HENRY (BLW)

COUNCIL, JAMES (BLW), died 8 Aug 1871, Southampton, VA; md (1) Parthenia ----, (2) 15 Mar 1858 Sarah M. Slade (P), Weldon, Halifax Co, NC. Her LNR Vicksville, Southampton Co, VA, 1885. On 4 Jan 1883, Sarah married Mr. Turner.

COUNCIL, JOEL (BLW)

COUNCIL, JOHN (BLW), died 22 Jul 1863, Portsmouth, VA; md 16 Aug 1823 Sarah Moore (P), Southampton Co, VA. Her LNR P.O. Franklin Depot, Southampton Co, VA, 1878

COUNSELMAN, PHILIP (P, BLW), MD militia, LNR P.O. Ipava, Fulton Co, IL, 1871; md 1846 Mary Lindsey, Brooke Co, VA

COUNTS/CONTE, GEORGE (P, BLW), LNR P.O. Sweet Springs, Monroe Co, WV, 1872

COURTNEY, LEONARD (BLW), died Jul 1860, Warsaw, VA; md 4 Nov 1812 Mary Alderson (P), Alderson, VA. Her LNR P.O. Warsaw, Richmond Co, VA, 1872

COUTTS, PATRICK (BLW), died 9 Apr 1829, Richmond, VA; md 3 May 1827 Sophia Kelly (P), Richmond, VA. Her LNR Richmond, VA, 1878

COWAN, WILLIAM R. (BLW), died 28 Oct 1868, Sullivan Co, TN; md (1) Nancy R. Dulaney, (2) 20 Nov 1823 Nancy Susong (P), Washington Co, VA. Her LNR P.O. Briston, Sullivan

COWAN (continued) Co, TN, 1878

COWEN, JOHN (BLW), died 10 Apr 1869, Rockingham Co, VA; md (1) Mary Pickering, (2) 22 Sep 1858 Martha (----) Stephens (P), Rockingham Co, VA. She died 27 Mar 1895, LNR P.O. Melrose, Rockingham Co, VA, 1887

COX, BERRYMAN (BLW), died 4 Jan 1866/67, Stafford Co, VA; md Jan 1818 Delila Payne (P), Falmouth, Stafford Co, VA. Her LNR Stafford Co, VA, 1878

COX, BEVERLY (P, BLW), died 8 Apr 1872, Willville, VA, LNR Willville, Nottoway Co, VA, 1871; md (1) Martha Foulks, (2) Mary Armistead, (3) Jane Blanton, (4) Dec 1855 Mary A. Blanton (P). Later, widow married Mr. Thompson.

COX, CHARLES (BLW), died 23 Sep 1862, Albemarle Co, VA; md (1) Maria Mooney, (2) 5 Jan 1844 Mildred L. Blackley (P), Charlottesville, Albemarle Co, VA. She died Feb 1907, LNR P.O. Arbor Hill, Augusta Co, VA, 1878

COX, HENRY (BLW), lieutenant

COX, HENRY (BLW), private

COX, ISAAC (BLW), died 4 Dec 1864, Doddridge Co, VA; md 29 Jul 1821 Frances Festor (P), Monroe Co, VA. She died 14 Jul 1894, LNR P.O. Fairmount, Marion Co, WV, 1887

COX, JACOB (P, BLW), LNR Old Providence Church, Augusta Co, VA, 1871; md 13 Mar 1813 Eva Stoner, Rockbridge Co, VA

COX, JAMES (P, BLW), KY militia, LNR P.O. New London, Ralls Co, MO; md 22 Dec 1815 Sarah E. Moore, Fayette Co, VA

COX, JAMES (P, BLW), died 27 Apr 1881, LNR Union Star, Breckenridge Co, KY; md 30 Apr 1819 Mary C. Cox, Bethel,

COX (continued)
Breckenridge Co, KY
COX, JESSE (P, BLW), USA,
died 4 Jan 1884, LNR P.O.
Lebanon, Russell Co, VA,
1871; md 27 Jul 1815 Thursa
Harper, Wilkes Co, NC
COX, JOHN (BLW), died Jan
1854, Cobb Hills, NC; md (1)
Patsy Figgs, (2) Feb 1834
Temperance Williams (P),
Northampton Co, NC. She died
10 Sep 1883, LNR Garysburg,
NC, 1880
COX, JOHN F. (BLW), died 15
Aug 1862, Winchester, VA; md
9 Jan 1852 Sarah Ann (Bryant)
Cox (P), Stafford Co, VA. She
died 22 Nov 1892, LNR Fal-
mouth, Stafford Co, VA, 1880
COX, JOSEPH whose widow Han-
nah applied for a pension
COX, LARKIN (P, BLW), TN
militia, LNR P.O. Monroe,
Overton Co, TN, 1871; md
Nancy Ray, Henry Co, VA
COX, LEVI (P, BLW), MD mi-
litia, died before 1 Mar 1887,
LNR Central Station, Dod-
dridge Co, WV, 1878; md 2 Jul
1817 Ann Hart, Baltimore, MD
COX, NATHAN (BLW), died 15
Sep 1845, Allen Co, OH; md
(1) Mary Steel, (2) 15 Sep 1842
Elizabeth (----) Ratcliff (P),
Chilicothe, Ross Co, OH. She
died 28 Mar 1884, Bluffton,
Wells Co, IN
COX, THOMAS (BLW), died 13
Nov 1864, Putnam Co, VA; md
18 May 1813 Joana/Annie
Stone (P), Mecklenburg Co,
VA. Her LNR Lincoln Co,
WV, 1871
COYNER, JACOB (P, BLW), died
28 Aug 1874, South River,
Augusta Co, VA; md 21 Dec
1815 Elizabeth Coyner (P), nr
Fisherville, Augusta Co, VA.
Her LNR P.O. Waynesborough,
Augusta Co, VA, 1878
COYNER, ROBERT (P, BLW),

COYNER (continued)
died 27 Jul 1874, Ross Co, OH;
md 20 Aug 1857 Frances Wallace (P), Ross Co, OH. She
died c1881, LNR P.O. Lyndon,
Ross Co, OH, 1878
CRABTREE, JOHN whose widow
Elizabeth applied for a pension
CRABTREE, RICHARD (BLW),
whose widow Betsey Ann applied for a pension
CRADDOCK, NATHANIEL whose
widow Joanna applied for a
pension
CRAFT, WILLIAM (BLW), died
3 Jan 1842, Botetourt, Bote-
tourt co, Va; md (1) Mary Be-
cker, (2) 25 Apr 1831 Elizabeth
Oiler (P), Black Creek, Bote-
tourt Co, VA. She died before
9 Jan 1885, LNR Blue Spring
Run, Allegany Co, VA, 1879
CRAIG, HENRY (BLW), died 7
May 1853; md cNov 1818
Mildred Medor (P), Bedford
Co, VA. She died c1888, LNR
Bedford Co, VA, 1878
CRAIG, JAMES (P, BLW), died
23 Feb 1887, Fayette Co, WV;
md 18 Dec 1825 Sarah M.
Blake (P), Kanawha Co, VA.
She died 29 Jul 1892, LNR
Coal Valley, Fayette Co, WV,
1887
CRAIG, JOHN (BLW), died 27
Apr 1865, Buffalo, Putnam Co,
Wv; md (1) Dorcas Handley,
(2) 25 Sep 1853 Sarah W. (---)
Rust (P), Winfield, WV. She
died 21 Jun 1886, Winfield,
Putnam Co, WV
CRAIG, JOHN applied for a pen-
sion
CRAIG, JOHN (P, BLW), died 3
Dec 1873, LNR P.O. Wood-
stock, Shenandoah Co, VA,
1872; md 3 Mar 1817 Elizabeth
Pence, Shenandoah co, VA
CRAIG, ROBERT (P, BLW), died
24 Jan 1872, LNR P.O.
Craigsville, Shenandoah Co,
VA; md 10 Jun 1819 Margaret

CRAIG (continued)
McCutchen, Middlebrook, VA

CRAIG, ROBERT (BLW), died 30 Aug 1866, Switzerland Co, IN; md 10 Apr 1814 Mary McGoreghan (P), Frederick Co, VA. Her LNR P.O. Enterprise, Switzerland Co, IN, 1871

CRAIGG, JAMES H. (P, BLW), died 4 May 1884, Montgomery Co, VA; md (1) Mary McManaway, (2) 10 Jun 1869 Margaret M. Foster (P), Bedford Co, VA. She died 21 Mar 1819, LNR P.O. Christiansburg, Montgomery Co, VA, 1884

CRAIN/CRANE, ARMISTEAD (P, BLW), died 5 Nov 1873, LNR P.O. Greencastle, Warren Co, KY; md 24 Feb 1824 Nancy White, Sumner Co, TN

CRALLE, SAMUEL (BLW), died Sep 1857, Richmond Co, VA; md 13 Sep 1832 Frances M. Belfield (P), Richmond Co, VA. She died 7 Jun 1885, Farmers fork, Richmond Co, VA

CRAMER/KRAMER, GEORGE (BLW), died 9 Apr 1874, Near Mt. Liberty, Knox Co, OH; md 26 Dec 1812 Elizabeth Moore, (P), Berkeley Co, VA. Her LNR nr Mt. Liberty, Knox Co, OH, 1871

CRAMER, JOHN (BLW), died 4 May 1846, Shelby Co, OH; md 16 Nov 1828/9 Priscilla Smoot (P), Hampshire Co, VA. She died before 10 Aug 1883, LNR Emerson, Gratiot Co, MI, 1878

CRANDALL, EDWARD (BLW), died 22 Mar 1818, Norfolk, VA; md 4 Sep 1813 Clorinda Charter (P), Richmond, VA. She died 22 Jan 1886, Ellington, CT, LNR Ellington, CT, 1878

CRANDOL/CRANDALL, JOHN (BLW), died Oct 1841, Warwick Co, VA; md (1) Susan Jones, (2) Oct 1834 Elizabeth Wood (P), Warwick Co, VA.

CRANDOL (continued)
She died 3 Nov 1892, Richmond, VA

CRANE, JOSEPH (BLW), died 9 Aug 1868, Mason Co, WV; md (1) Mary Gibbs, (2) Feb 1841 Mary (Board) Hendley (P), Mason Co, VA. Her LNR Arbuckle, Mason Co, WV, 1879

CRANE, THOMAS (BLW), died 20 May 1844, King and Queen Co, VA; md (1) Caty Penns, (2) May 1827 Mary Ann Cleavely (P), King and Queen Co, VA. Her LNR King William Courthouse, King William Co, VA, 1878

CRANFORD/CRAWFORD, JONAS (P, BLW), LNR P.O. Accotink, Fairfax Co, VA, 1872; md 22 Jun 1826 Susan Athey, Washington, DC

CRANK, GEORGE R. (P, BLW), died 20 Dec 1888, LNR P.O. Overton, Albemarle Co, VA; md Jan 1827 E. W. Bramhorn, Burwells, VA

CRANSTON, SAMUEL (P, BLW), USA, LNR Parkersburg, Wood Co, WV, 1871; md 1835 Cassee Ann Harris, Culpeper Co,VA

CRASK, JOHN whose widow Shady applied for a pension

CRAVEN, MAHLON (BLW), died 14 Jan 1849, Knox Co, OH; md 11 Mar 1810 Hannah Iden (P), Frederickstown, Frederick Co, MD. She died c1879, LNR P.O. Cardington, Morrow Co, OH, 1878

CRAVENS, JOHN (P, BLW), LNR Salem, Washington Co, IN, 1871; md 6 Jan 1818 Ann C. Newman, Rockingham Co, VA

ROLL NO. 23

CRAWFORD, CHARLES whose widow Lucy applied for a pension

CRAWFORD, JAMES E. (BLW),

102

CRAWFORD (continued)
died 11 May 1855, Augusta Co, VA; md (1) Mary Strubling, (2) 12 Apr 1823 Margaret A. Bell (P), Augusta Co, VA. She died 23 Oct 1886, Augusta Co, VA, LNR P.O. Staunton, Augusta Co, VA, 1880

CRAWFORD, JOHN (BLW), died 23 Sep 1862, Clarke Co, IA; md 20 Apr 1818 Sarah Rowlinson (P), Rockbridge Co, VA. Her LNR Woodburn, Clark Co, IA, 1878

CRAWFORD, JOHN D. (BLW), died 30 Aug 1869, Fayette Co, WV; md 18 Jan 1820 Amarilla Noell (P), Amherst Co, VA. She died 26 Mar 1888, LNR Fayette Co, WV, 1878

CRAWFORD, SAMUEL (P, BLW), LNR P.O. Cave Springs, Roanoke Co, VA, 1871

CRAWFORD, SAMUEL S. (BLW), died 7 Apr 1865, New London, VA; md 19 Jul 1800 Charlotte Austin (P), Bedford Co, VA. Her LNR Bedford Co, VA, 1871

CRAWFORD, WILLIAM (BLW), died 9 Jul 1833/4, Golconda, Pope Co, IL; md 9 Nov 1815 Charlotte Laing (P), Green Co, PA. Her LNR Moundsville, Marshall Co, WV, 1878

CRAWFORD, ZACHARIAH (P, BLW), died 18 Oct 1882, Winchester, VA; md 14 Sep 1861 Mary Ann Goss

CRAWLEY, JOHN B. whose widow Catharine applied for a pension

CREASEY, PLEASANT (BLW), died 10 Dec 1863, Perryville, Perry Co, AR; md 1 Mar 1822 Eliza W. Hill (P), Amherst Co, VA. She died before 18 Jan 1888, LNR Clark Co, IL, 1878. Pleasant substituted for brother Jordan in the War.

CREASY, JOHN (BLW), died 28 Mar 1869, Henry Co, VA; md

CREASY (continued)
(1) Rebecca Shackelford, (2) 12 Dec 1859 Polly Watkins (P), Henry Co, VA. She died before 8 Feb 1890, LNR Horse Pasture, Henry Co, VA, 1878

CREEKMORE, DEMPSEY (BLW), died 27 Oct 1870, Norfolk Co, VA; md (1) Betsy ----, (2) Eliza Flannagan, (3) 20 Dec 1855 Katy (----) Etheridge (P), Currituck Co, NC. Her LNR P.O. Lake Drummond, Norfolk Co, VA, 1878

CREEKMORE, PETER who applied for a pension

CREEL, DAVID (P, BLW), died c1878, LNR Chillicothe, OH, 1871; md (1) 8 May 1814 Elizabeth Naole, Wood Co, VA, (2) ?

CREEL, WORMLY (P, BLW), LNR P.O. The Plains, Fauquier Co, VA, 1871. Never married.

CREESY/CREASEY, ROBERT (P, BLW), LNR P.O. Edmonton, Metcalf Co, KY, 1871; md 20 Dec 1821 Mary E. Beck, Pittsylvania Co, VA

CREGER, JOHN P./PETER (BLW), died 10 Oct 1862, Rich Valley, Smythe Co, VA; md 1 Jan 1813 Polly Hounshell (P), Wytheville, Wythe Co, VA. Her LNR Rich Valley, Smythe Co, VA, 1872

CREMER, HENRY who applied for a pension

CRENSHAW, DAVID (P, BLW), LNR P.O. Thaxton, Bedfoed Co, VA, 1871. Not married.

CRENSHAW, FREEBORN G. (BLW), died 17 Feb 1826, Richmond, VA; md 14 Jan 1811 Elizabeth Crenshaw (P),

CRENSHAW (continued)
Charlotte Co, NC. She died 27 Sep 1881, LNR Richmond, Henrico Co, VA, 1878

CRENSHAW, WILLIAM (P,

CRENSHAW (continued)
BLW), died 24 Jul 1881, Albemarle Co, VA; md 7 Sep 1815 Mary Walker Twyman (P), Albemarle Co, VA. She died after 9 Nov 1881, LNR Richmond, Earlysville, Albemarle Co, VA.

CRESS, GEORGE (BLW), died 1 Sep 1851/2, Whitley Co, KY; md 11 May 1803 Nancy Reed (P), NC. Her LNR P.O. Speedwell, Claiborne Co, TN, 1872

CREW, CLARK (P, BLW), died 26 Dec 1879, Louisa Co, VA; md 23 Dec 1816 Sarah Gilbert (P), Louisa Co, VA. Her LNR P.O. Bells Crossroads, Louisa Co, VA, 1880

CREWS, ISAAC (P, BLW), LNR P.O. Martins Store, Halifax Co, VA, 1878; md 1 Jun 1809 Susan L. Sutherlin

CRIDER, JACOB (P, BLW), died c1878, LNR Lewistown, Fulton Co, IL; md 4 Jun 1816 Magdalene Waggoner, Rockingham Co, VA

CRIGLER, REUBEN W. (BLW), died 29 Aug 1869, Oxford, Henry Co, IL; md 18 Dec 1823 Anna Faulkner (P), Gallia Co, OH. She died 20 Mar 1887, New Windsor, Mercer Co, IL. Reuben was a substitute for Christopher Crigler in the War.

CRIM, JACOB whose widow Susanna applied for a pension

CRINER, JOHN (P, BLW), LNR Newport, Giles Co, VA, 1872

CRISLER, JONAS (BLW), died 2 Sep 1858, Boone Co, KY; md 31 Jul 1810 Betsey Price (P), Madison Co, VA. Her LNR P.O. Burlington, Boone Co, KY, 1872

CRISMOND, JOHN B. (BLW), died 31 Jul 1861, Spotsylvania, VA; md (1) Susan Hale, (2) 22 Mar 1830 Jane McDonald (P), Edge Hill, King George Co,

CRISMOND (continued)
VA. She died 19 Oct 1888, LNR P.O. Spotsylvania Courthouse, Spotsylvania Co, VA, 1879

CRIST, GEORGE (P, BLW), died 24 Aug 1875, Sullivan Co, MO; md 1 Oct 1848 Harriett B. Potts (P), Sullivan Co, MO. She died 23 Feb 1905, LNR Corbin, Summers Co, KS, 1887

CRITES, JONAS (P, BLW), LNR P.O. Lost Creek, Harrison Co, WV, 1871

CRITES, LEONARD (BLW), died 13 Mar 1869, Buckhannon, WV; md (1) Mary Formash, (2) 13 Mar 1817 Elizabeth Lewis (P), Buckhannon, VA. She died 28 Jan 1879, Buckhannon, Upshur Co, WV

CRITES/CRITZ, PHILIP (P, BLW), died 27 May 1879, New Canton, TN; md 14 Oct 1847 Ann (Kinkaid) Thurman (P), Hawkins Co, TN. She died 30 Sep 1879, New Canton, Hawkins Co, TN

CROCKER, GEORGE (P, BLW), LNR P.O. Smithfield, Isle of Wight Co, VA, 1873

CROCKETT, WHITTINGTON/ WHEATON (P, BLW), LNR P. O. Yorktown, York Co, VA, 1871; md 5 Feb 1848 Mary Hogge, York Co, VA

CROFT, JACOB (BLW), died 10 Jan 1864, Augusta Co, VA; md (1) Sarah Miller, (2) Lydia Brower, (2) 24 Dec 1829 Catharine Sanger (P), Rockingham Co, VA. She died c1891, LNR P.O. Staunton, Augusta Co, VA, 1879

CROFT, JACOB (BLW), died Aug 1865, Rockingham Co, VA; md (1) Polly Shotwell, (2) Apr 1838 Anna Jessee (P), Page Co, VA, 1878

CROMWELL, HIRAM (P, BLW), died 2 Dec 1879, LNR Crooked Fork, Morgan Co, TN, 1878;

CROMWELL (continued)
md 2 Jan 1822 Hennerts Sol-
mon, Kingston, Roane Co, TN
CRON/CRAWN, JOSEPH (BLW),
died 20 May 1867; md 17 Mar
1835 Jemima Clemens (P),
Delaware Co, IN. She died 5
Dec 1883, LNR Modina, Mer-
cer Co, MO, 1880
CRONE, GEORGE (P, BLW),
LNR P.O. Owensville, Cler-
mont Co, OH, 1871; md 22 Apr
1817 Catharine Shewy, Staun-
ton, Augusta Co, VA
CRONE, JACOB (P, BLW), LNR
P.O. Centreville, Wayne Co,
IN, 1871; md 11 Jan 1816
Polly Sours, Montgomery Co,
VA
CROOK, JOSEPH (BLW), died 20
Jan 1843, Rockingham Co, NC;
md 4 Dec 1807 Elizabeth G.
Colier (P), Brunswick Co, VA.
Her LNR P.O. Lebanon, Wil-
son Co, TN, 1872
CROOK, SAMUEL (P, BLW),
LNR P.O. New Lisbon, Co-
lumbiana Co, MO, 1871; md 25
Dec 1817 Margaret Lyden,
Loudoun Co, VA. Widower.
CROOKS, ABRAHAM (BLW),
died 24 Dec 1859, Boyd Co,
KY; md 19 Jan 1840 Mary Ann
Miller (P), Greenup Co, KY.
She died 15 Sep 1896, LNR
Ashland, Boyd Co, KY, 1879
CROOKS, JOSEPH B. (BLW),
died 12 Nov 1863, Orange Co,
VA; md 5 Jan 1815 Catharine
M. Hennesy (P), Orange Co,
VA. She died 23 Nov 1881,
Orange Courthouse, WV, LNR
Madison Mills, Orange Co,
VA, 1871
CROPP, WARNER L. applied for
a pension
CROSS, ABRAM (BLW), died 12
Oct 1837, Nansemond Co, VA;
md (1) Sarah Saunders, (2) 3
May 1832 Eliza Pitman (P),
Southampton Co, VA. She died
c1897, LNR Carrsville, Isle of

CROSS (continued)
Wight Co, VA, 1878
CROSS, ETHELRED (BLW), died
11 Jul 1854, Gates Co, NC; md
20 Dec 1825 Charity (Barnes)
Cross (P), Gates Co, NC. Her
LNR Gates Co, NC, 1878
CROSS, LEWIS (BLW)
CROSS, THOMAS (BLW), died
Sep 1857; md 1 Mar 1810 Mary
Tinsley (P), Hanover Co, VA.
Her LNR Richmond, VA, 1871
CROSS, WILLIAM B. applied for
a pension
CROSSLIN, EDWIN (P, BLW),
died 7 Aug 1875, Dobyville,
AR; md (1) Susan Daughtry, (2)
19 Feb 1843 Elizabeth (----)
Hall (P), Linden, Marengo Co,
AL. Her LNR P.O. Dobyville,
Clark Co, AR
CROUCH, JOHN (P, BLW), died
17 Jan 1878, Bedford Co, VA;
md (1) Basheba Overstreet, (2)
17 Jan 1859 Mary Ann Crowder
(P), Bedford Co, VA. She died
12 Feb 1899, LNR P.O. Thax-
ton, Bedford Co, VA, 1878
CROUCH, ROLLY whose widow
Jane applied for a pension
CROUCH, THOMAS H. (BLW),
died 5 Oct 1855, Richmond,
VA; md 25 Nov 1819 Molly
Brooks Temple (P), Ampel
Hil, Chesterfield Co, VA. Her
LNR P.O. Richmond, Henrico
Co, VA, 1878
CROUT, PETER C. (P, BLW),
died c1878, LNR Ross Co, OH,
1872; md 20 Aug 1818 Mar-
garet King, Preble Co, OH
CROW, GEORGE whose widow
Sarah applied for a pension
CROW, JACOB (P, BLW), LNR
P.O. West Alexander, Wash-
ington Co, VA, 1871
CROW, JOHN S. (P, BLW), LNR
P.O. Nebo, Hopkins Co, KY,
1871; md 22 May 1814 Nancy
Hutchinson, Mecklenburg Co,
VA
CROW, NATHANIEL S. (P,

CROW (continued)
BLW), LNR P.O. Boonville,
Prentiss Co, MS, 1873; md 5
Dec 1815 Nancy Buford John-
son, Lunenburg Co, VA

CROW, SAMUEL (BLW), PA mi-
litia, died 10 Oct 1842, Sunfish
Creek, VA; md 7 Jan 1815
Mary Deems (P), Pike Run
Township, Washington Co,
PA. Her LNR Pike Run,
Washington Co, PA, 1882

CROWDER, ARCHIBALD/AR-
CHER (P, BLW), LNR P.O.
Petersburg, Dinwiddie Co, VA,
1874

CROWDER, BARTLETT (P,
BLW), LNR Boydton, Meck-
lenburg Co, VA, 1871

CROWDER, ROBERT applied for
a pension

CROWDIS, MILES C. (BLW),
died 25 Dec 1861, New Kent
Co, VA; md 24 Dec 1822 Sarah
M. Taylor (P), James City Co,
VA. Her LNR Richmond, Hen-
rico Co, VA, 1879

CROWER/CROWDER, THEO-
THOLIS/THEOPHOLIS who
applied for a pension

CROWL, JOHN (P, BLW), died 4
Jan 1884, Mt. Vernon, Knox
Co, OH; md 4 Feb 1817 Sarah
Priest, Washington Co, MD

CROWL, JOSEPH (BLW), died 8
Sep 1865, Sangamon Co, IL;
md 1 Jan 1818 Mary A. Dillahunt (P), Washington Co,
MD. She died c1891, LNR
Rochester, Sangamon Co, IL,
1887

CROWLEY, JOHN (P, BLW),
died 13 Nov 1877, Coshocton
Co, OH; md (1) Mary Burns,
(2) 29 Mar 1838 Sarah
Humphrey (P), Walhonding,
Coshocton Co, OH. She died
c1881, LNR P.O. Canal
Lewisville, Coshocton Co, OH,
1878

CROXTON, RICHARD (BLW),
died 15 Oct 1848, Essex Co,

CROXTON (continued)
VA; md (1) Mary Clements, (2)
15 Mar 1826 Frances G. Ware
(P), Tappahannock, VA. She
died 28 Mar 1883, LNR Tappahannock, Essex Co, VA,
1879

CRUISE, JOHN (BLW), died 18
Mar 1866, Patrick Co, VA; md
(1) Mazy Martin, (2) 27 Jun
1861 Hannah Cockram (P),
Patrick Co, VA. She died
c1892, LNR P.O. Snake Creek,
Carroll Co, VA, 1878

CRUM, JOHN (BLW), died 7 Jul
1860, Franklin Co, VA; md 18
Jan 1816 Naoma Smith (P),
Franklin Co, VA. She died
Feb 1885 LNR Union Hall,
Franklin Co, VA, 1878

CRUMBAKER, JOHN (BLW),
died 23 Mar 1840, Muskingum
Co, OH; md 31 Jan 1813 Catharine Koehler (P), Loudoun Co,
VA. Her LNR P.O. Adams-
ville, Muskingum Co, OH,
1871

CRUMP, GEORGE (BLW), MD
militia, died 16 Feb 1847,
Fairfax Co, VA; md 11 Jul
1816 Jane Powell (P), Fairfax
Co, VA. She died c1885, LNR
Washington, DC, 1878

CRUMP, JESSE H./JAMES H./
HAMMON (P, BLW), LNR
P.O. Brownsville, Edmonson
Co, KY, 1871; md 14 Jan 1823
Cintha Ann Rountree

CRUMP, JOHN G. (P, BLW),
LNR Elm Wood, Boone Co,
AR, 1872; md 30 Apr 1827
Eliza G. Watkins, Jefferson
Co, TN

CRUMP, JOHN P. (BLW), died
28 Sep 1855, Dinwiddie,VA;
md 11 Dec 1832 Susan Wynn
(P), Dinwiddie, Dinwiddie Co,
VA. She died 17 Jan 1890,
LNR Baltimore, MD, 1878

CRUMP, JOSHUA P. (BLW),
died 9 Sep 1844, Charlotte Co,
VA; md (1) Martha Matthews,

CRUMP (continued)
(2) 24 Apr 1822 Margaret Clark (P), Charlotte Co, VA. She died 25 May 1893, LNR Smithville, VA, 1888

CRUMPACKER, JOHN (BLW), died 2 Mar 1854, VA; md (1) Elizabeth Hewitt, (2) Elizabeth Royalty, (3) 18 Oct 1840 Sarah (Smith) Wolf (P), Davis Co, MO. She died Nov 1880, Unionville, Putnam Co, MO

CRUTCHFIELD, BENJAMIN H. (BLW), died 17 Jun 1854, Louisa Co, VA; md 22 Dec 1831 Susan R. Amos (P), Goochland Co, VA. She died 23 May 1895, Goochland Courthouse, Goochland Co, VA

CUBBAGE, JACOB (BLW), died c1864, Page Co, VA; md Sep 1814 Nancy Nichols (P), Shenandoah Co, VA. She died 2 Feb 1888, LNR P.O. Alma, Page Co, VA, 1871

CULLERS, HENRY (BLW), died 22 Feb 1865, Shenandoah Co, VA; md 6 Jul 1817 Sarah Keyser (P), Shenandoah Co, VA. Her LNR Powells Fort, Shenandoah Co, VA, 1878

CULLY, GEORGE whose widow Elizabeth applied for a pension

CULP, JOHN FREDERICK (BLW)

CULTON, ALEXANDER (BLW), died 20 Apr 1840, Rockbridge Co, VA; md 13 Aug 1818 Ann R. Johnston (P), Rockbridge Co, VA. She died c1881, LNR Burnet, Burnet Co, TX, 1878

CUMBY/CUMBO, WILLIAM (BLW), died 9 Jul 1857, Scott Co, IL; md 20 Jan 1848 Ann Bell (P), Winchester, IL. She died 21 Mar 1901, LNR Glasgow, Scott Co, IL, 1887

CUMMINGS, JOHN (P, BLW), LNR P.O. Tazewell Courthouse, Tazewell Co, VA, 1878

CUMMINGS/CUMMINS, WILLIAM L. (BLW), died 4 Sep

CUMMINGS (continued)
1843, Jefferson Co, IA; md 9 Apr 1818 Sarah/Sally Cunningham (P), Rockbridge Co, VA. She died 5 Sep 1884, Fairfield, Jefferson Co, IA

CUMMINS, JOHN C. (P, BLW), LNR P.O. Staffords Store, Fauquier Co, VA, 1871; md Nov 1836 Lucy Phillips, Warrenton, Fauquier Co, VA

CUMPTON/COMPTON, JOHN (P, BLW), LNR P.O. Murfreesboro, Rutherford Co, TN, 1871

ROLL NO. 24

CUNDIFF, CHRISTOPHER (P, BLW), LNR P.O. Goodview, Bedford Co, VA, 1871

CUNDIFF, ISAAC (BLW), died 5 May 1861, Lancaster Co, VA; md (1) Mary R. Basye, (2) 7 Dec 1828 Pamala Carter (P), Lancaster Co, VA. She died 23 Apr 1887, Lancaster Co, VA, LNR P.O. Whitestone, Lancaster Co, VA, 1878

CUNNINGHAM, DAVID (BLW), died 22 Mar 1865, Marion Co, WV; md (1) Sarah Randall, (2) Jennie Haines, (3) 11 Feb 1861 Rebecca (Bolinger) Kelly (P). She died c1897, LNR P.O. Farmington, Marion Co, WV, 1883

CUNNINGHAM, EDWARD (P, BLW), died 10 Mar 1876, Sardis, WV; md 20 Nov 1816 Mary Hall (P), Harrison Co, VA. She died 1 Dec 1885, Sardis, WV, LNR Flag Run, Harrison Co, WV, 1878

CUNNINGHAM, ELIJAH (BLW), died 22 Oct 1868, Ritchie Co, WV; md 27 Jul 1815 Sarah Wagner (P), Harrison Co, VA. Her LNR P.O. Ellenboro, Ritchie Co, WV, 1878

CUNNINGHAM, GEORGE (P, BLW), died 29 Jan 1875,

CUNNINGHAM (continued)
Marion Co, WV; md (1) Sarah May, (2) 17 Apr 1849 Rachel Morgan (P), Marion Co, VA. She died c1900, LNR P.O. Fairmont, Marion Co, WV, 1878

CUNNINGHAM, JESSE (BLW), died 19 Nov 1823, Moorefield, VA; md (1) Betsey Hutton, (2) 17 Aug 1818 Martha Snodgrass (P), Moorefield, VA. She died 28 Sep 1888, LNR Moorefield, Hardy Co, WV, 1887

CUNNINGHAM, JESSE (P, BLW), died 18 Nov 1871, Lewis Co, WV; md 14 Apr 1816 Mary Jordan (P), Randolph Co, VA. She died 3 Jan 1883, Jacksonville, WV.

CUNNINGHAM, JOHN (P, BLW), died 29 Mar 1872, Montgomery Co, IN; md 17 Oct 1815 Mary Hall (P), Woodstock, Shenandoah Co, VA. She died 5 May 1885, LNR Crawfordsville, Montgomery Co, IN, 1878

CUNNINGHAM, JOHN whose widow Mary applied for a pension

CUNNINGHAM, RANDOLPH (P, BLW), LNR Franklin Co, VA, 1871; md Dec 1816 Martha G. Jones, Franklin Co, VA

CUNNINGHAM, REES (P, BLW), died 8 Aug 1871, Amherst Co, VA, LNR P.O. Amherst Courthouse, Amherst Co, VA, 1871. His Wife died c1861

CUNNINGHAM, ROBERT (P, BLW), died 17 Feb 1838, Nelson Co, VA; md 29 Aug 1816 Elizabeth Via (P), Nelson Co, VA. Her LNR Buckingham Co, VA, 1878

CUNNINGHAM, ROBERT (P, BLW), LNR P.O. Union Hall, Franklin Co, VA, 1873

CUNNINGHAM, ROBERT (BLW), died 13 Dec 1869, Harrison Co, WV; md 27 Jul 1815 Sarah Roby (P), Harrison Co, VA. She died 2 Jul 1885, LNR

CUNNINGHAM (continued)
P.O. Hessville, Harrison Co, WV, 1878

CUNNINGHAM, SILAS (P, BLW), LNR Sweet Home, Nodaway Co, MO, 1871; md 8 Mar 1821 Sarah Runion, Warren Co, OH

CUNNINGHAM, WILLIAM (P, BLW), LNR Little River, Floyd Co, VA, 1871; md 1816 Hannah Wilson, Bedford Co, VA

CUNNINGHAM, WILLIAM whose widow Rachel applied for a pension

CUNNINGHAM, WILLIAM (P, BLW), LNR McKenny's Mill, Rockbridge Co, VA, 1871. Not married.

CUNNINGHAM, WILLIAM (BLW), died 13 Sep 1840, Preble Co, OH; md 6 Dec 1810 Elizabeth Zolman (P), Botetourt Co, VA. Her LNR Preble Co, OH, 1873

CUPP, FREDERICK (BLW), died 24 Jan 1867, Rockingham Co, Va; md (1) Elizabeth Baker, (2), 26 May 1851 Elizabeth (Shaver) Carson (P), Rockingham Co, VA, widow of Isaac Carson. Her LNR P.O. Mt. Solon, Augusta Co, VA, 1879

CURD, JOHN whose widow Martha applied for a pension

CURD, RICHARD, alias Jones, Dick whose widow Susan applied for a pension

CURFMAN, CHRISTOPHER (P, BLW), MD militia, died 7 Apr 1882, Mt. Hoge, WV; md 9 Aug 1822 Rebecca Carman (P), Steubenville, Jefferson Co, OH. She died before 11 Jun 1883, LNR Mt. Hoge, Wirt Co, WV, 1882

CURRY, ANDREW (BLW), died 24 Sep 1865, Washington Co, PA; md 9 Jul 1814 Mary Williams (P), Hampshire Co, VA. She died 8 Feb 1886, Green

CURRY (continued)
Co, PA, LNR P.O. Strabane, Washington Co, PA, 1871

CURRY, JAMES (BLW), died 9 Sep 1855, Upshur Co, VA; md 11 Oct 1821 Sally Curry (P), Augusta Co, VA. She died 21 Sep 1892, LNR P.O. Rock Cave, Upshur Co, WV, 1881

CURRY, MABURY/MARBURY/MAYBERRY (P, BLW), died 30 Dec 1872, LNR P.O. Mill Gap, Highland Co, VA, 1871. Wife died c1869

CURRY, SAMUEL (BLW), whose widow was Mary

CURRY, THOMAS (BLW), whose widow was Margaret

CURTIS, CLAIBORNE (BLW), died 16 Nov 1868, Raleigh Co, WV; md (1) Nancy Smith, (2) Nov 1833 Martha L. Kirk (P), Mecklenburg Co, VA. She died 7 Mar 1898, LNR Prosperity, Raliegh Co, WV, 1881

CURTIS, JAMES who applied for a pension

CURTIS, JOHN (P-rejected, BLW), died 7 Mar 1874, Estill Co, KY; md 27 Mar 1836 Sydney Linsford (P), Estill Co, KY. She died before 3 Apr 1889, LNR P.O. Red River Ironworks, Estill Co, KY, 1878

CURTIS, MILES (BLW), died 26 May 1851, Warwick Co, VA; md 25 Dec 1816 Sarah K. Harwood (P), Warwick Co, VA. Her LNR P.O. Warwick Courthouse, Warwick Co, VA, 1878

CURTIS, ROBERT J. (P, BLW), PA militia, LNR Moundsville, Marshall Co, WV, 1871; md 24 Sep 1822 Anna A. Fox

CUSTER/CUSTARD/CUSTERD, JOSEPH (BLW), USA, died 3 Jun 1839, Henry Co, VA; md c1809 Martha Claig (P), Botetourt Co, VA. She died before 18 Feb 1885, LNR P.O. Big Lick, Roanoke Co, VA, 1871

CUSTER, RICHARD (BLW), died 14 Jun 1857, Brock's Gap, Rockingham Co, VA; md 28 Mar 1811 Elizabeth Trumbo (P), Brock's Gap, Rockingham Co, VA. She died 3 Dec 1873 LNR P.O. Cherry Grove, Rockingham Co, VA, 1872

CUTHRELL, MAXIMILIAN (P, BLW), died 1883, Marshalltown, Marshall Co, IA; md 1816/7 Margaret Cuthrell, Norfolk, VA

CUTLIP, ISAAC (P, BLW), died 1876, LNR P.O. Waverly, Pike Co, OH, 1871; md Apr 1809 Anna Wangburn, Greenbrier Co, VA

CUTRIGHT, JACOB (P, BLW), died 12 Oct 1874, Buckhannon, WV; md 7 Feb 1813 Elizabeth Westfall (P), Hanover Co, VA. Her LNR Buckhannon River, Upshur Co, WV, 1875

CUTRIGHT, PETER (BLW), died 3 May 1870, Upshur Co, WV; md 9 Dec 1816 Nancy Westfall (P), Harrison Co, VA. Her LNR P.O. Buckhannon, Upshur Co, WV, 1878

CYRUS/SYRES, WILLIAM (BLW), died 25 Mar 1867, Whites Creek, Wv; md (1) Rebecca Cyrus, (2) 13 Dec 1851 Leah Toney (P), Whites Creek, Wayne Co, VA. She died 14 Jul 1913, Whites Creek, WV

DABBS, LEMUEL (P, BLW), LNR Yanceyville, Caswell Co, NC, 1871; md 24 Apr 1821 Susan Coleman, Halifax Co, VA

DABNEY, HENRY (BLW), died 25 Mar 1870, Madison Co, IA; md (1) ?, (2) 21 Oct 1830 Maria Stanfield (P), Vermilion Co, IL. She died c1889, LNR Winterset, Madison Co, IA, 1878

DABNEY, JOSEPH F. whose widow Rachel B. applied for a

DABNEY (continued)
pension
DABNEY, MORDECAI B. (BLW),
died 6 Jun 1857, King William
Co, VA; md (1) Martha P.
Holmes, (2) 30 Sep 1852 Nancy
Phillips (P), King William Co,
VA. She died 29 Aug 1902,
LNR Richmond, VA, 1878
DABNEY, THOMAS S. applied for
a pension
DAGG, JOHN L. (P, BLW) died
11 Jun 1884, Haynesville,
Lowndes Co, AL
DAGG, SAMUEL D. (BLW), died
4 Oct 1821, Middleburg, Lou-
doun Co, VA; md 10 Apr 1817
Elizabeth Dutro (P), Loudoun
Co, VA. Her LNR P.O. Cross
Keys, Rockingham Co, VA,
1878
DAGGETT, DANIEL B. whose
widow Mary A. applied for a
pension
DAGGY, JOHN (P, BLW), died 2
Mar 1883, Rossville, Clinton
Co, IN, LNR P.O. Middlefork,
Clinton Co, IN, 1871; md
1817/8 Sarah McLaughlin,
Augusta Co, VA
DAILEY, JOHN (P, BLW), died
22 Jan 1881, LNR Johnson-
ville, Wayne Co, IL, 1878; md
5 Mar 1829 Talaifa Honnold,
Muskingum Co, OH
DAILEY, WILLIAM (P, BLW),
LNR P.O. Adamsville, Mus-
kingum Co, OH, 1871; md 1816
Eleanor Carr, Leesville, VA
DAILY/DALEY, JOHN (BLW),
died 8 Dec 1848, Londonberry,
Ross Co, OH; md 26 Sep 18--
or 8 Nov 1820 Rebecca Jane
Booth (P), Darksville,
Frederick Co, VA. She died 23
Feb 1885 Frankfort, Ross Co,
OH, LNR Chillicothe, Ross
Co, OH, 1884
DALLAS, TERRY whose widow
Mary A. applied for a pension
DALRYMPLE, JOHN (P, BLW),
MD militia, LNR P.O. Chil-

DALRYMPLE (continued)
licothe, OH, 1871; md Aug 1813
Elizabeth Miller, Shep-
herdstown, VA. Widower.
DAME, JOHN (BLW), TN mi-
litia, died 6 Feb 1866, Marion
Co, TN; md 17 Mar 18-- Eliz-
abeth Oyler (P), Franklin Co,
VA. Her LNR P.O. Jasper,
Marion Co, TN, 1871
DAMRELL, AUGUSTIN whose
widow Elizabeth applied for a
pension
DANCE, MATTHEW (BLW), died
30 Sep 1867, Cliaborne Parish,
LA; md (1) Mary Ann Adams,
(2) 10 May 1841 Rebecca Sim-
mons (P), Troup Co, GA. Her
LNR P.O. Athens, Claiborne
Parish, LA, 1889
DANDRIDGE, ROBERT A. whose
widow Ann O. applied for a
pension
DANFIELD/DANFELSER, WIL-
LIAM (P, BLW), PA militia,
died 1 Dec 1875, md 2 Mar
1815 Barbara Zumbro (P),
Pughtown, Hancock Co, VA.
Her LNR Reading, Berks Co,
PA, 1871
DANIEL, ABRAHAM S. (P,
BLW), LNR P.O. Marysville,
Campbell Co, VA, 1878; md 22
Dec 1822 Susan O. North,
Charlotte Co, VA
DANIEL, ALEXANDER (BLW),
died 5 Mar 1845, Jackson Co,
OH; md 28 Mar 1805 Nancy
Carwiles (P), Campbell Co,
VA. Her LNR P.O. Gallatin,
Daviess Co, MO, 1872'
DANIEL, ALSOP Y. (BLW), died
13 Jan 1841, Princeton, KY;
md 22 Oct 1826 Mary M. Har-
ris (P), Caldwell Co, KY. She
died 11 Oct 1883, LNR Prin-
ceton, Caldwell Co, KY, 1878
DANIEL, CARTER (BLW), died 5
Feb 1871, Montgomery Co,
KY; md 1809/10 Elizabeth
Kidd (P), Middlesex Co, VA.
She died 29 Apr 1880, Mont-

DANIEL (continued)
gomery Co, KY

DANIEL, CHESLEY (P, BLW), LNR Fork Willis, Cumberland Co, VA, 1871

DANIEL, JAMES (P, BLW), died 28 Jul 1875, Hillsboro, TN; md (1) Catherine Glass, (2) 31 Aug 1851 Eliza Smith (P), Huntsville, Madison Co, AL. She died 14 Aug 1806, Rocky Ford, Otero Co, CA. Her LNR Bairds Mills, Wilson Co, TN, 1883

DANIEL, JAMES G. (BLW), died 3 May 1861, Randolph Co, MO; md 27 Aug 1818 Elizabeth Reynolds (P), Lincoln Co, KY. She died 16 Jul 1885, Jacksonville, Randolph Co, MO

DANIEL, JOHN (BLW), died 12 Oct 1862, Rockbridge Co, VA; md (1) Nancy Newcomb, (2) 11 Feb 1841 Cassandra F. S. Haggett (P), South Buffalo, Rockbridge Co, VA. Her LNR P.O. Rapps Mill, Rockbridge Co, VA, 1878

DANIEL, JOSIAH (BLW), died 15 Mar 1852, Mason Co, VA; md 21 Feb 1833 Elizabeth White (P), Campbell Co, VA. She died 28 Nov 1886, Swann, Cabell Co, WV, LNR Union Ridge, Cabell Co, WV, 1879

DANIEL, LINDSAY (P, BLW), died 12 Oct 1874, Madison Co, VA; md 4 Apr 1822 Sarah C. Graves (P), Madison Co, VA. Her LNR P.O. Criglersville, Madison Co, VA, 1879

DANIEL, RICHARD (P, BLW), LNR P.O. Mt. Zion, Campbell Co, VA, 1871

DANNER, ISAAC (P, BLW), died c1879, LNR P.O. Bethlehem, Clark Co, IN, 1871; md 1863 Sovina Ryman, Switzerland Co, IN

DANSON, WILLIAM (BLW), died 15 Nov 1841, Lancaster Courthouse, VA; md (1) ?, (2) ?, (3)

DANSON (continued)
13 Oct 1831 Frances A. Tarkelson (P), Lancaster Co, VA. She died 10 Dec 1883, LNR Fredericksburg, Spotsylvania Co, VA, 1878

DARDEN, ELISHA (P, BLW), died 8 Jun 1878, Southampton Co, VA; md (1) Dicey Lawrence, (2) 31 Jan 1839 Priscilla (----) Lawrence (P), Southampton Co, VA. Her LNR Newsom's Depot, Southampton Co, VA, 1878

DARDEN, JEPTHAH (BLW), died 28 Jun 1856, Southampton Co, VA; md (1) ?, (2) 10 Sep 1851 Elizabeth Whitehead (P), Jerusalem, Southampton Co, VA. She died 14 Jan 1881, LNR P.O. Murfreesboro, Hertford Co, NC, 1879

DARNAL/DARNEL, LEVI (BLW), whose minor child was Louisa

DARNALL, JEREMIAH (BLW), died 9 May 1866, Morgan Co, OH; md Feb 1807 Narcissa Coppage (P), Culpeper Co, VA. Her LNR P.O. Hanover, Licking Co, OH, 1871

DARNEL, RICE (BLW)

DARNELL, JAMES F. (P, BLW), died before 6 Mar 1884, LNR Peaksville, Bedford Co, VA, 1875; md 15 Jan 1815 Elizabeth Wright, Albemarle Co, VA

DARR, PHILIP who applied for a pension

DASHIELL, THOMAS B. (BLW), died 30 Aug 1859, Westmoreland Co, VA; md 29 Mar 1825 Mary Ann Weston McCobb (P), Alexandria, VA. She died 12 Jan 1885, LNR Richmond, VA, 1878

DAUGHERTY, JOSHUA (BLW), died 8 May 1837 Rockingham Co, VA; md 25 Dec 1821 Hannah Turkeyhizer (P), North River, Rockingham Co, VA.

DAUGHERTY (continued)
She died 23 Apr 1888, LNR Calhoun, Barbour Co, WV, 1887

ROLL NO. 25

DAVENPORT, CHRISTOPHER (P, BLW), died 9 Jan 1888, Campbell Co, VA; md (1) Nancy Davenport, (2) 2 Dec 1855 Lydia M. (----) Doss (P), Campbell Co, VA. She died 10 Apr 1915, Lynchburg, VA, LNR P.O. Bedford Springs, Campbell Co, VA, 1888

DAVENPORT, EDMOND (BLW)

DAVENPORT, JOHN (P, BLW), died 17 Feb 1882, Spotsylvania Co, VA; md (1) Ellen Branchet Luck, (2) 19 Dec 1843 Harriet A. Hart (P), Spotsylvania Co, VA. She died c1900, LNR P.O. Post Oak, Spotsylvania Co, VA, 1882

DAVENPORT, MARTIN W. (BLW), died 19 Jan 1872, Lynchburg, VA; md 26 Jun 1838 Ann Eliza Thompson (P), Princeton, Mercer Co, NJ. She died c1883, Lynchburg, Campbell Co, VA

DAVENPORT, PUMPHREY (BLW), died 27 Jan 1870, Walnut Hill, King William Co, VA; md 20 Jan 1814 Elizabeth King (P), King William Co, VA. Her LNR P.O. Enfield, King William Co, VA, 1872

DAVIDSON, ALLEN (BLW), died 1 or 2 Oct 1839, Charlotte Co, VA; md 24 Dec 1818 Lucy A. Walker (P), Charlotte Co, VA. Her LNR P.O. Appomattox Courthouse, Appomattox Co, VA, 1878

DAVIDSON, DAVID (BLW), died 16 Feb 1859, Campbell Co, VA; md 2 Apr 1840 Caroline Lane (P), Campbell Co, VA, 1878. David was a substitute

DAVIDSON (continued)
for John Davidson in the War.

DAVIDSON, EDWARD (P, BLW), died 12 Nov 1873, LNR Santa Fe, Maury Co, TN, 1871

DAVIDSON, HENRY (P, BLW), LNR P.O. Spout Springs, Appomattox Co, VA, 1871; md 14 Sep 1851 Jane Wooten

DAVIDSON, JOHN whose widow Elizabeth applied for a pension

DAVIDSON, JOHN (BLW), died 18 Nov 1848, Washington Co, VA; md 25 Dec 1817 Tabitha Witten (P), Tazewell Co, VA. Her LNR, P.O. Abingdon, Washington Co, VA, 1878

DAVIDSON, WILLIAM (P, BLW), LNR Lexington, Rockbridge Co, VA, 1871. Widower.

DAVIES/DAVIS, HENRY L. (P, BLW), died 14 Sep 1875, Amherst Co, VA; md (1) Nancy Franklin, (2) 30 Nov 1847 Rebecca E. P. Thompson (P), Amherst Co, VA. She died Mar 1889, LNR Amherst, Amherst Co, VA, 1878

DAVIES, MAYO (P, BLW), LNR Bedford Co, VA, 1871; md 29 Feb 1816 Lucinda Talliaferro, Buffalo Springs, Amherst Co, VA

DAVIS, ABRAHAM W. (BLW)

DAVIS, ANANIAS (BLW), died 2 Mar 1836, Monongalia Co, VA; md 20 Feb 1823 Hanna Shafer (P), Monongalia Co, VA. She died c1881, LNR P.O. Maidsville, Monongalia Co, WV, 1878

DAVIS, ASA (BLW), died 26 Dec 1851, Wood Co, VA; md 15 Jul 1813 Content Davis (P), Hallsrun, Harrison Co, VA. She died 10 Jan 1887 Cherry Camp, Harrison Co, WV LNR P.O. New Salem, Harrison Co, WV, 1871

DAVIS, BARTLETT (BLW)

DAVIS, BENJAMIN (P, BLW), died 4 Jul 1866, Wheeling,

DAVIS (continued)
WV; md (1) ?, (2) 9 Aug 1858
Sarah Gladden (P), Greene Co,
PA. She died 22 Oct 1889,
LNR Waynesburg, Greene Co,
PA, 1887

DAVIS, CHAPMAN (BLW)

DAVIS, ELI (P, BLW), died 20
Feb 1881, LNR Pontiac,
Livingston Co, IL, 1871; md
c31 Dec 1814 ?, Frederick Co,
VA

DAVIS, ELIJAH who applied for a
pension

DAVIS, GEORGE (P, BLW), DC
militia, died 10 Mar 1879,
Washington, DC; md (1) Betsey Hill, (2) 1 Apr 1819 Sarah
E. Hickey (P), Alexandria, VA.
She died c1882, LNR Wash-
ington, DC, 1879

DAVIS, GEORGE A. (BLW), died
10 Nov 1867, Johnstown, WV;
md (1) Ville Middleton, (2) 1
Nov 1851 Sarah Talbott (P),
Raccoon Run, Barbour Co, VA.
Her LNR Johnstown, Harrison
Co, WV, 1878

DAVIS, HEZEKIAH A. whose
widow Frances T. applied for a
pension

DAVIS, HUCH C. applied for a
pension

DAVIS, ISAAC (BLW), USA, died
11 Oct 1854, Harrison Co, VA;
md 24 Sep 1835 Frances West.
Her LNR P.O. Janelew, Lewis
Co, WV, 1879

DAVIS, JAMES (P, BLW), LNR
P.O. Salem Center, Meigs Co,
OH, 1871; md 7 Apr 1856 Mary
Hampton, Meigs Co, OH. She
died c1876. Widower.

DAVIS, JAMES (BLW), died 18
Mar 1823, Norfolk Co, VA; md
16 Apr 1808 Sarah Wilkins (P),
Camden Co, NC. She died 15
Jan 1884, LNR Portsmouth,
Norfolk Co, VA, 1878

DAVIS, JAMES applied for a pension

DAVIS, JAMES whose widow Lida

DAVIS (continued)
applied for a pension

DAVIS, JESSE (BLW), died 3 Jul
1838, Occoquan, Prince William Co, VA; md 30 Aug 1810
Nancy Davis (P), Bardstown,
Nelson Co, KY. She died 7 Mar
1880, LNR Canton, Lewis Co,
MO, 1880

DAVIS, JOHN (BLW), died 19
May 1865, Hampshire Co, WV;
md 1813 Polly Brewer (P),
Hampshire Co, VA. Her LNR
Romney, Hampshire Co, WV,
1871

DAVIS, JOHN (P, BLW), died 24
Sep 1873, Weston, WV; md 28
Apr 1872 Bridget McAnan (P),
Lewis Co, WV. She died 25
May 1915, LNR Mt. Savage,
MD, 1915

DAVIS, JOHN (P, BLW), died 28
Mar 1876, Sand Run, WV; md
(1) Rachel Ward, (2) 28 Dec
1869 Susan Miller (P), Upshur
Co, WV. She died c1900, LNR
Sand Run, Upshur Co, WV,
1878

DAVIS, JOHN B. (BLW), died Jul
1851, Williamsburg, VA; md
21 Dec 1837 Jincy D.
McCauley (P), Albemarle Co,
VA. She died 2 Jun 1895, LNR
P.O. Free Union, Albemarle
Co, VA

DAVIS, JOHN F. (P, BLW), died
8 Nov 1878, Fulton Co, PA;
md 5 May 1818 Elisabeth
Boles (P), Hagerstown, Washington Co, MD. Her LNR P.O.
Harrisonville, Fulton Co, PA,
1878

DAVIS, JOHN H. (BLW), KY
militia, died 15 Jan 1848; md
14 Jan 1816 Martha H. Dixon
(P), Person Co, NC. Her LNR
Ringgold, Pittsylvania Co, VA,
1878

DAVIS, JORDAN R. (P, BLW),
LNR P.O. Manchester, Chesterfield Co, VA; md 25 Mar
1861 Martha Graham, Chester-

113

DAVIS (continued)
field Co, VA

DAVIS, JOSEPH whose former widow Mary Collier applied for a pension

DAVIS, JOSHUA (P, BLW), MA volunteers and USA, died before 8 May 1886, LNR Spring Grove, Surry Co, VA, 1871

DAVIS, JOSHUA (BLW), died 28 Nov 1861, East River, Mercer Co, VA; md 19 Dec 1822 Sarah French (P), Wolf Creek, Giles Co, VA. Her LNR Mercer Co, WV, 1879

DAVIS, JOSHUA J. (P, BLW), died 5 May 1873, Doddridge Co, WV; md (1) Catharine Maxson, (2) 12 Jun 1856 Delila Clark (P), New Salem, VA. She died 3 Apr 1898, LNR Doddridge Co, WV, 1878

DAVIS, LEWIS (BLW), died Oct 1863, Albemarle Co, VA; md 15 Feb 1814 Susan/Susannah B. Sandridge (P), Albemarle Co, VA. Her LNR P.O. Earleysville, Albemarle Co, VA, 1871

DAVIS, MATHIAS W. who applied for a pension

DAVIS, MATTHEWS, (BLW), died 22 Sep 1824 Buckingham Co, VA; md 1 Jan 1812 Susanna Faris (P), Buckingham Co, VA. Her LNR Central Plains, Fluvanna Co, VA, 1871

DAVIS, PARKS B. (BLW), died Mar 1854, King William Co, VA; md (1) ---- Meredith, (2) ?, (3) 19 Oct 1839 Sarah B. Slater (P), New Kent Co, VA. She died 14 Jun 1885, LNR P.O. Lanesville, King William Co, VA, 1878

DAVIS, PASCHAL (BLW), died 10 Mar 1862, Lawrence Co, OH; md 4 Nov 1812 Nancy L. Toon/Toone (P), Lunenburg, Lunenburg Co, VA. Her LNR P.O. Huntington, Cabell Co, WV, 1871

DAVIS, PAUL whose widow Mary applied for a pension

DAVIS, PETER (P, BLW), LNR Greenbrier Run, Doddridge Co, WV, 1871. He married twice, both wives deceased.

DAVIS, PETER (BLW)

DAVIS, REUBEN (BLW), died 17 Nov 1868, Piedmont, WV; md 1 Apr 1813 Eleanor Dean (P), Hampshire Co, VA. Her LNR Piedmont, Mineral Co, WV, 1871

DAVIS, RICHARD (BLW), died 18 May 1855, Albemarle Co, VA; md (1) Martha Michie, (2) 25 Oct 1831 Martha Harris (P), Albemarle Co, VA. Her LNR P.O. Free Union, Albemarle Co, VA, 1878

DAVIS, ROBERT S. (BLW), MD militia, died 14 Feb 1860 Marshall Co, VA; md Sep 1807 Elizabeth Harris (P), Baltimore, MD. Her LNR P.O. Glen Easton, Marshall Co, WV, 1871

DAVIS, ROBERT (P, BLW), died 19 Apr 1883, Cross Roads, Rockingham Co, VA, LNR Harrisonburg, Rockingham Co, VA, 1871; md 16 Mar 1815 Lucinda Grafton, Albemarle Co, VA. Widower.

DAVIS, ROBERT (BLW), died 1 Feb 1861, Buckingham Co, VA; md (1) Martha Gilliam, (2) Jan 1846 Sarah E. (----) Pankey (P), Buchingham Co, VA. She died c1890, LNR Buckingham Co, VA, 1878

DAVIS, SAMUEL (P, BLW), MD militia, died c22 Jul 1881, LNR P.O. Cherry Camp, Harrison Co, WV, 1871; md 18 Jan 1814 Julia Ann Wissman, Old Town, MD. She died c1880

DAVIS, SAMUEL (BLW), died 27 Oct 1826, Loudoun Co, VA; md 20 May 1820 Casandria M. Leeke (P), Carrolls Manor, Anne Arundel Co, MD. Her

114

DAVIS (continued)
LNR P.O. Hamilton, Loudoun Co, VA, 1878

DAVIS, SAMUEL whose widow Jane applied for a pension

DAVIS, SAMUEL whose widow Tabitha applied for a pension

DAVIS, SAMUEL (BLW), died 24 Sep 1868, Pickaway Co, OH; md 19 Jan 1819 Matilda Wamble (P), Wake Co, NC. She died c1880, LNR P.O. Atlanta, Pickaway Co, OH, 1878

DAVIS/DAVIES, SAMUEL C. (P, BLW), died 18 Jun 1878, Huntsville, MO; md 5 May 1857 Harriett Little (P), Roanoke, Howard Co, MO. She died 2 Feb 1907, LNR Huntsville, Randolph Co, OH, 1878

DAVIS, SPENCER (BLW), died 5 Jun 1854, Henderson Co, TN; md 24 Apr 1805 Nancy Davis (P), Lunenburg Co, VA. Her LNR Lone Elm, Henderson Co, TN, 1878

DAVIS, STEPHEN (BLW), died 9 Mar 1859, Dinwiddie Co, VA; md 27 Jan 1846 Susan E. Elder (P), Dinwiddie Co, VA. She died 21 Apr 1895, Petersburg, Dinwiddie Co, VA

DAVIS, THOMAS (P, BLW), died 22 Oct 1871, LNR P.O. Mathews Courthouse, Mathews Co, VA, 1871

DAVIS, THOMAS A. (BLW), died 31 Mar 1857 Luray, VA; md 1 Mar 1838 Sarah Hicks (P), Rappahannock Co, VA. She died 12 Feb 1888, Luray, Page Co, VA

DAVIS, THOMAS H. (P, BLW), died c1875, LNR P.O. Kingswood, Preston Co, WV, 1871; md 20 Oct 1816 Mary Hawley, Fairfax Co, VA. Thomas was a substitute for Barton D. Hawley in the War

DAVIS, THOMAS T. (BLW), died Mar 1857, Louisa Co, VA; md

DAVIS (continued)
(1) Elizabeth Gunnell, (2) Matilda Fleming, (3) Dec 1853 Sarah (Burton) Wright (P), Fluvanna Co, VA. She died 10 Dec 1871, Kents Store, Fluvanna Co, VA

DAVIS, WALTER (BLW), died 4 Aug 1863, Piqua, OH; md 28 Mar 1820 Sarah Shearer (P), Montgomery Co, OH. She died before 13 Oct 1885, LNR Winterset, Madison Co, IA, 1883

DAVIS, WILLIAM (BLW), DC militia, died 8 Jun 1837, Alexandria, VA; md 30 Aug 1812 Catharine McCatharine/ McCahan (P), Georgetown, DC. Her LNR Washington, DC, 1872

DAVIS, WILLIAM (BLW), USA, born in Fredericksburg, VA, and applied for a pension in NY

DAVIS, WILLIAM (BLW), died 20 Dec 1858, Southampton Co, VA; md 16 Mar 1828 Nancy/ Ann Joyner (P), Southampton Co, VA. Her LNR P.O. Berlin, Southampton Co, VA, 1878

DAVIS, WILLIAM F. (BLW)

DAWES/DAWS/DAVIS, INGRAM H. (P, BLW), died 10 Aug 1877, LNR Farmington, Marshall Co, TN, 1871; md 7 Jan 1815 Nancy Farrell, Carthage, Smith Co, TN

DAWKINS, THOMAS (BLW), died 2 Oct 1866 Wood Co, WV; md 25 Jun 1815 Susannah Barnett (P), Wood Co, VA. Her LNR Igger Flats, Wood Co, WV, 1878

DAWSON, BROOKS applied for a pension

DAWSON, GEORGE (P, BLW), LNR New Burlington, Clinton Co, OH, 1871. Not married.

DAWSON, HENRY (BLW), died 1 May 1853, Prince William Co, VA; md Feb 1818 Sarah Jewell (P), Stafford Co, VA.

DAWSON (continued)
Her LNR Woodbridge, Prince William Co, VA, 1878

DAWSON, HIRAM A. (P, BLW), LNR P.O. Jeffersonville, Tazewell Co, VA, 1871

DAWSON, HUDSON applied for a pension

DAWSON, JAMES (BLW), died 10 Feb 1830, Laurel Hill, Fairfax Co, VA; md 10 Jun 1810 Margaret Bates (P), Lebanon, Fairfax Co, VA. Her LNR P. O. Lorton Valley, Fairfax Co, VA, 1878

DAWSON, JEREMIAH, (BLW), died Mar 1850, Heathville, VA; md (1) ?, (2) 18 Jan 1849 Elizabeth (Pitman) Dawson (P), Heathville, Northumberland Co, VA. Her LNR Baileyville, Milan Co, TX, 1880. Her 1st husband was Nat Dawson.

DAWSON/DOSSON/DORSON, JOHN (BLW), died 11 Jul 1877, Cartwright Mills, Lawrence Co, OH; md 18 Apr 1852 Nancy Sanger (P), Scioto Co, OH. She died 3 Feb 1885, Powellsville, Scioto Co, OH

DAWSON, JOSEPH (P, BLW), died 8 Feb 1875, LNR P.O. Alexandria, Campbell Co, KY, 1871

DAWSON, LEMUEL (BLW), died 2 Apr 1853, Springfield, IL; md 19 Jun 1822 Mary Jane Garrison (P), Shelby Co, KY. She died 7 Jun 1884, Council Bluffs, IA, LNR Springfield, Sangamon Co, IL, 1878

DAWSON, NELSON (BLW), died 20 Dec 1831, Amherst Co, VA; md 10 Mar 1816 Frances L. Woodroff (P), Amherst Co, VA. She died 21 Dec 1888, LNR P.O. Lawyers, Campbell Co, VA, 1878

DAWSON, ROBERT M. (BLW), died 8 Aug 1848, Tuscawaras Co, OH; md 25 Mar 1831 Eliza

DAWSON (continued)
Ann Bukey (P), Ohio Co, VA. Her LNR P.O. Uhrichsville, Tuscawaras Co, OH, 1878

DAWSON, WILLIAM whose widow Frances applied for a pension

DAY, BALDWIN (BLW), died 27 Nov 1852, Warrenton, VA; md 20 Jan 1828 Lucretia Guthrie (P) Alexandria, VA. She died 26 Mar 1884, Warrenton, Fauquier Co, VA

DAY, JOHN (BLW)

DAY, RICHARD/DICK whose widow Sarah J. applied for a pension

ROLL NO. 26

DEAL, JARVIS whose widow Joice applied for a pension

DEALY, JOHN (BLW), died 20 Dec 1866, Champaign Co, IL; md Apr 1811 Mary Lewis (P), Woodstock, Shenandoah Co, VA. She died c1877, LNR Carysville, Champaign Co, IL, 1871

DEAN, GEORGE (P, BLW), LNR White Sulphur Springs, Greenbrier Co, WV, 1872; md May 1814 Margaret Dean, Pendleton Co, VA

DEAN, ISAAC (BLW), died 29 Jan 1870, Monongalia Co, WV; md (1) Mary Houston, (2) Zaney Saunders, (3) 24 Nov 1846 Anna F. Conaway (P), Monogalia Co, VA. She died 13 Nov 1908, LNR P.O. Maidsville, Monongalia Co, WV, 1878

DEAN, JOHN (P, BLW), died 18 Apr 1876, Buckhannon, WV; md 22 Mar 1814 Catharine Heavener (P), Pendleton Co, VA. Her LNR Buckhannon, Upshur Co, WV, 1876

DEAN, JOSEPH applied for a pension

DEAN, PHILIP (BLW), died 26

116

DEAN (continued)
Apr 1867, Jefferson Co, IN; md 29 Jul 1831 Alcy Smith (P), Marion Co, IN. Her LNR P.O. Greenwood, Johnson Co, IN, 1885

DEAN, ROBERT (BLW), died 8 Apr 1858, Brunswick Co, VA; md (1) Pattie Clements, (2) 9 Dec 1843 Mary Ann Holloway (P), Brunswick Co, VA. She died c1886, LNR P.O. Forest Hill, Brunswick Co, VA, 1879

DEAN, SAMUEL who applied for a pension

DEAN/DEEN, WILLIAM (P, BLW), died 8 Jun 1882, Falls Mills, WV, LNR P.O. Salt Lick Bridge, Braxton Co, WV, 1871; md Nancy Killingsworth, Pendleton Co, VA

DEAN, WILLIAM who applied for a pension

DEAN, WILLIAM (BLW), died 30 Jan 1857, Page Co, VA; md 9 Jun 1816 Mary Dean (P), Orange Co, VA. She died 27 Jan 1879, Rockingham Co, VA, LNR P.O. Roadside, Rockingham Co, VA, 1878

DEANE/DEAN, CHARLES (P, BLW), died c1883, LNR P.O. Mayfield, Graves Co, KY, 1871; md 1813-1815 Elizabeth Boston

DEANE, FRANCIS B., JR. (BLW), died 26 Nov 1868, Lynchburg, VA; md 16 Jan 1827 Ariana B. Cunningham (P), Goochland Co, VA. She died 18 Dec 1886, Lynchburg, Campbell Co, VA

DEANE, GEORGE (BLW), died 15 Jun 1842, Pulaski Co, VA; md (1) Polly Fisher, (2) 19 Feb 1828 Ann W. Askin (P), Montgomery Co, VA. She died c1886, LNR P.O. New River Bridge, Pulaski Co, VA, 1878

DEANS, REUBEN (P, BLW), died 17 Mar 1878, Benton Co, AR; md 15 Aug 1865 Elizabeth

DEANS (continued)
Hubbard (P), Beenton Co, AR. She died 1 Nov 1897 Sugar Creek, Benton Co, AR, 1871

DEARING, ALFRED (BLW), died 15 Mar 1856, near Flint Hill, Rappahannock Co, VA; md 17 Apr 1817 Anne Jackson (P), Culpeper Co, VA. She died Apr 1889, LNR P.O. Flint Hill, Rappahannock Co, VA, 1879

DEARING, JOHN (P, BLW), died Nov 1882, Daviess Co, MO, LNR Jameson, Daviess Co, MO, 1878; md 8 Jan 1818 Polly Nance ----, Bedford Co, VA

DEARING, WILLIAM L. S. (P, BLW), died 12 Jan 1876, Warren Co, TN; md (1) Mary T. Harrison, (2) 26 Feb 1868 Nellie (----) McGregor (P), Warren Co, TN. Her LNR P. O. Irving College, Warren Co, TN, 1878. William also served in the Florida War, 1837-1838

DEARING, WILLIAM R. (BLW), died 28 Feb 1836, Fauquier Co, VA; md 16 Mar 1819 Elizabeth Keith (P), Culpeper Co, VA. She died c1892, LNR Bridgeport, Harrison Co, WV, 1878

DEATLEY, HENRY L. (BLW), died 15 Apr 1857, Tollsboro, KY; md (1) Sarah Tate, (2) 1 Jan 1818 Elizabeth Rebecca Hobbs (P), Russell Co, VA. Her LNR P.O. Tollsboro, Lewis Co, KY, 1886

DEAVER, GEORGE (P, BLW), LNR North River Mills, Hampshire Co, WV. Never married.

DEBUSK, ELIJAH applied for a pension

DECKARD/DECKHARD, JOHN (P, BLW), LNR P.O. Smithville, Monroe Co, IN, 1871; md 5 Mar 1871 Polly Roach, Green Co, IN

DEEDS, VALENTINE (BLW),

DEEDS (continued)
died 15 Oct 1852, Augusta Co,
VA; md 14 Mar 1811 Catherine
Broofman (P), Fincastle,
Botetourt Co, VA. Her LNR
New London, Campbell Co,
VA, 1871

DEEM, JACOB (P, BLW), died
12 Jan 1884, Rockport, Wood
Co, WV; md (1) Margaret Hill,
(2) 23 Jul 1863 Elizabeth (---)
Florence (P), Wood Co, VA.
She died 5 Sep 1884, Rockport,
WV

DEEMS, ADAM (P, BLW), died
c1876, LNR P.O. Jackson
Courthouse, Jackson Co, OH,
1871; md 20 Apr 1813 Hannah
Deems, Wood Co, VA

DEER/DEARE, JOEL (BLW),
died 18 Aug 1861, Montgomery
Co, IN; md (1) Sarah Garnet,
(2) 11 Jan 1843 Susan Mallory
(P), Montgomery Co, IN. Her
LNR P.O. Waveland, Mont-
gomery Co, IN, 1887

DEER, MOSES (P, BLW), LNR
Middletown, Jefferson Co, KY,
1871; md May 1822 Martha
Clarke, Shelby Co, KY

DeFORD, BENNET M. applied for
a pension

DEHORT/DEHART, THOMAS
(P, BLW), LNR Benton Co,
IN, 1892; md 1815 Elizabeth
Howard, Chillicothe, Ross Co,
OH

DEJARNETTE, REUBEN H. (P,
BLW), LNR P.O. Green Bay,
Prince Edward Co, VA, 1871

DELAPLAINE, ELI (P-rejected,
BLW), died 3 Nov 1878,
Hampshire Co, WV; md (1)
Elizabeth Kurtz/Curts, (2) 27
Oct 1846 Emily Smith (P),
Hampshire Co, VA. She died
27 Sep 1905, Slanesville,
Hampshire Co, WV, LNR
Romney, WV, 1884

DELBRIDGE, WARREN (BLW),
died 22 Feb 1878, Brunswick
Co, VA; md (1) Elizabeth Phil

DELBRIDGE (continued)
lips, (2) 15 Dec 1816 Martha
Phillips (P), Northampton Co,
VA. She died c1889, LNR P.
O. Powellton, Brunswick Co,
VA, 1878

DELK, JEREMIAH (BLW), died
24 Jan 1864, Isle of Wight Co,
VA; md (1) Louisa Pleasants,
(2) 13 May 1827 Margaret Warren (P), Surry Co, VA. Her
LNR Hardy District, P.O.
Zuni, Isle of Wight Co, VA,
1878

DELLINGER, FREDERICK (P,
BLW), LNR P.O. Taylors Station, Franklin Co, OH, 1871;
md Mary Rye, Shenandoah Co,
VA

DELPH, ADAM (P, BLW), died
28 Mar 1876, Boone Co, KY;
md 3 Jun 1821 Catharine/Caty
Barlow (P), Boone Co, KY. She
died 20 Apr 1880, Boone Co,
KY

DELPH, CORNELIUS (P, BLW),
died 8 Sep 1872, LNR Madison
Courthouse, Madison Co, VA,
1871; md Betsey Racer, Madison Co, VA. Widower.

DELPH, SAMUEL (P, BLW),
LNR P.O. Burlington, Boone
Co, KY, 1871

DEMASTERS, JOHN (BLW), died
22 May 170, Nelson Co, VA;
md 18 Oct 1825 Mary Ann Coffey (P), Nelson Co, VA

DEMORY, WILLIAM applied for
a pension

DEMOSS, THOMAS (P, BLW),
LNR P.O. Noblesville, Hamil-
ton Co, IN, 1871; md Oct 1850
Lydia McDowell, Green Co,
OH

DENBY, SAMUEL (P, BLW),
died 26 Jun 1876, Cannon Co,
TN; md (1) Polly Lawrence,
(2) 24 Mar 1818 Mary Rogers
(P), Warren Co, TN. Her LNR
Cannon Co, TN, 1878

DENBY, WILLIAM (BLW), died
20 Nov 1861, Norfolk, VA; md

118

DENBY (continued)
8 Oct 1812 Mary DeShon (P),
Baltimore, MD. Her LNR Nor-
folk, VA, 1873
DENEALE, GEORGE (BLW),
died in the Service 1814
DENER/DEANER, GEORGE (P,
BLW), died 23 May 1873, LNR
P.O. Appomattox Courthouse,
Appomattox Co, VA, 1871
DENEUFVILLE/JOHN A. or
DENEAFRILL, AUGUSTIN (P,
BLW), dc1874, LNR Wil-
liamsburg, James City Co,
VA, 1871
DENNEY, SAMUEL B. (P, BLW),
LNR Staunton, Augusta Co,
VA, 1872; md 14 Dec 1815
Neomy Loving
DENNIS, ABSALOM and widow
Jane both applied for a pension
DENNIS, JOSEPH whose widow
Elizabeth applied for a pension
DENNY, JOHN (BLW), died 24
Mar 1861, Thomas Bridge, TN;
md (1) Mary Jones, (2) 7 Jan
1818 Margaret Swatz (P),
Frederick Co, VA. Her LNR
P.O. Blountsville, Sullivan Co,
TN, 1878
DENSON, WILLIAM (P, BLW),
died before 18 Nov 1885, LNR
P.O. Franklin, Southampton
Co, VA, 1878; md 23 Oct 1817
Nancy Barrett/Ballard, South-
ampton Co, VA
DENT, DUDLEY E. whose widow
Mahala applied for a pension
DENTON, ALLEN (BLW), died
12 Jul 1857, Henrico Co, VA;
md 11 Apr 1822 Sarah J. Toler
(P), Coochland Co, VA. Her
LNR P.O. Richmond, Henrico
Co, VA, 1878
DEPRIEST, RANDOLPH (P,
BLW), died 27 Jan 1879, LNR
P.O. Campbell Courthouse,
Campbell Co, VA, 1871. Ran-
dolph was a substitute for John
Depriest in the War
DEPRIEST, ROBERT H. (BLW),
died 28 Mar 1864, Augusta Co,

DEPRIEST (continued)
VA; md 1 Oct 1816 Jeminia
Ramsey (P), Staunton, VA. She
died 8 Aug 1879, August Co,
VA, LNR P.O. Staunton,
Augusta Co, VA, 1878
DEPRIEST, TURPIN (BLW), died
4 Jun 1832, Campbell Co, VA;
md 29 May 1811 Martha Wood,
(P), Campbell Co, VA. Her
LNR Campbell Co, VA, 1871
DEQUASIE, WILLIAM (P, BLW),
died 21 Sep 1878, Summers
Co, WV; md 1 Dec 1821 Eliz-
abeth Cary (P), Nelson Co,
VA. Her LNR P.O. Green Sul-
phur Springs, Summers Co,
WV, 1871
DERENBARGER/ DEREN-
BERGER, GEORGE alias
PETERS, GEORGE (BLW),
died 31 May 1855, Wood Co,
VA; md 20 Jan 1831 Peggy
Anderson (P), Wood Co, VA.
Her LNR P.O. Belleville,
Wood Co, WV, 1878
DERRY, CHRISTIAN (BLW), died
27 May 1858, Loudoun Co, VA;
md 21 Oct 1819 Susannah Karn
(P), Frederick, Frederick Co,
MD. She died 22 Jan 1884,
Loudoun Co, VA, LNR P.O.
Neersville, Loudoun Co, VA,
1878
DESHIELDS, JOSEPH (BLW),
died 17 Jul 1854, Heathsville,
VA; md (1) Mary Martin, (2)
Matilda Wade, (3) 6 Apr 1829
Emily C. Crewdson (P), War-
saw, Richmond Co, VA. Her
LNR Heathsville, Northumber-
land Co, VA, 1878
DESPER, AUSTIN (BLW), died
13 Nov 1862, Fluvanna Co,
VA; md 26 Sep 1816 Elizabeth
England (P), Louisa Co, VA.
She died Apr 1882, LNR P.O.
Kents Store, Fluvanna Co, VA,
1878
DEVAUGHN, JOHN (BLW), died
11 Aug 1839, Alexandria, VA;
md 21 Mar 1816 Nancy Coddy

DEVAUGHN (continued)
(P), Alexandria, VA. Her LNR Alexandria, Va, 1878
DEVAUGHN, THOMAS (BLW), died 6 Jun 1857, Baltimore, MD; md 14 Nov 1823 Nancy Harper (P), Alexandria, VA. Her LNR Baltimore, MD, 1879
DEVAULT, ABRAHAM whose widow Sarah applied for a pension
DEVAULT, ABRAHAM (BLW), died 29 Apr 1863, Monongalia Co, VA; md 4 Mar 1819 Mary Steele (P), Monongalia Co, VA. She died 2 Jan 1889, Smithtown, WV
DEVERS/DEAVERS/DEVRSE, AARON (P, BLW), died 8 Apr 1878, Mechanicsburg, OH; md (1) Catherine Davidson, (2) 4 Feb 1855 Mary Ann (----) Robuck (P), Champaign Co, OH. She died c1880, LNR Mechanicsburg, Champaign Co, OH, 1878. Mary Ann's first husband was James Robuck
DEVERS, THOMAS applied for a pension
DEVIN, CLAYTON (BLW), died 24 Nov 1868, Polk Co, MO; md 17 May 1820 Margaret West (P), Fayetteville, Lincoln Co, TN. She died c1888, LNR Bolivar, Polk Co, MO, 1878
DEWEES, SAMUEL (BLW)
DEWESE, PETER (BLW), died 23 Sep 1868, Floyd Co, VA; md (1) Easter Poff, (2) 7 May 1868 Nancy Byrd (P), Copper Hill, VA. She died 4 May 1893, LNR Graysville, Floyd Co, VA, 1884

ROLL NO. 27

DIAL, THOMAS (P, BLW), died 2 Jul 1886, Columbia City, IN; md 1818 Nancy Rogers, Hardy Co, VA
DIBRELL, EDWIN (P, BLW),

DIBRELL (continued)
LNR Richmond, Henrico Co, VA, 1871; md 31 Oct 1816 Martha Shrewsbury, Wayne Co, KY
DICE, REUBEN whose widow Eveline E. applied for a pension
DICE, WILLIAM (BLW), died 10 May 1859, Greene Co, OH; md 26 Dec 1811 Margaret Seldonridge (P), Staunton, Augusta Co, VA. She died c1877, LNR P.O. Alpha, Greene Co, OH, 1871
DICK, SOLOMON (P-rejected, BLW), MD militia, died 9 Oct 1876, Washington Co, OH; md Mar 1822 Barbary Moats (P), Wood Co, VA. She died 31 Mar 1884, Washington Co, OH, LNR P.O. Marietta, Washington Co, OH, 1873. Solomon was a substitute for Frederick Dick in the War
DICKENSON, ISAAC (BLW), died 18 Apr 1842, Cumberland Gap, Knox Co, KY; md 8 Dec 1814 Nancy Robinson (P), Lee Co, VA. She died 15 Mar 1885, LNR Somerset, Pulaski Co, KY, 1873
DICKENSON, JAMES whose widow Mary applied for a pension
DICKENSON, LEWIS/CADWALADER LEWIS (BLW), died 12 Oct 1850, Washington Co, VA; md 1808/9 Rebecca W. Bryan (P), Paperville, Sullivan Co, TN. Her LNR P.O. Abingdon, Washington Co, VA, 1871
DICKERSON, BARTLETT (P, BLW), LNR P.O. Davis Mills, Bedford Co, VA, 1871; md 1808 Sally Thompson, Bedford Co, VA
DICKERSON/DICKENSON, HEZEKIAH (P, BLW), died 5 Jul 1871, Breckinridge Co, KY, LNR Hudsonville, Breckinridge Co, KY, 1871; md 9 Feb 1815

DICKERSON (continued)
Frances McGeorge, Bedford Co, VA

DICKERSON/DICKENSON/DICKSON, JAMES (P, BLW), died c1880, LNR Sedalia, Pettis Co, MO, 1878

DICKERSON, JOHN (BLW), died 28 Dec 1837, Carroll Co, VA; md 5 Aug 1819 Mary Cock (P), Grayson Co, VA. She died c1890, LNR P.O. Hillsville, Carroll Co, VA, 1878

DICKERSON, JOHN (BLW), died 19 Sep 1867, Franklin Co, VA; md 11 Jul 1826 Serena Martin (P), Franklin Co, VA. She died c1885, LNR P.O. Rocky Mount, Franklin Co, VA, 1879

DICKERSON, LEONARD (BLW), died 17 Sep 1864, Floyd Co, VA; md 16 May 1826 Susannah Hytton (P), Floyd Co, VA. Her LNR Greasy Creek, Floyd Co, VA, 1878

DICKIE, JOHN (BLW), died 6 Oct 1856; md (1) ?, (2) 2 Nov 1851 Lucy C. (Haynes) Davis (P), Madison Co, TN. She died c1890, LNR P.O. Jackson, Madison Co, TN, 1878

DICKINSON, CHARLES whose widow Martha S. applied for a pension

DICKINSON/DICKENSON, EDMOND (P, BLW), died 11 Mar 1875, Russell Co, VA; md Apr 1817 Mary Honaker (P), Russell Co, VA. She died c1884, LNR Copper Creek, Russell Co, VA, 1878

DICKINSON/DICKERSON, ROBERT P. (P, BLW), LNR P.O. Elberton, Elbert Co, GA, 1871

DICKS, JOB (BLW)

DICKSON, JAMES whose widow Jane applied for a pension

DICKSON, JOHN (BLW), died 26 Jun 1826, Gosport, Norfolk Co, VA; md 20 Sep 1818 Selina White (P), New York City, NY.

DICKSON (continued)
She died 1 Jul 1887, Portsmouth, VA. Selina's 2nd husband was Robert Barclay

DIGGS, BLACKWELL (BLW), died 1828-1830 Mathews Co, VA; md 27 Sep 1821 Elizabeth Ripley (P), Mathews Co, VA. She died c1882, LNR P.O. Port Hayward, Mathews Co, VA, 1878

DIGGS, COLE (P, BLW), LNR P.O. Danville, Montgomery Co, MO, 1878; md 10 Feb 1820 Jane Pace, Madison Co, KY

DIGGS, ISAIAH (P, BLW), LNR Gloucester, Mathews Co, VA, 1873; md Mar 1830 Rachel; A. Belvin, Gloucester Co, VA

DIGGS, JOHN (BLW), died 8 or 18 Jan 1864, Mathes Co, VA; md Sep 1812 Susan Treacle (P), Mathews Co, VA. She died 12 Jul 1874, LNR P.O. Mathews Courthouse, Mathews Co, VA, 1871

DIGGS, WILLIAM (BLW), died 14 Mar 1837, Orange Co, VA; md 19 Jan 1825 Lucinda Cash (P), Culpeper Co, VA. Her LNR Fredericksburg, Spotsylvania Co, VA, 1878

DILL, ADOLPH (BLW), died 13 Aug 1867, Richmond, VA; md ()1) Hannah Heisler, (2) 2 Dec 1826 Hannah K. Gorgas (P), Philadelphia, PA. She died 12 Dec 1878, LNR Richmond, Henrico Co, VA, 1878

DILLARD, JAMES whose widow Polly applied for a pension

DILLARD, JAMES D. (BLW), died 20 Jun 1854, Spotsylvania Co, VA; md (1) Mrs. Mary Moon, (2) 8 Jun 1821 Emily Twyman (P), Spotsylvania Co, VA. Her LNR P.O. Twyman's Store; Spotsylvania Co, VA, 1878

DILLARD, JOHN (P, BLW), died 3 Apr 1878, Halifax Co, VA, LNR P.O. Halifax Courthouse,

DILLARD (continued)
Halifax Co, VA, 1871; md 26 May 1814 Alcy Guthrie, Halifax Co, VA

DILLARD, JOHN (BLW), whose widow was Matilda

DILLARD, RYLAND T. applied for a pension

DILLARD, WILLIAM whose widow Betsey applied for a pension

DILLE/DILLEY, MOSES (P, BLW), died c1876, LNR Chillicothe, Ross Co, OH, 1873; md Aug 1814 Jane Magill, Guernsey Co, OH

DILLION, JESSE (BLW), died 31 Mar or Apr 1871, Franklin Co, VA; md 4 Aug 1814 Polly Houseman (P), Franklin Co, VA. Her LNR P.O. Union Hall, Franklin Co, VA, 1874

DILLON, EDWARD (P, BLW), LNR Lunenburg Co, VA, 1871; md 31 dec 1813 Sally Doss, Prince Edward Co, VA

DILLON, SAMUEL (BLW), OH militia, died 23 Jun 1859, Sangamon Co, IL; md (1) ?, (2) ?, (3) 2 Apr 1812 Vashti Borton (P), Guernsey Co, OH. She died c1884, LNR Wheeling, Ohio co, WV, 1871

DILMAN, DANIEL (BLW), died Feb 1865, Botetourt Co, VA; md (1) Polly Dill, (2) Apr 1842 Mary Watkins (P), Botetourt Co, VA. She died 2 Jul 1903, LNR P.O. Tinker Knob, Botetourt Co, VA, 1878

DIMIT/DIMET, JACOB (P, BLW), died c1883, LNR Fowlers, Brooke Co, WV, 1871; md 3 Jul 1830 Sidney Buckey, Brooke Co, VA

DINGES/DENIS, DAVID applied for a pension

DINGLEDINE, PHILIP (P, BLW), LNR P.O. Terre Haute, Champaign Co, IN, 1871; md 26 Mar 1805 Mary Barrinton, Woodstock, Shenandoah Co, VA

DISHMAN, WILLIAM (P, BLW), LNR P.O. Abingdon, Washington Co, VA, 1872

DITTY, ABRAHAM (BLW), died 29 Dec 1869, nr Cookeville, TN; md (1) Jansie Fergus, (2) 19 mar 1857 Sarah C. (----) Dyer (P), Cookeville, TN. Her LNR Post Oak, White Co, TN, 1884

DIVERS, THOMAS (BLW), died 12 Nov 1848, Franklin Co, VA; md 12 Oct 1830 Lydia Plyborne (P), Franklin Co, VA. Her LNR P.O. Taylor's Store, Franklin Co, VA, 1878

DIVERS, WILLIAM R. (P, BLW), LNR P.O. Halesford, Franklin Co, VA, 1871; md Oct 1814 Margaret Weaver, Franklin Co, VA

DIVINE, WILLIAM (P, BLW), died 26 Mar 1884, Bloomfield, Loudoun Co, VA

DIX, JOHN (BLW), died 10 Jun 1866, Nashville, TN; md (1) Martha M. Edmundson, (2) 4 Jan 1855 Frances A. (----) Zuccarello (P), Nashville, TN. Her LNR West Nashville, Davidson Co, TN, 1878

DIXON, ADAM (BLW), died 27 Jul 1871, Maury Co, TN; md 24 Sep 1811 Hanna G. Irvine (P), Bedford Co, VA. She died 22 Feb 1876, LNR P.O. Bigby Mills, Maury Co, TN, 1873

DIXON/DICKSON, ARCHIBALD (BLW), died 30 Apr 1844, Licking Co, OH; md (1) Sarah Swisher, (2) 6 Sep 1821 Anna Burge (P), Licking Co, OH. She died c1885, LNR Salem, Knox Co, IL, 1879

DIXON, GEORGE (BLW), died 13 Apr 1854, Nansemond Co, VA; md (1) Sally Hall, (2) 12 Feb 1846 Nancy (----) Dixon (P), Nansmeond Co, VA. She died 22 Jun 1887, Everetts Bridge, Nansemond Co, VA

DIXON/DICKSON, JAMES

DIXON (continued)
(BLW), died 20 Dec 1866,
Licking Co, OH; md 19 Jul
1814 Sally Miller (P), Staunton, Augusta Co, VA. She died
c1875, LNR P.O. Homer, Licking Co, OH, 1871

DIXON, JAMES whose widow
Jane applied for a pension

DIXON, JOHN (P, BLW), LNR
P.O. Rush Creek, Union Co,
OH, 1871. Wife died Jun 1863

DIXON, STEPHEN (BLW), died
1842, OH; md 1 Oct 1814
Susan Dixon (P), Person Co,
NC. Her LNR Halifax Co, VA,
1872

DIXON, THOMAS (P, BLW), died
c1879, LNR P.O. Washington
Courthouse, Fayette Co, OH,
1871; md 28 Apr 1820 Margaret
Crautz, Bedford Co, VA

DIXON, TURLEY whose widow
Pamela applied for a pension

DIXON, WILLIAM applied for a
pension

DIXON, WILLIAM whose widow
Eliza Vaughn applied for a
pension

DOBSON, RICHARD (P, BLW),
died 7 Jan 1874, Lewis Co,
WV; md (1) Sally Jett, (2) 16
Apr 1857 Mary (Hodges)
Barnsgrove (P), Upshur Co,
VA. She died 4 Jan 1902, LNR
P.O. Weston, Lewis Co, WV,
1878

DODD, ELZY (P, BLW), died 9
Dec 1880, Palatine, WV; md
(1) Agnes A. Johnson, (2) 10
Nov 1839 Lucy A. Dodd (P),
Fauquier Co, VA. She died
c1887, LNR Palatine, Marion
Co, WV, 1887

DODD, WILLIAM whose widow
Elizabeth applied for a pension

DODD/DODS, JOHN (BLW), died
25 Jul 1856, Fulton Co, IL; md
(1) ?, (2) 28 Apr 1844
Elizabeth (Embertemer)
Thomas (P), Fayette Co, OH.
She died 23 Nov 1885, LNR

DODD (continued)
Isabel, Fulton Co, OH, 1883.
Elizabeth's 1st husband was
John Thomas

DODSON, CALEB whose widow
Martha applied for a pension

DODSON, HUGH H. (P, BLW),
died 15 Feb 1876, Pittsylvania
Co, VA; md (1) Susan Morris,
(2) 4 or 5 Jun 1871 Obedience
Newbell (P), Pittsylvania Co,
VA. She died 14 Jun 1897,
LNR Laurel Grove, Pittsyl-
vania Co, VA, 1878

DODSON, JETHRO applied for a
pension

DODSON, JOSIAH (P, BLW), died
20 May 1880, Marshall Co,
WV; md 28 Mar 1831 Hannah
A. Allen (P), Ohio Co, VA. Her
LNR P.O. Moundsville, Mar-
shall Co, WV, 1880

DODSON, STEPHEN (P, BLW),
died 17 Aug 1873, Surry Co,
NC; md (1) ---- Massey, (2)
25 Dec 1833 Sarah S. Gill (P),
Pittsylvania Co, VA. Her LNR
P.O. Rusk, Surry Co, NC, 1878

DODSON, WILLIAM C. (BLW),
died 9 May 1861, Patrick Co,
VA; md Aug 1818 Judith Dick-
son/Dixon (P), Pittsylvania
Co. VA. She died c1885, LNR
Patrick Co, VA, 1878

DODSON, WILLIAM (P, BLW),
LNR Charlotte, Dickson Co,
TN, 1871; md 23 Sep 1819
Catharine Davis, Pittsylvania
Co, VA

DOGGETT, ARMISTEAD whose
widow Mary/Polly applied for
a pension

DOGGETT, BENJAMIN (P,
BLW), died 2 May 1885, Tran-
quility, Adams Co, OH; md 20
Jul 1809 Mary/Polly Brimmer,
Stafford Co, VA. Widower.

DOGGETT, GEORGE W. (P,
BLW), died 19 Aug 1877,
Fayette Co, OH; md (1)
Lucinda Shepard, (2) 16 Feb
1843 Eliza Moon (P), Highland

DOGGETT (continued)
Co, OH. She died 12 Dec
1903, LNR P.O. New Mar-
tinsburg, Fayette Co, OH, 1878

DOGGETT, WILLIAM (P, BLW),
died 30 Nov 1877, Rushville,
IN; md 15 Apr 1816 Eliza Miller, Culpeper Co, VA

DOLD, SAMUEL M. (P, BLW),
died 9 Feb 1883, Lexington,
Rockbridge Co, VA; md 17 Oct
1820 Elizabeth M. Fadden,
Lexington, VA

DONAHOE, WILLIAM (BLW),
enlisted in Augusta Co, VA,
died 10 Dec 1857 Talladega,
AL; md 16 Jan 1810 Rebecca
Garvin (no claim for pension).
Her LNR Muscatine, IA, 1859

DONALD, JAMES F. applied for a
pension

DONALDSON, BALEE/BAILEY
(P, BLW), died c1880, LNR
Millersburg, Holmes Co, OH,
1879

DONALDSON, DAVID (P, BLW),
died c1875, LNR Burrow
Grove, Fountain Co, IN, 1871;
md 1 Mar 1810 Mary Miller,
Staunton, VA

DONALDSON, ROBERT applied
for a pension

DONALDSON, ROBERT (BLW),
died 19 Nov 1869/70, Alexandria, VA; md 5 Jan 1815
Elizabeth Burch (P), Alexandria, VA. She died c1885,
LNR Alexandria, VA, 1885

DONALDSON, THORNTON A.
(BLW), died 5 Jul 1848,
Washington, DC; md (1)
Catharine P. Barron, (2) 20
Dec 1855 Ann (Williams)
Faithfull (P), Washington, DC.
She died 22 Aug 1879, Bal-
timore, MD

DOOLEY, MICAJAH (BLW), died
29 Jan 1838, Clark Co, OH; md
4 Apr 1816 Elner Ellmore (P),
Winchester, Frederick Co, VA.
Her LNR Long Valley, Lassen
Co, CA, 1879

DOORES/DOORS, WILLIAM J.
(P, BLW), LNR P.O. Murray,
Calloway Co, KY, 1871. Wife
died 4 Feb 1857

DORAN, ROBERT L. (BLW), TN
militia, died 20 Sep 1868, md
19 May 1812 Elizabeth Lowry
(P), Washington Co, VA. Her
LNR P.O. Springfield, Greene
Co, MO, 1871

DORMAN, ANDREW (P, BLW),
died 16 Oct 1875, LNR P.O.
Harrisonburg, Rockingham Co,
VA, 1871

DORMAN, CHRISTIAN (BLW),
died 14 Mar 1864, Rockingham
Co, VA; md 26 Sep 1822 Bar-
bara Gates (P), Harrisonburg,
Rockingham Co, VA. Her LNR
Keezletown, Rockingham Co,
VA, 1878

DORMIN, WILLIAM (BLW)

DORRELL/DARRELL, JAMES
(P, BLW), LNR Neersville,
Loudoun Co, VA, 1871.
Widower.

DORSETT, FIELDER R. (P,
BLW), DC militia, LNR
Washington, DC, 1873; md 17
Jun 1817 Ann A. McRea,
Alexandria, VA. Widower.

DORSEY, JOSHUA (P, BLW), MD
militia, died 12 Jan 1881,
Wellsburg, WV; md 5 Dec
1839 Mary A. Shades (P),
Brooke Co, VA. Her LNR
Wellsburg, Brooke Co, WV,
1895. Joshua substituted for
Nicholas Dorsey in the War

DOSS, HARTWELL (P, BLW),
died 10 Feb 1872 Lynchburg,
Campbell Co, VA; md 1 May
1809 Martha Elam, Campbell
Co, VA

DOSS, JAMES whose widow
Lockey applied for a pension

DOSS, JAMES A. (BLW), died 31
Aug 1858, Macon Co, TN; md
16 Aug 1804 Sarah Hendley
(P), Pittsylvania Co, VA. Her
LNR P.O. Lafayette, Macon
Co, TN, 1878

DOSS, OVERSTREET whose widow Jane applied for a pension

DOSS, R. WALKER (BLW), died 10 Aug 1857, Appomattox Co, VA; md 27 Dec 1800 Mary Thomas (P), Buckingham Co, VA. She died 24 Jan 1874, LNR P.O. Oakville, Appomattox Co, VA, 1872

DOSS, STEPHEN (BLW), died 23 Jan 1866, Pittsylvania Co, VA; md c1810 Judith Hodges (P), Franklin Co, VA. Her LNR P.O. Chalk Level, Pittsylvania Co, VA, 1871

DOSSE, HENRY (P), died 18 Mar 1872; md 2 Sep 1858 Nancy Thomas (P), Washington Co, VA. She died 12 Jan 1899, LNR P.O. Loves Mills, Washington Co, VA, 1878

DOTSON, ELISHA (P, BLW), died 31 Aug 1871, Wood Co, WV; md (1) Nancy ----, (2) 3 Nov 1847 Ingaba (Louther?) Eustler/Utchler (P), West Union, Doddridge Co, VA. She died 2 Oct 1899, LNR P.O. Franklin, Warren Co, OH, 1889

DOTSON, RICHARD whose widow Mary applied for a pension

DOTSON, THOMAS (BLW), died 9 Dec 1870, Fayette Co, WV; md (1) Susannah ----, (2) 17 Jul 1862 Margaret (----) Jenkins (P), Nicholas Co, VA. She died c1908, LNR Palestine, Greenbrier Co, WV, 1886

DOTY, JAMES applied for a pension

DOUGHERTY, PHILLIP (BLW), died 27 Sep 1871, Monroe Co, WV; md 25 Nov 1819 Rachel ---- (P), Monroe Co, VA. She died c1890, LNR Monroe Co, WV, 1887

DOUGHTY, WILLIAM (P, BLW), died 20 Nov 1878, Knightstown, Henry Co, IN; md 3 Dec

DOUGHTY (continued) 1818 Elizabeth Gay (P), Centreville, Wayne Co, IN. She died before 31 Dec 1885, LNR Shelbyville, Shelby Co, IN, 1883

DOUGLAS, JOHN B. whose widow Elizabeth applied for a pension

DOUGLASS, DAVID (BLW), died 7 Aug 1843, Bedford Co, VA; md 19 Nov 1801 Sarah White (P), Bedford Co, VA. She died c1872, LNR P.O. Charlemont, Bedford Co, VA, 1872

DOUGLASS, JONATHAN (BLW), TN militia, died 20 Feb 1842, Overton Co, TN; md 5 Jan 1815 Sarah Smith (P), Washington Co, VA. Her LNR P.O. Netherland, Overton Co, TN, 1871

DOUGLASS, THOMAS whose widow Fanny applied for a pension

DOUGLASS, WILLIAM P. (P, BLW), LNR Fayette, Howard Co, MO, 1871

DOVE, JAMES (P, BLW), died 23 Apr 1878, Brocks Gap, VA, md (1) Catharine Fitzwaters, (2) 28 Oct 1838 Margaret Dove (P), Rockingham Co, VA. She died Jan 1889, LNR Dovesville, Rockingham Co, VA, 1882

DOVE, JOHN applied for a pension

DOVE, REUBEN (P, BLW),LNR Rockingham, Rockingham Co, VA, 1871; md 4 Jul 1818 Catharine Dare?, Rockingham Co, VA

DOVE, WILLIAM, died c1886, Pittsylvania Co, VA; md (1) Martha Irby, (2) Mary Irby, (3) 1870 Julia W. Payne (P), Pittsylvania Co, VA. She died 18 Aug 1895, LNR P.O. Dhalk Level, Pittsylvania Co, VA, 1890. Julia was erroniously pensioned as another William Dove's widow. A special ex-

DOVE (continued)

amination reported her husband to be a nephew of the other William. Her husband was not born until 1813, and thus was not a War of 1812 soldier

DOVE, WILLIAM (BLW), died 31 Aug 1853, Harding Co, TN; md 23 Jan 1816 Oney Sanders (P), Pittsylvania Co, VA. Her LNR Wayne Co, TN, 1855

DOVE, WILLIAM (BLW), died 20 May 1863, Pittsylvania Co, VA; md 18 or 25 Apr 1811 Polly/Mary Mustain (P), Pittsylvania Co, VA. She died c1880, LNR P.O. Chalk Level, Pittsylvania Co, VA, 1871. This William was the uncle of the William who died c1886, above

DOVEL, WILLIAM (BLW), died Nov 1860, Page Co, VA; md May 1816 Christena Long (P), Page Co, VA. Her LNR P.O. East Liberty, Page Co, VA, 1878

DOVER, JOHN (BLW)

DOWDY, ALLEN G. (P, BLW), died 27 Oct 1879, Campbell Co, VA; md 16 Dec 1815 Nancy Elder (P), Campbell Co, VA. Her LNR P.O. Rustburg, Campbell Co, VA, 1879

DOWDY, JABEZ (BLW), died Aug 1846, Montgomery Co, VA; md (1) Celia Hopkins, (2) 14 Nov 1819 Hannah (Bowles) Fagg (P), Franklin Co, VA. She died c1892, LNR Pearisburg, Giles Co, VA, 1883

DOWDY, JAMES (BLW), died 20 Jan 1860, Cumberland Co, VA; md 18 Apr 1822 Martha Smith (P), Cumberland Co, VA. Her LNR P.O. McCraes, Cumberland Co, VA, 1881

DOWDY, THOMAS (P, BLW), LNR Salem, Roanoke Co, VA, 1871; md 12 Feb 1818 Mary Hutson, Halifax Co, VA

DOWDY, WILLIAM B. (P,

DOWDY (continued)

BLW), died 15 Jan 1883, Rockbridge Co, VA, 1871

DOWELL, RICHARD (P, BLW), LNR Hatton, Shelby Co, KY, 1886

DOWELL, THOMAS (BLW), died 26 Nov 1869, Albemarle Co, VA; md 6 May 1813 Frances Collins (P), Albemarle Co, VA. Her LNR P.O. Stony Point, Albemarle Co, VA, 1872

DOWNER, JOHN W. (BLW), died 2 May 1828, Goochland Co, VA; md 27 Jan 1818 Maria Woodson, Dover Mills, Goochland Co, VA. Her LNR Richmond, Henrico Co, VA, 1878

DOWNING, RUFUS (BLW), died 2 Aug 1844, Caroline Co, VA; md 2 Sep 1813 Fanny Sale (P), Caroline Co, VA. Her LNR Bowling Green, Caroline Co, VA, 1871

DOWNS, WALTER (P, BLW), died c1875, LNR Janesville, Muskingum Co, OH, 1871; md 1812 Femity Wilson, Loudoun Co, VA

DOWNS, WILLIAM (P, BLW), LNR The Plains, Fauquier Co, VA, 1871; md 10 Dec 18-- Eleanor Archer, Middleburg, Loudoun Co, VA

DOYLE, DORRIS (P, BLW), LNR Amherst Co, VA, 1871; md (1) 15 Feb 1833 Mary Teake/ Lake, (2) 22 Dec 1851 Elizabeth Coflin, Amherst Co, VA

DOYLE, JOHN G. (BLW), died 4 Sep 1857, Newbern, Jersey Co, IL; md 23 Dec 1817 Elizabeth Haselton (P), Frederick, Frederick Co, MD. She died c1884, LNR Macoupin Co, IL, 1878

DOYLE, MICHAEL (BLW), died 20 Apr 1860, Highland Co, VA; md Oct 1827 Ann G. Sproul (P), Bath Co, VA. She died c1880, LNR P.O. Monterey, Highland Co, VA, 1878

DOYLE, WILLIAM (BLW), died

DOYLE (continued)
31 Dec 1851, Smithland, KY;
md 22 Sep 1812 Peachey Norvell (P), Amherst Co, VA. She
18 died Apr 1886, LNR Smithland, Livingston Co, KY, 1873
DOYLE, WILLIAM F. (P, BLW),
died 28 Jan 1882, Montgomery
Co, VA; md (1) Margaret Burgaydine, (2) Leanah Moses, (3)
20 May 1875 Hannay (Bradford)
Smith (P), Montgomery Co,
VA. Her LNR P.O. Chris-
tiansburg, Montgomery Co,
VA, 1883. Hannah's 1st husband was James Smith
DRAFFIN, WILLIAM (P, BLW),
LNR P.O. Wadesboro, Cal-
loway Co, KY, 1871; md Nancy
Foster, Calloway Co, KY
DRAKE, FRANCIS T. (P, BLW),
died before 23 May 1891, LNR
Leesburg, Loudoun Co, VA,
1878
DRAKE, JAMES (BLW), died 15
May 1845, Ritchie Co, vA; md
25 Sep 1815 Elizabeth Sinnett
(P), Wood Co, VA. Her LNR
Harrisville, Ritchie Co, WV,
1878
DRAKE, RIVERS/RIEVES whose
widow Elizabeth T. applied for
a pension
DRAKE, THOMAS (BLW), died
22 Sep 1853, Licking Co, OH;
md 27 Jan 1835 Jerusha
Baugham (P), Miskingum Co,
OH. She died c15 Mar 1884,
LNR Fallsburg, Licking Co,
OH, 1877
DRAKE, THOMAS B. (P, BLW),
LNR Hillsboro, Highland Co,
VA, 1871; md 7 Dec 1813 Mary
Newton, Buckingham Co, VA
DRAKE, WELLS (P, BLW), died
22 May 1880, Sussex Co, VA;
md (1) Mary Gay, (2) 8 Dec
1859 Mary Elizabeth Birdson
(P), Sussex Co, VA. She died
3 Oct 1892, LNR P.O. Wake-
field, Sussex Co, VA, 1880
DRAPER, THOMAS (P, BLW),

DRAPER (continued)
died 23 Dec 1873, Rush Co, IN;
md 17 Dec 1809 Mary Turner
(P), Southampton Co, VA.
Her LNR P.O. Carthage, Rush
Co, IN, 1874
DRENNEN, LAWRENCE applied
for a pension
DRESSLER, HENRY whose widow
Elizabeth applied for a pension
DREW, BENJAMIN L. (BLW),
died 22 Jul 1865, Belle Farm,
VA; md 11 Dec 1822 Lavinia
Hart (P), Belle Farm, VA. She
died 25 Sep 1884, LNR Belle
Farm, Southampton Co, VA,
1878
DREWRY, HENRY (BLW), died
28 May 1866, Chesterfield Co,
VA; md 28 Sep 1830 Martha
Amelia Davis (P), Chesterfield
Co, VA. She died 7 Jun 1886,
Centralia, Chesterfield Co,
VA, LNR Proctors Creek,
Chesterfield Co, VA, 1878
DREWRY/DRURY, JOHN (P,
BLW), died 18 Jul 1881, Bed-
ford Co, VA; md (1) Ferraby
Dowdy, (2) ?, (3) 3 Nov 1853
Charlotte Crouch (P), Bedford
Co, VA. She died 7 Sep 1905,
Mentow, VA, LNR Chestnut
Fork, Bedford Co, VA, 1899
DRINKARD, BEVERLY (BLW),
died 1 Dec 1875, Petersburg,
VA; md (1) Elizabeth A. F---,
(2) 2 Nov 1865 Jane E. (---)
Ellyson (P), Petersburg, VA.
She died c1894, LNR Peters-
burg, Dinwiddie Co, VA, 1878
DRINKARD, JOSHUA whose wi-
dow Polly applied for a pen-
sion
DRODDY, CHARLES (BLW), OH
militia, died 28 Aug 1865,
Walton, WV; md 1 May 1825
Sarah Grandee (P), Kanawha
Co, VA. She died 28 Jan 1883,
Walton, Roane Co, WV
DROWN, BENJAMIN (BLW)
DRUEN, DAVID applied for a
pension

127

DRUMHELLER, GEORGE (P, BLW), died 2 Sep 1876, Nelson Co, VA; md 7 Jan 1817 Jane A. Suthards (P), Albemarle Co, VA. Her LNR P.O. Orlando, Nelson Co, VA, 1878

DRUMMOND, GRIEVE (BLW), died 7 Nov 1844, Petersburg, VA; md (1) Elizabeth Starke, (2) 29 Sep 1836 Margaret (Henderson) Drummond (P), Glasgow, Scotland. Her LNR Petersburg, Dinwiddie Co, VA, 1878

DRUMMOND, PENDLETON whose widow Naomi applied for a pension

DRUMMOND, THOMAS (P, BLW), USA, LNR P.O. Castle Craig, Campbell Co, VA, 1871; md 25 Dec 1818 Catherine Hawkins, Bedford Co, VA

DRYDEN, DAVID (P, BLW), LNR Campbell, Coles Co, IL, 1871

DRYDEN, NATHANIEL (BLW), died 4 Feb 1858, Montgomery Co, MO; md 13 Sep 1811 Margaret Craig (P), Washington Co, VA. Her LNR P.O. High Hill, Montgomery Co, MO, 1871

DUCK, JACOB H. whose widow Nancy B. applied for a pension

DUDLEY, ABSALOM (BLW), died 30 Jun 1830, Pittsylvania Co, VA; md 25 Feb 1806 Elizabeth Joiner (P), Campbell Co, VA. Her LNR P.O. Castle Craig, Campbell Co, VA, 1871

DUDLEY, GEORGE F. (BLW), died 15 Sep 1839, Franklin Co, MO; md 23 Oct 1823 Jane T. Mann (P), Alleghany Co, VA. She died c1890, LNR Masters, Alleghany Co, VA, 1880

DUDLEY, JOSEPH whose widow Elizabeth Archer applied for a pension

DUDLEY, WILLIAM (BLW), died 11 Sep 1838, Staunton, VA; md 27 Jun 1809 Nancy Rankin (P),

DUDLEY (continued) Hagerstown, MD. Her LNR P.O. Churchville, Augusta Co, VA, 1871

DUERSON, JOHN F. (P, BLW), died 18 Jun 1899, Spotsylvania Co, VA, LNR P.O. Brokenburg, Spotsylvania Co, VA, 1878; md 1 Oct 1816 Nancy B. Holladay, Spotsylvania Co, VA

DUERSON, THOMAS applied for a pension

DUFFER, CHARLES S. (BLW), died 28 Feb 1860 or 28 Mar 1870; md (1) Sicely ----, (2) 28 Feb 1849 Elizabeth P. (----) Hannah (P), Graysville, IN. Her LNR Graysville, Sullivan Co, IN, 1878

DUFFLER, WILLIAM W. (P, BLW), died 29 Apr 1872, Jefferson Co, IL; md (1) Rebecca Hawkins, (2) 28 Jul 1863 Nancy M. (----) Shaner (P), Dodds, IL. She died c1888, LNR Dodds, Jefferson Co, IL, 1879

DUFFEY, JOHN whose widow Catherine applied for a pension

DUGGAN, WILLIAM (BLW) whose widow was Jane

DUGGER, HENRY (P, BLW), LNR P.O. Pulaski, Giles Co, TN, 1871; md 12 Aug 1821/22 Ann Eliza Clayton, Brunwick Co, VA

DUGLESS, LEVI (BLW)

DUKE, ARCHIBALD B. whose widow Sarah P. applied for a pension

DUKE, COSBY (BLW), died 17 Feb 1853, Hanover Co, VA; md (1) Elizabeth Mallory, (2) 14 Jun 1848 Martha Martin (P), Hanover Co, VA. She died c1882, LNR P.O. Rockville, Hanover Co, VA, 1879

DUKE, THOMAS (P, BLW), LNR P.O. Richmond, Henrico Co, VA, 1871; md 1826 Lucinda Shepherd, Henrico Co, VA

DULIN, JOHN (BLW)

DULIN, JOHN (BLW) whose widow was Sally

DULIN, JOHN (BLW), whose widow was Rebecca

DULIN, SMITH (P, BLW), died 8 Dec 1879, Webster City, IA; md (1) Frances ----, (2) 8 Jun 1863 Anna Maria (Woodard) Fisher (P), Webster City, IA. She died 27 Jul 1896, Homer, Hamilton Co, IA

DULIN, WILLIAM (BLW)

DULIN, WILLIAM whose widow Priscilla L. applied for a pension

DULTY/DULTZ, MICHAEL (P, BLW), died 15 Oct 1889, LNR Janesville, OH, 1881; md 4 Oct 1821 Sarah B. Scott, Putnam, Muskingum Co, OH

DUNAVANT, ABRAHAM (BLW), died 11 Jan 1867, Prince Edward Co, VA; md 25 Dec 1810 Nancy Dunavant (P), Prince Edward Co, VA. Her LNR Prince Edward Co, VA, 1872

DUNAVENT, JOHN (P, BLW), died 20 May 1876, LNR Ulysses, Butter Co, NE, 1875; md 1 Sep 1819 Jane Ellis, Shelby Co, KY

DUNAWAY, DRURY (P, BLW), died 10 Sep 1878, Paducah, McCracken Co, KY; md 1840 Mary Dunaway, Davidson Co, TN

DUNAWAY, JOSEPH applied for a pension

DUNBAR, WILLIAM died 1819/ 20, Mathews Co, VA; md Mar 1814 Nancy Dunston (P), Gloucester Co, VA. She died 2 Mar 1884, Mathews Co, VA, LNR P.O. Mathews Courthouse, Mathews Co, VA, 1879

DUNCAN, ABNER (BLW), died 2 Mar 1869, Cany Hollow, Lee Co, VA; md 19 Apr 1837 Mary Fulton (P), Abingdon, Washington Co, VA. She died c1888, LNR Cany Hollow, Lee Co, VA, 1878

DUNCAN, ABSALOM (BLW), died 31 Jul 1849, Staunton, IL; md 26 Dec 1816 Elizabeth Duncan (P),. Lincoln Co, NC. Her LNr Hornsby, Macoupin Co, IL, 1878

DUNCAN, CARY (BLW), died 10 Jun 1852, Buckingham Co, VA; md Fall 1815 Lucy Landrum (P), Buckingham Co, VA. Her LNR P.O. Roanoke, Lewis Co, WV, 1878

DUNCAN, CHARLES (BLW)

DUNCAN, DILLARD (BLW), died 30 Dec 1862, Logan Co, KY; md 2 Feb 1826 Elizabeth B. McCreary (P), Butler Co, KY. Her LNR Logan Co, KY, 1879

DUNCAN, GEORGE A. (BLW), died 6 Jul 1866, Conyersville, TN; md 10 Jul 1838 Mary Poe (P), Wilson Co, TN. She died 23 Aug 1883, Conyersville, Henry Co, TN

DUNCAN, GREENBURY/ GREENBERRY or DUNKIN, BERRY (BLW), died 12 May 1860, Carroll Co, VA; md 1809 Nancy Philips (P), Grayson Co, VA. She died 19 Feb 1882, LNR P.O. Dug Spur, Carroll Co, VA, 1878

DUNCAN, HENRY (P, BLW), LNR P.O. Normandy, St. Louis Co, MO, 1872; md 9 Jan 1843 America Ann Pearson, St. Louis Co, MO

DUNCAN, RICHARD C. (P, BLW), LNR P.O. Russellville, Logan Co, KY, 1871; md 4 Jun 1829 Mary Gilbert, Logan Co, KY

DUNCAN, WESLEY L. (P, BLW), died 30 Jun 1886, Bedford Co, VA; md (1) Sally W. Camden, (2) 13 Sep 1872 Susan Ramsey (P), Bedford Co, VA. She died 27 May 1914 Lynchburg, VA, LNR P.O. Liberty, Bedford Co, VA, 1886

DUNCAN, WILLIAM (P, BLW), LNR P.O. Fosterville, Ruther-

DUNCAN (continued)
ford Co, TN, 1871

DUNCANSON, ROBERT (P, BLW), died 19 Oct or Nov 1876, Nottoway Co, VA, LNR P.O. Blacks and Whites, Nottoway Co, VA, 1871; md 21 Dec 1838?. She died 1859

DUNDORE, ELIJAH (BLW), died 27 May 1860, Rockingham Co, VA; md 16 Jun 1834 Nancy Grove (P), Rockingham Co, VA. Her LNR P.O. Harrisonburg, Rockingham Co, VA, 1879

DUNFIELD, JOHN (BLW), died 29 Nov 1862, Ironton, Lawrence Co, OH; md 30 Apr 1810 Learma/Leanner Davis (P), Rockbridge Co, VA. Her LNR Ironton, Lawrence Co, OH, 1871

DUNFORD, PHILIP T. (P, BLW), LNR Richmond, Henrico Co, VA, 1871

DUNHAM, BENJAMIN A. (BLW), died 1 May 1839 Berkeley Co, VA; md 25 Apr 1813 Elizabeth Manor (P), Berkeley Co, VA. Her LNR Glengary, Berkeley Co, WV, 1871

ROLL NO. 29

DUNLAP, JAMES (BLW), whose former widow Hanay applied for a pension. Hannah married (2) Barton D. Hawley and received a BLW for his service. Her papers are in the folder of her second husband, also a War of 1812 soldier

DUNLAP, JAMES (P, BLW), LNR P.O. Milton Station, Mills Co, IA, after 1855; md (1) 5 Aug 1824 Ann Ligget, Brevard, Howard Co, MO; md (2) 5 Apr 1835 Rachel McJemeson, Bath Co, VA

DUNLAVEY, ROBERT W. whose widow Mary A. applied for a pension

DUNN, EDMUND (P, BLW), died 18 Jul 1871, Elkville, Wilkes Co, NC; md 1864 Sarah Jane Lippford, Wilkes Co, NC

DUNN, FONTAINE D. (BLW), died 1 Apr 1870, Albemarle Co, VA; md (1) Nancy Vice, (2) 7 Oct 1852 Mary F. McAlister (P), Albemarle Co, VA. She died 9 Jul 1894, Doylesville, VA, LNR P.O. Mechum's River, Albemarle Co, VA, 1879

DUNN, JAMES (BLW), died 3 Feb 1858, Pike Co, MO; md 19 Jul 1819 Nancy Norcutt (P), Amherst Co, VA. She died 1 or 7 Oct 1880, New Hartford, MO, LNR Middletown, Montgomery Co, MO, 1878

DUNN, JOHN (P, BLW), died before 23 May 1887, LNR Louisa Co, VA, 1880

DUNN, JOHN (BLW), died 22 Oct 1848, Albemarle Co, VA; md (1) Susan Maupin, (2) 7 Nov 1822 Elizabeth Johnson (P), Albemarle Co, VA. Her LNR P.O. Boonsville, Albemarle Co, VA, 1878

DUNN, MATHEW (BLW), died 13 Dec 1851, Pittsylvania Co, VA; md (1) Betsey Jackson, (2) 3 Feb 1844 Ailcy Johnson (P), Pittsylvania Co, VA. She died 4 Apr 1885, Whitmell, Pittsylvania Co, VA, LNR Pleasant Gap, Pittsylvania Co, VA, 1878

DUNN, THOMAS (P, BLW), died 1 Jan 1874, Monongalia Co, WV; md 5 Apr 1810 Temperance Pierpoint (P), Monongalia Co, VA. Her LNR P.O. Easton, Monongalia Co, WV, 1874

DUNNAVANT/DUNAVANT, HEZEKIAH (BLW), died 8 Aug 1858, Spotsylvania Co, VA; md (1) Mary Breeden, (2) 8 Mar 1854 Jane Bowling (P), Spotsylvania Co, VA. Her LNR

DUNNAVANT (continued)
Baltimore Co, MD, 1880
DUNNINGTON, RICHARD (P, BLW), LNR Malta, Morgan Co, OH, 1871; md 29 Feb 1844 Alsadana Stibbon, Morgan Co, WV
DUNSMORE, JOSEPH (BLW), died 8 Mar 1856, Monroe Co, VA; md (1) Jane Erskine, (2) 30 Aug 1836 Letitia M. Love (P), Monroe Co, VA. She died 25 Apr 1879, Wolf Creek, Monroe Co, WV
DUPREE, LITTLETON (BLW), died 20 Jul 1852, Greensville Co, VA; md 28 Sep 1848 Sarah B. Dunn (P), Northampton Co, TN. Her LNR Hicksford, Greensville Co, VA, 1878
DURELL/DARELL, BENJAMIN (P, BLW), LNR P.O. Drakes Branch, Charlotte Co, VA, 1871
DURHAM, DAVID (P, BLW), LNR P.O. Charlottesville, Albemarle Co, VA, 1871; md Mary James Burriss, Albemarle Co, VA
DURHAM, ISAAC (BLW), whose former widow Rebecca (----) Durham married (2) James Rose, a Revolutionary War veteran and received a BLW for his service. James Rose's RW pension file is #W27533
DURRETT, ROBERT D. (P, BLW), died 3 Mar 1882, Albemarle Co, VA; md (1) Mary D. Wood, (2) Martha H. Polk, (3) 24 Jul 1855 Eliza M. (----) Terrell (P), Albemarle, Albemarle Co, VA. She died c1890, LNR P.O. Earleysville, Albemarle Co, VA, 1887
DUST, JOHN E. applied for a pension
DUTTON, EDMOND (P, BLW), died 28 Dec 1882, Basham's Gap, Morgan Co, AL, LNR Lawrence Co, AL, 1871; md 11 Jul 1821 Margaret B. Ross,

DUTTON (continued)
Limestone Co, AL
DUTTON, SAMUEL (P, BLW), died 31 Dec 1874, Anson Co, NC; md 4 Dec 1822 Betsey/ Elizabeth R. Threadgill (P), Anson Co, NC. Her LNR Wadesboro, Anson Co, NC, 1878
DUVALL, GEORGE T. (P, BLW), LNR Weston, Lewis Co, WV, 1871; md 15 Sep 1811 Polly Godfrey, Harrison Co, VA
DYE, BENJAMIN (BLW), died 28 Dec 1882, Dallas Co, TX; md 1816 Sarah Crazier (P), Wood Co, VA. She died 24 May 1879, Dallas Co, TX, LNR P.O. Dallas, Dallas Co, TX, 1879
DYE, DENNIS (BLW), died 20 Jun 1866, Webbs Mills, Ritchie Co, WV; md 25 Dec 1823 Anna Webb (P), Webbs Mills, Ritchie Co, VA. She died c1888, LNR P.O. Smithville, Ritchie Co, WV, 1878
DYER, BENJAMIN (BLW), died 12 Jul 1823, Henry Co, VA; md Jul 1801 Mary Gravely (P), Henry Co, VA. Her LNR Dyers Store, Henry Co, VA, 1871
DYER, DAVID (BLW), died 8 Oct 1844, Lincoln Co, MO; md 8 Mar 1810 Nancy R. Salmon (P), Henry Co, VA. She died 1 Feb 1890, LNR Lincoln Co, MO, 1871
DYER, FRANCIS (P, BLW), LNR P.O. Ashland, Boyd Co, KY, 1871; md 22 May 1821 Jemima Robbins, Greenup Co, KY
DYER, ISHAM (BLW), died 10 Jan 1862, Nashville, TN; md 2 May 1810 Harriet Decker (P), NC. She died Oct 1884, LNR Washington, DC, 1871
DYER, JACOB (P, BLW), died 29 Apr 1874, Loda, IL; md 8 Mar 1819 Delilah Harrass (P), Hampshire Co, VA. She died c1883, LNR Parsons, Labette

DYER (continued)
Co, KS, 1879

DYER, MATHEW B. (BLW), died 21 Jul 1837, Fayette Co, TN; md (1) Ann W. Watkins, (2) 19 Aug 1824 Elizabeth Wersham (P), Dinwiddie Co, VA. Her LNR La Grange, Fayette Co, TN, 1879

DYER, WILLIAM H. (BLW), died 20 Jan 1862, St. Louis, MO; md 17 Feb 1814 Margaret Brydie (P), Richmond, VA. Her LNR St. Louis, St. Louis Co, MO, 1879

DYKE, JAMES (BLW), died 20 Dec 1853, Essex Co, VA; md 29 Nov 1813 Elizabeth Hundley (P), Essex Co, VA. Her LNR P.O. Montague, Essex Co, VA, 1871

DYSON, MANARD/MANOR/MANAN (P, BLW), died 19 Feb 1881, Point Eastern, Caroline Co, VA; md 28 Oct 1840 Agnes Long Demare (P), Richmond, Henrico Co, VA. Her LNR P.O. Point Eastern, Caroline Co, VA, 1881

DYSON, WILLIAM (BLW), died 18 Dec 1836, Chesterfield Co, VA; md 14 Aug 1817 Martha C. Howlett (P), Chesterfield Co, VA. Her LRN Petersburg, Dinwiddie Co, VA, 1878

EACHES, JOSEPH (BLW)

EADES, JOHN (P, BLW), USA, LNR P.O. Columbia, Fluvanna Co, VA, 1871; md but wife's name not given

EADES, THOMAS (P, BLW), LNR P.O. Kent Store, Fluvanna Co, VA, 1871; md Nov 1807 Catharine A. Parish, Goochland Co, VA

EADS, GEORGE W. applied for a pension

EAKLE, JOHN (P, BLW), died 23 Mar 1883, Wilsonville, VA, LNR Bath Co, VA, 1871; md 25 Sep 1825 Sarah Carpenter, Bath Co, VA

EANES, ISHAM (BLW), died 10 May 1857, Petersburg, VA; md 27 Apr 1826 Eliza Wilson (P), Chesterfield Co, VA. She died before 21 Feb 1884, LNR Petersburg, Dinwiddie Co, VA, 1878

EAREL, JAMES (BLW), died 6 Oct 1846 Columbus, Adams Co, IL; md 9 Feb 1826 Margaret Given (P), Nicholas Co, VA. She died 22 Dec 1885, Camp Point, Adams Co, IL

EAREY, JOHN (BLW), KY militia, died 14 Feb 1833, Greenbrier Co, VA; md 3 Dec 1818 Hannah Holcombe (P), Greenbrier Co, VA. She died c1890 Greenbrier Co, WV, LNR Lewisburg, Greenbrier Co, WV, 1878

EARLY, JACOB applied for a pension

EARLY, JOHN whose widow Phebe applied for a pension

EARSOM/EARSON, JACOB (BLW), died 17 Nov 1860, Carroll Co, IN; md 17 Oct 1831 Lucinda Hirschman/Tobridge (P), Oldtown, Grayson Co, VA. Her LNR Idaville, White Co, IN, 1885

EASLEY, HENRY (P, BLW), died 1 Feb 1878, Richmond, VA, LNR Richmond, Henrico Co, VA, 1871

EASLEY, JOHN S. (BLW), died 13 Nov 1869, Fayette Co, WV; md 8 Nov 1821 Agnes C. White (P), Pittsylvania Co, VA. She died 25 Jul 1891, LNR Cotton Hill, WV, 1879

EASTER, JOEL whose widow Lucy applied for a pension

EASTON, DAVID (BLW), NY militia, died 16 May 1863, Glen Easton, VA; md 22 Aug 1828 Mary T. White (P), Pittsburgh, Allegheny Co, PA. She died before 21 May 1887, LNR Glen Easton, Marshall Co, WV, 1878

132

EASTWOOD, JESSE, died 27 Aug 1837, Norfolk Co, VA; md 28 Feb 1825 Patience Spring (P), Portsmouth, VA. She died 26 Feb 1882, Norfolk Co, VA, LNR Portsmouth, Norfolk Co, VA, 1878

EASTWOOD, WILLIAM (BLW), died 20 May 1868, Gloucester Co, VA; md 16 Jan 1827 Susan (Jarvis) Hall (P), Gloucester Co, VA. She died before 28 Jul 1885, LNR P.O. Gloucester Courthouse, Gloucester Co, VA, 1879

EATON, ENOCH applied for a pension

EBERLY/EVERLY, GEORGE (P, BLW), LNR Strasburg, Shenandoah Co, VA, 1871

EBERLY, JACOB (BLW), died 25 Feb 1854, Shenandoah Co, VA; md (1) Leah Pitman, (2) 20 Dec 1839 Elizabeth Hockman (P), Shenandoah Co, VA. She died 21 Jun 1890, LNR P.O. Mt. Olive, Shenandoah Co, VA, 1878

ECHARD, PHILIP (BLW), USA, died 14 Feb 1856, Pendleton Co, VA; md 25 Dec 1820 Susannah Simmons (P), South Fork, Pendleton Co, VA. She died 12 Dec 1886, Sugar Grove, Pendleton Co, WV

ECHOLS, PEREGRINE (BLW), died 1 Mar 1870, New Haven, VA; md 18 Oct 1825 Sarah Carter (P), Pittsylvania Co, VA. She died 15 Feb 1879, Bedford Springs, Campbell Co, VA, LNR New London, Campbell Co, VA, 1878

ECKARD, ABRAHAM (P, BLW), LNR P.O. Franklin, Pendleton Co, WV, 1871; md 21 Dec 1814 Sally Ann Faint, Pendleton Co, VA

ECKARD/AKERT/ACRED/ACKERT, JOHN (P, BLW), died c1882/3, LNR P.O. Point Pleasant, Mason Co, WV,

ECKARD (continued) 1871; md 27 Nov 1818 Elizabeth Stewart, Mason Co, VA

ECKHARD/ACHARD/ECHARD, JOHN applied for a pension

ECKLES, CLEMENT (P, BLW), LNR P.O. Reidsville, Tattnall Co, GA, 1875; md Apr 1828 Mary Ann Warner, Macon, GA

ECLEBERY, VALENTINE (BLW), PA militia, died 12 Jun 1869, Wetzel Co, WV; md 10 Jun 1810 Alley Cumberledge (P), Greene Co, PA. Her LNR Wetzel Co, WV, 1871

EDDY, SAMUEL (P, BLW), LNR P.O. Peterstown, Monroe Co, WV, 1871; md 23 Mr 1814 Delilah Evans, Winchester, VA

EDENTON/ETHERTON, JAMES (BLW), died 13 Jul 1818, Spotsylvania Co, VA; md 13 Dec 1810 Nancy M. Crawford (P), Spotsylvania Co, VA. She died 4 Aug 1876, LNR Spotsylvania, Spotsylvania Co, VA, 1871

EDGAR, JAMES (BLW), died 15 Oct 1836, Florence, AL, md 19 Sep 1822 Margaret Thornton (P), Mason Co, KY. She died 30 Aug 1883, Bainbridge, Putnam Co, IN

EDGAR, JESSE whose widow Dorcus applied for a pension

EDGE, EDWARD (P, BLW), died c20 Sep 1877; md (1) Delany Rickets, (2) 5 Aug 1877 Elizabeth Braswell (P). She died 5 Apr 1912, LNR DeKalb Co, TN, 1878

EDGINGTON, THOMAS (BLW), whose widow was Sarah A.

EDIE, DAVID (BLW), died 15 Sep 1867, Hancock Co, WV; md 1 Nov 1814 Sarah Kritzer (P), Beaver Co, PA. Her LNR New Cumberland, Hancock Co, WV, 1871

EDINGS, HENRY (P, BLW), LNR

EDINGS (continued)
P.O. Coalburg, Kanawha Co, WV, 1871. Not married.

EDMONDS, ESOM (P, BLW), died 6 Sep 1878, Brownsville, Washington Co, MD; md 3 Jun 1819 Priscilla Hyatt (P), Charlestown, Jefferson Co, VA. Her LNR Martinsburg, Berkeley Co, WV, 1878

EDMONDS, NATHAN (P, BLW), LNR Bakersville, Washington Co, MD, 1871

EDMONDS, THOMAS (BLW), died 3 Apr 1854, Maysville, KY; md 8 Jan 1820 Ann Leftridge/Leftwich (P), Laurence Co, OH. Her LNR Maysville, Mason Co, KY, 1878

EDMONDS, WILLIAM (P, BLW), died 15 Sep 1872, Marshall Co, MS; md 8 Nov 1825 Lucinda Westmoreland (P), York District, SC. She died Jul 1884, Waterford, Marshall Co, MS

EDMONDSON, RICHARD (BLW), died 6 Nov 1859, Halifax Co, VA; md 15 May 1823 Susan H. Chastain (P), Halifax Co, VA. She died c1891, LNR P.O. Halifax Courthouse, Halifax Co, VA, 1878

EDMONDSON, WILLIAM (BLW), died 13 Oct 1866, Oak Point, IA; md 18 Aug 1831 Mary G. McCutchan (P), Augusta Co, VA. She died 27 Jan 1886, Milton, Van Buren Co, IA, LNR Oak Point, Van Buren Co, IA, 1878

EDMONSON, DAVID whose widow Hannah applied for a pension

EDMONSON, ROBERT S. (BLW)

EDMUNDS, PEYTON (P, BLW), LNR P.O. Gholonsville, Brunswick Co, VA, 1872

ROLL NO. 30

EDWARDS, AMOS (BLW), died 3 Nov 1864, Portsmouth, VA; md

EDWARDS (continued)
10 may 1817 Mary Ann Waughop (P), Portsmouth, VA. She died 8 Nov 1887, Portsmouth, Norfolk Co, VA

EDWARDS, ARTHUR (BLW), died 13 Nov 1829, Wirt Co, VA; md 18 Jan 1810 Mary Lewis (P), Mason Co, VA. Her LNR Kanawha Station, Wood Co, WV, 1877

EDWARDS, BARNETT (BLW), died 29 Dec 1831, Monroe Co, VA; md Sep 1818 Lucy Beverly Robinson (P), Amherst Co, VA. She died before 25 May 1883, LNR Sinks Grove, Monroe Co, WV, 1879

EDWARDS, BRICE (P, BLW), LNR Hallsville, Boone Co, MO, 1871; md 6 Mar 18-- Ann Dickinson, Albemarle Co, VA

EDWARDS, BRICE (BLW), died 28 Jan 1860, Patrick Co, VA; md Jane Rakes (P). Her LNR Edwards, Patrick Co, VA, 1871

EDWARDS, EDWARD (BLW), died 7 Jun 1863, Roane Co, TN; md (1) Mary Howlett, (2) 12 Sep 1848 Mary Ann McBriant (P), Bradley Co, TN. She died before 5 Jan 1883, LNR P.O. Coal Creek, Anderson Co, TN, 1878

EDWARDS, ENOCH applied for a pension

EDWARDS, GEORGE (P, BLW), LNR P.O. Roaring Run, Botetourt Co, VA, 1871. Not married.

EDWARDS, JACK/JACOB applied for a pension

EDWARDS, JAMES (BLW), died 31 Dec 1858, Richmond, VA; md 24 May 1826 Sophia Thomas (P), Richmond, VA. She died 28 Dec 1892, Richmond, VA

EDWARDS, JOHN (P, BLW), died 26 Nov 1873, Carroll Co, VA; md 13 Jun 1813 or 11 Apr 1816 Mary Hagne (P), Grayson

134

EDWARDS (continued)
Co, VA. She died 25 Mar 1881, LNR P.O. Hillsville, Carroll Co, VA, 1878

EDWARDS, JOHN (P, BLW), died 5 Jan 1880, Carroll Co, VA; md (1) Nancy Manskin, (2) 5 Feb 1840 or 1842 Roan King (P), Mt. Airy, Surry Co, NC. She died c1881, LNR St. Paul, Carroll Co, Va, 1880

EDWARDS, JOHN (BLW), died 26 Sep 1858, Southampton Co, VA; md Salley Joyner (P), Southampton Co, VA. She died c1889, LNR P.O. Berlin, Southampton Co, VA, 1878

EDWARDS, JOHN S. (BLW), died 5 Jun 1857, Brownsville, PA; md 25 Nov 1816 Catherine Cline (P), Leesburg, Loudoun Co, VA. She died before 12 May 1883, LNR Red Oak, Montgomery Co, VA, 1873

EDWARDS, RICHARD applied for a pension

EDWARDS, THOMAS (P, BLW), died 28 May 1879, Templeman Cross Roads, Westmoreland Co, VA; md (1) Elizabeth S. Templeman, (2) 2 Dec 1858 Virginia McKenny (P). She died 1 Apr 1892, LNR P.O. Montross, Westmoreland Co, VA, 1879

EDWARDS, THOMAS (P, BLW), LNR P.O. New Upton, Gloucester Co, VA, 1872

EDWARDS, THOMAS (BLW), whose widow was Eleanore

EDWARDS, THOMAS F. (BLW), whose widow Agness C. received a pension

EDWARDS, THOMAS G. (BLW) whose widow Sophia received a pension

EDWARDS, THORNTON whose widow Elizabeth applied for a pension

EDWARDS, WILLIAM (P, BLW), died Mar 1891, LNR P.O. Halifax Courthouse, Halifax Co,

EDWARDS (continued)
VA, 1871; md 25 Dec 1821 Rhoda R. Miller, Halifax Co, VA

EDWARDS, WILLIAM and his widow Mary both applied for a pension

EDWARDS, WILLIAM (BLW), died 28 Apr 1863, Caroline Co, VA; md (1) Sarah Rose, (2) 3 Dec 1841 Mary E. Collis (P), Spotsylvania Co, VA. She died 23 Jan 1901, LNR P.O. Port Toyal, Caroline Co, VA, 1878

EDWARDS, WILLIAM (BLW), died Nov 1870, Greene Co, VA; md 1857 Sarah Lamb (P), Stanardsville, VA. She died 20 Apr 1905, LNR P.O. Ruckersville, Greene Co, VA, 1878

EELLS, SAMUEL (P, BLW), NY militia, died 21 Jul 1873, Amherst Co, VA; md (1) Nancy B. Webster, (2) 21 May 1844 Sarah B. Leal (P), Delhi, Delaware Co, NY. She died before 4 Apr 1893, LNR P.O. Catskill, Greene Co, NY, 1881

EFFINGER, JOHN F. (BLW), died 6 Feb 1840, Harrisonburg, VA; md 18 Apr 1811 Mary Hite (P), Harrisonburg, VA. She died 18 Dec 1892, LNR Harrisonburg, Rockingham Co, VA, 1872

EGGLESTON, JOHN A. whose widow Lucinda applied for a pension

EGGLESTON, RICHARD B. whose widow Alvira applied for a pension

EGGLESTON, WILLIAM H. (BLW), died 4 Dec 1839, Wilkinson Co, MS; md 31 Oct 1832 Anne L. Poindexter (P), Woodville, Wilkinson Co, MS. Her LNR Amite Co, MS, 1880

EGGLETON, THOMAS (BLW), died 12 Dec 1849, Henry Co, VA; md 6 Sep 1826 Dorothy Pace (P), Henry Co, VA. Her LNR P.O. Martinsville, Henry

EGGLETON (continued)
Co, VA, 1882

EGLETON/EGGLETON,
GEORGE (BLW), died 22 Aug
1857 Henry Co, VA; md 25 Dec
1817 Nancy (----) Bouldin (P),
Henry Co, VA. She died 18
Aug 1885, Oak Hill, KS, LNR
Oak Hill, Clay Co, KS, 1881

EIKLEBERRY/EICHELBERRY,
ABRAHAM (P, BLW), PA
militia, died 19 Jan 1884; md
(1) Hannah Dawson, (2) 23 Oct
1871 Margaret (Hickman) Henthorn (P), Antioch, Monroe Co,
OH. She died c1895, LNR
Padens Valley, Wetzel Co,
WV, 1884

EKISS, HENRY M. (P, BLW),
died 30 Jun 1874, Montgomery
Co, VA; md 25 Jun 1807 Cath-
arine Kessler (P), Botetourt
Co, VA. Her LNR P.O. Mc-
Donalds Mill, Montgomery Co,
VA, 1874

ELAM, ANDERSON S. (P, BLW),
died 25 Sep 1878, Cleveland
Co, NC; md 10 Feb 1814
Lette/Latisha Weatherford
(P), Charlotte Co, VA. Her
LNR Shelby, Cleveland Co,
NC, 1879

ELAM, JOEL (P, BLW), LNR P.
O. Prospect Depot, Prince Edward Co, VA, 1872

ELAM, ROLAND (P, BLW), died
28 Mar 1878, Bent Creek, Appomattox Co, VA; md 23 Dec
1824 Nancy Dodson (P),
Amelia Co, VA. She died
c1890, LNR Bent Creek, Appomattox Co, VA, 1878

ELAM, THOMAS (P, BLW), died
15 Sep 1878, Milan, TN; md
(1) Martha Gregory, (2) 23 Apr
1863 Sarah J. Alden (P), Gibson Co, TN. She died before 13
Feb 1892, LNR Milan, Gibson
Co, TN, 1879

ELDER, JOHN S. (P, BLW), died
6 Jan 1880; md (1) Eliza A.
Jones, (2) 14 Nov 1861 Martha

ELDER (continued)
Johnson (P), Campbell Co, VA.
She died 23 Oct 1883,
Rustburg, Campbell Co, VA

ELDER, OLIVER (BLW), died 18
Jul 1867, Campbell Co, VA;
md 28 Mar 1864 Lidia Grishaw
(P), Campbell Co, VA. She
died 23 Jun 1893, Concord
Depot, Campbell Co, VA

ELDRIDGE, JOHN J. (BLW),
died 2 Jan 1855, Sussex Co,
VA; md (1) Agnes Lewis, (2)
12 Feb 1834 Mary S. Peebles
(P), Prince George Co, VA.
She died 17 Jan 1893, LNR
Petersburg, Dinwiddie Co, VA,
1878

ELEY, EXUM (BLW), died 12
Nov 1845, Isle of Wight Co,
VA; md (1) Polly Moody, (2)
13 or 14 Apr 1832 Martha (---)
Marshall (P), Isle of Wight
Co, VA. Her LNR Leesburg,
Loudoun Co, VA, 1878

ELGIN, GUSTAVUS (BLW), died
21 Jul 1860, Loudoun Co, VA;
md 11 Nov 1830 Elizabeth
Cross (P), Leesburg, VA. She
died 12 Aug 1887, Loudoun Co,
VA, LNR Leesburg, Loudoun
Co, VA, 1878

ELGIN, ROBERT (BLW)

ELKINS, JOHN H. (BLW) applied
for a pension

ELLINGTON, WILLIAM F. (P,
BLW), LNR P.O. Rices Depot,
Prince Edward Co, Va, 1871

ELLIOT, HENSON applied for a
pension

ELLIOT, JABEZ (BLW), died 14
Dec 1841, Ritchie Co, VA; md
9 Dec 1807 Elizabeth Wigner
(P), Harrison Co, VA. Her LNR
P.O. Webbs Mills, Ritchie Co,
WV, 1872

ELLIOTT, JOEL (P, BLW), LNR
Kiddville, Clark Co, KY, 1871;
md 6 Mar 1816 Margaret Fizen, Botetourt Co, VA

ELLIOTT, JOHN L., alias
LOWE, ISAAC, applied for a

ELLIOTT (continued)
pension

ELLIOTT, PHILIP (BLW), died 8 Aug 1865, Pittsylvania Co, VA; md 9 Jan 1815 Elizabeth W. Harness (P), Pittsylvania Co, VA. Her LNR P.O. Pittsylvania Courthouse, Pittsylvania Co, VA, 1871

ELLIOT, WILLIAM (BLW), died 20 Aug 1847, Pittsylvania Co, VA; md Mar 1805 Nancy Shaw (P), Rockingham Co, VA. She died before 24 Oct 1887, LNR P.O. Pittsylvania Courthouse, Pittsylvania Co, VA, 1871

ELLIOTT, WILLIS D. (BLW), died 12 Jan 1861, Campbell co, VA; md 26 Apr 1819 Martha Russell (P), Campbell Co, VA. Her LNR Campbell Courthouse, Campbell Co, VA, 1878

ELLIS, JAMES A. (BWL), died 24 Dec 1862, Gallatin Co, KY; md (1) Martha Rountree, (2) 13 Oct 1841 Maria (----) Bales (P), Gallatin Co, KY. Her LNR P.O. Warsaw. Gallatin Co, KY, 1879

ELLIS, JOHN (BLW)

ELLIS, JOHN (BLW)

ELLIS, JOHN S. (BLW) whose widow was Eliza

ELLIS, ROBERT (BLW) whose widow was Margaret W.

ELLIS, ROBERT (BLW) whose widow was Mary

ELLIS, THOMAS (P, BLW), LNR P.O. Hendricks Store, Bedford Co, VA, 1871; md 20 Jan 1820 Susan Meadows, Franklin Co, VA

ELLIS, WILLIAM (P, BLW), LNR Portsmouth, Norfolk Co, VA, 1871; md (1) Rebecca Denby, (2) 1822 Ritter Ann Mason

ELLIS, WILLIAM (BLW), died 18 Feb 1855, Lunenburg Co, VA; md 24 Jan 1809 Nancy Shuffield (P), Nottoway Co, VA. She died 17 Nov 1873,

ELLIS (continued)
LNR Lunenburg Co, VA, 1872

ELLISON, WILLIAM (P, BLW), LNR P.O. Braxton Courthouse, Braxton Co, WV, 1871; md 1812 Patsey Perdue, Franklin Co, VA. She died before Apr 1871

ELMORE, JAMES (P, BLW), LNR P.O. Barrow Store, Brunswick Co, VA, 1878

ELMORE, WILLIAM whose widow Frances applied for a pension

ELLMORE, JOHN (BLW), died 4 Apr 1871, Loucoun Co, VA; md 14 Apr 1833 Elizabeth Ann Rose (P), Loudoun Co, VA. She died 14 Dec 1896, LNR Farmwell Station, Loudoun Co, VA, 1878

EMANUEL, THORNTON (BLW), died 25 Nov 1854, Campbell Co, VA; md 26 Jan 1814 Elizabeth Powers (P), Campbell Co, VA. Her LNR P.O. Arnoldton, Campbell Co, VA, 1872

EMBREE, DANIEL (P, BLW), LNR P.O. Stafford Courthouse, Stafford Co, VA, 1871

EMBREY, ELI (P, BLW), whose wife Kitty also received a pension

EMBREY, THOMAS (P, BLW), LNR P.O. Mount Perry, Perry Co, OH, 1871; md 29 Nov 1831 Judah Perry, Culpeper Co, VA

EMBREY, WILLIAM (BLW), died 26 Jan 1854, Fauquier Co, VA; md Oct 1825 Elizabeth Brown (P), Fauquier Co, VA. Her LNR P.O. Rappahannock, Fauquier Co, VA, 1878

EMBRY, LEWIS applied for a pension

EMERSON, HARRISON (P, BLW), LNR West End, Fairfax Co, VA, 1876; md 6 Jan 1820 Jane Watson, Alexandria, VA

EMERSON/EMBEROON, JUD-
SON (P, BLW), died 18 May
1873, LNR Aldie, Loudoun Co,
VA, 1871; md 10 May 1812
Elizabeth Perry, Charles Co,
MD. She died before Dec 1871

EMERSON, RICHARD D./B. (P,
BLW), md (1) Catherine Williams, (2) Elizabeth R. Beeson

EMRY, THOMAS whose widow
Judy applied for a pension

ENDALEY/ENDAILY, DAVID (P,
BLW), died 18 Nov 1878, Jefferson Co, TN, LNR P.O.
Dandridge, Jefferson Co, TN,
1871

ENGLAND, EDWARD/JAMES
EDWARD whose widow Sarah
Ann applied for a pension

ENGLAND, GEORGE (BLW),
died 15 Feb 1869, Caroline Co,
VA; md 23 Apr 1827 Martha
Thacker (P), Stafford Co, VA.
Her LNR P.O. Ruther Glen,
Caroline Co, VA, 1878

ENGLAND, HENRY whose widow
Polly applied for a pension

ENGLAND, JOHN (P, BLW),
LNR Atlees Station, Hanover
Co, VA. Never married.

ENGLAND, JOHN whose widow
Polly applied for a pension

ENGLAND, JACOB applied for a
pension

ENGLISH, FRANCIS Y. (BLW),
died 3 Apr 1834 Southampton
Co, VA; md 27 Aug 1822
Phebe Wellons (P), South-
ampton Co, VA. Her LNR P.
O. Berlin, Southampton Co,
VA, 1878

ENGLISH, JAMES applied for a
pension

ENGLISH, JOHN whose widow
Mary applied for a pension

ENGLISH, NATHAN (BLW), died
10 Aug 1823, Southampton Co,
VA; md 3 Jan 1822 Martha
Corbett (P), Southampton Co,
VA. Her LNR P.O. Carrsville,
Isle of Wight Co, VA, 1879

ENNIS, JAMES (P, BLW), died

ENNIS (continued)
22 Dec 1875, Petersburg, VA;;
md 11 Feb 1868 Ann Eliza
Saunders (P), Petersburg, VA.
She died 14 Dec 1901, LNR
Springdale, VA, 1878

ENNIS, WILLIAM whose widow
Sally applied for a pension

ENNIS, WILLIAM (BLW), died
11 Mar 1859, Westmoreland
Co, VA; md (1) Peggy Brian,
(2) 22 Apr 1845 Jane McKinney
(P), Westmoreland Co, VA.
She died before 1 Oct 1889,
LNR P.O. Oldham, West-
moreland Co, VA, 1887

ENOS, GEORGE (BLW), whose
former widow Sarah A. (Enos)
Walden applied for a pension

ENOS, WARNER (P, BLW), LNR
Washington, DC, 1871; md 11
Dec 1841 Elizabeth Slater,
New Kent Co, VA

ENROUGHTY, NATHAN/
NATHANIEL (P, BLW), LNR
P.O. Curls Neck, Henrico Co,
VA, 1879

ENSOR, GEORGE (P, BLW), KY
Militia, LNR P.O. Camargo,
Douglas Co, IL, 1871; md 12
May 1812 Louisa Nelson,
Fauquier Co, VA

ENSOR, STEPHEN (P, BLW),
LNR P.O. Springfield, Wash-
ington Co, KY, 1871; md 19
Sep 1819 Fanny Wright,
Washington Co, KY

ENTLER, JOSEPH (P, BLW),
LNR Shepherdstown, Jefferson
Co, WV, 1873; md Sep 1817
Mary Rickard, Sharpsburg, MD.
She died before May 1873

ENSTMINGER/INCHMINGER,
JOHN (P, BLW), died 6 Dec
1873, Grant Co, IN; md (1)
Sarah Knick, (2) 15 Feb 1859
Martha J. Dixon (P), Buffalo
Forge, Rockbridge Co, VA. Her
LNR Jonesboro, IN, 1878

EPPERD/EPPARD, SAMUEL (P,
BLW), LNR P.O. Goshen
Bridge, Rockbridge Co, VA,

EPPERD (continued)
1873

EPPERLY, JOHN (BLW), died 25 Aug 1858, Floyd Co, VA; md 10 Mar 1814 Nancy Pharis/ Farris (P), Montgomrery Co, VA. She died 21 Jan 1881, LNR P.O. Floyd Courthouse, Floyd Co, VA, 1871

EPPERSON, LITTLEBERRY (BLW), died 1 Oct 1870, Knox Co, KY; md (1) Elizabeth Buys, (2) 31 Jan 1856 Sally Gray (P), Knox Co, KY. She died before 31 Jul 1886, LNR Flat Lick, Knox Co, KY, 1879

EPPS, DANIEL (BLW), died 6 Oct 1865, Halifax Courthouse, VA; md 29 Dec 1824 Nancy Dunn (P), Halifax Co, VA. Her LNR P.O. Halifax Courthouse, Halifax Co, VA, 1878

EPPS, HARTWELL (P, BLW), died 7 Feb 1872 or 1875, Campbell Co, VA; md 16 Apr 1822 Mary P. Jordan (P), Campbell Co, VA. She died before 26 Aug 1892, LNR P.O. Campbell Courthouse, Campbell Co, VA, 1878

EPPS, WILLIAM (BLW), died 12 May 1830, Prince George Co, VA; md 2 Oct 1817 Frances Easley (P), Rutledge, Granger Co, TN. She died 11 Dec 1883, Skaggston, Knox Co, TN, LNR P.O. Beans Station, Grainger Co, TN, 1878

ROLL NO. 31

ERAMBERT, HENRY (BLW), died 22 Mar 1868, Fayetteville, NC; md (1) ---- Cooper, (2) 15 Jul 1863 Eliza Mann (P), Richmond, VA. Her LNR Richmond, Henrico Co, VA, 1878

ERNST, JACOB (P, BLW), died c1878, LNR P.O. Morefield, Clarke Co, OH, 1878

ERSKINE, JAMES P. (P, BLW),

ERSKINE (continued)
died 9 Apr 1881, Quincy, IL; md 8 Jan 1834 Amelia D. Riggs (P), Philadelphia, PA. She died 24 Aug 1885, Quincy, Adams Co, IL

ERSKINE, MARTIN (P, BLW), LNR Philadelphia, PA, 1871; md 23 Feb 1816 Mary Alexander, Providence, RI

ERVINE, EDWARD (P, BLW), LNR P.O. Green Bank, Pocahontas Co, WV, 1871; md 30 Nov 1815 Polly Curry, Pendleton Co, VA

ERVINE/ERWIN, WILLIAM (P, BLW), died c1865, LNR P.O. Head Waters, Highland Co, VA, 1877; md 25 Dec 1817 Frances ----, Rockingham, Rockingham Co, VA

ERWIN, ROBERT whose widow Nancy applied for a pension

ESHON, THOMAS (BLW), died 6 Mar 1868, Northampton Co, VA; md 20 May 1845 Catherine Robins (P), Northampton Co, VA. She died 24 or 25 Mar 1880, Johnsontown, Northampton Co, VA

ESKEW, HENLEY (P, BLW), died 20 Jul 1876, Upshur Co, WV; md (1) Mary Wadkins, (2) 28 Sep 1853 Catharine Fletcher (P), Harrison Co, VA. She died 27 Oct 1890, LNR P.O. Sago, Upshur Co, WV, 1878

ESKRIDGE, RODHAM (BWL), died 10 Dec 1865, Fauquier Co, VA; md (1) Nancy Bridewell, (2) 22 May 1849 Ann Hickerson (P), Stafford Co, VA. She died Spring of 1883, Somerville, Fauquier Co, VA, LNR Stafford Co, VA, 1878

ESTERS/ESTES/EASTER, EPHRAIM (P, BLW), died 21 Apr 1875, Cumberland Co, KY; md 19 May 1843 Sallie (----) Cox (P), Cumberland Co, KY. Her LNR P.O. Burksville, Cumberland Co, KY, 1873

ESTES, ABRAHAM (BLW), died 27 Jun 1864, Dobson, NC; md 5 Mar 1820 Martha Farley (P), Coves, Halifax Co, VA. She died before 16 May 1889, LNR P.O. White Plains, Surry Co, NC, 1888

ESTES, CHRISTOPHER T./F. (BLW), died 1 Feb 1850, Lovingston, VA; md (1) Jane Howard, (2) 2 Jan 1838 Martha J. Morgan (P), Lovingston, VA. She died 15 Jan 1898, LNR Washington, DC, 1894

ESTES, EDWARD (P, BLW), died 3 Oct 1882, Castle Craig, Campbell Co, VA; md 23 Dec 1814 Catharine Hawkins, Bedford Co, VA

ESTES, JOHN C. (BLW), KY militia, died 18 Sep 1869, Edmonton, KY; md 7 Oct 1807 Susanah Butler (P), Culpeper Co, VA. She died 30 Apr 1879, Metcalf Co, KY, LNR P.O. Edmondton, Metcalfe Co, KY, 1880

ESTES, JOHN (P, BLW), died 27 Jul 1881, Marionville, MO, LNR Stone Co, MO, 1881; md 23 Dec 1818 Margaret Jones, Halifax Co, VA

ESTES/ESTIS, JOHN R. (P, BLW), died 30 May 1885, Yellow Springs, TN, LNR P.O. Tazewell, Claiborne Co, TN, 1871; md 25 Nov 1811 Ann Moore, Halifax Co, VA

ESTES, JOHN W. whose widow Nannie W. applied for a pension

ESTES, JOSIAH (BLW), died 17 Sep 1856, Giles Co, TN; md 9 Mar 1814 Elizabeth Chisholm (P), Halifax Co, VA. Her LNR P.O. Pulaski, Giles Co, TN, 1871

ESTES, WILLIAM (BLW), died 9 Apr 1871, Enterprise, MS; md 20 Apr 1820 Susan H. Shelton (P), Pittsylvania Co, VA. She died before 2 May 1884, LNR

ESTES (continued) Enterprise, Clarke Co, MS, 1878

ESTILL, BENJAMIN whose widow Patsey applied for a pension

EUBANK, GEORGE W. whose widow Mary C. applied for a pension

EUBANK, HEZEKIAH (BLW), died 18 Jul 1839, Richmond, VA; md (1) Frances Wilkinson, (2) Elizabeth Claxton, (3) 19 Jun 1824 Nancy Grimes (P), Richmond, VA. She died 28 Jul 1883, Richmond, Henrico Co, VA

EUBANK, JOHN (P-rejected, BLW), died 7 Nov 1872, Albemarle Co, VA; md 6 Nov 1829/30/31 Catharine Norvell (P), Albemarle Co, VA. Her LNR P.O. Fabers, Nelson Co, VA, 1884. John was a substitute for his brother Joseph in the War

EUBANK, JOHNSON whose widow Martha applied for a pension

EUBANK/EUBANKS, JOSEPH (P, BWL), died 20 Jan 1878, Jackson Co, OH; md (1) Catherine ----, (2) 7 Sep 1862 Elizabeth G. Melton (P), Jackson Co, OH. She died 21 Apr 1886, LNR Jackson, Jackson Co, OH, 1878

EUBANK, JOSEPH (BWL), died 22 Jul 1842, Columbia, KY; md 23 Dec 1824 Nancy M. Smith (P), Columbia, KY. She died before 26 Nov 1887, LNR P.O. Columbia, Adair Co, KY, 1881. Joseph's brother Thomas served as his substitute in the War

EUBANK, THOMAS (P, BLW), LNR P.O. Henderson, Rusk Co, TX, 1873; md 7 Mr 1816 Mary Gibson, Bedford Co, VA

EUBANK, WILLIAM (BLW), died 26 Oct 1864, Decatur Co, IN; md 16 Sep 1847 Mary Smothers

EUBANK (continued)
(P), Decatur Co, IN. Her LNR
P.O. Forest Hill, Decatur Co,
IN, 1879

EURIT, SAMUEL (BLW), died 17
Dec 1837 Elk Creek, VA; md 7
Nov 1816 Mary Angling (P),
Elk Creek, Harrison Co, VA.
Her LNR Pecks Run, Upshur
Co, WV, 1878

EVANS, BENJAMIN (BLW), died
15 Mar 1859; md Jun 1811
Sarah Walker (P), Mecklenburg
Co, VA. Her LNR P.O. Lom-
bardy Grove, Mecklenburg Co,
VA, 1871

EVANS/IVINS, DAVID whose widow Polly applied for a pension

EVANS, ELI (P, BLW), LNR P.O
Poplar Plains, Fleming Co,
KY, 1871; md 25 Nov 1852
Mary Armstrong

EVANS, ELIJAH whose widow
Elizabeth applied for a pension

EVANS, FRANCIS (BWL), died 5
Feb 1872, Daviess Co, KY; md
(1) ?, (2) 10 Aug 1842 Margaret
Skinner (P), Oldham Co, KY.
Her LNR P.O. Owensboro,
Daviess Co, KY, 1878

EVANS, HASTON/HASTING
(BLW), died Jan 1864, Logan
Co, VA; md (1) Norway Blair,
(2) 20 Nov 1852 Polly Chaffins
(P), Logan Co, VA. She died 8
Nov 1917, LNR Logan Co,
WV, 1879

EVANS, HENRY applied for a
pension

EVANS, JAMES (P-rejected,
BLW), died 28 Mar 1874,
Raleigh Co, WV; md 20 Oct
1814 Catharine Foster (P),
Monroe Co, VA. Her LNR
Raleigh, Raleigh Co, WV,
1883

EVANS, JAMES whose widow
Nancy applied for a pension

EVANS, JESSE whose widow
Peggy applied for a pension

EVANS, JESSE whose widow

EVANS (continued)
Mary applied for a pension

EVANS, JOHN (BLW), died 31
Jul 1869, Perry Co, OH; md
Jul 1821 Elizabeth Evans (P),
Loudoun Co, VA. She died 22
Jul 1887, LNR New Straits-
ville, Perry Co, OH, 1878

EVANS, JOHN (BLW), died 31
Oct 1867, Monroe Co, OH; md
Nov 1811 Sarah Crupper (P),
Fauquier Co, VA. She died 18
Aug 1881, LNR Ozark Monroe
Co, OH, 1871

EVANS, JOSEPH (P, BLW), died
23 Feb 1874, LNR Delhi,
Delaware Co, OH, 1871; md
Sep 1807 Mary Carpenter, Baltimore, MD. She died before
1871

EVANS, JOSEPH whose widow
Mary applied for a pension

EVANS, LEROY whose widow
Frances applied for a pension

EVANS, LUDWELL (BLW), died
2 Aug 1863/4, Rutherford Co,
TN; md 2 Sep 1813 Agnes W.
THompson (P), Mecklenburg
Co, VA. Her LNR P.O. Mur-
freesboro, Rutherford Co, TN,
1878

EVANS, MEREDITH (P, BLW),
LNR P.O. Bickleys Mills,
Russell Co, VA, 1871; md 2
Sep 1815 Sarah Skeen, Russell
Co, VA

EVANS, POINDEXTER (BLW),
died Jun 1866, Appomattox Co,
VA; md 24 Dec 1847 Polly Ann
Crews (P), Appomattox Co,
VA. She died c1893, LNR Ap-
pomattox Co, VA, 1878

EVANS, ROBERT (BLW), USA,
resided in Virginia and
Washington, DC

EVANS, SAMUEL whose widow
Nancy applied for a pension

EVANS, STERLING C. applied for
a pension

EVANS, TARLTON (BLW), died
6 Jul 1864, Nelson Co, VA; md
Jul/Aug 1811 Susan Hudson

EVANS (continued)
(P). Her LNR P.O. Amherst
Courthouse, Amherst Co, VA,
1873
EVANS, TRAVIS applied for a
pension
EVANS, WASHINGTON (BLW),
died 23 Aug 1853, Cumberland,
MD; md 20/21 Jul 1812 Maria
Maxwell (P), Martinsburg,
Berkeley Co, VA. She died
c1883, Cumberland, Allegany
Co, MD
EVANS, WILLIAM (P, BLW),
LNR P.O. Edmonton, Metcalf
Co, KY, 1871; md 7 Mar 1853
Nancy Rock, Metcalf Co, KY
EVANS, WILLIAM (BLW), died
27 Feb 1862, Greensburg,
Decatur Co, IN; md (1) Cath-
erine Stewart, (2) Ann
McGowan, (3) Jane B. Gowan,
(4) 28 Dec 1838 Ann Becroft
(P), Decatur Co, IN. Her LNR
P.O. Millhousen, Decatur Co,
IN, 1878
EVANS, WILLIAM B. (P, BLW),
died 10 Mar 1873, Union Co,
OH; md 12 Dec 1814 Elizabeth
Hester (P), Jefferso Co, VA.
She died c1875, LNR Rich-
wood, Union Co, OH, 1873
EVERETT, WILLIAM C. applied
for a pension
EVERLEY/EVERLY, JOHN H.
(BLW), died 20 Apr 1857,
Wardensville, VA; md 14 Feb
1819 Eliza B. Crebs (P), Win-
chester, Frederick Co, VA. Her
LNR P.O. Wardensville, Hardy
Co, WV, 1878
EVERLY, JAMES (BLW), died 7
Oct 1862, Marion Co, VA; md
9 Oct 1856 Rhoda (----) Con-
away (P), Fairmont, Marion
Co, VA. She died 23 Jun 1899,
Marion Co, WV, LNR Barrack-
sville, Marion Co, WV, 1887
EVERLY, PHILIP F. (P, BLW),
died 16 Jan 1879, Strasburg,
VA; LNR Strasburg, Shenan-
doah Co, VA, 1871

EVERSOLE, ABRAHAM (P,
BLW), LNR Moores Hill,
Dearborn Co, IN, 1871; md 14
Mar 1814 Elizabeth Allemong,
Jefferson Co, VA
EVILSIZER/EBELSISER, PHILIP
(P, BLW), LNR P.O. Green-
ville, Greene Co, TN, 1871;
md 1814 Anne Huffnow, Rock-
ingham Co, VA. She died
before 18 Mar 1871
EWELL, JAMES applied for a
pension
EVERS, JOSEPH (P-rejected,
BLW), md (1) Frances Alcock
(2) Polly H. Hudson (P)
EWING, CHARLES whose widow
Theresa applied for a pension
EWING, JAMES (BLW)
EWING, JAMES (BLW)
EWING, PATRICK (P, BLW),
LNR P.O. Hempstead, Cal-
laway Co, MO, 1871; md 15
Jun 1851 Ann Eliza Fisher,
Callaway Co, MO. Patrick also
claimed service in the Black
Hawk War, 1832
EYLENBURGH, JOHN (BLW),
PA militia, died 16 Dec 1864,
Pike Co, PA; md 2 May 1812
Mary Roberts (P), Monroe Co,
VA. She died 30 May 1880,
Orion, Oakland Co, MI, LNR
P.O. Egypt Mills, Pike Co,
PA, 1871
FACKLER, GEORGE (P, BLW),
LNR P.O. Pittsylvania Court-
house, Pittsylvania Co, VA,
1871; md 6 Sep 1810 Mary
White, Pittsylvania Co, VA
FADELY, HENRY (P, BLW),
died 22 Mar 1883, Mt. Clifton,
Shenandoah Co, VA; md 1 Jan
1816 Sarah Heaton, Shenandoah
Co, VA
FADLY, DAVID (BLW), died 28
Feb 1838 or 1840, Stony Creek,
VA; md 20 Mar 1810 Elizabeth
Coffman (P), New Market,
Shenandoah Co, VA. Her LNR
Stony Creek, Shenandoah Co,
VA, 1871

FAIR, HEZEKIAH (P, BLW),
died 27 Feb 1883, Henry Co,
VA; md (1) Martha McDaniel,
(2) 20 Dec 1854 Edy Olive
(Martin) Clark (P), Ayersville,
Stokes Co, NC. She died before
18 Oct 1887, LNR Nettle
Ridge, Patrick Co, VA, 1883
FAIRBANK, NOAH (P, BLW),
MD militia, died 1 Dec 1883,
Fredericksburg, VA, LNR
Caroline Co, VA, 1878; md 4
Jul 1845 Julia Ann Smith,
Philadelphia, PA
FAIRCHILD, AARON (P, BLW),
LNR P.O. Hoods Fork, John-
son Co, KY, 1871; md Rebecca
McSpaden, Washington Co, VA
FALLS, JOHN (P, BLW), LNR
Cartersburg, Hendricks Co,
MD, 1872; md Jun 1812 Eliz-
abeth Jenkins Fall, Botetourt
Co, VA
FALLS, PETER whose widow
Elizabeth applied for a pension
FALWELL, RICHARD whose for-
mer widow Margaret Snyder
applied for a pension
FANDREE, JAMES (P, BLW),
died 13 Jun 1876, Goochland
Co, VA; md (1) Frances Nuck-
ols, (2) 2 Oct 1853 Jane
Roundtree (P), Goochland Co,
VA. She died before 8 Nov
1887, LNR P.O. Johnsons
Springs, Goochland Co, VA,
1878
FANNON, BRIANT alias FAN-
NING, BRIAN (P, BLW), died
16 Apr 1872, Lee Co, VA; md
18 Feb 1812 Abigail Muncy
(P), Giles Co, VA. Her LRN
P.O. Stickleyville, Lee Co,
VA, 1872
FANT, JOHN L. (P, BLW), died
8 Jun 1874, Warrenton, VA;
md 14 Jun 1811 Lucy E. D. M.
Phillips (P), Travelers Rest,
Stafford Co, VA. Her LNR
Warrenton, Fauquier co, VA,
1874
FARIS/FERRIS, ARCHIBALD A.

FARIS (continued)
(BLW), died Sep 1837, Prince
Edward Co, VA; md Dec 1820
Mason/Mace Childris (P),
Prince Edward Co, VA. She
died before 10 Feb 1885, LNR
Curdsville, Buckingham Co,
VA, 1878
FARIS/FARRIS, CHARLES
(BLW), died 17 May 1871, Lo-
gan Co, IL; md (1) ?, (2) 1 Feb
1831 Eliza Fassett (P), Mays-
ville, KY. She died c1888,
Logan Co, IL, LNR P.O. Lin-
coln, Logan Co, IL, 1878
FARIS/FARRIS, JORDIN (P,
BLW), LNR Colusa, Colusa
Co, CA, 1882
FARIS, SAMUEL (BLW), died
1859, Fluvanna Co, VA; md
c1816 Nancy Griffin (P), Cum-
berland Co, VA. She died be-
fore 11 Jan 1886, LNR P.O.
Charlottesville, Albemarle Co,
VA, 1878
FARIS, WILLIAM (P, BLW)
FARIS, WILLIAM (P, BLW),
died 12 Apr 1872, Amherst Co,
VA; md 31 May 1821 Eliza M.
Daniel (P), Cumberland Co,
VA. She died c6 Jun 1896, P.
O. Allwood, Amherst Co, VA,
1878
FARISH/FARIS, STEPHEN M.
(P, BLW), LNR P.O. Char-
lottesville, Albemarle Co, VA,
1871. Wife died before 1871
FARISS, JACKSON (BLW), died
24 Jul 1841, Bedford Co, VA;
md Jul 1805 Rebecca Fariss
(P), Cumberland Co, VA. She
died cJan 1872, LNR P.O.
Wades, Bedford Co, VA, 1871
FARLEY, DANIEL (BLW), died
c1 Sep 1859, Powhatan Co,
VA; md 15 May 1808 Ann
Maria Winfree (P), NC. Her
LNR Powhatan Courthouse,
Powhatan Co, VA, 1871
FARLEY, STITH (BLW), died 31
Dec 1856, Prince Edward Co,
VA; md 7 Oct 1812 Maria Pin-

FARLEY (continued)
cham (P), Prince Edward Co,
VA. Her LNR Rices Depot,
Prince Edward Co, VA, 1871

FARMER, ARCHER (BLW), died
1855, Halifax Co, VA; md 16
Nov 1810 Nancy Wilson (P),
Halifax Co, VA. She died
c1876, LNR P.O. News Ferry,
Halifax Co, VA, 1872

FARMER, BENJAMIN (P, BLW),
LNR Ballard Co, KY, 1871; md
Sep 1811 Nancy Nunley, Ches-
terfield Co, VA

FARMER, BURWELL (BLW),
died 6 Apr 1814, Norfolk, VA;
md 10 Dec 1812 Edith ----
(P). Her LNR Davidson Co,
TN, 1866. Edith married on 2
Dec 1819 Adcock Hobson, also
a War of 1812 veteran

FARMER, DAVID (BLW), died
16 Jan 1862, Grayson Co, VA;
md Nov 1813 Catharine Ed-
wards (P), Ashe Co, NC. She
died after 9 Jul 1891, LNR
Grayson Co, VA, 1879

FARMER, ELI (P, BLW), died 6
Feb 1881, Bloomington, IN;
md (1) Matilda Allison, (2) 15
Jan 1828 Elizabeth W.
McClung (P), Crawfordsville,
Montgomery Co, IN. Her LNR
Bloomington, Monroe Co, IN,
1887

FARMER, MICHAEL applied for
a pension

FARMER, WILLIAM (P, BLW),
LNR P.O. Yellow Branch,
Campbell Co, VA, 1871; md
c1835 Martha Willard, Campbell Co, VA

FARRAR, BENNETT (BLW),
died 1 Jun 1837, Halifax Co,
VA; md 10 Feb 1833 Winney
B. Smith (P), Halifax Co, VA.
She died before 19 Aug 1886,
LNR Omega, Halifax Co, VA,
1878

FARRAR, CHARLES whose wi-
dow Sally applied for a pension

FARRAR, JESSE CARTER (P,
BLW), died 16 Oct 1878, At-
lanta, GA; md (1) Sarah G.
Shumate, (2) 31 Jan 1837
Nancy P. Johnson (P), DeKalb
Co, GA. Her LNR Atlanta,
Fulton Co, GA, 1878

FARRAR, JOHN (P, BLW), LNR
P.O. Haddock, Jones Co, GA,
1873; md 8 Feb 1821 Mary
Minter, Chatham Co, NC

FARRAR, JOHN S. (BLW), died
11 Apr 1832; md 21 Feb 1809
Sarah J. Grubbs (P), Louisa
Co, VA. Her LNR Snow Hill,
Albemarle Co, VA, 1871

FARRAR, STEPHEN (BLW), died
4 Jan 1870, Louisa Co, VA;
md 8 Jun 1820 Susan P. Duncan (P), Louisa Co, VA. Her
LNR P.O. Apple Grove, Louisa
Co, VA, 1878

FARRENS/FARNES, GEORGE
(P, BLW), USA, LNR P.O.
Pleasanton, Decatur Co, IA,
1871; md 15 Sep 1813 Sarah
Webb, Augusta Co, VA

FARRIS, EDWARD (P-rejected,
BLW), died 22 Dec 1876, md
(1) Mary Bishop, (2) 20 Jul
1858 Kisiah Blankenbeekler
(P), Smyth Co, VA. She died 4
Jan 1894, LNR Loudoun Co,
TN, 1878

FARRIS, WILLIAM, JR. (BLW),
died c1835, Manchester, Ches-
terfield Co, VA; md (1) Susan
McCullen, (2) c1819 Elizabeth
Higgins (P), New Kent Co, VA.
Her LNR Richmond, Henrico
Co, VA, 1878

FAUBER, CHRISTIAN (BLW),
whose widow Catharine re-
ceived a pension

FAULCONER, CARTER B.
(BLW), died 1 Mar 1853,
Orange Co, VA; md c27 Dec
1813 Nancy Faulconer (P),
Orange Co, VA. Her LNR Mad-
ison Run, Orange Co, VA, 1871

FAULCONER, HUGH (P, BLW),
died 16 Mar 1872, Orange Co,

FAULCONER (continued)
VA; md 23 May 1830 Susan Oakes (P), Orange Co, VA. She died c1890, LNR P.O. Mine Run, Orange Co, VA, 1878

FAULKNER, JAMES (BLW), died 28 Oct 1862, Halifax Co, VA; md 28 Dec 1837 Mary B. Averett (P), Halifax Co, VA. She died before Mar 1879, LNR P.O. Hyco, Halifax Co, VA, 1878

FAULKNER, KEMP (P, BLW), LNR P.O. McArthur, Vinton Co, OH, 1871; md 1 Apr 1819 Elizabeth H. Perry, Orange Co, VA. She died before Apr 1871

FAULKNER, OBADIAH (P, BLW), died 5 Mar 1875, Harmony, Halifax Co, VA; md 4 Jun 1817 Sarah B. Standfield, Person Co, NC

FAUT, GEORGE B. (BLW), died 20 Oct 1843, St. Charles, MO; md (1) Ann S. Ficklen, (2) 17 Nov 1831 Elizabeth Deatherage (P), Culpeper Co, VA. Her LNR P.O. Washington, Rappahannock Co, VA, 1878

FAWCETT/FOSSETT, JESSE (BLW), died 1 Jul 1870, Logan Co, OH; md 20 Apr 1815 Philadelphia Holloway (P), Winchester, Frederick Co, VA. She died c1880, LNR P.O. Rushsylvania, Logan Co, OH, 1878

FAYMAN, GEORGE (BLW), died 30 Apr 1871, Shepherdstown, WV; md 17 Oct 1822 Frances Keiffer (P), Franklin Co, PA. She died 8 Mar 1886, Shepherdstown, Jefferson Co, WV

ROLL NO. 32

FEARS, ROBERT (BLW), died 15 Oct 1866, Lee Co, MS; md 16 Dec 1828 Nancy Hays (P), Jasper Co, GA. She died before 29 Jul 1895, LNR P.O. Paris, Lamar Co, TX, 1892

FEASTER, ABRAHAM (P, BLW), died 3 Oct 1873, Grant Co, WV; md 27 Aug 1816 Elizabeth Crider (P), Rockingham Co, VA. Her LNR P.O. Grant Courthouse, Grant Co, WV, 1878

FEATHER, JOHN (BLW), died 25 Mar 1870, Crab Orchard, Preston Co, WV; md 19 Jun 1815 Mary Ervin (P), Preston Co, VA. She died 30 Sep 1878, Willey, Preston Co, WV

FEATHERLINE, GEORGE (P, BLW), died c1877, LNR Ross Co, OH, 1871; md 23 Mar 1815 Sarah Bly, Shenandoah Co, VA

FEATHERNAGLE, JOHN (BLW), died 26 Nov 1833, Warren Co, VA; md 5 Oct 1828 Mary Ramey (P), Shenandoah Co, VA. Her LNR Lewisville, Warren Co, VA, 1878

FEATHERS, JOHN L./LAWRENCE applied for a pension

FEATHERSTON, BURRELL (P, BLW), died 21 Feb 1875, LNR P.O. Bovina, Warren Co, MS, 1873; md 9 Dec 1808 Rebecca Adams, Dinwiddie, Dinwiddie Co, VA

FEATHERSTON, WILLIAM (P, BLW), LNR P.O. Springfield, Robertson Co, TN, 1871; md 9 Jan 1809 Elizabeth Jones, Nottoway Co, VA. She died Fall of 1867

FEATHERSTUN/FEATHERSTON, JOSHUA (BLW), died 3 Jul 1848, Lunenburg Co, VA; md 16 Oct 1821 Ann Wilkinson (P), Lunenburg Co, VA. Her LNR P.O. Hollydale, Lunenburg Co, VA, 1878

FEAZEL/FEAZELLE, AARON (BLW), died 2 Jul 1854, Henry Co, VA; md 2 Mar 1802 Martha St. Clair (P), Liberty, Bedford Co, VA. She died 9 Mar 1872, LNR P.O. Raleigh Courthouse, Raleigh Co, WV, 1871

FELTY, PETER whose widow

FELTY (continued)
Nancy applied for a pension

FENN, JOSEPH (BLW), died 4 Jan 1845, Petersburg, VA; md Dec 1825 Eliza Jackson (P), Dinwiddie Co, VA. Her LNR Petersburg, Dinwiddie Co, VA, 1873

FENNELL, BENJAMIN E. whose widow Eliza H. applied for a pension. Benjamin was a substitute for James Fennell in the War

FEREBEE, THOMAS (BLW), died 4 Aug 1846, Davidson Co, TN; md 30 Jun 1816 Sarah Poyner (P), Currituck Co, NC. She died before 8 Dec 1879, LNR Pegrams Station, Cheatham Co, TN

FERGESON, JOSEPH R. (P, BLW), LNR P.O. Danville, Yell Co, AR, 1871; md 25 Dec 1822 Janes Ayres, Buckingham Co, VA

FERGESS, JOHN E. whose widow Sarah E. applied for a pension

FERGUSON, ANDREW (BLW), died 10 Feb 1871, Russell Co, VA; md 27 Oct 1823 Margaret Kelly (P), Sullivan Co, TN. She died c1892, LNR P.O. Lebanon, Russell Co, VA, 1878

FERGUSON, ARCHIBALD (BLW), died 10 Apr 1867, Appomattox Co, VA; md 4 Feb 1801 Lucy Jennings (P), Prince Edward Co, VA. She died 30 Sep 1876, LNR P.O. Evergreen, Appomattox Co, VA, 1871

FERGUSON/FERGASON/FUR-GASON/FERGASSON, ED-MOND (BLW), died 5 Nov 1855, Calhoun Co, IL; md 22 Jul 1820 Lucinda Buckner (P), Albemarle Co, VA. She died Aug 1884, LNR Excelsior, Morgan Co, MO, 1878

FERGUSON, EDMUND (BLW), died 13 Aug 1866, Lawrence

FERGUSON (continued)
Co, OH; md 5 Nov 1815 Nancy Roberts (P), New Market, Nelson Co, VA. She died 20 Mar 1885, LNR P.O. Sheridan, Lawrence Co, OH, 1878

FERGUSON, FERGUS (BLW), died 11 Feb 1836, St. Louis, MO; md 22 Oct 1817 Elizabeth H. Gooch (P), Amherst Co, VA. She died c1890, LNR St. Louis, MO, 1882

FERGUSON, HAWKEY (BLW), died 22 Dec 1852, Albemarle Co, VA; md Apr 1803/4 Elizabeth Norris (P). Her LNR P.O. Free Union, Albemarle Co, VA, 1871

FERGUSON, JOHN whose widow Jane applied for a pension

FERGUSON, JOHN (BLW), died 27 Sep 1852, Montgomery Co, MO; md (1) Elizabeth Boaz, (2) 21 Jun 1831 Ann Nettle (P), Montgomery Co, MO. She died c1892, LNR Williamsburg, Calloway Co, MO, 1887

FERGUSON, KINDER (P, BLW), KY militia; died 11 Aug 1879, Holman Station, Scott Co, IN; md 1 Jun 1792 Mary Robbins, Franklin Co, VA

FERGUSON, SAMUEL whose widow Amy applied for a pension

FERGUSON, STEPHEN whose widow Ellen C. applied for a pension

FERGUSON, THOMAS (P, BLW), died 29 Aug 1872, LNR P.O. Glenmore, Buckingham Co, VA, 1872; md 16 Sep 1817 Elizabeth Maxey

FERGUSON/FERGESON, THOMAS (P, BLW), died 24 Dec 1874, Calloway Co, KY; md (1) ?, (2) 17 Dec 1867 Margaret (----) Tucker (P), Calloway Co, KY. She died 21 Sep 1894, Murray, Calloway Co, KY

FERGUSON, WILLIAM (BLW), died 1831; md 18 Feb 1811

FERGUSON (continued)
Mary Brodus (P), Fairfax Co, VA. She died 3 Sep 1880, Alexandria, VA

FERGUSON, WILLIAM H. (P, BLW), LNR P.O. Winterpock, Chesterfield Co, VA, 1871; md 1823 Elizabeth Davis

FERRELL, LEWIS W. (P, BLW), LNR Whites Camp, Upshur Co, WV, 1871

FERRELL/FARRELL, ROBERT (BLW), died 20 Oct 1867, Tyler Co, WV; md (1) ---- Jacobs, (2) 9 Jul 1857 Julia A. Fletcher (P), Tyler Co, VA. She died 20 Mar 1902, Alma, WV, LNR P.O. Middlebourn, Tyler Co, WV, 1878

FERRIS/FARIS, CHRISTIAN (P, BLW), died 17 Dec 1872, Dodson, OH; md Dec 1814 Nancy Campbell (P), Salem, Botetourt Co, VA. She died c1890, LNR Dodson, Montgomery Co, OH, 1879

FERRY, HUGH (BLW), died 12 May 1854, Indianapolis, IN; md 6 Jul 1826 Jane Brough (P), Newport, Washington Co, OH. She died 20 Apr 1888, LNR Indianapolis, Marion Co, IN, 1887

FICKES, JACOB (BLW), died 10 Oct 1864, Kilgore, Carroll Co, OH; md 12 Aug 1823 Maria Brown (P), Jefferson Co, OH. She died 12 Mar 1895, LNR Akron, Summit Co, OH, 1883

FIELD, JAMES (BLW), died 15 Jun 1854, Bedford Co, VA; md 13 Oct 1814 Elizabeth Burford (P), Bedford Co, VA. Her LNR P.O. Fancy Grove, Bedford Co, VA, 1871

FIELDING, JAMES (P, BLW), LNR Louisa Co, VA, 1871; md 20 Dec 1832 Matilda C. Gillespie, Louisa Co, VA

FIELDING, WILLIAM (BLW), died 19 Jan 1855, Limestone Co, AL; md 8 Dec 1831 Sarah

FIELDING (continued)
A. Thompson (P), Athens, AL. She died 6 Jan 1884, Athens, AL, LNR Limestone Co, AL, 1881

FIELDS, JOHN D. (BLW), died 29 Nov 1870, Wythe Co, VA; md 18 Feb 1822 Nancy Ann Williams (P), Wythe Co, VA. Her LNR Wytheville, Wythe Co, VA, 1878

FIELDS, MAJOR (BLW), died 2 Feb 1873, Washington Co, VA; md 11 Sep 1817 Sarah Wilder (P), Washington Co, VA. She died 9 Feb 1884, LNR P.O. Abingdon, Washington Co, VA, 1878

FIFE, ROBERT B. (P, BLW), died 8 Apr 1878, LNR Louisville, Jefferson Co, KY, 1871; md 10 Oct 1847 Sarah J. (----) Hopson, St. Louis, MO

FIFER, ABRAHAM (BLW), died 2 Apr 1857, Westchester, IN; md 20 Jul 1813 Lydia Fry (P), Rockingham Co, VA. Her LNR P.O. Westchester, Jay Co, IN, 1873

FILBATES, WILLIAM whose widow Mary applied for a pension

FILCHER/FLETCHER, PETER (P, BLW), died 20 Aug 1883, Frankfort, OH, LNR P.O. Chillicothe, Ross Co, OH, 1871; md 30 Apr 1816 Ann Inde, Richmond, VA. He served as a substitute in the War under the name of Peter Fletcher

FILSON, WILLIAM (P, BLW), died 20 Aug 1874, Canton, Stark Co, OH, LNR P.O. Leavitt, Carroll Co, OH, 1871; md Susan Elliot, Carrollton, Carroll Co, OH. She died 23 Feb 1876, Canton, OH

FINK, DANIEL applied for a pension

FINK, WILLIAM (P, BLW), died 30 Nov 1874, Drakesville, Davis Co, IA

FINKS, ELLIOT (BLW), died 20

FINKS (continued)
Aug 1865, Madison Co, VA; md 28 Sep 1802 Fanny Berry (P), Madison Co, VA. Her LNR P.O. Madison Courthouse, Madison Co, VA, 1871

FINKS, FIELDING (P, BLW), LNR Woodstock, Shenandoah Co, VA, 1871; md 27 May 1817 Frances B. Triplett, Culpeper Co, VA

FINLEY, WILLIAM (BLW), died 27 May 1834; md 18 mar 1812 Sarah Bailey (P), PA. Her LNR Doddridge Co, WV, 1878

FINN/FENN, ALLEN (BLW), died 14 Feb 1852, Petersburg, VA; md (1) Delila Butterworth, (2) 3 Aug 1836 Martha F. E. Scott (P), Dinwiddie Co, VA. She died before 26 Oct 1889, LNR Petersburg, Dinwiddie Co, VA, 1878

FINNALL/FINNEY, JAMES (P, BLW), LNR P.O. Comorn, King George Co, VA; md Aug 1816 Margaret Cox, Stafford Co, VA

FINNELL, CHARLES W., SR. (P, BLW), died 1 Sep 1878, Morgantown, WV; md (1) Elizabeth Thorn, (2) 27 May 1824 Lucinda Hoffman (P), Shenandoah Co, VA. Her LNR Morgantown, Monongalia Co, WV, 1878

FINNELL, JOHN (BLW), died 17 Sep 1862, Rappahannock Co, VA; md 19 Jan 1804 Elizabeth B. Thorn (P), Culpeper Co, VA. Her LNR P.O. Flint Hill, Rappahannock Co, VA, 1872

FINNEY, THOMAS W. (P, BLW), died 4 Oct 1873, Accomac Co, VA; md 25 Dec 1819 Sarah Fletcher (P), Accomac Co, VA. Her LNR P.O. Onancock, Accomac Co, VA, 1878

FINNEY, WILLIAM (BLW), died 21 Nov 1836 Powhatan Co, VA; md 3 Mar 1827 Elizabeth Chickton Wood (P), Henrico

FINNEY (continued)
Co, VA. She died c1891, LNR P.O. Jefferson, Powhatan Co, VA, 1881

FISHER, ADAM (P, BLW), died 18 Apr 1877, Poseyville, Posey Co, IN; md (1) Elizabeth Balsley, (2) 20 Aug 1846 Salome (----) (Duell) Abey (P), Poseyville, IN. Her LNR Evansville, Vanderburgh Co, IN, 1878

FISHER, HENRY (P, BLW), died 15 Oct 1880, Renick, Rahdolph Co, MO; md (1) Mary Ann Culps, (2) 10 Nov 1873 Nancy (Meadows) Greer (P), Akinsville, MO. She died c1881, LNR Akinsville, Morgan Co, MO, 1881

FISHER, JACOB (P, BLW), died before 2 Aug 1877, LNR P.O. Woodstock, Shenandoah Co, VA, 1871; md 15 Dec 1813 Isabella Lutz, Shenandoah Co, VA

FISHER, JACOB (BLW), died 28 Apr 1848, Floyd Co, IN; md 1820 Jane Thomas (P), Washington, MO. Her LNR P.O. Edwardsville, Floyd Co, MO, 1878

FISHER, JAMES (BLW)

FISHER, PHILIP (P, BLW), USA, LNR P.O. Columbus, Franklin Co, OH, 1871; md 22 Jun 1817 Sarah Houston, Wheeling, VA

FISHER, RICHARD applied for a pension

FISHER, SOLOMON applied for a pension

FISHER, THOMAS (BLW), died 10 Jan 1862, Bedford Co, VA; md 28 Aug 1816 Susan (----) McCraw (P), Bedford Co, VA. She died before 28 Feb 1883, LNR P.O. Liberty, Bedford Co, VA, 1878. Her first husband was Hugh McCraw

FISHER, WILLIAM (P, BLW), died 11 Oct 1873, Tazewell

FISHER (continued)
Co, VA, LNR P.O. Jackson's
Ferry, Wythe Co, VA, 1871;
md 1 May 1816 Amy Hudson,
Cripple Creek, Wythe Co, VA.
She died before 18 Mar 1871
FITTS, CORNELIUS (BLW), died
7 Jan 1865; md 1 Feb 1814
Sarah Randolph (P). Her LNR
P.O. Jonesville, Lee Co, VA
FITTS, SANFORD (P, BLW),
LNR P.O. Enon College,
Trousdale Co, TN, 1871; md
1817 Tabitha Hughes, Summer
Co, TN
FITZER, JACOB (BLW), died 14
Sep 1827, Gallipolis, OH; md
20 Oct 1818 Nancy Ward (P),
Mason Co, VA. She died 16
Feb 1895, LNR Parkersburg,
Wood Co, WV, 1878
FITZHUGH, HENRY W. (P,
BLW), LNR P.O. Woodville,
Rappahannock Co, VA, 1873;
md 21 Sep 1852 Augusta
Grundy, Baltimore, MD
FITZHUGH, JOHN whose widow
Ann G. applied for a pension
FITZHUGH, JOHN R. (P, BLW),
LNR Fredericksburg, Spotsyl-
vania Co, VA, 1878
FITZPATRICK, JOHN (P, BLW),
died 9 Nov 1879, McNairy Co,
TN; md (1) Mary Bellar/Bel-
lah, (2) 17 Sep 1865 Mary Jane
(Broome) Babb (P), McNairy
Co, TN. She died 19 Apr 1916,
Comanche Co, TX, LNR Gap,
Comanche Co, TX, 1871. John
also served in the TN militia
in the Seminole War in 1818
FITZPATRICK, THOMAS (BLW)
FITZPATRICK, WILLIAM whose
widow Polly applied for a pen-
sion
FITZWATER, GEORGE (BLW),
died 24 Apr 1835, Nicholas Co,
VA; md 23 Mar 1819 Nancy
Hamrick (P), Nicholas Co, VA.
She died 22 Apr 1885, Kesler's
Cross Lanes, Nicholas Co,
WV

FITZWATERS/FITZWATER,
ISAAC (P, BLW), died 13 Jan
1883, Kressler's Cross Lane,
Nicholas Co, WV, LNR P.O.
Nicholas Courthouse, Nicholas
Co, Wv, 1871; md 18 Aug 1814
Sarah Hamrick.   Her LNR
Peter's Creek, Nicholas Co,
WV, 1883
FIZER, HENRY whose widow
Elizabeth applied for a pension
FLAHERTY, MICHAEL (P,
BLW), LNR P.O. Brentsville,
Prince William Co, VA, 1871;
md Mar 1821 Kitty Cheek,
Stafford Co, VA
FLANAGAN, WILLIAM (P,
BLW), LNR P.O. Chris-
tiansburg, Montgomery Co,
VA, 1871; md 20 Jul 1823
Peggy Wall, Montgomery Co,
VA. She died before 29 Aug
1871
FLANNAGAN, WILLIAM (P,
BLW), died 24 Aug 1873,
Fluvanna Co, VA; md (1) Sarah
C. Johnson, (2) 10 May 1859
Ann E. Hughson (P), Fluvanna
Co, VA. She died c1889, LNR
P.O. Palmyra, Fluvanna Co,
VA, 1878

ROLL NO. 33

FLEEMAN, GEORGE (P, BLW),
LNR Cedar Co, MO, 1871; md
17 Jun 18-- Martha Pergeson,
Henry Co, VA
FLEENOR, ISAAC (P, BLW),
LNR P.O. Craigs Mills,
Washington Co, VA, 1871; md
18 Dec 1817 Susan ----,
Washington Co, VA
FLEGER, MICHAEL (P, BLW),
LNR Seafield, White Co, IN,
1878; md 10 Jun 1822 Eliz-
abeth McCrumb, PA
FLEMING, CARR (BLW), died
14 Feb 1868, Cumberland Co,
VA; md (1) Sally Spicer, (2) 3
Jan 1862 Martha M. Montague
(P), Cumberland Co, VA. She

149

FLEMING (continued)
died 16 Dec 1893, Cumberland Co, VA, LNR P.O. Flanagans Mills, Cumberland Co, VA, 1882. Carr was a substitute for his father Anthony Fleming in the War

FLEMING, DAVID applied for a pension

FLEMING, HENRY (BLW), whose widow was Sarah Foxwell

FLEMING, JAMES T. (BLW), died 7 Jan 1858, Gloucester Co, VA; md (1) Mary Bohannon, (2) 18 Sep 1842 Mary J. Williams (P), Gloucester Co, VA. She died c1890, LNR P.O. Gloucester Courthouse, Gloucester Co, VA, 1878

FLEMING, JESSE (BLW), died 16 Jun 1861, Page Co, VA; md (1) ?, (2) 24 Jul 1843 Nancy Hollingsworth (P), Page Co, VA. She died 15 Apr 1885, Luray, Page Co, VA

FLEMING, JOHN (BLW), whose widow was Ann

FLEMING, JOHN S. (BLW), died 31 Aug 1858, Goochland Co, VA; md 25 Jul 1833 Indiana B. Bowden (P), Petersburg, Dinwiddie Co, VA. Her LNR P.O. Goochland Courthouse, Goochland Co, VA, 1878

FLESHER, ISAAC whose widow Elizabeth applied for a pension

FLESHMAN, ABSALOM (BLW), died 1887, Louisville, KY; md 16 Nov 1819 Eleanor Callahan (P), Campbell Co, VA. She died c1887, LNR P.O. Mt. Zion, Campbell Co, VA, 1878

FLETCHER, GEORGE whose widow Mary applied for a pension

FLETCHER, THOMAS (P, BLW), LNR Porter, Van Buren Co, MI, 1871. Wife died before May 1871

FLETCHER, THOMAS (P, BLW), died 3 Jun 1876, Fauquier Co, VA; md 28 Jun 1864

FLETCHER (continued)
Elizabeth (----) Putnam (P), Warrenton, VA. She died 14 Nov 1907, Colvins Run, LNR P.O. Warrenton, Fauquier Co, VA, 1878

FLETCHER, TOWNSON/TOWN-SAND/TOWNSAN (BLW), died 6 Feb 1866, Bureau Co, IL; md Jan 1816 Susannah ---- (P), Fauquier Co, VA. She died c1887, LNR P.O. Warrenton, Fauquier Co, VA, 1871

FLETCHER, WILLIAM (BLW), died 6 Oct 1834, Fauquier Co, VA; md 29 Sep 1808 Nancy Caynor (P), Fauquier Co, VA. She died 3 Mar 1873, LNR P.O. Warrenton, Fauquier Co, VA, 1871

FLING, JAMES (BLW), died 4 Apr 1867, Marion Co, IN; md (1) Maria Biggs, (2) Sarah Taylor, (3) 5 Apr 1845 Rebecca Fluhart (P), Perry Co, OH. She died 5 Feb 1894, Ben Davis, Marion Co, IN

FLINN, CHARLES H. applied for a pension

FLINN, JOHN applied for a pension

FLIPPEN, FRANCIS (BLW), died 14 Apr 1851, Madison Co, AL; md 23 Dec 1823 Mary Hughes Douglass (P), Madison Co, AL. Her LNR Elora, Lincoln Co, TN, 1879

FLIPPIN/FLIPPEN, JOHN (P, BLW), died 23 Jul 1873, Stokes Co, NC; md 22 Jan 1813 Catharine Pell (P), Pittsylvania Co, VA. Her LNR P.O. Francisco, Stokes Co, NC, 1873

FLYNN, JOHN A. (P, BLW), LNR P.O. Palmyra, Fluvanna Co, VA, 1871

FLOOD, DANIEL (BLW), died 10 Oct 1850, Buckingham Co, VA; md 20 Jun 1812 Ann S. Coleman (P), Buckingham Co, VA. She died Sep 1871, LNR

FLOOD (continued)
P.O. Garys Store, Buckingham Co, VA, 1871

FLORENCE, JOHN L. alias LLOYD, JOHN and widow Ellen both applied for a pension

FLOWERS, BENJAMIN F. (P, BLW), died 2 Jun 1887, Pleasantville, OH; md (1) Jane Clark, (2) 8 Nov 1849 Hannah (Eyman) Hampson (P), Fairfield Co, OH. She died 24 Nov 1893, Pleasantville, Fairfield Co, OH

FLOWERS, CHARLES W. (BLW), died 27 Mar 1855, Jackson Co, AL; md (1) Eveline Coffey, (2) 26 May 1834 Sarah B. Watkins (P), Dandridge, Jefferson Co, TN. She died 1 Aug 1896, LNR P.O. Scottsboro, Jackson Co, AL, 1881. Charles also served in the Creek War in 1814

FLOWERS, JAMES whose widow Elizabeth applied for a pension

FLOWERS, JOEL (BLW), died 23 Dec 1862, Monroe Co, KY; md 15 Sep 1811 Elizabeth Branch (P), Buckingham Co, VA. Her LNR P.O. Mad Lick, Monroe Co, KY, 1875

FLOYD, SAMUEL and widow Susan E. both applied for a pension

FLOYD, THOMAS (P, BLW), LNR P.O. Martinsville, Clark Co, IL, 1871

FLOYD, THOMAS (P, BLW), died 31 Jan 1879, Locustville, VA, LNR P.O. Locustville, Accomac Co, VA, 1878

FLOYD, WILLIAM D. (P, BLW), LNR P.O. Lunenburg Courthouse, Lunenburg Co, VA, 1871; md 23 Oct 1816 Elizabeth Thompson, Lunenburg Co, VA

FLOYD, ZACHARIAH (BLW), died 8 Apr 1852, Mecklenburg Co, VA; md 6 Jun 1819 Christiana S. Stegall (P), Brunswick

FLOYD (continued)
Co, VA. Her LNR P.O. Lochleven, Lunenburg Co, VA, 1878

FLUART/FLUHART/FLEU-HART, WILLIAM (P, BLW), MD militia, died 7 Jan 1879 Suffolk, VA; md (1) Catharine Murphy, (2) 22 Dec 1866 Nancy Gaylord (P), Pantego, Beaufort Co, NC. Her LNR Suffolk, Nansemond Co, VA, 1879

FLUHARTY, DANIEL whose widow Mary applied for a pension

FOESE, JAMES F. (BLW), died 4 Oct 1865, Powhatan Co, VA; md 26 Aug 1826 Caroline Sublete (P), Powhatan Co, VA. She died before 26 Apr 1884, LNR Powhatan Courthouse, Powhatan Co, VA, 1878

FOGELSONG, JOHN (P, BLW), LNR Montrose, Henry Co, MO, 1871; md c1819 Mary Fox

FOLAND, JACOB (BLW), died 9 Sep 1846, Jefferson Co, TN; md Jan 1805 Elizabeth Hinkel (P), Shenandoah Co, VA. Her LNR P.O. Erie, Roane Co, TN, 1871

FOLAND, VALENTINE/VOLENTINE (P, BLW), LNR Greens Fork, Wayne Co, IN, 1871

FOLEY, ENOCH (BLW), died 25 Oct 1841, Fauquier Co, VA; md 1 Feb 1818 Nancy Brown (P), Fauquier Co, VA. She died before 10 Feb 1887, LNR P.O. Woodville, Rappahannock Co, VA, 1878

FOLEY, JEREMIAH applied for a pension

FOLK, GEORGE (BLW), PA militia, died 4 Sep 1851, Bel Air, Harford Co, MD; md 1 Aug 1872 Harriet McKewan (P), Winchester, Frederick Co, VA. Her LNR Washington, DC, 1878

FOLKES/FOLKS, ELIJAH (BLW), GA militia, died 26 Dec 1849, Richmond, VA; md

FOLKES (continued)
(1) Martha R. Austin, (2) 1 Dec 1840 Martha (----) (McDowell) McKenney (P), Richmond, VA. She died 21 Dec 1878, Richmond, Henrico Co, VA, 1878

FOLLEN, EDWARD (BLW), died 6 Dec 1865, California, MO; md 16 Aug 1813 Mary Ann Vermillion (P), Loudoun Co, VA. She died 28 Nov 1888, LNR California, Moniteay Co, MO, 1876

FOLLIN/FAULIN, THOMAS (BLW), PA militia, died after 1855, md 1 Aug 1807 Elizabeth Follin (P), Georgetown, DC. Her LNR P.O. Springvale, Fairfax Co, VA, 1871

FONTAINE, EDMOND whose widow Mary O. applied for a pension

FOOS/FLUSE, NICHOLAS whose widow Margaret applied for a pension

FORAN/FOREHAND, JOHN (BLW), USA, died 17 Jul 1861, Fort Spring, Greenbrier Co, VA; md 27 Dec 1814 Mary Agner (P), Rockbridge Co, VA. She died 10 Mar 1881, LNR P.O. Blue Sulphur Springs, Greenbrier Co, WV, 1879

FORBES, MURRAY (BLW), died 31 Jul 1863, Orange Co, VA; md 22 Jun 1815 Sally Innes Thornton (P), Spotsylvania Co, VA. She died 7 Feb 1886, Fredericksburg, Spotsylvania Co, VA

FORD, ALLISON (P, BLW), died c1891, LNR Warren Co, VA, 1872; md Mar 1818 Elizabeth Feagans, Fauquier Co, VA

FORD, ELISHA (BLW), died Jul 1865, Gilmer Co, WV; md 23 Mar 1810 Eleanor Warder (P), Harrison Co, VA. Her LNR P.O. Pruntytown, Taylor Co, WV, 1871

FORD, GERALD (BLW), died May 1846, Halifax Co, VA; md

FORD (continued)
27 Dec 1826 Keziah Witt (P), Halifax Co, VA. She died 1 Jun 1883, Hyco, Halifax Co, VA

FORD, HARBIN H. (BLW), died 27 Jan 1853, Monterey, Owen Co, KY; md (1) Margaret Grady, (2) 6 May 1840 Ann Maria Brooks (P), Frankfort, KY. Her LNR Franklin, Franklin Co, VA, 1878

FORD, JESSE (BLW), died 17 Aug 1856, LNR Halifax Co, VA, 1855; md 17 May 1813 Elizabeth S. Smith (P), Person Co, NC. Her LNR Halifax Co, VA, 1856

FORD, JOHN (P, BLW), LNR Urbana, Champaign Co, OH, 1871

FORD, JOHN whose widow Anna applied for a pension

FORD, JOHN C./CHANDLER (BLW), died 20 Aug 1866, Highland Co, OH; md 6 Dec 1849 Phebe (----) Tedroe (P), Highland Co, OH. She died 8 Dec 1893, Highland Co, OH, LNR Fairfax, Highland Co, OH, 1884

FORD, THOMAS applied for a pension

FORD, TIPTON (BLW), died 27 Mar 1869, Rockingham Co, VA; md Dec 1825 Mary Smith (P), Rockingham Co, VA. She died 30 Jun 1887, Runions Creek, Rockingham Co, VA

FORD, WILLIAM whose widow Nancy S. applied for a pension

FORD, WILLIAM (P, BLW), LNR P.O. Falmouth, Pendleton Co, KY, 1871; md 1818 Mary ----, Pendleton Co, KY

FORD, WILLIAM (P, BLW), LNR Richmond, Henrico Co, VA, 1871; md 19 Nov 1818 Martha Toddy, Richmond, VA

FORE, PETER (BLW), died Jul 1868, VA; md 17 May 1821 Sallie Richardson (P), Charlotte Co, VA. Her LNR P.O.

FORE (continued)
Fort Mitchell, Lunenburg Co, VA, 1878

FORE, PETER M. (P, BLW), died 24 Jan 1883, Linneus, Linn Co, MO; md 13 Sep 1829 Sarah Galloway, Cumberland Co, VA

FOREN/FORON, WILLIAM (BLW), died 25 Sep 1863, Cullen Co, TX; md Jan 1816 Elizabeth Martin (P), Rockbridge Co, VA. She died 28 Apr 1881, Macon, Decatur Co, IL

FORESTER, DAVID (P, BLW), LNR P.O. Locust Springs, Greene Co, TN, 1871; md 26 Dec 1830 Anne Olinger, Greene Co, TN

FORREST, ABRAM (P, BLW), LNR P.O. Francisco, Stokes Co, NC, 1872; md Mar 1819 Susan Holt

FORREST, JOHN (BLW) whose widow Parmelia A. received a pension

FORRESTER, NATHANIEL whose widow Elizabeth applied for a pension

FORSEE, JAMES applied for a pension

FORSYTHE, THORNTON (BLW), died 29 Mar 1851, Harpers Ferry, VA; md 5 Mar 1813 Hulda Foster (P), Fauquier Co, VA. She died 8 Sep 1879, Woodberry, Baltimore Co, MD

FORTNEY, HENRY whose widow Hannah applied for a pension

FORTUNE, JESSE (BLW), died 12 Oct 1868, Catlettsburg, KY; md 27 Dec 1836 Martha Hagar (P), Nelson Co, VA. Her LNR Catlettsburg, Boyd Co, KY, 1891. She was dropped from the pension rolls on 7 Mar 1897, having married William Miranda on 29 Jan 1871

FORTUNE, THOMAS applied for a pension

FORTUNE, THOMAS (BLW),

FORTUNE (continued)
died 14 Mar 1857; md 16 Sep 1810 Jane McAlexander (P). Her LNR P.O. Lovingston, Nelson Co, VA, 1871

FOSHER, MATHIAS applied for a pension

FOSTER, BENJAMIN (BLW), died 15 Aug 1841, Page Co, VA; md 16 Oct 1817 Sarah Young (P), Page Co, VA. Her LNR P.O. Stonyman, Page Co, VA, 1878

FOSTER, DANIEL applied for a pension

FOSTER, GEORGE DABNEY/ DABNEY (P, BLW), LNR Chattanooga, Hamilton Co, TN, 1872; md 30 Mar 1828 Rachel H. Rogers, Bledsoe Co, TN. She died 22 Sep 1864, Hamilton Co, TN

FOSTER, GEORGE N. (P, BLW), died 30 May 1877, Henry Co, TN; md (1) Lucy Manly, (2) 29 Aug 1874 Lucinda (----) Bradford (P), Henry Co, TN. She died 9 Sep 1898, LNR P.O. Paris Landing, Henry Co, TN, 1878

FOSTER, HAMPTON (BLW), died 7 Jan 1871, Elliott Co, KY; md 16 Jun 1818 Jemima Waggoner (P), Tazewell Co, VA. Her LNR P.O. Sandy Hook, Elliott Co, KY, 1879

FOSTER, JAMES (BLW), died Oct 1826, Albemarle Co, VA; md 22 Dec 1820 Lucy T. Rogers (P), Albemarle Co, VA. Her LNR Mount Meridian, Augusta Co, VA, 1878

FOSTER, JAMES P. (P, BLW), LNR Halifax Co, VA, 1871; md 19 Jul 1815 Pracilla Lawson, Halifax Co, VA

FOSTER, JOHN (BLW), died 1 Sep 1855, Greenup Co, KY; md (1) Martha Bradshaw, (2) 4 Nov 1824 Sarah Culp (P), Greenup Co, KY. She died 11 Jun 1893, Brooklyn, OH, LNR Greenup

FOSTER (continued)
Co, KY, 1878

FOSTER, JOHN (P, BLW), LNR
P.O. Rices Depot, Prince Edward Co, VA, 1873

FOSTER, JOHN (P, BLW), LNR
P.O. Wolf Creek, Monroe Co,
WV, 1872; md 20 Mar 1816
Mary Skaggs, Monroe Co, VA

FOSTER, JOHN, JR. (BLW), died
12 Jun 1852, Wirt Co, VA; md
7 Oct 1819 Amy Prebble (P),
Wood Co, VA. She died 22
Apr 1887, Newark, Wirt Co,
WV

FOSTER, JOHN H. applied for a
pension

FOSTER, JOHN PEYTON (BLW),
died 19 Dec 1847, Warren Co,
VA; md 23 Jan 1817 Mary
Hawley (P), Shenandoah Co,
VA. She died 28 Nov 1883,
Bentonville, Warren Co, VA

FOSTER, JOSHUA (P, BLW),
died c1882, Rockwell, TX,
LNR P.O. Kaufman, Kaufman
Co, TX, 1872; md 19 Feb 1819
Susan W. Adams, Prince Edward Co, VA. She died Sep
1868, Yell Co, AR

FOSTER, NELSON applied for a
pension

FOSTER, PATRICK H. (P,
BLW), LNR P.O. Clover
Depot, Halifax Co, VA, 1878

FOSTER, PETER B. (P, BLW),
died 17 Jan 1879, Cumberland
Courthouse, VA; md (1) Eliza
S. Jones, (2) Martha Hobson,
(3) 16 Mar 1837 Courtnay C.
Thornton (P), Cumberland Co,
VA. She died 10 Jul 1883,
Cumberland Courthouse, Cumberland Co, VA, 1879

FOSTER, PRESLEY whose widow
Lucresia applied for a pension

FOSTER, ROBERT D. (BLW),
died 6 Aug 1868, Richardsville, Culpeper Co, VA;
md 27 Dec 1820 Elizabeth
Mitchell (P), Spotsylvania Co,
VA. She died c1900, LNR

FOSTER (continued)
P.O. Ozark, Christian Co, MO,
1881

FOSTER, SAMUEL (P, BLW),
died 22 Dec 1872, Jackson Co,
IN; md (1) Mary Craig, (2) 24
Mar 1834 Margaret Critchlow
(P), Lawrence Co, IN. Her
LNR P.O. Medora, Jackson
Co, IN, 1887

FOSTER, THOMAS (BLW), died
20 Oct 1870, Washington, DC;
md 22 Nov 1830 Nancy (----)
Brown (P), Winchester, VA.
Her LNR Washington, DC,
1878

FOSTER, THOMAS K. applied for
a pension

FOSTER, WILLIAM (P, BLW),
LNR P.O. Fort Ritner, Lawrence Co, IN, 1871; md 12 May
1819 Sarah McCormick, Cabell
Co, VA

FOSTER, ZIPEARUS/ZIPEARIUS/ZIPERIUS (BLW), died 13
Apr 1864, Mathews Co, VA;
md Sep 1818 Catharine B.
Foster (P), Mathews Co, VA.
She died 1 Jan 1879, Mathews
Co, VA, LNR P.O. Port
Haywood, Mathews Co, VA,
1878

FOUCH, WILLIAM (BLW), died
29 Nov 1849, Warren Co, OH;
md 1 Jan 1818 Catharine Dunn
(P), Warren Co, OH. She died
c1878, LNR P.O. Defiance,
Defiance Co, OH, 1878

FOULKE, JACOB (P, BLW), died
before 30 Jan 1886, LNR Belleville, St. Clair Co, IL, 1855.
Pension papers lost after being
sent to House of Representatives

FOUSHEE, WILLIAM (BLW),
died 15 Aug 1839, Culpeper
Co, VA; md (1) Mildred J.
Thatcher, (2) 20 Jul 1831 Mary
Ann Pendleton (P), Winchester, Frederick Co, VA.
Her LNR Culpeper, Culpeper
Co, VA, 1878

FOUST, MICHAEL (P, BLW), LNR P.O. Pittsylvania Courthouse, Pittsylvania Co, VA, 1871; md 1818 Susanna Daniel, Pittsylvania Co, VA

FOUT, PHILIP (BLW), died 27 May 1836, Lawrence Co, OH; md 18 Mar 1818 Ann Tate (P), Lawrence Co, OH. She died 3 Jan 1889, LNR Russells Place, Lawrence Co, OH, 1878

FOUTS, JACOB (BLW), died 22 Apr 1836, Botetourt Co, VA; md 23 Dec 1824 Hetty Spickard (P), Botetourt Co, VA. She died before Sep 1887, LNR P.O. Blue Ridge Springs, Botetourt Co, VA, 1878

ROLL NO. 34

FOWLER, ASA (P, BLW), died 28 Aug 1875, Pike Co, MO; md (1) Mary Lane, (2) 12 Apr 1866 Elizabeth Neal (P), Ralls Co, MO. She died 24 Mar 1883, Pike Co, MO, LNr Spencersburg, Pike Co, MO, 1878

FOWLER, FOUNTAIN (P, BLW), LNR Petersburg, Dinwiddie Co, VA, 1872; md (1) ?, (2) Nov 1848 Elizabeth (----) Gill, Chesterfield Co, VA

FOWLER, JEREMIAH (BLW), died 8 Oct 1852, Henrico Co, VA; md (1) ---- Packet, (2) 13 Feb 1849 Martha Mathews (P), Henrico Co, VA. Her LNr Richmond, Henrico Co, VA, 1878

FOWLER, JOSHUA (BLW), died 1862, Putnam Co, VA; md 1811 Lovey Daggs (P), Mason Co, VA. Her LNR P.O. Fishers Point, Jackson Co, WV, 1872

FOWLER, KINGETH/KING (P, BLW), died 6 Aug 1879, Chesterfield Co, VA; md (1) ?, (2) 24 Nov 1853 Rebecca Martin (P), Chesterfield Co, VA. She died c1889, LNR P.O. Winter-

FOWLER (continued) pock, Chesterfield Co, VA, 1879

FOWLKES/FOWLKS, JOHN (BLW), died 26 Feb 1863, Campbell Co, TN; md (1) Anne Jones, (2) 18 Dec 1838 Melinda Brumley (P), Greene Co, TN. She died before 8 Jun 1865, LNR P.O. Greeneville, Greene Co, TN, 1878

FOWLKES/FULKS, REDFORD (BLW), died 16 Oct 1856, Prince Edward Co, VA; md 12 May 1811 Elizabeth Elliott (P), Prince Edward Co, VA. Her LNR P.O. Rices Depot, Prince Edward Co, VA, 1871

FOX, GEORGE whose widow Catharine applied for a pension

FOX, HENRY (BLW), died 6 Aug 1867, Knox Co, IN; md 17 Oct 1816 Catharine Snyder (P), Washington Co, VA. Her LNR P.O. Bruceville, Knox Co, IN, 1878

FOX, JAMES V. (P, BLW), died 19 Jul 1878, Tazewell Co, VA; md (1) Elizabeth ----, (2) 1842 Martha Moore (P), Logan Co, VA. She died c1889, LNR P.O. Tazewell Courthouse, Tazewell Co, VA, 1884

FOX, MANLEY R. whose widow Martha applied for a pension

FOXWELL, LEMUEL (BLW), died 17 Mar 1835, King and Queen Co, VA; md 24 Dec 1812 Peggy Coffey (P), Gloucester Co, VA. She died c1876, LNR P.O. Woodville, Adams Co, IL, 1871

FOXWORTHY, JOHN applied for a pension

FRANCE/FRANCIS, ABRAHAM (BLW), died 10 Jun 1861, Boone Co, IN; md 1 Jan 1818 Phebe Taylor (P), Botetourt Co, VA. Her LNR Ridge Farm, Vermilion Co, IL 1887

FRANCIS, HENRY (BLW), died 27 Jul 1840, Fairfax Co, VA;

FRANCIS (continued)
md 3 May 1823 Rebecca Saunders (P), Salem, Fauquier Co, VA. She died 4 Jan 1880, Loudoun Co, VA, LNR P.O. Waterford, Loudoun Co, VA, 1878

FRANCIS/FRANCE, HENRY (P, BLW), LNR Salem, Roanoke Co, VA, 1871; md 31 Mar 1809 Phoebe F. Morgan, Union, Monroe Co, VA. She died before 31 Mar 1871

FRANCIS, JOSEPH (P, BLW), died 3 Sep 1878, Itawamba Co, MS; md 13 May 1815 Sallie Raglin (P), Buckingham Co, VA. She died 26 Apr 1884, Lee Co, MS, LNR Itawamba Co, MS, 1878

FRANCIS, MILES (P-rejected, BLW), died 21 Oct 1875, Montgomery Co, VA; md (1) Jane R. Hall, (2) 19 Jan 1841 Melvina L. Simpkins (P), Montgomery Co, VA. Her LNR P.O. Christiansburg, Montgomery Co, VA, 1878

FRANCIS, WILLIAM, JR. (BLW), died 12 Sep 1868, Licking Co, OH; md 22 Oct 1818 Levinah Boylan (P), Licking Co, OH. She died 26 Apr 1889, LNR Newark, Licking Co, OH, 1878

FRANK, ADAM (P, BLW), died 16 Feb 1877, LNR High View, Frederick Co, VA; md 28 Nov 1815 Sarah Pugh, Winchester, VA. She died before 23 Jun 1871

FRANK, DANIEL (BLW), died 16 May 1870, North Mountain, Rockingham Co, VA; md Aug 1830 Elizabeth Bare (P), Brocks Gap, VA. She died 22 Mar 1883, Singers Glen, Rockingham Co, VA

FRANK, JOHN whose widow Priscilla applied for a pension

FRANKHOUSER, DANIEL (P, BLW), LNR Brandonville,

FRANKHOUSER (continued)
Preston Co, WV, 1871; md 15 May 1818 Elizabeth Moyers

FRANKLIN, EDWARD (BLW)

FRANKLIN, ELISHA/ELIJAH (P, BLW), died before 25 May 1883, LNR P.O. Lebanon, Russell Co, VA, 1879; md Dec 1840 Lucy Lester, Washington Co, VA

FRANKLIN, HENRY (P, BLW), LNR P.O. Lynchburg, Campbell Co, VA, 1871; md 1 Oct 1817 Sarah Gowin, Appomattox Co, VA

FRANKLIN, HENRY (BLW), died 26 Jul 1855, Amherst Co, VA; md 14 Dec 1809 Jane C. Moss (P), Amherst Co, VA. Her LNR P.O. Forks of Buffalo, Amherst Co, VA, 1872

FRANKLIN, JAMES (P, BLW), died 3 May 1872, Fayette Co, WV, LNR Fayette Courthouse, Fayette Co, WV, 1871; md Rhoda Ann Thomas, Charlotte Co, VA

FRANKLIN, PLEASANT (BLW), died 1 Sep 1859, Tazewell Co, VA; md (1) ?, (2) 14 Feb 1840 Elizabeth Helmandolar (P), Tazewell Co, VA. She died 25 Feb 1881, LNR P. O. Tazewell Courthouse, Tazewell Co, VA, 1878

FRANKLIN, STEPHEN (P, BLW), KY militia, LNR P. O. Edmonton, Metcalf Co, KY, 1871; md 11 Jun 1810 Nancy Clark, Henry Co, VA

FRANKLIN, WILLIAM (BLW), died 5 Oct 1847, Richmond, VA; md (1) Elizabeth Hooper, (2) 17 Jun 1839 Martha K Tucker (P), Richmond, VA. Her LNR Richmond, Henrico Co, VA, 1878

FRANKS, ISAAC whose widow Sarah applied for a pension

FRASER, ANTHONY R. (P, BLW), DC militia, LNR Alexandria, VA, 1878; md 23

FRASER (continued)
Oct 1823 Presha Lee, Leesboro, Montgomery Co, MD
FRAVEL, JACOB (P, BLW) LNR P. O. Bladensburg, Knox Co, OH, 1871; md 17 Oct 1822 Millie Lock, Woodstock, VA
FRAVEL/FRAVIL, JOHN (BLW) and his widow Jane A both received pensions
FRAVEL, JOSEPH (BLW), died 18 Aug 1865, Woodstock, VA; md c15 Apr 1814 Rosa Gochenour (P), Woodstock, VA. Her LNR Woodstock, Shenandoah Co, VA, 1871
FRAVIL, ISAAC (P, BLW)
FRAYSER, RODERICK (BLW), died 28 May 1869, Cumberland Co, VA; md (1) Nancy Edwards, (2) 25 Sep 1834 Maria C Flippen (P), Cumberland Co, VA. She died c1890, LNR P. O. Ashby, Cumberland Co, VA 1881
FRAZER, HERNDON (BLW) and his widow Martha L both received pensions
FRAZIER, HENRY (BLW), died 17 Sep 1853, Rockbridge Co, VA; md 21 Nov 1824 Eliza Wright (P), Alleghany Co, VA. She died 23 May 1880, LNR P. O. Goshen Bridge, Rockbridge Co, VA 1878
FRAZIER, JAMES (BLW), died 18 Apr 1842, Freericksburg, Spotsylvania Co, VA; md 3 Jun 1818 Sarah Long (P), Spotsylvania Co, VA. She died 15 Apr 1881, Washington, DC, LNR Washington, DC, 1878
FRAZIER, JOHN (BLW), died 15 Sep 1860, Muskingum Co, OH; md (1) Rebecca Jenkins, (2) Aug 1832 Elizabeth Aikin (P), Muskingum Co, OH. She died 30 Oct 1886, LNR P. O. Zeno, Muskingum Co, OH 1879
FRAZIER, PETER (P, BLW), died c1880, LNR P.O. Fillian, Vermilion Co, IL, 1871; md

FRAZIER (continued)
Elizabeth ----, Prince Edward Co, VA
FREDERICK, JOHN (BLW), died 16 Jun 1864, Long Run, Jefferson Co, KY; md 10 Sep 1816 Nancy Pugh (P), Bedford Co, VA. She died 11 Jul 1885, Eastwood, KY, LNR Taylors Station, Jefferson Co, KY, 1880
FREELAND, HALE T./HAIL (BLW), died 21 Nov 1829, Scottsville, VA; md 5 Dec 1816 Sarah A. Noel (P), Bent Creek, VA. She died c1880, LNR Buckingham Co, VA, 1878
FREEMAN, ALFRED applied for a pension
FREEMAN, DAVID (P, BLW), died before 18 Aug 1886, LNR P. O. Estillville, Scott Co, VA, 1871; md Nov 1825 Salitha Rhatuss, Scott Co, VA
FREEMAN, GARRETT (BLW), died c1835, Culpeper Co, VA; md 2 Mar 1813 Nancy Foster (P), Culpeper Co, VA. She died 4 Sep 1878, LNR Culpeper, Culpeper Co, VA, 1872
FREEMAN, JOHN H. (P, BLW), LNR P. O. Culpeper Courthouse, Culpeper Co, VA, 1873; md Nov 1805 Ann Robertson, Culpeper, VA. She died before 27 Feb 1873
FREEMAN, ROBERT (BLW), died 9 Oct 1836, Barren Co, KY; md 16 Aug 1815 Mary C. Parrish (P), Louisa Co, VA. Her LNR P. O. Glasgow, Barren Co, KY, 1878
FREEMAN, WILLIAM G. applied for a pension
FREEMAN, WILLIAM N. (P, BLW), died 5 Oct 1879, Seven Mile Ford, VA; LNR Seven Mile Ford, Smyth Co, VA, 1878; md Sarah Belshur
FREEZE, JACOB whose widow Elvira applied for a pension

FRENCH, GROVEY (BLW) whose widow Mary M. received a pension

FRENCH, JOHN (BLW), died 5 Oct 1868, Athens Co, OH; md 6 Mar 1823 Diana (Darling) Grubbs (P), Wood Co, VA.. Her LNR P. O. Floodwood, Athens Co, OH, 1878

FRENCH, REUBEN (BLW), died 10 Aug 1834

FRENCH, SAMUEL (BLW), died 7 Aug 1843, Lottsburgh, VA; md (1) Margaret Longley, (2) 7 Jan 1825 Elizabeth A. Haydon (P), Richmond, VA. She died c1892, LNR P. O. Lottsburgh, Northumberland Co, VA, 1881

FRENCH, WALTER (P, BLW), died 21 Jul 1880, LNR P. O. Hollansburg, Darke Co, OH, 1855; md Levina Bailey, Winchester, Frederick Co, VA

FRENCH, WILLIAM (P, BLW), died 13 Apr 1876, Franklin Co, KY; md (1) Lucy Deer, (2) 26 Apr 1860 Mildred P Vawter (P), Franklin Co, KY. She died 16 Mar 1911, LNR Franklin Co, KY

FRETWELL, JOHN (P, BLW), died 9 Jan 1877, Franklin Co, OH; md (1) Margaret Mars, (2) 13 May 1866 Elizabeth Walters (P), Franklin Co, OH. She died 25 May 1908, Clintonville, Franklin Co, OH

FRETWELL, RICHARD (P, BLW), died 23 Jul 1880, LNR P. O. Weston, Lewis Co, WV, 1871; md 1 Sep 1822 Sarah J. Barksdale, Albemarle Co, VA. She died 1852

FREY/FRY, ADAM (P, BLW), LNR P. O. Shanghai, Berkeley Co, WV, 1876. Never married

FRIDLEY, CHARLES whose widow Margaret applied for a pension

FRIEL, WILLIAM (BLW), died 13 Aug 1844, Bath Co, VA; md 29 Jun 1814 Jane Ann Stewart

FRIEL (continued) (P), Cow Pasture River, Bath Co, VA. Her LNR P. O. Frenchton, Upshur Co, WV, 1871

FRIEND, GEORGE applied for a pension

FRIEND, JOHN T. applied for a pension

FRISTOE, AMOS (P, BLW), LNR P.O. Georgetown, Pettis Co, MD, 1871

FRITTER, BAILEY/BARTLEY (P, BLW), died c1876, LNR P. O. Marshall, Clark Co, IL; md 20 May 1813 Dicey ----, Stafford Co, VA

FRITTER, BARNETT (P, BLW), LNR P. O. Stafford Courthouse, Stafford Co, VA, 1871; md 12 Aug 1820 Betsy Faut

FROST, JOHN (P, BLW), TN militia, died 30 Jun 1876, LNR P. O. Jeffersonville, Tazewell Co, VA, 1871

FRUSHOUR/FRESHOUR, GEORGE (BLW)

FRY/FRYE, HENRY (P, BLW), died 3 Aug 1871, Grant Co, WV, LNR P. O. Seymoursville, Grant Co, WV, 1871

FRY, ISAAC (BLW), died 19 Sep 1846, Guernsey Co, OH; md 5 Dec 1805 Hannah Cowgill (P), Loudoun Co, VA. Her LNR Noble Co, OH, 1871

FRY, JOHN (P, BLW), died c1889, LNR Mason Co, WV, 1871; md 1855 Kate Taylor, Mason Co, VA

FRY/FRYE, JOHN (BLW), 16 Feb 1867, Salem, VA; md 11 Feb 1819 Emily B. Crider (P), Middleburg, Loudoun Co, VA. Her LNR Salem, Fauquier Co, VA, 1878

FRY, JOHN (P, BLW), LNR P. O. Hamlin, Lincoln Co, WV, 1872; md 1816 Catherine Snodgrass

FRY, JOHN whose widow Frances applied for a pension

FRY, JOHN whose widow Polly applied for a pension

FRY/FRYE, JOHN (P, BLW), died 31 Mar 1873, Shenandoah Co, VA; md 11 Jun 1814 Catharine Grandstaff (P), Shenandoah Co, VA. Her LNR P. O. Edinburgh, Shenandoah Co, VA, 1877

FRY, JOSEPH whose widow Elizabeth A. applied for a pension

FRY, MATHIAS whose widow Rhoda A. applied for a pension

FRY, PETER (BLW), PA militia, died 22 Nov 1870, Greene Co, PA; md 14 Aug 1834 Elizabeth Taylor (P), Greene Co, PA. She died 25 Dec 1889, Calhoun Co, WV, LNR P. O. Big Spring, Calhoun Co, WV, 1889

FRY, VALENTINE whose former widow Mary C McRae applied for a pension

FRYER, JESSE (P, BLW), died 10 Apr 1879, Morgan Co, WV, LNR Berkeley Springs, Morgan Co, WV, 1871; md 1813 Mary Miller, Morgan Co, VA

FUDGE, JOHN (BLW), died 15 Sep 1868, Greene Co, OH; md 25 Feb 1846 Susan Barnett (P), New Jasper, Greene Co, OH. She died 16 Jun 1901, Bellbrook, Greene Co, OH

FUGATE, JOHN (BLW), KY militia, died 8 Apr 1857, Monroe Co, MO; md Dec 1813 Nancy A. Fugate (P), Wythe Co, VA. Her LNR P. O. Paris, Monroe Co, MO, 1871

FUGITT, BENJAMIN (BLW), died 7 Feb 1861, Greenbrier, Creek Co, KY; md 22 Feb 1840 Clarinda Roberts (P), Lawrence Co, KY. She died before 25 Aug 1883, LNR Louisa, Lawrence Co, KY, 1878

FUGITT, GUSTAVUS/GEORGE GUSTAVUS/AUGUSTA (BLW), died 17 Jun 1868, Alexandria, VA; md 1 Jun 1858 Ann Jourdan (P), Alexandria, VA. She

FUGITT (continued) died 26 Dec 1883, LNR Alexandria, VA, 1878

FULCHER, HENRY G (BLW), died 30 Mar 1849, Amherst Co, VA; md 19 Feb 1818 Delilah Fulcher (P), Lowesville, VA. She died before 20 Feb 1885, LNR P. O. Lowesville, Amherst Co, VA, 1878

FULCHER, PHILIP whose widow Saraphena applied for a pension

FULCHER, RODUM/RODHAM/ROWLAND (P, BLW), LNR P. O. Nellys Ford, Nelson Co, VA, 1871; md Jane Davis, Buckingham Co, VA. She died before 4 Apr 1871

FULKERSON, PHILIP (BLW), died 16 Sep 1860 Perry Co, OH; md (1) Polly Nicewarder, (2) 21 Jan 1837 Margaret (---) McCune (P), Zanesville, Muskingum Co, OH. She died Apr 1886, LNR P. O. Shawnee, Perry Co, OH, 1878

FULKERSON, ROBERT C. (P, BLW), LNR Danville, Montgomery Co, MO, 1871; md 17 Feb 1853 Margaret Davidson, Danville, MO. Robert was also a veteran of the Blackhawk War, being a member of the MO militia in 1832

FULLER, ALPHONSO T. F. (BLW), OH militia, died 28 Sep 1857, Lawrence Co, OH; md 11 Sep 1814 Mary Swain (P), Scioto Co, OH. She died 31 Mar 1883, Cox Landing, WV, LNR Cox Landing, Cabell Co, WV, 1879

FULLER, ELIJAH (P, BLW), died 11 Mar 1881, LNR Perry Co, KY, 1872; md 1822 Elizabeth Messer, Hazard, Perry Co, KY. She died c1850

FULLER, ISAIAH (P, BLW), died 3 Dec 1878, LNR P. O. Point Truth, Russell Co, VA, 1878

FULLER, JEREMIAH (BLW), died 6 Apr 1864, Staunton, VA; md 6 Apr 1813 Mary J Morrison (P), Chambersburg, PA. She died c1894, LNR Winchester, Frederick Co, VA, 1871

FULLER, JESSE applied for a pension

FULLER, JESSE (BLW), died 13 Oct 1834, Pittsylvania Co, VA; md 13 Jan 1818 Mary Hundley (P), Pittsylvania Co, VA. Her LNR P. O. Whitmell, Pittsylvania Co, VA, 1878

FULLER, JOHN (BLW), died 12 Oct 1858, Frederick Co, VA; md Oct 1829 Elizabeth Taylor (P), Frederick Co, VA. Her LNR Winchester, Frederick Co, VA, 1878

FULLER, WILLIAM applied for a pension

ROLL NO. 35

FULTON, JAMES (BLW), died 7 Mar 1863, Fultonham, OH; md (1) Elizabeth McGeorge, (2) 7 Aug 1833 Mary Ellen Newman (P), Prince William Co, VA. She died 16 Jan 1881, LNR Fultonham, Muskingum Co, OH, 1879

FULTON, JAMES (BLW), died 8 Aug 1870, Loudoun Co, VA; md Feb 1822 Sarah Stoneburner (P), Loudoun Co, VA. She died 25 Mar 1888, LNR Goresville, Loudoun Co, VA 1878

FULTON, MAHLON W. (BLW), died 16 Dec 1852, Adams Co, OH; md 16 Oct 1828 Jane S Jett (P), Loudoun Co, VA. She died 25 Feb 1894, Mound City, KS, LNR North Liberty, Adams Co, OH, 1878

FULTZ, GEORGE (BLW), PA Militia, died 7 Mar 1868, Highland Co, OH; md Jul 1814 Nancy Smith (P), Woodstock, VA. Her LNR P.O. Bourne-

FULTZ (continued) ville, Ross Co, OH, 1871

FULWIDER, GEORGE (BLW), died 11 Apr 1856, Bartholomew Co, OH; md 9 Aug 1814 Hannah Fix (P), Augusta Co, VA. Her LNR Hartsville, Bartholomew Co, OH, 1879

FULWIDER, JOHN (P, BLW), LNR Rochester, Cedar Co, IA, 1871

FULWILER, JOHN (P, BLW), died Jan or Mar 1869, Rockbridge Co, VA, LNR P.O. Collierstown, Rockbridge Co, VA, 1871; md 15 Dec 1808 Catherine Beaker, Botetourt Co, VA

FUNK, ISAAC (BLW), died 1 Jan 1828, Shenandoah Co, VA; md 28 Mar 1822 Priscilla Houck (P), Strasburg, VA. Her LNR Strasburg, Shenandoah Co, VA, 1878

FUNK, JACOB (BLW), died 29 Oct 1851, Pickaway Co, OH; md 8 May 1843 Mary Downs (P), Pickaway Co, OH. She died 30 Mar 1888, LNR P.O. Five Points, Pickaway Co, OH, 1887

FUNK, MICHAEL (P, BLW), died c1881, LNR P.O. New Holland, Pickaway Co, OH, 1871; md Jul 1820 Elizabeth Simpson, Clarksburgh, OH

FUNK, MICHAEL (P, BLW), died 12 Nov 1875, LNR P.O. Front Royal, Warren Co, VA, 1871; md 23 Sep 1807 Catherine Rittenour, Fort Shenandoah, VA

FUNK, SHEW (BLW), died 1 Dec 1827, Rockingham Co, VA; md 29 Oct 1803 Sarah Carrier (P), Shenandoah Co, VA. She died before Feb 1883, LNR P.O. Singers Glen, Rockingham Co, VA, 1871

FUNKHOUSER, JACOB (P, BLW), died c1881, LNR Brandonville, Preston Co, WV, 1883

FUNKHOUSER, JACOB (BLW), died 11 Mar 1839, Shenandoah Co, VA; md 15 Jun 1830 Elizabeth Long (P), Strasburg, Shenandoah Co, VA. She died 24 Feb 1887, Boone Co, IA, LNR Western College, Linn Co, IA, 1879

FUQUA, IRBY (BLW)

FUQUA, JAMES H (BLW) whose widow was Judith

FUQUA, JOHN (BLW)

FUQUA, JOSEPH (BLW) whose widow was Martha

FUQUA, JOSHUA (BLW) whose widow was Mary

FUQUA, SAMUEL (BLW)

FURBUSH, THOMAS (BLW), died 1824 New Kent Co, VA; md 18 Feb 1818 Elizabeth (----) Walker (P), New Kent Co, VA. She died 24 Nov 1881, LNR P.O. Chatham, Pittsylvania Co, VA, 1878

FURGUSSON/FARGUSSON/FARGUSON, NEWBY (P, BLW), died 22 Apr 1874, LNR P.O. Winterpock, Chesterfield Co, VA, 1871; md 1813 Prudence Pudue

FURR, ENOCH applied for a pension

FURR, EPHRAIM (P, BLW), LNR Buckhannon, Upshur Co, WV, 1871

FURR/FUR, MOSES (BLW), died 5 Jan 1867, Clarke Co, VA; md Nov 1818 Margaret Tracy (P), Warren Co, VA. Her LNR P.O. Paris, Fauquier Co, VA, 1878

FURROW, JACOB (P, BLW), died 22 Jan 1880, St. Paris, OH; md (1) Elizabeth Evans, (2) 14 Oct 1838 Amelia (Fletcher) Brooks (P), New Brighton, PA. She died 1 Apr 1904, LNR St. Paris, Champaign Co, OH, 1880

FURY, JOHN applied for a pension

FUTRILL/FUTRELL, JASON (P, BLW), LNR P.O. Rich Square, Northampton Co, NC, 1871; md 24 Nov 1818 Temperance Vinson

FYE, JOHN (BLW), died 10 Nov 1825, Butler Co, OH; md 3 Jun 1809 Catharine Baugher (P), Rockingham Co, VA. She died c1878, LNR P.O. Philanthropy, Butler Co, OH, 1871

GADD, BROAD C. (BLW) whose widow was Frances

GAINER, JOHN (P, BLW), died 6 May 1880, Barbour Co, WV; md (1) ?, (2) Susan Osler, (3) 13 Sep 1870 Fanny (----) Manier (P), Philippi, WV. She died before 4 Oct 1890, Philippi, Barbour Co, WV, 1880

GAINES, BENJAMIN P. (P, BLW), LNR P.O. Donnellsville, Clark Co, OH, 1871; md 10 Aug 1810 Magdalen Neff (PO, Shenandoah Co, VA. She died 12 May 1845

GAINES, JOHN (P, BLW), died 12 Dec 1853, Green Co, KY; md Sep 1828 Judith (----) White (P), Green Co, KY. Her LNR Louisville, Jefferson Co, KY, 1878

GAINES, NATHANIEL T. whose widow Harriet applied for a pension

GAINES, THOMAS H (P, BLW), died 29 Jul 1881, Roachville, KY; md (1) Elizabeth Jackson, (2) 18 Jun 1847 Mary Ann Buchanan (P), Green Co, KY. She died before 22 Dec 1893, LNR Roachville, Green Co, KY, 1881

GAINES, WILLIAM P. (BLW), died 30 Oct 1857, Fairfax Co, VA; md 17 Oct 1822 Euphama Holliday (P), Prince William Co, VA. She died 4 Sep 1881, LNR P.O. Philomont, Loudoun Co, VA, 1878

GAINES, WILLIAM (BLW), died c1840, Paynesville, Culpepper Co, VA; md 4 Mar 1804 Nancy Jasper (P), Georgetown, DC. She died 16 May 1882, Lexington, MO, LNR Lafayette Co, MO, 1872

GAITHER, GREENBURY (BLW), DC militia, died 3 Mar 1838, Washington, DC; md 18 May 1824 Margaret Brumley (P). Her LNR Falls Church, Fairfax Co, VA, 1878. Margaret elected to receive her pension based upon her son's Civil War service than on her husband's War of 1812 service. Her name was dropped from the War of 1812 widow pension rolls on 8 Jul 1882

GALLEHER, THOMAS H. (BLW), died 26 Feb 1859, Locust Bottom, VA; md (1) Martha Leith, (2) 27 Nov 1846 Sidney S Green (P), Prince William Co, VA. Her LNR P.O. Hickory Grove, Prince William Co, VA, 1878

GALLION, THOMAS alias SEXTON, THOMAS (P, BLW), LNR P.O. Grayson, Carter Co, KY, 1871; md 1818 Ruth Watson, Floyd Co, KY

GALLOWAY, JEHU/JOHN (BLW), died 26 Oct 1848, Baltimore, Md; md (1) Mary Little, (2) 13 Sep 1837 Augusta Kracht (P), Baltimore, MD. She died 19 Dec 1882, Baltimore, MD, LNR P.O. Finksburg, Carroll Co, MD, 1878

GAMES, ROBERT (P, BLW), died 25 Feb 1876, Delaware Co, OH; md (1) Mercy ----, (2) 7 May 1863 Elizabeth (---) Francis (P), Licking Co, OH. She died c1891, LNR Newark, Licking Co, OH, 1880

GAMMON, JAMES (BLW), died Dec 1848, Orange Co, IN; md Sep 1811 Elizabeth Harp (P), Pittsylvania Co, VA. She died

GAMMON (continued) 17 Nov 1872, Clay Co, IL, LNR P.O. Xenia, Clay Co, IL, 1871

GAMMON, ROBERT G. (P, BLW), LNR Zanesville, Muskingum Co, OH, 1871; md Aug 1820 Lizzie Bailey, Zanesville, OH

GANDER, GEORGE (P, BLW), died 24 Apr 1872, Muskingum Co, OH; md 20 Nov 1836 Elizabeth Grooves (P), Muskingum Co, OH. She died c1879, LNR P.O. Duncans Falls, Muskingum Co, OH, 1878

GUNNAWAY/GUNAWAY, THOMAS (P, BLW), LNR Appomattox Co, VA, 1871; md 15 Dec 1824 Catharine Routen, Buckingham Co, VA

GANNOWAY/GANAWAY, WARREN (P, BLW), LNR Lynchburg, Campbell Co, VA, 1871; md 3 Jun 1819 Elizabeth Snead, Lynchburg, VA

GANNAWAY, WILLIAM (BLW), KY militia, died 9 Mar 1816, Grayson Co, KY; md 23 Sep 1804 Sally Gannaway (P), Wythe Co, VA. She died 12 Aug 1881, LNR Pleasant Grove, Des Moines Co, IA, 1873

GANNAWAY, WILLIAM G. (BLW), died 27 Feb 1859, Appomattox Co, VA; md (1) Lydia Lascelles, (2) 15 Nov 1854 Ann Fore (P), Prince Edward Co, VA. She died c1888, LNR Farmville, Prince Edward Co, VA, 1878

GANT, JAMES (P, BLW), LNR P.O. Herndon, Fairfax Co, VA, 1878

GARARD/GARRARD, CALEB (P, BLW), died 26 Apr 1884, Harrison Co, WV; md (1) Sarah Murphy, (2) 4 Oct 1831 Elizabeth Pultz (P), Oldtown, Allegany Co, MD. She died 28 Jan 1903, LNR P.O. Sardis, Hampshire Co, WV, 1884

GARDNER, ANDREW applied for a pension

GARDNER, ASA B. (P, BLW), died 4 Oct 1876, Warren Co, KY; md (1) Amelia H Bowles, (2) Jane Keel, (3) 7 Mar 1850 America R. (Elam) Batts (P), Rutherford Co, TN. Her LNR P. O. Oakland Station, Warren Co, KY 1878

GARDNER, FRANCIS A. (BLW), died 22 Apr 1862, Montgomery Co, VA; md 26 Aug 1834 Zernah Hall (P), Floyd Co, VA. She died c1883, Jacksboro, TN, LNR Jacksboro, Campbell Co, TN, 1878

GARDNER, GEORGE (BLW), died 6 Dec 1856, Trigg Co, KY; md (1) ?, (2) 9 Nov 1837 Elizabeth Hawkins (P), Trigg Co, KY. Her LNR P. O. Cadiz, Trigg Co, KY, 1878

GARDNER, ISAAC R. (BLW), died 7 May 1863, Jackson Co, IN; md 23 Sep 1815 Comfort M. Rust (P), Winchester, Frederick Co, VA. Her LNR P.O. Seymour, Jackson Co, IN, 1878

GARDNER, JAMES (P, BLW), LNR P.O. Jamaica, Middlesex Co, IN, 1873. Wife died before 1871

GARDNER, JAMES (BLW), died 12 May 1858, Spotsylvania Co, VA; md (1) Mary Young, (2) 16 Feb 1848 Lucy T. Quisenbery (P), Rose Valley, Spotsylvania Co, VA. She died 25 Jan 1897, LNR P.O. Twyman's Store, Spotsylvania Co, VA, 1878

GARDNER, JOHN (BLW), died 15 Nov 1853, Montgomery Co, VA; md 21 Jan 1813 Elizabeth Page (P), Montgomery Co, VA. Her LNR Christiansburg, Montgomery Co, VA, 1872

GARDNER, JOHN (BLW), died 25 Jan 1861, Spotsylvania Co, VA; md 20 Dec 1818 Jane Grady (P), Louisa Co, VA.

GARDNER (continued) Her LNR P.O. Louisa Courthouse, Louisa Co, VA, 1878

GARDNER, WILLIAM (P, BLW), LNR Richmond, Henrico Co, VA, 1871. Married at least twice

GARLAND, CLIFTON applied for a pension

GARLAND, JAMES (P, BLW) whose wife was Sarah J. Burke

GARLAND, SAMUEL (BLW), died 9 Nov 1861, Coahoma Co, MS; md 26 Aug 1818 Mary L. Anderson (P), Bedford Co, VA. She died c1898, LNR Lynchburg, Campbell Co, VA, 1888

GARLAND, WILLIAM G. (BLW), died 1 Jun 1839, Richmond Co, VA; md 19 Dec 1816 Mary Leckie (P), Richmond, VA. She died c1888, LNR P.O. Warsaw, Richmond Co, VA, 1878

GARNER, DANIEL (BLW), died 15 Mar 1861, Culpeper Co, VA; md 23 Nov 1811 Elizabeth Howard (P), Warrenton, Fauquier Co, VA. She died before 22 Jun 1886, LNR P.O. Culpeper, Culpeper Co, VA, 1878

GARNER, JOHN (P, BLW), died 10 Dec 1878, Piqua, OH; md (1) Elizabeth Read, (2) 2 Nov 1842 Harriet A. Read (P), Rutland, Worcester Co, MA. She died 7 Feb 1904, LNR Piqua, Miami Co, OH, 1879

GARNER, LEWIS (BLW), died c1860; md 25 Jun 1812 Margaret Haga (P), Rockingham Co, VA. She died 3 Mar 1877, LNR P.O. Melrose, Rockingham Co, VA, 1871

GARNER, WILLIAM (BLW), died 18 Aug 1841, Williamsburg, VA; md 22 Sep 1825 Lucinda Doggett (P), Mecklenburg Co, VA. She died c1888, LNR P.O. Drapersville, Mecklenburg Co, VA, 1878

GARNER, WILLIAM (BLW), died 20 Dec 1868, Fentress Co, TN; md 12 Feb 1829 Lockey ---- (P), Fentress Co, TN. She died 17 Oct 1893, LNR Breathitt Co, KY, 1879

GARNER, WILLIAM A. applied for a pension

GARNETT, LARKIN whose widow Elizabeth J. applied for a pension

GARNETT, SMEDLEY (P, BLW), died 8 Jan 1875, Caroline Co, VA; md 13 May 1850 Sarah (----) Baldwin (P), Caroline Co, VA. She died 29 Jun 1895, Sparta, Caroline Co, VA

GARR, SOLOMON (P, BLW), died c1876, LNR P.O. Danville, Hendricks Co, IN, 1871; md 15 Sep 1817 Martha Chelf, Madison Co, VA

GARRET, CONRAD (P, BLW), LNR Hardy Co, WV, 1871; md 1816 Christina Gable, Shenandoah Co, VA

GARRETSON/GARRISON, FRENCH (BLW), died 7 Feb 1859, Tyler Co, VA; md 18 Jun 1825 Ellenor Ellis (P), Loudoun Co, VA. She died 18 Jan 1897, LNR Marietta, Washington Co, OH, 1887

GARRETSON/GARETSON, WILLIAM M. (BLW) whose widow Nancy received a pension

GARRETT, ANDREW (BLW), PA militia, died 22 Mar 1857, Hardy Co, VA; md 26 Nov 1830 Fanny Earles (P), Hardy Co, VA. She died 15 Feb 1882, LNR P.O. Wardensville, WV, 1879

GARRETT, IRA (BLW), died 26 Jul 1870, Charlottesville, Albemarle Co, VA; md 14 Mar 1817 Eliza J. Watson (P), Milton, Albemarle Co, VA. She died 22 Apr 1880, LNR Alexandria, VA, 1878

GARRETT, JOHN applied for a pension

GARRETT, REUBEN (BLW), died 28 Aug 1857, Kingston, Ross Co, OH; md 27 Dec 1813 Sarah Toombs (P), Essex Co, VA. She died c1878, LNR Hocking Co, OH, 1872

GARRETT, RICHARD (P, BLW), LNR P.O. Jane Lew, Lewis Co, WV, 1871; md 13 Oct 1871 ----

GARRETT, THOMAS (BLW), died 15 Mar 1870, Charlotte Co, VA; md 11 Oct 1826 Mary D. Crawley (P), Charlotte Co, VA. She died 19 Sep 1888, Charlotte Co, VA, LNR P.O. Drakes Branch, Charlotte Co, VA, 1878

GARRETT/GARRET, WILLIAM (P, BLW), LNR P.O. New Middleton, Smith Co, TN, 1871; md Anna Haley, Fauquier Co, VA

GARRETT, WILLIAM B. (P, BLW), died 3 May 1884, Portland, Callaway Co, MO; md 3 Jun 1824 Mary C. Ockerman (P), Buckingham Co, VA. She died c1892, LNR P. O. Portland, Callaway Co, MO, 1884

GARRISON, ALEXANDER (P, BLW), died 23 Mar 1875, LNR Mt. Olivet, Robertson Co, KY, 1871; md 1815 Resa Brashear, Bracken Co, KY

GARRISON, JOHN (BLW), died 20 Sep 1868, Jessamine Co, KY; md (1) Mary Alexander, (2) 18 Feb 1833 Isabella McNut (P). Her LNR P.O. Nicholasville, Jessamine Co, KY, 1887

GARTNER, PHILIP applied for a pension

GARVIN, ALEXANDER (BLW), died 15 Apr 1862, Appomattox Co, VA; md Dec 1809 Nancy S. Lack (P), Amherst Co, VA. She died 28 Oct 1873, LNR P.O. Amherst Courthouse, Amherst Co, VA, 1871

GATES, ELIAS (BLW), died Aug 1829, Alexandria, VA; md 14 May 1815 Susannah Simpson (P), Georgetown, DC. She died 1 Oct 1882, Washington, DC

GATES, JAMES R. (P, BLW), died 28 Jun 1871, Chesterfield Co, VA; md (1) ---- Forsee, (2) ---- Pinchbeck, (3) 21 May 1863 Ann O. (----) Mann (P), Petersburg, VA. She died before 24 Apr 1890, LNR Manchester, Chesterfield Co, VA, 1889

GATES, THOMAS (P, BLW), LNR P.O. Floyd Courthouse, Floyd Co, VA, 1872; md 17 Jan 1816 Sally Richerson, Pittsylvania Co, VA

GATES, WILLIAM (BLW), died 11 Jul 1860, Amelia Co, VA; md 13 Nov 1832 Ann E. Davis (P), Powhatan Co, VA. She died 26 Oct 1887, Richmond, VA, LNR Richmond, Henrico Co, VA, 1878

GATEWOOD, JOHN (BLW)

GATEWOOD, WILLIAM B. (P, BLW), LNR P.O. Chilesburg, Caroline Co, VA, 1878

GATHNEY, ROBERT S. (P, BLW), died 24 Feb 1878, Louisville, KY, LNR Louisville, Jefferson Co, KY, 1871; md Apr 1817 Deborah Able, Middletown, KY

GAULDEN, WILLIAM (P, BLW), LNR P.O. Ashland, Hanover Co, VA, 1871

GAUDLING/GOLDEN, SAMUEL (BLW), died 13 Feb 1858, Pittsylvania Co, VA; md (1) Chloe McDaniel, (2) Mar 1838 Mary M. Nance (P), Pittsylvania, VA. Her LNR P.O. Chatham, Pittsylvania Co, VA, 1878

GAWEN/GAWN, WILLIAM (BLW), died 17 Jan 1844, Westmoreland Co, VA; md 17 Dec 1818 Alice J Garner (P), Westmoreland Co, VA. She

GAWEN (continued) died c1882, LNR P.O. Tuckers Hill, Westmoreland Co, VA, 1878

GAY, EDWARD S. (BLW) died 11 Aug 1874, Staunton, VA; md 15 Dec 1840 Catherine (Tazewell) Ambler (P), Richmond, VA. Her LNR Richmond, Henrico Co, VA, 1878

GAY, GEORGE (P, BLW), died c1877, LNR Mason Co, WV, 1874; md Ruth Lot, Monongahela Co, PA. She died before Jun 1874

GAY, JOSEPH (P, BLW), LNR P.O. Weldon, Halifax Co, NC, 1871; md 4 Feb 1813 Elizabeth Deloach, Sussex Co, VA

GAY, VAN (P, BLW), died c 1882, LNR P.O. Cameron, Warren Co, IL, 1879; md Spring of 1818 Mary Mead, Bath Co, VA

GAYLE, ELIJAH (BLW), died 2 Sep 1863, Mathews Co, VA; md 24 Dec 1813 Mary Gayle (P), Mathews Co, VA. Her LNR P.O. Mathews Courthouse, Mathews Co, VA, 1871

GAYLE, JOHN M. applied for a pension

ROLL NO. 36

GEARHART/GEERHART, HENRY (BLW), died 6 Aug 1863, Montgomery Co, VA; md (1) Elizabeth Edwards, (2) 6 May 1823 Mary Mills (P), Franklin Co, VA. Her LNR P.O. Christiansburg, Montgomery Co, VA, 1878

GEE, ANDERSON/ANDREW (P, BLW), LNR P.O. Hopkinsville, Christian Co, KY, 1871

GEE, BENJAMIN (BLW), died 2 Nov 1852, Brunswick Co, VA; md 23 Dec 1812 Frances W Harper (P), Mecklenburg Co, VA. Her LNR Charlies Hope,

GEE (continued)
Brunswick Co, VA, 1872

GEE, HENRY (BLW), died 27 Apr 1845, Prince George Co, VA; md 30 Nov 1825 Mahala A Sturdivant (P), Prince George Co, VA. She died 18 Apr 1887, Petersburg, VA, LNR Petersburg, Dinwiddie Co, VA, 1878

GEE, JAMES (P, BLW), USA, died 7 Sep 1876, Amelia Co, VA; md 17 Nov 1846 Mary G (Fisher) Willis (P), Amelia Co, VA. Her LNR P.O Manboro, Amelia Co, VA, 1878

GEE, NELSON W (BLW), died 14 Feb 1859, Williamson Co, TN; md 15 Dec 1811 Catharine Byers (P), Lunenburg Co, VA. Her LNR P.O. Peytonsville, Williamson Co, TN, 1873

GEEDING, GEORGE A (BLW), died 10 Jan 1863, Augusta Co, VA; md 3 Sep 1818 Elizabeth Teaford (P), Augusta Co, VA. She died 26 Dec 1880, LNR Churchville, Augusta Co, VA, 1878

GEER, JOHN C applied for a pension

GEISENDOFFER, JOHN (BLW), MD and DC militia, died 22 May 1862, Alexandria, VA; md (1) Barbara Wilke, (2) 31 Oct 1839 Sabina Keene (P), Washington, DC. She died c 1890, LNR Washington, DC, 1878

GENTRY, JEHU (P, BLW), LNR P.O. Mechum River, Albemarle Co, VA, 1871. Not married

GENTRY, JOHN (BLW), died 8 Sep 1850 Richmond, VA; md (1) ---- Foulkes, (2) 1 Apr 1834 Mary Ann Willis (P), Richmond, VA. She died 28 Jun 1889, LNR Richmond, Henrico Co, VA, 1887

GENTRY, ROBERT (P, BLW)

GENTRY, WILSON applied for a pension

GEORGE, EDWARD (P, BLW), died 2 Jul 1875, LNR P.O. Fords, Dinwiddie Co, VA, 1871; md Mar 1856 Harriet George, Petersburg, VA

GEORGE, JESSE (P, BLW), LNR P.O. Maxville, Perry Co, OH, 1871; md c1816 Jemima ----, Shenandoah Co, VA

GEORGE, JOHN (P, BLW), USA, LNR Wilson Co, TN, 1871; md 5 Oct 1815 Elizabeth Atwood, Shenandoah Co, VA

GEORGE, PRESLEY whose widow Mary applied for a pension

GEORGE, REUBEN (BLW), died 27 Apr 1849, Fluvanna Co, VA; md 5 Nov 1828 Rebecca A Turner (P), Fluvanna Co, VA. Her LNR P.O. Shelbyville, Shelby Co, KY, 1878

GEORGE, WILLIAM (BLW), died 18 Aug 1836, Goochland Co, VA; md 14 Oct 1819 Susan W Holeman (P), Goochland Co, VA. Her LNR Goochland Co, VA, 1878

GEORGE, WILLIAM (BLW)

GEORGE, WILLIAM (BLW), died 31 Jan 1828, Goochland Co, VA; md 3 Mar 1813 Alice B Payne (P), Goochland Co, VA. Her LNR P.O. Caledonia, Goochland Co, VA, 1872

GEORGE, WILLIAM (BLW), died 7 Mar 1871, Mason Co, WV; md 24 Dec 1820 Nancy Eastham (P), Fauquier Co, VA. She died 1887, LNR P.O. Point Pleasant, Mason Co, WV 1878

GERRELL, BLAND (BLW), died 25 Mar 1855, Brockenburg, VA; md Aug 1845 Mary T Faulkner (P), Chilesburg, VA. She died c1893, LNR P.O. Chilesburg, Caroline Co, VA, 1878

GHISELIN, WILLIAM N. (BLW), died 28 Jan 1847, Norfolk, VA; md 28 FEb 1826 Mary B Wells (P), Princess Anne Co, VA. She died before 25 Jul 1884, LNR Norfolk, VA, 1878

GIBB, THOMAS whose widow Margaret applied for a pension

GIBBONS, ISAAC (P, BLW), died 31 Mar 1880, Hodgenville, KY, LNR Hodgenville, Larue Co, KY, 1871. Wife died 1850

GIBBS, CHARLES R (BLW), died 4 Apr 1872, Livingston, AL; md (1) Harriet Strother, (2) Mary G Trueheart, (3) 1 Dec 1836 Eleanor Stuart Thornton (P), Sumter Co, AL. She died 31 Oct 1888, P.O. Livingston, Sumter Co, AL, 1879

GIBBS, PHILLIP (BLW), died 31 Aug 1835 Simpson Co, KY; md 13 Apr 1812 Paulina/Perlina Jones (P), Campbell Co, VA. Her LNR P.O. Franklin, Simpson Co, KY 1871. Wife was pensioned as Perlina

GIBBS, SHELDON (BLW), died 26 Jan 1851, Coal Port, Meigs Co, OH; md 15 May 1813 Sarah Dashner (P), The Flats, Mason Co, VA. Her LNR Middleport, OH, 1871

GIBBS, THOMAS D. (BLW), died 1825, Fairfax Courthouse, Fairfax Co, VA; md 30 Nov 1815 Winifred Skinner (P), Fairfax Courthouse, Fairfax Co, VA. She died 18 Feb 1880, Wheaton, MD, LNR Wheaton, Montgomery Co, MD, 1878

GIBSON, DUDLEY (BLW), died Jun 1873, Kinsaille, Randolph Co, WV; md (1) ---- Armstrong, (2) 1852 Susan Kimbrau (P), Goochland Co, VA. She died 9 Jul 1907, Huttonsville, Randolph Co, WV

GIBSON, ISAAC (BLW), died 27 Feb 1862, Atchison Co, MO; md 1 Dec 1814 Mary Johnson (P), Russell Co, VA. Her LNR Atchison Co, MO, 1874

GIBSON, JAMES (BLW), PA militia, died 15 Sep 1859, New Albany, IN; md 19 Dec 1822 Mary F Mayo (P), Charlottes-

GIBSON (continued) ville, VA. She died 3 Mar 1883, New Albany, Floyd Co, IN

GIBSON, JESSE (P, BLW), LNR P.O. Middleburg, Loudoun Co, VA, 1871; md 4 Jul 1815 Catharine Bell, Fauquier Co, VA

GIBSON, JOHN (P, BLW), died 12 Aug 1876, Harrison Co, WV; md 27 Feb 1823 Lucinda Hoskins (P), Harrison Co, VA. She died Jan 1891, LNR P.O. Clarksburg, Harrison Co, WV 1878

GIBSON, JOHNSON M. (P, BLW), LNR P.O. Leavenworth, Crawford Co, IN, 1871; md Tempy Perkins, Mead Co, KY

GIBSON, JONATHAN (BLW), died 30 Sep 1834, Alexandria, VA; md 11 Jul 1813 Elizabeth Leonard (P), Cedarville, VA. Her LNR Stephensburg, Frederick Co, VA, 1871

GIBSON, JONATHAN C. (BLW), died 9 Dec 1849, Culpeper Co, VA; md 28 Dec 1824 Mary W Shackelford (P), Fairfax, Culpeper Co, VA. She died c1895, LNR P.O. Culpeper, Culpeper Co, VA, 1879

GIBSON, RICHARD (BLW), died 12 May 1866, Bracken Co, KY; md 6 Nov 1827 Polly Best (P), Augusta Co, VA. Her LNR Brooksville, Bracken Co, KY, 1878

GIBSON, WILLIAM whose widow Polly applied for a pension

GIBSON, WILLIAM (BLW), died 27 Aug 1865, Russell Co, VA; md 6 Jul 1820 Tabitha Dickenson (P), Temple Hill, Russell Co, VA. She died c1887, LNR P.O. Lebanon, Russell Co, VA, 1878

GIBSON, WILLIAM (BLW), died 23 Apr 1858, Richmond, VA; md 1817 Nancy Longest (P), King and Queen Co, VA. She

GIBSON (continued)
died c1890, LNR Richmond, Henrico Co, VA, 1887

GIDEON, GEORGE (P, BLW), died 7 May 1880, Clinton, IL; md 3 Oct 1866 Luann Rowley (P), Clinton, IL. Her LNR Clinton, DeWitt Co, IL, 1918

GIDEON, WILLIAM (P, BLW); md (1) Fannie Jacobs, (2) Easter (Conklin) (Green) Gideon (P)

GIDLEY, JOHN (BLW), died 12 Mar 1860, Monongalia Co, VA; md (1) ?, (2) Jun 1826 Rebecca Draper (P), Greene Co, PA. She died 12 Jul 1894, LNR Morgantown, Monongalia Co, WV, 1888

GIFFORD, ASAHEL/ASEL (BLW), died 27 Oct 1858, Sardis, VA; md 20 Feb 1817 Sarah Waldo (P), Booths Creek, Harrison Co, WV. She died before 17 Mar 1884, LNR Sardis, Harrison Co, WV, 1878

GILBERT, AQUILLA (BLW), died 5 Apr 1868, Breckinridge Co, KY; md (1) Elizabeth Hewitt, (2) 3 Feb 1839 Rachel Farmer (P), Perry Co, IN. Her LNR P.O. Stephensport, Breckinridge Co, KY, 1882

GILBERT, LYMAN alias CASE, NORMAN (P, BLW), CT militia, died 31 Dec 1882, Wetzel Co, WV; md c1852 Nancy Anderson (P). She died 1 Mar 1907, LNR Eagle Mills, Doddridge Co, WV, 1888. It is alleged that Lyman Gilbert served as a substitute for Norman Case in the War

GILBERT, SAMUEL (P, BLW), died 29 Oct 1877, Patrick Co, VA; md 5 Mar 1823 Lucy Sharp (P), Patrick Co, VA. Her LNR P.O. Patrick Courthouse, Patrick Co, VA, 1878

GILBERT, THOMAS (P, BLW), LNR P.O. Stony Point, Albemarle Co, VA, 1871

GILES, JAMES (P, BLW), OH and PA militia, died 20 Mar 1875, LNR P.O. Ravenswood, Jackson Co, WV, 1873; md 12 May 1817 Elizabeth Flesher, Jackson Co, VA

GILES, PERRIN/PERIN (BLW), died 25 Jun 1865, Gibson Co, TN; md 11 Nov 1813 Mary B. Abbott (P), Halifax Co, VA. Her LNR P.O. Kimball, Gibson Co, TN, 1874

GILES, THOMAS (BLW), died 2 Jun 1847, Rockingham Co, NC; md 1 May 1828 Sall T Ellington (P), Rockingham Co, NC. She died 31 Jul 1901, LNR P.O. Red Shoal, Stokes Co, NC, 1878

GILHAM, LEVI C. (P, BLW), died c1874, LNR Corydon, Harrison Co, IN; md 10 Jan 1813 Elizabeth Buker, Shenandoah Co, VA

GILHAM, PETER (P, BLW), died 19 Sep 1873, Frederick Co, VA; md 1 Oct 1822 Eliza Jackson (P), Frederick Co, VA. Her LNR Ottobine, Rockingham Co, VA, 1878

GILHAM, THOMAS (P, BLW), died 19 Mar 1875, Spencer Co, IN; md (1) Cythia Davis, (2) 29 Nov 1838 Mary Wiseman (P), Harrison Co, IN. Her LNR Newtonville, Spencer Co, IN, 1887

GILKERSON, JOHN whose widow Delilah applied for a pension

GILKERSON, THOMAS whose widow Nancy applied for a pension

GILKESON/GILKERSON, JAMES D. (P, BLW), LNR P.O. Moorefield, Hardy Co, WV

GILL, BOLLING, whose widow Mary L. applied for a pension

GILL, GARDNER (P-rejected, BLW), died 13 Sep 1876, Bethel, McNairy Co, TN; md 18 Sep 1818 Elizabeth Flournoy (P), Lawrenceburg, Law-

GILL (continued)
rence Co, TN. Her LNR Union City, Union Co, TN, 1879

GILL, GEORGE (BLW), died 7 Oct 1833, Northumberland Co, VA; md 1 Mar 1820 Sarah H. Jones (P), Northumberland Co, VA. She died 27 Nov 1887, LNR P.O. Marion Station, Somerset Co, MD, 1878

GILL, JAMES (P, BLW), died 2 Jan 1879, Meigs Co, OH; md 27 Oct 1829 Christena Derenberger (P), Reedsville, Meigs Co, OH. She died 18 Sep 1885, LNR P.O. Harrisonville, Meigs Co, OH, 1879

GILL, JOSEPH (P, BLW), died 7 Oct 1874, LNR Manchester, Chesterfield Co, VA, 1871; md 4 Apr 1810 Judith Henry

GILL, ROWLETT (P, BLW), died 22 Sep 1875, Chesterfield Co, VA; md (1) Martha Morris (2) 10 Oct 1853 Elizabeth (----) Tucker (P), Chesterfield Co, VA. She died 20 Sep 1888, LNR Petersburg, Chesterfield Co, VA. Her first husband was William Tucker, also a War of 1812 veteran, and she received a BLW for his service

GILL, TENEY/TENAGH/ TENAUGH (BLW) whose widow Maiza H. received a pension

GILL, THOMAS (BLW), died 30 Nov 1861, Hampshire Co, VA; md Aug 1817 Eilzabeth Young (P), Charlestown, Jefferson Co, VA. Her LNR P.O. Romney, Hampshire Co, WV, 1884

GILL, WILLIAM (BLW) whose widow Jane received a pension

GILLAM, JESSE (P, BLW), LNR Piketon, Pike Co, KY, 1876; md 15 Sep 1813 Elizabeth Fields, Russell Co, VA

GILLASPY/GALESPY, JAMES (P, BLW), died before Oct 1885, LNR P.O. Spruce Hill, Highland Co, VA, 1871; md 20

GILLASPY (continued)
May 1854 Elizabeth McGlaughlin, Highland Co, VA

GILLESPIE, HUGH W. applied for a pension

GILLESPIE/GILLASPIE, JOHATHAN H. (P, BLW), died 13 Mar 1873, Albemarle Co, VA; md (1) Matilda C. Breedlove, (2) 11 FEb 1858 Susan Margaret (----) (Smith) Hughes (P), Albemarle Co, VA. She died 2 Jun 1898, LNR Keswick Depot, Albemarle Co, VA, 1887

GILLESPIE, ROBERT (P, BLW), LNR Campbell Creek, Kanawha Co, WV, 1871

GILLESPIE, TARLTON (BLW), died 10 Mar 1868, Amherst, VA; md 27 May 1816 Mahala Reynolds (P), Bedford Co, VA. She died before 25 Sep 1883, LNR Amherst Co, VA

GILLESPIE/GILLASPIE/GILLASPY, WILLIAM applied for a pension

GILLESPIE, WILLIAM G./ GRANVILLE (BLW), died 3 Nov 1852, Alleghany Co, VA; md 18 Nov 1829 Mildred Franklin (P), Lexington, Rockbridge Co, VA. She died 10 Feb 1901, Kanawha Co, WV, LNR Poca, Putnam Co, WV 1887

GILLIAM, DREWRY (BLW), died 15 Sep 1829, Sussex Co, VA; md 11 Dec 1811 Sally Long (P), Sussex Co, VA. Her LNR P.O. Sussex Courthouse, Sussex Co, VA, 1872

GILLIAM, HARTWELL (P, BLW), died 17 Aug 1883, Clinton Co, OH; md (1) ?, (2) 3 Jan 1843 Sarah (Townsend) Routt (P), Darke Co, OH. She died 9 Nov 1907, LNR P.O. Blanchester, Clinton Co, OH, 1887

GILLIAM, JAMES (P, BLW), LNR P.O. Clarkesville, Red River Co, TX, 1872; md Nov

GILLIAM (continued)
1822 Harriet Bagby, Buckingham Co, VA
GILLIAM, STEPHEN (nickname Gilche) whose widow Edie applied for a pension
GILLIAN/GILLIAM/GILLEN, WILLIAM (BLW), died cJan 1815, Washington, DC; md 15 Jun 1809 Rosanna Kidd (P), Buckingham Co, VA. She died c1880, LNR McDonough Co, IL, 1871
GILLILAN, GEORGE R. (BLW), died 1 Aug 1854, Johnson Co, MO; md 9 Dec 1813 Martha Hill (P), Bath Co, VA. Her LNR P.O. Columbus, Johnson Co, MO, 1872
GILLILAND, JAMES H. (P, BLW), died 9 Jan 1889, Warren Co, NC; md 24 Dec 1822 Sallie Colly (P), Prince Edward Co, VA. Her LNR P.O. Warrenton, Warren Co, NC, 1889
GILLILAND, JOSEPH (BLW), died 31 Mar 1838, Alleghany Co, VA; md 11 Jun 1829 Mahaleth Griffith (P), Bath Co, VA. Her LNR P.O. Longdale, Alleghany Co, VA, 1878
GILLILAND/GILLELAND, SHEPERD/SHIPARD (P, BLW), LNR P.O. Long Dale, Alleghany Co, VA, 1874; md 6 Aug 1811 Jane H. Haynes, Alleghany Co, VA. He furnished James Gilliland as a substitute in the War
GILLISPIE, ROBERT J. (BLW), died 26 Jan 1868, Buckingham Co, VA; md (1) Elizabeth ---, (2) 21 Jun 1837 Marinda (Ransom) Baughan (P), Buckingham Co, VA. Her LNR Curdsville, Buckingham Co, VA, 1881
GILLS, PLEASANT (P, BLW), LNR P.O. Jetersville, Amelia Co, VA, 1872; md 26 Jan 1864 M.A. Hewey, Bibb Co, AL

GILLS, WILLIAM (P, BLW), died 5 Aug 1883, Prince Edward Co, VA, LNR Buckingham Co, VA, 1872
GILMORE, ROBERT (P, BLW), LNR P.O. Fairhaven, Preble Co, OH, 1871
GILMORE, THOMAS (P, BLW), LNR Effingham Co, IL, 1871; md 29 May 1815 Margaret Leach, Rockbridge Co, VA. She died Jan 1865
GIPSON/GIBSON, HENRY whose widow Mary applied for a pension
GISH, CHRISTIAN applied for a pension
GIST, THOMAS (BLW)
GITTINGS, MICHAEL D. (P-rejected, BLW), MD militia, died 24 Feb 1877, Clarksburg, WV; md (1) Mary P. Williams, (2) 2 Feb 1832 Sophia C. Jackson (P), Clarksburg, VA. She died 1882, LNR Clarksburg, Harrison Co, WV, 1878
GIVENS, JAMES (BLW), died 22 Dec 1835, Nicholas Co, VA; md 31 Jul 1806 Elizabeth Graham (P), Bath Co, VA. Her LNR Des Moines, Polk Co, IA, 1872
GIVEN, WILLIAM whose widow Elizabeth applied for a pension
GIVENS/GIVEN, DAVID (BLW), died 16 Dec 1850, Braxton Co, VA; md 3 Nov 1816 Catharine Laymaster (P), Kanawha Co, VA. She died 23 Jul 1885, Washington, KS, LNR Washington, Washington Co, KS, 1879
GIVIDEN, JOHN (BLW), died 1 Dec 1850, Trimble Co, KY; md 28 Nov 1816 Patsey Woodey (P), Buckingham Co, VA. She died 23 Jan 1887, Sulphur, Henry Co, KY, LNR Sulphur Fork, Henry Co, KY, 1878

GLADDON, JAMES whose widow Elizabeth applied for a pension

GLADSTUN, DANIEL (P, BLW), died 17 Aug 1886, Amissville, VA; md (1) Mary Heflin, (2) Elizabeth Creel, (3) 25 Oct 1869 Edna Goff (P), Rappahannock Co, VA. She died 26 Aug 1904, Amissville, Rappahannock Co, VA

GLADWELL, WILLIAM (P, BLW), died 27 Apr 1883, Greenbrier Co, WV; md (1) Betsey Dean, (2) 2 Dec 1852 Matilda A. Jones (P), Meadows Bluff, VA. She died 19 Dec 1895, LNR P.O. Williamsburg, Greenbrier Co, WV, 1887

GLAIZE, HENRY (P, BLW), LNR P.O. Winchester, Frederick Co, VA, 1871; md 23 Mar 1819 Annie Yeakley, Frederick Co, VA

GLASBURN/GLASSBURN, SAMUEL (P, BLW), died c1875, LNR Peru, Miami Co, IN

GLASS, AARON (BLW)

GLASS, BENJAMIN (BLW)

GLASS, DAVID (BLW) whose widow Rebecca received a pension

GLASS, DUDLEY (BLW)

GLASS, HENRY (BLW)

GLASS, JAMES (BLW), died 14 Oct 1847, Lee Co, VA; md (1) Johanna ----, (2) Sep 1821 Elizabeth Eagle (P), Wythe Co, VA. Her LNR P.O. Stickleyville, Lee Co, VA, 1883

GLASS, JAMES (BLW)

GLASS, JOHN (BLW), died 4 Oct 1860, Lynchburg, VA; md 4 Nov 1819 Susan Wilcox (P), Amherst Courthouse, VA. Her LNR Lynchburg, Campbell Co, VA, 1878

GLASS, MARTIN (BLW) whose widow was Nancy

GLASS, MORGAN (BLW), died 13 Mar 1846, Perry Co, OH; md 1 Apr 1815 Nancy Humphrey (P), VA. She died 7 Dec 1883, LNR P.O. New Lexington, Perry Co, OH, 1878

GLASS, RICHARD (P, BLW), LNR P.O. Scottsboro, Jackson Co, AL, 1871; md 1816 Polina Camlin, Rockbridge Co, VA

GLASS, THOMAS (BLW)

GLASS, THOMAS (BLW), died 13 Dec 1861, Frederick Co, VA; md (1) Catherine Wood, (2) 9 Nov 1848 Margaret M Cramer (P), Marion Co, VA. She died c1896, LNR Barracksville, Marion Co, WV, 1878

GLASS, THOMAS (BLW), died 13 Oct 1861, Hanover Co, VA; md (1) Fannie Martin, (2) 25 Dec 1823 Sally Butler (P), Hanover Co, VA. Her LNR P.O. Old Church, Hanover Co, VA, 1878

GLASS, THOMAS W. (BLW)

GLASS, WILLIAM (BLW)

GLASS, WILLIAM O. (BLW), USA

GLASSCOCK, ENOCH whose widow Mary applied for a pension

GLASSCOCK/GLASCOCK, JOHN (BLW), KY militia, died 5 Oct 1856, Breckinridge Co, KY; md 28 Dec 1813 Nelly Casey (P), Fauquier Co, VA. She died 7 Mar 1883, Long Grove, KY, LNR Cecelian Junction, Hardin Co, KY, 1878

GLASSCOCK, JOHN H. (BLW) whose widow Elizabeth received a pension

GLASSELL, ANDREW (P, BLW), LNR Los Angeles, CA, 1872

GLAZE, GEORGE (P, BLW), died 3 Jun 1876, Versailles, IL; md (1) Elizabeth Lynn, (2) 22 Feb 1846 Rachel (Rearden) Glaze (P), Scioto Co, OH. She died c1891 LNR Versailles, Brown Co, IL, 1878

GLASE, JOHN (BLW), died 20 Dec 1869, Highland Co, OH;

GLASE (continued)
md 13 Mar 1813 Anna Wolf (P), Wood Co, VA. She died c1879, LNR P.O. Hillsboro, Highland Co, OH, 1876

GLENDENING, GEORGE applied for a pension

GLENN, DAVID (P, BLW), died c1882, LNR P.O. Blandinsville, McDonough Co, IL, 1871

GLENN, TERRY (BLW), died 19 Dec 1854, Pittsylvania Co, VA; md 15 Nov 1821 Mary A. Whitehead (P), Pittsylvania Co, VA. She died 6 May 1888, LNR Pittsylvania Co, VA, 1878

GLISAN, SAMUEL (P, BLW), died 31 Oct 1875, Frederick Co, MD; md 24 Feb 1818 Eliza Poole (P), Frederick Co, MD. Her LNR P.O. Lingamore, Frederick Co, MD, 1878

GLOVER, JAMES (BLW), died 7 Jun 1871, Marshall Co, MS; md 8 Nov 1814 Mary Ann Parker (P), Windsor, NC. Her LNR P.O. Holly Springs, Marshall Co, MS, 1875

GLOVER, JESSE (P, BLW), died 28 Jun 1879, Callaway Co, MO; md (1) Eliza Anderson, (2) 4 May 1848 Susan Williamson (P), Callaway Co, MO. She died before 31 May 1897, LNR P.O. Fulton, Callaway Co, MO, 1879

GOAD, AARON (BLW), died 9 Dec 1858, Carroll Co, VA; md 26 Mar 1823 Ellenor Cock (P), Grayson Co, VA. She died 5 Mar 1888, Dugspur, Carroll Co, VA

GOAD, ANDREW (P-rejected, BLW), died 22 Nov 1871, Bedford Co, VA; md 26 Jul 1815 Mary Jacobs (P), Pittsylvania Co, VA. Her LNR White Rock, Bedford Co, VA, 1878

GOCHENOUR, SAMUEL (P, BLW), died 26 Oct 1873, LNR

GOCHENOUR (continued)
P.O. Hartford City, Blackford Co, IN, 1871; md Apr 1814 Catharine Wolgamoth, Shenandoah Co, VA

GODDARD/GODARD, JAMES (P, BLW), died c1877, LNR P.O. Marion, Williamson Co, IL, 1871; md (1) ?, (2) 13 Oct 1847 Cynthia Lewis, Williamson Co, IL

GODFREY, WILLIAM (P, BLW), died 22 Jan 1879, Norfolk Co, VA; md 5 times plus 1 Dec 1863 Mary Williamson (P), Portsmouth, VA. She died 20 Feb 1888, Berkley, Norfolk Co, VA, 1887

GODSEY, DRURY L. applied for a pension

GODSEY, HENRY (BLW), died Oct 1864, Campbell Co, VA; md 1 Oct 1810 Margaret Davidson (P), Campbell Co, VA. She died 17 May 1873, LNR Campbell Co, VA, 1871

GODSEY, SOLOMON (BLW), died 24 Dec 1850, Chesterfield CO, VA; md (1) Phebe Hancock, (2) Mar 1844 Elizabeth (----) Graves (P), Petersburg, Dinwiddie Co, VA. Her LNR P.O. Winterpock, Chesterfield Co, VA, 1878

GODSEY, THOMAS O. applied for a pension

GODWIN, DAVID (BLW), died 7 Mar 1841, Nansemond Co, VA; md (1) Eliza S. Bess, (2) 29 Sep 1819 Cherry G. Kelly (P), Nansemond Co, VA. She died 1883, LNR Portsmouth, Norfolk Co, VA, 1878

GODWIN/GOODWIN, ROBERT (BLW), LNR P.O. Valley Furnace, Barbour Co, WV, 1871; md 20 Mar 1816 Mary Barb, Morgan Glade, VA

GOFF, SALATHIEL (BLW), died 11 Jul 1863, Preston Co, VA; md (1) ? (2) 20 Nov 1819 Malinda Garner (P), Preston

GOFF (continued)
Co, VA. Her LNR Bowlesburg, Preston Co, WV, 1878

GOFF, WILLIAM applied for a pension

GOLD, JOHN (BLW)

GOLD, JOSIAH/JOSEPH (BLW)

GOLDEN, ENOCH (P, BLW), TN militia, LNR P.O. Sparta, White Co, Tn, 1871; md 1 Sep 1799 Lucy Gooch, Culpepper Co, VA

GOLLADAY/GALLADAY, DAVID (P, BLW), LNR P.O. Sandyville, Warren Co, IA, 1871; md 1816 Magdalin Dade, Shenandoah Co, VA

GOLLADAY, FREDERICK (P, BLW), LNR P.O. Troy, Miami Co, OH, 1871; md Mar 1814 Eliza Lowny, Norfolk, VA

GOLLADAY, JACOB (P, BLW), died 5 May 1872, LNR P.O. New Market, Shenandoah Co, VA, 1871; md Mar 1813 Margaret Funk. She died before 27 Mar 1871

GOLLIVER, JOHN whose widow Lydia Ann applied for a pension

GOLLOHORN, JOHN (BLW), died Mar 1862, Stafford Co, VA; md 20 MAr 1809 Penelope Hagan (P), Dumfrieds, Prince William Co, VA. She died 9 Jul 1872, LNR P.O. Stafford Courthouse, Stafford Co, VA, 1871

GOOD, ABRAHAM, (P, BLW), died 3 Nov 1872, LNR P.O. Christiansburg, Montgomery Co, VA, 1871; md 1822 Nancy Sullins. She died 1863

GOOD, FELIX (P, BLW), LNR P.O. Back Creek, Frederick Co, VA, 1871; md Nov 1820 Rachael Ordnorff, Frederick Co, VA

GOOD, JACOB (BLW), died 16 Jul 1863, Greene Co, MO; md (1) Eva Witicks, (2) 11 May 1843 Catharine Burnes (P),

GOOD (continued)
Page Co, VA. She died c1887, LNR P.O. Massanutton, Page Co, VA, 1878

GOOD, LEWIS (P, BLW), died 27 Jan 1877, LNR P.O. Grove Hill, Page Co, VA, 1871; md 1828 Susan Tanner, Madison Co, VA

GOOD, SAMUEL (P, BLW), died 6 Dec 1878, Rainsboro, Highland Co, OH; md (1) Mary Elizabeth Dettimore, (2) 17 Mar 1859 Arabella (----) Stevenson (P), Allen Co, OH. She died 7 Aug 1884, LNR P.O. Westminster, Allen Co, OH, 1882

GOODALL, FOUNTAIN (P, BLW), LNR P.O. Clendenen, Mason Co, WV, 1871; md 6 Nov 1816 Margaret Seel, Orange Co, VA

GOODALL, PHILANDER (P, BLW), died 27 May 1890, Madison Courthouse, VA; md (1) Mourning Marshall, (2) 27 Nov 1872 Mary Catharine Gallehugh, Madison Courthouse, VA

GOODE, EDWARD (P, BLW), LNR P.O. Milburn, Ballard Co, KY, 1871. Soldier in Capt. Benjamin Goode's Company

GOODE, EWING (BLW), died Jun 1839, Essex Co, VA; md 16 Feb 1816 Dorothy Patterson (P), King and Queen Co, VA. Her LNR P.O. Millers Tavern, Essex Co, VA, 1879

GOODE, JACOB (P, BLW), LNR P.O. Oak Level, Henry Co, VA, 1878

GOODE, MACK (BLW), died 25 Mar 1850, Mecklenburg Co, VA; md 25 Mar 1822 Mary Eliza Hayes (P), Greensboro, Mecklenburg Co, VA. Her LNR Union Level, Mecklenburg Co, VA, 1878

GOODE, PHILIP (P, BLW), died c1891, LNR P.O. Cambridge,

GOODE (continued)
Saline Co, MO, 1872; md 19
Dec 1819 Sarah P. Young,
Prince Edward Co, VA. She
died before Apr 1872

GOODIN/GOODWIN, THOMAS
(BLW), died 10 May 1853, Up-
shur Co, VA; md 21 Mar 1815
Susan Huffman (P), Page Co,
VA. She died before 12 May
1885, LNR P.O. Grimes Store,
Upshur Co, WV, 1878

GOODING, LEVI applied for a
pension

GOODING, SAMUEL applied for a
pension

GOODLING/GOODLAND,
THOMAS (P, BLW), MD
militia, LNR Newburgh, OH,
1871; md 11 Aug 1813 Elizabeth Finch, Loudoun Co, VA.
She died 15 Aug 1858, Jefferson Co, OH

GOODMAN, ACHILLES M. ap-
plied for a pension

GOODMAN, CHARLES M.
(BLW), died 1 Mar 1818,
Madison Co, KY; md 11 Jan
1816 Mary Barksdale (P), Albemarle Co, VA. She died
c1887, LNR Charlottesville,
Albemarle Co, VA, 1878

GOODMAN, DAVID (P, BLW),
died 19 Jun 1876, Hardin Co,
KY; md (1) Barbara Nico-
démus, (2) 7 Sep 1861 Mary E.
Lucas (P), Hardin Co, KY.
Her LNR P.O. Meeting Creek,
Hardin Co, KY, 1879

GOODMAN, GEORGE (BLW),
died 23 Sep 1858, Smyth Co,
VA; md 29 Jan 1818 Rachel
Wassom (P), Washington Co,
VA. Her LNR P.O. Seven Mile
Ford, Smyth Co, VA, 1878

GOODMAN, JAMES B. (P,
BLW), LNR P.O. Forest
Depot, Bedford Co, VA, 1872.
Wife died before 1872

GOODMAN, JESSIE W./M.
whose widow Philadelphia C.
applied for a pension

GOODMAN, JOHN (P-rejected,
BLW), died 18 Jan 1874,
Smyth Co, VA; md 25 Oct 1814
Mary Kinder (P), Washington
Co, VA. Her LNR Chilhowie,
Smyth Co, VA, 1878

GOODMAN, ROBERT (P, BLW),
died 4 Dec 1875, Osage Co,
MO, LNR P.O. Rich Fountain,
Osage Co, MO, 1871; md Dec
1818 Susan Mahan, Pittsylvania Co, VA

GOODNIGHT, CHRISTOPHER/
CHRISTIAN M. (BLW), died
12 May 1868 Clinton Co, IN;
md 7 Jan 1821 Jane Mason
(P), Frederick Co, VA. Her
LNR Clinton Co, IN, 1878

GOODRICH, GEORGE (BLW),
VA and DC militia, died Jun
1834/5, Georgetown, DC; md 1
Jun 1810 Dolly D Gates (P),
Georgetown, DC. Her LNR
Georgetown, DC, 1871

GOODRICH, JOHN B. (BLW),
USA, died 27 Aug 1865, Cen-
terburg, OH; md 1 Sep 1825
Ella Huffman (P), Lewisburg,
Greenbrier Co, VA. She died 1
Nov 1889, LNR Centerburg,
Knox Co, OH, 1878

GOODSON, GEORGE applied for a
pension

GOODSON, LEANDER L. applied
for a pension

GOODSON, WILLIAM (BLW),
died 24 Oct 1852, Floyd Co,
VA; md 8 Jan 1837 America
Sandefur (P), Patrick Co, VA.
She died c1891, LNR P.O.
Turtle Rock, Floyd Co, VA,
1878

GOODWIN, ALLEN (BLW), died
15 Apr 1827, Rockbridge Co,
VA; md 5 Dec 1811 Elizabeth
Hickman (P), Botetourt Co,
VA. Her LNR P.O. Rapps
Mills, Rockbridge Co, VA,
1871

GOODWIN, CHARLES (BLW),
died 7 Aug 1874, Raleigh
Springs, VA; md 21 Dec 1819

GOODWIN (continued)
Janet G Carmichael (P), Fredericksburg, Spotsylvania Co, VA. She died 24 Nov 1884, Baltimore, MD, LNR Baltimore, MD, 1878

GOODWIN, WILLIAM (BLW), died 8 May 1861, Occoquan, Prince William Co, VA; md 7 Feb 1818 Nancy A. Carter (P), Prince William Co, VA. She died 24 Jun 1885, Lorton Valley, VA, LNR Lorton Valley, Fairfax Co, VA, 1878

GOODWIN, WILLIAM (BLW), died 5 Apr 1863, Louisa Co, VA; md 8 May 1823 Frances Jane Goodwin (P), Louisa Co, VA. She died c1891, LNR P.O. Louisa Courthouse, Louisa Co, VA, 1878

GOODWYN/GOODWIN, JESSE T. (P, BLW), LNR P.O. Lebanon, DeKalb Co, AL, 1872; md 10 Dec 1810 Jincy Nance, Dinwiddie Courthouse, VA. She died before 1872

GOOLSBY, ALEXANDER (BLW), died Mar 1854, Amherst Co, VA; md (1) ?, (2) 3 Apr 1839 Abigail Lawhorn (P), Amherst Co, VA. She died before 24 Jun 1886, LNR Lynchburg, Campbell Co, VA, 1878

GOOLSBY, NATHANIEL D. whose widow Susan applied for a pension

GOORLEY, WILLIAM whose widow Mary applied for a pension. William was in Capt. John Goorley's Company

GORDAN, THOMAS (BLW), died 5 Oct 1854, Caswell Co, NC; md 2 Nov 1817 Nancy D. Hamlet (P), Person Co, NC. Her LNR Black Walnut, Halifax Co, VA, 1879

GORDON, ADISON M. (P, BLW), died 25 Feb 1881, Independence, WV; md 28 Jan 1819 Jane B. Triplett (P). She died before 5 Sep 1883, LNR Graf-

GORDON (continued)
ton, Taylor Co, WV, 1881

GORDON, ALEXANDER (BLW), died 12 Oct 1855, Louisville, KY; md 31 Jul 1838 Obedience Sallee (P), Jessamine Co, KY. She died 16 Jun 1880, Paris, MO, LNR Paris, Monroe Co, MO, 1878

GORDON, CHAPMAN whose widow Mary applied for a pension

GORDON, JOHN (BLW), died 24 Jun 1841, Augusta Springs, Augusta Co, VA; md 10 Sep 1812 Sarah Knowles (P), Staunton, VA. Her LNR Staunton, Augusta Co, VA, 1871

GORDON, JOHN L. (BLW), died 15 Sep 1855, Madison Co, VA; md (1) ---- Bradley, (2) 18 Jan 1845 Judy Carter (P), Madison Co, VA. She died 31 Mar 1888, LNR P.O. Madison Courthouse, Madison Co, VA, 1881

GORDON, JOHN W. (P, BLW), died 10 Nov 1877, LNR St. Louis, MO, 1871; md 23 Aug 1812 Delia McKinney

GORDON, OBEDIAH (BLW), died 14 Jul 1862, Appomattox Co, VA; md 15 Oct 1834 Mary Jane Pamplin (P), Nelson Co, VA. She died c1888, LNR P.O. Nebraska, Appomattox, Co, VA, 1878

GORDON, PHILIP (P, BLW), LNR P.O. Kobletown, Jefferson Co, WV, 1871; md (1) Mary Gordon, (2) Sep 1838 Elizabeth Harris, Jefferson Co, VA

GORE, JOSHUA (BLW), died Nov 1866, Happy Creek, Warren Co, VA; md (1) Frances Cochran, (2) 17 Dec 1816 Elizabeth Rountree (P), Culpeper Co, VA. Her LNR P.O. Front Royal, Warren Co, VA, 1878

GORSUCH, NICHOLAS (P, BLW), died 20 Oct 1877, LNR P.O. Duncan Falls, Muskin-

GORSUCH (continued)
gum Co, OH, 1871; md Oct
1804 Susanna Davis, Bal-
timore, MD

GOSS, HENRY, SR. applied for a
pension

GOUL, CHRISTIAN (BLW)

GOULD, AARON (BLW), died 3
May 1864, French Creek, VA;
md (1) ?, (2) ?, (3) 28 Nov
1841 Calysta Bartlett (P),
Morgan Co, OH. She died 23
Mar 1892, LNR French Creek,
Upshur Co, WV, 1878

GOULD, AMOS (BLW), died 4
Sep 1867, Sullivan, OH; md 17
Mar 1814 Polly Johnson (P),
Dover, Windham, CT. She
died 12 Oct 1885, Sullivan,
Ashland Co, OH, 1878

GOULD, GEORGE (BLW) whose
widow was Lydia

GOULD, GILBERT (P, BLW),
LNR Frenck Creek, Upshur Co,
WV, 1871

GOULD, JAMES (BLW)

GOUL, CHRISTIAN (BLW)

GOULD, AARON (BLW), died 3
May 1864, French Creek, VA;
md (1) ?, (2) ?, (3) 28 Nov
1841 Calysta Bartlett (P),
Morgan Co, OH. She died 23
Mar 1892, LNR French Creek,
Upshur Co, WV, 1878

GOULD, AMOS (BLW), died 4
Sep 1867, Sullivan, OH; md 17
Mar 1814 Polly Johnson (P),
Dover, Windham, CT. She
died 12 Oct 1885, Sullivan,
Ashland Co, OH, 1878

GOULD, GEORGE (BLW) whose
widow was Lydia

GOULD, GILBERT (P, BLW),
LNR French Creek, Upshur Co,
WV, 1871

GOULD, JAMES (BLW) whose
widow was Rhoda

GOURLEY/GARELY, ABEL (P,
BLW), LNR P.O. Oakdale,
Livingston Co, IL, 1871; md
Feb 1815 Elizabeth Richards,
Loudoun Co, VA. She died

GOURLEY (continued)
May 1868

GOURLEY, WILLIAM (BLW),
died 24 Jan 1860, Winchester,
Frederick Co, VA; md (1) Han-
nah Lewis, (2) 2 Oct 1845
Catherine Trenary (P), White
Post, Clark Co, VA. She died
Apr 1884, Milldale, Warren
Co, VA, LNR P. O. Nineveh,
Warren Co, VA, 1878

GOWAN/GOWEN, WILLIAM H.
(BLW), died 9 Dec 1870,
Goochland Co, VA; md 17 Dec
1812 Judith H. Atkinson (P),
Goochland Co, VA. Her LNR
P.O. Spring Creek, Madison
Co, VA, 1871

GOWIN/GOWING, SAMUEL (P,
BLW), LNR P.O. Big Island,
Bedford Co, VA, 1871; md (1)
Elizabeth Ferguson

GOWIN, WILLIAM P. (P, BLW),
died 4 Jun 1873, Gallia Co,
OH; md 23 Feb 1823 Anna
Amos (P), Buckingham, Buckingham Co, VA. She died
before 18 Aug 1886, LNR P. O.
Reedyville, Roane Co, WV,
1881

ROLL NO. 38

GRADY, EDWARD B. (BLW),
MA militia, died 8 Nov 1849,
Alexandria, VA; md 21 May
1809 Sarah Taylor (P), Upper-
vile, Loudoun Co, VA. Her
LNR Snickersville, Loudoun
Co, VA, 1871

GRAHAM, CHARLES (P, BLW),
LNR P. O. Benleyville, Breck-
enridge Co, KY, 1871; md 22
Jan 1818 Elizabeth Haynes,
Bedford Co, VA

GRAHAM, GABRIEL (BLW), OH
militia, died 6 Feb 1871,
Athens Co, OH; md 2 Apr 1815
Mary Bickle (P), Meigs Co,
OH. She died 8 Feb 1880,
Mason Co, WV; LNR New
Haven, Mason Co, WV, 1878

GRAHAM/GRAYHAM, ISAAC (P, BLW), died 10 Nov 1881, Bushby Run, WV; md (1) Mary Ann Barbary, (2) 29 Jul 1869 Lydia Ann Kimble (P), Grant Co, WV. Her LNR Bushby Run, Pendleton Co, WV, 1882

GRAHAM, JAMES (P, BLW), LNR P. O. Salem, Washington Co, IN, 1871. Wife died before May 1871

GRAHAM/GRAYHAM, THOMAS (P, BLW), died 31 Jul 1878, Wood Co, WV; md 27 Aug 1828 Elizabeth Reeder (P), Wood Co, VA. Her LNR P. O. Fountain Spring, Wood Co, WV, 1878

GRAHAM, THOMAS (BLW), died 6 Dec 1869, Highland Co, VA; md Mar 1849 Elizabeth/ Amanda E. Koontz (P), Highland Co, VA. She died 10 Sep 1909, LNR P.O. Clover Creek, Highland Co, VA, 1878

GRALEY/GRAYLEY, JAMES (P, BLW), LNR Lincoln Co, WV, 1871; md 4 Mar 18-- Sarah Trail, Montgomery Co, VA

GRANDSTAFF, BENJAMIN (P, BLW), died 22 Jan 1873, Shenandoah Co, VA; md 15 Oct 1820 Elizabeth Clinedinst (P), Shenandoah Co, VA. She died before 7 Feb 1885, LNR P.O. Edinburgh, Shenandoah Co, VA, 1878

GRANDSTAFF, GEORGE (P, BLW), LNR Edinburg, Shenandoah Co, VA, 1871; md 18 Mar 1810 Mary Reedy, Shenandoah Co, VA

GRANT, CHRISTOPHER (P, BLW), died 17 Jul 1876, Dekossa, Columbia Co, WI; md (1) ?, (2) 3 Feb 1844 Sarah Bowles (P), Solon, McHenry Co, IL. She died c1881, LNR Meridian, Dunn Co, WI, 1880

GRANT, GARDNER (BLW), died 10 Dec 1856, Washington Co, VA; md 23 Jan 1815 Hannah

GRANT (continued)
Gilliam (P), Washington Co, VA. She died 3 Jan 1877, Verona, MO, LNR Verona, Lawrence Co, MO, 1883 (sic)

GRANT, ISAAC whose widow Mary applied for a pension

GRANT, JAMES (BLW), died 20 Jan 1870, Callands, VA; md 19 Feb 1817 Mary Ann Swepston (P), Pittsylvania Co, VA. She died before Jun 1883, LNR Callands, Pittsylvania Co, VA, 1878

GRANT, SAMUEL (BLW) whose widow Mara applied for a pension

GRANT, STEPHEN (P-rejected, BLW), died 6 May 1873, Pekin, Jessamine Co, KY; md 10 Oct 1816 Nancy Forest (P), Halifax Co, VA. She died 18 Oct 1887, Jessamine Co, KY, LNR P.O. Nicholsville, Jessamine Co, KY, 1880

GRANT, STEWART (P, BLW), died 3 Aug 1877, LNR Winchester, Frederick Co, VA, 1871; md 1818 Elizabeth Fridley, Winchester, VA

GRANT, THOMAS G. (P-rejected, BLW), died 18 Apr 1875, Monroe Co, MO; md 20 Sep 1832 Lucy M. Allen, Boone Co, KY. She died c1890, LNR Renick, MO, 1887

GRANVILLE/GLANVILLE, PATRICK (BLW), USA, died 12 Feb 1857, Franklin Co, KS, LNR Preston Co, VA, 1854; md 25 Nov 1810 Frances Hartnett (P), Aghada, County Cork, Ireland. Her LNR Ottowa, Franklin Co, KS, 1871. Frances was pensioned as Fanny Granville

GRASS, JOHN (BLW), died 17 Apr 1843, Augusta Co, VA; md 30 Jun 1814 Sally/Sarah A. Haybarger (P), near Staunton, VA. She died c5 Feb 1879, Augusta Co, VA, LNR Sher-

GRASS (continued)
ando, Augusta Co, VA, 1871

GRASS, JOHN (P, BLW), died 29 Jun 1876, Port Andrew, WI; md 24 Feb 1820 Susan Cotton (P), Greenbrier Co, VA. She died 19 Aug 1878, Port Andrew, Richardson Co, WI

GRASTY, GEORGE whose widow applied for a pension

GRAVELY/GRAVELLY, JOSEPH (P, BLW), USA, died Z8 Feb 1873, LNR P.O. Hillsville, Carroll Co, VA, 1871; md Polly Higg

GRAVELY, LEWIS (P, BLW), LNR Leatherwood Store, Henry Co, VA, 1878

GRAVES, GEORGE B. (P, BLW), LNR P.O. Winchester, Frederick Co, VA, 1872; md 6 Apr 1843 Mary A. Speeny, Winchester, VA

GRAVES, JAMES H. (BLW), died 17 Jan 1850, Fredericksburg, VA; md 20 Oct 1819 Harriet Smith (P), Culpeper Co, VA. She died 26 Mar 1887, Richmond, VA, LNR Richmond, Henrico Co, VA, 1878

GRAVES, JAMES T. (BLW), died 1 May 1857, Columbia Mills, VA; md (1) ?, (2) 7 Sep 1845 Christina Sigler (P), Page Co, VA. She died c1887, LNR Honeyville, Page Co, VA, 1878

GRAVES, JOHN (BLW)

GRAVES, JOHN (BLW), died 12 Jul 1869, Prince George Co, VA; md (1) Adelia Graves, (2) 9 Jul 1863 Emma F. Hobbs (P), Surry Co, VA. Her LNR P.O. Garysville, Prince George Co, VA, 1878

GRAVES, LEWIS whose widow Fanny applied for a pension

GRAVES, RODHAM applied for a pension

GRAVES, THOMAS (BLW), died 28 Apr 1859, Huntsville, Randolph Co, MO; md (1) Judith Turner, (2) 27 Dec 1846 Eliz-

GRAVES (continued)
abeth Nalley (P), Lincoln Co, MO. She died c1895, LNR Moberly, Randolph Co, MO, 1887

GRAVES, WILLIAM L. (BLW), died 1 Sep 1853, Madison Co, TN; md 5 May 1811 Sarah H. Turner (P). Albemarle Co, VA. Her LNR P. O. Jackson, Madison Co, TN, 1871

GRAY, ALEXANDER (P, BLW). PA militia, died 19 May 1876, Jackson Co, WV; md 10 Nov 1857 Belinda Ward (P), Belmont Co, OH. She died 15 Aug 1908, LNR Toppins Grove, Jackson Co, WV, 1878

GRAY, ALEXANDER (BLW), TN militia, died 12 Feb 1859, Scott Co, VA; md 11 Sep 1834 Harriett Mason (P), Stanton Creek, Scott Co, VA. Her LNR P.O. Osborn's Ford, Scott Co, VA, 1880

GRAY, DANIEL (P, BLW), LNR Patrick Courthouse, Patrick Co, VA, 1878

GRAY, GEORGE (P, BLW), LNR P.O. Xenia Crossroads, Clark Co, OH, 1871; md 16 Aug 1810 Libby Burke, Bunkers Hill, VA. She died Jun 1866

GRAY, JAMES (BLW), died 17 May 1859, Harrisonburg, VA; md c1818 Sarah Moore (P), Buckingham Courthouse, Buckingham Co, VA. She died 26 Jun 1886, Harrisonburg, Rockingham Co, VA

GRAY, JOHN D. whose widow Mary M. applied for a pension

GRAY, WILLIAM whose widow Susan W. applied for a pension

GRAY, WILLIAM whose widow Mary applied for a pension

GRAY, WILLIAM W. (BLW), died 5 Apr 1865, Raleigh, NC; md 22 Jan 1816 Mary Ann Dunlop (P), Richmond, Henrico Co, VA. She died Dec 1882, Nashville, TN, LNR Nashville,

GRAY (continued)
Davidson Co, TN, 1881

GRAY, WILLIAM (P, BLW), died 10 Mar 1890, Cocke Co, TN; md (1) Phebe Fox, (2) 4 Feb 1874 Eliza Jane (----) Hannon (P), Cocke Co, TN. Her LNR Newport, Cocke Co, TN, 1891

GRAY, ZEBEDEE (P, BLW), LNR Berryville,Clarke Co, VA, 1871; md 18 Mar 1823 Nancy A. Dowell, Clarke Co, VA

GRAYSON, BENJAMIN (BLW), died 23 Mar 1850, New Creek, Hampshire Co, VA; md 3 May 1827 Mary Fout (P), Nobley Mountain, Hampshire Co, VA. She died c1892, LNR Washington, Washington Co, IA, 1887

GRAYSON, JOHN (BLW), died 14 Apr 1862, Logan Co, KY; md 7 Jul 1812 Susannah Britt (P), Albemarle Co, VA. Her LNR P.O. Adairville, Logan Co, KY, 1879

GRAYSON, THOMAS (BLW), died 21 Sep 1854, Lincoln Co, MO; md 4 Sep 1823 Rhoda Merritt (P), Albemarle Co, VA. She died 20 Apr 1883, Louisville, MO, LNR Ashby, Pike Co, MO, 1878

GREANER, WILLIAM (BLW), died 31 Dec 1868, Richmond, VA; md (1) Temperance Temple, (2) 9 Mar 1845 Sarah (----) Talbert (P), Richmond, VA. Her LNR Richmond, VA, 1879

GREEAR, NOAH whose widow Luticia applied for a pension

GREEN, ANDERSON (P, BLW), died 1 Jun 1883, Wadeville, NC, LNR P.O. Troy, Montgomery Co, NC, 1871; md 17 Nov 1819 Sarah Stone, Mecklenburg Co, VA. She died before 4 Sep 1871

GREEN, BENJAMIN (P, BLW), USA, LNR P. O. Elm Grove, Ohio Co, WV, 1871; md 5 Jun

GREEN (continued)
1828 Mary Ann Riley, Geauga Co, OH

GREEN, ELI (P, BLW), LNR P. O. Wellsburg, Brooke Co, WV, 1871; md 5 Nov 1812 Percilla Hood, Baltimore Co., MD

GREEN, GEORGE (BLW), USA, died 14 Oct 1854, Frederick Co, VA; md 20 Dec 1827 Nancy Ann Parmer (P), Fauquier Co, VA. She died c1883, LNR Cumberland, Alleghany Co, MD, 1879

GREEN, Isaam whose widow Jinsey applied for a pension

GREEN, JOHN (P, BLW), LNR P.O. Pittsylvania Court House, Pittsylvania Co, VA, 1871; md 20 Feb 1817 Sallie Clark, Rockingham Co, NC

GREEN, JOHN (BLW), died 2 Jul 1832, Washington Co, IN; md 25 Dec 1809 Rachel Kaylor (P), VA. Her LNR P.O. Mitchell, Lawrence Co, IN, 1871

GREEN, JOHN P. whose widow Dolly applied for a pension

GREEN, LAWRENCE applied for a pension

GREEN, LEWIS whose widow Ann Lewis Green applied for a pension

GREEN, MICHAEL (BLW), OH militia, died 4 Jul 1865, Muscatine, IA; md 26 Jun 1814 Elizabeth Glaze (P), Wood Co, VA. She died c1887, LNR Muscatine, IA, 1887

GREEN, THEOPHILUS F. (BLW), died 14 Apr 1862, Caroline Co, VA; md 24 Dec 1816 Patsey E. Walden (P). Caroline Co, VA. Her LNR P. O. Sparta, Caroline Co, VA, 1878

GREEN, THOMAS D. (BLW), MD militia, died 18 Aug 1841, Baltimore, MD; md 16 Dec 1813 Ann Kirgan (P), Baltimore, MD. Her LNR P.O. Modest Town, Accomac Co, VA, 1871

GREEN, WILLIAM whose widow Susan applied for a pension

GREEN, WILLIAM (BLW), died 16 Mar 1863, Rockville, Pike Co, IN; md 15 Jul 1820 Hannah Duncan (P), Russell Co, VA. She died c1898, LNR Topeka, Shawnee Co, KS, 1887

GREEN, ZACHARIAH (BLW), DC militia, died 9 Oct 1843, Salemdown, Fairfax Co, VA; md 27 Jul 1841 Ann R. Hubball (P), Fairfax Co, VA. She died 6 Nov 1886, LNR Washington, DC, 1878

GREENSTREET, GARNETT (BLW), died 16 Sep 1849, Essex Co, VA; md 26 Dec 1832 Rocksey Tate (P), Essex Co, VA. Her LNR P.O. Tunstalls Station, New Kent Co, VA, 1879

GREENSTREET, JOHN (BLW), died 20 May 1848, Caroline Co, VA; md 1829 Susan Bland (P), King and Queen Co, VA. She died 11 Jul 1888, Caroline Co, VA, LNR P.O. Sparta, Caroline Co, VA, 1878

GREER, JAMES (P, BLW), LNR P.O. Murphy, Cherokee Co, NC, 1871; md Jun 1818 Rachel Friesibes, Sevier Co, TN

GREER, JOSEPH applied for a pension

GREER, MATTHEW whose widow Rhoda applied for a pension

ROLL NO. 39

GREGG, HENRY whose widow Margaret applied for a pension

GREGG/GRIGG, PETER (P, BLW), died 6 Jul 1882; md (1) ---- Jones, (2) 15 Dec 1841 Catherine G. Epes (P), Nottoway Co, VA. She died 1891, LNR Chula Depot, Amelia Co, VA, 1882

GREGG, WILLIAM applied for a pension

GREGORY, ABEL (P, BLW), LNR La Belle, Lewis Co, MO, 1871

GREGORY, CHARLES applied for a pension

GREGORY, DAVID W. whose widow Elizabeth applied for a pension

GREGORY, FEW A. (P-rejected, BLW), died 18 Aug 1872, Monroe Co, TN; md 1 Jun 1841 Martha L. Reynolds (P), Monroe Co, TN. Her LNR P.O. Ocala, Marion Co, FL, 1878

GREGORY, JACOB (P, BWL), LNR P.O. Green Bay, Prince Edward Co, VA, 1871

GREGORY, JOHN (P, BLW), LNR P.O. Dalzell, Washington Co, OH, 1872; md 15 Feb 1812 Rachel Campbell, Nelson Co, VA. She died before 13 Mar 1872

GREGORY, JOHN (BLW), died 29 Dec 1850, Brown Co, OH; md 21 May 1850 Dulcena Berry (P), Brown Co, OH. She died 1 Sep 1884, LNR P.O. White Oak Station, Brown Co, OH, 1878

GREGORY, MATHEW (BLW), died 11 Jan 1856, Greenbrier Co, VA; md 1 Oct 1833 Dorcas Benston (P), Greenbrier Co, VA. Her LNR P.O. Lewisburg, Greenbrier Co, VA, 1878

GREGORY, ROBERT (BLW), died 17 May 1853, Martinsburg, Berkeley Co, VA; md 24 Feb 1807 Anna Stephens (P), Hagerstown, Washington Co, MD. Her LNR Piedmont, Mineral Co, WV, 1872

GREGORY, THOMAS (P, BLW), LNR P. O. Manchester, Chesterfield Co, VA, 1871; md 31 Oct 1820 Betsey Ann Chatham

GREGORY, UMBLETON whose widow Mary applied for a pension

GREGORY, WILLIAM (BLW), died 13 Jul 1875, Alexandria,

GREGORY (continued) VA; md 6 Mar 1838 Mary D. Long (P), Alexandria, VA. She died 6 Nov 1896, Alexandria, VA.

GREGORY, WILLIAM (P, BLW), LNR P.O. Hill Grove, Pittsylvania Co, VA, 1871; md 9 Apr 18-- Sally M. Kean, Pittsylvania Co, VA

GREGORY, WILLIAM (BLW), died 20 Jul 1859 Calloway Co, MO; md (1) Nancy ----, (2) 26 Mar 1829 Nancy Robinson (P), Campbell Co, VA. Her LNR P.O. Readville, Calloway Co, MO, 1887

GREGORY, WILLIAM (P, BLW), USA, died 11 Jan 1886, Dickinsons, VA; md (1) Mariah Bradner, (2) 29 Aug 1850 Mary Ann Massey Amos (P), Dickinsons, VA. She died before 21 Mar 1897, LNR Dickinsons, Franklin Co, VA, 1886

GREINER, JACOB (P, BLW), died c1876, LNR Dalson, Clark Co, IL, 1871

GRESHAM, ELIJAH (BLW), died 8 Apr 1859, Chesterfield Co, VA; md (1) Sarah Chatham, (2) ?, (3) 14 Aug 1822 Maria Goode (P), Chesterfield Co, VA. Her LNR Petersburg Dinwiddie Co, VA, 1878

GREYER, JOHN (BLW), died 5 Aug 1856, Rockingham Co, VA; md 19 Aug 1837 Elizabeth Alford (P), Rockingham Co, VA. She died c1891, LNR Goods Mill, Rockingham Co, VA, 1878

GRICE, CHARLES A. (BLW), PA militia, died 22 Jul 1870, Portsmouth, VA; md 22 Jul 1847 Eliza (----) Edwards (P), Portsmouth, VA. Her LNR Portsmouth, Norfolk Co, VA, 1878

GRIFFIN, AUSTIN (BLW), KY militia, died 9 Dec 1850, Clark Co, IL; md 30 Aug 1820 Ma-

GRIFFIN (continued) linda Wright (P), Nelson Co, VA. She died c1879, LNR P. O. Marshall, Clark Co, IL, 1878

GRIFFIN, BIRD (P, BLW), died 20 Apr 1872, LNR Lafayette, Christian Co, KY, 1871; md 4 Oct 1820 Ann Northington, Mecklenburg Co, VA

GRIFFIN, DANIEL G. (BLW), died 13 Apr 1879, Forsyth Co, NC; md c1815 Gemima Neale. She died c1859

GRIFFIN, JAMES (BLW), died 13 Oct 1871, LNR P. O. Franklin Depot, Southampton Co, VA, 1871

GRIFFIN, JAMES (BLW), died 2 Jul 1852, Richmond, VA; md (1) ---- Bowles, (2) 16 Oct 1844 Jane A. Barrett (P). Richmond, VA. She died 10 Aug 1888, LNR Richmond, Henrico Co, VA, 1888

GRIFFIN, JOHN N. (P, BLW). died c1878, Culpeper Co, VA, LNR P. O. Boston, Culpeper Co, VA, 1872; md Sep 1819 Eliza T. Withers, Culpeper Co, VA

GRIFFITH, DANIEL (P, BLW), LNR P.O. Longbranch, Franklin Co, VA, 1871; md 27 Dec 1809 Allay Sheridan, Franklin Co, VA

GRIFFITH, LITTLETON/LETER whose widow Mollie applied for a pension

GRIFFITH, SAMUEL applied for a pension

GRIFFITH, THOMAS whose widow Elender applied for a pension

GRIFFITH, THOMAS (BLW), died 22 Jul 1863, Loudoun Co, VA; md 23 May 1822 Sarah Elizabeth Van Horn (P), Loudoun Co, VA. She died 18 Feb 1896, LNR Charlestown, Jefferson Co, WV, 1879

GRIFFITTS/GRIFFITS/GRIF-
FITH, SAMUEL (BLW), died
29 Oct 1870, Hancock Co, IN;
md (1) Mary ----, (2) 27 Feb
1849 Mary Long (P), Rush Co,
IN. She died 12 Dec 1882,
Longwood, IN, LNR Leonard,
Fayette Co, IN, 1880

GRIGGS, JAMES (BLW), GA militia, died 8 Aug 1866, Glenville, AL; md 4 Jan 1825 Martha Marie Cox (P), Putnam Co,
GA. She died 4 Mar 1896,
LNR P.0. Folly Mills, Augusta
Co, VA, 1878

GRIGSBY, REDMOND/REDMAN
(P, BLW), LNR Chester, Warren Co, VA, 1871; md 18 Mar
1803 Catharine Weekley,
Chester's Gap, VA

GRIM, JACOB whose widow Martha applied for a pension

GRIM, JOHN (P, BLW), died 28
Jan 1872, Jasper Co, IA; md
20 Nov 1817 Rebecca Davis
(P), Hillsboro, Highland Co,
OH. She died Jan 1879, LNR
P.0. Vandalia, Jasper Co, IA,
1878

GRIM, JOHN H. applied for a
pension

GRIM, PHILIP (BLW)

GRIMM, JOSEPH (BWL), died
15 Dec 1870, Vanderburg Co,
IN; md (1) ?, (2) 5 Oct 1844
Elizabeth (----) (Reeves)
Sherry (P), Vanderburg Co, IN.
Her LNR Grand Tower, Jack-
son Co, IL, 1891

GRIMMETT, NICHOLAS (BLW),
died Aug 1859, Pike Co, OH,
LNR Louisiana, Pike Co, OH,
1871; md 1803 Peggy Cox

GRIMSLEY, ROBERT whose widow Dolly applied for a pension

GRINSTEAD, BARTHOLOMEW
(P, BLW), LNR P. 0. Bowling
Green, Warren Co, KY, 1871;
md Sep 1820 Nancy Totty,
Warren Co, KY

GRINSTEAD, JAMES (BLW),

GRINSTEAD (continued)
died 30 Jun 1850, Barren Co,
KY; md Oct 1812 Nancy Eu-
bank (P), Henrico Co, VA. Her
LNR Glasgow, Barren Co, KY,
1871

GRINSTEAD, JESSE (P, BLW),
died 27 Jun 1884, Pettis Co,
MO; md 6 Mar 1823 Elizabeth
Clopton (P), Madison Co, KY.
She died 15 Mar 1885, Pettis
Co, MO, LNR Longwood, Pet-
tis Co, MO, 1884

GRISBY, GEORGE whose widow
Massa applied for a pension

GROOM, WILLIAM (BLW), died
13 Jul 1831, Louisa Co, VA;
md 12 Sep 1811 Martha Butler
(P), Louisa Co, VA. She died
22 Jan 1874, LNR Louisa Co,
VA, 1871

GROSS, EDMOND (P, BLW), died
7 Apr 1871; md 1816 Hetty
Brock (P), Harlan Co, KY. She
died cFeb 1881, LNR P. O.
Harlan Courthouse, Harlan Co,
KY, 1879

GROSS, JOHN applied for a pension

GROSS, JOHN (P, BLW), died 15
Dec 1876, Ogden, IN; md 17
Apr 1820 Emily Purdy (P),
Gallia Co, OH. Her LNR
Knightstown, Henry Co, IN,
1878

GROSS, RICHARD whose widow
Margaret applied for a pension

GROVE, ABRAHAM (P, BLW),
LNR P.O. Woodstock, Shenandoah Co, VA, 1871; md 5 Dec
1815 Elizabeth Coffman, Shenandoah Co, VA

GROVE, ANDREW (BLW), died 3
Mar 1852, Philometh, Union
Co, IN; md 30 Sep 1830 Mary
Mallory (P), Botetourt Co, VA.
Her LNR Union Co, IN, 1878

GROVE, GEORGE whose widow
Lawrinda applied for a pension

GROVE, GEORGE W. whose widow Elizabeth applied for a
pension

GROVE, JOHN applied for a pension

GROVE, JOHN VANDORN applied for a pension

GROVE, JOHN W. (P, BLW), died 9 Feb 1873, Stevensburg, VA; md 31 Jan 1813 Jane Young (P), New Town Stevensburg, VA. She died before 9 Sep 1882, LNR P.O. New Town Stevensburg, Frederick Co, VA, 1879. John was a substitute for William Grove in the War

GROVE, PHILIP (BLW), MD militia, died 27 May 1858, Champaign Co, OH; md Feb 1817 Eve Demory (P), Loudoun Co, VA. She died c1881, LNR Catawba, Clark Co, OH, 1879

GROVE, WILLIAM H. (BLW), died 24 Mar 1863, Winchester, VA; md 14 Apr 1814 Mary Crockwell (P), Winchester, VA. Her LNR Winchester, Frederick Co, VA, 1871

GROVES, JAMES (P, BLW), died 9 Jul 1880, Culpeper Co, VA; md (1) Betsy Austin, (2) Oct 1824 Susan Tapp (P), Warrenton, Fauquier Co, VA. Her LNR P.O. Rixeyville, Culpeper Co, VA, 1880

GROVES, ZEBULON (BLW), died 7 Jul 1854, Wheeling, VA; md 10 Mar 1833 Deborah Russell (P), Morristown, Belmont Co, OH. She died 24 Feb 1887, LNR Wheeling, Ohio Co, WV

GROW, DANIEL (BLW), died Mar 1869, Taylor Co, WV; md 16 Sep 1813 Catherine Zimbro (P), Augusta Co, VA. Her LNR Taylor Co, WV, 1871

GRUBB, ANDREW W. (P, BLW), LNR Randolph, Randolph Co, MO, 1871; md 1815 Sally Hodges, Bedford Co, VA

GRUBB, EBENEZER (P, BLW), LNR P.O. Waterford, Loudoun Co, VA, 1871; md 22 Jun 1820 Leah Virtz, Lovettsville, VA.

GRUBB (continued) She died before Apr 1871

GRUBB, ELIJAH (BLW), died 25 Mar 1846, Pittsylvania Co, VA; md 4 Jul 1805 Polly Saunders (P), Bedford Co, VA. Her LNR Pittsylvania Courthouse, Pittsylvania Co, VA, 1871

GRUBB, JOHN (P, BLW), LNR Lovettsville, Loudoun Co, VA, 1871; md 28 Nov 1816 Elizabeth Jackson, Loudoun Co, VA

GRUBB, JOHN (BLW), died 6 Jun 1851, Chester Co, PA; md 27 Oct 1814 Magdalena Carl (P), Montgomery Co, PA. She died 25 Jun 1878, Vincent, Chester Co, PA

GRUBBS, JOHN whose widow Jemima applied for a pension

GRUBBS, THOMAS (BLW), died 10 Feb 1858, Campbell Co, VA; md 4 Jul 1811 Martha Mallory (P), Hanover Co, VA. She died 9 Apr 1872, LNR P. O. Castle Craig, Campbell Co, VA, 1871

GRUBER, JACOB (P, BLW), LNR P.O. Middleway, Jefferson Co, WV, 1871; md Martha Baughman. She died before 26 May 1871

GRUNLEE/GREENLEE, HENRY applied for a pension

GRIMES/GRYMES, EDMUND/EDWARD applied for a pension

GRYMES, PEYTON (P, BLW), LNR Selma, Orange Co, VA, 1873; md 5 Oct 1819 Harriet G. Dade

GUILL, AUGUSTUS applied for a pension

GUILL, BLUFORD whose widow Mary H. applied for a pension

GUILLIAMS, RICHARD (BLW), died 20 Mar 1854, Hendricks Co, IN; md 7 Aug 1814 Rosanna Scott (P), Franklin Co, VA. She died 18 Dec 1872,

183

GUILLIAMS (continued)
Cass Co, MO, LNR P.O.
Peculiar, Cass Co, MO, 1872
GULICK, WILLIAM whose widow
Ivy applied for a pension
GUNN, BURWELL whose widow
Mary S. applied for a pension
GUNNELL, HUGH W. (BLW),
died 7 Jul 1857, Fairfax Co,
VA; md 5 Nov 1839 Elizabeth
Trunnell (P), Fairfax Co, VA.
She died 24 Mar 1885, Vienna,
Fairfax Co, VA
GUNNELL, GEORGE W. (BLW),
died 8 Jan 1878, Fairfax Co,
VA; md (1) Lucy Ratcliffe, (2)
3 Oct 1839 Emmaline Young
(P), Fairfax Co, VA. She died
19 Nov 1887, LNR P.O.
Vienna, Fairfax Co, VA, 1878
GUNNELL, JAMES S. (BLW),
died 26 Mar 1852, Washington,
DC; md 13 Oct 1825 Helen M.
Mackall (P), Washington, DC.
Her LNR Washington, DC,
1859
GUNNELL, JOHN applied for a
pension
GUNNELL, NATHANIEL (BLW),
died 20 Mar 1857, Ray Co,
MO; md (1) ?, (2) 4 Jan 1848
Catharine (Saylor) Albert (P),
Ray Co, MO. Her LNR Rich-
mond, Ray Co, MO, 1878
GUNNELL, WILLIAM (BLW),
died 1 May 1848, Fairfax Co,
VA; md 5 Jan 1809 Elizabeth
Lanham (P), Fairfax Co, VA.
She died 2 Apr 1872, LNR P.
O. Fairfax Courthouse, Fairfax
Co, VA, 1871
GUSEMAN, ISAAC (P, BLW),
LNR P.O. Woodville, Adams
Co, IL, 1871; md 12 Dec 1819
Jane Reed, Monongalia Co, VA
GUSMAN, JOSEPH (P, BLW),
LNR Harrison Co, WV, 1871.
Not married.
GUSTER, JOHN (P, BLW), LNR
P.O. Elamsville, Patrick Co,
VA, 1871; md Aug 1813 Betsy
Junny

GUSTIN, JAMES W. whose widow
Hester applied for a pension
GUTHEREDGE/GUTHRIDGE,
PRESLEY (P, BLW), died 19
Aug 1874, LNR P.O. Spring-
hill, Livingston Co, MD, 1871.
GUTHRIE, EPHRAIM (P, BLW).
LNR P.O. Halifax Courthouse,
Halifax Co, VA, 1871; md 15
Dec 1811, Nancy Blackwell,
Halifax Co, VA
GUTHRIE, HENRY P. (BLW),
died 24 Nov 1869, Martins
Ferry, OH; md 19 Dec 1818
Mary C. Stedman (P), York Co,
VA. She died 30 Nov 1883,
LNR Martins Ferry, Belmont
Co, OH, 1878
GUTHRIE, JOHN (P, BLW), LNR
News Ferry, Halifax Co, VA,
1878; md 4 Jul 1821 Mary
New, Halifax Co, VA
GUTHRIE, ROBERT (P, BLW),
died 15 Jun 1874, Wetzel Co,
WV; md 12 Oct 1817 Castilla
Simpson (P), Glascow, PA.
She died 25 Apr 1879, Halls
Mills, Wetzel Co, WV
GUTHRIE, VINCENT (P-reject-
ed, BLW), died 27 Feb 1872,
Cerulean Spring, KY; md 28
Aug 1817 Sarah Stowe (P),
Person Co, NC. Her LNR Cer-
ulean Spring, Trigg Co, KY,
1879
GUY, JAMES applied for a pen-
sion
GUY/GUIE, MATHEW (BLW)
GWATHMEY, JOSEPH (BLW),
died 7 Dec 1843, Middletown,
KY; md 17 Feb 1820 Lucy Ann
Able (P), Jefferson Co, KY.
Her LNR Louisville, Jefferson
Co, KY, 1878
GWATHMEY, RICHARD whose
widow Lucy Ann applied for a
pension
GWINN, ANDREW (P, BLW),
LNR P.O. Mud Bridge, Cabell
Co, WV, 1871; md 1 Feb 1827
Rachel Harshburger, Cabell
Co, VA

HAAS, JOHN (BLW) whose widow was Sarah

HACKER, THOMAS S. (BLW), died 29 Sep 1858, Shelby Co, IN; md 17 Dec 1817 Margaret Keith (P), Lewis Co, VA. Her LNR P.O. Shelbyville, Shelby Co, IN, 1878

HACKNEY, THOMAS (P, BLW)

HACKWORTH, REUBEN (BLW), died 29 Mar 1863, Flat Woods, Boyd Co, KY; md 21 Dec 1815 Mary Hologan (P), Bedford Co, VA. She died 23 Aug 1887, Wayne Co, WV, LNR P.O. Ceredo, Wayne Co, WV, 1878

HADDOX, HENRY (P, BLW), USA & VA militia

HADEN, JAMES M. whose widow Sarah applied for a pension

HADEN/HEADEN, JOHN (BLW), died 10 Oct 1826 Bedford Co, VA; md 8 Sep 1796 Elizabeth Murphy (P), Bedford Co, VA. Her LNR P.O. Fancy Grove, Bedford Co, VA, 1871

HAFFNER, JACOB (BLW) whose widow Susanna received a pension

HAGA, DAVID whose widow Sarah received a pension

HAGISH, CHARLES whose widow Julia received a pension

HAIGH/HAY, GEORGE (BLW), MD militia, died Jan 1821, Norfolk, VA; md 5 Feb 1819 Elizabeth Carline (P), Norfolk, VA. Her LNR Norfolk, VA, 1878

HAIGLER, HENRY (P, BLW)

HAIGLER, JOHN (P, BLW)

HAIL, LEWIS, JR. (P-rejected, BLW) whose widow Celia Hall (per Mary A. Miller, her guardian), received a pension

HAIL, STEPHEN, Jr. (BLW) whose widow Lenora received a pension. Stephen served in Capt. Lewis Hail's Company

HAIL, STEPHEN, Sr. (BLW),

HAIL (continued) died 16 Feb 1854, Grayson Co, VA; md 22 Apr 1803 Frances Bourn (P), Grayson Co, VA. Her LNR Elk Creek, Grayson Co, VA, 1871. Stephen served in Capt. Lewis Hail's Company

HAIL/HALE, THOMAS LEWIS applied for a pension. Thomas served in Capt. Lewis Hail's Company

HAILE, MESHAK (BLW), died 10 Oct 1837, Lynchburg, VA; md 11 Jan 1816 Lucy Creasy (P), Bedford Co, VA. Her LNR P.O. Liberty, Bedford Co, VA, 1878

HAILE, THOMAS (P, BLW), died 21 Jun 1875, Carter Co, KY; md (1) ?, (2) ?, (3) 15 Jun 1825 Frances Oliver (P), Middlesex Co, VA. Her LNR P.O. Upper Tygart, Carter Co, KY, 1878

HAILEY/HALEY, BENJAMIN (BLW), KY militia, died 19 Mar 1846, Lincoln Co, KY; md 7 May 1802 or 1808 Nancy Sisk (P), Albemarle Co, VA. She died 5 Jul 1874, LNR Millidgeville, Lincoln Co, KY, 1871

HAILEY/HALEY, HENRY (BLW) whose widow Joana received a pension

HAIR, JAMES and widow Abigail received a pension

HAIR, JAMES (BLW), died 4 Jun 1860, Prince George Co, VA; md 11 Apr 18-- Nancy Lee (P), Prince George Co, VA. Her LNR Prince George Courthouse, Prince George Co, VA, 1872

HAIR, WILLIAM whose widow Elizabeth applied for a pension

HAIRSTON, SAMUEL applied for a pension

HAISLIP/HASLIP, ROBERT whose widow Mary T. received a pension

HALBERT, JAMES (BLW)

HALBERT, JOHN (P, BLW)

HALE, BENJAMIN applied for a pension

HALE, G./JEHU applied for a pension

HALE, ISAAC whose widow received a pension

HALE/HALL, KINCHEN applied for a pension

HALE, WILLIAM (P, BLW)

HALES, CORBIN (P-rejected) whose widow Emily received a pension

HALES, PETER (P, BLW)

HALEY, EDWARD applied for a pension

HALEY, MARK (P, BLW), died 24 Sep 1873, Fauquier Co, VA; md 29 Jan 1823 Harriet Garrett (P), Salem, Fauquier Co, VA. She died c1890, LNR P.O. Warrenton, Fauquier Co, VA, 1878

HALEY, STERLING S. whose widow Mary received a pension

HALEY, THOMAS whose widow Mary received a pension

HALEY, WILLIAM (P, BLW)

HALEY, WINSTON (BLW), died Jan 1866, Caroline Co, VA; md (1) Ann Wright, (2) Margaret Young, (3) 9 Jul 1851 Frances H. Bell (P), Caroline Co, VA. Her LNR P.O. Milford, Caroline Co, VA, 1878

HALL, ALEXANDER S. (BLW), died 23 Aug 1849, Staunton, VA; md 18 Aug 1818 Jane S. Paxton (P), Rockbridge Co, VA. Her LNR Staunton, Augusta Co, VA, 1878

HALL, ALFRED (P, BLW)

HALL, BENJAMIN (P, BLW)

HALL, CLARK (BLW)

HALL, DANIEL whose widow Nancy applied for a pension

HALL, DENNIS (P, BLW)

HALL, ELIJAH (P, BLW), died 1 Sep 1877, Montgomery Co, IN; md (1) Delila Reickman, (2) 23 May 1866 Nancy (----) Fields (P), Crawfordsville, IN. Her

HALL (continued) LNR Waynetown, Montgomery Co, IN, 1887

HALL, HENRY (BLW), died 9 Jul 1869, Lynchburg, VA; md 18 Jul 1822 Catharine W. Tompkins (P), Lynchburg, VA. Her LNR P.O. Lynchburg, Campbell Co, VA, 1878

HALL, HENRY J. whose widow Lucy W. received a pension

HALL, JAMES (P, BLW)

HALL, JAMES applied for a pension

HALL, JOHN applied for a pension

HALL, JOHN (BLW), died 4 Nov 1837, Dickson Co, TN; md 22 Feb 1809 Elizabeth Smith (P), Brunswick Co, VA. She died 31 Oct 1877, Dickson Co, TN, LNR P.O. Charlotte, Dickson Co, TN, 1873

HALL, JOHN B. (BLW), USA, died 1 Sep 1862, Fredericksburg, VA; md 23 Oct 1817 Harriet Stringfellow (P), Fredericksburg, VA. She died c1888, LNR Fredericksburg, Spotsylvania Co, VA, 1878

HALL, JOHN T. (BLW), died Jun 1857, Jackson Co, TN; md (1) Annie Simpson, (2) Sallie Scanland, (3) 1850 Telitha (Van Hoosir) Dodson (P), Jackson Co, TN. Her LNR P. O. Gainesboro, Jackson Co, TN, 1878

HALL, LEVI (BLW), USA, died 10 Jun 1829, Harpers Ferry, VA; md 29 Mar 1808 Sarah Bruce (P), Shepherdstown, VA. Her LNR Washington, DC, 1871

HALL, MARTIN E. applied for a pension

HALL, NATHAN (P)

HALL, NATHANIEL whose widow Rachel C. applied for a pension

HALL, PETER A. whose widow Lucinda S. received a pension

HALL, RICHARD (BLW), KY
militia, died 30 Nov 1831,
Hardensburg, KY; md Mar 1809
Martha Perrine (P), Bedford
Co, VA. Her LNR Meade Co,
KY, 1872
HALL, SAMUEL applied for a
pension
HALL, SAMUEL and widow Spicy
both received a pension
HALL, SIMEON (BLW), died 23
Aug 1862, Louisa Co, VA; md
11 Dec 1823 Mary H. Hall (P),
Louisa Co, VA. She died
c1890, LNR P.O. Bumpass,
Louisa Co, VA, 1871
HALL, SOLOMON whose widow
Morning received a pension
HALL, THOMAS (P)
HALL, THOMAS whose widow
Nancy applied for a pension
HALL, THOMAS whose widow
Ann received a pension
HALL, THOMPSON (BLW) and
widow Elizabeth both received
a pension
HALL, WILLIAM (P)
HALL, WILLIAM whose widow
Jane applied for a pension
HALLER, JOHN S. (P, BLW),
died 30 Dec 1876, Franklin,
OH; md (1) Ann Rossman, (2)
Hannah Winner, (3) 5 May
1839 Eliza Sill (P), Franklin,
OH. She died 28 Oct 1883,
Franklin, Warren Co, OH
HALLEY/HOLLEY, JOHN whose
widow Sarah E. received a
pension
HALSTEAD, FREDERICK (BLW)
HAM, WILLIAM (P, BLW)
HAM, WILLIS (P)
HAMBLEN/HAMBLIN, WIL-
LIAM HENRY (BLW), TN mi-
litia, died 17 Nov 1869,
Madison Station, TN; md 3 Jul
1817 Verrinia Hill Fowlkes
(P), Nottoway Co, VA. Her
LNR Madison Station, David-
son Co, TN, 1878
HAMBLIN, STEPHEN whose wi-
dow Sarah E. applied for a

HAMBLIN (continued)
pension
HAMBY, REUBEN, NC or VA
militia, applied for a pension
HAMERSLY, JAMES B. (P)

ROLL NO. 41

HAMILTON, JAMES (P)
HAMILTON, JAMES (P)
HAMILTON, JAMES (P)
HAMILTON, JAMES (P)
HAMILTON, JAMES whose widow
Margaret received a pension
HAMILTON, JAMES C. (P)
HAMILTON, JOHN (P), USA
HAMILTON, JOHN C. (P, BLW),
died 8 Oct 1877, Washington
Co, VA; md (1) Sarah E.
Moore, (2) 29 Nov 1859 Martha
Dinkins (P), Washington Co,
VA. She died before Apr 1903,
LNR P.O. Friendship, Wash-
ington Co, VA, 1887
HAMILTON, JOHN W. (BLW),
died 9 Feb 1824, Cumberland
Co, VA; md 1 Oct 1812 Re-
becca Boatwright (P), Cumber-
land Co, VA. Her LNR P. O.
Northside, Goochland Co, VA,
1871
HAMILTON, LEONARD (P)
HAMILTON, NATHANIEL
(BLW), died 15 Oct 1851,
Mathews Co, VA; md 2 Sep
1830 Ann Maria Callis (P),
Mathews Co, VA. Her LNR P.
O. Mathews Courthouse, Math-
ews Co, VA, 1878
HAMILTON, NELSON whose for-
mer widow Mary Jacobs ap-
plied for a pension
HAMILTON, ROBERT (BLW),
PA militia, died 31 Jan 1871,
Wheeling, WV; md 16 Nov
1815 Elizabeth McCartney (P),
Brownsville, PA. Her LNR
Wheeling, Ohio Co, WV, 1878
HAMILTON/HAMBLETON,
ROBERT M. (BLW), USN,
died 9 Aug 1859, Warrenton,
VA; md 6 May 1813 Mary Ann

187

HAMILTON (continued)
Armitage (P), Baltimore, MD. She died before 14 Jul 1891, LNR Warrenton, Fauquier Co, VA, 1871

HAMILTON, ROBINSON (BLW), KY militia, died 11 Jun 1871, Washington Co, IN; md 13 May 1814 Eliabeth Bough (P), Woodstock, Shenandoah Co, VA. She died c1876, LNR P. O. Salem, Washington Co, IN, 1871

HAMILTON, SCHUYLER (BLW)

HAMILTON, TILLMAN/TILMAN (BLW) whose widow was Nancy

HAMILTON, WILLIAM whose widow Elizabeth received a pension

HAMLETT/HAMLET, ELIAS whose widow Rebecca received a pension

HAMMACK, JOHN (P)

HAMMAN, JACOB whose widow Anna received a pension

HAMMER, JAMES (P)

HAMMER, JOHN whose widow Cynthia applied for a pension

HAMMILL, JOHN (BLW) whose widow was Elizabeth

HAMMON/HAMMOND/HAM-MAN, GEORGE and widow Regina both received a pension

HAMMONDS, LEWIS (BLW), died 18 Jan 1855, Lancaster Co, VA; md 16 Oct 1820 Lucy Lowery (P), Lancaster Co, VA. Her LNR Lancaster Co, VA, 1878

HAMMONTREE, ALEXANDER (P, BLW), died 28 Aug 1874, Buckingham Co, VA; md 16 Aug 1821 Judith Howell (P), Buckingham Co, VA. She died 25 Jun 1885, Buckingham Co, VA, LNR P.O. Gold Hill, Buckingham Co, VA, 1878

HAMPTON, JEREMIAH whose widow Pamela received a pension

HAMRICK, BENJAMIN (BLW),

HAMRICK (continued)
died 12 Jun 1863, Webster Co, VA; md 19 Apr 1811 Nancy Gregory (P), Kanawha Co, VA. Her LNR P.O. Webster Courthouse, Webster Co, WV, 1871

HAMRICK, DANIEL whose widow Amelia received a pension

HAMSLEY, HENRY (BLW), died Sep 1864; md 1809 Nancy Rhodes (P), Montgomery Co, VA. Her LNR P.O. New Albany, Floyd Co, IN

HAN/HAND, JAMES applied for a pension

HANAWAY, SAMUEL (P)

HANCHER, JOHN whose widow Nancy Ann received a pension

HANCOCK, HENRY (BLW), died 7 May 1847, Chesterfield Co, VA; md (1) Nancy Gibson, (2) Mary Burton, (3) 8 Apr 1845 Deniza B. Anderson (P), Chesterfield Co, VA. She died before 3 Mar 1884, LNR P.O. Crow Springs, Chesterfield Co, VA, 1878

HANCOCK, HIGGISON (BLW), died 20 Jan 1866, Richmond, VA; md 20 Oct 1819 Hannah Wooldridge Walthall (P), Chesterfield Co, VA. Her LNR P.O. Newtown, King and Queen Co, VA, 1878

HANCOCK, JOHN (BLW), died 30 Jun 1866, Bedford Co, VA; md 28 Feb 1813 Frances Rucker (P), Bedford Co, VA. Her LNR P.O. Liberty, Bedford Co, VA, 1871

HANCOCK, JOHN whose widow Nancy received a pension

HANCOCK, JOHN applied for a pension

HANCOCK, JOSEPH (P)

HANCOCK, SIMON (P)

HAND, JAMES whose widow Malinda received a pension

HANDEL, NICHOLAS (P)

HANDLEY, ISAAC applied for a pension

HANDY, JOHN (P)

HANEY, CHICHESTER (BLW), died 31 Dec 1815, Northumberland Co, VA; md 24 Aug 1812 Catharine Carter (P), Northumberland Co, VA. She died 15 Feb 1879, Columbus, OH, LNR Columbus, Franklin Co, OH, 1871

HANEY, JOHN applied for a pension

HANEY, JOHN whose widow Elizabeth received a pension

HANGER, FREDERICK (BLW), died 20 Jan 1869, Edwardsville, IN; md 1814 Margaret Cook (P), Augusta Co, VA. She died c1874, LNR P.O. Edwardsville, Floyd Co, IN

HANGER, GEORGE (BLW) whose widow Mary Ann received a pension

HANGER, JACOB (P, BLW)

HANGER, JOHN (BLW), died 3 Jul 1862, Augusta Co, VA; md 4 Apr 1822 Mary Allen (P), Augusta Co, VA. She died before 7 May 1887, LNR P. O. Waynesboro, Augusta Co, VA, 1878

HANKINS, WILLIAM (P, BLW), died 8 Jan 1873; md 27 Apr 1815 Susan Staples (P-rejected). She died 23 Apr 1878, LNR Wylliesburg, Charlotte Co, VA, 1878

HANKS, WILLIAM whose widow Elizabeth received a pension

HANLON, RICHARD (P, BLW), died 8 Mar 1878, Archers Fork, OH; md (1) Nancy French, (2) 27 Sep 1846 Margaret Williamson (P), Monroe Co, OH. She died c1882, LNR Archers Fork, Washington Co, OH, 1878

HANNA, JAMES (P-rejected) whose widow Ann received a pension

HANNA, WILLIAM (BLW), PA militia, died 28 Jan 1847, Richmond, VA; md 20 Feb 1831 Margaret Harris (P),

HANNA (continued) Richmond, VA. She died c1887, LNR Richmond, VA, LNR Richmond, Henrico Co, VA, 1878

HANNAH, JAMES applied for a pension

HANNAH, JAMES S. applied for a pension

HANNAH, JOHN R. (BLW), died 17 Apr 1871, Kanawha Co, WV; md 13 Dec 1822 Lucretia Black (P), Prince Edward Co, VA. Her LNR Carbonvale, Kanawha Co, WV, 1878

HANNAH, JOSEPH (P)

HANSBARGER, JACOB whose widow Elizabeth received a pension

HANSBARGER/HUNSBARGER, JOHN whose widow Rebecca applied for a pension

HANSBROUGH, ELIJAH (BLW), died 22 Aug 1857, Saline Co, MO; md 14 Aug 1806 Fanny C. Sampson (P), Frederick Co, VA. Her LNR P.O. Longwood, Pettis Co, MO, 1874

HANSELL, GEORGE whose widow Margaret applied for a pension

HANSELL, MORRIS (BLW), PA militia, died 11 Apr 1839, Philadelphia, PA; md 6 Nov 1820 Nancy Jamison (P), Lewisburg, Greenbrier Co, VA. She died c1878, LNR Philadelphia, PA, 1878

HANSFORD, JOHN (P-rejected, BLW), died Mar 1875, Portsmouth, VA; md Jul 1831 Mahala J. Adkins (P), Suffolk, VA. Her LNR Portsmouth, Norfolk Co, VA, 1878

HANSHAW, BENJAMIN (P)

HANSON, WILLIAM (BLW), died 28 Feb 1871, Greenbrier Co, WV; md 3 Apr 1817 Margaret Aery (P), Greenbrier Co, VA. Her LNR P.O. Asbury, Greenbrier Co, WV, 1878

HANUM/HANNUM, PETER and

HANUM (continued)
widow Mary both received a
pension
HARBOUR, THOMAS (BLW),
died 6 Nov 1837, Patrick Co,
VA; md 24 Aug 1820 Martha
Slaughter (P), Patrick Co, VA.
Her LNR P.O. Copeland, Surry
Co, NC, 1878
HARBOUT/HARBERT, PETER
whose widow Catharine applied
for a pension
HARDAWAY, WILLLIAM (P,
BLW), died 21 Feb 1873,
Amelia Co, VA; md (1) Eliz-
abeth Gibson, (2) 11 Nov 1833
Mary A. Berry (P), Amelia Co,
VA. She died 5 Nov 1895,
LNR Rodophile, Amelia Co,
VA, 1878
HARDBARGER, THOMAS applied
for a pension
HARDEN, CROCKER (BLW),
USN, died 30 Nov 1832, Wash-
ington, DC; md 4 Apr 1823
Frances C. Dameron (P), Nor-
folk, VA. Her LNR Norfolk,
VA, 1878
HARDESTY, ISAAC (P)
HARDESTY, WILLIAM (P,
BLW), died 2 Jan 1877, Akron,
OH; md 8 Feb 1816 Martha
McMullen (P), East Liberty,
PA. She died c1883, LNR
Copley, Summit Co, OH, 1878
HARDIMAN, JAMES E. (P)
HARDING, BENET applied for a
pension
HARDING, BENJAMIN (P)
HARDING, HIRAM applied for a
pension
HARDING, JOHN (BLW), died 11
Feb 1869, Lunenburg Co, VA;
md (1) Fanny Harper, (2) 1 Sep
1839 Julia Foulkes (P), Prince
Edward Co, VA. She died
before 18 Dec 1883, LNR
Lunenburg Co, VA, 1878
HARDING, MARK (P)
HARDING, RICHARD applied for
a pension
HARDING, THOMAS whose wi-

HARDING (continued)
dow Elizabeth W. received a
pension
HARDING, WILLIAM (P)
HARDING, WILLIAM (BLW),
died 1822, Richmond, VA; md
13 May 1810 Polly Farrar (P),
Goochland Co, VA. Her LNR
Richmond, Henrico Co, VA,
1871
HARDING, WILLIAM whose wi-
dow Sarah received a pension
HARDMAN, BENJAMIN (P)
HARDMAN, HENRY (BLW), OH
militia, died 2 Oct 1870,
Lewis Co, WV; md (1) Eliz-
abeth Hacker, (2) 14 Apr 1815
Julia Ann Rinehart (P), Har-
rison Co, VA. Her LNR P.O.
Gaston, Lewis Co, WV, 1878
HARDMAN, JAMES (P)
HARDWAY, ANDREW (BLW),
died 6 Jan 1871, Clark Co, IL;
md 1809 Margaret Sharrit (P),
Pendleton Co, VA. Her LNR
P.O. Martinsville, Clark Co,
IL, 1872
HARDWICK, BENJAMIN (P)
HARDY, BANISTER (BLW), died
8 Feb 1864, Pittsylvania Co,
VA; md (1) Alsey Yeates, (2)
20 Jan 1834 Evy Pigg (P), Pit-
tsylvania Co, VA. She died
c1888, LNR P.O. Chatham,
Pittsylvania Co, VA, 1878
HARDY, CHESLEY (P)
HARDY, WILLIAM applied for a
pension
HARDYMAN/HARDIMAN,
BEVERLEY (P)
HARE, JESSE (BLW), MD mi-
litia, died 14 Jan 1861,
Lynchburg, VA; md 11 Oct
1810 Catharine Welch (P),
Baltimore, MD. Her LNR
Lynchburg, Campbell Co, VA,
1871
HARE, WYATT (P)
HARFORD, HENRY (BLW), died
1858, Lebanon, OH; md 23 Jul
1818 Sally Rambo (P), Green-
brier Co, VA. Her LNR Le-

HARFORD (continued)
banon, Warren Co, OH, 1878
HARFORD, JAMES (P)
HARGRAVE, DAVID (BLW), died
18 Jan 1850, Richmond, Hen-
rico Co, VA; md 2 Mar 1826
Catharine B. Parker (P), Cabin
Point, VA. She died 28 May
1888, Cabin Point, Surry Co,
VA
HARGRAVE, JOHN (P)
HARGROVE, GARLAND applied
for a pension
HARGROVE, JOSEPH (P)
HARGROVE, NELSON (P)
HARGROVE, WILLIAM (BLW),
died c15 Jul 1830, Hanover Co,
VA; md 15 May 1819 Martha
G. Mason (P), Hanover Co,
VA. She died before 5 Jan
1883, LNR Auburn Mills, Han-
over Co, VA, 1877
HARKLESS/HARTLESS, BEN-
JAMIN, SR., whose widow
Mary L. received a pension
HARL, JAMES (BLW), died 6
Oct 1834, Beardstown, Cass
Co, IL; md 22 Jan 1816 Susan
F. Shoemaker (P), Frederick
Co, MD. She died 31 May
1883, LNR Chicago, Cook Co,
IL, 1879
HARLAN/HARLING, LEVI (P,
BLW), MD militia, died 21
Mar 1872, Winchester, IL; md
(1) Frances Eliza Street, (2) 15
Sep 1835 Mary E. Evans (P),
Martinsburg, Berkeley Co, VA.
She died c1896, LNR Win-
chester, Scott Co, IL, 1878
HARLAN, WILLIAM G. and wi-
dow Adaline R. both received a
pension
HARLESS, ABRAHAM and widow
Lucy both received a pension
HARLOW, JESSE (P)
HARLOW, PLEASANT (BLW),
died 6 Dec 1844, Albemarle
Co, VA; md 11 Sep 1833 Mar-
tha Ferguson (P), Albemarle
Co, VA. Her LNR P.O. Stony
Point, Albemarle Co, VA, 1878

HARLOW, THOMAS (BLW), died
9 Feb 1869, Louisa Co, VA;
md 18 Mar 1829 Rosanna Butler (P), Louisa Co, VA. She
died before 19 Jul 1889, LNR
P.O. Cobham Depot, Albe-
marle Co, VA, 1878
HARLOW, WILLIAM whose wi-
dow Maria received a pension
HARMAN, ANTHONY (P)
HARMAN, HENRY (P)
HARMAN, JAMES K. whose widow Nancy K. received a pen-
sion
HARMAN, THOMAS (BLW), died
9 Apr 1853, VA; md 1820 Lucy
Blankenship (P), Franklin Co,
VA. She died before 26 Feb
1890, LNR P.O. Taylors Store,
Franklin Co, VA, 1878
HARMAN/HARMON, WILLIAM
and widow Elizabeth both
received a pension
HARMANSON, WILLIAM
(BLW), died 12 Nov 1876, Nor-
thampton Co, VA; md 22 Dec
1825 Margaret C. Mapp (P),
Northampton Co, VA. She died
c1887, LNR P.O. Eastville,
Northampton Co, VA, 1878
HARMANSON/HANNANSON,
WILLIAM applied for a pen-
sion
HARMON, JOHN whose widow
Susannah C. recevied a pen-
sion
HARMON, JOHN SAMUEL and
widow Nancy both received a
pension
HARMON, JOSEPH (P)
HARMON, WILLIAM (of John)
whose widow Margaret re-
ceived a pension

ROLL NO. 42

HARNED, NATHAN (BLW), died
9 Oct 1854, New York City,
NY; md 24 Mar 1846 Mary Ann
Morrison (P), New Orleans,
LA. She died 2 Dec 1887,
Jenkintown, PA, LNR Jenkin-

HARNED (continued)
town, Montgomery Co, PA, 1878
HARPER, CLAIBORNE (BW) whose widow Mary applied for a pension
HARPER, GEORGE W. S. (BLW), died 7 May 1865, Louisa Co, VA; md (1) Angelina McGelvee, (2) 20 Aug 1860 Martha A. Hester (P). Louisa Co, VA. She died 23 May 1919, LNR P.O. Trevilians, Louisa Co, VA, 1878
HARPER, HENSON (BWL), died 13 Jun 1865, Wood Co, WV; md May 1808 Nancy Pettit (P), Fairfax Co, VA. She died 6 Mar 1883, Wood Co, WV, LNR P.O. Claysville, Wood Co, WV, 1871
HARPER, JOEL J. (BLW), DC militia, died 18 Oct 1864, Fauquier Co, VA; md Fall of 1820 Frances McCoull (P), Stamford, Spotsylvania Co, VA. Her LNR P.O. Upperville, Fauquier Co, VA, 1878
HARPER, THOMAS (P, BLW), died 10 Jan 1874, New Lexington, OH; md 21 Mar 1811 Elizabeth Kinsale (P), Fauquier Co, VA. She died c1876, LNR P.O. New Lexington, Perry Co, OH, 1874
HARPOLD, SOLOMON (BLW) and widow Margaret both received a pension
HARRAH, THOMAS whose widow Elizabeth applied for a pension
HARRELL, JAMES (BLW)
HARNESS, ADAM whose widow Eunice received a pension
HARRIS, BENJAMIN widow Rebecca applied for a pension
HARRIS, CHARLES whose widow Abbie applied for a pension
HARRIS, DANIEL H. (BLW), died 13 Apr 1852, Pittsylvania Co, VA; md 12 Jul 1827 Jane S. Wilson (P), Henry Co, VA. She died 18 Mar 1880, Kansas

HARRIS (continued)
City, MO, LNR Kansas City, Jackson Co, MO, 1878
HARRIS, DAVID whose widow Mary received a pension
HARRIS, DAVID applied for a pension
HARRIS, DAVID W. (BWL), died 2 Mar 1871, Porcelaine, VA; md 6 Jun 1820 Elizabeth Newcomb (P), Albemarle Co, VA. She died 25 Dec 1888, LNR P. O. Ellington, Nelson Co, VA, 1878
HARRIS, GEORGE and widow Catharine both received a pension
HARRIS, HENRY and widow Jane W. both received a pension
HARRIS, HENRY T. whose widow Mary W. applied for a pension
HARRIS, HIRAM (BLW), died 9 May 1867, Powhatan Co, VA; md (1) ---- Christians, (2) ---- Urlson, (3) Elizabeth Garthright, (4) 13 Oct 1853 Frances G. Gordon (P), Powhatan Co, VA. Her LNR Ballsville, Powhatan Co, VA, 1878
HARRIS, JABAL whose widow Sallie Wood received a pension
HARRIS, JAMES whose widow Lucy A. applied for a pension
HARRIS, JAMES WRIGHT whose widow Mary applied for a pension
HARRIS, JESSE (P-rejected, BLW), OH militia, died 20 Dec 1871, Jefferson Co, IL; md 25 Jul 1809 Sarah Davis (P), Hardy Co, VA. She died 1 Apr 1873, LNR P.O. Mt. Vernon, Jefferson Co, IL, 1872
HARRIS, JESSE (BLW)
HARRIS, JESSE (BLW)
HARRIS, JOHN (BLW), died 7 Feb 1848, Marion Co, VA; md 21 Jun 1819 Sarah Powell (P), Greene Co, PA. She died 17 Mar 1885, LNR Palatine, Mar-

HARRIS (continued)
ion Co, WV, 1878

HARRIS, JOHN whose widow Drusilla applied for a pension

HARRIS, JOHN (P)

HARRIS, JOHN whose widow Mary received a pension

HARRIS, JOHN M. applied for a pension

HARRIS, JOSEPH B. whose widow Rachel received a pension

HARRIS, JOSHUA (BLW), died 18 Jul 1859, Lawrence Co, IN; md 10 Jun 1812 Jane Badger (P), Middletown, Fayette Co, PA. Her LNR P.O. Tunnelton, Lawrence Co, IN, 1878

HARRIS, NATHAN (P)

HARRIS, NATHANIEL D. whose widow Martha received a pension

HARRIS, PETER whose widow Mary applied for a pension

HARRIS, PETER whose widow Elizabeth applied for a pension

HARRIS, PEYTON applied for a pension

HARRIS, ROBERT (BLW), died 8 Dec 1851, Johnson Co, IL; md 25 Dec 1816 Nancy Goen/Goin (P). She died 6 Nov 1886, Johnson Co, IL, LNR Johnson Co, IL, 1871-1886

HARRIS, SAMUEL I. (P) whose widow applied for a pension

HARRIS, SAMUEL J. whose widow Sally applied for a pension

HARRIS, THOMAS applied for a pension

HARRIS, THOMAS (P)

HARRIS, THOMAS whose widow Ann received a pension

HARRIS, WILLIAM (P)

HARRIS, WILLIAM (BLW), died 19 Mar 1845, Charlotte Co, VA; md 22 Aug 1811 Martha Fitzpatrick (P), Charlotte Co, VA. She died 23 Aug 1888, Keysville, Charlotte Co, VA

HARRIS, WILLIAM whose widow Mary received a pension

HARRIS, WILLIAM B. whose wi-

HARRIS (continued)
dow Elizabeth T. received a pension

HARRIS, WILLIAM H. (P)

HARRIS, WILLIAM O. (BLW), died 27 Mar 1861, Louisa Co, VA; md 14 Dec 1825 Mary Ann Tyler (P), Louisa Co, VA. She died 17 Feb 1895, LNR P.O. Apple Grove, Louisa Co, VA, 1878

HARRIS, WILLIAM W. whose widow Mary received a pension

HARRISON, CARTER H. (BLW), died 21 Oct 1843, Bremo, Fluvanna Co, VA; md 16 Jan 1819 Janetta R. Fisher (P), Richmond, Henrico Co, VA. She died 18 Apr 1886, Fredericksburg, VA, LNR Woodlawn, Stafford Co, VA, 1878

HARRISON, CHARLES whose widow Mary F. received a pension

HARRISON, FREDERICK T. (P)

HARRISON, GEORGE P. whose widow Leonora received a pension

HARRISON, HENRY T. (P)

HARRISON, JAMES (BLW), died 16 Oct 1852, Fredericksburg, VA; md 23 May 1839 Susan P. Helmstatter (P), Fredericksburg, VA. She died before 11 Dec 1896, LNR Fredericksburg, Spotsylvania Co, VA, 1878

HARRISON, JAMES applied for a pension

HARRISON, JAMES (BWL), died 15 Mar 1835, King George Co, VA; md 10 Mar 1815 Margaret Farmer (P), Essex Co, VA. She died before 31 May 1883, LNR P.O. Shiloh, King George Co, VA, 1878

HARRISON, JAMES M. (BLW), died 17 Aug 1845, Monroe Co, OH; md 9 Mar 1807 Elizabeth Mazena (P), West Alexander, Washington Co, PA. She died c1878, LNR P.O. Round Bot-

HARRISON (continued)
tom, Monroe Co, OH, 1872
HARRISON, JESSE (P)
HARRISON, JOHN (P)
HARRISON, JOHN (P-rejected, BLW), died 24 Dec 1877, Todd Co, KY; md 17 Sep 1822 Lucinda Gorin (P), Todd Co, KY. Her LNR P.O. Elkton, Todd Co, KY, 1878
HARRISON, JOHN whose widow Penelope received a pension
HARRISON, JOHN C. applied for a pension
HARRISON, JOSEPH whose widow Mary applied for a pension
HARRISON, MALCOLM/MALCOM/MALCOMB (P-rejected) whose widow Mary A. received a pension
HARRISON, SAMUEL whose widow Caroline applied for a pension
HARRISON, SELDEN P. whose widow Mary B. received a pension
HARRISON, STEPHEN P. (BLW), died 10 Sep 1865, Suffolk, VA; md (1) ?, (2) 12 Jan 1820 Ann Coleburn (P). Suffolk, Nansemond Co, VA. Her LNR Nansemond Co, VA, 1878
HARRISON, WILLIAM (BLW)
HARRISON, WILLIAM H. (BLW) whose widow was Sally
HARRISS/HARRIS, MOSES (P, BLW), died 5 Nov 1873, Patrick Co, VA; md (1) ?, (2) 2 Oct 1866 Lucinda Clardy (P), Patrick Co, VA. She died c1900, LNR P.O. Patrick Courthouse, Patrick Co, VA, 1878
HARROW, CHARLES A. (BLW), died 2 Mar 1874, Spotsylvania Co, VA; md 25 Jun 1829 Ellen S. Hove (P), King George Co, VA. She died 8 Mar 1881, Spotsylvania Co, VA, LNR P.O. Fredericksburg, Spotsylvania Co, VA, 1878
HARRUF, JONATHAN (P)

HARRY, ELI (P)
HARRY, JOHN (BLW) and widow Caroline both received a pension
HART, ARCHIBALD applied for a pension
HART, HENRY S. whose widow Elizabeth received a pension
HART, MOSES and widow Margaret both received a pension
HART, SAMUEL (P)
HART, WILLIAM whose widow Rebecca received a pension
HARTER, ADAM whose widow Margaret applied for a pension
HARTMAN, ABRAHAM (BLW), died 16 Jan 1853, Rockingham Co, VA; md 15 Nov 1810 Susanna Long (P), Augusta Co, VA. Her LNR P.O. Harrisonburg, Rockingham Co, VA, 1871
HARTSOOK, PETER (BLW), died 21 Feb 1864, Madison Co, IA; md 3 Jun 1821 Ann Wooten (P), Gallia Co, OH. She died 29 Apr 1895, Winterset, Madison Co, IA
HARVEY, ANDREW (BLW), died 13 Jan 1853, Laporte, IN; md 27 Mar 1825 Prudence Owen (P), Clarke Co, OH. Her LNR Laporte, Laporte Co, IN, 1878
HARVEY, GIDEON (P)
HARVEY, GLOVER (BLW), died 7 Jan 1871, Appomattox Co, VA; md 9 Feb 1811 Judy Wooldridge (P), Prince Edward Co, VA. Her LNR P.O. Appomattox Co, VA, 1871
HARVEY, ISHAM (BLW), died 25 Dec 1864, Harvey's Store, VA; md 4 Sep 1812 Elizabeth Harris (P), Spring Creek, Charlotte Co, VA. Her LNR P.O. Charlotte Courthouse, Charlotte Co, VA, 1873
HARVEY, ISHAM (P)
HARVEY, ZACHARIAH (BLW), died 10 Feb 1868, Jefferson Co, IL; md (1) Betsey Ward, (2) Sarah Tyler, (3) 12 Oct

HARVEY (continued)
1852 Ellen (----) Dukes (P),
Jefferson Co, IL. She died 15
May 1887, LNR P.O. Mount
Vernon, Jefferson Co, IL, 1878
HASLEWOOD, WILLIAM (P)
HASTINGS, JOHN (P)
HASTINGS, SIMEON (BLW), died
3 Dec 1869, Kanawha Co, WV;
md 24 Dec 1818 Sarah Martin
(P), Kanawha Co, VA. Her
LNR Coalburg, Kanawha Co,
WV, 1878

ROLL NO. 43

HATCHELL, OBEDIAH (P)
HATCHER, BENJAMIN (BLW),
died 14 Jan 1853, Harpersville,
AL; md 23 Dec 1830 Lucinda
B. Flippin (P), Cumberland
Co, VA. Her LNR Har-
persville, Shelby Co, AL, 1878
HATCHER, JOHN whose widow
Martha received a pension
HATCHER, JULIUS W. (P)
HATCHER, WILLIAM (BLW),
died 31 May 1866, Williamson
Co, TN; md 21 Dec 1815 Lucy
Rucken (P), Bedford Co, VA.
Her LNR P.O. College Grove,
Williamson Co, TN, 1876
HATCHET, WILLIAM whose wi-
dow Tabitha applied for a pen-
sion
HATCHETT, ARCHIBALD
(BLW), died 25 Jul 1857, LNR
Barren Co, KY, 1855; md 17
Feb 1817 Elizabeth Love (P),
Danville, NC. She died c1889,
LNR P.O. Edmonton, Metcalf
Co, KY, 1884
HATCHETT, EDWARD (P)
HATFIELD, JAMES whose widow
Zerrilda received a pension
HATTEN/HATTON, ELIJAH
(BLW), died Aug 1866, Wayne
Co, WV; md 12 Feb 1818
Elizabeth McGinnis (P),
Cabell Co, VA. Her LNR P.
O. Round Bottom, Wayne Co,
WV, 1878

HATTEN, PHILIP applied for a
pension
HATTON, BOLING (P)
HATTON, WILLIAM (P, BLW)
HAUGHT/HAUT, JOSEPH (P,
BLW), died 24 Nov 1876,
Washington Co, OH; md 19
Feb 1815 Ann Elizabeth
Haught (P), Fayette Co, VA.
She died c1878, LNR P.O.
Lawrence, Washington Co,
OH, 1878
HAVANS, CHARLES whose wi-
dow Nancy applied for a pen-
sion
HAVELY, ISAAC B. (BLW), died
21 Oct 1852, Knoxville, Knox
Co, TN; md 4 Jun 1918
Elizabeth Crider (P), Abind-
gon, Washington Co, VA. She
died c1886, LNR P.O. Nash-
ville, Davidson Co, TN, 1878
HAVENS, ELISHA (BLW), died
26 May 1869, Twin Township,
Preble Co, OH; md 1 Mar 1810
Sarah Davis (P), VA. Her LNR
Twin Township, Preble Co,
OH, 1871
HAVNER, JOSEPH (P)
HAWKES/HAWKS, JOHN (P)
HAWKINS, ALEXANDER whose
widow Nancy received a pen-
sion
HAWKINS, ELLIOTT (P) and
widow Nancy received a pen-
sion
HAWKINS, JAMES (BLW),
whose widow was Christena/
Christiana
HAWKINS, JOHN and widow
Susanna both received a pen-
sion
HAWKINS, JOHN (P)
HAWKINS, THOMAS (P, BLW),
died 28 Apr 1878, Cabell Co,
WV; md 24 Dec 1816 Mary
Perry (P), Orange Co, VA. She
died c1891, LNR P.O. Milton,
Cabell Co, WV, 1887
HAWKINS, WILLIAM applied for
a pension
HAWKINS, WILLIAM whose

195

HAWKINS (continued)
widow Calley applied for a pension

HAWKS, RANDOLPH applied for a pension

HAWLING, ISAAC (BLW), died 24 Sep 1854, Loudoun Co, VA; md 16 Oct 1817 Frances Best (P), Loudoun Co, VA. Her LNR P.O. Leesburg, Loudoun Co, VA, 1878

HAWSE, CHRISTIAN (P)

HAY, DAVID (BLW), whose widow Barbary received a pension

HAY, JOHN (P)

HAY, RUBIN (P)

HAYBERGER, JACOB whose widow Elizabeth applied for a pension

HAYES/HAYSE, GEORGE (BLW), died 11 Nov 1865, Beaver Creek, Randolph Co, WV; md 2 Dec 1824 Mary Vanscoy (P), Beverly, Randolph Co, VA. She died c1890, LNR Beaver Creek, Randolph Co, WV, 1878

HAYHURST, BENJAMIN and widow Eliza J. both received a pension

HAYHURST, JOSEPH (P)

HAYMAN, CALEB (P)

HAYMOND, CYRUS (BLW), died 14 Sep 1870, Quiet Dell, WV; md (1) Jane Somerville, (2) 17 Nov 1851 Mary Carpenter (P), Stevens Run, Harrison Co, VA. She died c1890 LNR Quiet Dell, Harrison Co, WV, 1878

HAYNES, ARCHIBALD whose widow Sarah Ann applied

HAYNES, AUSTIN (P)

HAYNES, DRURY (P)

HAYNES, JAMES B./J.B.W. (BLW), died 20 Aug 1869, Richwood, OH; md (1) Susan Floyd, (2) 21 May 1857 Mary R. Converse (P), Union Co, OH. She died 12 Aug 1897, Highland Park, TN, LNR Richwood, Union Co, OH, 1878

HAYNES, PATRICK whose widow Mary A. received a pension

HAYNES, PETER and widow Amanda both received a pension

HAYNES, WILLIAM C. (BLW), died 18 Dec 1852 Charles City, VA; md 26 Dec 1832 Elizabeth Pulley (P), Charles City, VA. She died before 17 Aug 1886, LNR Washington, DC, 1874

HAYNIE, AUSTIN (BLW), died 11 Nov 1860, Northumberland Co, VA; md 26 Nov 1845 Mary A. (Hagaman) (Lampkin) Garner (P), Northumberland Co, VA. Her LNR P.O. Kilmarnock, Lancaster Co, VA 1878. Mary also received a BLW for the War of 1812 service of her first husband Griffin Lampkin who died 1 May 1822

HAYNIE, CHARLES and widow Sarah both received a pension

HAYNIE, CYRUS (P)

HAYS, WILLIAM whose widow Harriet applied for a pension

HAYS, WILLIAM (BLW), died 18 Nov 1848, New Providence, Augusta Co, VA; md (1) Jane Surface, (2) 16 Jun 1841 Rachel Strong (P), Augusta Co, VA. She died c1890, LNR P. O. Middlebrook, Augusta Co, VA, 1878

HAYTER, ABRAHAM applied for a pension

HAYTER, ISRAEL (P-rejected, BLW), died 29 Aug 1873, DeKalb Co, MO; md 17 Jan 1814 Margaret Gregory (P), Washington Co, VA. She died 23 Jan 1883, Stewartsville, DeKalb Co, MO

HAYTH, THOMAS whose widow Mary applied for a pension

HAYZLETT, JAMES whose widow Mahala applied for a pension

HAZELGROVE, BENJAMIN (BLW), died 19 Apr 1858, Hanover Co, VA; md (1) Eliz-

HAZELGROVE (continued)
abeth Cross, (2) 12 Jun 1844
Martha A. Archer (P), Hanover
Co, VA. Her LNR P.O. Atley
Station, Hanover Co, VA, 1878
HAZELL, BENNETT and widow
Nancy both received a pension
HAZELRIGG, JOHN (BLW), died
4 Dec 1845, Wood Co, VA; md
15 Feb 1810 Abigail/Abagail
Jemason (P), Marietta, OH.
She died c1899, LNR nr Wil-
liamstown, Wood Co, WV,
1871
HAZELWOOD, MITCHEL (P)
HAZZARD, RAWLEIGH (BLW)
whose widow was Elizabeth
HEABERLIN, ANDREW whose
widow Elizabeth received a
pension
HEADLEY, George O. (P)
HEATH, HARTWELL whose wi-
dow Eliza Cureton Heaton ap-
plied for a pension
HEATH, JOSEPH whose widow
Catharine applied for a pension
HEBB, THOMAS (BLW), died 25
Nov 1839, Preston Co, VA; md
1 Oct 1819 Ann E. Caricow
(P), Preston Co, WV. She
died c20 Sep 1884, Hannah-
ville, WV, LNR Hannahville,
Tucker Co, WV, 1878
HEDGES, CHARLES applied for a
pension
HEDGES, SILAS (P)
HEDRICK, HENRY applied for a
pension
HEDRICK, NICHOLAS (BLW),
died 3 May 1842, Ross Co,
OH; md 15 Jan 1815 Elizabeth
Johnson (P), Hardy Co, VA.
She died c1878, LNR P.O.
Colmar, McDonough Co, IL,
1872
HEDRICK, PHILIP (BLW), died
6 Feb 1857, Putnam Co, VA;
md 16 Jul 1813 Catherine Debo
(P), Pittsylvania Co, VA. Her
LNR P.O. Winfield, Putnam
Co, WV, 1874

HEFFERTON, ELIJAH B.
(BLW), died 18 May 1846,
Norfolk, VA; md 23 Mar 1820
Catharine D. Tucker (P),
Richmond, VA. She died 29
Mar 1886, Richmond, Henrico
Co, VA
HEFFLIN, WILLIAM (P)
HEFFNER, JOHN (P)
HEFLIN/HELFIN, ALEXANDER
W. and widow Sarah both
received a pension
HEIZER, EDWARD whose widow
Elizabeth received a pension
HELBERT, GEORGE whose wi-
dow Sarah received a pension
HELLRIGLE, JACOB C. (BLW),
MD militia, died 5 Mar 1847,
Dayton, OH; md 12 May 1803
Ann Maria Jackson (P),
Alexandria, VA. She died 10
Dec 1883, Dayton, Montgomery
Co, OH
HELMICK, JOHN M. (P)
HELMICK, PHILIP (BLW), died
8 May 1870, Pendleton Co,
WV; md 1815 Sarah (Wil-
liams) (Calhoun) Vandevander
(P), Pendleton Co, VA. Her
LNR P.O. Franklin, Pendleton
Co, WV, 1878
HELMICK, PHILLIP (P)
HELMICK, SAMUEL (P, BLW),
died 1 Mar 1872, Laporte Co,
IN; md 25 Jan 1814 Anna Min-
nis (P), Pendleton Co, VA.
She died before Apr 1888, LNR
Rolling Prairie, Laporte Co,
IN, 1875
HELMICK, URIAH whose widow
Jane received a pension
HELMS, WILLIAM (P)
HELSLEY, JACOB (P, BLW),
USA, died 20 Apr 1872, Shen-
andoah Co, VA; md 4 Apr 1821
Mary G. Helzel (P), Shenan-
doah Co, VA. Her LNR P.O.
Strasburg, Shenandoah Co, VA,
1878

197

HELVESTINE/HELVISTON, HIRAM (P, BLW), died 1 Nov 1875, Frederick Co, VA; md 13 Apr 1819 Nancy Caldwell (P), Hagerstown, Washington Co, MD. She died 17 Mar 1885, Frederick Co, VA, LNR P.O. Stephenson Depot, Frederick Co, VA, 1878

HEMELWRIGHT, HENRY (P)

HEMMICK, DAVID whose widow Catherine received a pension

HEMPENSTALL, ABRAM/ ABRAHAM applied for a pension

HENAGE, GEORGE (BLW), died 25 Oct 1826, Scott Co, KY; md 19 Jan 1809 Catharine Jones (P), Spotsylvania Co, VA. She died 19 Oct 1876, Scott Co, KY, LNR Stone Wall, Scott Co, KY, 1871

HENDERSON, BENNETT whose widow Catherine received a pension

HENDERSON, DAVID whose widow Jane applied for a pension

HENDERSON, EDWARD (BLW), died 5 Dec 1841, Halifax Co, VA; md 17 Dec 1807 Elizabeth Clark (P), Halifax Co, VA. She died before 4 Dec 1886, LNR P.O. News Ferry, Halifax Co, VA, 1871

HENDERSON, JOHN applied for a pension

HENDERSON, JOHN (P)

HENDERSON, JOHN G. applied for a pension

HENDERSON, ROBERT applied for a pension

HANDERSON, SAMUEL (P)

HENDERSON, TARLTON T. applied for a pension

HENDERSON, THOMAS whose widow Anna applied for a pension

HENDERSON, WILLIAM (P)

HENDREE, GEORGE (BLW), died 8 Jul 1834, Richmond, VA; md 5 Feb 1814 Sarah A. Tinsley (P), Hanover Co, VA.

HENDREE (continued) Her LNR Tuskegee, Macon Co, AL, 1871

HENDREN, ROBERT whose widow Sallie received a pension

HENDRICK, DAVID (BLW), died 23 Feb 1872, Cumberland Co, VA; md (1) Sally Palmore, (2) 22 Nov 1835 Eliza G. Steyer (P). Amelia Co, VA. Her LNR P.O. Cumberland Courthouse, Cumberland Co, VA, 1878

HENDRICK, JOSEPH C. and widow Judith Ann both received a pension

HENDRICK, RICHARD BROWN (P)

HENING, WILLIAM H. (BLW), died 12 May 1848, Powhatan Co, VA; md 4 May 1826 Eliza Parke Scott (P), Powhatan Co, VA. Her LNR P.O. Powhatan Courthouse, Powhatan Co, VA, 1878

HENLEY, CHARLES whose widow Elizabeth received a pension

HENLEY, RICHARDSON (BLW), died 28 Apr 1864, James City Co, VA; md 18 Nov 1813 Catharine N. Lightfoot (P), James City Co, VA. Her LNR P.O. Williamsburg, James City Co, VA, 1872

HENLEY, THOMAS whose widow Frances received a pension

HENLEY, WILLIAM and widow Sarah both received a pension

HENRY, HIRAM (P)

HENRY, JOHN (BLW), NJ militia, died 7 Jul 1850, Norfolk, VA; md 20 Aug 1814 Elizabeth Ryno (P), New Brunswick, NJ. She died 25 Apr 1881, Norfolk, VA

HENRY, JOHN, SR. (P)

HENRY, PETER (BLW), died 2 Sep 1857, Morgan Co, VA; md 17 Dec 1811 Mary Ambrose (P). Her LNR P.O. Berkeley Springs, Morgan Co, WV, 1871

HENRY, WILLIAM applied for a

HENRY (continued)
pension (from Caldwell Co, LA)

HENRY, WILLIAM applied for a pension (from Caldwell Co, LA). Served in different unit than previous William Henry

HENRY, WILLIAM whose former widow Rachel Jenkins applied for a pension

HENSELL, DANIEL (P)

HENSLEY, BENJAMIN, SR. (P)

HENSLEY, JAMES (P, BLW), died 23 May 1873, Jefferson Co, MO; md Fall of 1811 Sarah Bailey (P), Albemarle Co, VA. Her LNR P.O. Hillsboro, Jefferson Co, MO, 1874

HENSLEY, JESSE (BLW), died 11 Apr 1858, Owen Co, IN; md 1 Sep 1813 Susan Peters (P), Sullivan Co, TN. Her LNR P. O. Quincy, Owen Co, IN, 1871

HENSLEY, JOHN whose widow Liddy received a pension

HENSLEY, JOHN whose widow Lydia received a pension

HENSLEY, THOMAS (P)

HENSLEY, WILLIAM Mc. applied for a pension

HENSLEY, ZACHARIAH (P)

HENSLEY, ELIJAH applied for a pension

HENSON, BARTLETT (BLW), died 22 May 1848, Louisa Co, VA; md 25 Dec 1807 Lucy Pulliam (P). Her LNR P.O. Poindexters Store, Louisa Co, VA, 1871

HENSON, JAMES (BLW), KY militia, died 15 Jun 1869, Elliott Co, KY; md 1 Aug 1812 Mary Lewis (P), Goose Creek Salt Works, VA. Her LNR P. O. Martinsburg, Elliott Co, KY, 1871

HENTON/HINTON, PETER whose widow Lurenna received a pension

HENTON, SILAS (P)

HEPLER, HENRY (BLW), died 9 Apr 1863, Mill Creek, VA; md

HEPLER (continued)
11 Dec 1809 Elizabeth Kessler (P), Botetourt Co, VA. Her LNR P.O. Troutville, Botetourt Co, VA, 1871

HERBERT, WILLIAM (BLW), whose widow was Maria

HEREFORD, WILLIAM applied for a pension

HERNDEN/HERNDIN/ HERNDON, JOHN (P)

HERNDON, BENJAMIN (BLW)

HERNDON, DAVID (P)

HERNDON, EDWARD (BLW)

HERNDON, ELISHA (BLW)

HERNDON, FIELDING (BLW) whose widow was Mildred

HERNDON, GEORGE (P)

HERNDON, GEORGE T. and widow Melinda both received a pension

HERNDON, JACOB S. (P, BLW), died 25 May 1875, Warren Co, TN; md (1) Jane West, (2) 11 Jan 1850 Charlotte Brown (P), Warren Co, TN. She died 29 Nov 1899, LNR P.O. Smartts Station, Warren Co, TN, 1887

HERNDON, JACOB W. (BLW) whose widow was Mary

HERNDON, JOSEPH (BLW), died 18 Jun 1857, Albemarle Co, VA; md 26 Dec 1825 Lourena Cave (P), Orange Co, VA. She died c1905, LNR P.O. Waynesboro, Augusta Co, VA, 1878

HERNDON, SOLOMON (BLW)

HERNDON, WILLIAM (P)

HERNDON, WILLIAM (BLW), whose widow was Elizabeth A.

HERNDON, WILLIAM (BLW), whose widow was Mary

HERNDON, WILLIAM (BLW), whose widow was Sarah

HERRING, GEORGE (BLW), and widow Lucy both received a pension

HERRON, ALEXANDER (BLW), died 15 Nov 1868, Albemarle Co, VA; md 22 Oct 1812 Jane Colvin (P), Albemarle Co, VA.

HERRON (continued)
Her LNR P.O. Batesville, Albemarle Co, VA, 1871
HERRON, ANDREW applied for a pension
HERRON, WILLIS and widow Abigale both received a pension
HESKET/HESKETT, JAMES whose widow Henrietta received a pension
HESKETT, SPICER whose widow Nancy applied for a pension
HESS, PETER (BLW), died June 1857, Rockingham Co, VA; md 31 Mar 1826 Elizabeth Romake (P), Shenandoah Co, VA. She died 10 Mar 1888, LNR P.O. Coates Store, Rockingham Co, VA, 1882
HESSER, JONATHAN (P)
HESSER, EDWARD (BLW), KY militia, died 21 Feb 1866, Mount Washington, KY; md 22 Mar 1807 Catherine Venable (P), Middletown, Frederick Co, VA. Her LNR Mount Washington, Bullitt Co, KY, 1872
HEVENER/HEAVENOR/HEAVNER, GEORGE, Sr. (P)
HEVNER/HEVENER, WILLIAM (BLW)
HEYWOOD/HAYWOOD, ROBERT S. whose widow Ann B. received a pension

ROLL NO. 45

HICK, ELIJAH (P)
HICKEL, SAMUEL (P)
HICKEY, WILLIAM and widow Harriet both received a pension
HICKLE, STEPHEN (P, BLW), died 19 Mar 1874, Fairfield Co, OH; md 16 Oct 1816 Hannah Sigler (P), Mount Jackson, Shenandoah Co, VA. She died 12 Dec 1884, LNR P.O. Marcy, Fairfield Co, OH, 1878
HICKMAN, ASA whose widow Elizabeth applied for a pension
HICKMAN, JACOB V. (BLW)

HICKMAN, JOHN T. (P)
HICKMAN, JOSEPH whose widow Lucinda applied for a pension
HICKMAN, PETER whose widow Catherine received a pension
HICKMAN, ROBERT (P)
HICKOK, JOHN whose widow Sally A. applied for a pension
HICKOK, MORRIS (P)
HICKS, BENJAMIN (BLW), died 14 Apr 1845, Gallia Co, OH; md 22 Nov 1814 Jane McBane (P), Gallia Co, OH. She died c1876, LNR nr Downington, Meigs Co, OH, 1871
HICKS/HIX, BENJAMIN whose widow Clarissa received a pension
HICKS, BENJAMIN A. (BLW), died 22 Apr 1861, Richmond, VA; md 10 Nov 1835 Sarah B. Sale (P), Caroline Co, VA. She died c1890, LNR Richmond, VA, 1878
HICKS, CHARLES (P)
HICKS, JEREMIAH (BLW), died 1834, Franklin Co, VA; md 6 Sep 1810 Mary Williams (P). Her LNR Coopers, Franklin Co, VA, 1873
HICKS, JOHN whose widow Frances applied for a pension
HICKS, JOHN whose widow Rebecca applied for a pension
HICKS, JOHN (BLW), died 1 Jan 1857, Russell Co, VA; md 28 Mar 1805 Nancy Hamly (P), Russell Co, VA. Her LNR P.O. Lebanon, Russell Co, VA, 1871
HICKS, JOHN G. and widow Mary both received a pension
HICKS, PASCAL (BLW), died 3 May 1853, Brunswick Co, VA; md 29 Apr 1807 Lucy Hall (P), Brunswick Co, VA. She died 21 Apr 1873, LNR P.O. Charlie Hope, Brunswick Co, VA, 1871
HICKS, REUBEN whose widow Nancy received a pension
HICKS, REUBEN and widow

HICKS (continued)
Nancy both received a pension.
Served in a different unit than
the previous Reuben Hicks
HICKS, THOMAS whose widow
Sally E. applied for a pension
HICKS, THOMAS S. (BLW), died
12 Oct 1870, Spotsylvania Co,
VA; md 30 Jul 1823 Ann A.
Bradford (P), Scott Co, KY.
She died before 26 Jul 1884,
LNR Spotsylvania Courthouse,
Spotsylvania Co, VA, 1878
HICKS, WASHINGTON (P)
HIDACRE/HIDECKER, JACOB
(P, BLW), died 13 Oct 1876,
Barbour Co, WV; md (1)
Frances Woodford, (2) 23 Feb
1854 Christina Mace (P), Bar-
bour Co, VA. She died c1896,
LNR P.O. Belington, Barbour
Co, WV, 1887
HIETT, JOSEPH (BLW), died 2
Mar 1842, Franklin Co, VA;
md (1) Susan Ferguson, (2)
Nancy Forbes, (3) 17 Aug 1828
Elizabeth Ann Waid (P),
Franklin Co, VA. Her LNR P.
O. Rocky Mount, Franklin Co,
VA, 1878
HIGGANBOTHAM, ROBERT (P)
HIGGINBOTHAM, JAMES G.,
alias LAMBAG, JOSEPH
whose widow Isabella Higgin-
botham received a pension
HIGGINS, ISAAC (BLW), NJ
militia, died 15 May 1841,
Chester, PA; md 25 Dec 1817
Elizabeth Evans (P), Chester,
Delaware Co, PA. She died 31
Dec 1878, Fairfax Co, VA
HIGGINS, JOHN J. applied for a
pension
HIGGINS, JOSIAH (BLW), died
26 Aug 1850, Springfield, New
Kent Co, VA; md 21 May 1807
Elizabeth H. Pollard (P), New
Kent Co, VA. Her LNR
Springfield, New Kent Co, VA,
1871
HIGH, JACOB (P)
HIGH, SAMUEL (P, BLW), died

HIGH (continued)
24 Jan 1876, Rockingham Co,
VA; md (1) Frances Shoemaker
(2) 23 Feb 1872 Mary Ann
(Mitchell) Shoemaker (P),
Rockingham Co, VA. She died
c1896, LNR P.O. Fulks Run,
Rockingham Co, VA, 1882
HILBRANT, JOHN whose widow
Nancy applied for a pension
HILDEBRAND, JOHN whose wi-
dow Susannah applied for a
pension
HILDERBRAND, HENRY whose
widow Susannah applied for a
pension
HILL, FRANCIS whose widow
Emeline applied for a pension
HILL, JAMES (BLW), USA, died
25 Jul 1844, Botetourt Co, VA;
md 25 Dec 1804 Elizabeth
Pannell (P), Amherst Co, VA.
Her LNR P.O. Middlebrook,
Augusta Co, VA, 1871
HILL, JAMES (BLW), died 7 Oct
1858, Stokes Co, NC; md 15
Jan 1824 Sophronia M. Lake
(P), Stokes Co, NC. She died
c1894, LNR P.O. Francisco,
Stokes Co, NC, 1878
HILL, JOHN whose widow Sarah
H. received a pension
HILL, JOHN applied for a pen-
sion
HILL, JOHN A. (P)
HILL, JOHN P. applied for a
pension
HILL, JOSEPH D. (BLW), died
28 Aug 1859, nr Morgantown,
Monongalia Co, VA; md 22 Sep
1814 Sarah Houston (P), Mon-
ongalia Co, VA. Her LNR
Morgantown, Monongalia Co,
WV, 1871
HILL, LEVI (BLW), USA, died
Aug 1844, Charlestown, VA;
md 26 Oct 1841 Sarah Pennell
(P). Her LNR North East,
Cecil Co, MD, 1878
HILL, LEVI whose widow Mary
applied for a pension
HILL, RICHARD (BLW), died 31

HILL (continued)
Mar 1855, Madison Co, VA;
md 25 Sep 1798 Elizabeth Hill
(P), Albemarle Co, VA. She
died 26 May 1876, LNR P.O.
Harrisonburg, Rockingham Co,
VA, 1871

HILL, RICHARD applied for a
pension

HILL, THOMAS (BLW), died 14
Oct 1866, Stafford Co, VA; md
26 Jan 1812 Mary Hill (P),
Pelmorth Grove, VA. Her LNR
P.O. Stafford Courthouse, Staf-
ford Co, VA, 1871

HILL, WILLIAM (P)

HILL, WILLIAM (P)

HILLDRUP/HILDRUP, ROBERT
(P, BLW), died 7 Dec 1872,
Spotsylvania Co, VA; md 7 Oct
1819 Elizabeth L. Powers (P),
Port Royal, Caroline Co, VA.
She died 4 Feb 1881, Spotsyl-
vania Co, VA, LNR P.O.
Fredericksburg, Spotsylvania
Co, VA, 1878

HILLER, EDWARD (P), USN

HILLHOUSE/HILLIS, DAVID
(BLW), died 20 Jan 1858,
Logansport, IN; md 26 Nov
1822 Mary Ann Collings (P),
Chillicothe, OH. She died
before 13 Dec 1888, LNR
Logansport, Cass Co, IN, 1878

HILLHOUSE, HUGH and widow
Lucy both received a pension

HILLIARD, JACOB (BLW), died
9 Apr 1864, Page Co, VA; md
(1) Betsy Taylor, (2) 1842
Phebe Elliott (P), Frederick
Co, VA. She died before 8 Jan
1883, LNR P. O. Grove Hill,
Page Co, VA, 1878

HILLIARD, WILLIAM (P)

HILLIARY/HILLEARY, ELIJAH
(P-rejected, BLW). died 9 Oct
1873, Perry Co, OH; md 18
Aug 1818 Eleanor Freeman
(P), Georgetown, MD. She
died 18 Jan 1885, LNR P.O.
Maxville, Perry Co, OH, 1878

HILLMAN, SIMEON (BLW),

HILLMAN (continued)
USN, died 18 Apr 1860,
Frederick Co, VA; md 11 Jun
1829 Charlotte Copenhaver (P),
Winchester, VA. She died 1
Dec 1892, LNR P.O. Win-
chester, Frederick Co, VA,
1878

HILLMAN/HILMAN, SQUIRE
(P)

HINCHEN, WILLIAM H. (BLW),
died 28 Mar 1849, Cass Co,
IL; md 23 Apr 1812 Margaret
Barley (P), Rockingham Co,
VA. Her LNR P.O. Hagly,
Cass Co, IL, 1871

HINER, ALEXANDER (P)

HINES, CHARLES J. (BLW),
died Feb 1837 Mary C.
Thomas (P), Louisa Co, VA.
She died before 17 Sep 1884,
LNR P.O. Kents Store, Flu-
vanna Co, VA, 1878

HINES, JACOB (BLW), died 10
May 1863, Grayson Co, VA;
md 16 Sep 1805 Hannah Briles
(P), Forsyth Co, NC. She died
11 Feb 1875, LNR P.O. Elk
Creek, Grayson Co, VA, 1872

HINES, JAMES whose widow
Nancy R. received a pension

HINES, JOHN whose widow
Hester applied for a pension

HINES, JOHN W. whose widow
Aurora B. applied for a pension

HINES, WILLIAM (P)

HINKLE, JOHN (P, BLW), died
11 Oct 1873, Stony Creek, TN;
md 30 Nov 1834 Elizabeth Arrowood (P), Stony Creek, TN.
Her LNR Stony Creek, Carter
Co, TN, 1878

HINKLE, RANDOLPH and widow
Charlotte both received a pension

HINKLEY, JOHN, USN, and widow Sarah A. both received a
pension

HINTON, DAVID whose widow
Polly applied for a pension

HIPES, SAMUEL whose widow
Catherine received a pension

HIPKINS, JOHN (P)
HISER/HIZER, ADAM (P)
HISER/HIZER, GEORGE whose
widow Elizabeth received a
pension
HISER, SAMUEL (P, BLW), died
19 Jun 1878, Fort Defiance,
VA; md 19 Jul 1823 Catharine
Showalter (P), Rockingham Co,
VA. Her LNR P.O. Fort De-
fiance, Augusta Co, VA, 1878
HISEY, JACOB whose widow
Abigail received a pension
HISSOM, DAVID and widow
Elizabeth both applied for a
pension
HITAFFER/HIGHTEFFER,
JOHN (P, BLW), died 22 Jul
1871, North Fork, VA; md 20
Jul 1820 Sarah Dutroe (P),
Loudoun Co, VA. Her LNR
Leesburg, Loudoun Co, VA,
1878
HITCH, GARNER B. (BLW),
died 25 Aug 1840, St. Louis,
MO; md 10 Dec 1815 Mary
Barbee (P), Fauquier Co, VA.
She died 11 Feb 1882, LNR P.
O. Wentzville, St. Charles Co,
MO, 1878
HITCHCOCK, GEORGE A. (P)
HITE, ANDREW (P)
HITE, JOSEPH (BLW) whose
widow Magdaline Jones ap-
plied for a pension
HITE, VINCENT whose widow
Rebecca received a pension
HITE, WILLIAM whose widow
Sarah received a pension
HITT, DANIEL (P, BLW), KY
militia, died May 1862,
Livingston Co, MO; md (1)
Mary Lafferty, (2) 26 Apr 1825
Joanna Murdock Jett (P),
Fauquier Co, VA. Her LNR
Osborn, DeKalb Co, MO, 1879
HITT, JOHN (BLW), died 15 Dec
1851, Culpeper Co, VA; md 22
Feb 1822 Elizabeth M.
Vaughan (P), Culpeper Co, VA.
Her LNR P.O. Culpeper, Cul-
peper Co, VA, 1878. John was

HITT (continued)
a substitute for Joseph Hitt in
the War
HITT/HILL, THADDEUS (P-rejected, BLW), died 18 Jun
1877, Elizabeth, IL; md 29 Jul
1831 Rebecca Brown (P),
Rushville, Schuyler Co, IL.
She died c1892, LNR Eliz-
abeth, Jo Daviess Co, IL,
1878. Thaddeus also served in
the Blackhawk War, 1832
HITT, WILLIAM whose widow
Polly applied for a pension
HITTSON, THOMAS (P)
HIVELY, JOHN and widow Mar-
tha E. both received a pension
HIX, ACHILLES (P, BLW), died
17 Mar 1874, Putnam Co, WV;
md (1) Delila Lykins, (2) 19
May 1844 Harriet Jenkins (P),
Fayette Co, VA. She died 29
Apr 1895, LNR P.O. Winfield,
Putnam Co, WV, 1887
HIX, DRURY whose widow Sophia
received a pension
HIX, HOWARD G. whose widow
Sarah H. applied for a pension
HIX, SAMUEL (BLW), died 17
Apr 1870, Richmond, VA; md 3
Sep 1819 Catharine Mullen (P),
Richmond, VA. She died be-
fore 18 Aug 1890, LNR Rich-
mond, Henrico Co, VA, 1878
HIXSON, JONATHAN (BLW),
died 21 Sep 1853, Prince Wil-
liam Co, VA; md 20 Jun 1820
Priscilla Woodyard (P). Prince
William Co, VA. She died
c1880, LNR P.O. Manassas,
Prince William Co, VA, 1878
HIZER, JOSHUA whose widow
Jemima received a pension

ROLL NO. 46

HOBACK, JACOB (BLW) and
widow Cynthia both received a
pension
HOBBS, EDMOND (P, BLW)
HOBBS, JOHN whose widow
Elizabeth/Betsy applied for a

203

HOBBS (continued)
pension

HOBBS, NATHAN (P, BLW), died 24 Dec 1872, Scott Co, VA; md (1) Mary Smith, (2) Eliza Olinger, (3) Eliza (----) Taylor (P-rejected), Mill Point, Sullivan Co, TN. Her LNR Scott Co, VA, 1878

HOBDAY, WILLIAM applied for a pension

HOBSON, ADCOCK (BLW), died 11 Aug 1830, Davidson Co, TN; md 2 Dec 1819 Edith (----) Farmer (P), Cumberland Co, VA. Her LNR P.O. Nashville, Davidson Co, TN, 1878. Edith also pensioned as former widow of Burwell Farmer, also an 1812 veteran

HOBSON, JOHN whose widow Louisa W. received a pension

HOCKER, ALEXANDER whose widow Sarah Darrah applied for a pension

HODGES, ELISHA applied for a pension

HODGES, ISHAM whose widow Mary Jane received a pension

HODGES, JAMES H. and widow Lucinda both received a pension

HODGES, JOHN and widow Harriet both received a pension

HODGES, JOHN (BLW), died 17 Feb 1859, Halifax Co, VA; md Mar 1823 Sarah Bomar (P), Halifax Co, VA. She died 28 Apr 1884, Halifax Co, VA, LNR Whitesville, Halifax Co, VA, 1878

HODGES, JOSIAH whose widow Mary T. received a pension

HODGES, LEWIS whose widow Carolina received a pension

HODGES, PEYTON (P-rejected, BLW), died 10 Apr 1876, Franklin Co, VA; md 10 Apr 1816 Elizabeth Hall (P), Franklin Co, VA. Her LNR Rocky Mount, Franklin Co, VA, 1878

HODGKIN, ROBERT (P, BLW), died 27 Mar 1876, Alexandria, VA; md (1) Clara Taylor, (2) 28 Jun 1831 Elizabeth Fraser (P), Alexandria, VA. Her LNR Washington, DC, 1879

HOES/GOES, NICHOLAS (BLW), died 14 May 1865, Friendship, WI; md 27 Sep 1811 Eunice Kellum (P), Kenderhook Landing, NY. Her LNR Fairmount, Marion Co, WV, 1871

HOFF, WILLIAM whose widow Martha received a pension

HOFFMAN, JACOB and widow Elizabeth both received a pension

HOGAN, RICHARD H. and widow Martha both received a pension

HOGELAND/HOGELIN, ISRAEL C. whose widow Jane received a pension

HOGG, JOHN whose widow Julia received a pension

HOGG, MUHLENBURG and widow Mary E. both received a pension

HOGWOOD, MORTICE alias WARSHAM, HENRY whose widow Amelia Hogwood received a pension

HOKE, WILLIAM (P)

HOLBROOK, JOHN THOMPSON/THOMAS W. whose widow Mary received a pension

HOLCOMB, GEORGE whose widow Frances B. applied for a pension

HOLDEN, ALEXANDER C. whose widow Sarah received a pension

HOLDER, TALIAFERRO/TOLIVER applied for a pension

HOLDER, WILLIAM and widow Nandy both received a pension

HOLDERBY, ROBERT (BLW) whose widow was Susan A.

HOLDERBY, WILLIAM (BLW), died 24 Dec 1870, Lawrence Co, OH; md 12 Feb 1809 Re-

HOLDERBY (continued)
becca Hoskins (P). Her LNR
P.O. Aid, Lawrence Co, OH,
1871
HOLDRON/HOLDREN, BAR-
THOLOMEW and widow Jane
both received a pension
HOLDRYDE/HOLDRIGHT,
JOHN D. (BLW), died 29 Aug
1856, Cabell Co, VA; md 2
Feb 1819 Sarah Chapman (P).
Cabell Co, VA. Her LNR P.
O. Cabell Courthouse, Cabell
Co, WV, 1878
HOLEMAN, WILLIAM (P)
HOLLAND, HENRY (BLW),
whose widow was Margaret
HOLLAND, LAWSON F. (BLW),
whose widow was Polly
HOLLAND, RICHARD (P)
HOLLAND, WILLIAM whose wi-
dow Christina applied for a
pension
HOLLEMAN, JONATHAN whose
widow Nancy applied for a
pension
HOLLEMAN, JORDAN (P)
HOLLENBACK, MARTIN (BLW),
died 27 Jan 1849, Cabell Co,
VA; md 1 Sep 1811 Elenor
Hampton (P), Cabell Co, VA.
Her LNR P.O. Huntington,
Cabell Co, WV, 1872
HOLLEY, JOEL (BLW), died 28
Feb 1863, Orange Co, IN; md
14 Jun 1810 Sophia Smith (P),
Pittsylvania Co, VA. She died
5 Oct 1875, LNR P.O. In-
graham, Clay Co, IL, 1871
HOLLIDAY, ROBERT B. (P)
HOLLIDAY, SAMUEL (BLW),
died 11 Nov 1857, Fairfax Co,
VA; md 17 Oct 1815 Ann P.
McDonough (P). Fairfax Co,
VA. Her LNR P.O. Spring-
vale, Fairfax Co, VA, 1878
HOLLINS, JOHN whose widow
Mary applied for a pension
HOLLINS, RICHARD (P)
HOLLINS, RICHARD L. (P)
HOLLINSWORTH, WILLIAM
whose widow Elizabeth re-

HOLLINSWORTH (continued)
ceived a pension
HOLLOWAY, DAVID (P)
HOLLOWAY, GEORGE whose
widow Jane received a pension
HOLLOWAY, JAMES (BLW)
HOLLOWAY, JOSEPH HAYNES
(BLW), died 14 May 1849,
Mason Co, VA; md 17 or 18
Aug 1813 Mary S. Hinton/ Hen-
ton (P), Botetourt Co, VA. Her
LNR Mason Co, VA, 1855
HOLLOWAY, NATHAN (P)
HOLLOWAY, THOMAS (BLW)
HOLLOWAY, WILLIAM whose
widow Margaret received a
pension
HOLLY/HAWLEY/HOLLEY,
JAMES (P, BLW), LNR P. O.
Christiansburg, Montgomery
Co, VA, 1871; md 1815
Catharine Cofer, Montgomery
Co, VA
HOLLY/HOLLEY, JAMES
(BLW), died 15 Oct 1860; md
2 Nov 1809 Betsy Ralph (P),
Pittsylvania Co, VA. Her LNR
Franklin Co, VA, 1875
HOLMAN, JAMES (P)
HOLMES, JAMES (BLW), MD
militia, died 13 Aug 1851, Nor-
folk, VA; md 14 Oct 1835
Elizabeth S. Ryan (P), Norfolk,
VA. She died 23 Aug 1891,
LNR Norfolk, VA, 1852-1878
HOLMES, JAMES (BLW), MS
militia, died 9 Dec 1869,
Kanawha Co, WV; md 25 Sep
1814 Elizabeth B. Horton (P),
Lincoln Co, TN. Her LNR
Kanawha Courthouse, Kanawha
Co, WV, 1871
HOLMES, NATHANIEL (P)
HOLMES, SAMUEL (P)
HOLESAPPLE/HOLSAPPLE/
HOLSHOPPLE, HENRY
(BLW), and widow Elizabeth
both received a pension
HOLSOPPLE, HENRY (BLW),
whose widow was Susannah
HOLSTEIN/HOLSTEN,
STEPHEN (BLW), died 10 Dec

HOLSTEIN (continued)
1856, Lens Creek, Kanawha
Co, VA; md Jan 1808 Jane
Wilson (P), Craigs Creek,
Botetourt Co, VA. Her LNR P.
O. Peyton, Boone Co, WV,
1871
HOLSTINE/HOLSTIN, THOMAS
J. whose widow Martha applied
for a pension
HOLT, EDWARD (P)
HOLT, MILES (BLW), died 20
Jun 1851, Pittsylvania Co, VA;
md (1) Sally Fowlkes, (2) 13
May 1841 Wilmoth Bradley
(P), Pittsylvania Co, VA. Her
LNR Laurel Grove, Pittsyl-
vania Co, VA, 1878
HOLT, ROBERT whose widow
Winifred M. applied for a pen-
sion
HOLT, WILLIAM (BLW)
HOMAN, MARK and widow
Rachel both received a pension
HOMES, JOSEPH (BLW)
HONAKER, JACOB whose widow
Anna received a pension
HONEYMAN, JOHN (P)

ROLL NO. 47

HOOD, JESSE (P)
HOOD, JONAH (P)
HOOD, NATHANIEL whose wi-
dow Nancy received a pension
HOOD, ROBERT (P)
HOOE, JOHN whose widow Vir-
ginia received a pension
HOOK, ROBERT S. (P)
HOOKE, ROBERT (BLW), died
25 Jan I858 Rockingham Co.
VA; md Z5 Dec I82I Elizabeth
Fisher (P), Null Creek, VA.
She died 13 Dec 1882, Port
Republic, Rockingham Co, VA
HOOVER, EMANUEL (BLW)
HOOVER, HENRY (BLW), whose
widow Barbara applied for a
pension
HOOVER, JACOB (P, BLW)
HOOVER, JOHN applied for a
pension

HOOVER, JOHN DIDEN whose
widow Elizabeth received a
pension
HOPE, JAMES T. (P)
HOPE, WILLIAM P. (P)
HOPKINS, ARTHUR alias POL-
LARD, ARTHUR H. whose
widow received a pension
HOPKINS, CALEB (P)
HOPKINS, GEORGE B. applied
for a pension
HOPKINS, JAMES whose widow
Mary applied for a pension
HOPKINS, JAMES M. whose
widow Ann E. received a pen-
sion
HOPKINS, JOHN (BLW), died 16
Mar 1872, Henderson Co, IL;
md (1) Jane E. Ervine, (2)
Nancy Andrews, (3) 3 Aug 1848
Dorothy Proctor Choate (P),
Oquawka, Henderson Co, IL.
She died 12 Jan 1894, Mon-
mouth, IL, LNR Monmouth,
Warren Co, IL, 1889
HOPKINS, JOHN (BLW)
HOPKINS, JOHN (BLW)
HOPKINS, JOHN P. (BLW), died
4 May 1841, Surry Co, NC; md
22 Jan 1823 Patsey Bailey (P),
Surry Co, VA. Her LNR Surry
Courthouse, Surry Co, VA,
1878
HOPKINS, JOSHUA D. applied for
a pension
HOPKINS, JOSHUA L. (BLW),
died Jun 1871, Norfolk, VA;
md (1) Fanny Morely, (2) 10
Apr 1857 Susan (Kelles) Ross
(P), Norfolk, Norfolk Co, VA.
She died 12 Jul' 1885,
Portsmouth, Norfolk Co, VA
HOPKINS, NATHAN G. (BLW)
HOPKINS, NELSON (BLW), died
10 May 1846, Smyth Co, VA;
md 30 Dec 1802 Polly Mat-
thews (P), Louisa Co, VA. She
died 4 Mar 1877, LNR Little
Fox Creek, Grayson Co, VA,
1871
HOPKINS, RUFUS applied for a
pension

HOPKINS, THOMAS (BLW), died 31 Jan 1836, Jefferson Co, OH; md 15 Sep 1834 Elizabeth Perry (P), Wellsburg, Brooke Co, VA. She died 31 May 1881, LNR P.O. Smithfield, Jefferson Co, OH, 1872

HOPKINS, THOMAS (BLW), died 11 Feb 1854, Philadelphia, PA; md 29 May 1817 Mary Ann Patton (P), Philadelphia, PA. She died before 21 Feb 1883, LNR Philadelphia, PA, 1878

HOPKINS, WILLIAM (BLW), died 30 Nov 1853, Fairfax Co, VA; md 6 Jun 1812 Nancy Wells (P), Prince William Co, VA. She died 10 May 1880, Fairfax Co, VA, LNR P.O. Fairfax Courthouse, Fairfax Co, VA, 1871

HOPKINS, WILLIAM R. (P)

HOPPER, JOHN (BLW), whose widow was Martha

HOPPER, JOHN whose widow Elizabeth B. applied for a pension

HORD/HOARD, WILLIAM (P, BLW)

HORD, WILLIAM (BLW), whose widow Elizabeth applied for a pension

HORN, EDWARD (BLW), died Sep 1854, Montgomery Co, IN; md 12 Jan 1809 Nancy Tolly (P). Her LNR P.O. Crawfordsville, Montgomery Co, IN, 1871

HORN, JESSE (BLW), LNR Sussex Co, VA, 1855

HORN, JOHN whose widow Nancy received a pension

HORN, JOHN R. (BLW), whose widow was Ann

HORNER, MAJOR (BLW), died 8 Mar 1867, Randolph Co, MO; md 7 Nov 1812 Keturah Morgan (P), Chesterfield Co, VA. She died 4 Jan 1884, Columbia, MO. Her LNR Columbia, Boone Co, MO, 1871

HORNER, RICHARD T. (P)

HORNOR, JAMES Y. (P, BLW), died 9 Aug 1872, Clarksburg, WV; md (1) Dolly O. Hornor, (2) 1 Apr 1834 Mary A. Robinson (P), Lumberport, Harrison Co, VA. Her LNR Clarksburg, Harrison Co, WV, 1878

HORTON, HEGRON whose widow Elizabeth received a pension

HORTON, JOSEPH (P)

HOSCHAR, ANDREW (BLW), died 29 Apr 1865, Mason Co, WV; md 9 Sep 1813 Susan Pritchett (P), Harrison Co, VA. She died Jul 1884, Point Pleasant, WV, LNR Point Pleasant, Mason Co, WV, 1871

HOSSENFLUCK/HAUSENFLUCH, JOHN (P, BLW), died 9 Aug 1874, Shenandoah Co, VA; md (1) Catharine Roland, (2) 18 Jan 1866 Mary (----) Spigle (P). Shendandoah Co, VA. Her LNR P.O. Maurertown, Shenandoah Co, VA, 1878

HOST, PETER (BLW), died 4 Apr 1840, Dinwiddie Co, VA; md Sep 1816 Angelina Gibbs (P), Dinwiddie Co, VA. Her LNR Dinwiddie Courthouse, Dinwiddie Co, VA, 1855-1878

HOSTETER, JOHN (BLW)

HOSTETTER, ANDREW (BLW), died 22 Jul 1864, Rockbridge Co, VA; md 12 Sep 1811 Nancy Standoff (P), Rockbridge Co, VA. She died 26 Oct 1877, LNR P.O. Collierstown, Rockbridge Co, VA, 1873

HOTTEL, JOSEPH whose widow Catharine received a pension

HOTTEL, PAUL (BLW)

HOUCK, GEORGE applied for a pension

HOUGH, GARRET (BLW), died 27 Mar 1851, Waterford, Loudoun Co, VA; md 5 Jul 1841 Mary Moore (P), Loudoun Co, VA. Her LNR Frederick City, Frederick Co, MD, 1878

HOUGH, JOHN whose widow Mary S. received a pension

HOUSE, HENRY (BLW), died 22 Jan 1849, Brunswick Co, VA; md 20 May 1820 Lucy S. Owen (P), Brunswick Co, VA. She died before 25 Feb 1889, LNR P.O. Lawrenceville, Brunswick Co, VA, 1878

HOUSE, JOHN (BLW), died 24 Sep 1852, Rush Co, TX; md 15 Aug 1821 Elizabeth Perkins (P), Smith Co, TN. Her LNR P.O. Carthage, Smith Co, TN, 1878

HOUSEHOLDER, JOHN and widow Ann both received a pension

HOUSERIGHT, JAMES whose widow Malinda received a pension

HOWARD, ALLEN (P)

HOWARD, BENJAMIN whose widow Eliza applied for a pension

HOWARD, GEORGE (P)

HOWARD, GEORGE (BLW), died 22 Oct 1860, Henrico Co, VA; md (1) ?, (2) 2 Apr 1838 Sarah Roberts (P), Henrico Co, VA. She died 28 Jan 1897, Richmond, Henrico Co, VA

HOWARD, HARVEY (P)

HOWARD, JAMES (P)

HOWARD, JOHN (BLW), died 11 May 1868, Richmond, VA; md 20 Mar 1810 Nancy S. Dickerson (P), Richmond, VA. She died 22 Jun 1884, LNR Richmond, Henrico Co, VA, 1877

HOWARD, JOHN (BLW)

HOWARD, JOHNSTON applied for a pension

HOWARD, RICHARD (P)

HOWARD, SAMUEL and widow Sarah B. both received a pension

HOWARD, SYLVANUS (BLW), died 22 Jan 1853, Centerville, Bedford Co, VA; md (1) ?, (2) 29 Aug 1825 Mary P. Rhodes (P), Bedford Co, VA. She died

HOWARD (continued) 1884, LNR Liberty, Bedford Co, VA, 1878

HOWARD, THOMAS (P, BLW), died 30 Mar 1875, Campbell Co, VA; md 19 Dec 1816 Mary Clark (P), Charlotte Co, VA. She died before 19 Sep 1883, LNR P.O. Hat Creek, Campbell Co, VA, 1878

HOWDERSHELT, DANIEL (BLW), died 22 Nov 1846, Barbour Co, VA; md (1) Katy Foreman, (2) 30 Dec 1844 Mary (----) Walters (P). Barbour Co, VA. She died 20 Sep 1895, LNR Meadowville, Barbour Co, WV, 1878

HOWELL, DANIEL (BLW), died 3 Dec 1856, Tuscawaras Co, OH; md Oct 1808 Margaret George (P), Clarksburg, VA. She died 7 Mar 1880, Tuscawaras Co, OH, LNR P.O. New Comerstown, Tuscarawas Co, OH, 1871

HOWELL, DAVID (P)

HOWELL, JONATHAN whose widow Elizabeth applied for a pension

HOWELL, KINCHEN (P, BLW), died 31 Oct 1872, Gates Co, NC; md (1) ?, (2) ?, (3) ?, (4) 27 Jun 1848 Julia Jordan (P), Gates Co, NC. She died 7 Apr 1886, Gates Co, NC

HOWELL, SPICER whose widow Namoie K. received a pension

HOWELL, THOMAS (P)

HOWELL, WILLIAM whose widow Elizabeth received a pension

HOWELL, WILLIAM whose widow Chrissey received a pension

HOWERTON, PHILIP (P)

HOWEY, JAMES M. (P)

ROLL NO. 48

HOYE, ISSAC (P)

HUBBARD, BENJAMIN (BLW),

208

HUBBARD (continued)
died 30 Mar 1853, Buckingham Co, VA; md Nancy (----) Talbert (P), Buckingham Co, VA. Her LNR P.O. Garys Store, Buckingham Co, VA, 1878

HUBBARD, BOLER/BOWLER whose widow Pamelia Jane received a pension

HUBBARD, JAMES O. T. (P)

HUBBARD, JOEL and widow Margaret H. both received a pension

HUBBARD, JOHN (BLW)

HUBBARD, THOMAS K. (P, BLW)

HUDDLE, ABRAHAM applied for a pension

HUDDLE, CHRISTIAN (P)

HUDGIN, JAMES whose widow Milly applied for a pension

HUDGINGS, THOMAS and widow Lucy E. both received a pension

HUDGINS, FRANCIS and widow Sarah both received a pension

HUDGINS, GABRIEL (BLW), died Oct 1844, Mathews Co, VA; md 24 Dec 1810 Frances Brooks (P), Mathews Co, VA. Her LNR P.O. Mathews Courthouse, Mathews Co, VA, 1871

HUDGINS, JOHN and widow Anna both received a pension

HUDGINS, JOHN F. whose widow Agnes B. applied for a pension

HUDGINS, WILLIAM (BLW), died 6 Jan 1839, Mathews Co, VA; md 18 Mar 1808 Mary Pugh (P), Mathews Co, VA. Her LNR Mathews Courthouse, Mathews Co, VA, 1871

HUDNALL, RICHARD whose widow Mary A. applied for a pension

HUDNALL, STANLEY S. (BLW)

HUDSON, ALLEN (P, BLW), died 4 Sep 1877, Marysville, MD; md (1) ?, (2) 18 Oct 1860 Parthenia (----) Smith (P), Ripley Co, IN. Her LNR Sharpsville, Tipton Co, IN,

HUDSON (continued)
1888

HUDSON, ANDERSON (BLW), died Jul 1864, Kanawha Co, VA; md 1807 Sarah Clark (P), Kanawha Co, VA. She died 27 Nov 1878, Kanawha Co, WV, LNR P.O. Kanawha Courthouse, Kanawha Co, WV, 1871

HUDSON, CHRISTOPHER (BLW), died 12 Dec 1861, Goochland Co, VA; md 17 Jan 1837 Judith R. Holland (P). Goochland Co, VA. She died c1887, LNR Hardensville, Goochland Co, VA, 1878

HUDSON, DAVID (P, BLW), died 19 Oct 1874, Charlotte Co, vA; md 4 Apr 1828 Dicey Toombs (P), Charlotte Co, VA. Her LNR P.O. Red Oak Grove, Charlotte Co, VA, 1878

HUDSON, DAVID whose widow Ann applied for a pension

HUDSON, EDWIN (P)

HUDSON, ELI and widow Lucretia both received a pension

HUDSON, GEORGE V. R. alias **HUTSON, GEORGE V. C.** whose widow Mary applied for a pension

HUDSON, HIRAM/HYRAM (BLW), died 10 Oct 1867, Halifax Co, VA; md 22 Nov 1832 Nancy E. Vanhook (P), Person Co, NC. Her LNR P. O. Mt. Carmel, Halifax Co, VA, 1878

HUDSON, JOHN and widow Grizell both received a pension

HUDSON, JOSHUA (BLW), whose widow was Mary H.

HUDSON, JOSIAH T. (BLW), whose widow Mary E. received a pension

HUDSON, RUSH (BLW), died 20 Aug 1849; md 4 Nov 1804 Parmelia Hudson (P), Amherst Co, VA. Her LNR P.O. Amherst Courthouse, Amherst Co, VA, 1871

HUDSON, VALENTINE B. applied for a pension

HUDSON, WILLIAM (BLW), died 13 Aug 1864, Fluvanna Co, VA; md (1) Nancy Chiles, (2) Malinda Vawter, (3) 22 Apr 1831 Lavinia P. P. Bryant (P), Fluvanna Co, VA. She died 10 Oct 1880, Albemarle Co, VA, LNR P.O. Hunters Lodge, Fluvanna Co, VA, 187

HUDSON, WILLIAM C. whose widow Jane received a pension

HUDSON, WILLIAM T. (BLW), died 2 Sep 1854, Lunenburg Co, VA; md 20 Jun 1816 Mary Ann Hardwick (P), Halifax Co, VA. Her LNR P.O. Ft. Mitchell, Lunenburg Co, VA, 1878

HUFF, GEORGE whose former widow Elizabeth Crane applied for a pension

HUFF, JAMES (P), died 15 Mar 1885, LNR Davis Co, IA, 1871; md 19 Sep 1819 Mary T. -

HUFF, JAMES (P), died 10 Feb 1879, LNR Wayne Co, WV, 1871; md (1) 1816 Anna Pennington/Pendleton, (2) 1869 Mahala Wells (P)

HUFF, JAMES C. (BLW), died 7 May 1870, Salem, VA; md (1) Jane G. Godwin, (2) 3 Jan 1847 Harriet D. Noble (P), Salem, VA. She died 31 Jan 1896, LNR Salem, Roanoke Co, VA, 1888

HUFF, JOSHUA applied for a pension

HUFF, POWELL H. and widow Eliza Ann received a pension

HUFF, JACOB (P)

HUFFMAN, ABRAHAM (P, BLW)

HUFFMAN, ANDREW (BLW), died 4 Apr 1847, Shenandoah Co, VA; md 21 Mar 1834 Rebecca (Hackman) Miley (P), Shenandoah Co, VA. Her LNR Edinburg, Shenandoah Co, VA, 1878

HUFFMAN, ANDREW (P)

HUFFMAN, ARCHIBALD whose widow Elizabeth received a pension

HUFFMAN, ELISHA (BLW), died 15 Aug 1840, Madison Co, VA; md 14 Nov 1806 Elizabeth Scales (P), Madison Co, VA. She died c1886, LNR P.O. Madison Courthouse, Madison Co, VA, 1871

HUFFMAN, ENOS (BLW), died 19 Apr 1856, Preble Co, OH; md 7 Sep 1820 Jane George (P), Greenbrier Co, VA. Her LNR Greenbrier Co, WV, 1878

HUFFMAN, JACOB (BLW), died 28 Dec 1863, Sinking Creek, Craig Co, VA; md 12 Oct 1809 Parmelia Lake (P), Botetourt Co, VA. Her LNR P.O. Simmondsville, Craig Co, VA, 1871

HUFFMAN, JOHN (P, BLW), died 16 May 1872, Craig Co, VA; md 15 Nov 1807 Priscilla Gray (P), Botetourt Co, VA. Her LNR Craig Co, VA, 1873

HUFFMAN, JOHN (P, BLW), died 24 Nov 1874, Fauquier Co, VA; md 21 Jun 1825 Dillyla Embrey (P), Fauquier Co, VA. Her LNR P.O. Somerville, Fauquier Co, VA, 1878

HUFFMAN, WILLIAM applied for a pension

HUGHES, ABNER (P)

HUGHES, ANDERSON whose widow Delilah applied for a pension

HUGHES, CHARLES (BLW), died 20 Jun 1871, Halifax Co, VA; md 27 Mar 1822 Judith Soy Ars (P), Pittsylvania Co, VA. She died 24 Jun 1897, Hyco, Halifax Co, VA, LNR P. O. Black Walnut, Halifax Co, VA, 1878

HUGHES, EDWARD (BLW), died 27 Sep 1853, Mathews Co, VA; md (1) Fanny Davis, (2) 8 Nov 1849 Joice Chenault (P), Mathews Co, VA. She died 28

HUGHES (continued)
Feb 1892, LNR P.O. Mathews Courthouse, Mathews Co, VA, 1878

HUGHES, EDWARD (BLW)

HUGHES, EDWARD P. whose widow Martha C. received a pension

HUGHES, ISAAC whose widow Nancy received a pension

HUGHES, JEREMIAH (BLW), died 22 Sep 1822, Halifax Co, VA; md 24 Dec 1817 Nancy Hall (P), Halifax Co, VA. Her LNR P.O. Scottsburg, Halifax Co, VA, 1878

HUGHES, JESSE (BLW), died 28 Apr 1864, Appomattox Co, VA; md 22 Oct 1807 Mary Cheadle (P), Oakley, Prince Edward Co, VA. She died 13 Jul 1875, LNR Appomattox Co, VA, 1871

HUGHES, JOHN (P)

HUGHES, JOHN applied for a pension

HUGHES, JOHN (P)

HUGHES, JOHN (BLW) died 22 Feb 1853, Prince Edward Co, VA; md (1) Mary S. Wright, (2) 3 Aug 1836 Mary M. Tredway (P), Prince Edward Co, VA. She died 14 Aug 1885, LNR P. O. Hampden Sidney, Prince Edward Co, VA, 1878

HUGHES, JACOB whose widow Susannah applied for a pension

HUGHES, JOSEPH F. whose widow Mary received a pension

HUGHES, LEWIS whose widow Letecia received a pension

HUGHES, MADISON R. (P)

HUGHES, PETER (P)

HUGHES, SAMUEL, Sr. (P)

HUGHES, THOMAS, in Indian War 1791, whose widow Nancy applied for a pension

HUGHES, THOMAS whose widow Elizabeth applied for a pension

HUGHES, WILLIAM applied for a pension

HUGHES, WILLIAM whose widow Polly received a pension

HUGHES, WILLIAM applied for a pension

HUGHES, WILLIAM whose widow Elizabeth received a pension

HUGHLETT, THOMAS whose widow Virginia F. received a pension

HUGHS, BOLAN whose widow Rhoda applied for a pension

HUGHSON, ELLIS G. (P)

HUGHTON/HOUGHTON, ELIJAH (P)

HUGILL, WILLIAM (P)

HUGLEY, SAMUEL applied for a pension

HULL, JAMES B. applied for a pension

HULL, JOHN H. (P)

HULL, MARTIN whose widow Anne M. applied for a pension

HUMBER, EDWARD (P)

HUMMER, LEVI whose widow Martha received a pension

HUMMER, WILLIAM whose widow Julia received a pension

HUMPHREY, JOHN G. (BLW), applied for a pension

HUMPHREY, JOHN G whose widow Sarah C. received a pension

HUMPHREY, JONAH whose widow Elizabeth applied for a pension

HUMPHREY, RICHARD and widow Matilda both received a pension

HUMPHREY, WILLIAM and widow Rutha both received a pension

HUMPHREYS, CHARLES (P)

HUMPHREYS, EDWARD whose widow Margaret applied for a pension

HUMPHREYS, JOHN whose widow Elizabeth W. received a pension

HUMPHREYS, RICHARD (BLW), died 25 Mar 1869, Putnam Co, MO; md 4 Jun 1814 Sarah G. Humphreys (P), Greenbrier Co, VA. She died 9

211

HUMPHREYS (continued)
Mar 1882, Putnam Co, MO,
LNR P.O. Shoneytown, Putnam
Co, MO, 1871
HUMPHRIES, HENRY (BLW),
died 19 Nov 1814, Norfolk, VA;
md 19 Mar 1812 Elizabeth
Howard (P), Botetourt Co, VA.
Her LNR P.O. Fortville, Han-
cock Co, IN, 1871
HUMPHRIES, REUBEN (P-re-
jected, BLW), died 18 Apr
1872, Roanoke Co, VA; md 20
Feb 1823 Mary Smith (P),
Botetourt Co, VA. Her LNR P.
O. Alleghany Spring, Mont-
gomery Co, VA, 1878
HUMPHRIES/HUMPHREY,
THOMAS (BLW) and widow
Susan both received a pension
HUNDLEY, JOHN (BLW), died
11 May 1860, Fayette Co, VA;
md 15 Jul 1811 Mary Thomas
(P), Fayette Co, VA. She died
13 Sep 1879, Mountain Cove,
Fayette Co, WV, LNR Char-
leston, Kanawha Co, WV, 1871
HUNDLEY, RANDOLPH (P)
HUNDLEY/HUNLEY, THOMAS
(P, BLW), died 25 Jul 1874,
Fayetteville, WV; md c16 Oct
1812 Elizabeth Hensley (P),
Albemarle Co, VA. Her LNR
P.O. Oak Hill, Fayette Co,
WV, 1875
HUNDLEY, WILLIAM (BLW),
and widow Tabitha both re-
ceived a pension
HUNDLY, LARKIN (P)
HUNLEY, RICHARD (BLW),
whose widow was Elizabeth

ROLL NO. 49

HUNT, ELIJAH (P)
HUNT, ELISHA (BLW), USA,
died May 1842, Rockbridge Co,
VA; md 4 Jan 1817 Sally But-
ler (P), Fluvanna Co, VA. She
died 23 Jun 1879, Rockbridge
Co, VA, LNR P.O. Timber
Ridge, Rockbridge Co, VA,

HUNT (continued)
1878
HUNT, EUSTACE (BLW), died
Sep 1845, Pittsylvania Co, VA;
md Eliza A. ----. She later
md ---- Williamson
HUNT, JAMES D. whose widow
Maria received a pension
HUNT, JOHN (BLW), died 22
Feb 1867, Fleming Co, KY;
md 2 Jan 1814 Nancy Chandlor
(P), Prince William Co, VA.
Her LNR Elizaville, Fleming
Co, KY, 1871
HUNT, JOHN whose widow Sarah
applied for a pension
HUNT, LEWIS (P)
HUNT/HURT, MUNFORD L.
(BLW), died 16 Jun 1867,
Pleasnt Grove, VA; md 22 Dec
1825 Dianisha Johns (P), Lun-
enburg Co, VA. Her LNR
Pleasant Grove, Lunenburg Co,
VA, 1879
HUNT, SAMUEL J. whose widow
Sallie J. received a pension
HUNT, WILLIAM (P-rejected)
whose widow Jane received a
pension
HUNTER, DAVID and widow
Frances both received a pen-
sion
HUNTER, JOHN whose widow
Margaret W. received a pen-
sion
HUNTER, ROBERT (P)
HUNTON, LUDWELL A. (BLW),
died 9 Jul 1860, Warren Co,
KY; md Apr 1824 Fannie
Washington (P), Prince Wil-
liam Co, VA. Her LNR Bowl-
ing Green, Warren Co, KY,
1878
HUPMAN, JOHN (P)
HUPP, GEORGE F. (P),
paymaster VA militia
HURN, JAMES (BLW), died 3
Feb 1854, Limestone Co, AL;
md (1) ---- Marks, (2) 27 Jun
1830 Nancy C. Robinson (P),
Limestone Co, AL. She died
before 8 Mar 1888, LNR P.O.

212

HURN (continued)
Athens, Limestone Co, AL, 1878
HURSEY, JOHN and widow Margaret E. both received a pension
HURST, DANIEL and widow Elenor both received a pension
HURST, NATHANIEL (P)
HURST, SAMUEL applied for a pension
HURST, WILLIAM (BLW), died 14 Oct 1857, Mathews Co, VA; md 17 Nov 1808 Sarah Hall (P), Mathews Co, VA. Her LNR P.O. Mathews Courthouse, Mathews Co, VA, 1871
HURST, WILLIAM whose widow Sarah applied for a pension
HURT, BARNETT (P, BLW), died 5 Nov 1871, Appomattox Co, VA; md 16 Aug 1831 Frances Gregory (P), Buckingham Co, VA. She died before 29 Jul 1889, LNR P.O. Hixburg, Appomattox Co, VA, 1878
HURT, GEORGE whose widow Rebecca received a pension
HURT, HARRISON H. (BLW)
HURT, MARTIN whose widow Louisa received a pension
HURT, MEKIN S. whose widow Elizabeth received a pension
HURT, WILLIAM D. (BLW), died 22 Feb 1847, Russell Co, VA; md (1) Elizabeth Price, (2) 2 Oct 1844 Ann Clark (P), Washington Co, VA. She died 14 May 1891, LNR P.O. Abingdon, Washington Co, VA, 1878
HUSHOUR, PETE (P)
HUSTON, ARCHIBALD whose widow Margaret G. received a pension
HUSTON, SAMUEL (BLW), died 28 Dec 1846, Lincoln Co, MO; md 12 Sep 1802 Catharine Savage (P), Shenandoah Co, VA. Her LNR Troy, Lincoln Co, MO, 1871

HUTCHERSON, NATHAN (BLW), died 16 Oct 1848, Pittsylvania Co, VA; md (1) Polly Pigg, (2) 21 Sep 1836 Elizabeth B. Price (P), Pittsylvania Co, VA. Her LNR P.O. Chatham, Pittsylvania Co, VA, 1878
HUTCHESON/HUTCHINSON, THOMAS (P)
HUTCHINGS/HUTCHINS, ROBERT and widow Mary both received a pension
HUTCHINS, CALEB D. whose widow Mindwell received a pension
HUTCHINSON, THOMPSON (BLW), died 17 Jul 1854, Washington, DC; md (1) ?, (2) 19 May 1846 Martha Sampson (P), Washington, DC. She died before 7 Mar 1892, LNR Washington, DC, 1878
HUTCHINSON, WILLIAM whose widow Mary received a pension
HUTCHINSON, WILLIAM whose widow Margaret received a pension
HUTCHINSON, ENOCH whose widow Abigail received a pension
HUTCHISON, SANFORD M. whose widow Frances M. applied for a pension
HUTSELL, GEORGE and widow Margaret both received a pension
HUTSELL, JOHN whose widow Mary Ann applied for a pension
HUTSON, EDMOND applied for a pension
HUTTON, JAMES whose widow Nancy applied for a pension
HUTTON, THOMAS applied for a pension
HYATT, JOHN (BWL), died 17 Jun 1869, Harpers Ferry, WV; md (1) Ann Morrow, (2) 26 Mar 1833 Mary Ann Lamon (P), Charlestown, Jefferson Co, VA. She died before 13 May 1895, LNR Washington, DC,

HYATT (continued)
1891
HYDEN/HIDON, HIRAM (P)
HYLES, ARCHIBALD applied for a pension
HYSLOP, JOHN C. (P)
I'ANSON/ANSON, MACKIE D. whose widow Jane T. received a pension
IDEN, JONATHAN (P)
IDLE, HENRY whose widow Susannah applied for a pension
IMBODEN, GEORGE and widow Isabella both received a pension
IMBODEN, SAMUEL (P)
INGE, CHARLES (P)
INGE, CHESLEY L. whose widow Frances M. received a pension
INGRAM, ROWLAND whose widow Nancy received a pension
INGRAM, SYLVANUS whose widow Alice L. received a pension
INGRAM, VALENTINE, USA, whose widow Nancy received a pension. Also minor child Melinda/Margaret was pensioned in Spotsylvania Co, VA
INGYEARD, LEWIS, USA & VA militia, whose widow Catharine applied for a pension
INNES, ROBERT whose widow Catharine received a pension
INSCO, DANIEL (P)
INSKEEP, JOEL whose widow Mary A. applied for a pension
INSLEY, NABOTH whose widow Mary Ann received a pension
IRBY, JOHN STEWART (P)
IRELAND, GEORGE applied for a pension
IRELAND, WILLIAM whose widow Sarah applied for a pension
IRESON, JAMES whose widow Mary A. received a pension
IRONMONGER, CHARLES B. applied for a pension
IRVIN, BENJAMIN H. whose widow Jane S. received a pension
IRVIN/IRVINE, EUGENE whose

IRVIN (continued)
widow Isabella P. applied for a pension
IRVIN, JOHN (P)
IRVINE/IRWINE, JOHN whose widow Selina A. C. received a pension
IRVING, CHARLES and widow Mary both received a pension
IRVING, GEORGE N. whose widow Frances A. received a pension
IRWIN, SAMUEL and widow Leanna both applied for a pension
ISAACS, GABRIEL, alias LLEWELLYN, JOHN whose widow Caroline Isaacs applied for a pension
ISBELL, JAMES T. (P)
ISBELL, JOHN W. whose widow Celia Ann received a pension
ISENER, SALATHIEL (P, BLW)
ISHON/ESHION, SAMUEL applied for a pension
ISLER, JACOB whose widow Martha L. received a pension
ISLER, JOHN JEREMIAH whose widow Sarah received a pension
IVEY, STERLING L. applied for a pension
IVIE, JOHN (P, BLW). died 6 Dec 1875, Calloway Co, KY; md 20 Aug 1816 Elizabeth Wells (P), Henry Co, VA. She died cJan 1880, LNR P.O. Murray, Calloway Co, KY, 1878
IVY/IVEY, HARDMAN S. (BLW), whose widow Elizabeth P. received a pension.

REEL NO. 50

JACK, JEREMIAH (P)
JACKSON, ABEL whose widow Elizabeth received a pension
JACKSON, CLEMENT applied for a pension
JACKSON, DANIEL whose widow Mary applied for a pension

JACKSON, ELI (P)
JACKSON, ELIJAH/ELISHA (P)
and widow Elizabeth both
received a pension. Also a
contesting widow Julia applied
for a pension
JACKSON, GREEN whose widow
Temperance received a pension
JACKSON, JAMES whose widow
Rachel received a pension
JACKSON, JOHN and widow
Rhoanna both received a pension
JACKSON, JOHN (P)
JACKSON, JOHN R. whose widow
Martha R. applied for a pension
JACKSON, LEROY/ROY (P)
JACKSON, MATHEW W. (P,
BLW), died 11 Mar 1880,
Charlotte Co, VA; md 18 Jun
1878 Lucy Lewis (P-rejected),
Rough Creek Church, Charlotte
Co, VA. Her LNR P.O. Hat
Creek, Campbell Co, VA, 1880
JACKSON, WILLIAM and widow
Nancy M. both received a pension
JACKSON, WILLIAM whose widow Martha B./Mary received
a pension
JACOBS, CHRISTIAN (P)
JACOBS, GREENBERY/GREEN-
BURY (P)
JACOBS, THOMAS whose widow
Malinda received a pension
JAMIESON/JAMESON, JOHN,
USA, whose widow Charlotte
received a pension. Residence
was in VA
JAMES, CYRUS B. whose widow
Mary received a pension
JAMES, ISAAC E. whose widow
Betsey received a pension
JAMES, JOHN whose widow
Catherine T. received a pension
JAMES, JOSEPH S. applied for a
pension
JAMES, SAMUEL whose widow
Elizabeth applied for a pension

JAMES, SAMUEL whose widow
Mary received a pension
JAMES, THOMAS whose widow
Mary received a pension
JAMES, THOMAS D. (P)
JAMESON, GEORGE applied for
a pension
JAMESON, JAMES whose widow
Rebecca received a pension
JAMESON, SAMUEL (P) whose
widow was Rebecca
JAMIESON, JOHN (BLW), whose
widow was Maria C.
JANEGAN/JENNIKEN/JAN-
NEGAN/JARNEGAN, HENRY
and widow Nancy Janegan both
received a pension
JANNEY/JENNIE, ISAAC whose
widow Mary applied for a pension
JARRATT, GREGORY and widow
Sally both received a pension
JARRETT, DAVID whose widow
Elvira E. received a pension
JARROTT/JARRETT, YOUNG
(BLW)
JARVIS, AMOS whose widow
Elizabeth received a pension
JARVIS, DANIEL whose widow
Mary received a pension
JARVIS, JOHN whose widow Margaret received a pension
JARVIS, JOSEPH whose widow
Sally received a pension
JASPER, SAMUEL whose widow
Lucy A. G. applied for a pension
JEFFERS, JAMES (P), not in
War of 1812 but in USN in War
with Tripoli. Residence in VA
JEFFERSON, HENRY whose widow Elizabeth received a pension
JEFFERSON, JAMES (P, BLW)
JEFFERSON, THOMAS applied
for a pension
JEFFRIES, GEORGE whose widow Sally received a pension
JEFFRIES, HOWELL whose widow Anna M. applied for a
pension
JEFFRIES, JAMES applied for a

JEFFRIES (continued)
pension

JEFFRIES, RICHARD whose widow Martha B. L. received a pension

JEFFRIES, SMITH S. and widow Elizabeth both received a pension

JEFFREIS, WILLIS (P) whose widow was Kitty

JELT, FRANCIS whose widow Elizabeth applied for a pension

JENKINS, ANDERSON whose widow Martha received a pension

JENKINS, ARMISTEAD (P)

JENKINS, DANIEL and widow Jane E. both received a pension

JENKINS, DANIEL applied for a pension

JENKINS, EDWARD (BLW)

JENKINS, ELISHA whose widow Elizabeth applied for a pension

JENKINS, EVAN (P)

JENKINS, GEORGE (P)

JENKINS, GEORGE and widow Tulip both received a pension

JENKINS, JAMES whose widow Charity received a pension

JENKINS, JONATHAN whose widow Rosanna received a pension

JENKINS, LEWIS whose widow Sally received a pension

JENKINS, OBADIAH C./OBEDIAH C. (P)

JENKINS, ROBERT (P)

JENKINS, STEPHEN (BLW)

JENKINS, WESLEY (P)

JENKINS, WILLIAM whose widow Jemima received a pension

JENNELLE, LEWIS (P)

JENNINGS, ANDERSON whose widow Nancy K. received a pension

JENNINGS, JAMES whose widow Mary received a pension

JENNINGS, JESSE whose widow Rebecca received a pension

JENNINGS, JOHN L. whose widow Mary C. applied for a

JENNINGS (continued)
pension

JENNINGS, WILLIAM whose widow Frances B. received a pension

JESSE, THOMAS whose widow Fanny received a pension

JETER, IRA applied for a pension

JETT, BIRKETT/BERKETT (P, BLW)

JETT, JAMES whose widow Julia M. received a pension

JETT, JOHN whose widow Nancy received a pension

JETT, WILLIAM JOHN MARSHALL (P)

JIMERSON/JAMESON, DANIEL (P)

ROLL NO. 51

JOHNSON, ANDERSON whose widow Nancy received a pension

JOHNSON, BARTON whose widow Phebe applied for a pension

JOHNSON, BENJAMIN (P)

JOHNSON, BENJAMIN (P)

JOHNSON, BENJAMIN whose widow Sally received a pension

JOHNSON, BENJAMIN whose widow Sally received a pension

JOHNSON, BURREL whose widow Martha received a pension

JOHNSON, CHARLES and widow Elizabeth both received a pension

JOHNSON, DAVID (P)

JOHNSON, DAVID whose widow Elizabeth received a pension

JOHNSON/JOHNSTON, EDMUND and widow Letitia both received a pension

JOHNSON, ELIAS whose widow Eliza received a pension

JOHNSON, GEORGE whose widow Mary A. received a pension

JOHNSON, GEORGE whose widow Sary received a pension

JOHNSON, GEORGE A. W.

JOHNSON (continued)
whose widow Elizabeth R.
received a pension
JOHNSON, HARTWELL whose
widow Liddie received a pen-
sion
JOHNSON, HENRY (P)
JOHNSON, HICKERSON (P)
JOHNSON, JACOB (P)
JOHNSON, JAMES T. whose wi-
dow Ann M. received a pension
JOHNSON, JESSE (P)
JOHNSON, JOHN/JAMES whose
widow Nancy F. applied for a
pension
JOHNSON, JOHN (P)
JOHNSON, JOHN whose widow
Behethland received a pension
JOHNSON, JOHN (P)
JOHNSON, JOHN (P)
JOHNSON, JOHN and widow
Catharine both received a pen-
sion
JOHNSON, JOHN and widow Anne
both received a pension
JOHNSON, JOHN (P)
JOHNSON, JOHN C. (P)
JOHNSON, LARKIN applied for a
penson
JOHNSON, LEMUEL (BLW)
JOHNSON, LEVI whose widow
Elizabeth received a pension
JOHNSON, LEWIS W. whose wi-
dow Susannah B. received a
pension
JOHNSON, LITTLEBERRY
whose widow Mary T. applied
for a pension
JOHNSON, MARTIN and widow
Lockey both received a pen-
sion
JOHNSON, REUBEN whose wi-
dow Elizabeth received a pen-
sion
JOHNSON, REUBEN F. whose
widow Anna received a pension
JOHNSON, ROBERT whose wi-
dow Sarah Ann received a pen-
sion
JOHNSON, ROBERT whose wi-
dow Sarah received a pension
JOHNSON, ROBERT and widow

JOHNSON (continued)
Lucy Ann both received a pen-
sion
JOHNSON, SAMUEL whose wi-
dow Elizabeth received a pen-
sion
JOHNSON, STANHOPE whose
widow Susannah received a
pension
JOHNSON, STEPHEN whose wi-
dow Nancy received a pension
JOHNSON, THOMAS (P)
JOHNSON, THOMAS (P)
JOHNSON, THOMAS (P)
JOHNSON, THOMAS (BLW)
JOHNSON, WALSON whose wi-
dow Nancy L. received a pen-
sion
JOHNSON, WILLIAM (P)
JOHNSON, WILLIAM (P, BLW)
JOHNSON, WILLIAM (P,BLW)
JOHNSON, WILLIAM whose wi-
dow Hardenia received a pen-
sion
JOHNSON, WILLIAM and widow
Hannah both received a pen-
sion
JOHNSON, WILLIAM whose wi-
dow Jane E. received a pen-
sion
JOHNSON, WILLIAM (P, BLW),
died 4 Jan 1874, Noble Co, IN;
md (1) Mary K. Wood, (2) 2
Jun 1839 Phebe Myers (P),
Tiffin, Seneca Co, IA. She
died 1 Apr 1880, Christian Co,
MO, LNR Christian Co, MO,
1878
JOHNSON, WILLIAM whose wi-
dow Mary H. received a pen-
sion
JOHNSON, WILLIAM whose wi-
dow Margaret applied for a
pension
JOHNSON, WILLIAM and widow
Sally both received a pension
JOHNSON, WOODSON V. (BLW)
JOHNSTON/JOHNSON, ARTHUR
whose widow Zellen received a
pension
JOHNSTON, BALDWIN (P)
JOHNSTON, HUGH (P) whose

217

JOHNSTON (continued)
widow was Sally Hogan Colley
JOHNSTON, JAMES and widow
Sallie both received a pension
JOHNSTON, OLIN C. (P)
JOHNSTON, REUBEN/REUBIN
(P)
JOHNSTON, WILLIAM ST.
CLAIR applied for a pension
JOHNSTON, ZACHARIAH applied
for a pension
JOLLIFFE, JOHN whose widow
Fanny applied for a pension

ROLL NO. 52

JONAS, DANIEL (BLW), died 18
Jan 1869, Wythe Co, VA; md
14 Feb 1814 Elizabeth New-
comer (P), Rockbridge Co, VA.
Her LNR Rockbridge & Wythe
Co, 1814-1886
JONES, ALLEN (BLW), died 7
Aug 1824, Stafford Co, VA; md
6 Jan 1803 Frances/Fanny
Walters (P), Stafford Co, VA.
She died 17 May 1871, LNR
Stafford Courthouse, Stafford
Co, VA, 1871
JONES, ALLEN whose widow
Harriet W. applied for a pen-
sion
JONES, ASHER whose widow
Mary E. applied for a pension
JONES, AUGUSTIN whose widow
Ruth received a pension
JONES, BENJAMIN (BLW) ap-
plied for a pension
JONES, CHARLES whose widow
Phebe received a pension
JONES, CHARLES S. whose
widow Sarah K. received a
pension
JONES, DAVID and widow Polley
E. both received a pension
JONES, DAVID (P-rejected)
whose widow Elizabeth re-
ceived a pension
JONES, EDWARD (P)
JONES, ELIAS A. (BLW), whose
widow Elizabeth received a
pension

JONES, FIELDING (P)
JONES, GABRIEL whose widow
Mary P. received a pension
JONES, GEORGE W. G. applied
for a pension
JONES, HENRY whose widow
Lucy applied for a pension
JONES, HENRY whose widow
Elizabeth applied for a pension
JONES, HEZEKIAH whose widow
Virginia received a pension
JONES, JABISH (P)
JONES, JAMES and widow Rachel
P. both received a pension
JONES, JAMES and widow Julia
Ann both received a pension
JONES, JAMES (P) whose widow
was Elanor
JONES, JAMES whose widow
Mary S. received a pension
JONES, JAMES whose widow
Milly received a pension
JONES, JAMES whose widow
Luanna M. applied for a pen-
sion
JONES, JAMES GORDON whose
widow Jane Ann received a
pension
JONES, JAMES L. whose widow
Lucinda received a pension
JONES, JEREMIAH (P, BLW)
JONES, JESSE whose widow El-
len K. received a pension
JONES, JOHN whose widow Susan
received a pension
JONES, JOHN and widow Jane
both received a pension
JONES, JOHN (P)
JONES, JOHN and widow Malinda
both received a pension
JONES, JOHN G. whose widow
Susan L. received a pension
JONES, JOHN L. (P, BLW)
JONES, JOSEPH (P)
JONES, JOSEPH whose widow
Nancy received a pension
JONES, JOSEPH (BLW), died 10
Jun 1859, Point Pleasant, VA;
md 22 Dec 1815 Nancy W.
Yates (P), Culpeper Co, VA.
Her LNR Point Pleasant, WV,
1878

218

JONES, JOSIAH (P) whose widow was Catherine

JONES, LEWIN/LEVIN whose widow Jane received a pension

JONES, LEWIS whose widow Rebecca received a pension

JONES, MICAJAH (P)

JONES, MINITREE and widow Celia both received a pension

JONES, MOSIAS

JONES, NATHANIEL whose widow Delilah applied for a pension

JONES, PHILIP (P)

JONES, RICHARD and widow Mary both received a pension

JONES, RICHARD (P)

JONES, RICHARD (BLW), whose widow Elizabeth C. received a pension

JONES, RICHARDSON (P)

JONES, ROBERT and widow Lucy both received a pension

JONES, ROBERT and widow Amanda G. both received a pension

JONES, ROBERT W. whose widow Molsey received a pension

JONES, ROWLAND applied for a pension

JONES, SAMUEL whose widow Margaret received a pension

JONES, SAMUEL P. (P)

JONES, SIDNEY (P)

JONES, TALBERT (P)

JONES, TANDY whose widow Sally received a pension

JONES, THOMAS (P)

JONES, THOMAS (P, BLW)

JONES, THOMAS (P)

JONES, THOMAS (BLW), died 1 May 1854, Hollowayville, Bureau Co, IL; md 10 Aug 1812 Hannah Brown (P), Loudoun Co, VA. Her LNR Fremont Co, IA, 1871

JONES, THOMAS whose widow Elizabeth received a pension

JONES, THOMAS (BLW) and widow Martha both received a pension

JONES, THOMAS R. and widow

JONES (continued) Ann Jane both applied for a pension

JONES, WATTS (BLW)

JONES, WILLIAM and widow Catherine/Kitty both received a pension

JONES, WILLIAM whose widow Jane received a pension

JONES, WILLIAM whose widow Patsy received a pension

JONES, WILLIAM applied for a pension

JONES, WILLIAM (P)

JONES, WILLIAM (P)

JONES, WILLIAM (P)

JONES, WILLIAM B. and widow Mary W. both received a pension

JONES, WILLIAM D. (P-rejected, BLW) whose widow Judith B. received a pension

JONES, WILLIAM G. (BLW)

JONES, WILLIAM whose widow Susan A. applied for a pension

JONES, WILLIAM THORNTON (P)

JONES, WILLIAM W. whose widow Elizabeth received a pension

JONES, WILLIAM W. whose widow Frances E. applied for a pension

JONES, WILLIE whose widow Catharine P. received a pension

JONES, WOOD applied for a pension

JOPLING, BENJAMIN (P)

JOPLING, THOMAS (P) whose widow was Patience

JORDAN, ELIJAH whose widow Martha E. applied for a pension

JORDAN, JOHN whose widow Joanna received a pension

JORDAN, JOHN (P)

JORDAN, JOSEPH whose widow Mary Ann applied for a pension

JORDAN, LEWIS (P) whose widow was Elizabeth

JORDAN, MERIT and widow

JORDAN (continued)
Paulina both received a pension
JORDAN, MICHAEL whose widow Elizabeth received a pension
JORDAN, PLEASANT whose widow Polly received a pension
JORDAN, THOMAS whose widow Mary applied for a pension
JORDAN, WILLIAM whose widow Margaret received a pension
JORDEN/JORDAN, ANDREW (P–rejected, BLW), whose widow Catharine received a pension
JOSEPH, DANIEL (BLW), whose widow Annis applied for a pension
JOYNER, ELIJAH whose widow Martha/Patsy received a pension
JOYNER, ELISHA whose widow Jane received a pension
JOYNER/JOINER, ELY whose widow Diza applied for a pension
JOYNES, LEVIN S. whose widow Maria S. received a pension
JUDKINS, FREDERICK J. whose widow Rebecca applied for a pension
JUSTICE, LEWIS (P)
JUSTICE, SWREN/SUREN whose widow Sarah received a pension

ROLL NO. 53

KABRICK, JOHN (BLW), whose widow Susan applied for a pension
KALAR, MICHAEL whose widow Jane received a pension
KARNES, MOSES and widow Jane both received a pension
KAY, JOHN whose widow Lucy received a pension
KAYLOR, PETER (P)
KEAN/KAIN/CAIN, SAMUEL whose widow Hannah Kean received a pension
KEATTS, WILLIAM C. (P)
KECKLEY, JACOB whose widow

KECKLEY (continued)
Leah received a pension
KEELING, HENRY whose widow Fanny applied for a pension
KEELING, NATHANIEL whose widow Martha R. received a pension
KEEMLE, CHARLES whose widow Mary received a pension
KEEN, MATHIAS (P)
KEENE, BENJAMIN and widow Margaret both received a pension
KEESEE, JACOB (P)
KEETON, LARKIN whose widow Annie received a pension
KEEZEL, GEORGE whose widow Amanda F. received a pension
KEFFER, GEORGE whose widow Lucy received a pension
KEISTER, GEORGE whose widow Mary C. received a pension
KELLAM, JOHN whose widow Eliza applied for a pension
KELLAM, NATHANIEL (P)
KELLAM, THOMAS H. whose widow Harriet B. D. received a pension
KELLER, JOHN whose widow Dorothy received a pension
KELLER, LEWIS whose widow Elizabeth received a pension
KELLEY/KELLY, ABEL W. (P)
KELLEY/KELLY, GEORGE W. and widow Nancy Kelly both received a pension
KELLEY/KELLY, JAMES (P)
KELLEY, JOHN whose widow Mary received a pension
KELLY, ELIJAH whose widow Sarah P. received a pension
KELLY/KELLEY, JOHN (P)
KELLY, THOMAS S. (P)
KELLY, WESTCOAT/WESCOAT and widow Mary R. both received a pension
KEMP, GREGORY applied for a pension
KEMP, MATTHEW W. whose widow Mary G. received a pension
KEMPER, GEORGE W. whose

220

KEMPER (continued)
widow Matilda applied for a pension
KENDALL, CHARLES (P)
KENDALL, JESSE whose widow Mary/Polly received a pension
KENDALL, JOHN E. whose widow Roxy A. received a pension
KENDALL, JOHN S. applied for a pension
KENDALL, JOSEPH C. whose widow Elizabeth A. received a pension
KENDRICK, FRANCIS E. whose widow Nancy L. received a pension
KENDRICK, WILLIAM and widow Margaret both received a pension
KENNEDY, THOMAS whose widow Ruth received a pension
KENNER, RODHAM F. (P-rejected) whose widow Eliza J. received a pension
KENNERLY, JACOB whose widow Amanda F. received a pension
KENNETT, BARNABAS (P)
KENNETT, THOMAS (P)
KENNEY, JOSEPH whose widow Sarah applied for a pension
KENNON, JOHN (BLW)
KERLIN, DAVID whose widow Barbara received a pension
KERNELL, RICHARD whose widow Elizabeth received a pension
KERNES/KEARNES, JEREMIAH whose widow Mary received a pension
KERNS, ABNER and widow Mildey both applied for a pension
KERR, ABNER R. whose widow Sally N. received a pension
KERR/CARR, JAMES M. (P)
KERR/CARR, JOHN (P)
KERR, THOMAS (P)
KERSEY, HENRY T. whose widow Sally received a pension
KERSEY, JOHN whose former widow Catharine Tate applied

KERSEY (continued)
for a pension
KESLER, HENRY whose widow Elizabeth received a pension
KESLER, JACOB and widow Catherine both received a pension
KESSLER, JACOB (P)
KESSLER, JOHN whose widow Elizabeth applied for a pension
KESSLER, JOHN (P)
KESTERSON, WILLIS whose widow Catherine received a pension
KETTERMAN, JACOB whose widow Sarah received a pension
KETTERMAN, JUSTUS whose widow Mary Ann received a pension
KEY, PLEASANT (BLW) whose widow Elizabeth applied for a pension
KEY, ROBERT whose widow Mary A. R. received a pension
KEYES, HUMPHREY whose widow Jane H. received a pension
KEYS, JAMES (P)

ROLL NO. 54

KIBBE, GAINS (P)
KIBLER, JACOB (P)
KIDD, ALEXANDER whose widow Charity received a pension
KIDD, COLEMAN W. (P)
KIDD, JAMES (P)
KIDD, JAMES (P)
KIDD, JOHN whose widow Lucy received a pension
KIDD, WILLIAM (P, BLW)
KIDD, WILLIAM (P)
KIDDY, LEWIS and widow Lucinda both received a pension
KIDWELL, JOHN and widow Emeline E. both received a pension
KIZER, ANDREW (P)
KIGER, GEORGE W. whose widow Anna J. received a pension
KIGER, HENRY and widow Polly

221

KIGER (continued)
both received a pension
KIGER, ISAAC (BLW) whose widow was Lydia
KILBY, HENRY whose widow Susan B. applied for a pension
KILBY, LEROY whose widow Sallie L. received a pension
KILE, JOHN (P)
KILGORE, HIRAM whose widow Lucy received a pension
KILGROW, WILLIAM whose widow Verressa received a pension
KILLINGSWORTH, WILLIAM whose widow Rebecca received a pension
KIMBERLIN, NATHANIEL (P, BLW)
KIMBLER, WILLIAM whose widow Nancy received a pension
KIMBROUGH, JOHN P. whose widow Nancy applied for a pension
KIMBROUGH, WILLIAM whose widow Susan received a pension
KIMLER, DANIEL (P)
KINCADE, JOSEPH applied for a pension
KINCAID/KINKAID, WILLIAM whose widow Elizabeth received a pension
KINCANON/KINCANNON, SAMUEL (P, BLW)
KINCHELOW, DANIEL whose widow Courtney Ann received a pension
KINDER, HENRY whose widow Mary received a pension
KINDRED, WILLIAM applied for a pension
KING, ABRAHAM whose widow Linia received a pension
KING, ALEXANDER (P)
KING, AUGUSTINE whose widow Verlinda received a pension
KING, AVERETT and widow Elizabeth V. both received a pension
KING, DANIEL (P)
KING, ELIAS applied for a pen-

KING (continued)
sion
KING, ELIAS (P)
KING, ELIAS whose widow Margaret applied for a pension
KING, GRIFFIN T. whose widow Ann H. received a pension
KING, JAMES (BLW)
KING, JOHN (P)
KING, JOHN (BLW), and widow Elizabeth Jane both received a pension
KING, JOSEPH whose widow Catharine applied for a pension
KING, MILES whose widow Mary (Little) King applied for a pension
KING, MOSES and widow Polly both received a pension
KING, PETER (P)
KING, REUBEN whose widow Elizabeth applied for a pension
KING, ROBERT whose widow Catherine received a pension
KING, WILLIAM (P)
KINGRED/KINGREY/KINGRY, ABRAHAM and widow Sarah Kingred received a pension
KINGREE/KING, REUBEN whose widow Sarah Kingree received a pension
KINGSTON, FRANCIS applied for a pension
KININGHAM/KINNINGHAM, IRA (P)
KINKAID/KINCAID, JOHN and widow Mary both received a pension
KINKEAD, JOHN L. and widow Henrietta both received a pension
KINNARD, DAVID whose widow Lavinia received a pension
KINNEAR, JAMES (BLW) whose widow was Martha/Patty
KINNINGHAM/KININGHAM, WILLIAM and widow Jane both received a pension
KIOUS/KIAS, JACOB (BLW) whose widow Susanna received a pension
KIPPER, JOHN whose widow

222

KIPPER (continued)
Jane received a pension
KIPPS/KIPS, JACOB (P)
KIPPS, JOHN whose widow Mary
received a pension
KIRACOFE, GEORGE and widow
Mary A. both received a pension
KIRBY, ANDERSON (P)
KIRBY, BENNETT whose child
Elizabeth A. Huagins applied
for a pension
KIRBY, JOHN (P, BLW), OH
militia, whose widow was
Cecelia. Residence in VA
KIRBY, JOHN (P, BLW)
KIRBY, ---- (BLW), whose widow Elizabeth received a pension
KIRK, ISAAC (P)
KIRK, ISAAC applied a pension
KIRK, JAMES (P)
KIRK, WILLIAM (P) whose widow was Sallie
KIRK, WILLIAM applied for a pension
KIRKLAND, WILLIAM and widow
Abetha E. both received a pension
KIRKPATRICK, THOMAS and widow Polly both received a pension
KIRLIN, WILLIAM (P)
KISER/KEYSER, EPHRAIM (P)
KISLING, WILLIAM and widow
Nancy both received a pension
KITCHEN, WESTON applied for
a pension
KITCHENS, THOMAS (P)
KITCHIN, WILLIAM whose widow Elizabeth I. applied for a
pension
KLEIN, JACOB whose widow Esther applied for a pension
KLIEN/KLEIN, LEWIS whose
widow Elizabeth received a
pension
KLIPSTEIN, JOHN A. and widow
Elizabeth both received a pension
KNAPP, JOHN R. applied for a
pension

KNAPP, WILLIAM and widow
Almira both applied for a pension

ROLL NO. 55

KNIGHT, BAILEY whose widow
Frances applied for a pension
KNIGHT, BENJAMIN (P)
KNIGHT, BRANSON whose widow
Ann Gorsuch applied for a pension
KNIGHT, JOHN and widow Sarah
both received a pension
KNIGHT, JOHN ESSLEY, alias
KNIGHT, ESSLEY, whose widow Louise M. received a pension
KNIGHT, MATHEW L. whose
widow Sophia W. received a
pension
KNIGHT, THOMAS whose widow
Elizabeth applied for a pension
KNIGHT, TISCHARNER applied
for a pension
KNISELEY/KNICELY, JOHN
whose widow Barbara Kniseley
received a pension
KNISELY, DAVID whose widow
Polly applied for a pension
KNOPP/KNAPP, ABRAHAM and
widow Cathrine Knopp both
received a pension
KNOTTS, JONATHAN applied for
a pension
KNOWLES, ARCHIBALD S.
whose widow Nancy received a
pension
KNOWLES, JOSHUA whose widow Jane received a pension
KNOX, JAMES (P)
KNOX, JOHN applied for a pension
KNOXVILLE/KNOX, JOHN whose
widow Mary Knoxville received
a pension
KOGER, JOHN whose widow
Polly applied for a pension
KOONCE/COUNCE, NICHOLAS
whose widow Elizabeth Koonce
received a pension
KOONTZ, JACOB whose widow

KOONTZ (continued)
Elizabeth received a pension
KOONTZ, JOHN whose widow
Mary J. received a pension
KREMER, GEORGE applied for a
pension
KUMP, JACOB and widow Julia
Ann both received a pension
KUNKLE, JACOB whose widow
Mary M. received a pension
KURLEY, DAVID whose widow
Mary Ann B. received a pension
KYLE, HENRY (P)
KYLE, JAMES whose widow Harriet received a pension
LACEY, WILLIAM S. and widow
Julia A. both received a pension
LACK, WILLIAM (P)
LACKS/LAX, ROBERT (P)
LACKS, TIMOTHY whose widow
Tabitha applied for a pension
LACKS, WILLIAM (P)
LACKY/LACKEY, NATHAN
whose widow Elizabeth applied
for a pension
LACY/LACEY, JAMES HORACE
(P)
LACY, JOSIAH whose widow Ann
received a pension
LACY, PLEASANT whose widow
Zippora applied for a pension
LACY, SHADRACK whose widow
Martha received a pension
LAFORCE, MONCIER (BLW),
whose widow was Catharine
LAFONG, GEORGE B. whose
widow Cassandra received a
pension
LAIDLEY, JAMES G. whose
widow Harriet received a pension
LAIN, JEREMIAH whose widow
Mary received a pension
LAIRD, WILLIAM P. and widow
Mary A. both received a pension
LAKE, DANIEL whose widow
Elizabeth received a pension
LALEY, JOHN whose widow Mary
received a pension

LALLIS/LOLLIS, AUGUSTUS applied for a pension
LAMB, BENJAMIN whose widow
Susan applied for a pension
LAMB, JOHN F. whose widow
Susanna received a pension
LAMB, MICHAEL (BLW), died
26 Mar 1868, Pendleton Co,
WV; md 27 Oct 1812 Barbara
Simmons (P), Pendleton Co,
VA. Her LNR nr Franklin,
Pendleton Co, WV, 1871
LAMB, PHILIP whose widow
Polly received a pension
LAMBIRTH, JOHN whose widow
Malinda received a pension
LAMEUSE, RENE/PETER applied for a pension
LAMME/LAMB, ISAAC (P)
LAMPKIN, JOHN and widow Ellen both received a pension
LANCASTER, JAMES and widow
Sarah Jane both received a
pension
LANCASTER, JOHN A. whose
widow Adelaide M. received a
pension
LANCASTER, LEWIS whose widow Nancy received a pension
LANCASTER, WILLIAM P. and
widow Drusilla R. both received a pension
LAND, MESHAK whose widow
Rachel received a pension
LAND, ZACHARIAH whose widow
Millie received a pension
LANDES, DANIEL (P)
LANDES, HENRY whose widow
Elizabeth applied for a pension
LANDES, JACOB (P)
LANDIS, SAMUEL whose widow
Elizabeth received a pension
LANDRUM, JAMES F. whose widow Patience received a pension
LANDRUM, JOSEPH whose widow Rachel received a pension

ROLL NO. 56

LANE, ISHAM H. whose widow
Theodocia received a pension

224

LANE, JAMES B. (P)

LANE, JOHN W. and widow Sarah both received a pension

LANE, LEWIS whose widow Lucinda received a pension

LANE, ROBERT (P)

LANE, THOMAS (BLW), TN militia, died 22 May 1859, Williamson Co, TN; md 1 Aug 1811 Catherine Utley (P), Goochland Co, VA. Her LNR Nolensville, Williamson Co, TN, 1871

LANGFITT, JOHN TL (BLW), died 3 Jun 1834, Wood Co, VA; md 8 Jun 1812 Canzada Pilcher (P), Wood Co, VA. She died before 29 Dec 1884, LNR Claysville, Wood Co, WV, 1871

LANGFORD, JAMES H. (P)

LANGHORNE, WILLIAM whose widow Charlotte L. received a pension

LANGLEY, WALTER whose widow Susanna applied for a pension

LANHAM, ENOS (BLW)

LANHAM, JACKSON, alias LANNAN, JOHN (BLW) whose widow Betsy Lanham received a pension

LANIER, LEWIS and widow Martha both received a pension

LANKFORD, PLEASANT whose widow Elender applied for a pension

LAPRADE, ANDREW whose widow Lina received a pension

LAREW, JACOB and widow Margaret W. both received a pension

LARGENT/SARGENT, JOSEPH applied for a pension

LARIMORE/LARMER, JOHN applied for a pension

LARIMORE, ROBERT (BLW), whose widow Susan A. applied for a pension

LARIMORE, SAMUEL (BLW), applied for a pension

LARRANCE, WILLIAM O. whose

LARRANCE (continued) widow Elizabeth received a pension

LARSON/LAWSON/LOSSON, WILLIAM applied for a pension

LASLEY, IVY and widow Willia C. both received a pension

LASLEY, JOHN B. whose widow Susan P. received a pension

LATHAM, JOHN whose widow Lucy received a pension

LATHAM, JOHN and widow Juliet A. both applied for a pension

LATHAM, ROWZEE (P)

LATHAM, WILLIAM (P)

LATIMER/LATTIMER, GEORGE whose widow Elizabeth Latimer received a pension

LAUCK, JACOB (BLW) and widow Catherine both received a pension

LAUGHERY/LOUGHERY, WILLIAM applied for a pension

LAVELL/LAVEL, ABRAHAM and widow Lucy A. both received a pension

LAVEN/LAVIN, BENJAMIN and widow Frances both received a pension

LAVENDER/LAVINDER, WILLIAM whose widow Sallie received a pension

LAVINDER, CHILTON/SHELTON whose widow Mary Ann applied for a pension

LAW, NATHANIEL whose widow Sally applied for a pension

LAWHORN, JAMES whose widow Margaret received a pension

LAWLACE/LAWLESS, BENJAMIN and widow Elizabeth Lawlace both received a pension

LAWLER, MARTIN whose widow Nancy A. received a pension

LAWLER, LAZARUS appiled for a pension

LAWLESS, JAMES applied for a pension and widow Polly

LAWLESS (continued)
received a pension

LAWLESS, LELAND whose widow Prudence T. received a pension

LAWLESS, LEWIS whose widow Sarah received a pension

LAWRENCE/LORRANCE, JAMES and widow Charlotte Lawrence both received a pension

LAWRENCE, JAMES applied for a pension

LAWRENCE, JOHN G. whose widow Hannah G. received a pension

LAWRENCE, LEWIS (P)

LAWRENCE, ROBERT whose widow Elizabeth received a pension

LAWSON, BENJAMIN (P)

LAWSON, GEORGE W. and widow Rachel both applied for a pension

LAWSON, ISAAC (BLW)

LAWSON, JOHN alias BOULL-ING, JOHN applied for a pension

LAWSON, JOHN (BLW) whose widow Eve received a pension

LAWSON/LOSSON, WILLIAM and widow Delia both received a pension

LAWWILL/LOWWILL, JAMES (P)

LAYCOCK, JACOB and widow Rebecca A. both received a pension

LAYMAN, DANIEL whose widow Barbara received a pension

LAYMAN, PHILIP and widow Christena both received a pension

LAYNE, HNERY whose widow Susanna received a pension

LAYNE, JOEL (P)

LAYNE, JOHN S. and widow Dilecia T. both received a pension

LAYNE/LANE, PLEASANT whose widow Elizabeth received a pension

LAYNE/LAIN, WILSON whose widow Matilda C. Layne received a pension

LAYTON, CHARLES whose widow Sarah received a pension

LAZEAR, JOSEPH (P)

LEA, THOMAS whose widow Mary received a pension

LEACH, LEWIS (BLW), and widow Sarah both received a pension

LEACH, PHILEMON W. whose widow Mary received a pension

LEACH, SAMUEL (P, BLW), USA, whose wife was Mary. Residence in VA

LEACH, THOMAS, Jr. (BLW), and widow Nancy both received a pension

LEACH, THORNTON K. (P)

LEACH, WILLIS whose widow Mary received a pension

LEADBETTER, ISAAC (BLW), whose widow Jane W. received a pension

LEAK, ROBERT whose widow Sarah received a pension

LEAMON, JACOB (P)

LEAPLY, JACOB whose widow Louisa received a pension

LEATH, EPPS whose widow Nancy Chappell received a pension

LECKIE, GRIFFIN L. whose widow Emily S. received a pension

LECKLIGHTER/LICKLIGHTER, GEORGE whose widow Ann Lecklighter received a pension

ROLL NO. 57

LEE, ARTHUR (BLW), died 18 Nov 1847, Lancaster Co, VA; md 13 Jan 1814 Sarah Haggoman (P), Lancaster Co, VA. Her LNR P.O. Kilmarnock, White Stone Township, Lancaster Co, VA, 1871

LEE, BROOKING whose widow Polly received a pension

LEE, DAVID (P)

LEE, ELISHA (P, BLW)

LEE, JEREMIAH whose widow Ann J. received a pension

LEE, JOEL (BLW), whose widow Catharine received a pension

LEE, JOHN whose widow Mary P. received a pension

LEE, JOHN R. (BLW), whose widow was Elizabeth

LEE, JOSEPH whose widow Polly received a pension

LEE, RICHARD H. (P, BLW)

LEE, RICHARD K. applied for a pension

LEE, ROBERT T. and widow Mary both received a pension

LEE, SAMUEL and widow Jane R. both received a pension

LEE, THOMAS whose widow Rachael received a pension

LEE, THOMAS whose widow Sally received a pension

LEE, THOMAS whose widow Elizabeth received a pension

LEE, WILLIAM and widow Sarah both received a pension

LEE, WILLIAM and widow Hannah A. both received a pension

LEE, WILLIAM HENRY whose widow Susan Harwood received a pension

LEE, ZACHARIAH (P)

LEEP/LEAP, GABRIEL (P, BLW)

LEEPER, WILLIAM whose widow Martha received a pension

LEFFEW, JOSIAH (P)

LEFOE, GRAVETT (P)

LEFTRICH/LEFTWICH, JACK H. whose widow Jane Leftrich received a pension

LEFTWICH, AUGUSTINE and widow Elizabeth Williams both received a pension

LEFTWICH, JABEZ (BLW)

LEFTWICH, JABEZ (P,BLW)

LEFTWICH, JOEL whose widow Sarah applied for a pension

LEFTWICH/LEFTWICK, NICODEMUS whose widow Margaret Leftwich received a pension

LEFTWICH, THOMAS L. whose widow Mildred O. received a pension

LEFTWICH, WILLIAM whose widow Charlotte C. received a pension

LEGAN, CHARLES whose widow Nancy received a pension

LEGG, HARRISON whose widow Nancy received a pension

LEGG, THOMAS (BLW), and widow Hannah C. both received a pension

LEIGH, BENJAMIN W. whose widow Julia received a pension

LEIGH, JOHN D. whose widow Damaris received a pension

LEIGH, NATHANIEL (BLW), entered service from Campbell Co, VA. Residence in Noble Co, IN, 1851 and 1855

LEITCH, JAMES whose widow Frances M. received a pension

LEMAY, JOHN (P)

LEMLEY, JACOB (P)

LEMLEY, MICHAEL (BLW), died 18 Dec 1821, Stephensburg, Frederick Co, VA; md 22 Dec 1802 Rosanna Slusher (P), Frederick Co, VA. She died 31 Mar 1873, LNR Stephensburg, Fredericksburg, VA, 1871

LEMON, GEORGE whose widow Nancy applied for a pension

LEMON, JACOB applied for a pension

LEMON, PETER (BLW), whose widow was Eleanor

LENEVE, JOHN whose widow Permelia applied for a pension

LENOX, THOMAS whose widow Sarah received a pension

LEONARD, ABRAHAM whose widow Levina R. received a pension

LEONARD/LEANARD, FREDERICK whose widow Annie received a pension

LEONARD, GEORGE (P)

LEONARD, GEORGE (P)

LEONARD, HENRY whose widow Elizabeth received a pension

LEONARD, MICHAEL (BLW) whose widow Phebe received a pension

LEONARD, WILLIAM whose widow Mary H. applied for a pension

LESTER/LUSTER, GEORGE whose widow Sally received a pension

LESTER, JOHN (BLW), and widow Annie both received a pension

LESTER, MOSES applied for a pension

LE SUEUR, MYRTLE whose widow Martha applied for a pension

LETT, JOSEPH whose widow Susan received a pension

LEVANT, THOMAS W. alias DEVAUGHN, THOMAS W. whose widow Celeste Levant applied for a pension

LEVERT, EUGENE applied for a pension

LEVICK, GEORGE applied for a pension

LEVY, JOHN B (P)

LEWARK, JOSEPH (P, BLW)

LEWELLEN, ASA whose widow Catherine received a pension

LEWIS, ANDREW whose widow Harriet applied for a pension

LEWIS, BURTON R. whose widow Louisa received a pension

LEWIS, CHARLES whose widow Jane received a pension

LEWIS, CHARLES whose widow Polly received a pension

LEWIS, DAVID (P)

LEWIS, EDMUND whose widow Jane received a pension

LEWIS, EDWARD (BLW), whose widow was Ann

LEWIS, FIELDING whose widow Elizabeth received a pension

LEWIS, HENRY (P)

LEWIS, JACOB applied for a pension

LEWIS, JAMES whose widow Cassandra received a pension

LEWIS, JAMES B. whose widow

LEWIS (continued) Elizabeth applied for a pension

LEWIS, JOHN applied for a pension

LEWIS, JONATHAN (P, BLW), LNR P.O. New England, Athens Co, OH, 1871; md 28 Aug 1816 Nancy Randolph (P-rejected), Belmont Co, OH. She died 31 Jan 1879, New England, OH

LEWIS, JOSEPH (P)

LEWIS, LEWIS (P)

LEWIS, NACY (P)

LEWIS, RICHARD and widow Mary both received a pension

LEWIS, ROBERT died in service 1813. Former widow Mary White applied for a pension

LEWIS, SAMUEL whose widow Mary received a pension

LEWIS, SAMUEL (P)

LEWIS, SAMUEL whose widow Susan R. received a pension

LEWIS, SAMUEL M. whose widow Frances applied for a pension

LEWIS, WARNER whose widow Joicy received a pension

LEWIS, WARNER whose widow Maria Isabella received a pension

LEWIS, WILLIS whose widow Catherine received a pension

ROLL NO. 58

LICHLITER, ADAM and widow Catharine both received a pension

LICHLITER, CONRAD whose widow Sarah applied for a pension

LICHLITER/LICKLITER, DANIEL whose widow (unnamed) received a pension

LICKLITER, CONRAD (P)

LIGHT, JOHN S. whose widow Hannah applied for a pension

LIGHTBURNE, ROBERT (BLW)

LIGON, HENRY whose widow Sarah A. received a pension

LIGON, MATTHEW (BLW), whose widow was Jane

LIKENS, LEONARD whose widow Ruth received a pension

LILLER, HENRY applied for a pension

LILLER/LILLEN, JACOB applied for a pension

LILLER, JOHN applied for a pension

LILLY, JOSEPH (P)

LINEBAUGH, WILLIAM (P, BLW), MD militia, died 28 Oct 1881, Rockingham Co, VA, LNR Harrisonburg, Rockingham Co, VA; md (1) Betsy Wise, (2) 2 Jan 1852 Fanny E. Moore (P-rejected), Melrose, Rockingham Co, VA. She died 13 Apr 1885, Hagerstown, MD

LINCH/LYNCH, JAMES (P)

LINCOLN, DAVID (BWL), whose widow Catherine received a pension

LINDEMOOD, JACOB and widow Christina both received a pension

LINDSAY, HENRY and widow Frances D. both received a pension

LINDSAY/LINDSEY/LINDZY, JEREMIAH whose widow Nancy Lindsay received a pension

LINDSAY, LUNSFORD (BLW), and widow Elizabeth both received a pension

LINDSEY, JOHN (BLW), died in service 7 Oct 1814; md Elizabeth Rambo. She later md John Wilson, Revolutionary War veteran of NC and received a pension and bounty land warrant based upon his service.

LINDSEY, JOHN whose widow Tabitha received a pension

LINDSEY/LINDSY, PHILIP/PHILIPS (P)

LINE, GEORGE and widow Elizabeth both received a pension

LINEAWEAVER, PHILIP applied

LINEAWEAVER (continued) for a pension

LINEWEAVER, JACOB (P)

LINEWEAVER, JOHN and widow Catherine both received a pension

LINEWEAVER, JOHN (P)

LINK, DAVID (BLW), and widow Rebecca both received a pension

LINK, JOHN (BLW) whose widow Barbara received a pension

LINKONS/LINKUS, ADAM whose widow Margaret Linkons received a pension

LINN/LYNN, PETER (P)

LINTON, JAMES N. (BLW), whose widow Rachael M. received a pension

LIPFORD, AMOS whose widow Elizabeth received a pension

LIPP, DANIEL whose widow Frances received a pension

LIPPS, DANIEL whose widow Barbary applied for a pension

LIPSCOMB, IRA E. whose widow Ann F. received a pension

LIPSCOMB, JAMES and widow Anna M. both received a pension

LIPSCOMB, THOMAS applied for a pension

LIPSCOMB, WARREN whose widow Elizabeth received a pension

LIPTRAP/LIPSTRAP, THOMAS alias BRIGHT, THOMAS (P, BLW), died 19 Jan 1873, Dry Fork, WV; md 1821 Margaret Cox (P-rejected), Rockbridge Co, VA. She died Sep 1879, LNR P.O. Black Fork, Tucker Co, WV

LITCHFORD, JOHN and widow Sarah A. both received a pension

LITTEN, THOMAS whose widow Nancy received a pension

LITTERAL, HUTSON whose widow Sarah received a pension

LITTERAL, JOHN whose widow Elizabeth applied for a pension

LITTLE, JAMES and widow Mary both received a pension

LITTLE, JOHN A. applied for a pension

LITTLEJOHN, ABRAHAM whose widow Sarah received a pension

LITTRELL, THOMAS whose widow Frances received a pension

LIVELY, HENRY P. and widow Ophelia both received a pension

LIVELY, JAMES (P)

LIVESAY, JAMES whose widow Leathy received a pension

LIVESAY, THOMAS (P-rejected) whose widow Rebecca received a pension

LLOYD, ANDERSON whose widow Agnes applied for a pension

LLOYD, GEORGE E. (BLW), died 22 Feb 1852, Kalamazoo, MI; md 20 Apr 1815 Ruth Dunkin (P), Union, Loudoun Co, VA. She died 12 Feb 1880, Kalamazoo, MI

LLOYD, JOSEPH A. (P)

LLOYD, THOMAS whose widow Ann received a pension

LOCHMILLER, ISAAC (P)

LOCKE, LUDWELL L. whose widow Sarah Cox applied for a pension

LOCKER, JEPTHA B. whose widow Frances received a pension

LOCKET, FOREST whose widow Mary applied for a pension

LOCKETT, RICHARD (BLW), whose widow Sarah received a pension

LOCKHART, JAMES (P)

LOCKRIDGE, ANDREW (P)

LOGAN, BENJAMIN (P)

LOGAN, WILLIAM (P)

LOGAN, WILLIAM whose widow Rebecca received a pension

LOHR, JOHN and widow Margaret both received a pension

LONDON, WIATT and widow

LONDON (continued) Rachel M. both received a pension

LONG/LANG, GEORGE W. applied for a pension

LONG, HENRY (P)

LONG, JAMES and widow Elizabeth both applied for a pension

LONG, JAMES whose widow Lucy applied for a pension

LONG, JEREMIAH whose widow Mary E. received a pension

LONG, JOHN (P)

LONG, JOSHUA and widow Frances both received a pension

LONG, PAUL (P)

LONG, VALENTINE C. (P)

LONG, WYRE whose widow Nancy received a pension

ROLL NO. 59

LOOKADO, WILLIAM applied for a pension

LOONEY, JOSEPH (BLW)

LOONEY, ROBERT (BLW)

LOSH, DANIEL (P)

LOTT, ROBERT whose widow Martha received a pension

LOTTS, JOHN whose widow Eve applied for a pension

LOUDENBACK, JOSEPH whose widow Eve applied for a pension

LOUGH, PHILIP whose widow Sally received a pension

LOUGHERY, AARON (P)

LOVE, BENJAMIN whose widow Teliza received a pension

LOVE, DANIEL W. (BLW), and widow Cynthiana both received a pension

LOVE, HENRY whose widow Caty received a pension

LOVE, SAMUEL (P)

LOVE, THOMAS (BLW)

LOVELESS, THOMAS (BLW), and widow Elizabeth both received a pension

LOVELL, EDMOND/EDWARD received a pension

LOVELL, JOHN J. whose widow Rhoda received a pension
LOVERN, PATRICK H. applied for a pension
LOVIN/LOVING, PITMAN whose widow Maria Lovin received a pension
LOVING, CHRISTOPHER whose widow Leah received a pension
LOVING, DAVID (BLW), whose widow Henrietta R. received a pension
LOVING, RICHARD whose widow Anna received a pension
LOVING, RICHARD whose widow Elizabeth applied for a pension
LOVING, THOMAS whose widow Mary received a pension
LOW, JESSE whose widow Easter applied for a pension
LOW, JOHN and widow Elizabeth both received a pension
LOWDER, JESSE and widow Ann both received a pension
LOWE, HENSON (P)
LOWE, JESSE whose widow Wilsey received a pension
LOWE, JOHN H. (P)
LOWE, JOSEPH (P)
LOWE, JOSHUA (P)
LOWE, MATHEW whose widow Eliza applied for a pension
LOWER, WILLIAM applied for a pension
LOWHORN, THOMAS whose widow Sarah Jane received a pension
LOWMAN, GEORGE whose widow Susannah applied for a pension
LOWRIE, WILLIAM (P)
LOWRY, ANDERSON (P)
LOWRY, EDWARD whose widow Polly received a pension
LOWRY, WALKER whose widow Rebecca received a pension
LOWTHER, ALEXANDER whose widow Rachel M. received a pension
LOWTHER, ROBERT whose widow Mary applied for a pension
LOY, WILLIAM (BLW), whose

LOY (continued) widow Magdalen received a pension
LOYD, HENRY whose widow Nancy received a pension
LOYD, JOHN whose widow Mary received a pension
LOYD, LEVI and widow Harriet A. both received a pension
LOYD, PAYTON/PEYTON whose widow Sarah received a pension
LOYD, WILLIAM KIRTLEY alias LLOYD, WILLIAM KERTLY (P)
LUCAS, GEORGE (BLW), whose widow Elizabeth received a pension
LUCAS, LEVI whose widow Elizabeth received a pension
LUCAS, ROBERT (P)
LUCAS, WILLIAM (P)
LUCK, DIGGS (P, BLW)
LUCK, LARKIN whose widow Elizabeth received a pension
LUCK, SAMUEL P. applied for a pension
LUCK, TARLTON (P)
LUCKADOO/LUCCADO, WILLIAM applied for a pension
LUCKETT, HORACE whose widow Louise A. received a pension
LUDWICK, GEORGE whose widow Mary received a pension
LUDWICK, SOLOMON (P)
LUDWIG, JOHN (P)
LUFFMIRE, HENRY whose widow Elizabeth received a pension
LUKE, ISAAC V. (P)
LUKE, JAMES whose widow Permelia received a pension
LUKE, JOHN (P)
LUKE, WILLIAM whose widow Sophronia received a pension
LUMKIN, ROBERT W. (P)
LUMPKIN, JOSEPH applied for a pension
LUMPKIN, ROBERT (P)
LUNCEFORD/LUNSFORD, LAVENDER (BLW)

LUNDY, AMOS (BLW), whose widow Mary received a pension
LUNSFORD, REUBEN (P)
LUSHER, GEORGE applied for a pension
LUSHER, JOHN applied for a pension
LUTER/LUTHER, BLAND whose widow Sarah Luter received a pension
LUTES, DAVID and widow Mary both received a pension
LUTTRELL, JAMES whose widow Elizabeth received a pension
LUTZ, EPHRAIM whose widow Elizabeth applied for a pension
LUTZ, JACOB (P)
LYLE, JOHN F. whose widow Jane received a pension
LYNCH, DANIEL whose widow Sarah received a pension
LYNCH, JAMES whose widow Jane received a pension
LYNCH, JOHN W. (BLW), whose widow Nancy received a pension
LYNCH, MEREDITH whose widow Mary received a pension
LYNCH, ROBERT (P)
LYNCH, SAMUEL whose widow Sally received a pension
LYNCH, WILLIAM C. whose widow Mary received a pension
LYNN, MOSES (BLW), whose widow Elizabeth received a pension
LYON, ALEXANDER whose widow Jane received a pension
LYON, ELISHA (BLW), enlisted in Franklin Co, VA, died 4 Apr 1842, Patrick Go, VA; md 2 Aug 1792 Rhoda Hatcher. Her LNR Patrick Co, VA, 1855
LYON, JACOB whose widow Eliza received a pension
LYON, WILLIAM whose widow Elenor H. received a pension
LYONS, DANIEL (P)
LYONS, JOHN applied for a pension
LYONS, ROBERT (P)

MABERRY, JOSHUA whose widow Mary Ann received a bounty land warrant and pension
MABRY, JOEL whose widow Sally received a pension. Their minor child Edward G. applied for a pension
MACDANIEL, MARTIN NORRIS whose widow Ann received a pension
MACE, SEBASTIAN whose widow Hannah applied for a pension
MCABOY/MCOBOY, JOHN (P)
MCALLISTER/MCALISTER/MCCALLISTER, GARLAND whose widow Naba/Neba McAllister applied for a pension
MCALLISTER/MCCALLISTER, JAMES (P)
MCARTOR, WILLIAM applied for a pension
MCBEE, WILLIAM (P, BLW)
MCBRIDE, ROBERT whose widow Elizabeth applied for a pension
MCBUCKNER/BUCKNER, PATRICK (P)
MCCABE, JAMES whose widow Mary received a pension
MCCABE, JOHN (P, BLW)
MCCAFFRY, WILLIAM (P)
MCCALLISTER/MCALLISTER, WILLIAM whose widow Mary McCallister received a pension
MCCAMMANT, ANDREW whose widow Rebecca received a pension
MCCANN, JAMES (BLW), whose widow Margaret applied for a pension
MCCANN/MCCAN, WILLIAM whose widow Sarah Ann applied for a pension
MCCARTY, GEORGE, Jr. (P)
MCCARTY/MCCARTHY, JAMES C. (P)
MCCARTY, WILLIAM M. whose widow Mary B. received a pension

MCCAULEY, GEORGE whose widow Julia A. applied for a pension

MCCAULEY, PETER (BLW), died 1 May 1852, Albemarle Co, VA; md c6 Jan 1807 Agnes Garrison (P), Albemarle Co, VA. Her LNR nr Union, Albemarle Co, VA, 1871

MCCLAIN/MCLANE, THOMAS (BLW), whose widow Sarah McLain received a pension

MCCLAIN/MCLAIN, WILLIAM whose widow Martha received a pension

MCCLANAHAN, ELIJAH (BLW). Residence in Roanoke Co, VA

MCCLANAHAN, JOHN (BLW), whose widow Sallie A. received a pension

MCCLANAHAN, JOHN whose widow Emily Nevil McClanahan received a pension

MCCLANAHAN, SAMUEL H., USA, and widow Charity both received a pension. Samuel was born in VA and later resided in TN

MCCLANAHAN, WILLIAM whose widow Margaret received a pension

MCCLANE/MCCLAIN, JOHN whose widow Mary applied for a pension

MCCLANEN, GEORGE whose widow Sarah received a pension

MCCLAREN, CHARLES (P)

MCCLARREN/MCCLANNON, HENRY (P)

MCCLELLAND, SAMUEL whose widow Margaret Ann received a pension

MCCLINTIC, ARCHIBALD (P)

MCCLUNG/MCCLUN, ABSALOM B. (BLW), whose widow Margaret McClung received a pension

MCCLUNG, BENJAMIN S. whose widow Maria received a pension

MCCLUNG, EDWARD (P, BLW)

MCCLUNG, JOSEPH (BLW), whose widow Esther received a pension

MCCLUNG, WILLIAM whose widow Jane applied for a pension. Residence was in WV. William served in the Indian Wars 1795-1800

MCCLURE, MORDECAI (P, BLW), LNR Parke Co, IN, 1871. Enlisted in Botetourt Co, VA

MCCLURE, SAMUEL applied for a pension

MCCLURE, WILLIAM and widow Ruth both received a pension

MCCOMAS, ISAAC and widow Nancy both received a pension

MCCOMB, SAMUEL whose widow Sallie received a pension

MCCOMB, WILLIAM and widow Sally L. both received a pension

MCCOMMACK, ANDERSON applied for a pension

MCCOMMACK, JOHN (P)

MCCONNELL, ABRAM (BLW), whose widow Susan B. received a pension

MCCONNELL, RODDY applied for a pension

MCCONNELL, THOMAS (BLW), whose widow Louisa C. received a pension

MCCOOK, NEIL (BLW), died 9 Oct 1850, Richmond, VA; md 9 Dec 1814 Mary/Polly Shelton (P), Hanover Co, VA. Her LNR Richmond, VA, 1871

MCCORD, WILLIAM (BLW), whose widow Sarah received a pension

MCCORKLE, ABNER whose widow Susan received a pension

MCCORMACK, JOHN applied for a pension

MCCORMACK, WILLIAM whose widow Polly received a pension

MCCORMICK, GEORGE and widow Grissell both received a pension

MCCORMICK/MCCORMACK, HENRY A. (P)

MCCORMICK, THOMAS (BLW), whose widow Elizabeth received a pension

MCCORMICK, THOMAS (P)

MCCOWN, JAMES (BLW), and widow Mourning both received a pension

MCCOWN, JAMES (BLW), and widow Elizabeth E. both received a pension

MCCOWN, JOHN W. (P, BLW)

MCCOY, ARTHUR (P)

MCCOY, ENOS whose widow Elizabeth J. applied for a pension

MCCOY, HENRY whose widow Ann received a pension

MCCOY, THOMAS (BLW), whose widow Dorcas French, nee Adley, applied for a pension

MCCOY, WLLLIAM whose widow Sally A. received a pension

MCCRAY, ALEXANDER whose widow Druzilla received a pension

MCCRAY, GEORGE W. whose widow Isabell applied for a pension

MCCUAN, ISAAC (P)

MCCULLOCH/MCCULLOCK, SAMUEL whose widow Martha A. McCulloch received a pension

MCCULLOCH, WILLIAM A. whose widow Mary C. received a pension

MCCULLOCK, ROBERT (BLW), died 12 Jun 1853, Cooper Co, MO; md 18 Sep 1806 Patsy Mills (P), Albemarle Co, VA. Her LNR Clarks Fork, Cooper Co, MO, 1871

MCCUSKEY, GEORGE applied for a pension

MCCUTCHAN, CHARLES C. whose widow Elizabeth received a pension

MCCUTCHAN, SAMUEL (P)

MCCUTCHEN, JOHN whose

MCCUTCHEN (continued) widow Elizabeth received a pension

MCCUTCHEN, JOSEPH whose widow Elizabeth received a pension

ROLL NO. 61

MCDADE, JOHN/JACK whose widow Rebeckah/Rebecca/Becky applied for a pension

MCDANIEL, JOHN (P)

MCDANIEL, JOHN (BLW), whose widow Polly received a pension

MCDANIEL, TIMOTHY (P)

MCDANIEL, WILLIAM applied for a pension

MCDANIEL, ZACHARIAH (P)

MCDONALD, GABRIEL applied for a pension

MCDONALD, HUGH (P, BLW), whose widow Phebe applied for a pension

MCDONALD, JOHN (BLW) applied for a pension

MCDONALD, WILLIAM (P)

MCDORMANT, JOHN whose widow Elizabeth received a pension

MCELHANY, ROBERT whose widow Miriem received a pension

MCELHANEY, SAMUEL whose widow Margaret received a pension

MCELROY, SAMUEL, USA, whose widow Juliet received a pension. Residence in WV

MCELWAIN, GEORGE whose widow Elizabeth received a pension

MCFADDEN, JOHN whose widow Sallie applied for a pension

MCGEE, THOMAS (BLW), whose widow Ruth received a pension

MCGEHEE, DELFORD whose widow Eilzabeth applied for a pension

MCGEHEE, JOHN (P)

MCGEHEE, MICAJAH whose

MCGEHEE (continued)
widow Martha A. received a pension

MCGEORGE, CORNELIUS alias GEORGE, CORNELIUS M. and widow Amanda E. McGeorge both received a pension

MCGHEE, NELSON whose widow Susan applied for a pension

MCGHEE, WILLIAM F. whose widow Mary M. received a pension

MCGLASSON/MCGLASSEN, IRA whose widow Mary applied for a pension

MCGLAUGHLIN, WILLIAM whose widow Nancy received a pension

MCGLOTHIAN/MCGLAUGH-LIN, HENRY whose widow (unnamed) received a pension

MCGOWN, DANIEL (P, BLW)

MCGRAW, MARTIN whose widow Sarah J. received a pension

MCGRUDER, SUBLETT (BLW), whose widow was Mary L.

MCGRUDER/MAGRUDER, WADE S. (P)

MCGUINN, WILLIAM whose widow Asenath received a pension

MCGUIRE, DANIEL (BLW), and widow Eliza both received a pension

MCGUIRE, ROBERT (P)

MCHENRY, LAWRENCE whose widow Magdaline applied for a pension

MCINTIRE, JOHN (BLW), whose widow was Polly

MCINTOSH, JOSEPH whose widow Sarah N. applied for a pension

MCINTOSH, THOMAS applied for a pension

MCKAY, LEWIS (P)

MCKEE, JAMES whose widow Sarah received a pension

MCKEE, SILAS applied for a pension

MCKENNEY, HIRAM whose wi-

MCKENNEY (continued)
dow Rebecca A. received a pension

MCKENNEY/MCKINNEY/MCKENNY, JOHN (P), USA. Residence in PA and VA

MCKENNIE, JAMES whose widow Louisa R. received a pension

MCKENZIE, JOHN (P)

MCKINLEY, JOHN whose widow Martha received a pension

MCKINLEY, WILLIAM (P)

MCKINLEY, BRACKSON applied for a pension

MCKINNEY, WILLIAM whose widow Polly/Mary received a pension

MCKNIGHT, HAYDEN (P)

MCKNIGHT/MCNIGHT, JAMES (BLW), and widow Caltha McKnight both received a pension

MCKNIGHT, JOHN whose widow Sarah applied for a pension

MCKNIGHT, JOHN whose widow Eliza received a pension

MCKNIGHT, THOMAS applied for a pension

MCKNIGHT, WILLIAM (BLW), whose widow Agnes received a pension

MCKNIGHT, WILLIAM (BWL), whose widow Margaret received a pension

ROLL NO. 62

MCLANE, CHARLES (P, BLW)

MCLAREN, DANIEL whose widow Susan applied for a pension

MCLAUGHLAN/MCLAUGHLIN, HENRY whose widow Mary McLaughlan received a pension

MCLAUGHLIN, WASHINGTON (P)

MCMAHON, WLLLIAM whose widow Mary applied for a pension

MCMANAWAY, ANDREW and

MCMANAWAY (continued)
widow Mary Jane both received a pension

MCMANNUS, HARTWELL whose widow Sarah received a pension

MCMASTERS, JOHN (P)

MCMILLAN, WILLIAM (P)

MCMORROW, WILLIAM whose widow Margaret received a pension

MCMULLIN, ANDREW B. whose widow May received a pension

MCNAIR, JOHN (P)

MCNEELY, GEORGE whose widow Elizabeth received a pension

MCNEMAR / MCNEMAROW, FELIX (P)

MCNEW, JOHN (P)

MCNIEL, JOHN (BLW)

MCREYNOLDS, JOHN and widow Hannah both received a pension

MCVAY, JACOB and widow Mary both received a pension

MCWHIRT, WILLIAM applied for a pension

MCWHORTER, JOHN (P, BLW), USA. Also service in VA and MD militia

MCWILLIAMS, JOHN and widow Isabella A. both received a pension

MCWILLIAMS, PEACHY H. applied for a pension, and his widow Julia received a pension

MADDEN, WILLIAM applied for a pension

MADDING, SCARLETT (P)

MADDOX, BENNETT (BWL), whose widow Elizabeth received a pension

MADDOX, WALTER whose widow Mary received a pension

MADEN/MAIDEN, WILLIAM and widow Sarah H. Maden both received a pension

MADERA, NICHOLAS B. (BLW)

MADISON, DABNEY (P)

MADISON, GEORGE and widow Elizabeth both received a

MADISON (continued)
pension

MADISON, JOHN Jr. whose widow Nancy T. applied for a pension

MADISON, THOMAS applied for a pension

MAGEE, BENJAMIN (P)

MAGEE, HENRY M. (P)

MAGEE, WYLEY/WILLEY whose widow Sally applied for a pension

MAGGARD, DAVID (BLW), whose widow was Ellenor

MAGSON, JOHN M. (P)

MAHANES, LEWIS and widow Virginia A. both received a pension

MAHONEY, WILLIAM G. (P) and widow Eliza applied for a pension

MAIDEN, JACOB and widow Julia both received a pension

MAJOR, JAMES whose widow Nancy applied for a pension

MALCOM, JOHN whose widow Sarah received a pension

MALICH, DAVID (P)

MALIN, JOSEPH applied for a pension and widow Harriet received a pension

MALLOR, ICHABOD (BLW), whose widow Mary Jane received a pension

MALLORY, JESSE H. (P)

MALLORY, JOHN F. whose widow Judith received a pension

MALLORY, JOHN H. applied for a pension and widow Nancy received a pension

MALLORY, ROGER (BLW), whose widow Elizabeth C. applied for a pension

MALLOW, GEORGE (P)

MALONE, THOMAS and widow Rebecca both received a pension

MANESS/MANIS/MANOS, JACOB (BLW) whose widow was Susannah

MANGES, JACOB and widow Mary both received a pension

MANKIN, CHARLES whose widow Elizabeth applied for a pension

MANKIN, ISAAC and widow Judith both received a pension

MANLEY, RICHARD A. alias MANLEY, ENSELM (P)

MANLEY, ROBERT whose widow Malinda received a pension

MANN, ABNER whose widow Edith received a pension

MANN, ANDREW and widow Mary W. both received a pension

MANN, CHASTAIN whose widow Nancy received a pension

MANN, JOHN whose widow Susannah applied for a pension

MANN, LEVI whose widow Mary received a pension

MANN, ROBERT whose widow Susan D. applied for a pension

MANN, WALTER H. (P)

MANN, WILLIAM H. whose widow Nancy/Frances received a pension

MANNING, CALEB whose widow Rebecca applied for a pension

MANNING, WRIGHT whose widow Catharine received a pension

ROLL NO. 63

MANSFIELD, BENJAMIN whose widow Elizabeth received a pension

MANSFIELD, WILLIAM H. (BLW), and widow Selina both received a pension

MANSPILE, THOMAS whose widow Ushey/Ursula received a pension

MANTIPLY, SAMUEL (BLW)

MANUEL, ANDERSON whose widow Malinda received a pension

MAPHIS, GEORGE applied for a pension

MAPP, SAMUEL whose widow Critty applied for a pension

MARABLE, BENJAMIN whose

MARABLE (continued) widow Fanny A. received a pension

MARABLE, CHAMP C. M. and widow Rebecca T. both received a pension

MARABLE, WILLIAM H. whose widow Elizabeth received a pension

MARCH, JOHN P. whose widow Sarah received a pension

MARCUM, JACOB and widow Rody both applied for a pension

MARCUM, JOSIAH whose widow Mary received a pension

MARICLE, JACOB (BLW), whose widow Sarah received a pension

MARK, JOHN (P, BLW)

MARK, JOSEPH whose widow Ellen K. received a pension

MARKHAM, NATHANIEL (P, BLW)

MARKHAM, OWEN (BLW), and widow Nancy both received a pension

MARKS, STEWARD/STEWART applied for a pension

MARLATT, BURGOIN applied for a pension

MARLER, WILLIAM whose widow Jane received a pension

MARLING, ELIJAH (P)

MARLOTT, ABRAHAM (P)

MARLOW, JAMES applied for a pension

MARNEY, JONATHAN whose widow Ann P. received a pension

MARPLE, ENOCH (P)

MARPLE/MARPOLE, MORGAN H. (P)

MARQUESS, JOHN applied for a pension

MARQUESS, WILLIAM K. (BLW), whose widow Polly received a pension

MARR, JOHN whose widow Catharine F. received a pension

MARRS, JAMES whose widow Sarah applied for a pension

MARSH, JAMES (P)

MARSH, MATHIAS whose widow
Amelia received a pension.
Her application was submitted
by Richard A. Marsh, com-
mittee

MARSHALL, COLEMAN (P,
BLW)

MARSHALL, DAVID and widow
Lucy B. both received a pension

MARSHALL, HENRY and widow
Julia both received a pension

MARSHALL, HENSON whose widow Massy received a pension

MARSHALL, JAMES (P-rejected) whose widow Susan re-
ceived a pension

MARSHALL, JAMES P. applied
for a pension

MARSHALL, JOHN F. whose widow Henrietta applied for a
pension

MARSHALL, JOHN W. whose
widow Mary applied for a pension

MARSHALL, SAMUEL applied
for a pension

MARSHALL, SAMUEL, USN, not
War of 1812 service, but in
war with France. He died in
1800 in hospital in Norfolk, VA

MARSHALL, WILLIAM whose
widow Harriett received a pension

MARSHALL, WILLIAM whose
widow Malinda received a pension

MARSHALL, WILLIAM whose
widow Julia received a pension

MARTIN, ABRAM/ABRAHAM
whose widow Frances received
a pension

MARTIN, ALFRED and widow
Lucinda both received a pension

MARTIN, ASA whose widow Nancy received a pension

MARTIN, BALEY/BAILEY (P)

MARTIN, CHARLES (P)

MARTIN, CHARLES (BLW),
whose widow Elizabeth re-
ceived a pension

MARTIN, CHARLES J. applied
for a pension

MARTIN, DAVID (P)

MARTIN, EDWARD whose widow
Kissey received a pension

MARTIN, FRANCIS whose widow
Polly received a pension

MARTIN, GILES whose widow
Sarah received a pension

MARTIN, HENRY whose widow
Frances W. received a pension

MARTIN, HUMPHREY H. whose
widow Mary Ann received a
pension

MARTIN, ISAAC whose widow
Susanna applied for a pension

MARTIN, JACOB whose widow
Sophia received a pension

MARTIN, JACOB and widow
Mary both received a pension

MARTIN, JAMES whose widow
Maria A. received a pension

MARTIN, JAMES G. (P)

MARTIN, JAMES W. whose widow Elizabeth received a pension

MARTIN, JESSE (P, BLW)

MARTIN, JOHN whose widow
Nancy M. received a pension

MARTIN, JOHN (P)

MARTIN, JOHN whose widow Ellen received a pension

MARTIN, JONATHAN applied for
a pension

MARTIN, JOSEPH applied for a
pension

MARTIN, LEWIS G. (P)

MARTIN, LITERAL whose widow
Lucy applied for a pension

MARTIN, MALLORY and widow
Telitha J. both received a pension

MARTIN, PLEASANT (P, BLW)

MARTIN, STEPHEN WOODSON
(P)

MARTIN, THOMAS P. whose widow Mary F. applied for a pension

MARTIN, William applied for a
pension

MARTIN, WILLIAM whose wi-
dow Rosa/Rosey received a

MARTIN (continued)
pension
MARTIN, WILLIAM and widow
Mary both received a pension
MARTIN, WILLIAM C. whose
widow Sarah applied for a pen-
sion
MARTIN, WILLIS (BLW), died
Mar 1859, Campbell Co, VA;
md 18 Feb 1810 Mary Wood
(P), Campbell Co, VA. She
died c1888, LNR P.O. Mt.
Zion, Campbell Co, VA, 1871
MARTIN, WOODY and widow
Docia both received a pension
MARTZ, JACOB and widow Eliz-
abeth both received a pension
MARYE, JOHN L. whose widow
Jane Hamilton Marye received
a pension
MASLING, WILLIAM whose wi-
dow Elizabeth received a pen-
sion
MASON, BURWELL (BLW),
whose widow Lucinda received
a pension. Samuel was a sub-
stitute for Joseph Mason in the
War.
MASON, CARTER W. whose wi-
dow Elizabeth W. received a
pension
MASON, DAVID applied for a
pension and widow Susannah
received a pension
MASON, GEORGE whose widow
Sally E. received a pension
MASON, JAMES applied for a
pension
MASON, JAMES F. applied for a
pension
MASON, JOHN whose widow
Annie received a pension
MASON, JOHN (P)
MASON, JOHN A. (P)
MASON, JOSEPH whose widow
Susan received a pension
MASON, JOSEPH whose widow
Elizabeth received a pension
MASON, MILES whose widow
Fannie received a pension
MASON, PEYTON whose widow
Sally applied for a pension

MASSEY, JAMES O. (P)
MASSEY, JUBAL applied for a
pension
MASSIE, JESSEE (P)
MASSIE, LEWIS D. whose widow
Elizabeth received a pension
MASSIE, THOMAS (BLW), whose
widow Nancy S. received a
pension
MASSIE, WILLIAM A. whose widow Sarah received a pension
MASSIE, WILLIAM W. (BLW),
and widow Frances both received a pension
MASTIN, FRANCIS T. whose
widow Ann Eliza Caroline received a pension

ROLL NO. 64

MATHENY, DANIEL and widow
Mary both received a pension
MATHENY/MATHENA/METH-
ENY, DANIEL (BLW), whose
widow was Margaret
MATHERLY, BAZZEL whose
widow Rhoda received a pen-
sion
MATHEWS, GEORGE (P)
MATHEWS, WILLIAM whose
widow Margaret Susan received
a pension
MATHEWS, WILLIAM (P)
MATTHEW/MATHEWS, JOHN
(P)
MATTHEWS, EDWARD (P)
MATTHEWS/MATHEWS,
WASHINGTON whose widow
Christian Matthews received a
pension
MAUK, FREDERICK and widow
Eva both received a pension
MAUND/MOUND, MALCOLM
(BLW), whose widow was An-
nis
MAUPIN, JOHN whose widow
Rosanna applied for a pension
MAUPIN, JOHN D. (P)
MAUPIN, MARTIN (P)
MAUPIN, THOMAS G. (P, BLW)
MAURY, HUDSON whose widow
Peggy applied for a pension

239

MAURY, RICHARD B. whose widow Ellen received a pension

MAUZY, JOSEPH whose widow Christina received a pension

MAWYER, JOHN (P)

MAXWELL, BEDWELL (BLW), whose widow was Nancy

MAXWELL, MOSES (P)

MAXWELL, THOMAS (P)

MAY, ABRAHAM (P)

MAY, ALLEN and widow Mary both received a pension

MAY, ANDREW whose widow Margaret received a pension

MAY, JACOB (P, BLW)

MAY, JOHN (P)

MAY, JOSEPH and widow Nancy C. both received a pension

MAY, THOMAS and widow Mary E. both received a pension

MAYER, ISAAC whose widow Catherine received a pension

MAYES/MAYS, STERLING and widow Mary both received a pension

MAYHEW, DRURY (P)

MAYHUGH, AMOS whose widow Deidamia received a pension

MAYHUGH, WILLIAM (BLW), but warrant was cancelled because solder died at time of issue

MAYNARD, EVEN (P)

MAYO, ELIAS L. whose widow Frances D. applied for a pension

MAYO, PHILIP whose widow Caroline E. received a pension

MAYO, THOMAS whose widow Elizabeth D. received a pension

MAYS, FLEMING B. whose widow Mary M. received a pension

MAYS, GEORGE W. alias MAYO, WASHINGTON and widow Catherine both received a pension

MAYS, JAMES whose widow Sarah applied for a pension

MAYS, JOHN (P)

MAYS, LEWIS (P)

MAYS, MORGAN (P)

MAYS, NELSON L. and widow Polly both received a pension

MAYS, THOMAS (P)

MAYS, WILLIAM (P)

MAYS, WILLIS (BLW), and widow Manerva E. both received a pension

MAYSE, JOHN (P)

MEACHAM, JAMES C. whose widow Mary O. received a pension

MEAD, EBENEZER whose widow Ann applied for a pension

MEADE, MADISON (P)

MEADE/MEAD, MAYO (BLW)

MEADOR, DANIEL (BLW), whose widow Nancy received a pension

MEADOR, WILSON (BLW), and widow Mary both received a pension

MEADOWS, GABRIEL whose widow Frances received a pension

MEADOWS, OSBORNE (P)

MEADOWS, SAMUEL whose widow Nancy received a pension

MEALEY, JAMES whose widow Eliza received a pension

MEANLY, WILLIAM R. whose widow Ann M. received a pension

MEANS, EPHRAIM and widow Huldah S. received a pension

MEARS, WILLIAM W. (BLW), whose widow Mary Ann received a pension

MEAUX, THOMAS whose widow Cornelia C. received a pension

MEDLEY, AMBROSE whose widow Malinda received a pension

MEDLEY, JAMES B. (P, BLW)

MEDLEY, JAMES T. (P)

MEDLEY, JAMES whose widow Nancy C. received a pension

MEEK, ARCHIBALD whose widow Anna applied for a pension

MEEK, ROBERT A. (BLW), whose widow Susan received a pension

MEEKINS, JAMES whose widow
Catherine applied for a pension
MEEKS, SYLVANUS (P)
MEGGINSON, WILLIAM whose
widow Amanda M. received a
pension
MELONE, JOHN applied for a
pension
MELONE, WILLIAM applied for
a pension
MELSON, CABB applied for a
pension
MELSON, THOMAS (P)
MENCER, CONRAD whose widow
Nancy applied for a pension
MENEFEE, JOHN M. (P)
MERCER, DANIEL (P)
MERCER, JOB whose widow
Sarah applied for a pension
MERCER, WILLIAM (BLW),
whose widow was Elizabeth
MEREDITH, ELISHA applied for
a pension
MEREDITH, JOSEPH B. applied
for a pension
MEREDITH, REUBEN whose wi-
dow Mary L. received a pen-
sion
MEREDITH, WILLIAM A. ap-
plied for a pension
MERRILL, REUBEN whose wi-
dow Mercy received a pension
MERRIMAN, THOMAS and wi-
dow Nancy both received a
pension
MERRITT, VALENTINE (P)

ROLL NO. 65

MESMER, JACOB whose widow
Ann Smith Mesmer applied for
a pension
METCALF/MIDCALF, JESSE
and widow Tabitha both
received a pension
METCALFE, ROBERT (P)
METHENY, JAMES (BLW), ap-
plied for a pension
METTAUER, JOHN P. and widow
Mary E. both received a pen-
sion
MEUX, THOMAS T. (BLW),

MEUX (continued)
whose widow Eliza E. received
a pension
MICHAEL, CHRISTIAN whose
widow Sarah received a pen-
sion
MICHAEL, DANIEL whose wi-
dow Catherine received a pen-
sion
MICHAEL, DAVID whose widow
Sarah applied for a pension
MICHAEL, JOHN whose widow
Elizabeth applied for a pension
MICHAEL, PETER and widow
Mary both received a pension
MICHAELS, JOHN whose widow
Mason received a pension
MICHIE, JAMES F. whose widow
Mary A. received a pension
MICHIE, MARTIN D. applied for
a pension
MICK, GEORGE whose widow
Ruth received a pension
MIDDLETON, ISAAC whose
widow Joanna/Johanna re-
ceived a pension
MIDDLETON, JACOB (BLW),
whose widow was Mary
MIDDLETON, JEREMIAH
(BLW), whose widow was
Nancy
MIDDLETON, JESSE (P)
MIDDLETON, JOHN R. (BLW)
MIDDLETON, WILLIAM (BLW)
MIDDLETON, WILLIAM (BLW),
whose widow was Elizabeth
MIERS/MEYERS, PETER and
widow Sallie Miers both re-
ceived a pension
MIEURE, THOMAS whose widow
Catherine received a pension
MILBURN/MILBOURN, DAVID
whose widow Mary Milburn
received a pension
MILEM, LEWIS (P)
MILES, ARMSTEAD J. applied
for a pension
MILES, CHARLES (BLW)
MILES, DRURY (BLW), whose
widow Rebecca received a
pension
MILES, HENRY (P, BLW), died

MILES (continued)
18 Apr 1873, Buckingham Co,
VA; md Jul 1814 Delila Taylor
(P), Buckingham Co, VA. Her
LNR Buckingham Co, VA,
1873. Delila was daughter of
James Taylor
MILES, JAMES whose widow
Nancy applied for a pension
MILES, JAMES S. (BLW), whose
widow was Hannah
MILES, SAMUEL applied for a
pension
MILES, WILLIAM M. whose wi-
dow Susan M. applied for a
pension
MILHORN, HENRY whose widow
Sarah received a pension
MILLER, ABSALOM applied for
a pension
MILLER, ABSLOM applied for a
pension. His substitute David
Moreland performed all of
Abslom's service
MILLER, ARMISTEAD whose
widow Mary/Polly received a
pension
MILLER, BRICE (P)
MILLER, CHRISTLY (P)
MILLER, DANIEL (P)
MILLER, DAVID (P)
MILLER, DAVID (P)
MILLER, DAVID and widow Ann
C. both received a pension
MILLER, FRANCIS (BLW),
whose widow was Margaret
MILLER, GEORGE whose widow
Elizabeth received a pension
MILLER, GEORGE whose widow
Hannah received a pension
MILLER, HENRY whose widow
Mary received a pension
MILLER, HENRY and widow
Rebecca both received a pen-
sion
MILLER, HENRY (P)
MILLER, HENRY whose widow
Nancy received a pension
MILLER, JACOB (P)
MILLER, JACOB whose widow
Dosha applied for a pension
MILLER, JAMES applied for a

MILLER (continued)
pension and widow Elizabeth
received a pension
MILLER, JAMES and widow
Sarah both received a pension
MILLER, JAMES and widow
Anna both received a pension
MILLER, JESSE whose widow
Polly received a pension
MILLER, JOHN (P)
MILLER, JOHN (P)
MILLER, JOHN (P) whose widow
Amanda J. applied for a pen-
sion
MILLER, JOHN whose widow
Amy received a pension
MILLER, JOHN (BLW), whose
widow Elizabeth received a
pension
MILLER, JOHN whose widow
Hannah received a pension
MILLER, JOHN and widow Ma-
linda both received a pension
MILLER, JOHN and widow Han-
nah both received a pension
MILLER, JOHN whose widow
Mary applied for a pension
MILLER, JOBN whose widow
Polly received a pension
MILLER, JOHN whose widow
Sarah received a pension
MILLER, JOHN whose widow
Sarah received a pension
MILLER, JOHN J. whose widow
Elizabeth received a pension
MILLER, JOHN W. whose widow
Elizabeth applied for a pension
MILLER, JOSEPH (P)
MILLER, MICHAEL whose wi-
dow Phoebe received a pension
MILLER, NATHANIEL M. (P),
USN and VA militia
MILLER, ROBERT R. whose
widow Jane S. received a pen-
sion
MILLER, SAMUEL (P)
MILLER, SAMUEL D. (P)
MILLER, THOMAS applied for a
pension
MILLER, THOMAS (P)
MILLER, TIMOTHY whose
widow Julia Ann received a

MILLER (continued)
pension
MILLER, WILLIAM whose widow Elizabeth applied for a pension
MILLER, WILLIAM (P)
MILLESON, JESSE (BLW), applied for a pension
MILLNER, OWEN whose widow Clarissa P. received a pension
MILLS, DANIEL M. whose widow Elizabeth T. received a pension
MILLS, JOHN whose widow Susan received a pension
MILLS, JOSEPH W. and widow Ellen Jane both received a pension
MILLS, LEVI applied for a pension
MILLS, SAMUEL whose widow Nancy received a pension
MILLS, WILLIAM W. whose widow Mary S. received a pension

ROLL NO. 66

MILSTEAD, JOHN applied for a pension
MILSTEAD, PETER whose widow Elizabeth received a pension
MILSTEAD, WILLIAM (BLW), whose widow was Sally
MINER, THOMAS E. (P)
MINNICK, JACOB whose widow Elizabeth received a pension
MINNICK, JACOB (P)
MINOR, HUBBARD T. (P)
MINOR, JAMES, USA, whose widow Lucy A. received a pension
MINOR, JOHN applied for a pension
MINOR, SMITH (P)
MINOR, SPENCER whose widow Mary Ann received a pension
MINOR, WILLIAM (BLW), whose widow Catharine received a pension
MINSON, THOMAS whose widow

MINSON (continued)
Mary E. received a pension
MINTER, CHARLES whose widow Nancy applied for a pension
MINTER/WATSON, OBEDIAH whose widow Frances W. Minter received a pension
MINTER, OTHNEAL whose widow Mary received a pension
MINTER, THOMAS whose widow Mary received a pension
MINTON, JOHN (BLW)
MINTON, MERIT (BLW)
MINTON, PETER (BLW), whose widow was Lydia
MINTON, PHILIP whose widow Polly received a pension
MINTON, RICHARD (P)
MIRACLE/MARKLE, WILLIAM and widow Lucinda Miracle both received a pension
MISENER/MIZNER, JACOB (P)
MITCHAM, HARGROVE whose widow Mary F. received a pension
MITCHELL, CHARLES and widow Mary J. both received a pension
MITCHELL, DANIEL, USA, applied for a pension. VA residence
MITCHELL, DANIEL whose widow Sarah received a pension
MITCHELL, EDWARD (P)
MITCHELL, HORACE, USA, and widow Sarah Ann both received a pension. Residence in VA.
MITCHELL, JAMES, USA and VA militia, applied for a pension
MITCHELL, JAMES applied for a pension
MITCHELL, JAMES H. (P)
MITCHELL, JOHN whose widow Nellie received a pension
MITCHELL, JOHN whose widow Elizabeth applied for a pension
MITCHELL, JOHN G. and widow Obedience both received a pension
MITCHELL, LEWIS whose wi-

MITCHELL (continued)
dow Elizabeth M. received a
pension

MICTHELL, SAMUEL whose widow Susan received a pension

MITCHELL, STEPHEN C.
(BLW)

MITCHELL, TARPLEY B.
whose widow Polly C. received
a pension

MITCHELL, THOMAS whose widow Peggy received a pension

MITCHELL, WILLIAM whose
widow Lucinda applied for a
pension

MITCHELL, WILLIAM whose
widow Elizabeth applied for a
pension

MIX, WILLIAM P. whose widow
Mary Ann received a pension

MODENA, HENRY whose widow
Lucy A. E. received a pension

MOFFATT, JAMES whose widow
Phebe applied for a pension

MOFFETT, ANDERSON whose
widow Margaret E. H. received
a pension

MOGNET, DAVID (P)

MOHLER, JOHN (P, BLW)

MOHON, CURTIS applied for a
pension

MOHON, JOHN whose widow
Elizabeth received a pension

MOLER, JACOB whose widow
Evelina received a pension

MONCURE, JOHN applied for a
pension

MONROE, ALEXANDER applied
for a pension

MONROE, ALEXANDER, Sr. applied for a pension

MONROE, JOHNSON whose wi-
dow Jane E. received a pension

MONROE, LEWIS (P)

MONROE, ROBERT applied for a
pension

MONROE, WILLIAM and widow
Hannah both applied for a pension

MONTAGUE, HENRY B. whose
widow Mary Ann received a

MONTAGUE (continued)
pension

MONTAGUE, JAMES whose wi-
dow Catharine received a pension

MONTAGUE, THOMAS and wi-
dow Sally both applied for a
pension

MONTAGUE, WILLIAM L.
whose widow Hannah F. ap-
plied for a pension

MONTGOMERY, ANDREW C.
and widow Rebecca M. both
received a pension

MONTGOMERY, JOHN whose
widow Sarah P. applied for a
pension

MONTGOMERY, JOHN applied
for a pension

MONTGOMERY, ROBERT whose
widow Sarah applied for a pension

MOODY, WILLIAM W. whose
widow Mareekle P. received a
pension

MOODY, WILSON whose widow
Eliza B. received a pension

MOOITY, JESSE (P)

MOOMAN, JACOB applied for a
pension

MOON, ARCHIBALD whose wi-
dow Nancy received a pension

MOON, JESSE whose widow Lucretia received a pension

MOON, JOHN whose widow Mary
E. received a pension

MOON, RANSOM whose widow
Lydia G. received a pension

MOON, SAMUEL H. whose widow
Sallie applied for a pension

MOONEY, EDWARD and widow
Anna both received a pension

ROLL NO. 67

MOOR/MOORE, JOHN whose
widow Catharine Moor received
a pension

MOOR, PLEASANT whose widow
Nancy received a pension

MOOR, WILLIAM S. PAGE
whose widow Hannah applied

MOOR (continued)
for a pension
MOORE, ABNER whose widow
Elizabeth F. received a pension
MOORE, ALLEN whose widow
Mary received a pension
MOORE, AMOS applied for a
pension
MOORE, ASA (P)
MOORE, AZARIAH whose widow
Letitia S. applied for a pension
MOORE, BAGWELL whose widow Marian applied for a pension
MOORE, BARNET B. whose widow Lydia M. received a pension
MOORE, BENJAMIN whose widow Elizabeth received a pension
MOORE, BENJAMIN whose widow Rebecca received a pension
MOORE, DANIEL (P)
MOORE, DAVID (P)
MOORE, DAVID (P)
MOORE, ELI (P)
MOORE, ELIJAH whose widow
Frances received a pension
MOORE, HALEY whose widow
Mary received a pension
MOORE, JAMES applied for a
pension
MOORE, JOHN whose widow
Catherine applied for a pension
MOORE, JOHN (P)
MOORE, JOHN (P)
MOORE, LEVI applied for a pension
MOORE, MATHEW whose widow
Martha applied for a pension
MOORE, MELON applied for a
pension
MOORE, MERRETT S. whose
widow Virginia R. received a
pension
MOORE, PETER applied for a
pension and widow Rebecca
received a pension
MOORE, PHILIP applied for a
pension

MOORE, RANDOLPH (BLW),
died 19 Sep 1845, Miami Co,
OH; md 12 Jun 1810 Mary
Porter (P), Barbersville, VA.
She died 23 Feb 1878, LNR
Elizabeth Township, Miami
Co, OH, 1871
MOORE, SAMUEL whose widow
Eliza Ann received a pension
MOORE, SAMUEL H. whose widow Hannah received a pension
MOORE, SAMUEL W. whose widow Nancy B. received a pension
MOORE, THOMAS (P)
MOORE/MOOR, WILLIAM
whose widow Rebecca Moore
received a pension
MOORE, WILLIAM and widow
Sophia both received a pension
MOORE, WILLIAM whose widow
Mary received a pension
MOORE, WILLIAM P. (P)
MORAN, NELSON whose widow
Sally received a pension
MORECOCK, EDWARD (BLW),
whose widow Mary E. received
a pension
MOREFIELD, HENRY whose widow Elizabeth applied for a
pension
MOREFIELD/MOOREFIELD,
JOHN R. whose widow Sally
Morefield received a pension
MOREHEAD, GEORGE (P)
MORELAND/MOULDING, EDWARD whose widow Mary
Moreland received a pension
MORELAND, NICHOLAS whose
widow Martha applied for a
pension
MOREN/MOORNEY, JOHN and
widow Mary Moren both received a pension
MORGAN, JOHN whose widow
Martha P. received a pension
MORGAN, JOHN G. (P, BLW)
MORGAN, PHILIP and widow
Mary both received a pension
MORGAN, ROBERT whose widow
Sarah received a pension
MORGAN, WILLIAM (BLW)

MORGAN, ZACKVILLE/ZACQUILLE/ ZAQUILLE (BLW), USA, whose widow was Elizabeth. Residence in VA

MORING, CASWELL and widow Emily H. both received a pension

MORING, HENRY (P)

MORING, JOHN whose widow Nancy received a pension

MORMAN/MORMAND, JAMES (BLW), whose widow was Elizabeth

MORRIS, CHARLES whose widow Emily T. received a pension

MORRIS, ELISHA whose widow Phoebe received a pension

MORRIS, FRISBY (BLW), USA and VA militia

MORRIS, JOHN (P)

MORRIS, JOHN (BLW), and widow Sarah E. both received a pension

MORRIS, LELAND and widow Mildred both received a pension

MORRIS, MAHLON (P)

MORRIS, MORGAN whose widow Eleanor (then an imbecile, with Samuel McFadden as guardian) received a pension

MORRIS, OSBORNE whose widow Polley received a pension

MORRIS, PHARIS whose widow Agness E. received a pension

MORRIS, SAMUEL (BLW)

MORRIS, SAMUEL F. whose widow Mary B. applied for a pension

MORRIS, WILLIAM whose widow Louisa received a pension

MORRIS, WILLIAM whose widow Elizabeth W. received a pension

MORRIS, ZACHARIA (P)

MORRISON, ALEXANDER (P)

MORRISON, ANDREW whose widow Mary received a pension

MORRISON, DAVID and widow Elizabeth C. both received a pension

MORRISON, JOHN whose widow Malinda received a pension

MORRISON, JOHN (P)

MORRISON, JOHN F. whose widow Roxana S. applied for a pension

MORRISON, SAMUEL and widow Eliza both received a pension

MORRISS/MORRIS, WYATT and widow Mary Seward Morriss both received a pension

ROLL NO. 68

MORTIMER, WILLIAM (P)

MORTON, DAVID whose widow Elizabeth applied for a pension

MORTON, JAMES whose widow Lucy H. applied for a pension

MORTON, JOHN whose widow Margaret applied for a pension

MORTON, THOMAS T. alias MORTON, THROCKMORTON (USA) and widow Denicie both received a pension. Thomas enlisted in VA and was later a WV resident

MOSBY, WILLIAM H. (BLW)

MOSELY, JOHN (BLW), whose widow Lucy A. received a pension

MOSELEY, RICHARD (BLW), died Oct 1858, Albemarle Co, VA; md 29 Dec 1813 Martha Bentley (P), Fluvanna Co, VA. Her LNR Charlottesville, Albemarle Co, VA, 1871

MOSELEY, RICHARD J./DICK (BLW), whose widow Mary E. received a pension

MOSELEY/MOSELY, 'ROBERT W. (BLW)

MOSELY, WILLIAM (BLW), and widow Mary both received a pension

MOSELY, CUTHBERT (BLW), whose widow Nellie received a pension

MOSELY, HARDAWAY (BLW), whose widow Harriet received a pension

MOSELY, THOMAS (BLW)

MOSELY (continued)
whose widow Jane M. received
a pension
MOSER, SOLOMON whose widow
Christena received a pension
MOSES, JONATHAN whose widow Mercy received a pension
MOSLEY, JAMES (BLW)
MOSS, FRANCIS whose widow
Mary received a pension
MOSS, GEORGE (P)
MOSS, GREEN applied for a pension
MOSS, JOHN whose widow Elizabeth received a pension
MOSS, JOSHUA (P)
MOSS, STEPHEN (P)
MOSS, WILLIAM whose widow
Susannah received a pension
MOTLEY, JOEL (P)
MOTT, RANDOLPH applied for a pension
MOTT, SYLVESTER W. whose widow Sarah received a pension
MOUNT, EZEKIEL (P, BLW)
MOUNT, STEPHEN R. (P)
MOUNTCASTLE, SONES M. whose widow Mary A. received a pension
MOUNTSTEVENSON, CHARLES applied for a pension
MOWERY, JOHN (P)
MOWLES, HENRY whose widow
Nancy A. received a pension
MOYER, JOHN whose widow
Nancy received a pension
MOYER, LEWIS whose widow
Mary received a pension
MOYERS, JOHN (P)
MOYERS, JOSEPH (P)
MOZENEY, DENNIS (BLW), and widow Rachel both received a pension
MOZINGO, BENJAMIN (P, BLW)
MOZINGO, MORGAN and widow
Nancy both received a pension
MUCKELWEE/MCILWEE, JOHN (P)
MULL, GEORGE whose widow
Mary received a pension

MULLANAX/MILLANAX, JOSEPH whose widow Mary A. Mullanax received a pension
MULLENAX, WILLIAM whose widow Anna received a pension
MULLENIX, NATHAN whose widow Catherine received a pension
MULLINS, JOEL whose widow
Silvy O. received a pension
MULLINS, JOHN (P)
MULLINS, JOSEPH applied for a pension and widow Elizabeth received a pension
MULLINS, PAUL (P)
MULLINS, WILLIAM and widow
Nancy both received a pension
MULLINS, WILLIAM WERLEY (P)
MUMAW/MOOMAUGH, DAVID (P)
MUMMEY, JOSHUA whose widow Catherine received a pension
MUMMY, SAMUEL whose widow
Anne received a pension
MUNCY/MUNSEY, JACOB whose widow Mary Muncy received a pension
MUNCY, JOHN (BLW), whose widow Susan received a pension
MUNCY, LEVI whose widow
Elizabeth received a pension
MUNDAY, BURRUSS (P)
MUNDAY, JOHN (P)
MUNDAY, MEREDITH/MERIDAY whose widow Susan H. received a pension
MUNDAY, WILSON whose widow
Nancy received a pension
MUNDEN/MEDLIN, ---- whose widow Sarah Munden applied for a pension
MUNSELL, ASA H. (P)
MURCHIE, ROBERT D. whose widow Judith A. received a pension
MURDUCK, ELIJAH whose widow Louisa received a pension
MURPH, CONRAD applied for a pension

MURPHY, BENNETT M. whose widow Lucinda received a pension

MURPHY, DANIEL C. (P)

MURPHY, JAMES applied for a pension

MURPHY, JOHN (BLW)

MURPHY, JOHN (BLW)

MURPHY, JOSEPH applied for a pension and widow Polly received a pension

MURPHY, JOSEPH whose widow Margaret applied for a pension

MURPHY, MARSHALL and widow Mary both received a pension

MURPHY, STEPHEN (P)

MURPHY, TRAVIS applied for a pension

MURPHY, WILLIAM whose widow Nancy received a pension

MURRAY, ALEXANDER (BLW) applied for a pension and widow Hepsey A. received a pension

MURRAY, ANDREW applied for a pension

MURRAY, ARCHIBALD (BLW)

MURRAY, GARLAND H. (BLW), died 3 Sep 1842, Albemarle Co, VA; md 7 May 1810 Jane/ Jinney Rea (P), Albemarle Co, VA. She died c1885, LNR Fauqier Co, VA, 1871

MURRAY, JAMES (BLW)

MURRAY, JOSHUA (P)

MURRAY, PHILIP (P)

MURRAY, REUBEN (BLW), whose widow Judith received a pension

MURRELL/MURRILL, THOMAS (P, BLW)

MURRER, JAMES (BLW), whose widow was Mary

MURREY, JOHN whose widow Susan Henderson applied for a pension

MURRILL, CHARLES (BLW), whose widow Eliza Ann received a pension

MURROW, ISAAC (BLW), whose widow Sally received a pension

MURTLE, JAMES J. whose widow Catharine received a pension

MUSE, HENRY whose widow Ann received a pension

MUSE, JOHN whose widow Susannah received a pension

MUSE, THOMAS S. whose widow Eliza M. received a pension

MUSSELMAN, JESSE (BLW), whose widow Delila received a pension

ROLL NO. 69

MYERS, AARON whose widow Catherine applied for a pension

MYERS, ADAM whose widow Ruth applied for a pension

MYERS, HENRY whose widow Christina received a pension

MYERS, JACOB (BLW), whose widow Mary received a pension

MYERS, JAMES applied for a pension

MYERS, JOHN applied for a pension

MYERS, LEONARD (P)

MYERS, LEWIS whose widow Elizabeth applied for a pension

MYERS, MICHAEL (BLW), whose widow Margaret received a pension

MYERS, MYER (P) whose widow Judith applied for a pension

MYERS, PETER (P)

MYERS, WILLIAM whose widow Mary applied for a pension

MYRICK, BENJAMIN and widow Anne Eliza both received a pension

MYRICK, WALTER whose widow Mary received a pension

NACE, GEORGE (P)

NALLE, JESSE whose widow Nancy received a pension

NALLE, LEWIS (P)

NALLEY, BENNETT (P)

NANCY, JEREMIAH (P)

NANCE, JOEL and widow Sarah both received a pension

NANCE, PEYTON S. whose wi-

NANCE (continued)
dow Elenor N. received a pension
NANNEY, DANIEL (P)
NAPIER/NAPPER, JOHN whose widow Spicey received a pension
NAPIER/NAPIER, MICAJAH/MCCAGER (BLW), and widow Rody/Rhoda Napier both received a pension
NASH, HENRY whose widow Emily received a pension
NASH, JOHN W. whose widow Mary F. received a pension
NASH, REUBEN whose widow Kesiah received a pension
NASH, WILLIAM (BLW), died Apr 1822, Richmond, VA; md Dec 1811 Catherine/Caty Hinson (P), Westmoreland Co, VA. Her LNR Richmond, VA, 1871
NASH, WILLIAM (P)
NASH, WILLIAM D. (BLW), whose widow Mary F. received a pension
NEAL, CHARLES whose widow Sarah A. received a pension
NEAL, JOEL whose widow Usley received pension
NEAL, JOHN whose widow Eliza applied for a pension
NEAL, LITTLEBERRY/LITTLE-BURY (P)
NEAL, STEPHEN Y. (P)
NEALE, CHRISTOPHER whose widow Virginia C. received a pension
NEAR, CONRAD whose widow Mary Ann received a pension
NEBLETT, STERLING whose widow Ann S. received a pension
NEECE, HENRY whose widow Mary applied for a pension
NEECE/NEACE, JOSEPH (P)
NEELEY, WILLIAM whose widow Mary applied for a pension
NEELY, JAMES applied for a pension
NEELY, JOSEPH (BLW), whose widow Jemimah received a

NEELY (continued)
pension
NEELY, WILLIAM B. (BLW), died 15 Mar 1865, Washington Co, IN; md 24 May Judith Pool (P), Washington Co, VA. Her LNR Kossuth, Washington Co, IN, 1871
NEER, JOHN (P)
NEER, NATHAN whose widow Eliza received a pension
NEFF/NAFF, JACOB (BLW), and widow Margaret Neff both received a pension
NEIGHBORS, JAMES whose widow Catharine applied for a pension
NEIGHBOURS, WILLIAM R. (P)
NEILL, STEPHEN (BLW)
NEILSON, HALL whose widow Mary Archer Neilson received a pension
NELMS, CHARLES and widow Mildred J. both received a pension
NELSON, JOHN (BLW), whose widow Frances E. received a pension
NELSON, REUBEN applied for a pension
NELSON, WILLIAM (BLW), whose widow Martha L. received a pension
NELSON, WILLIAM M. whose widow Margaret received a pension
NESMITH, HENRY (BLW), and widow Margaret both received a pension
NESMITH, JOSEPH whose widow Elizabeth applied for a pension
NESSELRODT/NAZELROD/NAZZLEROD, SAMUEL (P)
NESTER, FREDERICK (BLW), and widow Sarah Ann both received a pension
NETHERLAND, GEORGE S. (BLW), and widow Nancy both received a pension
NETHERY, DANIEL whose widow Sarah applied for a pension

NETHERY, JOHN whose widow Elizabeth received a pension

NEVIL, REUBEN J. (BLW), whose widow Frances received a pension

NEVILLE, JOSEPH (P). Service in Capt. Jeth Neville's company

NEW, JOHN C. applied for a pension

NEWBY, JAMES whose widow Sally received a pension

NEWBY, JOHN (P) whose wife was Elizabeth

NEWBY, WILLIAM whose widow Phebe received a pension

NEWCOMB, THOMAS whose widow Polly received a pension

NEWCOMB, WILLIAM L. whose widow Polly T. received a pension

NEWELL, JACOB whose widow Fanny received a pension

NEWHOUSE, JAMES A. whose widow Rebecca J. received a pension

NEWLAN/NEWLON, DAVID whose widow Rachel received a pension

NEWLAND, ABRAHAM whose widow Margaret applied for a pension

NEWLON/NEWLAND, JACOB and widow Sarah Newlon both received a pension

NEWLON, WILLIAM and widow Elizabeth both received a pension

NEWMAN, ALBERT applied for a pension

NEWMAN, ALEXANDER whose widow Rebecca J. received a pension

NEWMAN, ALEXANDER R. applied for a pension

NEWMAN, CALEB (P)

NEWMAN, JAMES whose widow Mary A. applied for a pension

NEWMAN, JOHN whose widow Celia applied for a pension

NEWMAN, JOHN whose widow Martha received a pension

NEWMAN, REUBEN and widow Nancy both received a pension

NEWMAN, WALTER whose widow Eleanor S. applied for a pension

NEWTON, GEORGE (BLW), and widow Sarah Ann both received a pension

NEWTON, JOHN whose widow Sophia received a pension

NEWTON, RANDOLPH (P, BLW)

ROLL NO. 70

NIBLETT/NEBLETT, JOHN L. (P)

NICHOLLS, EDWARD (BLW), and widow Sacarisa both received a pension

NICHOLS, DUDLEY (P)

NICHOLS, ISAAC (P)

NICHOLS, JACOB (BLW), whose widow Rebecca received a pension. Residence in WV

NICHOLS, JAMES whose widow Magdalen applied for a pension

NICHOLS, THOMAS (P)

NICKLIN, JACOB whose widow Mary received a pension

NICODEMUS, JOHN (BLW), whose widow Margaret received a pension

NIMMO, JAMES R. (BLW), died 31 Dec 1841, Norfolk, VA; md 20 Dec 1810 Eliza T. McCandish (P), Williamsburg, James City Co, VA. Her LNR Norfolk, VA, 1871

NISEWANGER, ABRAHAM whose widow Lucinda applied for a pension

NIXON, GEORGE whose widow Mary A. received a pension

NIXON, JOHN whose widow Jane received a pension

NIXSON/NICKSON, DRURY (BLW), whose widow Mary P. received a pension

NOAKES, REDMAN whose widow Sarah received a pension

NOEL, ACHILLES applied for a pension

NOEL, RICHARD (P)

NOEL, STEPHEN whose widow Judith received a pension

NOEL, WILLIAM T. whose widow Hetta received a pension

NOELL, CALEB SR. (P)

NOLAN, CHARLES whose widow Lucy A. applied for a pension

NOLIN/NOWLAND/NOLAND, THOMAS whose widow Susannah D. Nolin received a pension

NOOE, ZEPHANIAH (BLW). Of Culpeper or Loudoun Co, VA

NORDYKE, ABRAM (P)

NORFLEET, JOHN (P)

NORFORD, ISAAC (P)

NORMAN, DANIEL whose widow Elizabeth applied for a pension

NORMAN, THOMAS whose widow Mildred F. received a pension

NORRIS, CALEB whose widow Allie received a pension

NORRIS, RICHARD (P)

NORRIS, SAMUEL (P)

NORRIS, WILLIAM whose widow Susannah received a pension

NORTH, JOHN R. and widow Mary Ann B. both received a pension

NORTHCRAFT, HEZEKIAH applied for a pension

NORTHCRAFT, WILLIAM F. whose widow Ann Hill Northcraft received a pension

NORTHCUTT, WOODSON whose widow Mary received a pension

NORTHINGTON, JOHN W. S. whose widow Mary H. received a pension

NORTON, JACOB (P)

NORTON, LEMUEL (P)

NORVELL, BENJAMIN (BLW)

NORVELL, JAMES applied for a pension

NORVELL, SENECA (P, BLW)

NORVELL, THOMAS W. whose widow Elizabeth M. received a pension

NORVELL, WILLIAM W. whose widow Ann M. applied for a pension

NOTTINGHAM, JOSEPH R. whose widow Elizabeth B. applied for a pension

NOTTINGHAM, SMITH whose widow Esther S. B. received a pension

NOWELL/NOEL, JOHN whose widow Martha Nowell applied for a pension

NOWLIN, THOMAS W. applied for a pension and widow Ann T. received a pension

NOWLING, JOSEPH (P) whose widow Mary applied for a pension

NUCKOLS, JOSEPH whose widow Phebe applied for a pension

NUGENT, EDMUND/EDMOND R./EDWARD (BLW), and widow Amanda both received a pension

NUNN, HENRY S. (P, BLW)

NUNN, JOHN whose widow Deborah applied for a pension

NUNNALLY, EDWARD whose widow Nancy H. received a pension

NUNNALLY, JAMES applied for a pension

NUNNALLY, WILLIAM B. whose widow Mary H. received a pension

NUNNERY, CHRISTOPHER whose widow Polly received a pension

NUZUM, RICHARD (BLW), and widow Esther both received a pension

ROLL NO. 71

OAKES, THOMAS K. whose widow Malinda received a pension

OAKES/OAKS, WILLIAM whose widow Sallie/Sally received a pension

OAKLEY, JOHN (P)

OAKLEY, JOHN (P)

OAKS/OKES, JESSE (P-rejected) whose widow Mary received a pension

OAKS, THOMAS (P)
OBENSHAIN, JOHN (BLW)
OBENSHAIN, PETER (P, BLW)
O'BRIANT, HALCOLM alias O'BRYAN, HARREL (P, BLW)
O'BRIEN/O'BRYON, JOHN applied for a pension
O'CONNER, BRITTEN whose widow Susanah applied for a pension
O'CONNER, JOHN (BLW), whose widow Elizabeth received a pension
ODELL, ELIJAH (BLW), whose widow Delilah received a pension
ODEWALT, JOBN H. applied for a pension
O'DONOVAN/DONAVAN, JAMES HAYES (BLW), whose widow Mary received a pension
ODWALT, JOHN H. applied for a pension
O'FERRALL, IGNATIUS alias OFERREL, NATHAN (P)
OGBURN, STERLING and widow Nancy M. both received a pension
OGDEN, ANDREW whose widow Elizabeth received a pension
OGDEN, CORNELIUS whose widow Matilda received a pension
OGDEN, JAMES whose widow Sarah received a pension
OGDON/OGDEN, JAMES (P, BLW)
OGILBY, PETER F. (BLW). Residence in Gallatin Co, IL, in 1855
OGILVIE, JOHN (BLW), whose widow Elizabeth A. received a pension
OGLE, THOMAS whose widow Sarah applied for a pension
OLD, KADER P. whose widow Fannie C. received a pension
OLDHAM, JOHN whose widow Polly received a pension
OLDNER, MALACHI whose widow Elizabeth applied for a pension

OLEAR/OHLEAR, WILLIAM C. whose widow Nancy received a pension
OLINGER, PHILIP whose widow Elizabeth received a pension
OLIVER, CHARLES whose widow Mary received a pension
OLIVER, CHARLES whose widow Nancy G. received a pension
OLIVER, JAMES (P)
OLIVER, JOHN applied for a pension
OLIVER, JOSEPH (P)
OLIVER, WILLIAM (BLW), and widow Martha A. both received a pension
OLLER, GEORGE (P)
OMOHUNDRO, ELLIS P. whose widow Mary D. applied for a pension
ORNDORFF, JOHN (P)
ORNDORFF, PHILIP (BLW), and widow Christena both received a pension
ORR, FINDLEY applied for a pension
ORR, JAMES whose widow Ann E. applied for a pension
ORR, JOSEPH whose widow Nancy W. received a pension
ORR, THOMAS (P)
ORR/ORE, WILLIAM (BLW). Enlisted at Leesburg, VA
ORR, WILLIAM whose widow Sarah received a pension
ORRISON, MATHEW (BLW), whose widow Elizabeth Ann received a pension
OSBORN, SAMUEL whose widow Rebecca received a pension
OSBORNE, THOMAS whose widow Martha received a pension
OSBURN/OSBORN, ENOS (BLW), whose widow Sarah received a pension
OSBURN, LEONARD whose widow Elizabeth applied for a pension
OSLIN, JOHN A. whose widow Frances received a pension
OSTER, GEORGE (BLW)
OTEY, THOMAS whose widow

OTEY (continued)
Rebecca received a pension
OTT, FIDILLAS/PHIDILLAS and widow Mary both received a pension
OURS/OUERS/OWERS, HENRY applied for a pension
OURS, JOHN (P)
OUTTEN, SHADRACK W. (BLW), whose widow Nancy received a pension
OVERBEY, JOHN (P)
OVERBEY/OVERBY, OBEDIAH (BLW), and widow Harriet Overbey both received a pension
OVERBY, ANDERSON (P, BLW)
OVERBY/OVERBEY, WILLIAM (P, BLW)
OVERFIELD, PETER (BLW), whose widow Deborah received a pension
OVERHOTS/OVERHOLTS, JOHN (BLW), whose widow Barabara received a pension
OVERHOLTZER/OVERHOLTS, CHRISTIAN (BLW), whose widow Rebecca Overholter received a pension
OVERSHINER, GIDEON (BLW), whose widow Barbara received a pension
OVERTON, BENJAMIN (P, BLW)
OWEN, ARMISTEAD (BLW), and widow Elizabeth both received a pension
OWEN, DAVID (P, BLW)
OWEN, DAVID (BLW), whose widow Elizabeth received a pension
OWEN, EDMUND (BLW) whose widow Nancy L. received a pension
OWEN, HENRY (BLW) whose widow Frances received a pension
OWEN, JOHN (P, BLW)
OWEN/OWENS, JOHN (P, BLW) ·
OWEN, JOHN (BLW), whose widow Sarah E. R. received a pension
OWEN, JOHN (BLW), whose

OWEN (continued)
widow Sallie received a pension
OWEN, NATHAN (BLW), and widow Elizabeth both received a pension
OWEN, ROBERSON (BLW), whose widow Maria B. received a pension
OWEN, THOMAS (BLW), and widow Eilzabeth both received a pension
OWEN, WILLIAM B. (BLW), and widow Rebecca both received a pension
OWENS, JESSE (BLW), whose widow Mary received a pension
OWENS, JOHN TURNER (BLW), whose widow Susan received a pension
OWENS, OWEN (P, BLW)
OWENS, THOMAS (BLW), whose widow Judith applied for a pension
OWENS, ZACHARIAH (P, BLW)
OXLEY, AARON (P, BLW)
OXLEY/OXLY, THOMAS (BLW), applied for a pension

ROLL NO. 72

PACE, THOMAS (BLW), whose widow Parthenia received a pension
PACE, WILLIAM (P, BLW)
PECK, JAMES (BLW), whose widow Martha received a pension
PACKER, JOSHUA applied for a pension
PADGETT, DEMPSEY (BLW), whose widow Sarah received a pension
PADGETT, HENRY G. (BLW), whose widow Mary W. received a pension
PADGIT, JAMES A. (BLW), whose widow Margaret received a pension
PAGE, BARNET O. (BLW), whose widow Mary W. received a pension
PAGE, BENJAMIN (P, BLW)

253

PAGE, JOHN (BLW)
PAGE, JOHN C. (BLW), whose widow Sarah E. received a pension
PAGE, JOSIAH (P, BLW)
PAGET, LEWIS B. whose widow was Eliza. Lewis was a sailing master and was in the service in 1826. Old Navy widow file
PAGE, SAMUEL (BLW), whose widow Hannah received a pension
PAGE, SAMUEL (BLW), whose widow Christina received a pension
PAGE, WILLIAM B. (BLW), whose widow Lucy A. received a pension
PAINE, WESLEY (BLW), whose widow Mary received a pension
PAINTER, ADAM whose widow Elizabeth received a pension
PAINTER, JAMES whose widow Nancy received a pension
PALMER, EDWIN N. (P, BLW)
PALMER, ELIAS (P)
PALMER, ELIJAH (BLW), whose widow (unnamed) received a pension
PALMER, HENRY C. (BLW), and widow Mary M. both received a pension
PALMER/PARMER, JOHN applied for a pension
PALMER, JOHN (BLW), whose widow Polly received a pension
PALMER, REUBEN D. (BLW), whose widow Sarah E. received a pension
PALMER, SAMUEL (BLW), applied for a pension
PALMER, THOMAS L. (P, BLW)
PALMER/HARBETT, WILLIAM (BLW), KY and VA militia, whose widow Margaret Palmer received a pension
PALMER/PERMAR, WILLIAM whose widow Elizabeth Palmer applied for a pension. Ekney Moran was guardian of widow

PALMER, WILLIAM whose widow Hannah received a pension
PALMORE/PALMER, CHARLES (P)
PANGLE, JACOB whose widow Ann received a pension
PANGLE, VANCE (BLW), died 15 Sep 1835, Putnam Co, OH; md 14 Aug 1799 Rebecca Longacre (P), Frederick Co, VA. She died c1880, LNR near Delphos, Allen Co, OH, 1871
PANKEY, SAMUEL (P)
PARDUE/PERDUE, JESSE (P, BLW)
PARE, JOHN (BLW), whose widow Elizabeth received a pension
PARHAM, WILLIAM and widow Mary F. both received a pension
PARISH, ARMISTEAD E. applied for a pension
PARISH, WILLIAM (BLW), whose widow Sarah received a pension
PARK, ABRAHAM (P, BLW)
PARK, JACOB (BLW), whose widow Nancy Ann received a pension
PARKER, ARCHIBALD (P, BLW), and widow Louisa B. both received a pension
PARKER, CLAWSON (BLW), whose widow Rebecca received a pension
PARKER, ELIJAH (BLW), whose widow Permelia received a pension
PARKER, ELISHA whose widow Christian applied for a pension
PARKER, FARLING/FARLAND B. (BLW), whose widow Clarissa received a pension
PARKER, GEORGE S. (BLW), whose widow Hardenia L. received a pension
PARKER, HENRY E. whose widow Tamasa applied for a pension
PARKER, JABEZ (BLW), whose widow Eliza received a

PARKER (continued)
pension
PARKER, JACOB G. whose widow Annie G. applied for a pension
PARKER, JOHN whose widow Ann E. applied for a pension
PARKER, JOHN (BLW), whose widow Mary received a pension
PARKER, JOHN E. (P, BLW)
PARKER, NATHANIEL (BLW), whose widow Elizabeth received a pension
PARKER, ROBERT L./S. (BLW), whose widow Susannah received a pension
PARKER, THOMAS (BLW), whose widow Harriett applied for a pension
PARKER, WARREN (BLW), and widow Careen F. H. both received a pension
PARKER, WILLIAM (BLW), applied for a pension
PARKERSON/PARKINSON, JOSEPH (BLW)
PARMER/PALMER, JOHN (P, BLW)
PARR, RICHARD (BLW), whose widow Almeda received a pension
PARRISH, BENJAMIN (BLW), whose widow Mary A. received a pension
PARRISH, COLLIN whose widow Elizabeth applied for a pension
PARRISH, JOHN B. whose widow Elizabeth S. received a pension
PARRISH, JOHN W. (BLW), and widow Jane H. both received a pension
PARRISH/PARISH, JOSHUA (P, BLW)
PARRISH, URIAH (BLW), whose widow Elizabeth A. received a pension
PARRISH, VALENTINE (P, BLW)
PARRISH, WILLIAM (BLW), and widow Louisa both received a pension

PARSELL, JOHN (BLW), whose widow Drewsillar received a pension
PARSONS, BENNETT G. (BLW), whose widow Mary received a pension
PARSONS, DAVID (P, BLW)
PARSONS, ELIJAH (BLW), whose widow Sarah M. received a pension
PARSONS, FREDERICK whose widow Sarah applied for a pension
PARSONS, HARTWELL (P, BLW)
PARSONS, ISAAC (BLW)
PARSONS, JOB (BLW), and widow Sarah both received a pension
PARSONS, JOHN (P, BLW)
PARSONS, JOHN F. applied for a pension
PARSONS, SOLOMON (P), son of James
PARSONS, SOLOMON whose widow Mary received a pension
PARSONS, THOMAS whose widow Frances received a pension
PARSONS, WILLIAM (BLW)

ROLL NO. 73

PATE, EDMUND, USA, whose widow Sally applied for a pension. Residence in VA
PATE, WILLIAM THOMAS (BLW), and widow Eliza A. both received a pension
PATES/PATE, AUGUSTUS (BLW), whose widow Elizabeth received a pension
PATESEL, JOHN (P)
PATRAM, DANIEL whose widow Lucy received a pension
PATRAM, FRANCIS whose widow Elizabeth received a pension
PATRAM, GEORGE whose widow Barbara applied for a pension
PATRICK, ROBERT (BLW), and widow Mary both received a pension

PATTEN, WILLIAM (P)

PATTERSON, AARON (BLW), whose widow Lucinda received a pension

PATTERSON, ANDREW (BLW), whose widow Elizabeth received a pension

PATTERSON, CHAMBERS (BLW), and widow Cynthia both received a pension

PATTERSON, CHARLES C. (BLW), whose widow Jane received a pension

PATTERSON, JOHN (P)

PATTERSON, JOHN W. whose widow Lally O. applied for a pension

PATTERSON, ROBERT whose widow Nancy applied for a pension

PATTERSON, THOMAS (P)

PATTERSON, WILLIAM whose widow Elizabeth applied for a pension

PATTON, ELLIOTT and widow Maria both received a pension

PATTON, JAMES whose widow Ann received a pension

PATTON, JOHN whose widow Elizabeth S. received a pension

PATTON, ROBERT (BLW), whose widow Phebe S. received a pension

PATTON, THOMAS and widow Sally both received a pension

PATTON, WILLIAM (P)

PAUGH, JAMES applied for a pension

PAUL, WILLIAM (BLW), whose widow Jane received a pension

PAUL, NIMROD (P)

PAULETT, RICHARD (BLW), whose widow Sarah received a pension

PAULEY/PAWLEY, JOHN (BLW), whose widow Margaret received a pension

PAXTON, DAVID C. (BLW), whose widow Lucy S. received a pension

PAYNE, BENJAMIN C. (BLW),

PAYNE (continued) and widow Nancy both received a pension

PAYNE, ISHAM (BLW), whose widow Patsey received a pension

PAYNE, DANIEL (BLW), whose widow was Nancy

PAYNE, DANIEL (BLW), whose widow was Susan

PAYNE, FRANCIS whose widow Margaret E. applied for a pension

PAYNE, JOHN W. (BLW), whose widow Nancy received a pension

PAYNE, JOHN (P)

PAYNE, JOHN (BLW), whose widow was Cesy

PAYNE, JOHN (BLW), whose widow was Rosa

PAYNE, JOHN W. (BLW), whose widow was Mary C.

PAYNE, LED G. (P, BLW)

PAYNE, MATTHEW whose widow Jane applied for a pension

PAYNE, RICHARD (BLW), whose widow Nancy received a pension

PAYNE, ROBERT A. (BLW), whose widow Polly received a pension

PAYNE, ROBERT B. and widow Frances G. both received a pension

PAYNE, THOMAS (P, BLW)

PAYNE, THOMAS (BLW), and widow Ann both received a pension

PAYNE, THOMAS (BLW), applied for a pension and widow Catharine M. received a pension

PAYNE, THOMAS G. (BLW), and widow Susan A. both received a pension

PAYNE, TRAVIS and widow Eliza J. both applied for a pension

PAYNE, WALTER (P)

PAYNE, WILLIAM A. (P, BLW)

PAYNE, WILLIAM O. (BLW), whose widow Martha A. re-

PAYNE (continued)
ceived a pension

PAYNTER/PAINTER, JOHN (BLW), whose widow Catherine received a pension

PAYTON, BENJAMIN (P)

PEACEMAKER, JACOB (P, BLW)

PEACHER, EDMUND whose widow Lucy A. applied for a pension

PEAD/PEEDE, JAMES whose widow Cena received a pension

PEAK, BOOKER whose widow Obediance received a pension

PEAL, JOSEPH whose widow Martha received a pension

PEALE, JONATHAN whose widow Margaret M. applied for a pension

PEARCE, SAMUEL (BLW), died 1855-1861, Floyd Co, VA; md Feb 1801 Mary Page (P), nr Christiansburg, Montgomery Co, VA. She died 12 Feb 1877, LNR Christiansburg, VA, 1871

PEARCE/PIERCE, WILLIAM (P)

PEARCY, CHARLES (BLW), and widow Joanna both received a pension

PEARCY/PEARSEY, JOHN Jr. (P)

PEARMAN, JESSE (P)

PEARMAN, PLEASANT (BLW), and widow Sarah both received a pension

PEARRILL/PERRILL/PARRELL /POUND, JOSEPH (BLW), whose widow Isabella Pearrill received a pension

PEARSON, BENJAMIN W. (P, BLW)

PEARSON, CUMBERLAND (BLW)

PEARSON, GEORGE applied for a pension

PEARSON, JOHN M. whose widow Ann received a pension

PEARSON, MASTIN whose widow Rachel received a pension

PEARSON, PASCHAL (P, BLW)

PEARSON, WILLIAM B. (P, BLW)

PEARSON, WILLIAM M. whose widow Catharine received a pension

PEATROSS, JAMES W. (BLW), whose widow Eliza Ann received a pension

PEATT, JAMES (P)

PECK, JACOB C. (BLW)

PECK, JACOB F. (P, BLW)

PECK, JOSIAH and widow Sarah both received a pension

PEDDICORD/PETTICORD, PERRY (P)

PEDIGO, JOHN (BLW), and widow Amy T. both received a pension

PEEBLES, JOHN (BLW), whose widow Mary received a pension

PEEBLES, JOHN (BLW), whose widow Mary W. received a pension

PEEK, SAMUEL whose widow Mary applied for a pension

PEEL/PEAL, RICHARD (P)

PEELER/BEELER, JOHN (P)

PEER, DAVID (P)

PEER, JACOB (P)

PEERMAN, JOHN (P)

PEERS, ALEXANDER (P, BLW)

PEERS, THOMAS R. (P)

PEERY/PERRY, DAVID and widow Jane both received a pension

PEERY, THOMAS whose widow Jane received a pension

PEETE, SAMUEL (P)

PEGG, RANSDELL (P)

PEGRAM, EDWARD (P)

PEGRAM, HENRY D. whose widow Ciscelia F. received a pension

PELL, RICHARD whose widow Rebecca received a pension

PELL, THOMPSON (P, BLW)

PEMBERTON, JOHN (BLW), whose widow Margaret W. received a pension

PENCE, ISAAC (BLW), whose widow Patsey received a pension

PENCE, JACOB (BLW), and widow Harriet both received a pension
PENCE, JACOB (P)
PENDLETON, EDMUND A. (BLW), and widow Mildred both received a pension
PENDLETON, HENRY applied for a pension
PENDLETON, JOHN whose widow Mary received a pension
PENDLETON, MICAJAH (P)
PENDLETON, PRIOR whose widow Louisa received a pension
PENINGER, WILLIAM whose widow Martha applied for a pension
PENN, MOSES (P)
PENN, ROBERT C. whose widow Lucinda applied for a pension
PENNINGTON, WILLIAM applied for a pension
PENTECOST, WILLIAM (BLW), whose widow Obedience received a pension

ROLL NO. 74

PEPPER, JACOB (BLW), whose widow Martha received a pension
PERDUE, DANIEL whose widow Harriet received a pension
PERDUE, ZACHARIAH applied for a pension
PERKINS, BENJAMIN whose widow Eliza A. received a pension
PERKINS, EDWARD (P)
PERKINS, ELIJAH and widow Frances both received a pension
PERKINS, JOHN H. whose widow Lucy applied for a pension
PERKINS, JONATHAN whose widow Martha Newell applied for a pension
PERKINS, PETER (BLW), whose widow Nancy received a pension
PERKINS, ROBERT (BLW), and widow Elizabeth C. both re-

PERKINS (continued) ceived a pension
PERKINS, THOMAS whose widow Margaret applied for a pension
PERKINS, WHITNEY whose widow Rosie M. received a pension
PERKS, JOSEPH P. whose widow Mary Ann received a pension
PERKS, STARK applied for a pension
PERRILL, JOSEPH whose widow Isabella applied for a pension
PERRILL, NATHAN whose widow Christina received a pension
PERRIN/PERRYM, CHARLES whose widow Cyrene received a pension
PERRIN/PERIAN, JOHN (BLW), and widow Elizabeth A. both received a pension
PERROW, JOHN F. (P)
PERRY, BENJAMIN H. (BLW), whose widow Catharine applied for a pension
PERRY, JOSEPH (BLW), and widow Nancy A. both received a pension
PERRY, JOSHUA (BLW), and widow Mariah both received a pension
PERRY, NICHOLAS (BLW), and widow Elizabeth both received a pension
PERRY, THOMAS (BLW), and widow Elizabeth both received a pension
PERSINGER, ALEXANDER (P)
PERSINGER, GEORGE whose widow Elizabeth received a pension
PERSINGER, WILLIAM whose widow Barbary received a pension
PETERS, HENRY (BLW), whose widow Susan received a pension
PETERS, JOHN (BLW), and widow Catharine both received a pension
PETERS, JORDAN N. (BLW),

PETERS (continued)
and widow Rachel both received a pension
PETERS, WARNER (P, BLW)
PETERS, WILLIAM applied for a pension
PETERSON, JOHN applied for a pension
PETERSON, WILLIAM applied for a pension
PETICREW/PETTICREW, WILLIAM (P)
PETTET/PETTIT, SAMUEL whose widow Fanny S. received a pension
PETTETT, WILLIAM (BLW), whose widow Elizabeth received a pension
PETTIT, HUGH (BLW), and widow Elizabeth A. both received a pension
PETTUS, HENRY (P)
PETTY, HUGH whose widow Lucy applied for a pension
PETTY, JAMES (BLW), whose widow Lucinda received a pension
PETTY, TRAVIS whose widow Mary Ann received a pension
PEUE, ANDREW whose widow Sarah applied for a pension
PEW, JOHN applied for a pension
PEYTON, ISAAC whose former widow Sarah Johnson applied for a pension
PEYTON, ISAAC (BLW), whose widow Helen received a pension
PEYTON, JAMES whose widow Eliza applied for a pension
PEYTON, JEREMIAH (BLW), and widow Elizabeth both received a pension
PEYTON, THOMAS whose widow Sarah applied for a pension
PHELPS, ISHAM whose widow Elizabeth received a pension
PHELPS, JOHN P. (P)
PHELPS, JOHN W. whose widow Dixy received a pension
PHELPS, WILLIAM C. whose widow Eliza A. F. received a

PHELPS (continued)
pension
PHIELDING, WILLIAM D. applied for a pension
PHILLIPPE, GEORGE (P)
PHILLIPS, EMANUEL E. whose widow Elizabeth applied for a pension
PHILLIPS, GEORGE whose widow Sarah received a pension
PHILLIPS, JAMES applied for a pension
PHILLIPS, JAMES applied for a pension
PHILLIPS/PHILIPS, JAMES Sr. (P)
PHILLIPS, JOHN G. (P)
PHILLIPS, JONATHAN whose widow Susan received a pension
PHILLIPS, RANDOLPH B. applied for a pension
PHILLIPS, RICHARD (P)
PHILLIPS, S. F. G. (P)
PHILLIPS, WESLEY and widow Frances both received a pension
PHILLIPS, WILLIAM (P)
PHILLIPS, WILLIAM (P)
PHILLIPS, WILLIAM (BLW), and widow Polly both received a pension
PHILLIPS, WILLIAM and widow Nancy B. both received a pension
PHILPOTT/PHILPOT, ADDISON (P)
PHILPOTTS, JOHN whose widow Mary A. S. received a pension
PHIPPS/PHIPS, ISAAC whose widow Mary (Catherine?) applied for a pension
PICKEL, SOLOMON whose widow Margaret applied for a pension
PICKEL/PICKLE, THOMAS applied for a pension
PICKERELL/PICKEREL, BURGSDELL (P)
PICKERING, WILLIAM (P)
PICKETT, CHARLES whose widow Jane received a pension

PICKLE/PICKEL, JACOB (P, BLW)

PIERCE, JOHN (P)

PIERCE/PEIRCE, JOHN (P)

PIERCE, JOHN whose widow Frances W. received a pension

PIERCE, JOHN (BLW), whose widow Sarah received a pension

PIERCE, RICE B. (P, BLW)

PIERCE, WILLIAM (P, BLW)

PIERCY, NATHANIEL (BLW), whose widow Elizabeth received a pension

PIERCY, WILLIAM (P)

PIERMAN, JAMES (BLW), and widow Polly both received a pension

PIERPOINT, FRANCIS whose widow Isabel received a pension

PIERSON/PINSON, GILBERT (P, BLW)

PIFER, ADAM (P, BLW)

PIGOTT, EDWARD (P, BLW)

PIKE, WILLIAM whose widow Martha received a pension

PILCHER, GEORGE P. whose widow Lucy E. received a pension

PILCHER, WINSLOW whose widow Averilla received a pension

PILLON, JOSEPH B. whose widow Martha applied for a pension

PILLOW, JOSEPH (P, BLW) died 8 May 1872, LNR Henry Co, TN, 1871; md 28 Jan 1820-22 Mary Webb (applied for pension), Campbell Co, VA. Her LNR Parris, TN, 1872

PINNELL, EDWARD and widow Martha A. both received a pension

PIPPIN, RICHARD and widow Elizabeth both received a pension

PITCHFORD, LABAN whose wi-

PITCHFORD (continued) dow Mary received a pension

PITMAN, DANIEL whose widow Catharine applied for a pension

PITMAN, PHILIP (P)

PITT, HENRY whose widow Nancy received a pension

PITTS, ELISHA whose widow Elizabeth applied for a pension

PITTS, PITMAN whose widow Mary C. received a pension

PITTS, ROBERT whose widow Nancy B. received a pension

PITTS, THOMAS H. (BLW). In Capt. Thomas D. Pitts company

PITZER, JACOB whose widow Nancy received a pension

PLATT, JONAS D. (BLW), died 9 Feb 1851, Alexandria, VA; md 4 May 1812 Rhoda Hyde (P), Clinton, Duchess Co, NY. Her LNR Lockport, NY, 1871

PLEASANTS, ABNER whose widow Eliza J. received a pension

PLEASANTS, RICHARD S. whose widow Zipporah applied for a pension

PLEASANTS, ROBERT whose widow Kesiah received a pension

PLEASANTS, THOMAS W. whose widow Nancy received a pension

PLOTNER, DANIEL (BLW), died 20 Jan 1860, Hocking Co, OH; md 12 May 1807 Sarah Crowl (P), Berkeley Co, VA. She died c1877, LNR Perry Township, Hocking Co, OH, 1871

PLOTT, ABRAHAM whose widow Mary/Polly received a pension

PLUM, GEORGE whose widow (unnamed) received a pension

POAGE, JOHN (BLW)

POAGUE/POAGE, ANDREW whose widow Polly E. A. received a pension

POE, HASTEN (P)

POE, JOHN (P)

POE, JOHN G. applied for a pension

POINDEXTER, EDWIN W. and widow Frances A. both received a pension

POINDEXTER, JOHN B. (P)

POINDEXTER, LEWIS/LOUIS and widow Mary L. both received a pension

POINDEXTER, RICHARD whose widow Lucy T. received a pension

POLING, JOHN whose widow Mary received a pension

POLING, MARTIN D. whose widow Mary received a pension

POLING, SAMUEL (P)

POLLARD, GEORGE J. (BLW), whose widow Philadelphia received a pension

POLLARD, JESSE (P)

POLLARD, JOHN (BLW), and widow Elizabeth M. both received a pension

POLLARD, JOHN H. (BLW), whose widow Mary A. B. received a pension

POLLARD, WOODSON (P, BLW)

POLLOCK, MAYOR whose widow Cecily received a pension

POLLOCK, WILLIAM T. A. (BLW), died Feb 1841-44, Harpers Ferry, VA; md 29 Sep 1813 Elizabeth Keffer (P), Frederick, Frederick Co, MD. Her LNR Rising Sun, Ohio Co, IN, 1871

POMEROY, ALEXANDER whose widow Elizabeth received a pension

POMEROY, SPENCER and widow Elizabeth both received a pension

POMEROY, WILLIAM (BLW), died c1830; md Mary Scott (P), Fairfax Co, VA. Her LNR Morgantown, Monongalia Co, WV, 1871

POOL, DAVID whose widow Patty received a pension

POOL, GEORGE (P, BLW)

POOL, PETER whose widow

POOL (continued) Elizabeth P. received a pension

POOL/PETTYPOOL, THOMAS whose widow Lavinia received a pension

POOL, WILLIAM and widow Alice both received a pension

POPKINS, THOMAS (P)

PORCH, JAMES applied for a pension

PORTER, JAMES (BLW)

PORTER, JOHN whose widow Hannah K. received a pension

PORTER, JOHN (BLW)

PORTER, JOHN C. whose widow Helena A. received a pension

PORTER, MORRIS whose widow Maria E. applied for a pension

PORTER, SAMUEL Jr. (BLW), and widow Anna both received a pension

PORTER, SAMUEL SR (P, BLW)

PORTER, SAMUEL whose widow Elizabeth received a pension

PORTERFIELD, ALEXANDER (P, BLW)

PORTERFIELD, JOHN S. whose widow Julia A. received a pension

ROLL NO. 76

POSEY, ASHFORD/ASHELL (P)

POSEY, WILLIAM applied for a pension

POSTLETHWAIT, RICHARD whose widow Lydia applied for a pension

POTTER, LEWIS whose widow Cassander applied for a pension

POTTS, DAVID (BLW), applied for a pension

POULTON, REED (P)

POWELL, EDWARD (BLW), whose widow Mary received a pension

POWELL, GEORGE and widow Sarah A. both received a pension

POWELL, HARTWELL F./T. (P)

POWELL, JOHN applied for a pension

POWELL, JOHN whose widow Margaret M. received a pension

·POWELL, JOHN whose widow Dorcas Ann received a pension

POWELL, JOSIAH (BLW), whose widow Catharine received a pension

POWELL, MOSES whose widow Charity Ann received a pension

POWELL, ROBERT whose widow Ann received a pension

POWELL, SAMUEL (BLW), and widow Elizabeth both received a pension

POWELL, THOMAS C. whose widow Elizabeth received a pension

POWELL, WILLIAM (BLW), and widow Matilda both received a pension

POWELL, WILLIAM whose widow Rachel applied for a pension

POWELL, WILLIAM whose widow Catharine applied for a pension

POWELL, WILLIAM whose widow Elizabeth received a pension

POWERS, EDWARD whose widow Selah received a pension

POWERS, HENRY whose widow Sina received a pension

POWERS, JAMES whose widow Rhoda received a pension

POWERS, JAMES W. (BLW), whose widow Fanny applied for a pension

POWERS, JOHN S. whose widow Lorena M. received a pension

POWERS, RICHARD whose widow Elizabeth received a pension

POWNALL/POWELL, JONATHAN applied for a pension

POYNER/POYNOR, CHARLES and widow Elizabeth both received a pension

PRATER, ARCHIBALD/ARCHLISS/ARCHILISS/ARCHELISS (BLW)

PRATER, JAMES (BLW), whose widow Phebe received a pension

PRATER/PRAYTER, NEHEMIAH (BLW)

PRATT, WILLIAM S. whose widow Martha received a pension

PREBBLE, HENRY whose widow Martha W. received a pension

PRENTIS, JOHN B. whose widow Catharine received a pension

PRENTISS, STANTON (P, BLW)

PRESTON, FRANCIS (BLW)

PRESTON, STEPHEN whose widow Frances received a pension

PRESTON, THOMAS (BLW)

PREWETT, ALLEN whose widow Nancy applied for a pension

PREWITT/PRUIT, JOSEPH applied for a pension

PRIBBLE, HIRAM (P)

PRICE, ABRAHAM whose widow Elizabeth received a pension

PRICE, ALEXANDER whose widow Sarah received a pension

PRICE, BARNETT M. whose widow Elizabeth applied for a pension

PRICE, GEORGE (P)

PRICE, JACOB (P)

PRICE, JOHN (BLW), whose widow Cynthia received a pension

PRICE, JOHN A. (BLW)

PRICE, JOSIAH M. whose widow Mary Mead Price received a pension

PRICE, PHILIP B. (BLW), whose widow was Mary

PRICE, STEPHEN (P)

PRICE, THOMAS whose widow Martha received a pension

PRICE, WILLIAM (P, BLW)

PRICE, WILLIAM M. (BLW), whose widow Mary received a pension

PRICHARD, JAMES and widow Elizabeth both received a

262

pension
PRICHARD, REES and widow Arabell both received a pension
PRIDDY, JAMES (P)
PRIDDY, JOHN S. and widow Scitty both received a pension
PRIDE, JOHN whose widow Amelia received a pension
PRIEST, JOHN applied for a pension
PRIEST, STEPHEN (P)
PRIEST, WILLIS whose widow Ann N. received a pension
PRIM, WILLIAM applied for a pension
PRINCE, DAVID whose widow Elizabeth received a pension
PRINCE, PHILIP (BLW)
PRITCHETT, JEREMIAH (P)
PRITCHETT, JOHN (BLW), whose widow Sarah H. received a pension. John was in Capt. W. Pritchett's company
PROCTOR, THOMAS (BLW), whose widow Frances received a pension
PROFFITT, JESSE S. whose widow Jane S. received a pension
PROPHET, JACOB whose widow Dorothea received a pension
PROPHET/PROFFITT, OBEDIAH (P)
PROPST, JACOB whose widow Esther applied for a pension
PRUDEN, AARON (P)
PRUETT, WILSON whose widow Rebecca received a pension
PRUNTY, JAMES whose widow Tabitha received a pension
PRYOR, SAMUEL T. and widow Lucie J. both received a pension
PRYOR, WILLIAM whose widow Louisa Jane received a pension
PRYOR, WILLIAM B. whose widow Jane B. received a pension. William was in Capt. Philip Pryor's company

PUCKET, DODSON (P)
PUCKETT, ISOM whose widow Mary applied for a pension
PUCKETT, JAMES whose widow Susannah received a pension
PUCKETT/PUCKET, JOHN (P)
PUCKETT, JOHN H. and widow Frances W. both received a pension
PUCKETT, STEPHEN C. and widow Perlina D. both received a pension
PUFFENBERGER/PUFFENBURGER, JACOB whose widow Ellen Puffenberger received a pension
PUGH, DAVID whose widow Mary received a pension
PUGH, ENOS and widow Nancy both received a pension
PUGH, JAMES and widow Catharine both received a pension
PUGH, JESSE J. (BLW)
PUGH, JOHN B. and widow Ann S. both received a pension
PUGH, WILLIAM D. and widow Martha both received a pension
PULLEN, THOMAS and widow Margaret both received a pension
PULLER, JAMES whose widow Mary A. received a pension
PULLER, JAMES whose widow Mary Ann received a pension
PULLIAM, GEORGE S. (BLW), whose widow Lucy S. applied for a pension
PULLIAM, GEORGE W. (BLW), whose widow was Nancy
PULLIAM, GEORGE W. (BLW)
PULLIAM, SAMUEL G. (BLW), whose widow was Mary H.
PULLIAM/POOLUM, WILLIM P. whose widow Betsy G. Pulliam received a pension
PULLIAM, WILLIAM P. whose widow Nancy R. received a pension
PULLIN/PULLEN, ABRAHAM/ABRAM B. (BLW), whose wi-

PULLIN (continued)
dow Charlotte received a pension
PUMMILL, JOHN whose widow Margaret received a pension
PUMPHREY, JOSEPH whose widow Elizabeth applied for a pension
PURCELL/PURSELL, GEORGE applied for a pension and widow Martha Purcell received a pension
PURDOM/PURDAM, JOHN whose widow Sarah Purdom received a pension
PURDUE, ASA (P)
PUSSELL, SAMUEL whose widow Mary E. Douglas applied for a pension
PURVIS, FRANCIS (P)
PURYEAR, BENJAMIN H. whose widow Mary applied for a pension
PURYEAR, SEYMOUR (P)
PYRTLE, BARTON whose widow Millie received a pension
QUARLES, JAMES whose widow Martha received a pension
QUARLES, JOHN whose widow Elizabeth received a pension
QUARLES, PETER whose widow Mary E. received a pension
QUEEN, WALTER applied for a pension
QUESINBERRY, THOMAS applied for a pension
QUICK, CHARLES and widow Nancy both received a pension
QUICK, JOHN (P)
QUICK, TUNIS (BLW), whose widow was Jane
QUICKLE, PETER whose widow Mary applied for a pension
QUINN, EDMOND (P)
QUISENBERRY, DANIEL whose widow Mary received a pension
QUISENBERRY, VIVION whose widow Elizabeth received a pension
QUISENBERY, JAMES applied for a pension
RACER, GEORGE M. (P)

RACER, JOHN (P, BLW)
RACER, THOMAS (P)
RACHEL/POCHEL/PACHEL, ALEXANDER applied for a pension
RADCLIFF, STEPHEN (P, BLW)
RADER, ABRAHAM (BLW), whose widow Barbara received a pension
RADER, ADAM (P)
RADER, GEORGE (BLW), whose widow Nancy received a pension
RADER, HENRY (BLW), and widow Catharine both received a pension
RADER, JOHN (BLW), and widow Permelia both received a pension
RADER, JOSEPH (BLW), and widow Martha both received a pension
RADER, MICHAEL (BLW), whose widow Catharine received a pension
RADFORD, JOHN (P)
RADFORD, JOSHUA whose widow Sarah F. applied for a pension
RADFORD, ROBERT whose widow Ellender applied for a pension
RAGAN/REAGEN, JOEL B. (P)
RAGAN, JOHN and former widow Alice Marcum both received a pension
RAGLAND, DABNEY whose widow Harriet B. received a pension
RAGLAND, PETTUS whose widow Helen C. received a pension
RAGSDALE, EDWARD (P)
RAGSDALE, THOMAS (BLW), whose widow Lucy B. received a pension
RAILSBACK, THOMAS F. whose widow Louisa V. received a pension
RAINEY, ISAAC whose widow Elizabeth H. received a pension
RAINS, FIELDING whose widow

RAINS (continued)
Elizabeth applied for a pension
RAINS, ISAAC whose widow
Catharine A. applied for a pension
RAKES, HENRY whose widow Ara Annah received a pension
RALLS, JOHN (P)
RALSTON, JOHN H. (P)
RALSTON, SAMUEL whose widow Ann received a pension
RAMEY, JOHN F. (P, BLW)
RAMSBOTTOM, JAMES whose widow Elizabeth received a pension
RAMSEY, JAMES whose widow Eliza received a pension
RAMSEY, JAMES whose widow received a pension
RAMSEY, JOEL whose widow Mary applied for a pension
RANDABOUGH, JACOB applied for a pension
RANDALL, AUSTIN applied for a pension
RANDALL, GEORGE (P, BLW)
RANDOLPH, GEORGE T. whose widow Hannah applied for a pension
RANDOLPH, WILLIAM B. (P)
RANDOLPH, WILLIAM FITZHUGH whose widow Jane C. received a pension
RANEY, JOHN whose widow Catherine received a pension
RANEY, ROBERT whose widow Sallie applied for a pension
RANEY, SAMUEL whose widow Charlotte received a pension
RANEY, THOMAS H. whose widow Elizabeth I. received a pension
RANKIN, JAMES (BLW), whose widow Nancy received a pension
RANKIN, WILLIAM whose widow Mary M. received a pension
RANKINS, GEORGE applied for a pension
RANNELLS, WILLIAM (P)
RANSBOTTOM, THOMAS (P)
RANSDELL, WILLIAM P. whose

RANSDELL (continued)
widow Caroline M. received a pension
RAPER, JOHN (BLW), IN militia, died 10 Mar 1864, Boston Township, Wayne Co, IN; md 2 Feb 1808 Elizabeth Keesling (P), Wythe Co, VA. Her LNR Boston Township, Wayne Co, IN, 1871
RARDON, DAVID whose widow Elizabeth received a pension
RATCLIFF/RATLIFF, VALENTINE (P)
RATCLIFFE, FRANCIS whose widow Mary Ann received a pension
RATLIFF, NUBEL whose widow Eddie received a pension
RATLIFF/RATCLIFF, SILAS K. applied for a pension
RATLIFF, WILLIAM whose widow Martha H. applied for a pension
RATTLIFF, PENDLETON whose widow Elizabeth received a pension
RAWLES/ROWLS, HARDY (P)
RAWLET/ROLETH, REUBEN whose widow Eliza Rawlet received a pension
RAWLINGS, DANIEL whose widow Clarissa Ann applied for a pension
RAWLINGS, JAMES (P)
RAWLINS, WILLIAM M. (P)
RAWLS, JOHN whose widow Mary Ann Woodson applied for a pension
RAWLS, WILLIAM (P)
RAY, EDWARD whose former widow Elizabeth Smith applied for a pension
RAY, JESSE whose widow Sarah received a pension
RAY, JOSEPH (P, BLW)
RAY, SWANAGAN whose widow Catharine received a pension
RAY, WILLIAM (BLW), and widow Martha Y. both received a pension
RAY, WILLIAM whose widow

RAY (continued)
Mary applied for a pension
RAYMOND, GARRETT V. applied for a pension

ROLL NO. 78

REA, DANIEL (P)
REA, JAMES whose widow Jane received a pension
REA, JAMES C. (P)
REA, REYNARD (P)
READ, BEVERLY G. whose widow Elizabeth Y. received a pension
READ/REED, DAVID (BLW), died 5 Dec 1866, Pecks Run, Upshur Co, WV; md 20 Feb 1814 Nancy A. Romine (P), Harrison Co, VA. Her LNR Washington Township, Upshur Co, WV, 1871
READ, FRANCIS whose widow Hannah received a pension
READ, JOHN whose widow Margaret D. received a pension
READ, NOAH whose widow Rebecca D. received a pension
REAGER, LEONARD whose widow Mary received a pension
REAM, SAMUEL (P)
REAMY, JAMES whose widow Sarah applied for a pension
RECE, ABIA (P)
RECTOR, BENNETT whose widow Susan received a pension
RECTOR, ELI (P)
REDDISH, JOSEPH (BLW), applied for a pension
REDMAN, DANIEL whose widow Emily J. received a pension
REDMAN, ELI whose widow Catharine received a pension
REDMAN, HENRY whose widow Olive applied for a pension
REED, DAVID whose widow Mary received a pension
REED, HENRY L. and widow Charlotte both received a pension
REED, JAMES whose widow Lydia received a pension

REED, JESSE applied for a pension
REED, ROBERT B. whose widow Adeline W. applied for a pension
REED, THOMAS whose widow Mary applied for a pension
REEDER, EDWIN applied for a pension
REEDER, WILLIAM B. (BLW)
REEL, JOHN M. whose widow Mary W. received a pension
REES, ABEL (BLW)
REESE, GEORGE whose widow Phoebe Ann received a pension
REESE, JOHN, USA and VA militia, whose widow Mary A. F. Chandler applied for a pension
REESE, JOHN W. (P)
REESE, JOSEPH A. whose widow Mary E. received a pension
REESE, STEPHEN whose widow Nancy received a pension
REESER, PETER whose widow Elizabeth received a pension
REEVES, NATHAN whose widow Rachel applied for a pension
REEVES, REUBEN (P)
REEVES, REZIN R. (BLW), whose widow Eliza G. received a pension
REGER, ABRAM (P)
REID, ANDREW whose widow Mary J. received a pension
REID, ARCHIBALD (P)
REID, CHRISTOPHER whose widow Martha received a pension
REID, JOHN B. and widow Mariah both received a pension
REID, JONATHAN whose widow Ann applied for a pension
REID, PEYTON whose widow Ann received a pension
REID/REED, SAMUEL (P)
REID, WILLIAM whose widow Lydia received a pension
REINS/RAINS, RICHARD whose widow Susan Ellen applied for pension
RENNOLDS/REYNOLDS, JOHN T. whose widow Eleanor/ Elanor Rennolds received a

RENNOLDS (continued)
pension

REXROAD, JOHN whose widow Phebe received a pension

REXROAD, ZACHARIAH applied for a pension

REXRODE, ADAM whose widow Elizabeth Ann applied for a pension

REXRODE, CHRISTIAN (P)

REXRODE, SAMUEL alias PECK, JOHN whose widow Sarah Rexrode received a pension

REYNOLDS, HENRY whose widow Elizabeth received a pension

REYNOLDS, HUMPHREY and widow Lockey both received a pension

REYNOLDS/RENNOLDS, JAMES whose widow Sophia Reynolds received a pension

REYNOLDS, JOHN whose widow Sarah R. received a pension

REYNOLDS, JOHN (P)

REYNOLDS, JOHN S. whose widow Ruth received a pension

REYNOLDS, TANDY (P)

REYNOLDS, THOMAS whose widow Fanny Ann applied for a pension

REYNOLDS, THOMAS whose widow Priscilla received a pension

REYNOLDS, WILLIAM whose widow Mary Ann received a pension

REYNOLDS, WILLIAM R. whose widow Elizabeth applied for a pension

RHINEHART, ABRAHAM (P)

RHOADES, JOHN (P, BLW)

RHODES, CLIFTON whose widow Elizabeth applied for a pension

RHODES/ROADES, DAVID whose widow Jane Margaret received a pension

RHODES, GEORGE (BLW) whose widow Jane received a pension

RHODES, JACOB whose widow Elizabeth received a pension

RHODES/RHOADS, JOEL (P)

RHODES, SAMUEL whose widow Parthenia received a pension

RHODES, WILLIAM whose widow Charity received a pension

RHYMER, JACOB applied for a pension

RIAN/RYAN, JOHN whose former widow Margaret Crisler applied for a pension

RICE, ADAM whose widow Margaret applied for a pension

RICE, JAMES (BLW), and widow Anna both received a pension

RICE, JOHN W. whose widow Anna M. received a pension

RICE, LEMUEL whose widow Dicey received a pension

RICE, RANDALL, whose widow Dolly R. applied for a pension

RICE, THOMAS whose widow Martha received a pension

RICE, THOMAS J. whose widow Sarah applied for a pension

ROLL NO. 79

RICH, WILLIAM whose widow Sarah received a pension

RICHARD, JACOB (P)

RICHARDS, EDWARD whose widow Jane received a pension

RICHARDS, GEORGE B. whose widow Catharine R. applied for a pension

RICHARDS, GEORGE W. whose widow Catharine applied for a pension

RICHARDS, JOHN (P)

RICHARDS, JOHN whose widow Mary A. Margaret received a pension

RICHARDS, PAYTON (P)

RICHARDS, RICHARD Sr. and widow Mahala both received a pension

RICHARDS, THOMAS whose widow Nancy received a pension

RICHARDS, WESLEY (P)

RICHARDS, WILLIS and widow Judith both received a pension

267

RICHARDSON, ARCHER C. whose widow Martha Ann received a pension

RICHARDSON, DAVID whose widow Jane G. received a pension

RICHARDSON, HENRY whose widow Louisa applied for a pension

RICHARDSON, JAMES (P)

RICHARDSON, JAMES whose widow Elizabeth received a pension

RICHARDSON, JAMES whose widow Sarah Ann Downing applied for a pension

RICHARDSON, JAMES whose widow Sarah received a pension

RICHARDSON, JOHN P. (BLW), whose former widow was Elizabeth M. Marshall

RICHARDSON, JONATHAN and widow Nancy both received a pension

RICHARDSON, JOSHUA whose widow Ann applied for a pension

RICHARDSON, THOMAS P. and widow Catherine both received a pension

RICHARDSON, WALTHALL (BLW)

RICHARDSON, WILLIAM (P) whose widow was Nancy

RICHARDSON, WILLIAM H. applied for a pension

RICHARDSON, WILLIAM R. whose widow Mary Ann received a pension

RICHARDSON, WILLIAM S. (P), USA. Residence in VA

RICHEY, JOHN (P)

RICHMAN/RICHMOND, HENRY whose widow Rebecca received a pension

RICKARD / RICKHART, MICHAEL and widow Mary Rickard both received a pension

RICKETTS, WILLIAM whose widow Mary applied for a pension

RICKMAN, HUBBARD applied for

RICKMAN (continued) a pension

RICKMAN, THOMAS whose widow Elizabeth received a pension

RIDDELL, ARCHIBALD applied for a pension

RIDDELL, JOHN and widow Anna both applied for a pension

RIDDICK, MILLS whose widow Mary applied for a pension

RIDDLE, JAMES and widow Ruth both received a pension

RIDDLE, JEREMIAH whose widow Margaret received a pension

RIDDLEBURGER, DAVID (P)

RIDENOUR, ADAM whose widow Mary M. received a pension

RIDGEWAY, JAMES whose widow Mary A. received a pension

RIDGEWAY, PEYTON whose widow Sophia received a pension

RIDGWAY, ROBERT whose widow Mary applied for a pension

RIDOUT, BENJAMIN B. whose widow Eliza D. received a pension

RIDOUT, THOMAS and widow Elizabeth A. both received a pension

RIFE, HENRY whose widow Mildred applied for a pension

RIFE/RIFFE, JACOB whose widow Nancy received a pension

RIFE, JOHN and widow Elizabeth both received a pension

RIFFE, COONROD whose widow Sally received a pension

RIFFLE, GEORGE whose widow Susannah B. applied for a pension

RIFFLE/KIFFLE, JACOB whose widow Margaret Riffle applied for a pension

RIGG, ADDISON applied for a pension

RIGGS, JAMES whose widow Matilda received a pension

RIGGS, TOWNLEY whose widow Elizabeth received a pension

RIGGS, WILLIAM whose widow Sarah applied for a pension

RIGSBY, SAMUEL whose widow Nancy received a pension

RILEY, ALEXANDER (P)

RILEY, JOHN R. (P)

RILY/RILEY, JOHN applied for a pension

RINE, DANIEL (BLW), whose widow Hester Ann received a pension

RINEHART, ABRAHAM (P)

RINEHART, ADAM whose widow Mary received a pension

RINEHART, JOHN whose widow Rosanna received a pension

RINER, AARON and widow Catherine both received a pension

RINER, JOHN (P)

RING, SHALINGTON alias KING, WILLIAM applied for a pension

RINGER, JACOB whose widow Nancy received a pension

RINGLESBY/RINGSBURY, CHRISTOPHER (P)

RION, JOHN whose widow Margaret applied for a pension

RIORDAN/REARDEN, GEORGE whose widow Sarah D. Riordan received a pension

RIPLEY, JACOB applied for a pension

RIPLEY, WILLIAM (BLW), whose widow Elizabeth Murray Ripley received a pension. LNR St. Clair, IL

RIPPETOE, JOHN B. whose widow Susan W. received a pension

RISSLER, THOMAS whose widow Margery received a pension

RITTENHOUSE, SAMUEL (P)

RIVERS, JOHN S. whose widow Sallie Ann received a pension

RIVES, WILLIAM MASON whose widow Sarah Ann received a pension

ROACH, GERARD whose widow Maria A. W. received a pension

ROACH, HENRY M. alias BARNARD, SOPEL B. whose widow Sophia Roach applied for a pension

ROACH, JESSE whose widow Pracilla received a pension

ROACH, THOMAS C. (P)

ROACH, WILLIAM whose former widow Elizabeth Almond applied for a pension

ROACH, WILLIAM whose widow Delilah received a pension

ROADCAP, EMANUEL whose widow Elizabeth applied for a pension

ROANE, JOHN J. whose widow Mary M. received a pension

ROARK, BERRY alias BARNETT, WILLIAM alias SHORT, WILLIAM whose widow Lockey Roark applied for a pension

ROBB, PATRICK C. (BLW), whose widow was Maria

ROBBINS, ELIJAH whose widow Mary E. B. received a pension

ROLL NO. 80

ROBERSON, JAMES and widow Mary A. both received a pension

ROBERSON, JOSEPH whose widow Fannie F. applied for a pension

ROBERTS, BENJAMIN (BLW), died 14 May 1868, near New Lexington, OH; md 30 Jan 1814 Mary Dulany (P), Culpeper, VA. Her LNR near New Lexington, Perry Co, OH, 1871

ROBERTS, BENJAMIN (P)

ROBERTS, BENJAMIN (P)

ROBERTS, HENRY G. and widow Elvina both received a pension

ROBERTS, HOWELL and widow Elizabeth both received a pension

ROBERTS, JESSE (P)

ROBERTS, JOHN (P)

ROBERTS, JOHN (P)

ROBERTS, JOSEPH and widow

ROBERTS (continued)
Ann both received a pension
ROBERTS, RICHARD whose widow Anna received a pension
ROBERTS, SAMUEL whose widow Mary received a pension
ROBERTS, SAMUEL (P)
ROBERTS, THOMAS whose widow Ann M. received a pension
ROBERTS, THOMAS (P)
ROBERTS, THOMAS whose widow Judith C. received a pension
ROBERTS, WILLIAM applied for a pension
ROBERTS, WILLIAM (P)
ROBERTS, WILLIAM (P)
ROBERTSON, AARON P. whose widow Ann D. received a pension
ROBERTSON, ANDREW (P)
ROBERTSON, CHRISTOPHER applied for a pension
ROBERTSON, CYRUS whose widow Sally received a pension
ROBERTSON, DAVIS (BLW), whose widow Eliza S. received a pension
ROBERTSON, DAVID M. whose widow Eleanor received a pension
ROBERTSON, EDWARD (BLW), whose widow Nancy R. F. received a pension
ROBERTSON, ELISHA applied for a pension
ROBERTSON, FREDERICK N. (P)
ROBERTSON, JAMES applied for a pension
ROBERTSON, JAMES whose widow Frances L. received a pension
ROBERTSON, JOHN whose widow Ann received a pension
ROBERTSON, JOHN A. whose widow Mary B. received a pension
ROBERTSON, JORDAN (P)
ROBERTSON, JOSEPH (P)
ROBERTSON, JOSIAH (BLW), whose widow Eliza M. re-

ROBERTSON (continued)
ceived a pension
ROBERTSON, LEWIS (BLW), whose widow Martha E. received a pension
ROBERTSON, ROBERT B. and widow Elizabeth C. both received a pension
ROBERTSON, SAMUEL whose widow Elizabeth received a pension
ROBERTSON, THOMAS whose widow Miriam applied for a pension
ROBERTSON, WILLIAM (P)
ROBERTSON, WILLIAM H. whose widow Martha M. applied for a pension
ROBERTSON, WILLIAM M. whose widow Elizabeth M. received a pension
ROBINETT, JESSE whose widow Elizabeth received a pension
ROBINETT, SAMPSON/SAMSON whose widow Selah received a pension
ROBINS/ROBBINS, SOLOMON T. whose widow Mary F. Robins received a pension
ROBINSON, ARCHIBALD whose widow Mary M. received a pension
ROBINSON, DANIEL whose widow Clara applied for a pension
ROBINSON, DAVID whose widow Mary A. received a pension
ROBINSON, DAVID whose widow Sarah received a pension
ROBINSON, GEORGE whose widow Sarah S. received a pension
ROBINSON, HARRISON I. and widow Elizabeth M. both received a pension
ROBINSON, JAMES and widow Elizabeth both received a pension
ROBINSON, JAMES whose widow Sarah received a pension
ROBINSON, JOHN whose widow Sarah received a pension

ROBINSON, JOHN applied for a pension

ROBINSON, JOHN W., USA, whose widow Elizabeth received a pension. Residence in VA

ROBINSON, JONATHAN P. whose widow Sarah received a pension

ROBINSON, PETER B. applied for a pension

ROBINSON, PRESTON and widow Polly both received a pension

ROBINSON, RICHARD P. whose widow Mary received a pension

ROBINSON, ROBERT S. and widow Maxa A. both received a pension

ROBINSON, SIMEON W. whose widow Sarah Ann received a pension

ROBINSON, THOMAS (P)

ROBINSON, THOMAS (P)

ROBINSON, WILLIAM (P, BLW)

ROBINSON, WILLIAM (P)

ROBINSON, WILLIAM whose widow Rebecca J. M. applied for a pension

ROBINSON, WILLIAM A. (P)

ROBINSON, WINSLOW applied for a pension

ROBION/ROBIO, BENONI/BEN (P)

ROBISON/ROBINSON, THOMAS whose widow Mary Robison received a pension

ROCK, THOMAS whose widow Sallie received a pension

RODEBAUGH/RADEBAUGH, GEORGE and widow Isabella both received a pension

RODEFFER, PHILIP and widow Rebecca both received a pension

RODEHEAVER, JACOB (P)

RODES, THOMAS (P)

RODGERS, ALVERI whose widow Mary received a pension

RODGERS, JOHN applied for a pension

RODGERS, JOHN WORSHAM whose widow Susan received a

RODGERS (continued) pension

RODGERS, NATHANIEL KERR (BLW), whose widow Elizabeth received a pension

RODGERS, PHILIP B. (P, BLW)

RODGERS, THOMAS H. whose widow Mary applied for a pension

RODGERS/ROGERS, WILLIAM and widow Jane Rogers both received a pension

ROE, JAMES whose widow Frances received a pension

ROE, WILLIAM (P)

ROGERS, ARNOLD (P)

ROGERS, JAMES (BLW), KY & VA militia, whose widow Lucy received a pension

ROGERS, JOHN applied for a pension

ROGERS, JOHN whose widow Phoebe received a pension

ROGERS, JOHN whose widow Mary received a pension

ROGERS, JOSEPH whose widow Margaret received a pension

ROGERS, JOSEPH (BLW), whose widow Lucy received a pension

ROGERS, LUDWELL L. whose widow Harriet P. received a pension

ROGERS, RHODUM/RHODAM E. whose widow Eleanor applied for a pension

ROGERS, ROBERT whose widow Milly received a pension

ROGERS, ROBERT A. and widow Lucy G. both received a pension

ROGERS, ROBERT B. whose widow Margaret J. received a pension

ROGERS, WILLIAM (P)

ROGERS, WILLIAM H. (BLW), whose widow Mary P. received a pension

ROLAND, ROBERT whose widow Mary applied for a pension

ROLAND, THOMAS (P)

ROLLER, DANIEL applied for a pension

ROLLER, FREDERICK (P)
ROLLER, MICHAEL (P)
ROLLINS, ELIJAH J. whose widow Sophiah received a pension
ROLLS, DANIEL whose widow Mary Catharine received a pension
ROLSTON, ARCHIBALD whose widow Maria received a pension
ROLSTON, NATHAN (P)

ROLL NO. 81

ROMACK, JOHN applied for a pension
ROOF, JOHN (P, BLW)
ROOF, MARTIN (P) whose wife was Margaret Zirkle
ROOKER, JOHN whose widow Elizabeth received a pension
ROOKWOOD, HIRAM (P) whose widow Mary applied for a pension
ROOT, JACOB and widow Margaret both received a pension
ROPER, JOHN M. applied for a pension
RORER, JOHN D. and widow Frances both received a pension
ROSAR/ROSER, ANDREW whose widow Margaret received a pension
ROSE, CHARLES applied for a pension
ROSE, HENRY whose widow Jane received a pension
ROSE, HENRY applied for a pension and widow Margaret E. received a pension
ROSE, JAMES E. (P)
ROSE, WASHINGTON (BLW)
ROSE, WILLIAM (P)
ROSEBROUGH, MOSES R. whose widow Rebecca received a pension
ROSIER/ROSER, LAWRENCE whose widow Esther received a pension
ROSS, JAMES whose widow

ROSS (continued)
Frances H. received a pension
ROSS, JOHN whose widow Elizabeth received a pension
ROSS, JOHN (P)
ROSS, WILLIAM (P)
ROSSER, JESSE whose widow Elizabeth applied for a pension
ROSSER, JOHN applied for a pension
ROSSER, THOMAS whose widow Christine E. received a pension
ROTTENBERRY, PRESLEY whose widow Elizabeth received a pension
ROTTENBERRY, WILLIAM and widow Jane both received a pension
ROUSE, NICHOLAS (P)
ROUSH, ABRAHAM (P, BLW)
ROUSH, DANIEL (BLW), died 2 Sep 1866, Mason Co, WV; md 2 Jan 1810 Catharine Yeager (P), Pleasant Flats, VA. She died 28 Jul 1886, LNR Graham Township, Mason Co, WV, 1871
ROUSH, GEORGE whose widow Judam applied for a pension
ROUTON, JESSE whose widow Lucy W. received a pension
ROW, KEELING whose widow Fannie received a pension
ROW, PETER whose widow Anna received a pension
ROWAN, MANUS whose widow Fannie P. applied for a pension
ROWE, JACOB whose widow Elizabeth received a pension
ROWE, LANSON whose widow Elizabeth received a pension
ROWE, WILLIAM (P)
ROWELL, HOWELL (P)
ROWLAND, CAGER/OURY/ HENRY whose widow Winnie M. applied for a pension
ROWLAND, HENRY B. whose former widow Wilmoth A. Groome applied for a pension
ROWLAND, JOHN whose widow

ROWLAND (continued)
Eliza Jane applied for a pension

ROWLAND, NATHANIEL H. (P)

ROWLAND, PETER H. whose widow Nancy applied for a pension

ROWLAND, REASON whose widow Elender received a pension

ROWLETT, DANIEL whose former widow Mary Sutton applied for a pension

ROWSEY/ROWSEN, JOHN (P)

ROY, JAMES (BLW), whose widow was Martha

ROY, JOHN (BLW)

ROY, MCCARTY D. (BLW)

ROYAL, WILLLIAM applied for a pension

ROYALL, JOHN B. whose widow Pamela W. received a pension

ROYALL, JOSEPH (P)

ROYALL, JOSEPH E. whose widow Mary E. received a pension

ROYALL, LITTLEBERRY whose widow Susan J. received a pension

ROYER, JOHN (P, BLW)

ROYSTER, BANISTER (P)

ROYSTER, GEORGE (P)

RUBLE, APPOLOS/POSER (BLW), died 10 May 1865, Wood Co, WV; md 23 May 1809 Anna Masters (P), Wood Co, VA. She died 20 Mar 1885, Fountain Springs, WV, LNR Tygatt Towship, Wood Co, WV, 1871

RUBLE, GEORGE (P)

RUBLE, JACOB whose widow Maryan applied for a pension

RUBLE, JAMES (BLW), whose widow Sarah applied for a pension

RUBLE, JOSEPH whose widow Nancy received a pension

RUCKER, ANTHONY (BLW), whose widow was Margaret

RUCKER, ELZAPHEN whose widow Fanny applied for a

RUCKER (continued)
pension

RUCKER, JARVIS (BLW), whose widow was Milly

RUCKER, JOHN F. whose widow Mary applied for a pension

RUCKER, WILLIAM whose widow Mary J. received a pension

RUCKER, WILLIAM whose widow Tabitha received a pension

RUDD, ARCHIBALD applied for a pension

RUDY, JOHN whose widow Sarah received a pension

RUFFIN, JOHN alias OVERBY, JOHN B. whose widow Ann Ruffin received a pension

RUFFNER, REUBEN whose widow Ann received a pension

RULEY, JACOB T. whose widow Sally received a pension

RUMBOUGH, JACOB (P, BLW)

RUMBURG, ELIA whose widow Mary received a pension

RUNION, JAMES (P)

RUNION, JAMES applied for a pension

RUPERT/RUPART, CHRISTIAN and widow Rebecca Rupert both received a pension

RUSH, DAVID whose widow Susan received a pension

RUSH, JOB/JOEL whose widow Nancy received a pension

RUSH, JOHN (P)

RUSH, PETER H. whose widow Susan received a pension

RUSH, THOMAS whose widow Nancy received a pension

RUSMISEL, ADAM whose widow Sally received a pension

RUSMISEL, CHRISTIAN whose widow Martha received a pension

RUSSELL, BARTLETT whose widow Ann applied for a pension

RUSSELL, CALLIHAM/ CALAHAN whose widow Dorcas received a pension

RUSSELL, CHARLES and widow Sarah both received a pension
RUSSELL, HENRY whose widow J. Louisa received a pension
RUSSELL, HEZEKIAH (P)
RUSSELL, ISAAC whose widow Eliza A. received a pension
RUSSELL, JAMES (BLW), whose helpless child Nellie M. applied for a pension
RUSSELL, JOHN (BLW), USA. Born in VA
RUSSELL, JOSEPH whose widow Celia received a pension
RUSSELL, LEWIS (P)
RUSSELL, ROBERT whose widow Mary received a pension
RUSSELL, ROBERT whose widow Mary applied for a pension
RUSSELL, STEPHEN whose widow Sarah received a pension
RUSSELL, WILLIAM whose widow Margaret applied for a pension
RUSSELL, JOHN whose widow Elizabeth received a pension
RUTHERFORD, WILLIAM whose widow Polly received a pension
RUTTER, ALFRED whose widow Chloe applied for a pension
RYAN, BERRY whose widow Millinder received a pension
RYAN, DABNEY whose widow Nancy applied for a pension
RYAN, GEORGE (P)
RYAN, JAMES whose widow Elizabeth received a pension
RYAN, JESSE whose widow Delilah received a pension
RYAN, WILLIAM alias DAMRON, WILLIAM R. (BLW), whose widow Sallie Ryan received a pension
RYE, JOHN W. whose widow Elizabeth H. received a pension
RYHN/RYANT, GEORGE and widow Barbara A. Ryhn received a pension
RYLES, ALEXANDER/ELLIOTT alias RYALLS, ELLIOTT (P)

RYMAN, HENRY (P)
RYMAN, JACOB and widow Sarah both received a pension
RYMAN, JOSEPH (P)
RYON, HENRY applied for a pension

ROLL NO. 82

SADDLER, JESSE whose widow Ann received a pension
SADDLER, THOMAS (P)
SADDLER, WILLIAM T. (P)
SADLER, JOHN and widow America H. both received a pension
SADLER, ROBERT C. whose widow Wilmoth received a pension
SADLER, WILLIAM (P)
ST. CLAIR, ARCHER whose widow Sarah applied for a pension
ST. CLAIR, ISAAC whose widow Jane applied for a pension
ST. CLAIR, ISAAC B. applied for a pension
ST. CLAIR/SINKLER, WILLIAM whose widow Mary St. Clair received a pension
ST. JOHN, ABRAHAM whose widow Dicy received a pension
SALE, BENJAMIN whose widow Polly T. applied for a pension
SALE, SAMUEL L. whose widow Jane received a pension
SALISBURY, ELIJAH whose widow Keziah received a pension
SALLE, GEORGE F. and widow Julia B. both received a pension
SALLEE, BARTLEY (P)
SALMON/SALAMON/SOLOMON, JAMES (BLW), whose widow Dicey Salmon received a pension
SALMON, JOHN whose widow Eliza J. received a pension
SALMON, WILLIAM whose widow Evelina P. received a pension
SAMFORD, WATKINS (BLW),

274

SAMFORD (continued)
and widow Susan A. E. both
received a pension
SAMMONS, GEORGE applied for
a pension
SAMPLE, JAMES whose widow
Mary received a pension
SAMPSON, ROBERT (BLW),
died 1828, whose widow was
Agnes Poore Sampson, LNR
Goochland Co, VA
SAMPSON, ROBERT (BLW),
died 1824, whose widow was
Ann Keyes Sampson, LNR
Middlesex Co, VA
SAMPSON, SAGE (P)
SAMPSON, WILLIAM applied for
a pension
SAMS, JAMES whose widow Bar-
bara received a pension
SAMS, JOHN whose widow Nancy
received a pension
SAMUEL, HERNDON (P)
SAMUELS, MISHACK/MESHACK
(P)
SAMUELS, SHADRACK whose
widow Margaret received a
pension
SANDERS, BENJAMIN applied for
a pension
SANDERS/SAUNDERS, GEORGE
(P)
SANDERS, HIRAM (P)
SANDERS, JACOB (BLW), en-
listed in Pittsylvania Co, VA,
died 18 Sep 1849, Williamson
Co, IL; md 27 Jun 1839 or
1849 Sarah Hartwell, Franklin
Co, IL. Her LNR Williamson
Co, IL, 1856
SANDERS, JAMES (P)
SANDERS, JOSEPH whose widow
Margaret applied for a pension
SANDERS, MAHLON (P)
SANDERS, PRESLEY whose wi-
dow Lana received a pension
SANDERS, THOMAS and widow
Melviny S. both received a
pension
SANDERS, WILLIAM and widow
Sally both received a pension
SANDERSON, GEORGE G. (P)

SANDERSON, JOHN (P)
SANDERSON/SAUNDERSON,
ROBERT whose widow Eliz-
abeth R. Sanderson received a
pension
SANDIDGE, ANDERSON whose
widow Catharine received a
pension
SANDIDGE/LANDRIDGE/ LAN-
DIDGE, DUDLEY whose widow
Belinda Sandidge received a
pension
SANDIDGE, JAMES (BLW), DC
militia, died 18 Apr 1856,
Loudoun Co, VA; md 9 Jun
1808 Mary Herbert (P),
Loudoun Co, VA. Her LNR
Washington, DC, 1871
SANDS, CHARLES whose widow
Sarah received a pension
SANDS, GEORGE whose widow
Elizabeth received a pension
SANDS, JOHN and widow Mary
both received a pension
SANDY, THOMAS whose widow
Rebecca received a pension
SANDY, VINCENT whose widow
Anne received a pension
SANFORD, WILLIAM HENRY
and widow Mary Jane both re-
ceived a pension
SANGSTER, GEORGE applied for
a pension
SARGENT, ABNER O. whose
widow Elizabeth applied for a
pension
SARGENT, HENRY E. whose wi-
dow Palmyra received a pen-
sion
SARVER, ISAAC whose widow
Frances received a pension
SARVER, JAMES (P, BLW)
SATCHELL, JOHN (BLW)
SATCHELL, THOMAS
STOKELEY (BLW), whose wi-
dow was Mary G.
SATTERFIELD, JEMMA (P)
SAUM, CHRISTIAN (P)
SAUNDERS, DAVID (BLW)
SAUNDERS, JAMES whose widow
Mary received a pension
SAUNDERS, JAMES and widow

SAUNDERS (continued)
Elizabeth C. received a pension

SAUNDERS, JAMES whose widow Ann M. received a pension

SAUNDERS, JESSE W. whose widow Joanna received a pension

SAUNDERS, JOHN G. whose widow Catharine received a pension

SAUNDERS, JOHN H. whose widow Sally D. received a pension

SAUNDERS, LITTEBERRY whose widow Sarah F. received a pension

SAUNDERS, NIMROD whose widow Sarah Ann applied for a pension

SAUNDERS, SAMUEL S. whose widow Elizabeth received a pension

SAUNDERS, WILLIAM whose widow Catharine applied for a pension

SAUNDERS, WILLIAM L. applied for a pension and widow Sarah received a pension

SAURBAUGH, JOHN applied for a pension

SAVAGE, CHAMPION H. applied for a pension

SAVAGE, JAMES whose widow Elizabeth applied for a pension

SAVAGE, KENDAL whose widow Polly received a pension

SAVAGE, LEVIN whose widow Nancy/Ann received a pension

SAYRE/SEIRS, EPHRAIM (P)

SEABERRY/SEARBERRY, WILLIAM (P)

SCARBOROUGH, BRITTON whose widow Margaret G. applied for a pension

SCARFF, WILLIAM C. and widow Mary B. both received a pension

SCOTES, ZACHARIAH whose widow Martha received a pension

SCATTERDAY, AARON (BLW) and widow Ann M. both received a pension

SCATTERDAY (continued)
ceived a pension

SCHAFFER/SHAVER, JOHN whose widow Susan Schaffer received a pension

SCHAPPART, JACOB (BLW), died 25 Apr 1867, Berkeley Co, WV; md 22 May 1806 Mary Miller (P), Martinsburg, Berkeley Co, VA. Her LNR Martinsburg, WV, 1871

SCHOOLS, THOMAS whose widow Nancy received a pension

SCHOONOVER, DANIEL (P, BLW)

SCHROCK/SHROCK, CHRISTOPHER (BLW), whose widow Sarah received a pension

SCHROFFE, CHARLES M. (P)

SCHWARTZ, GEORGE alias BLACK, GEORGE (P)

SCISSOR, ROBERT T. applied for a pension

ROLL NO. 83

SCOTT, ANDERSON M. alias SCOTT, ANDREW M. applied for a pension

SCOTT, FLEMING (P)

SCOTT, GEORGE (P)

SCOTT, GEORGE (P)

SCOTT, GEORGE W. (P)

SCOTT, HENRY and widow Elizabeth both received a pension

SCOTT, JEREMIAH whose widow Annie received a pension

SCOTT, JOHN whose widow Ruth received a pension

SCOTT, JOHN T./L. applied for a pension

SCOTT, MORGAN whose widow Catharine applied for a pension

SCOTT, MOSES A. (P), USA. Residence in VA

SCOTT, NATHANIEL and widow Sarah E. both received a pension

SCOTT, SAMUEL (P, BLW)

SCOTT, SAMUEL D. (BLW), whose widow Polly received a pension

SCOTT, THOMAS, USA and VA militia, whose widow Mary received a pension

SCOTT, WILLIAM C. and widow Mary both received a pension

SCOTT, WILLIAM T. whose widow Juliet received a pension

SCOTT, WILLIAM W. (P)

SCOTT, WILLIAM W. whose widow Elizabeth M. received a pension

SCRIVNER/SCRONER, BENJAMIN (P)

SCRIVNER, WILLIAM applied for a pension

SCRIVNER/SCRIGLER/ SCRIGNER, WILLIAM applied for a pension

SCRUGGS, BENJAMIN whose widow Lucy received a pension

SCRUGGS, JAMES and widow Nancy both received a pension

SCRUGGS, JOHN whose widow Frances received a pension

SCRUGGS, WILLIAM (P)

SCYOC/SEYOC, ABEL and widow Nancy both received a pension

SEABURN/SEABORN, JACOB and widow Mary/Polly Seaburn both received a pension

SEAL, JOHN whose widow Susanah received a pension

SEARES, THOMAS whose widow Mary received a pension

SEARGENT, JOHN and widow Nancy both received a pension

SEARS, WESLEY (P)

SEARS, WILLIAM whose widow Mary received a pension

SEAVER, JACOB (P)

SEAY, ABRAHAM (BLW), whose widow Sarah received a pension

SEAY, ABRAM/ABRAHAM B. whose widow Susan received a pension

SEAY, AUSTIN and widow Sally A. both received a pension

SEAY, CARR W. whose widow Jane applied for a pension

SEAY, ELISHA whose widow Susan received a pension

SEAY, GEORGE B. (P, BLW)

SEAY, JAMES whose widow Elizabeth received a pension

SEAY, JESSE (P)

SEAY, JOSEPH whose widow Elizabeth received a pension

SEAY, LEONARD whose widow Lucy received a pension

SEAY, STEPHEN W. and widow Lucy B. both received a pension

SEAY/SEARY, WOODSON (P)

SEBASTIAN, BENJAMIN (BLW), whose former widow was Elizabeth Davis

SEBASTIAN, WILLIAM applied for a pension

SEBRELL, FREDERICK whose widow Margaret applied for a pension

SEBRELL, JOHN whose widow Sarah applied for a pension

SECREST, ABRAHAM (P)

SECRIST, GEORGE whose widow Mary received a pension

SEE, GARRED whose widow Florence applied for a pension

SEE, JACOB whose widow Nancy received a pension

SEE, MICHAEL (BLW)

SEE, MICHAEL (BLW), died 1827, whose widow was Nancy G.

SEEMAN, JOHN (P)

SEES/CEASE, CHRISTOPHER (P)

SEESE/CEESE, JACOB and widow Catharine both received a pension

SEEVERS, JAMES (P)

SEIBERT, CHRISTIAN whose widow Mary received a pension

SEIBERT, GEORGE (P)

SEIBERT, MICHAEL whose widow Elizabeth received a pension

SELBY, JOHN whose widow Hannah received a pension

SELDEN, JAMES M. whose widow Mary E. received a pension

SELDEN, WILLIAM (P)

SELF, JOHN whose widow Nancy received a pension

SELLARS, JOHN and widow Elizabeth both received a pension

SELLERS, JOHN whose widow Delila received a pension

SEMMENS, THOMAS (P)

SENNETT, JOHN whose widow Elizabeth applied for pension

SEPARD, WILLIAM applied for a pension

SERGEANT, CHAPMAN (P)

SESLER, SAMUEL applied for pension

SETTERS, URIAH whose widow Elizabeth applied for a pension

SETTLE, FRANKLIN/FRANCIS (BLW), whose widow Nancy received a pension

SETTLE, MARTIN whose widow Ann applied for a pension

SETTLE, WILLIAM P. whose widow Polly received a pension

SEVERNS, JOHN (P) and widow Catharine both received a pension

SEWALL, CHARLES whose widow Sarah received a pension

SEWELL, JOSEPH (BLW)

SEWER/SEWERT, WILLIAM (P)

SEXTON, CHARLES (P)

SEXTON, THORNTON applied for a pension

SEYMOUR, JESSE (P) and widow Margaret both received a pension

SEYMOUR/SEYMORE, WILLIAM whose widow Eliza Seymour received a pension

SHACKELFORD, JOHN whose widow Ann applied for a pension

SHACKELFORD, SATTERWHITE whose widow Courtney Ann received a pension

SHACKELFORD, SEAMOUR whose widow Nancy applied for a pension

SHACKELFORD, WARNER whose widow Lydia received a pension

SHACKLEFORD, WILLIAM and widow Frances both received a pension

SHADE, PETER whose widow Mary received a pension

SHAFER, CONRAD (BLW), whose widow Mary received a pension

SHAFER/SHAVER, JOHN (P, BLW)

SHAFER/SHAVER, JOHN (BLW), whose widow Mary M. received a pension

SHAFER, JOHN (BLW), whose widow Mary A. received a pension

SHAFFER, ABRAHAM (BLW), whose widow Margaret received a pension

SHAFFER/SHAVER, ABRAHAM (BLW), whose widow Mary received a pension

SHAFFER, GEORGE (BLW), applied for a pension

SHAFFER/SHAVER, ISRAEL (BLW), and widow Polly both received a pension

SHAFFER, JACOB (BLW), applied for a pension

SHAMBAUGH, DANIEL (BLW), LNR DeKalb Co, MO, 1855

SHAMBAUGH, ISAAC (BLW), and widow Nancy both received a pension

SHANDS, AUGUSTINE whose widow Sarah C. applied for a pension

SHANK, GEORGE (P)

SHANK, JACOB whose widow Margaret received a pension

SHANK, PETER whose widow Ann Mary received a pension

SHANNON, BENJAMIN P. whose widow Mary applied for a pension

SHANNON, JOHN whose widow Margaret received a pension

SHARP, DAVID H. (P)

SHARP, JACOB L. whose widow Evaline L. received a pension

SHARP, JOHN (P, BLW)

SHARP, JOHN (BLW)

SHARRITTS, DANIEL whose widow Elizabeth received a pension
SHARTZER/SHATZER, JACOB (P)

ROLL NO. 84

SHAUHOLTZER, JACOB applied for a pension
SHAULL/SHAWL, DAVID and widow Mary both received a pension
SHAVEN, PETER and widow Nancy applied for a pension
SHAVER, GEORGE (BLW), whose widow Isabella received a pension
SHAVER, GEORGE (P, BLW)
SHAVER, JOHN (BLW), and widow Josina both received a pension
SHAVER, LEVI (BLW), whose widow Barbara received a pension
SHAVER, PETER (P, BLW)
SHAVER, WILLIAM (BLW), and widow Josina both received a pension
SHAW, CHARLES whose widow Jane received a pension
SHAW, JAMES whose widow Catharine received a pension
SHAW, JAMES whose widow Judy received a pension
SHAW, JAMES (P, BLW)
SHAW, WILLIAM and widow Edith both received a pension
SHAWEN, GEORGE W. applied for a pension
SHAWHAN, DAVID (BLW)
SHAWVER, JOHN (P)
SHAY, THOMAS whose widow Phebe A. received a pension
SHEALER/SHELER, JOHN applied for a pension
SHEAR, PHILLIP (P)
SHEARER, JAMES (P)
SHEETS, GEORGE (P)
SHEETS, GEORGE whose widow Mary applied for a pension
SHEETS, HENRY (P)

SHEETS, HENRY whose widow Elizabeth applied for a pension
SHEETS, JOHN whose widow Susan received a pension
SHEETZ, JOHN and widow Mary both received a pension
SHELBERN, PETTUS whose widow Mary J. received a pension
SHELDON/SHELDEN, JOHN applied for a pension
SHELDON, TRUMAN (P)
SHELL, GEORGE whose widow Elizabeth received a pension
SHELL, GEORGE W. whose widow Mary B. Roberts applied for a pension
SHELL, JOHN and widow Margaret both received a pension
SHELOR, JACOB whose widow Anna received a pension
SHELTON, ABRAHAM whose widow Anna received a pension
SHELTON, CHARLES IRBY whose widow Jane A. received a pension
SHELTON, GEORGE G. whose widow Lucinda applied for a pension
SHELTON, HUDSON and widow Lucy both received a pension
SHELTON, JAMES (BLW), whose widow was Frances S.
SHELTON, JOSEPH whose widow Matilda received a pension
SHELTON, LEWIS C./G. whose widow Jane B. received a pension
SHELTON, MACKEY whose widow Nancy received a pension
SHELTON, MERIT (P)
SHELTON, NOAH (P)
SHELTON, PETER R. whose widow Eleasure P. received a pension. Peter served in Capt. Tunstall Shelton's Company
SHELTON, RICHARD P. (P), served in Capt. Tunstall Shelton's company
SHELTON, ROBERT H. (P)
SHELTON, THOMAS L. (BLW), died 6 Jan 1859, Albemarle

SHELTON (continued)
Co, VA; md 10 Dec 1807
Susanna/Mary Susan Ballard
(P), Albemarle Co, VA. Her
LNR nr Mechum River, Albemarle Co, VA, 1871
SHELTON, VINCENT and widow
Nancy both received a pension.
Vincent served in Capt.
Tunstall Shelton's company
SHELTON, VINCENT H. (P)
SHELTON, WILLIAM and widow
Anna/Amy both received a pension
SHEPHERD, BENJAMIN whose
widow Susan E. received a pension
SHEPHERD, BYRD/BIRD (P)
SHEPHERD, EDWARD and widow Sarah both received a pension
SHEPHERD, WILLIAM whose
widow Martha G. received a pension
SHERLEY, JOSEPH whose widow
Eliza Ellett Shirley received a pension
SHERMAN, JESSE whose widow
Sallie received a pension
SHERMAN, THOMAS (BLW)
SHIELD, CHARLES H. whose widow Cornelia A. received a pension
SHIELD/SHIELDS, JOHN (P)
SHIELDS, JAMES whose widow
Jane applied for a pension
SHIELDS, PRESTON and widow
Delila both received a pension
SHIFFIELD, LEONARD whose
widow Lucy O. received a pension
S H I F F L E T / S H I F L E T T /
SHIFLET, MORDECAI applied
for a pension
S H I F F L E T / S H I F L E T, ST.
CLAIR (BLW), applied for a
pension
SHIFFLET, THOMAS (P)
SHIFFLET, WINSTON and widow
Mildred both received a pension
SHIFFLETT, MICAJAH whose

SHIFFLETT (continued)
widow Charlotte received a
pension
SHIFFLETT, THOMAS whose
widow Lucy received a pension
SHIFFLETT, WINSTON whose
former widow Mary Amiss applied for a pension
SHIFLET, JOHN and widow Eliza
both received a pension
SHIFLETT/SHIFFLETT, ARCHIBALD (P)
S H I F L E T T, BENNETT whose
widow Pollie received a pension
SHIFLETT, EDWARD whose widow Joice received a pension
SHIFLETT, NATHANIEL (BLW),
whose widow Elizabeth received a pension
SHILLINBURG/SHILLINGBURY,
HUGH (P)
S H I P, JAMES and widow Mary
Jane both received a pension
SHIP, MACK (P)
S H I P E, JOHN whose widow
Elizabeth received a pension
SHIPMAN, JOHN whose widow
Jane received a pension
SHIPP, JOHN (P, BLW)
SHIRK, ADAM (P)
S H I R K, HENRY whose widow
Rebecca received a pension
SHIRKEY, JOHN whose widow
Mary Shirkey/Sharkey received
a pension
SHIRLEY/SHYRAY, DANIEL (P)
SHIVELY, PHILIP (P)
S H I V E R D E C K E R / S C H O E N-
D E C K E R, LUKE and widow
Sally Shiverdecker both received a pension
SHOCKEY, BAZIL (P)
S H O E M A K E R, CHRISTIAN
whose widow Eve received a
pension
SHOEMAKER, JEREMIAH (P)
SHOEMAKER, JOHN whose widow Nancy received a pension
SHOEMAKER, LANDY (P)
SHOEMAKER, WILLIAM (P)
SHORE/SHOER, SIMON whose

SHORE (continued)
widow Susan applied for a pension

SHORES, WILSON whose widow Martha C. received a pension

SHORT, ANDERSON (P)

SHORT, CHARLES and widow Ruthia both received a pension

SHORT, FREDERICK whose widow Eliza received a pension

SHORT, GEORGE applied for pension

SHORT, JAMES (P)

SHORT, JAMES C. applied for a pension

SHORT, JOEL (P)

SHORT, THOMAS whose widow Jemina received a pension

SHOTWELL, JEREMIAH whose widow Sarah received a pension

SHOTWELL, LEWIS (BLW), whose widow Sedam applied for a pension

SHOWALTER, DAVID whose widow Agnes received a pension

SHOWALTER, HENRY whose widow Lydia received a pension

SHOWEN, HENRY (P)

SHRADER, JOHN whose widow Christina received a pension

SHRECK, CONRAD whose widow Catharine received a pension

SHREVE, DANIEL applied for a pension

SHREVES/SREVES, JACOB R. (P)

SHRIVER, JACOB (P)

SHUE, DANIEL (P)

SHUEY, DANIEL whose widow Elizabeth received a pension

SHUFFLEBARGER, JOHN whose widow Vina applied for a pension

SHULL, JACOB whose widow Margaret received a pension

SHULTZ, BENJAMIN applied for a pension

SHULTZ, GEORGE whose widow Rachel received a pension

SHUMAKER, JACOB and widow

SHUMAKER (continued)
Sarah both received a pension

SHUMATE, WILLIAM and widow Peggy T. both received a pension

SHY, EDWARD (P)

ROLL NO. 85

SIBERT, FREDERICK whose widow Margaret received a pension

SIBERT/SYBERT, JOSEPH (P)

SIBOLD, JAMES whose widow Lydia applied for a pension

SIBOLE, ICHABOD applied for a pension

SICKELS, BENJAMIN whose widow Hannah received a pension

SIDEBOTTOM, JOHN whose widow Elizabeth applied for a pension

SIDELS, FRANCIS whose widow Catherine applied for a pension

SILCOTT, WILLIAM whose widow Agnes received a pension

SILLINGS, DAVID and widow Nancy both received a pension

SILMAN, BENJAMIN P. whose widow Nancy received a pension

SIMMONS, DANIEL whose widow Katie received a pension

SIMMONS, DANIEL W. whose widow Rebecca received a pension

SIMMONS, DAVID whose widow Martha received a pension

SIMMONS, EPHRAIM (BLW), whose widow Ruth received a pension

SIMMONS, FREDERICK, SR. applied for a pension

SIMMONS, HENRY (P)

SIMMONS, JOHN T. whose widow Ann received a pension

SIMMONS, STEPHEN (P)

SIMMONS, THOMAS whose widow Theresa Ann received a pension

SIMMONS, WELTSHIRE (P)

SIMMS, HEZEKIAH whose widow

SIMMS (continued)
Caroline applied for a pension
SIMMS, JAMES L. (P)
SIMMS, JOHN (P)
SIMMS, JOHN H. whose widow
Martha A. received a pension
SIMMS, SILAS whose widow
Sarah L. received a pension
SIMPKINS, JOHN (P)
SIMPKINS, JOHN (P) whose wi-
dow Delilah received a pension
SIMPSON, ALFRED (P)
SIMPSON, ELCANIA/KAIN
whose widow Belama applied
for a pension
SIMPSON, DEMARCUS L. ap-
plied for a pension
SIMPSON, FRENCH (BLW),
whose widow was Ann
SIMPSON, FRENCH (BLW),
whose widow was Elizabeth
SIMPSON, JOHN applied for a
pension
SIMPSON, JOHN applied for a
pension
SIMPSON, JOHN whose widow
Henrietta received a pension
SIMPSON, JOHN M. (P)
SIMPSON, PRESLEY (P, BLW)
SIMPSON, SANFORD (BLW),
died May 1868, Knox Co, TN;
md 16 Jun 1812 Hope Poston
(P), Henry Co, VA. She died
28 Feb 1880 nr Knoxville, TN,
LNR Knox Co, TN, 1871
SIMPSON, SOLOMON B. applied
for a pension and widow
Patience received a pension
SIMPSON, WILLIAM applied for
a pension
SIMS, CHAPMAN whose widow
Sarah received a pension
SIMS, ROBERT T. (BLW), whose
widow was Harriet S.
SIMS, WILLIAM B. (P)
SINCLAIR, GEORGE B. (P)
SINCOX, JESSE (P)
SINES, HENRY (BLW), whose
widow Amanda A. received a
pension
SINGER, LEWIS whose widow
Jane F. received a pension

SINGLETON, DAVID whose widow Mary received a pension
SINGLETON, HAZZEL/HAZEL
whose widow Lavinia B. re-
ceived a pension
SINGLETON, HENRY whose wi-
dow Marsena received a pen-
sion
SINGLETON, JOHN whose widow
Joicey K. received a pension
SINGLETON, JOHN F. (BLW),
whose widow Lucinda received
a pension
SINGLETON, WASHINGTON G.
whose widow Maria A. applied
for a pension
SINKS/ZINK, PETER and widow
Mary Sinks both received a
pension
SINOR, JOHN whose widow Nancy
applied for a pension
SIPE, JACOB whose widow
Catharine applied for a pension
SIPPLE, HENRY applied for a
pension
SIRK, ABRAHAM whose widow
Mary Ann received a pension
SISEMORE, WILLIAM whose wi-
dow Anna applied for a pension
SISSON, BALDWIN L. whose wi-
dow Sarah A. E. applied for a
pension
SISSON, JOHN B. (P)
SISSON, ROBERT T. whose wi-
dow Nancy E. received a pen-
sion
SIZEMORE, ANDERSON whose
widow Margaret received a
pension
SIZEMORE, BIRD whose widow
Sarah Jane received a pension
SIZEMORE, THOMAS (P)
SIZER, JOHN (BLW), whose wi-
dow Elizabeth received a pen-
sion
SKELTON, MOSES (P)
SKIDMORE, JAMES whose widow
Elizabeth applied for a pension
SKIDMORE, SAMUEL (P)
SKINNER, PRICE (P)
SKINNER, WILLIAM whose wi-
dow Elizabeth applied for a

SKINNER (continued)
pension
SLACK, ABRAHAM (BLW), whose widow Maria applied for a pension
SLACK, JAMES applied for a pension
SLACK, JOHN whose widow Siggarina received a pension
SLACK, SIMON applied for a pension
SLAGLE, ABSALOM applied for a pension
SLAGLE, GEORGE and widow Mary both received a pension
SLATER, ANTHONY (P)
SLATER, JOHN whose widow Frances received a pension
SLATES, FREDERICK/FREDRICK whose widow Rebecca applied for a pension
SLAUGHTER, ANDREW D. (P)
SLAUGHTER, THOMAS (P)
SLAYDON/SLAYTON, WILLIAM (P)
SLOAN, DAVID and widow Catharine both received a pension
SLOAT, JOHN whose widow Rebecca received a pension
SLONE, JACOB and widow Elizabeth both received a pension
SLUSHER/SLUSSER, SOLOMON (P)
SLUSSER, PETER whose widow Mary received a pension
SMALLMAN, ALEXANDER and widow Nancy both received a pension
SMALLWOOD, GRIFFIN W. whose widow Delilah applied for a pension
SMALS/SMALTS, GEORGE (BLW), died 31 Aug 1850, Bridgewater, Rockingham Co, VA; md 24 Sep 1807 Catherine Rader (P), Rockingham Co, VA. Her LNR Bridgewater, VA, 1871
SMAW, DANIEL G. whose widow Ann W. received a pension
SMELL, PETER whose widow Hannah received a pension

SMELL, PHILIP (P)
SMILEY, JAMES whose widow Barbara received a pension

ROLL NO. 86

SMITH, ABRAHAM (P)
SMITH, AMOS (BLW), whose widow Eliza M. received a pension
SMITH, ANTHONY W. whose widow Ann M. received a pension
SMITH, ARCHER N. (P)
SMITH, AUSTIN H. whose widow (unnamed) received a pension
SMITH, BALLARD applied for a pension
SMITH, BRADFORD whose widow Nancy received a pension
SMITH, BURNLEY D. and widow Martha W. both received a pension
SMITH, DANIEL A. and widow Elizabeth both received a pension
SMITH, DAVID and widow Elizabeth both received a pension
SMITH, DUDLEY applied for pension
SMITH, ELIJAH whose widow Martha received a pension
SMITH, ELIJAH F. (P)
SMITH, ENOCH applied for a pension
SMITH, EPHRAIM W. whose widow Nancy received a pension
SMITH, EZEKIEL whose widow Mildred W. received a pension
SMITH, FIELDING whose widow Rhoda received a pension
SMITH, GARRETT/JARRETT whose widow Elizabeth received a pension
SMITH, GEORGE (P, BLW)
SMITH, GEORGE (P)
SMITH, GEORGE (P)
SMITH, GEORGE B. whose widow Polly received a pension
SMITH, GRIFFIN L. whose widow Sallie G. received a pension

SMITH, HENRY (P)

SMITH, HENRY and widow Elmina both received a pension

SMITH, HENRY (P, BLW)

SMITH, HENRY and widow Mary both received a pension

SMITH, HENRY C. whose widow Melissa received a pension

SMITH, HENRY applied for a pension

SMITH, HENRY M. (P)

SMITH, HENRY W. whose widow Elizabeth received a pension

SMITH, HEZEKIAH (P)

SMITH, ISAAC (P)

SMITH, ISAAC whose widow Julia A. received apension

SMITH, JACOB applied for a pension

SMITH, JACOB (P)

SMITH, JACOB whose widow Geneva Ann M. received a pension

SMITH, JAMES, USA, whose widow Ann received a pension. VA residence

SMITH, JAMES (P)

SMITH, JAMES (P)

SMITH, JAMES (BLW), whose widow Sarah received a pension

SMITH, JAMES (P)

SMITH, JAMES whose widow Elizabeth K. received a pension

SMITH, JAMES and widow Anna both received a pension

SMITH, JAMES W., USA and VA militia, and widow Elizabeth A. both received a pension

SMITH, JAMES whose widow Jane applied for a pension

SMITH, JAMES whose widow Sally applied for a pension

SMITH, JAMES R., DC and VA militia, applied for a pension

SMITH, JAMES W. whose widow Catharine K. received a pension

SMITH, JAMES W. whose widow Elizabeth S. received a pension

SMITH, JAREORRIGIN D. whose widow Mary G. received a pension

SMITH, JESSE whose widow Amy received a pension

SMITH, JOHN and widow Mary R. V. both received a pension

SMITH, JOHN whose widow Sarah received a pension

SMITH, JOHN (P)

SMITH, JOHN (P)

SMITH, JOHN (BLW), whose widow Elizabeth received a pension

SMITH, JOHN whose widow Elizabeth R. received a pension

SMITH, JOHN whose widow Rebecca K. received a pension

SMITH, JOHN whose widow Elizabeth applied for a pension

SMITH, JOHN whose widow Lucy applied for a pension

SMITH, JOHN whose widow Lucy received a pension

SMITH, JOHN whose widow Lucy received a pension

SMITH, JOHN and widow Catharine both received a pension

SMITH, JOHN B. whose widow Nellie received a pension

SMITH, JOHN H. (BLW), whose widow Elizabeth received a pension

SMITH, JOHN R. (P)

SMITH, JOHN R. whose widow Sarah S. received a pension

SMITH, JOHN S. applied for a pension

SMITH, JORDEN whose widow Lucinda received a pension

SMITH, JOSEPH alias DORMAN, ANDREW (served as substitute for Andrew Dorman in the War). LNR Council Grove, Morris Co, KS, 1879. Residence in Switzerland Co, IN, in 1851

SMITH, JOSEPH applied for a pension

SMITH, JOSHUA (P)

SMITH, JOSHUA and widow Mar-

SMITH (continued)
tha both received a pension
SMITH, LEANDER applied for a
pension
SMITH, LEVI and widow Doro-
thea both received a pension
SMITH, MATHIAS whose widow
Sinah received a pensoin
SMITH, MICHAEL whose widow
Susannah received a pension
SMITH, NATHAN whose widow
Elizabeth received a pension
SMITH, PETER (P)
SMITH, PETER (BLW), whose
widow Rachel received a pen-
sion
SMITH, PETER, SR. (P)
SMITH, PETER J. whose widow
Jane applied for a pension
SMITH, PHILIP whose widow
Polly received a pension
SMITH, RALPH whose widow
Viola received a pension
SMITH, RALPH whose widow
Barbara received a pension
SMITH, REUBEN whose widow
Elizabeth received a pension
SMITH, RICHARD whose widow
Martha A. received a pension
SMITH, RICHARD whose widow
Patsy Ann received a pension
SMITH, RICHARD L. whose wi-
dow Louisa received a pension
SMITH, ROBERT (BLW)
SMITH, ROBERT (BLW)
SMITH, ROBERT (BLW) whose
widow Polly received a pen-
sion
SMITH, ROBERT (BLW)
SMITH, ROBERT (BLW)
SMITH, ROBERT applied for a
pension
SMITH, ROBERT (BLW), whose
widow Catharine received a
pension
SMITH, ROBERT, JR. and widow
Martha S. both received a pen-
sion
SMITH, ROBERT N. applied for
a pension

ROLL NO. 87

SMITH, SAMPSON and widow
Elizabeth both received a pen-
sion
SMITH, SAMUEL (P)
SMITH, SAMUEL and widow
Eleanor both received a pen-
sion
SMITH, SAMUEL (P)
SMITH, SOLOMON (P)
SMITH, THOMAS whose widow
Mary P. received a pension
SMITH, THOMAS M. whose wi-
dow Cary Ann applied for a
pension
SMITH, WILLIAM whose widow
Martha received a pension
SMITH, WILLIAM applied for a
pension
SMITH, WILLIAM (P)
SMITH, WILLIAM applied for a
pension
SMITH, WILLIAM (P)
SMITH, WILLIAM whose widow
Agnes M. received a pension
SMITH, WILLIAM whose widow
Nancy H. received a pension
SMITH, WILLIAM (P)
SMITH, WILLIAM and widow
Polly both received a pension
SMITH, WILLIAM D. and widow
Delilah both received a pen-
sion
SMITH, WILLIAM L. whose wi-
dow Joicy R. received a pen-
sion
SMITH, WILLIAM P. whose wi-
dow Frances received a pen-
sion
SMITH, WILLIAM R. whose wi-
dow Lucy received a pension
SMITH, ZACHARIAH (P)
SMITHER/SMITHEY, EDMUND
(BLW), applied for a pension
SMITHERS, JOHN whose widow
Nancy applied for a pension
SMITHEY, WILLIAM and widow
Martha both received a pension
SMITHSON, HEZEKIAH P.
whose widow (unnamed) re-
ceived a pension
SMITHSON, WILLIAM whose
widow Elvira received a

SMITHSON (continued)
pension
SMITHY, THOMAS whose widow
Sallie received a pension
SMOCK, ESME whose widow
Sarah H. received a pension
SMURR, GEORGE applied for a
pension
SMYTH, JOHN (P)
SMYTHE, ALEXANDER H.
whose former widow Mary C.
Dodd applied for a pension
SNAPP, JOHN (P)
SNARR, JACOB whose widow
Magdalena received a pension
SNAVELY, JACOB received a
pension
SNEAD, CARY (BLW), whose wi-
dow Elizabeth M. received a
pension
SNEAD, JACOB whose widow
Polly received a pension
SNEAD, JOHN (P)
SNEAD, JOHN H. whose widow
Susan received a pension
SNEAD, WILLIAM (BLW)
SNEED, BENJAMIN (BLW),
whose widow Mary Jane re-
ceived a pension
SNEED, JAMES R. whose widow
Lucy received a pension
SNEED, MICAJAH whose widow
Rachel applied for a pension
SNELLING, SAMUEL whose wi-
dow Sarah applied for a pen-
sion
SNELLING, WILLIAM whose wi-
dow Elizabeth received a pen-
sion
SNELSON, JOHN (BLW), whose
widow Jemima received a pen-
sion
SNELSON, WILLIAM R. (P)
SNIDER, JACOB (P)
SNIDER, JAMES (BLW), and
widow Mary both received a
pension
SNIDER, JOHN (P)
SNIDER/SNYDER, LEVI whose
widow Abigail applied for a
pension
SNIDER, MICHAEL (BLW)

SNIDER/SNYDER, PRICE (P)
SNIDER, VALENTINE and widow
Harriet both received a pension
SNODGRASS, DAVID applied for a
pension
SNODGRASS, ROBERT whose wi-
dow Nancy received a pension
SNODGRASS, WILLIAM B.
(BLW), whose widow Mary ap-
plied for a pension
SNODY/SNODDY, WILLIAM
whose widow Virlinda Snoddy
applied for a pension
SNOW, LEWIS (BLW), died 4
Mar 1871, Albemarle Co, VA;
md 3 Jan 1811 Polly Dunn (P),
Albemarle Co, VA. Her LNR
Free Union, Albemarle Co,
VA, 1871
SNOWDEN, ISAAC (P, BLW)
SNYDER, JACOB and widow
Frances S. both received a
pension
SNYDER, JAMES (BLW), whose
widow was Sarah
SNYDER, JOHN (BLW), died 27
Apr 1847, Shepherdstown, VA;
md before 17 Feb 1815
Nancy/Ann Rightstine (P),
Shepherdstown, VA. She died
Dec 1874, LNR Shepherdstown,
WV, 1871
SNYDER/SNIDER, JOHN applied
for a pension and widow Hester
received a pension
SNYDER, JOSHUA whose widow
Elizabeth received a pension
SNYDER, WILLIAM K. and wi-
dow Henrietta both received a
pension
SOMERVILLE, SAMUEL (BLW),
died 4 Oct 1869, Robison
Township, Mason Co, WV; md
17 Oct 1811 Margaret Eckard
(P), Point Pleasant, VA. She
died 21 Nov 1884, LNR Robi-
son Township, Mason Co, WV,
1876
SOMMERVILLE, JAMES (BLW),
applied for a pension
SONGER, JOHN (P)
SOPHER, JAMES (P)

SORREL, REUBEN applied for a pension

SORRELL, JOHN whose widow Eliza received a pension

SORRELL, JOHN and widow Cassandra both received a pension

SORRELL, WILLIAM applied for a pension

SOTES, JOHN H. applied for a pension

SOURS, ADAM whose widow Sarah received a pension

SOUTHALL, CARY and widow Polly both received a pension

SOUTHALL, JOHN (BLW), died 13 Jul 1835, Richmond, Henrico Co, VA; md 28 Apr 1813 Phebe Harris (P), Richmond, VA. Her LNR Richmond, VA, 1872

SOUTHALL, JOHN T. (BLW). Residence in Sussex Co, VA, 1855

SOUTHALL, TURNER (BLW), whose widow Martha received a pension

SOUTHARD, LEWIS whose widow Mary received a pension

SOUTHERLAND, WILLIAM P. (BLW), died 10 Jun 1877; md Clementine A. (P). William lived in Linn Co, MO, 1855

SOWDER, DANIEL (BLW), whose widow was Martha

SOWERS, JACOB applied for a pension

SOWERS, JACOB whose widow Mary A. received a pension

SPAIN, RICHARD whose widow Lucy applied for a pension

SPAIN, ROYAL applied for a pension

SPAIN, WILLIAM, Sr. and widow Mary both received a pension

SPANGLER, CHARLES applied for a pension

SPANGLER, GEORGE applied for a pension and widow Sarah received a pension

SPANGLER, MICHAEL (P)

SPANGLER, SAMUEL (P)

SPARKS, REUBEN H. (BLW),

SPARKS (continued) died 15 Jul 1855, Jonesboro, TN; md 14 Sep 1807 Sarah L. McClellan (P), Blountville, TN. She died 21 Jun 1875, LNR Jonesboro, Washington Co, TN, 1871

SPARKS, THOMAS (P)

SPARR, SAMUEL (P)

SPARROW, LABAN whose widow Nancy received a pension

SPEAKER/SPRAHER/SPRAYER, JACOB whose widow Experience Speaker received a pension

SPEAKES, JAMES (BLW), whose widow Sarah Ann received a pension

SPEARS, JOHN whose widow Anna received a pension

SPEED, JOHN H. whose widow Susan M. received a pension

SPEELMAN, PETER whose widow Eva/Evan applied for a pension

SPEER, JOSHUA (P)

SPEER, ROBERT and widow Rebecca both received a pension

SPENCER, MANN whose widow Virginia received a pension

SPENCER, SAMUEL whose widow Nancy received a pension

SPENCER, SION G. (P)

SPENCER, THOMAS F. whose widow Emma received a pension

SPENCER, THOMAS J. whose widow Ann E. received a pension

SPENCER, JAMES (BLW), died 12 Feb 1837, Parkersburg, VA; md 20 Jan 1811 Mary Derrenberger (P), Bellville, Wood Co, VA. Her LNR Coolville, Athens Co, OH, 1871

SPENCER, JAMES, Sr. applied for a pension

SPENCER, JAMES and widow Sarah both received a pension

SPENCER, JOHN whose widow Delila received a pension

SPERRY, JOSEPH whose widow

SPERRY (continued)
Martha A. received a pension

SPIERS/SPIRES, ADAM whose
widow Polly W. received a
pension

SPIERS, JESSE whose widow
Martha received a pension

SPILLER, PATRICK (BLW),
whose widow was Louisa

SPILMAN, PHILIP J. whose
widow Mary received a pension

SPINDLE, DAVID whose widow
Mary received a pension

SPOONER, ALDEN B. whose widow M. W. received a pension

SPOTTS, EPHRAIM (P)

SPOTTS, JACOB whose widow
Mary A. received a pension

SPRADLING/SPALDING,
PLEASANT (P)

SPRAGINS, JOHN H. (P)

SPRAGINS, STITH B. whose widow Eliza A. applied for a
pension

SPRATLEY, BENJAMIN whose
widow Johanna received a pension

SPRATT, ISAAC (P, BLW)

SPRING, ADAM whose widow
Elizabeth applied for a pension

SPRING, CASPER whose widow
Elizabeth received a pension

SPRING, JOHN whose widow
Mary received a pension

SPRING, PETER whose widow
Mary received a pension

SPRINGER, JOB whose widow
(unnamed) received a pension

SPROUSE, JOHN (BLW), died 1
Apr 1848, Albemarle Co, VA;
md 2 Jul 1804 Rachel Wood
(P), Albemarle Co, VA. She
died 7 Jan 1875, LNR nr Charlottesville, VA, 1871

SPROUSE, ELIJAH (P)

SPROUSE, JAMES whose widow
Polly applied for a pension

SPROUSE, MARTIN and widow
Polly both received a pension

SPROUSE, PETER whose widow
Patsey received a pension

SPROUSE, TANDY (P)

SPURLOCK, BURWELL applied
for a pension. Captain of a
company of militia from
Cabell Co, VA

SQUIRES, ELIJAH whose widow
Elizabeth applied for a pension

SQUIRES, WILLIAM whose widow Catharine received a pension

STAFFORD, RALPH and widow
Polly both received a pension

STAFFORD, RALPH and widow
Margaret both received a pension

STAFFORD, WILLIAM whose
widow Jane received a pension

STAFFORD, WILLIAM whose
widow Lydia received a pension

STAINBACK, PETER W. (P)

STAIR, JOHN (P, BLW)

STALEY, JACOB applied for a
pension

STALLARD, JOSEPH B. (P)

STALNAKER, FERDINAND
whose widow Sarah received a
pension

STALNAKER, SAMUEL whose
widow Isabel received a pension

STAMPER, JAMES whose widow
Martha J. applied for a pension

STANFORTH, JAMES (P)

STANLEY, ABSALOM whose widow Elizabeth applied for a
pension

STANLEY, LUKE A. whose widow Tabitha received a pension

STANLEY, THOMAS (P)

STANLEY, WILLIAM M. whose
widow Elizabeth received a
pension

STAPLES, JAMES whose widow
Louisa received a pension

STAPLES, JOHN (BLW)

STARCHER, JOHN whose widow
Charity applied for a pension

STARKE, WILLIAM (BLW),

STARKE (continued)
whose widow Susan L. received a pension
STARKEY, GABRIEL whose widow Mary received a pension
STARKEY, ISAAC whose widow Sabina received a pension
STARKEY, JOHN whose widow Mary received a pension
STARKEY, JOHN and widow Nancy G. both received a pension
STARR, MOSES whose widow Sarah N. received a pension
STATEN, JOHN (P)
STATEN, WILLIAM (P)
STAYLEY/STALEY, DANIEL (BLW), whose widow Isabella Stayley received a pension
STEADMAN, JOHN (BLW), whose widow was Margaret
STEADMAN, THOMAS (BLW)
STEBAR, ISAAC (P)
STEED/STEAD, JOHN (P)
STEED, SION applied for a pension
STEEL, DORA HARRISON whose widow Mary applied for a pension
STEEL, GEORGE whose widow Nancy received a pension
STEELE, CHARLES, VA & DC militia, whose widow Ann W. received a pension
STEELE, JOHN HENRY alias STEEL, JOHN HARRY and widow Elizabeth both received a pension
STEELE, LEWIS whose widow Leah received a pension
STEELE, SAMUEL (P, BLW)
STEEPLE, JOHN W. (P)
STEFFY, JOSEPH whose widow Mary received a pension
STEGER, JOHN H. whose widow Sarah J. received a pension
STEGER, WILLIAM (BLW), whose widow Frances E. received a pension
STEP/STEPP/STOOP, JOHN whose widow Polly received a pension

STEPHENS, BRIANT and widow Harriet both applied for a pension
STEPHENS, DAVID whose widow Phebe applied for a pension
STEPHENS, GEORGE applied for a pension
STEPHENS, GEORGE whose widow Theodosia W. received a pension
STEPHENS, HENRY whose widow Mary A. received a pension
STEPHENS, HUGH (P)
STEPHENS, JACOB (P)
STEPHENS/STEVENS, JAMES P. whose widow Sally Stephens received a pension
STEPHENS, SILAS whose widow Mary received a pension
STEPHENS, WILLIAM whose widow Chloe Ann received a pension
STEPHENSON, JAMES and widow Mary both received a pension
STEPHENSON, JAMES (P)
STEPHENSON, JOHN and widow Mary both received a pension
STEPHENSON, JOHN whose widow Elizabeth received a pension
STEPHENSON, JOHN and widow Louisa G. both received a pension
STEPHENSON, JOHN G. (BLW)
STEPHENSON, JOSHUA whose widow Nancy received a pension
STEPHENSON, ROBERT whose widow Courteney Ann received a pension

ROLL NO. 89

STERLING, JOHN whose widow Ellen applied for a pension
STERLING/STALLIONS, THOMAS (P)
STEVENS, GEORGE whose widow Catherine applied for a pension
STEVENS, JACOB (P)

STEVENS, JAMES O. whose widow Elizabeth received a pension

STEVENS, JOHN applied for a pension

STEVENS, JOHN whose widow Elizabeth received a pension

STEVENS, JOHN W. (P)

STEVENS, SAMUEL whose widow Nancy received a pension

STEVENS, THOMAS (P). Served in Capt. J. B. Stevens company

STEVENS, WILLIAM (P)

STEVENS/STEPHENS, WILLIAM (P)

STEWART, JAMES (P)

STEWART, JOHN (BLW), died 23 Oct 1822, Warren Township, Washington Co, OH; md 31 Oct 1802 Susanna Hutchinson (P), Williamsport, Wood Co, VA. She died 15 Jan 1884, California, OH, LNR Columbus, Hamilton Co, OH, 1876

STEWART, JOHN (P)

STEWART, JOHN (P)

STEWART, JOSEPH whose widow Susan M. received a pension

STEWART, ROBERT (BLW)

STEWART, ROBERT (P)

STEWART, ROBERT whose widow Isabel received a pension

STICKEL/MICHAEL, SIMON applied for a pension

STICKELMAN, GEORGE whose widow Nancy received a pension

STICKLEY, GABRIEL whose widow Rebecca received a pension

STIFF, HENRY and widow Chaney both received a pension

STIGGLEMAN, PHILLIP (BLW), whose widow Susan received a pension

STILL, CLAIBORN whose widow Sally applied for a pension

STILL, CREED whose widow Elizabeth received a pension

STILL/STELL, JEREMIAH whose widow Sarah Still received a pension

STILL, JOHN (P, BLW)

STILLIONS/STALIONS, WILLIAM (P)

STINNETT, BENJAMIN (P)

STINNETT, RICHARD whose widow Elizabeth applied for a pension

STINSON, GEORGE (P)

STINSON, JAMES whose widow Julia A. received a pension

STINSON, STEPHEN whose widow Mazy Ann received a pension

STIVERS, EDWARD (BLW), whose widow Elizabeth B. received a pension

STOCKDALE, JOHN and widow Catharine both received a pension

STOCKDALE, ROBERT and widow Sally both received a pension

STOCKS/STALKS, WILLIAM (P, BLW)

STOKES, JOHN W. (BLW), whose widow Barbary received a pension

STONE, DANIEL (P)

STONE, DAVID applied for a pension

STONE, JACOB (P)

STONE, JAMES whose widow Susannah received a pension

STONE, JOEL applied for a pension

STONE, JOHN (BLW), whose widow Eliza Jane received a pension

STONE, JOHN whose widow Matilda received a pension

STONE, JOHN whose widow Susan received a pension

STONE, JOHN B. whose widow Susan Cemantha applied for a pension

STONE, SAMUEL whose widow Mary A. received a pension

STONE, SAMUEL whose widow Phebe H. received a pension

STONE, THOMAS S. whose widow Sarah A. received a pension
STONEBERGER, JOHN (P)
STONEBURNER, HENRY applied for a pension and widow Sarah received a pension
STONER, JOHN, Jr. applied for a pension
STONNELL, RICHARD (BLW)
STONNELL, VINCENT applied for a pension
STOOTS, WILLIAM whose widow Sally applied for a pension
STORER, BARTLET (P)
STORY, ZACHEUS whose widow Mary received a pension
STOTTS, JOHN whose widow Ruth applied for a pension
STOUT, HENRY and widow Kizziah both received a pension
STOUT, JAMES S. (P)
STOUT, JONATHAN A. whose widow Lucy W. received a pension
STOUT, SAMUEL (P)
STOVALL, WILLIAM (P)

ROLL NO. 90

STRAIN, EBENEZER (P)
STRAIT, WILLIAM (P)
STRALEY, JOHN (P)
STRANGE, GIDEON A. whose widow Mary B. received a pension
STRANGE, HENRY (P)
STRANGE, HUDSON whose widow Sally received a pension
STRANGE, JAMES (P)
STRANGE, JOHN whose widow Sarah received a pension
STRATON, JAMES and widow Harriet both received a pension
STREAM, JACOB whose widow Susannah received a pension
STREET, DANIEL whose widow Polly applied for a pension
STREET, WILLIAM N. whose widow Malinda received a pension
STRICKLAND/STRICKLING/STRICLING, JAMES B. (P)

STRICKLAND, JOSEPH whose widow Catherine received a pension
STRICKLER, JOSEPH applied for a pension
STRICKLING, JOSEPH (P)
STRIDER, SAMUEL whose widow Eliza Jane received a pension
STRINGFELLOW, JAMES (P)
STROBIA, JOHN H. (BLW), died 5 Oct 1860, Richmond, VA; md 10 Jun 1810 Ann Maria Lambert (P), Richmond, VA. Her LNR Richmond, VA, 1871
STROLE, JACOB whose widow Evy received a pension
STRONG, SAMUEL (BLW), whose former widow Elizabeth Cox applied for pension
STROSNIDER, JOHN applied for a pension and widow Rachel received a pension
STROTHER, BENJAMIN whose widow Nancy received a pension
STROTHER, JOHN whose widow Elizabeth received a pension
STROUP, PETER whose widow Elizabeth received a pension
STROUSE, DAVID whose widow Ann received a pension
STRUTHERS, JAMES (P, BLW)
STRUTTON, JOHN whose widow Elizabeth applied for a pension
STUART, ARCHIBALD whose widow Elizabeth L. received a pension
STUART, HENRY (P)
STUART, JAMES (P)
STUART/STEWART, JAMES (P)
STUART, JOHN (P)
STUART, JOHN R. whose widow Lucy M. received a pension
STUART, LEWIS (BLW), whose widow Maria H. received a pension
STUART, WILLIAM applied for pension
STUBBLEFIELD, GEORGE W. (P), LNR Jackson Co, MO, 1871. Wife Nancy Riggs was deceased in 1871

291

STUBBLEFIELD, THOMAS L. whose widow Mary applied for a pension

STUCKEY, JACOB whose widow Nancy received a pension

STUCKEY/STOCKEY, SAMUEL and widow Margaret C. Stuckey both received a pension

STULL, HENRY whose widow Rebecca G. applied for a pension

STURDIVANT, GEORGE (P)

STURM, HENRY (BLW), whose widow Susan received a pension

STUTLER, ELIAS whose widow Rebecca received a pension

SUBLETT, JOSEPH and widow Nancy both received a pension

SUBLETT, WILLIAM and widow Mary both received a pension

SUDDARTH, JAMES whose widow Elizabeth received a pension

SUDDATH, HENRY applied for a pension

SUDDITH, JOHN B. applied for a pension

SUDSBURY, JOSEPH whose widow Frances received a pension

SULLIVAN, BENJAMIN whose widow Lucy applied for a pension

SULLIVAN, DANIEL V., NC, GA, or VA militia, whose widow Eilzabeth A. applied for a pension

SULLIVAN, FRANCIS B. whose widow Frances received a pension

SULLIVAN, JEREMIAH and widow Frances both received a pension

SULLIVAN, JOHN whose widow Jane received a pension

SULLIVAN, JOHN (P)

SULLIVAN, MARMION whose widow Susan received a pension

SULLIVAN, RODNEY (P)

SULLIVAN, SPENCER S. whose widow Mary M. received a

SULLIVAN (continued) pension

SULLIVAN, WILLIAM (BLW)

SULLIVANT, JOHN whose widow Cordelia received a pension

SUMMERFIELD, DAVID (P)

SUMMERS, ANDREW J. whose widow Phebe Ann received a pension

SUMMERS, DAVID whose widow Margaret received a pension

SUMMERS, GEORGE whose widow Elizabeth applied for a pension

SUMMERS, JOHN (P)

SUMMERS, RICHARD, USA, applied for a pension. Residence in VA

SUMMERSON, WILLIAM (P)

SUMNER, MARK whose widow Lucy received a pension

SUMNER, NEHEMIAH whose widow Mary A. received a pension

SUMNER, OWEN whose widow Lucinda applied for a pension

SUMNER, WILLIAM whose widow Catharine received a pension

SUTHARD, WILLIAM (BLW), and widow Elizabeth H. both received a pension

SUTHERS/ELLERS, JAMES applied for a pension

SUTPHIN, HENRY whose widow Mary received a pension

SUTPHIN, OWEN and widow Sarah both received a pension

SUTTENFIELD, JAMES (BLW), whose widow Cynthia received a pension

SUTTLE, FRANCIS whose widow Lucy received a pension

SUTTLE, JOHN (P)

SUTTON, FRANCIS/FRANS V. (P)

SUTTON, NORBORNE E. and widow Mary Jane both received a pension

SWALLOM, GEORGE and widow Phoebe both received a pension

292

SWALLOM, HENRY (P)
SWALLUM, JOHN (P)
S W A N , GEORGE whose widow Nancy received a pension
SWANN, JEFFERSON whose widow Martha B. received a pension
SWANSON, WILLIS (BLW), died 2 Sep 1823 or 1 Sep 1829, Harrisonburg, VA; md 7 Feb 1812 Mary Breedlove (P), Rockingham Co, VA. She died 28 Dec 1881, LNR Harrisonburg, Rockingham Co, VA, 1871
S W A R T , WILLIAM R. whose widow Elizabeth applied for a pension
SWARTZ, CHRISTIAN whose widow Mary applied for a pension
SWATZ/SWATS, JOHN (P)
SWECKER/SWICHARD, BENJAMIN (P)
SWEENEY, HENRY (BLW), and widow Elizabeth both received a pension
SWEPSTON, JOHN A. (P, BLW)
SWIFT, EDMUND (P, BLW)
SWIFT, WILLIAM whose widow Eliza A. received a pension
SWIGER, JERIAH applied for a pension
S W I G E R , JESSE whose widow Cassa applied for a pension
SWINDLER, CLAITON (BLW), whose widow Lucy received a pension
S W I N K , ENOS whose widow Rachael M. received a pension
SWINK, JOHN and widow Sarah both received a pension
SWINK, WILLIAM whose widow Margaret received a pension
SWISHER, JACOB whose widow Catharine received a pension
S W I S H E R , JACOB and widow Margaret both received a pension
SWISHER, SOLOMON (P)
SWISHER/SWITZER, STEPHEN and widow Rebecca Swisher both received a pension
S W O R D , HENRY applied for a

SWORD (continued)
pension
SWORD, JOHN and widow Margaret both received a pension
SWORDS, WILLIAM (P)
SYDNOR, RICHARD H. (P)
S Y D N O R , RICHARD M. whose widow Mary Ann received a pension
SYDNOR, WILLIAM (P)
SYFERD, PHILIP (P)
S Y L O R , PETER H. and widow Sarah both received a pension
SYMPSON, CARRINGTON whose widow Decy received a pension
SYMS, JOHN (P)
SYRON, NATHANIEL (P)

ROLL NO. 91

TABB, PHILIP M. whose widow Martha T. received a pension
T A B O R , DANIEL whose widow Mary received a pension
TACKETT, ENOCH (P)
TACKETT, JOHN W. (BLW), and widow Irena both received a pension
T A D E , JOSEPH applied for a pension
TALBOTT, JOHN whose widow Permelia received a pension
TALIAFERRO, HAY whose widow Rebecca Seymour Taliaferro received a pension
T A L I A F E R R O , LAWRENCE whose widow Eliza received a pension
TALLEY, BILLY whose widow Elizabeth received a pension
TALLEY, JOSEPH whose widow Sarah D. received a pension
T A L L E Y , LARKIN and widow Nancy both received a pension
TALLEY, PEYTON whose widow Holly received a pension
TALLEY, WILLIAM and widow Stacey both applied for a pension
TALMAN, JOHN and widow Sarah both received a pension
TANKERSLEY, REUBEN whose

293

TANKERSLEY (continued)
widow Cynthia received a pension
TANNER, BENJAMIN whose widow Lucy received a pension
TANNER, BIRD L. whose widow Eunice applied for a pension
TANNER, JOEL H. (P)
TANNER, JOHN O. applied for a pension and widow America received a pension
TANNER, MICHAEL whose widow Margaret received a pension
TANNER, THOMAS and widow Judith both received a pension
TAPPERMAN, JOHN applied for a pension
TAPPEY, JAMES (P)
TARGGRET, HUGH whose widow Nancy applied for a pension
TARLTON, KALBY/KELVEY alias KALBY, TARLTON (P)
TARMAN, GEORGE W. (BLW), whose widow Mary received a pension
TARPLEY, WILLIAM H./HENRY applied for a pension
TARR, DANIEL (P)
TARR, JOHN S. and widow Eliza both received a pension
TARRANT, RICHARD, USA, whose widow Elizabeth received a pension. Residence in VA
TASKER, RADDY (P)
TATE, HENRY F. and widow Minnie both received a pension
TATE, JOSEPH (BLW), died 26 Apr 1841, Hampshire Co, VA; md 2 Jan 1811/12 Margaret Horn (P), Winchester, VA. She died 31 Apr 1883, Palmyra, OH, LNR Marion Co, MO, 1871
TATE, NATHANIEL whose widow Lucy received a pension
TATE, WADDY and widow Mary both received a pension
TATE, WILLIAM L. and widow Nancy both received a pension
TATSAPAUGH, HENRY, DC mi-

TATSAPAUGH (continued)
litia, whose widow Margaret received a pension
TATUM, THOMAS received a pension and widow Mary Ann applied for a pension
TAULBEE, JAMES whose widow Elizabeth applied for a pension
TAYLOR, ALLEN (P)
TAYLOR, AMANDRAS whose widow Eliza Ann applied for a pension
TAYLOR, ANDREW and widow Martha both received a pension
TAYLOR, BENJAMIN and widow Elizabeth both received a pension
TAYLOR, CHRISTOPHER C. applied for a pension
TAYLOR, DANIEL whose widow Louisa B. received a pension
TAYLOR, DANIEL and widow Jane both received a pension
TAYLOR, DAVID PRESTON (P, BLW)
TAYLOR, EDMOND (P)
TAYLOR, EDMOND/EDMUND (P)
TAYLOR, EDMUND G. whose widow Nancy received a pension
TAYLOR, FRANCIS G. (P)
TAYLOR, GEORGE whose widow Hennie P. received a pension
TAYLOR, GEORGE whose widow Elizabeth B. received a pension
TAYLOR, GEORGE W. whose widow Fanny received a pension
TAYLOR, HENRY whose widow Catharine applied for a pension
TAYLOR, JAMES whose widow Elizabeth applied for a pension
TAYLOR, JAMES whose widow Dosha received a pension
TAYLOR, JAMES whose widow Sofa applied for a pension
TAYLOR, JAMES whose widow Permelia received a pension
TAYLOR, JAMES whose widow Tabetha applied for a pension
TAYLOR, JAMES D. whose wi-

TAYLOR (continued)
dow Nancy received a pension
TAYLOR, JESSE whose widow
Nancy received a pension
TAYLOR, JOEL (P)
TAYLOR, JOHN (BLW), whose
widow was Polly/Mary Ann
TAYLOR, JOHN (P)
TAYLOR, JOHN (P, BLW) was a
substitute for his brother William in the War
TAYLOR, JOHN (BLW), whose
widow was Nancy
TAYLOR, JOHN (BLW), whose
widow Elizabeth applied for a
pension
TAYLOR, JOHN and widow Mary
both received a pension
TAYLOR, JOHN whose widow
Mary E. received a pension
TAYLOR, JOHN whose widow
Sarah applied for a pension
TAYLOR, JORDAN (P)
TAYLOR, JOSEPH and widow
Mary both received a pension
TAYLOR, LUDY whose widow
Elizabeth S. received a pension
TAYLOR, MARK and widow Elizabeth P. both received a pension
TAYLOR, MICHAEL whose widow Sarah applied for a pension
TAYLOR, NATHANIEL whose
widow Martha received a pension
TAYLOR, NICHOLAS H. applied
for a pension
TAYLOR, NIMROD (P)
TAYLOR, SAMUEL whose widow
Elizabeth C. received a pension
TAYLOR, SAMUEL (P)
TAYLOR, SAMUEL (P, BLW),
LNR Roane Co, TN, 1871; md
4 Sep 1816 Elizabeth S. Dickey
TAYLOR, SAMUEL whose widow
Emily received a pension
TAYLOR, SAMUEL N. whose widow Kerziah applied for a pension

TAYLOR, TARLTON (P)
TAYLOR, THOMAS whose widow
Mary Ann received a pension
TAYLOR, THOMAS (P)
TAYLOR, THOMAS L. and widow
Sally McC. both received a
pension
TAYLOR, THOMAS O. applied for
a pension
TAYLOR, THORNTON (P)
TAYLOR, TIMOTHY whose widow Harriet B. received a pension
TAYLOR, WILLIAM (P)
TAYLOR, WILLIAM applied for a
pension
TAYLOR, WILLIAM whose widow Susannah Glenn applied
for a pension
TAYLOR, WILLIAM whose widow Mary received a pension
TAYLOR, WILLIAM whose widow Lucy P. received a pension
TEAFORD, JACOB and widow
Sophia Catharine both received
a pension
TEANEY, DANIEL (P)
TEANEY, MILES whose widow
Eve received a pension
TEMPLETON, DAVID (P)
TEMPLETON, JOHN I. whose
widow Sarah applied for a pension
TENISON/TENNISON,
SHADRACH (P)
TENNANT/TENNENT/TENENT,
ABRAHAM (P)
TENNANT, JACOB (P)
TENNANT, JOSEPH (P, BLW)
TENNANT, WILLIAM (BLW)
TENNIS, JOSEPH received a pension and widow Mary applied
for a pension
TENNIS, RICHARD (BLW)
TERRELL, ALFRED whose widow Frances C. received a
pension
TERRELL, JOHN whose widow
Mary J. received a pension
TERRELL, JOHN (P)
TERRELL, RICHARD (P)

TERRELL, WILLIAM and widow Mary Ann both received a pension

TERRELL, JOHN and widow Elizabeth E. both received a pension

TERRY, CHAMPION and widow Jane both received a pension

TERRY, ELISHA whose widow Margaret applied for pension

TERRY, HENRY whose widow Sarah received a pension

TERRY, JAMES whose widow Elizabeth W. received a pension

TERRY, JAMES whose widow Sarah received a pension

TERRY, JAMES A. (P)

TERRY, JOSEPH R. and widow Bethena both received a pension

TERRY, ROYAL (P)

TERRY, THOMAS whose widow Elizabeth applied for a pension

TERRY, THOMAS R. (P)

TERRY, WILLIAM (P)

TERRY, WILLIAM whose widow Elizabeth received a pension

THACKER, AMOS (P)

THACKER, CHESLEY whose widow Polly/Mary applied for a pension

THACKER, EMANUEL E. (P)

THACKER, JOEL (BLW)

THACKER, JOHN whose widow Abigail applied for a pension

THACKER, PLEASANT and widow Sarah G. both received a pension

THACKER, WILLIAM whose widow Sarah applied for a pension

THACKSTON, FRANCIS (P)

THACKSTON, JAMES whose widow Mary S. received a pension

THACKSTON, JOHN whose widow Martha H. received a pension

THARP, ISAAC applied for a pension

THARP, JAMES whose widow

THARP (continued) Nancy received a pension

THARP, JESSE whose widow Elizabeth received a pension

THARPE, WILLIAM whose widow Susanna received a pension

THATCHER, EVAN (BLW), and widow Rachel both received a pension

THATCHER, HADEN/HAYDEN/ HADDAM whose widow Vilinda applied for a pension

THAXTON, BENJAMIN D. whose widow Malinda L. received a pension

ROLL NO. 92

THOMAS, ALLEN whose widow Maria applied for a pension

THOMAS, ARCHIBALD whose widow Catharine received a pension

THOMAS, ARCHIBALD whose widow Catherine E. received a pension

THOMAS, ARCHIBALD (BLW), whose widow Sarah received a pension

THOMAS, BENJAMIN (BLW), whose widow Lucy received a pension

THOMAS, CHARLES whose widow Elizabeth M. received a pension

THOMAS, CHARLES and widow Lottie both received a pension

THOMAS, DAVID whose widow Susan received a pension

THOMAS, DAVID whose widow Lucy received a pension

THOMAS, EDWARD (P)

THOMAS, EDWARD (P)

THOMAS, EDWARD whose widow Frances received a pension

THOMAS, HARRISON M. whose widow Margaret Helen received a pension

THOMAS, ISAAC (BLW), whose widow Jemima received a

THOMAS (continued)
pension
THOMAS, JACOB and widow
Sarah both received a pension
THOMAS, JAMES whose widow
Polly received a pension
THOMAS, JAMES whose widow
Nancy received a pension
THOMAS, JAMES (BLW), whose
widow Elizabeth received a
pension
THOMAS, JAMES whose widow
Mary Ann S. received a pension
THOMAS, JAMES (P)
THOMAS, JAMES and widow
Jane both received a pension
THOMAS, JESSE whose widow
Mahala received a pension
THOMAS, JESSE whose widow
Rebecca received a pension
THOMAS, JOHN whose widow
Catharine received a pension
THOMAS, JOHN applied for a
pension
THOMAS, JOHN (P)
THOMAS, JOHN B. whose widow
Catharine S. received a pension
THOMAS, JOHN R. whose widow
Sophia received a pension
THOMAS, JOHN W. and widow
Margaret E. both received a
pension
THOMAS, JONATHAN (P)
THOMAS, KEMP whose widow
Nancy received a pension
THOMAS, LEWIS whose widow
Nancy received a pension
THOMAS, LEWIS whose widow
Ann received a pension
THOMAS, MERIWEATHER
F./J. (BLW)
THOMAS, PASCAL (P)
THOMAS, REUBEN whose widow
Rachel applied for a pension
THOMAS, RICHARD whose wi-
dow Matilda recieved a ˈ pen-
sion
THOMAS, SAMUEL whose widow
Margaret M. received a pen-
sion

THOMAS, SAMUEL whose widow
Susan received a pension
THOMAS, SAUL applied for a
pension
THOMAS, SIMEON C. whose
widow Elizabeth received a
pension
THOMAS, STITH whose widow
Rebecca J. received a pension
THOMAS, THOMAS and widow
Sirena C. both received a pen-
sion
THOMAS, WARNER whose wi-
dow Mary A. received a pen-
sion
THOMAS, WILLIAM whose wi-
dow Fanny C. applied for a
pension
THOMAS, WILLIAM and widow
Amanda J. both received a
pension
THOMAS, WILLIAM (P, BLW)
THOMAS, WILLIAM (P)
THOMAS, WILLIAM (P)
THOMAS, WILLIAM whose wi-
dow Biddy received a pension
THOMAS, WILLIAM N. (P)
THOMAS, YOUNGER whose wi-
dow Judiah received a pension
THOMER/TOMAW, MOSES (P)
THOMPSON, CAREY (P)
THOMPSON, CHARLES WIL-
LIAM whose widow Cynthia
Ann received a pension
THOMPSON, GEORGE W. and
widow Fannie both received a
pension
THOMPSON, HORATIO whose
widow Lucy applied for a pen-
sion
THOMPSON, ISRAEL whose wi-
dow Lucretia received a pen-
sion
THOMPSON, JAMES applied for
a pension
THOMPSON, JAMES whose wi-
dow Catharine received a pen-
sion
THOMPSON, JAMES P. (P,
BLW)
THOMPSON, JOHN whose widow
Cynthia received a pension

THOMPSON, JOHN (P)

THOMPSON, JOHN E. whose widow Rachel Amanda received a pension

THOMPSON, JOSEPH whose widow Mahala received a pension

THOMPSON, JOSIAH whose widow Margaret received a pension

THOMPSON, PYRANT (BLW), and widow Jane both received a pension

THOMPSON, RANDOLPH whose widow Mary W. applied for a pension

THOMPSON, RAWLEY whose widow Ann D. received a pension

THOMPSON, SAMUEL and widow Ann both received a pension

THOMPSON, VINCENT (BLW), whose widow was Mary

THOMPSON, WADDY (P)

THOMPSON, WILLIAM (P)

THOMPSON, WILLIAM whose widow Nancy received a pension

THOMPSON, WILLIAM (BLW), whose widow Elizabeth received a pension

THOMPSON, WILLIAM whose widow Mary received a pension

THOMPSON, WILLIAM (BLW), and widow Nancy both received a pension

THOMPSON, WILLIAM E. (P)

THOMPSON, WILLIAM S. whose widow Avis O. received a pension

THOM, JOB and widow Tamsy Jane both received a pension

THORNBERRY, DANIEL (BLW), and widow Frances both received a pension

THORNBURG, DAVID applied for a pension

THORNHILL, BRYANT whose widow Rachel applied for a pension

THORNHILL, JAMES (BLW), whose widow Polly received a

THORNHILL (continued) pension

THORNHILL, THOMAS P. applied for a pension

THORNHILL, THOMAS J. whose widow Agnes received a pension

THORNHILL, THOMAS W. whose widow Martha received a pension

THORNHILL/THORNELL, WILLIAM whose widow Jeanette C. Thornhill received a pension

THORNIBY/THORNLEY/THORNILEY, JOHN (BLW), OH militia, died 17 Aug 1844 Marietta Township, Washington Co, OH; md 10 Jul 1810 Mary/Polly Compton (P), Wood Co, VA. She died c1875, LNR Marietta, OH, 1871

THORNTON, CHARLES whose widow Elizabeth received a pension

THORNTON, FRANCIS (P)

THORNTON, FRANCIS (P)

THORNTON, JOHN whose widow Nancy received a pension

THORNTON, JOHN H. whose widow Nancy received a pension

THORNTON, JOSEPH (P)

THORNTON, PHILIP whose widow Caroline H. received a pension

THORP, JAMES (BLW), USA. Residence in VA

THRASHER, ELIAS (P)

THRIFT, DAVID (P)

THRUSH/THRASH, ANDREW applied for a pension

THURMOND, ELISHA (BLW), and widow Letitia both received a pension

THURSTON, GEORGE W. whose widow Ruth Nancy received a pension

THURSTON, WILLIAM R. whose widow Polly received a pension

THWEATT, PHILIP B. (BLW)

TIBBS, JACOB whose widow Nancy Jane received a pension

TICE/TIES, MANASSAH whose widow Cynthia Tice applied for a pension

TICHNOR, AARON (P)

TILL, WILLIAM whose widow Libby received a pension

TILLETT, ERASMUS G. whose widow Martha G. received a pension

TILLETT, SAMUEL and widow Pleasant both received a pension

TILLETT, SAMUEL G. and widow Elizabeth both received a pension

TILLMAN, EMANUEL (BLW)

TILMAN, THOMAS W. (BLW), whose widow Teresa received a pension

TIMMS, JOHN whose widow Nancy received a pension

TIMMS, JOHN D. and widow Hannah both received a pension

ROLL NO. 93

TINDALL, POWHATAN BOLLING (P)

TINDER, EPHRAIM applied for a pension

TINDER, JAMES (BLW), and widow Emily both received a pension

TINDER, STEPHEN (P)

TINGLE, JACOB (BLW), whose widow Barbara received a pension

TINKER, JOHN H. whose widow Mary A. applied for a pension

TINSLEY, ANDERSON whose widow Scynthia received a pension

TINSLEY, BENNETT whose widow Parmelia received a pension

TIPTON, JOSEPH whose widow Rebecca received a pension

TIPTON, JOSHUA (P)

TISDALE, DAVID whose widow Maria D. received a pension

TITCOMB, WILLIAM B. whose widow Abigail received a pension

TITMARSH, ROBERT whose widow Nancy applied for a pension

TODD, ANDREW (P)

TODD, BENJAMIN (P)

TOLBERT, CHARLES (BLW)

TOLER, HOPEFUL whose widow Ann Atkinson Toler received a pension

TOLER, JAMES (P)

TOLLEY, EZEKIEL whose widow Mary received a pension

TOLLEY, WILLIAM whose widow Elizabeth received a pension

TOLSON, BENJAMIN (P)

TOMBLIN, THOMAS whose widow Ann received a pension

TOMBLINSON/TOMLIN, WILLIAM whose widow Elizabeth Tomblinson received a pension

TOMBLISON, HENRY whose widow Catherine received a pension

TOMERSON, ARTHUR whose widow Caroline M. received a pension

TOMLINSON, NATHANIEL whose widow Margaret applied for a pension

TONEY, EDMUND (P)

TONEY, WILLIAM (BLW), died 31 Mar 1865, Powhatan Co, VA; md 10 Sep 1806 Clarkey Jones (P), Powhatan Co, VA. She died 26 Apr 1874, LNR Powhatan Co, VA, 1871

TOOL, ADAM (P)

TOOMBS, CHARLES (P)

TOOMIRE, JOHN (BLW), whose widow Sarah received a pension

TOOTHMAN, JOHN whose widow Betsy applied for a pension

TOSH/DOSH, GEORGE and widow Lucy Tosh both received a pension

TOTTY, THOMAS whose widow Dorothy received a pension

TOTTY/TOLTY, THOMAS T. and widow Frances both received a pension

TOUCHSTONE, SAMPSON (P)

TOWELL, HENRY whose widow Cynthia S. received a pension

TOWLER, JAMES and widow Sally L. both received a pension

TOWLER, JOHN whose widow Sarah received a pension

TOWLER/TOLER, WILLIAM whose widow Abigail received a pension

TOWLES, HENRY (P)

TOWLES, OLIVER (P, BLW)

TOWNER, JAMES whose widow Harriet C. received a pension

TOWNES, STEPHEN C. and widow Sarah both received a pension

TOWNES, WILLIAM (P)

TOWNLEY, KALITA B. whose widow Mary Jane received a pension

TOWNSEND, ORSTON/CLEMENTS whose widow Mary received a pension

TOWNSEND, THOMAS and widow Mary both received a pension

TOWNSEND, WILCHEN J. L. whose widow Jane applied for a pension

TRACY, BENJAMIN (P)

TRACY, EVERIT (P)

TRADER, PARKER (P)

TRAIL, WILLIAM applied for a pension

TRAINUM, COLEMAN whose widow Sarah received a pension

TRAMMEL, JAMES (P)

TRANBARGER/TRANBOYER, DAVID whose widow Christena Tranbarger applied for a pension

TRAVIS, WILLIAM L. whose widow Mary A. received a pension

TRAYLOR, ARCHER (BLW), whose widow was Martha A.

TRAYLOR (continued) Stowe

TRAYLOR, BEDFORD whose widow Sophia received a pension

TRENNER, JACOB (P)

TRENT, ALEXANDER (BLW)

TRENT, B. B. whose widow Sarah applied for a pension

TRENT, JOHN whose widow Mary Thompson received a pension

TRESSLAR, JOHN applied for a pension

TREVEY, JOSEPH Y. whose widow Rebecca received a pension

TREVILLIAN, GIDEON C. (P)

TREZVANT, THEODORE whose widow Martha D. received a pension

TRIAL, JOHN G. whose widow Elizabeth received a pension

TRIBBEY, GEORGE (P)

TRIBBLE, GEORGE applied for a pension and widow Margaret received a pension

TRIBLE, JAMES whose widow Mary Ann received a pension

TRICE, THOMAS J. (P)

TRIMBLE, JOHN (BLW)

TRIMBLE, JOSEPH (BLW)

TRIMMER, OBEDIAH whose widow Elizabeth received a pension. Obediah was born in Hanover Co, VA, and enlisted at Richmond. Residence in TX

TRINKLE, STEPHEN whose widow Sarah applied for a pension

TRIPLETT, BURR and widow Eliza Ann both received a pension

TRIPLETT, NATHANIEL whose widow Susan applied for a pension

TRIPLETT, SINNETT (BLW), whose widow Elizabeth R. received a pension

TRIPLETT, WILLIAM H. (P)

TRIPLETT, WILLIS F. whose widow Rachel G. received a pension

TRIPETT, CALEB whose widow Elizabeth received a pension. Residence in WV

TROTT, HENRY whose widow Nancy received a pension

TROUT, ANTHONY and widow Ann E. both received a pension

TROUT, ISAAC applied for a pension

TROUT, JOHN (P)

TROUT, JOSEPH (BLW), died 26 Mar 1850, Port Republic, Rockingham Co, VA; md 24 Dec 1812 Sarah Whitesides (P), Staunton, Augusta Co, VA. She died 15 Aug 1873, LNR Port Republic, VA, 1871

TRUE, JAMES H. (BLW), applied for a pension and widow Nancy Ann received a pension

TRUE, JAMES M. applied for a pension

TRUMAN, JOHN R. (P) whose widow was Nancy

TRUMAN/TRUEMAN, THOMAS and widow Elizabeth both received a pension

TRUMBO, MATHIAS (P)

TUCK, GEORGE W. applied for a pension

TUCK, JAMES whose widow Nancy applied for a pension

TUCK, MOSES and widow Mary both received a pension

TUCK, THOMAS whose widow Jane received a pension

TUCKER, BERRYMAN T. whose widow Frances applied for a pension

TUCKER, CREED H. whose widow Luvina received a pension

TUCKER, ELI B. (P)

TUCKER, GEORGE whose widow Polly received a pension

TUCKER, GEORGE whose widow Lucy received a pension

TUCKER, GEORGE whose widow Sally O. applied for a pension

TUCKER, JOEL applied for a pension

TUCKER, JOHN whose widow Sallie/Sally received a pension

TUCKER, JOHN (P)

TUCKER, JOSEPH J. G. and widow Louisa R. both received a pension

TUCKER, RICHARD and widow Nancy both received a pension

TUCKER, THOMAS (P)

TUCKER, WILLIAM (BLW), died 31 Aug 1846, Amelia Co, VA; md 22 Oct 1832 Elizabeth Perkinson (P), Amelia Co, VA. Her LNR Chesterfield Co, VA, 1855. Elizabeth was also pensioned as widow of Rowlett Gill of VA

TUCKER, WILLIAM whose widow Emily received a pension

TUCKER, WILLIAM whose widow Permela W. received a pension

TUCKER, WILLIAM E. applied for a pension

TUDOR, LEWIS whose widow Charlotte received a pension

TUGGLE, WILLIAM WALKER applied for a pension

TUNE, JOHN P. and widow Jinnie both received a pension

TUNE, LEWIS (P)

TUNING, WILLIAM applied for a pension

TUNSTILL, STOKES (P)

ROLL NO. 94

TURLEY, SAMPSON (P)

TURLEY, SAMPSON (P)

TURLINGTON, LEVIN whose widow Elizabeth received a pension

TURNER, BENJAMIN whose widow Catharine A. received a pension

TURNER, DANIEL whose widow Mary A. received a pension

TURNER, GEORGE applied for a pension

TURNER, HENRY whose widow Agnes C. received a pension

TURNER, JAMES whose widow Polly T. applied for a pension

TURNER, JAMES (P)

TURNER, JAMES whose widow Elizabeth L. received a pension

TURNER, JOHN (P)

TURNER, JOHN B. and widow Mary Frances both received a pension

TURNER, JOHN B. whose widow Almira received a pension

TURNER, JOSEPH (P, BLW)

TURNER, LEMUEL (P)

TURNER, LEWIS whose widow Jemima received a pension

TURNER, LEWIS whose widow Lucretia applied for a pension

TURNER, LEWIS (P)

TURNER, LITTLEBERRY whose widow Mary Ann received a pension

TURNER, SAMUEL whose widow Matilda received a pension

TURNER, SHORES P. whose widow Adelphi received a pension

TURNER, SMITH whose widow Nancy received a pension

TURNER, STEPHEN whose widow Martha received a pension

TURNER, THOMAS and widow Ann both received a pension

TURNER, THOMAS (BLW) and widow Rachel P. both received a pension

TURNER, THOMAS C. whose widow Nancy G. applied for a pension

TURNER, WILLIAM S. whose widow Frances J. received a pension

TURPIN, HENRY whose widow Lucy F. received a pension

TURPIN, JOHN and widow Mary M. both received a pension

TURPIN, PHILIP (P)

TURVEY, DANIEL (P)

TUSINGER, MICHAEL (P)

TUTT, CHARLES R. whose widow Ann M. applied for a pension

TUTT, PHILIP applied for a pension

TYE, ABNER B. whose widow

TYE (continued) Henrietta received a pension

TYLER, EDMUND whose widow Mary K. received a pension

TYLER, JOHN (BLW)

TYLER, JOHN (BLW), whose widow Julia Gardner received a pension. John was a president of the US

TYLER, JOSEPH applied for a pension

TYLER, SEATON whose widow Louisa V. received a pension

TYNES, JAMES N. whose widow Judith M. received a pension

TYREE, THOMAS J. whose widow Charlotte received a pension

TYREE, WILLIAM whose widow Martha E. received a pension

UHL, GEORGE H. (P)

UNDERHILL, JOHN whose widow Nancy B. received a pension

UNDERWOOD, ISAAC (P)

UNDERWOOD, JACOBUS and widow Hannah both received a pension

UNDERWOOD, SAMUEL applied for a pension

UNDERWOOD, WILLIAM (BLW)

UNDERWOOD, WILLIAM O. whose widow Margaret applied for a pension

UPDEGRAFF/UPDEGRAFFE, AMBROSE whose widow Catharine Updegraff received a pension

URTON, JOHN applied for a pension

UTLEY, WILSON whose widow Rhoda applied for a pension

UTZ, BENJAMIN whose widow Rosanna applied for a pension

UTZLER/EUTSLER/UTSLER, CHRISTIAN whose widow Mary Ann Utzler received a pension

VADEN, BRADDOCK G. alias YODDER, GOODWIN (P)

VADEN, HENRY (P)

VADEN, MICHAEL (P)

VADEN, THOMAS whose widow Ann Eugenia received a

VADEN (continued)
pension
VADEN/VARDEN, WILEY and widow Susan both received a pension. Susan later received a mother's pension for her son Jasper N. Vaden's service in the MO Infantry, Civil War
VAIDEN, ISAAC whose widow Caroline received a pension
VAIDEN, SIMS whose widow Elizabeth P. applied for a pension
VALENTINE, ELZEY applied for a pension
VALENTINE, GEORGE W. (P)
VALERY, WILLIAM (BLW), USN, died 1 Jul 1865, Philadelphia, PA; md 13 Apr 1814 Ann Tate (P), Norfolk, VA. She died 1 Jul 1876, LNR Washington, DC, 1872
VAN CAMP, JOHN whose widow Margaret applied for a pension
VANCE, THOMAS and widow Chloe both received a pension
VANDEGRIFT, JOHN whose widow Barbara received a pension
VANDERVORT, PAUL (BLW), whose widow Mary received a pension
VANDEVANDER, GEORGE whose widow Susan received a pension
VANDIVER, JACOB applied for a pension
VANHISE, JAMES (P)
VANHORN, ELI whose widow Margaret received a pension
VANHORN, WILLIAM H. (BLW), whose widow Nancy received a pension
VANLEAR, JACOB (P)
VANMETER, DAVID whose widow Hannah received a pension
VANMETER, JOSEPH and widow Damaris both received a pension
VANNOY, FRANCIS whose widow Mary received a pension
VANPELT, BENJAMIN (BLW),

VANPELT (continued)
died 21 Apr 1862, Harrisonburg, VA; md 2 Nov 1808 Mary Ragan (P), Harrisonburg, VA. Her LNR, Harrisonburg, Rockingham Co, VA, 1871
VANPELT, JACOB whose widow Arthela received a pension

ROLL NO. 95

VANSCYOC, JAMES whose widow Jerusha received a pension
VANSICKLES, HENRY (BLW). Served in Capt. Vansickles company as pvt.
VANZANT, JAMES (BLW), OH & VA militia, volunteered at Point Pleasant, VA, and in Gallia Co, OH, died 10 Sep 1854, Cheshire, Gallia Co, OH; md 9 Jun 1814 Margaret/Peggy Guy (P), Addison, Gallia Co, OH. Her LNR Gallia Co, OH, 1855
VANZANT, JOHN (P)
VARNUM, BARTLETT W. alias WEEKS, BARTLETT (BLW), whose widow Rebecca Varnum received a pension
VASS, LELAND whose widow Mary R. received a pension
VASS, WALKER (P)
VASSER, JAMES whose widow Mary received a pension
VAUGHAN/VAUGHN, ARCHIBALD applied for a pension
VAUGHAN, COLEMAN A. and widow Lucinda both received a pension
VAUGHAN, JOHN (BLW), and widow Ruth both received a pension
VAUGHAN, JOSEPH (BLW), whose widow Nancy received a pension
VAUGHAN, MATTHEW (BLW), whose widow was Lucy
VAUGHAN, PETER whose widow Jane received a pension
VAUGHAN, RANDOLPH (BLW)

303

VAUGHAN, RICHARD (BLW), whose widow was Narcissa G.

VAUGHAN, THEODORICK whose widow Jane received a pension

VAUGHAN, WILLIAM whose widow Mary received a pension

VAUGHAN, WILLIAM B. L. whose widow Sallie received a pension

VAUGHAN, WILLIAM H. whose widow Mason J. received a pension

VAUGHN, AVERETT M. applied for a pension

VAUGHN, GEAREY applied for a pension and widow Lydia received a pension

VAUGHN, JORDAN (BLW)

VAUGHN, JOSEPH (BLW)

VAUGHN, MITCHELL (BLW) whose widow was Nancy

VAUGHN, NATHANIEL (P)

VAUGHN, WILLIAM (P)

VAUGHN, WILLIAM whose widow Nancy received a pension

VAUGHT, ABRAHAM (BLW), whose widow Martha received a pension

VEACH, DORMAN (P)

VEATCH/VEACH, ELIJAH (BLW), whose widow Charlotte received a pension

VERMILION/VERMILLION, HANSON/HENSON applied for a pension

VERMILLION, CHARLES (P)

VERMILLION, JAMES and widow Elizabeth both received a pension

VERMILLION, JESSE whose widow Obedience received a pension

VERNON, THOMAS (BLW), whose widow Nancy E. applied for a pension

VEST, EDMUND/EDWARD (P)

VIA, RICHARD (P)

VIA, THOMAS C. (P)

VICK, WILSON whose widow Mary received a pension

VIER, ROBERT applied for a pension

VINCENT, EDWARD whose widow Rebecca received a pension

VINCENT, FREDERICK and widow Susan both received a pension

VINCENT, JOHN (P)

VINEYARD, WILLIAM (P)

VINT, JOHN whose widow Delilah received a pension

VIRTS/WERTS, CONRAD and widow Elizabeth Virts both received a pension

VOLENTINE, CHARLES applied for a pension

VOWLES, JAMES (P)

WADDEL, JAMES whose widow Catharine applied for a pension

WADDELL, JAMES B. (P)

WADDLE/WEDDLE, JOHN (BLW), died 16 Mar 1828, Pleasantville, Jackson Co, IN; md 14 Nov 1811 Lucy Hubbard (P), Patrick Co, VA, or Hawkins Co, TN. Her LNR Little York, Washington Co, IN, 1871

WADDLE, MICHAEL (P)

WADDY, GARLAND T. whose widow Sophia A. received a pension

WADE, BRUNT whose widow Easter received a pension

WADE, DREWRY F. whose widow Sarah A. received a pension

WADE, DRURY and widow Nancy A. both received a pension

WADE, FARLEIGH and widow Louisa both received a pension

WADE, GEORGE W. (P)

WADE, ISAAC (P)

WADE, JOHN whose widow Aoma received a pension

WADE, JOHN whose widow Dulceana applied for a pension

WADSWORTH, THOMAS applied for a pension

WAGGENER, ANDREW (BLW)

WAGGENER, REUBEN and widow Mary both received a pension

WAGGONER, JACOB whose wi-

WAGGONER (continued)
dow Elizabeth received a pension
WALCUTT, JAMES (P)
WALDEN, BILLY applied for a pension
WALDEN, ELISHA whose widow Elizabeth received a pension
WALDEN, JOHN and widow Virginia F. both received a pension
WALDEN, TERRY (P)
WALDEN, WILLIAM (P)
WALDON, JOHN (P)
WALDRIP, JAMES (BLW)
WALDROP, RICHARD whose widow Charlotte H. received a pension
WALE, GEORGE (BLW), died 10 Oct 1821, Stevensburg, Culpeper Co, VA; md 23 Jan 1815 Patsey Hansborough (P), Stevensburg, VA. Her LNR Stevensburg, VA, 1871. Her previous husband was George Petty
WALKER, ARCHIBALD and widow Susannah both received a pension
WALKER, AUSTIN (BLW)
WALKER, BAYLOR (P)
WALKER, CHRISPI AMOS alias WALKER, C. H. AMOS and widow Frances both received a pension
WALKER, DANIEL (BLW), and widow Elizabeth both received a pension
WALKER, DANIEL (P)
WALKER, DANIEL and widow Catherine both received a pension
WALKER, DAVID whose widow Elizabeth received a pension
WALKER, EDWARD whose widow Sarah L. received a pension
WALKER, FREDERICK (P)
WALKER, HENRY (P)
WALKER, JAMES whose widow Charlotte C. received a pension

WALKER, JAMES applied for a pension
WALKER, JESSE whose widow Elizabeth received a pension
WALKER, JOEL (P)
WALKER, JOHN (P)
WALKER, JOHN whose widow Ann received a pension
WALKER, JOHN whose widow Elizabeth received a pension
WALKER, JOHN whose widow Martha S. received a pension
WALKER, JOHN whose widow Anne received a pension
WALKER, JOSEPH whose widow Minty received a pension
WALKER, NATHANIEL and widow Susan J. both received a pension
WALKER, ROBERT whose widow Nancy received a pension
WALKER, SAMUEL (BLW), USA. Born in VA
WALKER, THOMAS whose widow Sarah applied for a pension
WALKER, THOMAS whose widow Fanny applied for a pension
WALKER, THOMAS whose widow Anna received a pension
WALKER, WILLIAM whose widow Harriet received a pension
WALKER, WILLIAM whose widow Sina received a pension
WALKER, WILLIAM and widow Sarah both received a pension
WALKUP, JOHN (P)
WALKUP, JOSEPH (P)
WALKUP, SAMUEL whose widow Margaret received a pension

ROLL NO. 96

WALL, DRURY whose widow Tabitha T. received a pension
WALL, ISAAC applied for a pension
WALL, ROBERT (P)
WALL, THOMAS (P)
WALLACE, BENJAMIN whose widow Letta received a pension

305

WALLACE, CHRISTOPHER (P, BLW)
WALLACE, HUGH (P)
WALLACE, HUGH (P)
WALLACE, JAMES whose widow Catharine applied for a pension
WALLACE, JOHN (P)
WALLACE, JOHN and widow Adelia J. both received a pension
WALLACE, MOSES whose widow Elizabeth received a pension
WALLACE, THOMAS (P, BLW) whose widow Ann C. received a pension
WALLACE, USSERY whose widow Elizabeth W. received a pension
WALLACE, WILLIAM H. (P)
WALLACE, WILLIS applied for a pension
WALLAR, JOSEPH (P)
WALLAR, SAMUEL (BLW), died 25/26 Jan 1833, Cambridge Township, Guernsey Co, OH; md 27 Feb 1806 Margaret Graham (P), Monongalia Co, VA. Her LNR Cambridge, Guernsey Co, OH, 1871
WALLAR, WILLIAM whose widow Sarah received a pension
WALLER, EDMUND whose widow Maria/Mariah received a pension
WALLER, JAMES (BLW), whose widow Elizabeth received a pension
WALLER, RICHARD whose widow Sarah received a pension
WALLER, ROBERT and widow Julia W. both received a pension
WALLER, THOMAS whose widow Nancy applied for a pension
WALLIS, WYATT applied for a pension
WALLTON/WALTON, JOSHUA whose widow Hannah Wallton received a pension
WALSH, BAKER (P)
WALTER, MICHAEL (P)
WALTERS, LEMUEL whose wi-

WALTERS (continued) dow Elizabeth received a pension
WALTERS, THORNTON (P)
WALTHALL, HENRY whose widow Elizabeth received a pension
WALTHALL, JOHN (BLW), whose widow Sarah received a pension
WALTHALL, THOMAS H. whose widow Sarah A. received a pension
WALTMAN, DAVID (P, BLW)
WALTON, EDMUND P. whose widow Lutitia applied for a pension
WALTON, HENRY W. whose widow Luraney/Luaney P. received a pension
WALTON, JAMES (P)
WALTON, JESSE R. and widow Nancy both received a pension
WALTON, JOHN F. whose widow Rhody T. received a pension
WALTON, MATTHEW P. whose widow Susan received a pension
WALTON, PETER W. whose widow Mary F. received a pension
WALTON, SIMEON whose widow Demarius received a pension
WALTON, SOLOMON whose widow Nancy H. received a pension
WALTON, WILLIAM O. and widow Martha M. both received a pension
WAMPLER, CHRISTIAN (P)
WAMPLER, JEREMIAH (P)
WAMSLEY, ISAAC whose widow Susannah received a pension
WANSTURFF, JACOB whose widow Catharine applied for a pension
WARBERTON, BENJAMIN whose widow Catharine G. received a pension
WARD, ANDREW (BLW), USA. Born in VA
WARD, ASA whose widow Susan

WARD (continued)
received a pension

WARD, DANIEL whose widow Ellen received a pension

WARD, JAMES whose widow Susan recieved a pension

WARD, JOHN and widow Zippora both received a pension

WARD, LANGSTON (BLW), died 25 Aug 1832, Kanawha Co, VA; md 13 Oct 1807 Martha C. Wilson (P), Kanawha Co, VA. Her LNR Galliapolis, OH, 1871

WARD, MOSES whose widow Mary applied for a pension

WARD, ROBERT (P)

WARD, SAMUEL applied for a pension

WARDEN, THOMAS applied for a pension

WARDER, NOAH (P)

WARE, GEORGE applied for a pension

WARE, ROBERT whose widow Jane G. received a pension

WARFORD / WOLFORD, ABRAHAM (P)

WARFORD, JOHN whose widow Rebecca received a pension

WARREN, ABIJAH whose widow Sarah received a pension

WARREN, MICHAEL S. whose widow Elizabeth B. received a pension

WARRICK, JOHN (P)

WARRICK, ROBERT whose widow Mary received a pension

WARRINER, WILLIAM whose widow Elizabeth received a pension

WARWICK, JAMES whose widow Polly C. received a pension. Polly later married Mr. Newsan

WASHINGTON, GEORGE (colored) applied for a pension

WASHINGTON, HENRY whose widow Louisa W. received a pension

WASHINGTON, MILES applied for a pension

WASHINGTON, PERRIN whose

WASHINGTON (continued)
widow Hannah F. received a pension

WASHINGTON, SOLOMON (P)

WATERFIELD, JAMES G. and widow Elizabeth Amanda both received a pension

WATERS, JAMES Jr. whose widow Judy W. received a pension

WATERS, WILLIAM whose widow Catherine T. received a pension

WATKINS, FRANK whose widow Elizabeth W. received a pension

WATKINS, HENRY N. whose widow Mildred S. received a pension

WATKINS, JOHN whose widow Patsey received a pension

WATKINS, JOHN (P)

WATKINS, JOHN R. whose widow Lucy A. C. received a pension

WATKINS, JOSEPH whose widow Sally received a pension

WATKINS, MILES SELDEN (BLW), whose widow Sally Davis Watkins received a pension

WATKINS, OVERTON and widow Jane both received a pension

WATKINS, PHILLIP and widow Margaret both received a pension

WATKINS, PHILIP whose widow Eliza received a pension

WATKINS, REUBEN L. (P)

WATKINS, RICHARD (BLW)

WATKINS, SAMUEL and widow Margaret both received a pension

WATKINS, THOMAS whose widow Judith received a pension

WATKINS, THOMAS applied for a pension

WATKINS, WALKER (P)

WATKINS, WILLIAM (P)

WATKINS, WILLIAM whose widow Rebecca applied for a pension

WATKINS, WILLIAM M. and

WATKINS (continued)
widow Jane both received a
pension
WATLINGTON, CLEVER whose
widow Elizabeth R. received a
pension
WATLINGTON, NATHANIEL
whose widow Martha S.
received a pension
WATSON, ABRAHAM and widow
Ruth both received a pension
WATSON, ALEXANDER and wi-
dow Sarah both received a pen-
sion
WATSON, BENJAMIN N. (BLW)
WATSON, GEORGE whose widow
Anne received a pension
WATSON, GEORGE E. whose wi-
dow Mary Ann received a pen-
sion
WATSON, JAMES applied for a
pension
WATSON, JAMES B. whose wi-
dow Sarah applied for a pen-
sion
WATSON, JAMES B. (P)
WATSON, JOSEPH A. applied for
a pension
WATSON, JOSIAH (BLW), whose
widow Martha received a pen-
sion
WATSON, SAMUEL whose widow
Permelia P. received a pen-
sion
WATSON, THOMAS and widow
Nancy both received a pension

ROLL NO. 97

WATTS, CURTIS whose widow
Nancy received a pension
WATTS, MOUNTZION whose wi-
dow Mary received a pension
WATTS, OVERTON BUCKNER
(P)
WATTS, PHILIP H. (P)
WATTS, THOMAS whose widow
Catharine received a pension
WAUGH, ALEXANDER and wi-
dow Polly both received a pen-
sion
WAUGH, GOWRY applied for a

WAUGH (continued)
pension
WAUGH, JAMES applied for a
pension
WAUGH, RODERICK whose wi-
dow Editha Ann received a
pension
WAUGHOP, JAMES F. whose
widow Harriet received a pen-
sion
WAULISS, WILLIAM whose wi-
dow Nancy received a pension
WAYLAND, JEREMIAH (P,
BLW)
WAYMAN, HENRY (P)
WAYNE, LEONARD whose widow
Judith received a pension
WEADON, JOHN (P)
WEAKLEY, FRANCIS (P)
WEAKLEY, WILLIAM (P)
WEANE, ISAAC applied for a
pension
WEANNING/WEAN, JOHN whose
widow Sarah Weanning re-
ceived a pension
WEAR/WARE, RICHARD C. (P)
WEAVER, ADAM whose widow
Katharine received a pension
WEAVER, CHARLES whose wi-
dow Susan received a pension
WEAVER, GEORGE whose widow
Mary received a pension
WEAVER, JACOB whose widow
Hannah received a pension
WEAVER, JAMES (P)
WEAVER, JOHN whose widow
Nancy received a pension
WEAVER, JOHN P. whose widow
Elizabeth received a pension
WEAVER, LEWIS (P)
WEAVER, WILLIAM whose wi-
dow Elizabeth applied for pen-
sion
WEBB, ABRAHAM/ABRAM
whose widow Mary received a
pension
WEBB, BENJAMIN (P)
WEBB, DAVID and widow Cath-
arine both received a pension
WEBB, EWELL S. whose widow
Nancy received a pension
WEBB, GEORGE (P)

WEBB, GEORGE whose widow Rebecca R. received a pension

WEBB, HOWEL and widow Temperance E. both received a pension

WEBB, JAMES A. whose widow Rebecca applied for a pension

WEBB, JAMES E. (P)

WEBB, JOHN (P)

WEBB, JOHN (BLW), whose widow Hannah received a pension

WEBB, JOHN (P)

WEBB, LEWIS applied for a pension

WEBB, PLEASANT whose widow Margaret applied for a pension

WEBB, REUBEN whose widow Nancy A. applied for a pension

WEBB, ROBERT H. whose widow Margaret S. received a pension

WEBB, SYLVESTER (P)

WEBB, THOMAS applied for a pension

WEBB, WENTWORTH (P)

WEBB, WESLEY whose widow Sarah received a pension

WEBB, WILLIAM whose widow Catharine applied for a pension

WEBB, WILLIAM whose widow Mary received a pension

WEBB, WILLIAM whose widow Frances F. applied for a pension

WEBBER, JOHN whose widow Catharine C. received a pension

WEBBER, WILLIAM B. whose widow Eliza C. received a pension

WEBER, GEORGE (P)

WEBSTER, ABRAHAM whose widow Margaret H. applied for a pension

WEBSTER, CHARLES whose widow Rachel applied for a pension

WEBSTER, GEORGE whose widow Margaret applied for a pension

WEBSTER, HEZEKIAH whose widow Catherine applied for a pension

WEBSTER, REUBEN whose widow Mary received a pension

WEEDON, THOMAS W. (P, BLW)

WEEKLY, JAMES (BLW)

WEEKLY, JOHN (P, BLW)

WEEKS, EMANUEL whose widow Lucy received a pension

WEEKS, WILLIAM whose widow Sina applied for a pension

WEEKS, WILLIAM L. (P)

WEIR, WILLIAM J. whose widow Louisa received a pension

WEISIGER, JOHN W. whose widow Catherine received a pension

WEITSEL/WHITEZEL, JOHN whose widow Betsey Weitsel received a pension

WELCH, BENJAMIN applied for a pension

WELCH, BENJAMIN whose widow Aria received a pension

WELCH, EDWARD (P)

WELCH, ROBERT whose widow Mary received a pension

WELCH, SAMUEL (P)

WELCH, WILLIAM (P)

WELCHHAUS/WELCHHENTZ, WILLIAM (P)

WELLARD, ANTHONY whose widow Elizabeth received a pension

WELLER, JOSEPH (P)

WELLMAN, JEREMIAH whose widow Julia Ann received a pension

WELLONS, WILLIS whose widow Eliza received a pension

WELLS, AUGUSTIN whose widow Elizabeth applied for a pension

WELLS, BENJAMIN (P) whose widow was Elizabeth

WELLS, DANIEL whose widow Mary R. applied for a pension

WELLS, HALEY applied for pension

WELLS, JOHN (P)

WELLS, JOHN (P)

WELLS, PATRICK H. whose widow Susan V. received a pension

WELLS, WILLIAM (P)
WELLS, WILLIAM whose widow Martha received a pension
WELSH, JOHN, USA, whose widow Nancy received a pension. Residence in VA
WELSH/WELCH, THOMAS (P)
WELSH, WILLIAM (P)
WENNER, WILLIAM (P)
WERTENBAKER, WILLIAM and widow Louisiana both received a pension
WESCOAT, GEORGE E. whose widow Mary A. received a pension
WESLEY, PAUL (P)
WEST, CHARLES (P)
WEST, JAMES whose widow Jane received a pension
WEST, JAMES G. and widow Mary A. both received a pension
WEST, OBEDIAH (P)
WEST, SAMUEL and widow Annie both received a pension
WEST, THOMAS (P)
WEST, THOMAS E. whose widow Sarah R. applied for a pension
WEST/MOONEY, WILLIAM R. and widow Emeline West both received a pension
WESTBROOK, ABRAHAM P./H. applied for a pension
WESTFALL, JAMES whose widow Elizabeth received a pension
WESTFALL, STEPHEN whose widow Elizabeth received a pension
WESTLAKE, JOSEPH applied for a pension
WESTMORELAND, WILLIAMSON whose widow Mary D. received a pension

ROLL NO. 98

WETHERHOLTZ, JOHN whose widow Elizabeth received a pension
WETZEL/WETSEL/WHETZEL, JACOB whose widow Mary

WETZEL (continued) Wetzel received a pension
WHALEY, BENJAMIN whose widow Sarah applied for a pension
WHARTON, BENJAMIN whose widow Lucy received a pension
WHARTON, JOHN applied for a pension
WHEATS, DORY whose widow Mary received a pension
WHEELER, CLEMENCE/CLEMENT (BLW), whose widow was Sarah
WHEELER, IGNATIUS/NACY (BLW)
WHEELER, JOHN whose widow Sarah received a pension
WHEELER, JOSEPH whose widow Anna received a pension
WHEELER, JOSHUA (P)
WHEELER, MALCOLM/MACON (P)
WHEELER, ROBERT applied for a pension
WHEELER, SAMUEL (P)
WHEELER, THOMAS (P, BLW). Pensioned in VA transferred to MD
WHEELER, WILLIAM applied for a pension
WHETZEL, DAVID applied for a pension
WHIDBEE, WILLIAM R. and widow Susan both received a pension
WHISMAN, PHILIP applied for a pension
WHISSON/WHISTON, JOSEPH (BLW), died 27 Jan 1840, Shenandoah Co, VA; md 12 Feb 1812 Elizabeth Carr (P), Frederick Co, VA. Her LNR Rockford, Winnebago Co, IL, 1871
WHITACRE/WHITAKER/WHITTACRE, ROBERT (P)
WHITAKER/WHITTAKER, DANIEL and widow Camilla Ann Whitaker both received a pension

WHITAKER, JOSEPH (BLW) whose widow Alice received a pension

WHITE, ABRAHAM (P)

WHITE, ABRAM and widow Martha J. both received a pension

WHITE, ADAM (P)

WHITE, ANDERSON and widow Lucinda both received a pension

WHITE, AUSTIN and widow Margaret both received a pension

WHITE, BENJAMIN applied for a pension

WHITE, CHARLES and widow Temperance both received a pension

WHITE, CLAYBORNE W. and widow Susan C. both received a pension

WHITE, DAVID (P)

WHITE, GEORGE whose widow Rebecca received a pension

WHITE, GEORGE applied for a pension

WHITE, JAMES whose widow Lucy received a pension

WHITE, JAMES and widow Polly both received a pension

WHITE, JAMES H. whose widow Eliza R. received a pension

WHITE, JAMES H. (P)

WHITE, JESSE (P)

WHITE, JOHN (P)

WHITE, JOHN applied for a pension

WHITE, JOHN (P)

WHITE, JOHN and widow Sarah both received a pension

WHITE, JOHN J. (P)

WHITE, JOHN M. whose widow Lucinda received a pension

WHITE, JOHN Y. whose widow Lucy received a pension

WHITE, JOSEPH whose widow Clary received a pension

WHITE, JOSEPH (P)

WHITE, MOSES (P)

WHITE, RANSOM whose widow Elizabeth applied for a pension

WHITE, RICHARDSON (P)

WHITE, THOMAS (P, BLW)

WHITE, WARNER whose widow Harriet received a pension

WHITE, WILLIAM applied for a pension

WHITE, WILLIAM (P)

WHITE, WILLIS applied for a pension

WHITEHEAD, LITTLEBERRY S. and widow Nancy W. both received a pension

WHITEHEAD, MARLOW (P)

WHITEHORN, JOHN M. whose widow Elizabeth received a pension

WHITELAW, JAMES whose widow Mary received a pension

WHITELY, FRANCIS whose widow Elizabeth applied for a pension

WHITEMAN, JAMES whose widow Rebecca S. received a pension

WHITESIDES, THOMAS (P)

WHITFIELD, ELISHA whose widow Nancy received a pension

WHITLOCK, JOHN N. whose widow Hannah received a pension

WHITLOCK, SAMUEL (P)

WHITLOW, MATHEY whose widow Polly applied for a pension

WHITMORE, BURWELL T. applied for a pension

WHITMORE, GEORGE whose widow Rachel received a pension

WHITMORE, JAMES whose widow Elizabeth received a pension

WHITTAKER, JOSEPH (P)

WHITTEN, JOSEPH whose widow Jane P. received a pension

WHORLEY, WILLIS whose widow Huldah W. received a pension

WIATT, VINCENT H. and widow Ellenor both received a pension

WIBLIN, WILLIAMSON whose widow Deborah received a pension

WICKHAM, ROBERT applied for a pension

WICKLINE, JACOB applied for a pension

WICUFF, CORNELIUS (BLW)

WIDENER, SAMUEL whose widow Patience received a pension

WIDMEYER, WILLIAM (P, BLW)

ROLL NO. 99

WIGGENTON/WIGGINTON, GEORGE (P)

WIGGINTON, PETER applied for a pension

WIGGINTON, WILLIAM whose widow Margaret received a pension

WIGNER, DANIEL (P)

WIGNER, JOHN (P)

WILBOURN, ROBERT L. whose widow Ann E. applied for a pension

WILBOURN, JOHN whose widow Sarah W. received a pension

WILBUN/WILBOURN, GUNNERY S. whose widow Sarah M. Wilbun received a pension

WILCHER, JOHN alias PEACOCK, JOHN (BLW)

WILCHER/WILLCHER, JOSIAH and widow Rachel both received a pension

WILCHER, RICHARD H. (BLW)

WILCOX, THOMAS W. whose widow Hannah H. received a pension

WILDMAN, ENOS (BLW), whose widow Jane D. received a pension

WILDMAN, JOSEPH and widow Sarah E. both received a pension

WILES, RANSOM and widow Adaline both received a pension

WILES, THOMAS and widow Frances both received a pension

WILEY, ALEXANDER whose widow Catherine received a pension

WILEY (continued)
dow Catherine received a pension

WILEY, JEREMIAH whose widow Sinah applied for a pension

WILEY, MOSES whose widow Sarah received a pension

WILEY, ROBERT whose widow Rebecca received a pension

WILEY, WILSON (P)

WILHELM, GEORGE and widow Martha both received a pension

WILHELM, JACOB A. (P)

WILHELM, PHILIP (BLW), and widow Ruhanna both received a pension

WILHELM, SOLOMON (P)

WILHITE, DAVID whose widow Polly received a pension

WILHOITE, BENJAMIN (BLW), whose widow Katy received a pension

WILKERSON, CHARLES W. whose widow Mary R. received a pension

WILKERSON, NICHOLAS whose widow Polly applied for a pension

WILKES, BENJAMIN (P)

WILKES, PEYTON (P, BLW)

WILKEY, JOHN (BLW), whose widow was Elizabeth

WILHELM, JAMES whose widow Hannah applied for a pension

WILKINS, JAMES and widow Susan R. both received a pension

WILKINS, NICHOLAS whose widow Dinah received a pension

WILKINS, THOMAS (BLW), whose widow Catharine received a pension

WILKINS, WILLIAM whose widow Nancy received a pension

WILKINS, WILLIAM (P)

WILKINS, WILLIS J. whose widow Judith S. received a pension

WILKINSON, IZARD whose widow Emeline H. received a pension

WILKINSON, JOHN G. (P)

WILKINSON, JOSEPH whose widow Rachel received a pension
WILKINSON, JOSEPH whose widow Martha J. received a pension
WILKINSON, RICHARD whose widow Amarylles Feliciama received a pension
WILKINSON, SAMUEL (BLW)
WILKINSON, SAMUEL (BLW)
WILKINSON, WILLIAM whose widow Susan W. received a pension
WILL, PHILIP ADAM whose widow Elizabeth received a pension
WILLET, WILLIAM whose widow Mary received a pension
WILLEY, WILLIAM (BLW), died 1 Jan 1857, Perry Township, Licking Co, OH; md 1803 Anna Butler (P), Culpeper Co, VA. She died c1875, LNR nr Rocky Fork, Licking Co, OH, 1871
WILLIAMS, ARTHUR whose widow Elizabeth applied for a pension
WILLIAMS, BENJAMIN (P)
WILLIAMS, COMMELIUS/ COMLIUS W. applied for a pension
WILLIAMS, DANIEL applied for a pension
WILLIAMS, DANIEL whose widow Mary A. received a pension
WILLIAMS, DAVID applied for a pension
WILLIAMS, EDWARD (P, BLW)
WILLIAMS, EDWARD whose widow Martha/Patsy received a pension
WILLIAMS, ELI whose widow Judith received a pension
WILLIAMS, ELIAS whose widow Eve received a pension
WILLIAMS, ELIJAH (P)
WILLIAMS, GREGORY whose widow Priscilla received a pension
WILLIAMS, HAZAEL (P)
WILLIAMS, ISAAC N. whose wi-

WILLIAMS (continued) dow Sarah G. applied for a pension
WILLIAMS, JACOB (P)
WILLIAMS, JACOB applied for a pension
WILLIAMS, JACOB (P)
WILLIAMS, JAMES whose widow Fanny applied for a pension
WILLIAMS, JAMES and widow Sarah both received a pension
WILLIAMS, JAMES and widow Mary B. both received a pension
WILLIAMS, JAMES whose widow Mary received a pension
WILLIAMS, JAMES (P)
WILLIAMS, JAMES F. (BLW), whose widow was Rebecca
WILLIAMS, JAMES L. whose widow Eliza received a pension
WILLIAMS, JESSE (P)
WILLIAMS, JOHN (BLW). Born in VA
WILLIAMS, JOHN (BLW), whose widow Elizabeth received a pension
WILLIAMS, JOHN whose widow Martha A. received a pension
WILLIAMS, JOHN whose widow Rebecca received a pension
WILLIAMS, JOHN E./S. whose widow Christiana P. received a pension
WILLIAMS, JOHN M. whose widow Elizabeth received a pension
WILLIAMS, JOHN M. whose widow Elizabeth M. applied for a pension
WILLIAMS, LARKIN whose widow Rhoda received a pension
WILLIAMS, RICHARD whose widow Ann received a pension
WILLIAMS, RICHARD and widow Elizabeth T. both received a pension
WILLIAMS, ST. CLAIR and widow Lucinda both received a pension
WILLIAMS, SAMUEL whose wi-

WILLIAMS (continued)
dow Martha C. applied for a pension
WILLIAMS, THOMAS applied for a pension
WILLIAMS, THOMAS whose widow Esther received a pension
WILLIAMS, THOMAS and widow Judith both received a pension
WILLIAMS, THOMAS whose widow Mary J. applied for a pension
WILLIAMS, THOMAS whose widow Juliet applied for a pension
WILLIAMS, WILLIAM (P)
WILLIAMS, WILLIAM whose widow Elizabeth received a pension
WILLIAMSON, ABRAHAM whose widow Barbary received a pension
WILLIAMSON, CHARLES whose widow Rhoda received a pension
WILLIAMSON, CORNELIUS whose widow Hannah received a pension
WILLIAMSON, CUTBIRTH (P)
WILLIAMSON, JOSEPH whose widow Elmira received a pension
WILLIAMSON, MOSES applied for a pension
WILLIAMSON, ROBERT whose widow Jane R. received a pension
WILLIAMSON, WILLIAM (P)
WILLIAMSON, WILLIAM whose widow Caroline applied for a pension
WILLIAMSON, WILLIAM whose widow Mary H. received a pension
WILLIAMSON, WINGO (P)
WILLIS, EDWIN and widow Matilda both received a pension
WILLIS, HENRY whose widow Nancy A. applied for a pension
WILLIS, JOSHUA (P, BLW)
WILLIS, SAMUEL (BLW), and

WILLIS (continued)
widow Jane both received a pension
WILLIS, WILLIAM whose widow Rhoda received a pension
WILLIS, WILLIAM C. and widow Elzira both received a pension
WILLIS, WILLIAM S. whose widow Malinda received a pension

ROLL NO. 100

WILLMORE, AMBROSE (P)
WILLOUGHBY, JOSEPH whose widow Susan received a pension
WILLOUGHBY, WALLACE (P, BLW)
WILLS, JESSE (P)
WILLS, MILES C. whose widow Rebecca M. received a pension
WILLS, ROBERT and widow Elizabeth T. both received a pension
WILLS, WILLIS C. whose widow Mary received a pension
WILLS, WOODSON and widow Julia A. both received a pension
WILLSON, WILLIAM H. applied for a pension
WILLYARD, FREDERICK (P)
WILSHER, WILLIAM whose widow Nancy applied for a pension
WILSON, ALEXANDER (BLW)
WILSON, ALEXANDER (BLW), whose widow was Elizabeth. Residence in OH
WILSON, ANDREW (BLW), whose widow Elizabeth received a pension
WILSON, AQUILLA whose widow Mary received a pension
WILSON, ARMISTEAD (P, BLW)
WILSON, ASA whose widow Emily received a pension
WILSON, AZARIAH (P)
WILSON, BAZZEL and widow Sarah both received a pension
WILSON, BENJAMIN whose wi-

314

WILSON (continued)
dow Anna received a pension

WILSON, EDLY whose widow Rebecca received a pension

WILSON, EDWARD whose widow Mary A. received a pension

WILSON, GEORGE L. (BLW), whose widow was Catharine R.

WILSON, HENRY and widow Clarissa both received a pension

WILSON, HORACE and widow Elizabeth A. both received a pension

WILSON, ISAAC (BLW), whose widow Mary B. received a pension

WILSON, JACOB whose widow Mary applied for a pension

WILSON, JACOB whose widow Catharine received a pension

WILSON, JAMES (BLW)

WILSON, JAMES B. whose widow Anne H. applied for a pension

WILSON, JAMES and widow Amelia both received a pension

WILSON, JAMES and widow Frances both received a pension

WILSON, JAMES (P)

WILSON, JAMES E. whose widow Sarah Ann applied for a pension

WILSON, JAMES F. and widow Emaline B. both received a pension

WILSON, JOHN (BLW), whose widow was Sarah M.

WILSON, JOHN and widow Ann R. both received a pension

WILSON, JOHN (P)

WILSON, JOHN (BLW)

WILSON, JOHN (BLW), whose widow was Catharine

WILSON, JOHN B. applied for a pension

WILSON, JOHN F. alias MORECOCK, EDWARD and widow Mary A. Wilson both received a pension

WILSON, JOHN F. applied for a

WILSON (continued)
pension

WILSON, JOHN H. (P, BLW)

WILSON, JOHN W. Sr. (P)

WILSON, JOSEPH (P)

WILSON, JOSEPH whose widow Rebecca received a pension

WILSON, JOSEPH whose widow Louisa applied for a pension

WILSON, MARCUS applied for a pension and widow Susannah received a pension

WILSON, MATTHEW whose widow Martha A. received a pension

WILSON, NATHANIEL whose widow Mary received a pension

WILSON, NATHANIEL B. and widow Polly M. both received a pension

WILSON, PETER and widow Susan both received a pension

WILSON, RALPH applied for a pension

WILSON, ROBERT whose widow Lydia received a pension

WILSON, ROBERT (P)

WILSON, ROBERT (BLW), whose widow Lucy D. received a pension

WILSON, SAMUEL applied for a pension

WILSON, SAMUEL K. whose widow Mary received a pension

WILSON, SAMUEL P. and widow Elizabeth both received a pension

WILSON, SHEROD whose widow Stacy received a pension

WILSON, THOMAS whose widow Mary received a pension

WILSON, WALLAR (P)

WILSON, WILLIAM (BLW)

WILSON, WILLIAM (BLW)

WILSON, WILLIAM (BLW)

WILSON, WILLIAM (BLW)

WILSON, WILLIAM (BLW)

WILSON, WILLIAM (BLW)

WILSON, WILLIAM (BLW)

WILSON, WILLIAM (BLW), whose widow was Elizabeth

WILSON, WILLIAM (BLW),

WILSON (continued)
whose widow was Elizabeth
WILSON, WILLIAM C. whose former widow was Stacia Gill
WILSON, WILLIAM H. whose widow Sarah received a pension
WILY, JOHN F. whose widow Mary received a pension
WIMER, ABRAHAM (P)
WIMER, HENRY and widow Elizabeth Ann both received a pension
WIMER, JACOB (P)
WIMMER, WILLIAM (P)
WINDLE, TEMPLE whose widow Sarah T. received a pension
WINDSOR, WILLIAM (P, BLW)
WINE, GEORGE whose widow Margaret received a pension
WINE, JOHN whose widow Elizabeth received a pension
WINEBURGH, SAMUEL applied for a pension
WINES, HEDGMAN (P)
WINFIELD, WILLIAM whose widow Nancy received a pension
WINFREE, MARVEL whose widow Elizabeth received a pension
WINFREE, OBADIAH whose widow Louisa received a pension
WINFREE, THOMAS whose widow Mary A. received a pension
WINFREE, WILLIAM (BLW), died 15 Nov 1834, Richmond, VA; md 11 Apr 1809 Lucy Boss/Bass (P), Chesterfield Co, VA. Her LNR Chesterfield Co, VA, 1871
WINGFIELD, CHARLES (P)
WINGFIELD, ROBERT whose widow Elizabeth E. received a pension
WINGFIELD, WILLIAM H. (BLW), whose widow was Eliza
WINN, BANNISTER whose widow Nancy received a pension
WINN, CHARLES whose widow Elizabeth received a pension

WINN, JAMES (BLW), and widow Sarah both received a pension
WINN, JOHN S. (BLW), whose widow Ann Jennet received a pension
WINN, RICHARD (P)
WINN, RICHARD (P, BLW), USA. Born in VA. Residence in TN
WINN, WILLIAM (BLW), whose widow Eliza received a pension
WINNIFORD, DAVID (P)
WINSTEAD, JAMES applied for a pension
WINSTON, PHILIP B. whose widow Jane D. received a pension
WINSTON, VIA (P)
WINTER, WILLIAM whose widow Martha received a pension
WINTZ/WINCE, JOSEPH whose widow Polly received a pension
WIRE, DAVID whose widow Catharine E. received a pension
WISDOM, THOMAS G. (P)
WISE, ADAM whose widow Elizabeth received a pension
WISE, HUGH H. (P, BLW)
WISE, JOHN I. whose widow Harriet A. received a pension
WISE, SAMUEL (P)
WISE, WILLIAM (P)
WISEMAN, JOHN (P, BLW)
WISMAN, JACOB (P)
WISMAN, JOSEPH and widow Anna both received a pension
WISOR, ADAM applied for a pension
WITCHER, JAMES (BLW), VA & GA militia (Cherokee Indian War), died 9 Feb 1873, Polk Co, GA; md 1813 Gilley Edwards (P), Pittsylvania Co, VA. She died 21 Dec 1882, LNR Polk Co, GA, 1878
WITCHER, VINCENT applied for a pension
WITHERS, WILLIAM (BLW), whose widow Sarah received a

WITHERS (continued)
pension
WITHROW, DAVID (P)
WITT, DANIEL whose widow
Martha W. applied for a pension
WITT, RICHARD (BLW), whose
former widow was Nancy
McPherson
WITT, SANDERS whose widow
Vily received a pension
WITT, WILLIAM whose widow
Frances received a pension
WITT, WILLIAM (P)
WOLF, DAVID whose widow
Elizabeth received a pension
WOLF, HENRY whose widow
Catharine received a pension
WOLF, JACOB (P)
WOLF, JONATHAN H. applied
for a pension
WOLF, PHILIP and widow Drusilla both received a pension
WOLF, ROLAND whose widow
Elizabeth L. received a pension
WOLFE, DANIEL (P)
WOLFE, GEORGE F. whose widow Celia A. received a pension
WOLFE, PETER whose widow
Clara received a pension
WOLFF, JOSEPH (P)
WOLTZ, JOHN whose widow
Margaret applied for a pension
WOLVERTON, CHARLES applied
for a pension
WOMACK, HUBBARD whose
daughter Jane A. E. received a
pension
WOMACK, LILLIOUS D. whose
widow Sarah C. received a
pension
WOMACK, WILLIAM whose widow Martha J. received a pension

ROLL NO. 101

WOOD, DAVID (P)
WOOD, FLEMING whose widow
Lucy A. received a pension

WOOD, Isaac W. whose widow
Lucinda received a pension
WOOD, Isaiah whose widow
Sophia received a pension
WOOD, JAMES (BLW), whose
widow was Margaret
WOOD, JAMES M. and widow
Mary Jane both received a
pension
WOOD, JEREMIAH whose widow
Elizabeth applied for a pension
WOOD, JESSE and widow Mary
H. both received a pension
WOOD, JOHN whose widow
Janetta received a pension
WOOD, JOHN whose widow Sarah
A. received a pension
WOOD, JOHN whose widow
Elizabeth received a pension
WOOD, JOHN D. whose widow
Ann E. applied for a pension
WOOD, JOHN J. (P)
WOOD, JOSEPH whose widow
Amanda J. received a pension
WOOD, REUBEN and widow
Martha/Patsey M. both received a pension
WOOD, ROBERT whose widow
Elizabeth applied for pension
WOOD, SILAS whose widow
Nancy received a pension
WOOD, THOMAS whose widow
Susan applied for a pension
WOOD, WILLIAM whose widow
May E. received a pension
WOOD, WILLIAM (P)
WOOD, WILLIAM whose widow
Margaret S. received a pension
WOOD, WILLIAM D. whose widow Sarah received a pension
WOODALL, DANIEL H. applied
for a pension
WOODALL, JAMES H. (P)
WOODALL, JOHN whose widow
Elizabeth received a pension
WOODALL, SAMPSON whose widow Sally received a pension
WOODARD/WOODWARD,
CHARLES whose widow Nancy
received a pension
WOODFIN, GEORGE whose widow Martha E. received a

317

WOODFIN (continued)
pension
WOODHOUSE, HENRY B. applied for a pension
WOODRUFF, ROBERT W. (P)
WOODS, CHARLES whose widow Catharine received a pension
WOODS, DAVIDS whose widow Elizabeth received a pension
WOODS, JAMES and widow Maria both received a pension
WOODS, JOHN (P)
WOODS, MOSES whose widow Hannah applied for a pension
WOODS, MOSES (P)
WOODS, ZACHARIAH applied for a pension
WOODS, ZACHARIAH and widow Elizabeth both received a pension
WOODSON, AUGUSTIN whose widow Nancy received a pension
WOODSON, CHARLES F. (P)
WOODSON, GEORGE (BLW)
WOODSON, HUGHES (BLW), whose widow Sarah M. received a pension
WOODSON, JAMES B. (P)
WOODSON, TARLTON (P)
WOODSON/WOODSAM, WILLIAM whose widow Nancy R. received a pension
WOODWARD, EPHRAIM (P)
WOODWARD, JOSHUA and widow Sarah both received a pension
WOODY, SAMUEL whose widow Mary Ann received a pension
WOODY, WILLIAM (P)
WOODYARD, HENRY/HENLY/HENDLEY (BLW), died 30/31 Aug 1847, Lubeck, Wood Co, VA; md 3 Nov 1814 Sally Wiseman (P), Harrison Co, VA. She died 27 Aug 1886, Lubeck, Wood Co, WV
WOOLDRIDGE, EDMUND B. (P)
WOOLDRIDGE, JOHN (P)
WOOLDRIDGE, WILLIAM B. (P)
WOOLDRIDGE, WILLIAM C. whose widow Elizabeth R.

WOOLDRIDGE (continued)
received a pension
WOOLF, HENRY (P)
WOOTON/WOOLTON/ WOOTTEN, SIMON (BLW), whose widow Mary W. Wootton received a pension
WOOTTON, WILLIAM whose widow Sallie C. applied for a pension
WORKMAN, JOSEPH (P)
WORLEY/WHORLEY, CHARLES whose widow Mary received a pension
WORLEY, HENRY whose widow Frances received a pension
WORNAL, JOHN and widow Mary J. both received a pension
WORRELL, BENJAMIN (P)
WORRELL, CAREY (BLW), died 1 Feb 1844, Southampton Co, VA; md 18 Dec 1806 Sarah Council (P), Southampton Co, VA. Her LNR Berlin, Southampton Co, VA, 1871
WORRELL, PETER whose widow Martha applied for a pension
WORRELL, SHADRICK (P)
WORSHAM, DANIEL whose widow Emeline received a pension
WORSHAM, WILLIAM and widow Lucretia both received a pension
WORSTELL, JOHN whose widow Ann received a pension
WORSTER, TAPLEY (BLW), whose widow Nancy received a pension
WORT/WIRT, SAMUEL and widow Margaret Wirt both received a pension
WORTMAN, ISAAC whose widow Sarah J. received a pension
WRAY, ADAM whose widow Mary received a pension
WRAY, ANDERSON whose widow Nancy Ann received a pension
WRAY, CREED T. whose widow Lucy received a pension
WRAY, JACOB K. whose widow Aphia W. applied for a pension

WRAY, JOHN (BLW), died 26 Nov 1860, Rome Township, Lawrence Co, OH; md 10 Sep 1808 Agnes Pillow (P), Lynchburg, Campbell Co, VA. Her LNR Sheridan, Lawrence Co, OH, 1871

WRAY, JOHN whose widow Mary G. received a pension

WRAY, NATHANIEL whose widow Nancy received a pension

WREN, EDWARD and widow Mary M. both received a pension

WREN, WILLIAM D. whose widow Mary Ann received a pension

WRENN, JOHN (BLW), whose widow Ester received a pension

WRENN, JOHN (BLW)

WRENN, THOMAS applied for a pension

WRENN/WREN, WILLIAM (P)

WRIGHT, ANDREW whose widow Ruhanna received a pension

WRIGHT, ANTHONY (P)

WRIGHT, BENJAMIN whose widow Sarah Ann applied for a pension

WRIGHT, BRYANT and widow Charity both received a pension

WRIGHT/RIGHT, DANIEL (P)

WRIGHT, EDWARD (P)

WRIGHT, GEORGE whose widow Nancy received a pension

WRIGHT, GEORGE whose widow Ellinder applied for a pension

WRIGHT, GEORGE C. (P)

WRIGHT, GEORGE M. whose widow Caty M. P. received a pension

WRIGHT, JAMES (P)

WRIGHT, JAMES whose widow Jane received a pension

WRIGHT, JAMES and widow Judith both received a pension

WRIGHT, JAMES whose widow Martha received a pension

WRIGHT, JAMES and widow

WRIGHT (continued) Mary both received a pension

WRIGHT, JAMES (P), USA. Residence in VA

WRIGHT, JEREMIAH whose widow Morning received a pension

WRIGHT, JESSE and widow Elizabeth both received a pension

WRIGHT, JOHN whose widow Christiana received a pension

WRIGHT, JOHN whose widow Elizabeth received a pension

WRIGHT, JOHN whose widow Terissa received a pension

WRIGHT, JOHN S. whose widow Charlotte C. received a pension

WRIGHT, JOHN W. whose widow Nancy A. received a pension

WRIGHT, JONATHAN whose widow Sarah received a pension

WRIGHT, JOSEPH applied for a pension

WRIGHT, JOSEPH Y. whose widow Tabitha received a pension

WRIGHT, LEWIS whose widow Hannah C. received a pension

WRIGHT, LUTHER (P)

WRIGHT, MERRITT whose widow Mary B. received a pension

WRIGHT, NELSON (P)

WRIGHT, NEWTON (BLW), whose widow Sarah received a pension

WRIGHT, ROBERT and widow Mary both received a pension

WRIGHT, ROBERT and widow Ellen both received a pension

WRIGHT, RUBEN/REUBEN whose widow Martha received a pension

WRIGHT, SAMUEL and widow Frances both received a pension

WRIGHT, SAMUEL A. whose widow Barbara G. received a pension

WRIGHT, SOLOMON whose wi-

WRIGHT (continued)
dow Sarah received a pension
WRIGHT, THOMAS whose widow
Mary Ann received a pension
WRIGHT, THOMAS (P)
WRIGHT, THOMAS and widow
Catharine W. both received a
pension
WRIGHT, WESLEY and widow
Ann Jane both received a pension. Wesley was a substitute
for James D. Wright in the
War
WRIGHT, WILLIAM (P)
WRIGHT, WILLIAM whose widow Leah received a pension
WRIGHT, WILLIAM A. whose
widow Charlotte received a
pension
WRIGHT, WILLIAM R. and widow Elizabeth both received a
pension
WRIGHT, WILLIAM S. and widow Rhoda both received a
pension
WRIGHT, WILLIS whose widow
Mary A. F. received a pension

ROLL NO. 102

WYANT, DANIEL and widow
Nancy T. both received a pension
WYANT, JOHN (P)
WYATT, EDMOND, USA, whose
widow Mary A. received a pension. Residence in VA
WYATT/WIATT, JAMES (BLW),
whose former widow was Susan
Blasingham
WYATT, JOHN whose widow
Jane applied for a pension
WYATT, MOSES and widow Mary
L. both received a pension
WYATT, RICHARD (P)
WYATT, THOMAS (BLW), whose
widow Susana received a pension
WYATT, YOUNGER whose widow
Mary applied for a pension
WYKLE, JACOB applied for a
pension

WYLIE, THOMAS (BLW), whose
widow Rhoda received a pension
WYNANS/WININGS, EZEKIEL
and widow Margaret both
received a pension
WYNN, JAMES (BLW), USA.
Residence in VA
WYNN/WYNE, JOHN whose widow Jane received a pension
WYNN, JOHN M. whose widow
Susan applied for a pension
WYNN, PETER whose widow
Mary received a pension
WYRICK, JOHN applied for a
pension
WYSONG, JAMES whose widow
Lucie S. received a pension
YAGER, NICHOLAS W. (BLW),
whose widow Christina W.
received a pension
YAGER, SALATHIEL W. and widow Ann both received a pension
YANCEY, FRANCIS G. whose widow Harriet received a pension
YANCEY, WILLIAM (P)
YANCY, JAMES (P)
YANCY, JOHN S. whose widow
Sarah W. applied for a pension
YARBOROUGH, JOHN whose widow Lucy A. applied for a pension
YARBOROUGH, THOMAS
(BLW), whose widow was
Citivia
YARRINGTON, JAMES S. (P)
YATES, ABSALOM whose widow
Catharine received a pension
YATES, ANDREW and widow
Hester both received a pension
YATES, BENJAMIN G. applied
for a pension and widow Catharine received a pension
YATES, GARRETT whose widow
Frances received a pension
YATES, JOHN H. and widow
Peggy both received a pension
YATES, WILLIAM P. whose widow Elizabeth received a pension
YEATMAN, JOHN H. whose wi-

320

YEATMAN (continued)
dow Mary applied for a pension
YEATTS, WILLIAM whose widow
Frances applied for a pension
YEOMANS, PLEASANT whose
widow Mary received a pension
YERBY, THOMAS whose widow
Harriet received a pension
YERBY, WILLIAM G. (P)
YERKES/YERKEE, JOSHUA (P)
YOAKUM, JACOB (BLW), and
widow Margaret both received
a pension
YOKOM, SAMUEL whose widow
Elizabeth received a pension
YONAS, STUFFLE whose widow
Mary received a pension
YOST, JOHN whose widow
Elizabeth received a pension
YOST, PETER applied for a pen-
sion
YOUNG, ANDREW (P)
YOUNG, DANIEL (BLW), whose
widow Ann C. received a pen-
sion
YOUNG, HENRY (P)
YOUNG, JOHN, USA, whose wi-
dow Susannah received a pen-
sion. Residence in WV
YOUNG, JOHN whose widow
Nancy received a pension
YOUNG, JOHN applied for a pen-
sion
YOUNG, JOHN whose widow Mary
received a pension
YOUNG, JOHN Y. whose widow
Elizabeth applied for a pension
YOUNG, JONATHAN whose wi-
dow Sophia received a pension
YOUNG, WILLIAM (P)
YOUNG, WILLIAM P. (BLW)
YOUNGER, ANTHONY (P)
YOWELL, WILLIAM whose wi-
dow Simphronica received a
pension

ZACHARY, BENJAMIN whose
widow Martha received a pen-
sion
ZEIGLER, MARK (P)
ZICKEFOOSE/ZECKEFOOSE/
ZICKAFOOSE, GEORGE (P)
ZICKEFOOSE, SAMPSON applied
ZICKEFOOSE (continued)
for a pension
ZIGLER, PHILIP (P)
ZIMBRO, JACOB (P)
ZIMMERS, CHRISTIAN and wi-
dow Mary Ellen both received
a pension
ZINN, ALEXANDER whose widow
Jane Heatherly applied for a
pension
ZOLLMAN, ADAM whose widow
Polly received a pension

INDEX

This index lists women with their married and maiden names, when known, and men who are not the subject of an entry.

ALLEN (continued)
5 24 Hannah A 123 Jane 5
Julia 4 Lavicy F 4 Lucy 4
Lucy M 177 Lydia 5 Margaret
(---) 4 Marie E 4 Martha 4 5
Martha (---) 5 Martha A (---)
5 Martha Scutt 5 Mary 4 189
Nancy 4 5 Patsey W 4 Phoebe
Ann 4 Polly 4 Rebecca W 5
Sarah 4 Susan 4 5
ALLEY, Martha 33 Sarah 5
ALLIMONG, Christina 5
ALLISON, Elizabeth 5 Ellen 5
Elsey 5 Jane Campbell 5
Lucinda 5 Mary 5 Mary Selena
5 Matilda 144 Rosannah 74
Sarah 6
ALLTON, Nancy H 6 Samuel 6
ALMAN, Nancy (---) 6
ALMOND, Elizabeth 269 Joica 6
ALPINE, Mahala Farmer (---) 6
ALSOP, Lucy M 6 Robert 6
ALTICK, Elizabeth 6
ALVERSON, Lucy 6
ALVIS, Lucy 14 Mary S 6
Zephaniah 14
AMBLER, Catherine (Tazewell)
165 Lucy H 6
AMBROSE, Linney 67 Mary 198
Susanna 68
AMBURN, Ester 17
AMICK, Jane 6 Rachael 6
AMISS, Mary 280 Mary T (---) 6
AMMONS, Elizabeth H 6 Sarah 6
AMONETT, Juliet 6
AMOS, Anna 176 Mary Ann Mas-
sey 181 Nancy 6 Sally 60 Sarah
60 Susan R 107
AMSPOKER, Mary Ann 6
ANCELL, Frances 7
ANDERSON, --- 3 Abigail 8 Ann
68 Ann P 7 Ann W 8 Carrol 8
Catharine B 7 Catherine 8
Deniza B 188 Elenor 66 Eliza
172 Elizabeth 7 8 Emily H 7
Jane 7 Jane S 8 John B 7 Leah
7 Margaret 8 Margery 7 Maria
7 Maria D 7 Martha M 7 Mary
8 Mary C 7 Mary F 8 Mary L
163 Mary M 3 Melcon 8
Mildred A (---) 7 Missaniah
87 Nancy 7 8 168 Nancy (---)

ANDERSON (continued)
7 Nancy W 8 Peggy 119 Per-
melia 7 Rebecca 8 Sally 8
Sophia A 8 Tabitha 7 Unetta 8
ANDERTON, Lucy 8
ANDRESS, Mary 8
ANDREWS, Cassandra (---) 8
Margaret T 9 Martha G 9 Mary
A 8 Mary W 9 Mason 9 Nancy
206 Rebecca B 9 Sally 28
Sophia Ann 9
ANGLEA, Eliza 9 Mary E 9
ANGLIN, Elizabeth 42
ANGLING, Mary 141
ANGUS, Betsey 9 Elizabeth 9
ANKERS, Harriet A 9
ANKROM, Clarissa 62
ANNETT, Catharine 9
ANSON, Jane T 214
ANTHONY, Emelia 9
ANTON, Hugh 12 Jane 12
APPELBERRY, Eliza 9
APPERSON, Evelina 9 Jane 9
Martha 9 Sarah H 83 Sidney 9
APPLEWHITE, Mary Ann 9
ARBGASS, Martha 28
ARBOGAST, Jane G 10 Sarah 9
ARCHER, Eleanor 126 Elizabeth
10 128 Jane S 8 Martha A 197
Priscilla 10 Prudence Ann 10
Sarah H 30
ARDINGER, Ann 78
ARGABRITE, Catharine 10
ARGENBRIGHT Christina "Tiny"
10 Eva 25
ARIE, Nancy 10
ARINGTON, Grizzia J 30
ARISMAN, Malinda 10
ARISON, Catherine 10
ARMENTROUT, Amy 10 Barbara
10 Mary 10 Priscilla 10
ARMISTEAD, Eliza 11 Elizabeth
D 10 Harriet J 11 Mary 47 100
Sarah 10
ARMITAGE, Mary Ann 187 188
ARMSTRONG, 167 Achsah 11
Cynthia D 11 Frances A 11
Jane 11 Mary 11 141 Patsy
Ann 11 Peggy 11 Sarah 11
ARNALL, Catharine S 11 Richard
11
ARNETT, Ann 11 Frances L 11

BAKER (continued)
Christina "Tiny" 10 Eleanor 18
Elizabeth 18 76 108 Harriet A
18 Jane 17 John 17 Leah 93
Margaret 45 Mary 18 88
Matilda (---) 18 Nancy 17
Permelia 18 Rebecca 17 Rhoda
18 Sarah 18 Savilla 17
BALCKWELL, Nancy 184
BALDEN, Malinda 18
BALDERSON, Elizabeth 18 Fanny
B 94 Henry 94 Rebecca 18
BALDWIN, Caroline 54 Martha 18
Mary (---) 18 Nancy 18 Portia
Lee 18 Sally 18 Sarah (---)
164
BALES, Joanah 18 Maria (---)
137 Presley 33
BALL, Ann 19 Athaline 19
Catharine 19 Louisa 19 Martha
18 Tempey 71
BALLARD, Louisa S 19 Lucy 19
Mary Ann 19 Mary Susan 279
280 Nancy 19 119 Phebe ---
19 Ruth 19 Sarah 19 Susanna
279 280 Ursula 19
BALLENTINE, Nancy 19
BALLEW, Martha 42
BALLINGER, Lovel 19 Sally 19
BALLOW, Parmelia J 19
Rebecca A 19
BALSLEY, Elizabeth 148 Martha
Ann 19 Nancy 19
BALTHIS, Sarah Ann 20
BANDAY, Mary 20 Polly 20
BANDY, Elizabeth 20 Nancy 20
BANE, Louisa 20
BANKET, Charles L 20 Mary Ann
20
BANKHEAD, Mary Ann 20
BANKS, Frances Elizabeth 20
BANTON, Elizabeth 20
BARB, Mary 172
BARBARY, Mary Ann 177
BARBEE, Lucy 20 Margaret 20
Mary 203 Sallie 20
BARBER, Eliza 20 Elizabeth 20
Mourning 20 Tabitha 20
BARBOUR, Elizabeth I M 20
Nancy 46
BARCLAY, Robert 121 Selina 21
Selina White Dickson 121

BARDON, Ann Elizabeth 65 Cloyd
65
BARE, Christina 21 Elizabeth 156
Felty 21 Valentine 26
BARGDALL, Christina 21
Elizabet (---) 21
BARGER, Ann 21 Mary 21
BARKER, Annie Jane 21
Elizabeth (---) 21 Margaret B
21 Mary 21 Mary S 21 Mildred
21 Milly 21 Nancy 21 Rebecca
22 Sarah 21 Susan 21
BARKSDALE, Ann P 21 Elizabeth
21 Mary 174 Rebecca F L 21
Sarah J 158
BARLEY, Margaret 202 Phoebe
22 Sally M 23
BARLOW, Catharine 118 Caty
118
BARNER, Catharine C 22
BARNES, Charity 105 Charlotte
22 Eliza 22 Elizabeth 22
Elizabeth J 22 Letitia Ann 22
Lucy A 22 Mary 22 Mary A
(---) 22 Nancy 22 Rebecca 22
Sarah 22 48
BARNETT, Anna 53 Elizabeth 22
Jane (---) 59 Lucy 22 Nancy
22 Rebecca 22 Sarah 22 Susan
159 Susannah 22 115
BARNHART, Nancy 22
BARNS, Frances H 22
BARNSGROVE, Mary (Hodges)
123
BARR, Elizabeth 23 Lydia 23
BARRACK, Mary 23
BARRETT, Clarissa B 23
Elizabeth 23 Jane A 181 John
23 Martha 23 Mildred 23 Nancy
119
BARRICK, Mary 23
BARRINTON, Mary 122
BARRON, Catharine P 124 Mary
B 23
BARROT, Elizabeth 23
BARROTT, Mary 23
BARROW, Mary J 23
BARTAS, Mary Ann 43
BARTEE, Ellen (---) 23 Mary 23
BARTEN, Roxey Ann 13
BARTHALL, Christina 21
Elizabeth (---) 21 Solomon 21

BARTLETT, Calysta 176 Sarah 23

BARTON, Magdalene 23 Nancy M 23 Polly 70 Sallie C 23 Sally 23

BARTUM, Rebecca 23

BASCUE, Rachel 23

BASETT, Ann R 24 Mary 24

BASHAM, Ellen 24 Ellender 24 Elizabeth H 24 Polly 24

BASKET, Jesse 24 Mary W 24 Sallie T 24 Susan C 24

BASKETT, Lucy 24 Mary (---) 24 Mildred 24 Sallie T 24 Sarah 24 Susan C 24

BASS, Ann 24 Lucy 316 Martha 24 Mary A 24

BASSETT, Alexander H 24 Ann R 24 Mary 24

BASYE, Hannah 24 Mary R 107 Sallie E C 24

BATCHE, Elizabeth 64

BATEMAN, Elizabeth 24 Susan 24

BATES, Ann 24 Catharine 24 Eliza 24 Margaret 116 Nancy 24 Susan G 24

BATTIN, Anna 25

BATTS, America R (Elam) 163

BAUGH, Elizabeth H 25 Mahala A 72 Mary T 27

BAUGHAM, Jerusha 127 Marinda (Ransom) 170

BAUGHAN, Sidner 25

BAUGHER, Catharine 161 Rachel 25

BAUGHMAN, Ann 25 Dorothy 25 Martha 183 Sarah 25

BAVEN, Elizabeth 42

BAVINGTON, Selina 85

BAXTER, Elizabeth 25 Rebecca 25 Sarah 25

BAYES, Polly 25

BAYLES, Elizabeth 25

BAYLIS, Catherine 25 Mary K 25

BAYLOR, Eva 25 Lucy Page 51

BAYLY, Caroline I 2 Jane O 2 25 Margaret 25 Sallie 25 Thomas M 2

BAYNES, Elizabeth 40

BAYS, Nancy 25 Tabitha 62

BAYTOP, Sarah E S 77

BEACH, Elizabeth 25 Elizabeth B 26 Ester 25

BEADLE, Sarah 26

BEAHM, Christina 26

BEAKER, Catherine 160

BEAL, Ann E 91 Nancy 26 Sally 26 Susan 26 Temperance 26

BEALE, Ann M 26 Hannah 26 Jane B 26 Margaret 26 Mary 26 Mary H 26 Rebecca 26 Richard 26 Susan 26

BEALL, Catharine 26 Mary 26

BEALS, Margaret 26

BEAMAN, Martha A (---) 22

BEAN, Sarah 26

BEAR, Christina 21 Elizabeth 26 Felty 21 Valentine 21

BEARD, Elizabeth 26 Margaret E 26 Mary 27

BEASLEY, Frances 27 Martha 27 Mary T 27 Susan 36 T U 27

BEATIE, Thomas 25

BEATLEY, Elizabeth 27

BEATON, Hannah 27

BEATTY, ELizabeth 27 Rachel 27

BEATY, Elizabeth 27

BEAZLEY, Amanda 87 Elizabeth 27 Frances 27 Susannah 27 Valentine 27

BEAZLY, Laura L 27 Lucy B 27

BECHTOL, Mary Ann 27

BECK, Elizabeth 28 Judith T 27 Margaret 28 Mary E 103

BECKER, Mary 101

BECKETT, Amy 28

BECKNER, Margaret 28 Nancy 28

BECKOM, Elizabeth 15 Mathias 15

BECKWITH, Sally Eleanor 28

BECON, Mary A 46

BECROFT, Ann 142

BEDDO, Ellen 28 Sarah Ann 28

BEDDOW, Ellen 28 Nathaniel 28 Sarah Ann 28

BEEDLE, Letitia 28 Nancy 28

BEEL, Richard 26

BEELER, Martha 28

BEEM, Christina 26 Martin R 26

BEESON, Elizabeth R 138

BEHEN, Emenetia 28

BEHER, Eliza 28

BELCHER, Abigail 29 Amy 28
Keziah 80 Martha 29 Permelia
29 Sally 28 Tabitha 28
BELFIELD, Fanny F 29 Frances
M 102 Mary B 29
BELILES, Peggy 29
BELISLE, Jesse 29 Peggy 29
BELKNAP, Emsey 29 Mary 29
BELL, Ann 107 Catharine 167
Elizabeth 29 Elizabeth N 29
Frances H 186 Frances M 30
Grizzia J 30 Jane (Atwood) 30
Margaret A 103 Martha 29
Mary 29 30 Mary J 85 Mason
29 Nancy 29 58 Nancy B 29
Rebecca 29 Richard 26 Roda
29 Sarah 29
BELLAH, Mary 149
BELLAR, Mary 149
BELSHUR, Sarah 157
BELVIN, Rachel A 121
BENDER, Elizabeth 30 Rebecca
30
BENEDUM, Mary 30
BENN, Nancy 30 Sarah 30
BENNETT, Catherine 30 Charity
31 Elizabeth M A 31 Frances
30 Jane (---) 30 Lucy 30
Lydia 30 Malinda 31 Margaret
30 Martha 30 Mary 30 Rachel
30 Sally 30 Sarah 29 Sarah H
30
BENSON, Lusander 31 Sarah L 31
BENSTON, Dorcas 180
BENT, Margaret 31 Mary 31
BENTER, Mary 45
BENTHALL, Martha 31
BENTLEY, Martha 246
BERDICK, Elizabeth 63 John 63
Lucinda 63
BERKELEY, Nancy D 31
BERLIN, Sarah Jane 31
BERREY, Drucilla (---) (Taylor)
31 Elizabeth 31 Mildred 31
BERRY, Catherine 32 Dulcena
180 Elisabeth 32 Elizabeth 31
Elizabeth (---) 31 Fanny 148
Frances 32 Harriet 32 James
31 Kitty 32 Mary A 1 190
Rachel W 32 Sally 31 Soreno
32
BESS, Eliza S 172

BEST, Elizabeth D 32 Frances
196 Polly 167
BETS, Sally 32
BETSY, Norris 34
BETTS, Ann 32 Elizabeth A 32
Fanny H 32 Parthenia C 32
BIAS, Elizabeth 68 James 67
BIBB, Cynthia Ann 32
BIBBINS, Ann 3 Anna 3
BIBLE, Mary 32 Polly 32
BICKEL, Elizabeth 32
BICKERS, Mary 33
BICKERTON, Polly 33
BICKLE, Dinah 32 Elizabeth 32
George 32 Mary 176
BIGBIE, Frances W 33 Lucy G 33
BIGERS, Permelia 29
BIGGS, Maria 150 Mary 33
BIGHAM, Jane 58
BILLER, Hannah 33
BILLINGS, Calva 33 Jane 33
BILLS, Martha 33
BILLUPS, Ann 33 Louisa 33 Lucy
(---) 33 Lusy 33
BINGHAM, Eliza M 17 Obedience
A 33
BINNS, Amelia D 80
BIRAM, Hannah 33
BIRCH, Ann 34 Jane M 83 Mary
33 Sarah 33 Susan 33
BIRD, Betsy 34 Elizabeth 34
Hannah M 34 Lucy 34
BIRDSON, Mary Elizabeth 127
BIRDSONG, Mary (Foster) 34
Peggy 34 Winaford 34
BISHOP, Aquila 34 Euphemia 13
Levina 34 Margaret 34 Martha
34 Mary 34 144 Mary Ann 34
Mary C 34
BIUS, Elizabeth 68 James 67
BLACK, Elizabeth 35 Johanna 35
Joseph 35 Lucretia 189 Lucy
35 Martha P 35 Mary 34 66
Mary A 56 Matilda 35 Mildred
A 34 Rosanna 35
BLACKBURN, Jane 35 Mary Ann
H 35 Nancy 35
BLACKEMORE, Polly 35
BLACKFORD, Caroline 35
BLACKLEY, Mildred L 100
BLACKMAN, Eliza 35 Owen 35
BLACKMORE, Eliza 35

BLACKSTOCK, Permelia 35
BLACKWELL, Catharine 35
Elizabeth 35 Mary A 35
Rebecca 35
BLADEN, Millie 35
BLAIN, Hannah 36
BLAINE, Eliza A 36 Elizabeth 36
BLAIR, Clarissa W 36 Dianah 36
Mary 36 Nancy 39 Norway 141
Polly 36
BLAKE, Anna R 36 Cynthia A
(---) 97 Elizabeth 36 Helen 36
Margaret 36 Mary P 36 Sarah
36 Sarah M 101
BLAKELY, Dicy A 36
BLAKEMORE, Elizabeth W 36
Joseph 35 Polly 35 36
BLALOCK, Mary C 36
BLANCHETT, Mary 36 Stacy 36
Susan 36
BLAND, Adeline 37 Elizabeth 37
Martha 37 Martha Elizabeth 37
Mary 37 Mary B 37 Sarah 37
Susan 180
BLANFORD, Sarah 37
BLANKENBECKLER, Amanda 37
BLANKENBEEKLER, Kisiah 144
BLANKENSHIP, Lucy 191 Nancy
37 Permelia 37 Polly 37 Sally
37 Susan 37
BLANKHALL, Martha M 39
Robert 38 39
BLANKINSHIP, Permelia 37
Sarah 37
BLANKS, Amanda M F 38
BLANN, Elizabeth 38
BLANTON, Elizabeth 38 Gilly 38
James 92 Jane 100 Mary A 100
Nancy 38 Sally 85
BLASINGHAM, Susan 320
BLAUCET, Sally 38
BLEDSOE, Julia 38 Sidney 38
BLESS, Ann 38 Caroline 38 Chris-
tian Henry 38 Elizabeth 38
Priscilla 38
BLESSER, Jane 95
BLISS, Ann 38 Caroline 38 Chris-
tian Henry 38 Henry 38 Pris-
cilla 38 Stephen 38
BLIZZARD, Margaret W 38 Mary
W 38
BLOCK, Margaret 38 Mary 38

BLOXSOM, Elizabeth 16
BLOXUM, --- 16
BLUFORD, Elizabeth 38
BLUME, Elizabeth 38
BLUNKALL, Martha M 39
BLY, Sarah 145
BLYTHE, Susan 26
BOALES, Jacob 45 Susan 46
BOAN, David 45 Elizabeth 45
BOAR, John H 64 Susannah 64
BOARD, Cleopatra A 39 Elizabeth
39 Mary 39 102 Mary A 39
Nancy 39 Sally 39
BOATWRIGHT, Judith 39 Judith
W 52 Mary 39 Nancy 39
Rebecca 187 Richard 39
BOAZ, Elizabeth 146 Martha 39
BOBBETT, Nancy 53
BOBBIT, Lucy 92
BOBBITT, Dicey 39 Jemimah 39
Mildred 39 Nancy 39
BOBLETT, Elizabeth Ann 39
BODINE, Catherine 39 Nancy 94
BOGARTH, Anna 85
BOGGS, Nancy 40 Rebecca 74
BOHANNAH, Polly 40
BOHANNON, Elizabeth 40 Franky
40 Maria 40
BOHANON, Mary 150
BOHON, Athaliah 40 Eliza 40
BOICE, Rebecca 40
BOLEN, Mary 40
BOLES, Elisabeth 113 Peggy 40
BOLIN, Mary 40 Mary T 40
Samuel 40
BOLING, Margaret 40 Nancy 40
Polly 46 Sarah 40 Thomas 46
BOLINGER, Rebecca 107
BOLLING, Nancy 40 Rebecca 40
BOLLINGER, Lea 99
BOLT, Elizabeth 40
BOLTON, Elizabeth W 41
Frances 41 Hannah M 41 Har-
riet 32 Margaret 40
BOMAR, Sarah 204
BOMBACK, Mary Ann 41
BOMBAUGH, Andrew 41 Mary
Ann 41
BOND, Edith 41 Elizabeth 29
Emily 41 Henehie 41 Jane 41
Margaret 41 Mary 41 Nancy 41
Prudence 41 Sarah 64

BONDURANT, Marcia L 41
BONHAM, Anna 41
BONNELL, Hannah 41
BONNER, Elizabeth 41 Mary 41
　Sarah 41
BONNET, Margaret 73
BONNETT, Sarah 42
BOOKER, Ann F 42 Catherine 42
　Claramond 42 Elizabeth 42
　Margaret 42 Martha 42 Martha
　A 42 Mary 42 Matilda 42
　Pinkethman D 42 Sarah 42
　Selena 42
BOOP, Sarah A 46
BOOTEN, Elizabeth 40
BOOTH, Alley 42 Deborah 42
　Elizabeth 42 Keziah 43 Mary D
　42 Mary E 42 Mary W 42
　Rachel 42 Rebecca Jane 110
BOOTHE, Dolly 43 Dorothy 43
　Mary F 43
BOOZ, Matilda 43
BORAKER, Mary Ann 43
BORDEN, Mary 43
BORER, Jacob 43 Sarah 43
BOROUGH, Sarah 43
BORRER, Jacob 43 Sarah 43
BORTON, Vashti 122
BORUM, Eliza A 43
BOSHER, --- 55 Elizabeth 82
　·Gabrilla H 43 Unity 43 Verity
　43
BOSMAN, Nancy 43
BOSS, Lucy 316
BOSSERMAN, Catharine 43 Mar-
　garet 43
BOSSLEMAN, Catharine 43
　George 43
BOSTIC, Sarah 43
BOSTON, Elizabeth 117
BOSWELL, Ellen J 44 Katie 43
　Nancy 43
BOTKIN, Elizabeth 44 Malinda 44
　Sarah 44
BOTTOM, Jane 44 Mary A 95
BOTTS, Emily 44
BOUGH, Eliabeth 188
BOUGHTON, Susan 44
BOULDIN, Catharine 44 Catharine
　C 44 Celia 44 Nancy (---) 136
　Sarah B 44
BOULTON, Joel 91 Margaret 44

BOULWARE, Mary Ann 44
BOURN, Frances 185 Milla 44
　Polly 44
BOURNE, Mary 44 Nancy 44
BOUSE, Annis 44
BOUTZ, Margaret 45 Mary 45
BOWDEN, Indiana B 150 Mildred
　45
BOWEN, Elizabeth 45 Frances S
　45 Jeanette J 45 Nancy 45
　Rebecca 45 Sarah 45 Sarah J
　45
BOWERS, Barbara 45 Catharine
　45 Lydia 45 Martha T 45 Mary
　45 Rachel 45
BOWIE, Sarah A 45
BOWLEN, Fannie 45
BOWLER, Caroline V 45 Frances
　T 45 Martha 37
BOWLES, 181 Amelia H 163
　Caleb 40 Elizabeth 8 Hannah
　126 Judith 46 Judy 46 Mary
　Page 46 Peggy 40 Sarah 177
　Susan 46
BOWLEY, John 40
BOWLIN, Nancy 46 Polly 46
BOWLING, Caroline V 45 Jane
　130
BOWLWARE, Marie E 4
BOWMAN, Eva Catharine 46 Gil-
　bert 46 Isaac 41 Mary 46 Mary
　A 46 Mickey 46 Nancy 46
　Polly 46 Polly S 46 Sally 46
　Sarah A 46
BOWRY, Bettie 84 Eliza W Dur-
　fey 46 Sarah Ann 46
BOWSEL, Jane K 46
BOWSELL, Jane K 46 Matthew
　46
BOWYER, Elizabeth A 47
　Elizabeth F 47 Purmelia 47
　Rebecca 47
BOYD, Ann 24 Elizabeth 47 Jane
　M 47 Martha (---) 5 Mary L 47
　Sarah E 47 John 68 Margaret
　47 Rachel 47
BOYERS, Elizabeth 47
BOYLAN, Levinah 156
BOYLE, Caleb 40 Eliza 24 Peggy
　40
BOYLES, Margaret 47
BOZMAN, Edward 43 Nancy 43

BRACKETT, Frances 30
BRADFIELD, Elizabeth L 47
Maria 47 Nancy 82 Susannah
47
BRADFORD, Ann 47 Ann A 201
Elizabeth 47 Hannay 127 Leah
47 Lucinda (---) 153 Margaret
47 Mary 47 Peggy 47
BRADLEY, 175 Elizabeth 48
Mary 4 48 55 Mary C 48 Polly
48 Sally 48 Wilmoth 206
BRADNENR, Mariah 181
BRADS, Eleanor 51
BRADSHAW, Amy 48 Frances S
48 Lucy Ann 48 Mancy A 48
Margaret 48 Martha 153 Mary
48 Permelia 48 Rhoda Ann 48
Sarah 48
BRADY, Elizabeth 20 Lucinda 48
Nancy 48 Susanna 48 William
20
BRAGG, Eliza S 49 Judith 49
Judy 49 Maria A 49 Nancy 49
Sallie H 49 Susannah 48
BRAITHWAITE, Maria 49 Susan
49
BRAME, Cary Happy 75
BRAMEL, John 49 Sarah 49
BRAMHAM, Elizabeth H 24
BRAMHORN, E W 102
BRAMMELL, Sarah 49
BRAMMER, Frances 49 Mary 49
BRANAMAN, Elizabeth 49 Mary
A 49
BRANCH, Elizabeth 151 Emma
49 Harriet T 49 Mary 49 Mary
C 91 Matilda Archer 49
Winiford 49
BRAND, Sarah 50
BRANDOM, Francis 50
BRANDON, Jane 50
BRANHAM, Jemima 50 Sarah 50
BRANIGAN, Lucy F 50
BRANIJIN, John 50 Lucy F 50
BRANNON, Elizabeth 50 Ruth 50
Sally 50
BRANSCOM, Tabitha 50
BRANSCOMB, Francis 50 Hannah
50
BRASFIELD, Sophia 50
BRASHEAR, Resa 164
BRASWELL, Elizabeth 133

BRATHWAIT, Benjamin 49 Maria
49
BRATTON, Hannah 50 Mary 50
Sarah 50
BRAWLEY, Frances 50
BRAWNER, Mary 50
BRAY, Mary S 51
BREARDY, Nancy 51
BREEDEN, Mary 130
BREEDLOVE, Eleanor 51 Mary
293 Matilda C 169
BRELSFORD, Mary E 51
BRENNON, Elizabeth 51
BRENT, Ann N 51 Elizabeth 51
Julia 4 Lucy Page 51
BRENTON, Martha E 59
BRESSIE, Elizabeth Ann 51
BREWBAKER, Anne 51
BREWER, Anna 51 Benjamin 51
Elizabeth 51 Litha 51 Polly
113 Rebecca 53 Susan A 51
Tabitha W 51 Wiley 51 Wil-
liam 51
BRIAN, Peggy 138
BRIANT, Sarah 51
BRICKHEAD, Mary 52
BRICKHOUSE, Ann J 52
BRIDEWELL, Nancy 139
BRIDGES, Ann R 52 Elizabeth 52
BRIDWELL, Mary 52 Milly 55
BRIGGS, Lucy 8 Nancy 52
Rebecca 52
BRIGHAM, Cassandra 52 Mary 52
BRIGHT, Dorcas 52 Ester 60 Es-
ther 60 John 60 Sarah 52
BRIGHTWELL, Judith W 52
Peggy 60 Sally 52
BRILES, Hannah 202
BRILL, Mary 52 Mary Catharine
52 Polly 52 Rebecca 52 Sarah
Elizabeth 52
BRIMER, Lucy 52
BRIMMER, Lucy 52 Mary 123
Polly 123 Zachariah 52
BRINNON, Chilton 51 Elizabeth
51 Shelton 51
BRISCOE, Eliza H 53 Juliet
Wood 52
BRISTER, George 53 Susan 53
BRISTOR, Susan 53
BRITT, Anna 53 Eleanor 82
Jemimah 53 Lois O 53 Mar

BRITT (continued)
garet 53 Martha J 53 Mary 53
Polly 53 Susannah 179
BRITTON, Elizabeth H 58 Martha
J 53 Nancy 53 Patty 53
Rebecca 53 Sarah B 44
BROACH, Polly 96
BROAD, James 31 Mary 31
BROADBELT, James 31 Mary 31
BROADBENT, James 31 Mary 31
BROADDUS, Hannah 1
BROADIE, Nancy 53
BROADUS, Sarah 63
BROADWATER, Margaret 53
BROADY, Ellen 53 Nancy 53 Wil-
liamson 53
BROCK, Hetty 182
BROCKENBROUGH, Sarah Jane
93
BROCKETT, Elizabeth 53
BROCKMAN, Lucy A 53 Lucy E
53
BRODUS, Mary 147
BRODY, Nancy 53 Williamson 53
BROILES, Melevy 93
BROMLEY, Mildred M 54
BRONAUGH, Judith 54 Mary C 54
BROOFMAN, Catherine 118
BROOKE, Elizabeth W 36
BROOKES, Ellen H 54 Esther
Jane 54 Sarah Taliaferro 54
BROOKOVER, June 54
BROOKS, Amelia (Fletcher) 161
Ann 54 Ann Maria 152 Caroline
54 Eliza 54 Elizabeth 54 55
Elizabeth M 54 Elvira A 55
Fanny 54 Frances 209 Maria
54 Martha 55 Mary 54 55 Milly
55 Nancy A 57 Phebe 54 Rhoda
54 Sarah 54 55 Stacey A 54
Susan 44 Zachariah 54
BROOME, Mary Jane 149
BROTHERS, Emily 55
BROUGH, Jane 147
BROUGHMAN, Elizabeth 55
BROWDER, Fanny 55 Mary J 23
BROWER, Lydia 104
BROWN, Adelaide 56 Agnes 56
Amelia 56 Ann Maria 57
Casandra 58 Catharine 8 56 72
Charlotte 199 Edith 56 Effie 58
Elizabeth 10 56 57 58 137

BROWN, (continued)
Elizabeth (---) 21 Elizabeth H
58 Gracie 57 Hannah 57 219
Harriet I 57 Jane 55 Jane
Arena 55 Judith 58 Julia A 56
Lettie 57 Malinda 56 Malinda
U 57 Margaret (---) 4 Maria
147 Martha 55 58 Martha H 57
Mary 30 55 56 60 Mary A 56
Mary Ann 57 Mary H 95 Mary
M 57 Mary W 24 Mercy 56
Nancy 55 58 151 Nancy (---)
154 Nancy A 57 Polly 56 92
Polly R 55 Rebecca 71 203
Sagey G 67 Sallie 56 Sally 56
58 Sarah 56 Sarah H 57 Susan
57 Susanna 56 74 Virginia 56
William 56 58 Winnafred 57
BROWNE, Alford 57 Mary Ann 57
BROWNING, Samantha 58 Sarah
58
BROWNLEE, Nancy 58
BROWNLEY, Jane 58 Sarah 58
BROWNLOW, Martha Maria
Robert 58
BRUBECK, Catharine 43
BRUCE, Jane B 59 Maria 59 Sally
59 Sarah 186 Sophronia 59
BRUDEN, Winney 83
BRUE, Ridley 59
BRUFFLER, Susan 59
BRUFFY, Polly 53
BRUGH, Abraham 59 Elizabeth 81
Harman 59 Ridley 59
BRUMFIELD, Jane 59 Letitia 59
Susanna 59
BRUMLEY, Margaret 162 Melinda
155 Sarah 59
BRUNER, Priscilla 3 Sarah 59
BRUNNEMER, Catharine 59 Mar-
tha E 59
BRUNTY, Elizabeth 59 Mary E 59
BRUSE, Matilda Archer 49
BRYAN, Calista 59 Martha W 59
Mary 60 Nelson 60 Percia 60
Rebecca W 120
BRYANT, Ann M 60 Cynthia Ann
60 Frances 60 Lavinia P P 210
Martha 60 Nancy 60 Sally 60
Sarah 60 Sarah Ann 101
BRYARLY, Mary 60
BRYDIE, Margaret 132

BRYTE, Ester 60 Esther 60
BUCHANAN, Frances 60 Mary
 Ann 161 Nancy 60 Peggy 60
 Phebe 87 Rachel 60
BUCK, Eliza T 60 Hannah 60
 Mary C 60 Nancy 39 Rebecca
 R 13
BUCKER, Abraham 60
BUCKEY, Sidney 122
BUCKHANAN, Lucretia 60
BUCKHANON, James 60 Lucretia
 60
BUCKLES, Rachel 23
BUCKLEY, Fannie 61 Nancy 61
BUCKNER, Adeline M 61 Lucinda
 146 Mary 61 Mildred 61
BUFKIN, Mary 61
BUFORD, Frances A 61
BUGG, Frances 61 Martha 61
BUKER, Elizabeth 168
BUKEY, Eliza Ann 116
BUKLE, Anthony 32 Dinah 32
BULEY, Hester 90
BULGER, Sarah 61
BULL, Jane 61
BULLARD, Lucy A F 61
BULLINGTON, Ann 62
BULLMAN, Clarissa 62
BULLOCK, Eliza 62 Susan 59
BUMGARDNER, Ruth 91
BUMGARNER, Rebecca 62
BUNCH, Elizabeth 62 Porency 62
 Sarah 62
BUNCHETT, Elizabeth 41
BUNDRANT, Lucy 62 Tabitha 62
BUNNER, Nancy 62
BUNTIN, Susan 62
BUNTING, Ann 62 Ann Maria 62
 Nancy 62
BUR, John H 64 Susannah 64
BURACHER, Henry 43 Mary Ann
 43
BURACKER, John 65
BURBECK, Margaret 43
BURCH, Cynthia 62 Elizabeth 124
 Frances H 22 Harriet 62 Jane
 30 John 33 Louisa 62 Mary 33
 62 Sarah 33 Susan 33
BURCHETT, Margaret 62
BURDETT, Matilda 63 Nancy 63
 Sarah 63
BURDICK, Elizabeth 63 John 63

BURDICK, (continued)
 Lucinda 63
BURDITT, Catharine 10 Elizabeth
 63 Lucinda 63
BURFORD, Elizabeth 147
BURGAYDINE, Margaret 127
BURGE, Anna 122 Bradford 63
 Eliza N 63 Frances E 63
 Keziah 63 Nancy 63
BURGES, Polly 40
BURGESS, Elizabeth 14 Mary 63
 Matilda 63
BURGIN, Susannah 63
BURK, Jane C 63 Lucinda 63
 Lucy 63 Mary 63 Sophia 63
BURKE, Ann 11 Libby 178
 Mahala 63 Nancy 63 Rebecca
 63 Sarah J 163 Zeviah 63
BURKHART, Elizabeth 63
BURKS, Demaris 64 Harriet B 64
 Remelia Anna 64 Sarah A 92
BURLEY, Elizabeth 64 Sarah 64
BURNER, Pris'cilla 3 Susannah 64
BURNES, Catharine 173
BURNETT, Eliza 64 Elizabeth 64
 Frances 64 Keziah 43 Margaret
 64 Martha 18 Mary Ann 64
BURNHAM, Mary E 64 Sophia 64
BURNS, Elender 64 Elizabeth 64
 Mary 106 Peachy E 64 Thursea
 70
BURR, Mary C 48 Susannah 64
BURREYS, George S 65
BURRIS, Nancy 18 Sarah 65
BURRISS, Mary James 131
BURROUGHS, Elizabeth W 65
 Katherine G 65 Leanna M 65
 Zachariah 65
BURROW, Ann Elizabeth 65
BURROWS, Sarah 50
BURSON, Sarah 65
BURTON, Catharine 65 Elizabeth
 65 Elizabeth C 65 Frances 93
 Maria 65 Mary 188 Nany 65
 Sally T 65 Sarah 115 Susanna
 65 Thena 65 Winney 65
BURWELL, Sally 65 Sally E 65
BUSBY, Elizabeth 38 Mary 66
BUSH, Elizabeth D 66 Mary A 66
 Sarah 66
BUSHONG, Elizabeth 56
BUSSABARGER, Elizabeth 66

BUSSEAR, Sarah 66
BUSSELL, Elizabeth 55 Lucy Ann 66 Mary 66
BUSSEY, Julia A 66
BUTCHER, Christina 66 Elenor 66
BUTLER, Alsa 75 Anna 313 Catharine 67 Catharine S 11 Catherine 39 E Rod 66 Elizabeth 66 Frances 67 Linney 67 Lucy 66 Margaret 67 Martha 182 Mary 67 Mildred 67 Nancy 66 67 Rosanna 191 Sally 66 67 171 212 Susan Ann 67 Susan H 66 Susanah 140
BUTT, Elizabeth 67 Mahala 67 Mary M 67 Mary P 67
BUTTERFIELD, Nancy 88
BUTTERWORTH, Delila 148 Lucy 67 Sally 67
BUTTS, Margaret 67 Mary Ann 67
BUXTON, Frances 67 Sagey G 67 Sary 67
BUYS, Elizabeth 139
BYAS, Elizabeth 68
BYBEE, Nancy 29
BYER, John 47 Margaret 47
BYERS, Catharine 166
BYRAM, Ellen 68
BYRD, Ann 68 Elizabeth 68 Esther 68 Lavinia 68 Nancy 68 120 Sarah 68
BYRNE, Elizabeth 68
BYRNS, Martha 68 William 68
BYWATERS, Sarah G Hudson 68
CACKLEY, Francie 68 Jane 68
CAIN, Anna N 68 Hannah 220 Nancy 68 Susanna 68
CAINES, Margaret 31
CAKELY, Catherine 68
CALBREATH, Ann 4
CALDWELL, Ann 68 Betsy Saxton 93 James 93 Mary Magdaline 69 Nancy 198 Ruth 68
CALE, Rachel 69
CALES, Elizabeth 69
CALHOUN, Elizabeth 69 Sarah (Williams) 41 197 313
CALLAHAM, Mary 16
CALLAHAN, Claramond 42 Cynthia 69 Eleanor 150 Jane S 69 Sarah 66 Sebastian 69 Sebeston

CALLAHAN (continued) 69
CALLAWAY, Margaret 69
CALLIHAN, Sally 67
CALLIHOM, Sally 67
CALLIS, Ann Maria 187 Lucy Weston 69
CALVERT, Jane K 46
CAMDEN, Sally W 129
CAMERON, Jane 69 Margaret 69 Martin 71 Sarah 71
CAMERSON, Elvina 69 Mary 69
CAMERY, Nancy 69
CAMLIN, Polina 171
CAMM, Ann W 8 Nancy W 8
CAMMERON, Ruthie 69
CAMON, Martin 71 Sarah 71
CAMP, Maria 70 Sarah 26 Thursea 70
CAMPBELL, Anguish 71 Ann 70 Anna M 71 Belinda 71 Cena Jane 70 Demartha 70 Dorcas 70 Eleanor 70 Ellen 70 Frances L 13 Jane 5 71 Jemima 70 Lucinda G 70 Malinda 70 Mary 49 71 Mary C 70 Milly 70 Moses 49 Nancy 70 71 147 Orphia 70 Polly 70 Rachel 180 Rebecca 71 Sallie Ann 71 Sarah 70 Sarah Ann 71 Sarah Wallace Lyle 70 Sency Jane 70 Sophia 70
CAMPER, Fannie 71
CAMRON, Daniel 69 Ruthie 69 Sarah 71
CANADA, Annie 71 John 71 Maria 71
CANNON, Nancy 25
CANTLEY, Mary 71 Mary (Ball) 71
CAPITO, Elizabeth 68
CAPLINGER, Catharine 71
CAPPER, Malinda E 71
CARAWY, Amy Sykes 71
CARBIERE, Harriet 72
CARDEN, Judith 72 Nancy 72
CARDER, Frances 72 Priscilla C 72
CARDIN, Frances E 72 Marandy S 72
CARDOZO, Mahala A 72
CARDWELL, Jane M 72 Lucy 72

CARDWELL (continued)
Mary L P 72 Sarah 72 Susanna
P 95
CARICO, Louisa 72
CARICOW, Ann E 197
CARL, Magdalena 183
CARLINE, Elizabeth 185
CARLISLE, Catharine 72 Jane 72
CARLTON, Eliza 72 Lucy 95
Nancy 72 Rachel 72
CARLYLE, Catharine 72 Robert
72
CARMAN, Rebecca 108
CARMICHAEL, Janet G 175
CARMICHIEL, Nancy 73
CARMICLE, John 73 Nancy 73
CARNAHAN, Eleanor 17
CARNAL, James 73 Mary M 73
Nancy D 73
CARNALL, Hannah 73
CARNE, Mary Ann Cleavely 102
CARNEAL, James 73 Mary M 73
CARNELL, Elizabeth 73
CARNES, Catharine 98
CARNEY, Margaret 73 Nancy F
73 Susan 73
CARNICLE, Jacob 73
CARNOL, Mary M 73
CARPENTER, Ann 73 Elizabeth
M 73 John 73 Malinda 73 Mar-
garet 73 Mary 141 196 Mary A
49 Polly 73 Sarah 132
CARPER, Jane Maria 73 Kitty 73
Margaret 73 Mary 81
CARR, Deborah W 74 Eleanor 110
Elizabeth 310 Martha 27 Mary
30 Penelope 74 Rebecca 74
Sally 74 Sarah 56 Susanna 74
Tamar 74
CARREL, Sarah (Dowell) 37
CARRIER, Sarah 160
CARRINGTON, Judith A 74
CARROL, Catharine H 74
CARROLL, Ann (Follin) 74
Dempson 74 Elizabeth 74
Juliet 74 Lydia 74 Nancy 74
CARRON, Joseph 99 Nancy Wall
P 99
CARSON, Elizabeth (Shaver) 108
Jane 74 Margaret 74 Margaret
K 74 Nancy 74 Polly 74
Rosannah 74

CARTER, Alsa 75 Amelia 75 Ann
75 Ann Parthena 89 Bains 75
Cary Happy 75 Catharine 76
189 Eliza 20 75 Eliza A 76
Elizabeth 75 76 Elizabeth F 76
Fanny A 75 Hellen 75 Jane 75
76 Judy 77 175 Julia 75 Julia
A 76 Littleberry 76 Mahala 75
Margaret 75 Martha 76 92 Mar-
tha K 75 Mary 75 Mary A 75
Mary Ann 76 Mary S 77 Nancy
76 Nancy A 175 Pamala 107
Phebe 75 Pollie 76 Sally 76
Sarah 133 Sarah Jane 75 Susan
75 Theodoric 76 Theodorick 76
Winney Maria 76
CARTHRAE, Julia A (---) 56
Mary Ann 20
CARTY, Catherine 77 Parthana 77
CARUTHERS, Ann R 77 Margaret
30
CARVER, Ann 19 Catharine 77
John Jr 77 Nancy 77
CARWILES, Nancy 110
CARY, Elizabeth 119 Mary Ann
77 Rebecca 77 Sarah E S 77
CASE, Norman 168 Penelope 77
CASEBOLT, Mary 77
CASEY, Jane 77 Mary A 77 Nelly
171 Sarah W 77 William 77
CASH, Belinda 71 Cynthia 77
Lucinda 121
CASHWELL, Sophia 78
CASKEY, Ann 78
CASON, Adaline 78 Maria E 78
Rebecca L 78
CASSADAY, Mary Ann 78
CASSELL, Lucy 78
CASTELOW, U 78
CASTER, Nancy 8
CASTLE, Sarah A 78
CASTLEN, Eliza 78
CASTLIN, Eveline 78 Nancy 78
CASTLOW, John 78 U 78
CASTO, Magdalena 78 Mary 78
Sidney 78
CASTOR, Susan 78
CATLETT, Mary W 78 Pheraby
78
CATLIN, Betsey 79 Elizabeth 79
Thomas 79
CATLING, Betsey 79 Elizabeth

335

CATLING (continued)
79
CATTERTON, Nancy 79
CAVE, Elizabeth 79 Lourena 199
Sarah 79
CAVENDISH, Jenette 79
CAW, Marthey 79
CAWOOD, Mary 79 Sally R 79
CAWTHARN, Mary Hickle 99
Thomas 99
CAWTHON, Elizabeth 79
CAYNOR, Nancy 150
CAYTON, Nancy 79
CEAN, Catharine Heavener 116
CEESE, Catharine 277
CEMANTHA, Susan 290
CERTAIN, Rebecca 79 Susan 79
CHADDUCK, Mary 79
CHAFFIN, Nancy 79 Tabitha 79
CHAFFINS, Polly 141
CHALFANT, Sarah 97
CHALKLEY, China W 16
Rebecca 79
CHAMBERLAIN, Catherine 80
CHAMBERLAYNE, Martha B 80
CHAMBERLIN, Malinda E 71
CHAMBERS, Amelia D 80 Ann 80
Ellen Maria 80 Julia H 88
Mary Ann 80
CHAMBLIN, Mary 78 Sarah 80
CHAMBLISS, Evelena B 80 Lucy
80 Mary 2
CHAMPION, Rebecca 80
CHAMPLIN, Rachel 80
CHANCELLOR, Fannie L 80
CHANDLER, Hannah 36 Hervey
80 Julia Ann 80 Keziah 80
Mary 80 Mary A F 266 Sarah
80 Susanna 81
CHANDLOR, Nancy 212
CHANDOIN, Eliza 81
CHANEY, Dicey 81 Elizabeth 81
Frances 81 Mary 81 Nancy 81
Sally 81 Sarah 81 Serena A 81
CHAPELAER, Nancy 82 William
A 82
CHAPELIER, Nancy 82 William
A 82
CHAPMAN, Chason 81 Elizabeth
81 Lucy 81 Mary 81 Reity 81
Sarah 205 Susanna 81 Susannah
81

CHAPPALEAR, Susan 82
CHAPPEL, Lucinda 82
CHAPPELL, Elizabeth (---) 21
Nancy 226 Susan 94
CHAPPLEAR, Nancy 82
CHARLTON, Araminta 82 Jane 82
Malinda Jane 82 Polly 37
Rebecca 82
CHARTER, Clorinda 102
CHASTAIN, Eleanor 82 Eliza A
43 Susan H 134
CHATHAM, Betsey Ann 180 Sarah
181
CHEADLE, Mary 210
CHEATHAM, Martha 82 Mary Ann
82 Nancy 82 Patsey 91
CHEEK, Kitty 149 Mary (---) 18
CHELF, Martha 164 Virenda 82
CHENAULT, Ann 82 Elizabeth 82
Joice 210
CHENNAULT, Sarah 82
CHERRY, Casandra 58 Elizabeth
82
CHESER, Sarah 82
CHESSER, Samuel 82 Sarah 82
CHEUVRRONT, Sarah 83
CHEVERONT, Amos 83 Sarah 83
CHEWNING, Delilah 83 Elizabeth
83 Lucy 83 Nancy 83 Susan 83
CHICOATE, Parmelia 99
CHILCOT, John 83 Rachel 83
CHILCOTT, Rachel 83
CHILDERS, Mary 83
CHILDRESS, Jane 83 Jane M 83
Nancy 83 Sarah H 83 Sophia 83
Winney 83
CHILDRIS, Mace 143 Mason 143
CHILDS, Nancy 66 Rachel A 84
CHILES, Lucy F 83 Nancy 210
CHISHOLM, Elizabeth 140
CHISMOND, John 84 Sarah 84
CHITTUM, Betsy 83
CHITTURN, Sarah Ann 83
CHOATE, Dorothy Proctor 206
CHOWNING, Cordelia 84
CHRISMAN, Dorothy 84 Thirza
Ann E 84
CHRISMOND, Sarah 84
CHRISTIAN, Bettie 84 Caroline M
84 Susan 84
CHRISTIANS, 192
CHUMBLY, Patsy 84

CHUMNEY, Nancy Larkin 84
CIRCLE, Martha L 84
CLAIBORNE, Martha 84 Sallie A
84
CLAIG, Martha 109
CLAPTON, Nancy 60
CLARDY, Lucinda 194
CLARE, Eliza 84 Virginia J 84
CLARK, Ann 84 213 Ann C 84
Ann J 85 Barbara 86 Benete 85
Catharine 84 Cindarilla 85
Delila 114 Edy Olive (Martin)
143 Eliza C 85 Eliza J 84
Elizabeth 85 86 198 Elizabeth
H 86 Elizabeth J 85 Harriet 86
Jane 85 151 Jane C (---) 63
Jane R 85 Lettice 84 Levina
34 Margaret 26 107 Margaret M
86 Mary 85 86 208 Mary Ann F
86 Mary J 85 Mildred H 86
Nancy 5 85 156 Patsey 85
Peggy 86 Phebe F 85 Phebe
Howson 16 Polly 84 Rachel A
84 Rebecca 85 86 Rhoda C 85
Sallie 179 Sally 85 Sarah 84 86
209 Selina 85 Susan 16
Susanna 86 Thomas 86 Wil-
liam 86
CLARKE, Elizabeth 96 Elizabeth
H 86 Margaret M 86 Martha
118 Mary E 86 Matilda 86
Minerva J 86 Nancy 85 Sarah
86 William 86
CLARKSON, Mary E 64 Nancy 79
CLATOR, Coleman 87 Elizabeth
87 Phebe 87
CLAXTON, Elizabeth 140
CLAY, Jordon 86 Marthy 86 Per-
melia 86 Susan 86
CLAYBROOK, Daisy 87 Mis-
saniah 87
CLAYPOOL, Melinda 87
CLAYTON, Ann Eliza 128 Martha
87 Patsy 87 Susanna 87
CLAYTOR, Amanda 87 Elizabeth
87 Julia 87 Martha Ann 19
Phebe 87
CLEATON, Frances 87
CLEAVELAND, Ann 33
CLEAVELY, Mary Ann 102
CLEFT, Delila Martin 88 George
W 88

CLEGHORN, Rachel 87
CLEIN, George 88 Susan
Didowick 88
CLELLAND, Jane (---) 30
CLEM, Sarah 58
CLEMENS, Jemima 105 Polly J 4
CLEMENT, Cary 87 Isham 87
CLEMENTS, Cary 87 Elizabeth
87 Martha J 87 Mary 106
Pattie 117 Polly J 4 Sally 87
Virginia 87
CLEMINGS, Matilda 87
CLERENGER, Elizabeth 88
CLEVELAND, Ann 34
CLICE, Sarah Triplett 88
CLIENTINCK, Lydia Holler 88
CLIFT, Delila Martin 88
CLIFTON, Sarah Miller 88
CLINE, Catherine 135 Elizabeth
88 Elizabeth Coffee 88 Julia H
Chambers 88 Lane Pugh 88
Mary Baker 88 Sarah (---)
McPeak 88 Susan Didowick 88
CLINEDINST, Elizabeth 177
Isaac 88 Lydia Holler 88
CLIPPARD, Nancy Henry 88
CLISER, Sarah Fletcher 88
CLOE, Charles B 88 Harriet
Wyatt 88
CLOPTON, Cornelia H Palmer 88
Elizabeth 182 Sarah S G
Skinker 88
CLOUCH, Mary 34
CLOUD, Nancy Butterfield 88
CLOWE, Harriet Wyatt 88
CLOWER, Mary 89
CLUTTER, Catherine 89 Rebecca
71
CLYBORN, Mahala Pettis 89
CLYSER, Martin 88 Sarah Flet-
cher 88
CLYZER, Martin 88 Sarah Flet-
cher 88
CNSALVO, Elizabeth 38
COALTER, Mary 89
COAN, Littleton 94 Nancy Cul-
peper 94 Patient Ann Jones 90
William 90
COATES, Mary R Smith 89 Nancy
Shipp 89
COATS, James 89 Mary R Smith
89 Nancy Howell 89

COBB, Martha R 89
COBBS, Ann Parthena Carter 89
Cynthia 62 Mary L 47 Nancy
Woods 89
COCHRAN, Frances 175 Susannah
Richardson 89
COCK, Ellenor 172 Jane Philips
89 Louisa J Day 89 Mary 121
COCKE, Cecelia Ann Russel 89
Harriet W Holland 89 James
89 Mary 75 Rebecca Richards
89
COCKERELL, Anna Leetman 89
COCKRAM, Allen 89 Hannah 106
Nancy L Waller 89
COCKRAN, Mariah R 89
COCKRHAN, Nancy L Waller 89
COCKRILL, Catharine Riley 90
CODDY, Nancy 119
COE, Anna Sherwood 90 Margaret
Wright 90
COEN, Grace McCulley 90
Patient Ann Jones 90 Susanna
90
COFER, Catharine 205
COFFEE, Elizabeth 88 Jane 5
COFFEY, Eveline 151 Jane 5
Mary Ann 118 Peggy 155
COFFLAND, Eleanor Potts 90
COFFMAN, Elizabeth 142 182
Elizabeth Fadeley 90 Emily R
Porter 90 Hester Buley 90
COGAR, Eve Spillman 90
COGBILL, Elizabeth Cole 90
COGER, Elizabeth Kingery 90
Margaret Mollohan 90
COGHILL, Mary Samuel 90 Polly
Samuel 90
COHAGAN, Catharine Fling 90
COHEN, Mary W Heath 90
COIL, Dolly 91 Elvina 69
COLBERT, Joseph 91
COLBY, Gilly 38
COLE, Ann E Beal 91 Anna
Freeman 91 Catharine 91 Eliza
91 Elizabeth 90 Hannah 91
Hannah Rogor 91 Liza 91
Lydia Perry 91 Martha Ket-
chum 91 Nancy Wharton 91
Patsey Cheatham 91 Polly
Todd 91 Priscilla Roler 91
Rebecca (Thompson) Lambert

COLE (continued)
91 Ruth Bumgardner 91
COLEBURN, Ann 194
COLEMAN, Ann S 150 Catharine
(---) Smith 93 Judida Duncan
91 Lucy Stewart 91 Martha 14
Martha G 9 Mary C Branch 91
Mary Headen 92 Mary King 92
Nancy 43 92 Polly Watkins 91
Robert 93 Sally Mills 92 Sarah
Cruise 92 Sarah Dunnavant 92
Susan 109
COLEY, Elizabeth McClain 92
Ridley 59
COLIER, Elizabeth G 105
COLLETT, Elizabeth Davis 92
COLLEY, Margaret (Stidlen)
Stratton 92 Martha Carter 92
Polly Brown 92 Sallie Willis
92 Sally Hogan 218 Sarah A
Burks 92
COLLIER, Frances 92 Lucy Bob-
bit 92 Mary 114
COLLINGS, Mary Ann 202
COLLINS, Abie 92 Agnes Max-
well 93 Catherine 92 Catherine
Jesse 92 Christina 92
Elizabeth Fisher 92 Elizabeth
Selock 93 Frances 126 Mary A
92 Nancy Hancock 92 Zilpha
Cornel 93
COLLIS, Mary E 135
COLLISON, Cynthia Robinson 93
COLLY, Sallie 170 Sarah 30
COLMAN, Catharine (---) Smith
93
COLP, Catharine 71
COLSTON, Jane Marshall 93
Sarah Jane Brockenbrough 93
COLVERT, Harriet Weedon 93
COLVILLE, Leah Baker 93
COLVIN, Jane 199 Louisa Plem-
mons 93 Margaret Youill 93
Melevy Broiles 93
COLWELL, Betsy Saxton 93
COMBS, Anna M Milner 94 Fanny
Harrison 94 Jane Rogers 93
Margaret A Pritchett 93
COMER, Catharine Godber 94
Elizabeth Strob 94 Elizabeth
Strole 94 Rachel Jones 94
Susan T Dunkley 94

338

COMPTON, Anna (---) Johnson 94 John 107 Mary 298 Polly 298 Susan Chappell 94
CONANT, Mary McClallan 94
CONAWAY, Anna F 116 Nancy Bodine 94 Rhoda (---) 142
CONDREY, Catharine Ford 94 Judith W Goode 94
CONE, Littleton 94 Nancy Culpeper 94 Samuel 94
CONELY, Fanny B (---) Balderson 94 Lucy Hazard 94 Robert 94
CONGROVE, Elizabeth Taylor 94
CONKLIN, Easter 168
CONLEY, Asona Romine 94 Martha Ann Sheppard 95 Nancy Middleton 94
CONNALLY, --- 44
CONNELL, Polly 36
CONNELLEE, Fanny B (---) Balderson 94 Lucy Hazard 94 Robert 94
CONNELLY, Fanny B (---) Balderson 94 Jesse 95 Lucy Hazard 94 Martha Ann Sheppard 95 Mary A Botton 95
CONNER, Anna (---) Crook 95 Lucy Carlton 95 Martha Ann 95 Martha T Scales 95 Mary 52 Polly 52 Rachel More 95 Rebecca Powell 95 Susanna P Cardwell 95
CONNOR, Ailcy 99
CONRAD, Elizabeth Copenhaver 95 Eunice Mace 95 Jane Blesser 95 Mary Ann Richards 95 Mary H Brown 95
CONROD, Jane Blesser 95 Mary H Brown 95 Peter 95 Solomon 95
CONTE, George 100
CONVERSE, Mary R 196
CONWAY, Daniel 94 Harriet E Thornton 95 Martha E Stanfield 95
COOK, Catharine A Croft 96 Elizabeth Clarke 96 Elizabeth Mayers 96 Elizabeth O Darrows 96 Hannah Neff 96 Jane Philips 89 John 89 Louisa J Day 89 Margaret 189 Margaret

COOK (continued) M 86 Mary Harford 96 Nancy Martin 96 Parthena Wilson 96 Polly Broach 96 Salley (---) Harvey 96 Sallie Pennington 96 Sarah 96 Sarah (---) Harvey 96
COOKE, Ann Norris 96 Lucy Harper 96 Margaret L Harrison 96
COOKSEY, Sarah D Watson 96
COOLEY, Betsy Ford 96 Elizabeth Ford 96 Jemima Walden 96
COONROD, Sally 4
COONS, Hannah Jones 97
COOPER, 139 Cynthia A (---) Blake 97 Elenor Daley 97 Elizabeth 97 Elizabeth (---) Wilson 97 Elizabeth Lavanard 97 Elizabeth Quales 97 Elizabeth Suggs 97 Ellen 68 Hester 97 Margaret M 97 Mary H Wingfield 97 Mary S Atwell 97 Polly Thompson 97 Sarah Chalfant 97
COPELAND, Jane 97
COPENHAVER, Barbara Philipy 97 Charlotte 202 Elizabeth 95
COPIN, Annie 97
COPPAGE, John H 98 Mary 33 Narcissa 111 Sarah Vaughn 98
COPPEDGE, Rebecca 98 Sarah Vaughn 98
COPSEY, Sarah (Green) 44
CORBAN, Catherine 98
CORBETT, Martha 138 Martha Guy 98 Mathew 98
CORBIN, Jane 98 Nancy Scott 98 Rebecca J Nicholson 98 Sarah Davis 98
CORBINS, Rebecca Williams 98
CORBITT, Martha Guy 98
CORDELL, Catharine Carnes 98
CORDER, Frances 98 Jane 98 Susan Gorder 98
CORDOW, Susan 46
CORE, Jane Johns 98 Sarah 56
CORKER, Nancy Martin 98 Nancy Olns 98
CORLEY, Christine Wince 98 Elizabeth 98
CORNEL, Zilpha 93
CORNELL, Elcy Spencer 99

CORNELL (continued)
Elizabeth 73
CORNETT, Reuben 99
CORNUTT, Elizabeth S (---)
Roberts 99 John 99
CORNWELL, Betsy Yeaman 99
Clarissa Postlaw 99 Judy
Reese 99 Letitia Dodd 99 Lucy
A Pullin 99 Mary E Guant 99
Nancy Posey 99 Thomas 99
CORRELL, Frances 15
CORRICK, Parmelia Chicoate 99
CORRON, Ailcy Connor 99
Elizabeth McDade 99 Nancy
Wall 99
COSNER, Catharine Henline 99
COTHRON, Mary Hickle 99
COTTELL, Margaret 73
COTTERILL, Lea (Bollinger)
Wilson 99 Polly Mathas 99
COTTON, Sophia 50 Susan 178
COTTRELL, Margaret 73 Mary 99
Samuel 99
COTTRILL, Sarah A Gratehouse
99
COUCH, Elizabeth Harrison 100
Rachel 100 Elizabeth 223
COUNCIL, Elizabeth 100 Par-
thenia 100 Sarah 318 Sarah M
Slade 100 Sarah Moore 100
COUNSELMAN, Mary Lindsey
100
COURTNEY, Mary Alderson 100
COUTTS, Samuel 97 Sophia Kelly
100
COWAN, Nancy R Dulaney 100
Nancy Susong 100
COWARD, Jane O 2 25
COWDERY, Samantha 58
COWELL, Elizabeth 35
COWEN, Martha (---) Stephens
100 Mary Pickering 100
COWGILL, Hannah 158
COX, Ann Hart 101 Annie Stone
101 Deborah W 74 Delila
Payne 100 Elizabeth 28 55 291
Elizabeth (---) Ratcliff 101
Eva Stoner 100 Frances Festor
100 Hannah 101 Jane Blanton
100 Joana Stone 101 Margaret
148 229 Maria Mooney 100
Martha Foulks 100 Martha

COX (continued)
Marie 182 Mary A Blanton 100
Mary Armistead 100 Mary C
100 Mary Steel 101 Mildred L
Blackley 100 Nancy Ray 101
Patsy Figgs 101 Peggy 182
Sallie (---) 139 Sarah 230
Sarah A 45 Sarah Ann (Bryant)
101 Sarah E Moore 100 Tem-
perance Williams 101 Thursa
Harper 101
COYNER, Elizabeth 101 Frances
Wallace 101 Margaret 48
CRABTREE, Betsy Ann 101
Elizabeth 101 Pheraby (---) 78
CRADDOCK, Joanna 101
CRAFT, Elizabeth Oiler 101 Mary
Becker 101
CRAFTON, Elizabeth 5
CRAIG, Dorcas Handley 101
Elizabeth Pence 101 Margaret
128 Margaret McCutchen 101
102 Mary 154 Mary
McGoreghan 102 Mildred
Medor 101 Sarah M Blake 101
Sarah W (---) Rust 101
CRAIGG, Mary McManaway 102
CRAIN, Nancy White 102
CRALLE, Frances M Belfield 102
CRAMER, Elizabeth Moore 102
Margaret M 171 Priscilla
Smoot 102
CRANDALL, Clorinda Charter 102
Elizabeth Wood 102 John 102
Susan Jones 102
CRANDOL, Elizabeth 102
Elizabeth Wood 102 Susan
Jones 102
CRANE, Armistead 102 Caty
Penns 102 Elizabeth 210 Mary
(Board) Hendley 102 Mary
Gibbs 102 Nancy White 102
CRANFORD, Susan Athey 102
CRANK, E W Bramhorn 102
CRANSTON, Cassee Ann Harris
102
CRASK, Shady 102
CRAUTZ, Margaret 123
CRAVEN, Hannah Iden 102
CRAVENS, Ann C Newman 102
CRAWFORD, Amarilla Noell 103
Charlotte Austin 103 Charlotte

CRAWFORD (continued)
Laing 103 Jane 41 Jonas 102
Lucy 102 Margaret A Bell 103
Mary Ann Goss 103 Mary Stru-
bling 103 Nancy M 133 Pur-
melia 47 Rebecca 29 Ritter 2
Sarah 37 Sarah Rowlinson 103
Susan Athey 102
CRAWLEY, Catharine 103 Mary
D 164
CRAWN, Jemima Clemens 105
Joseph 105
CRAZIER, Sarah 131
CREASEY, Eliza W Hill 103 Jor-
dan 103 Mary E Beck 103
Robert 103
CREASY, Lucy 185 Polly Wat-
kins 103 Rebecca Shackelford
103
CREBS, Eliza B 142
CREECH, Mary 52
CREEKMORE, Betsy 103 Eliza
Flannagan 103 Katy (---)
Etheridge 103
CREEL, Elizabeth 171 Elizabeth
Naole 103 Mary Ann 44
CREESY, Mary E Beck 103
CREGER, John Peter 103 Polly
Hounshell 103
CREMORE, Catharine 56
CRENSHAW, Elizabeth 103 Mary
Walker Twyman 104
CRESS, Nancy Reed 104
CREW, Sarah Gilbert 104
CREWDSON, Emily C 119
CREWS, Polly Ann 141 Susan L
Sutherlin 104
CRIDER, Elizabeth 145 195
Emily B 158 Magdalene Wag-
goner 104
CRIGLER, Anna Faulkner 104
Christopher 104
CRIM, Susanna 104
CRISLER, Betsey Price 104 Mar-
garet 267
CRISMOND, Jane McDonald 104
Susan Hale 104
CRISP, Mary Jeffers 84 Nancy 38
CRIST, Catharine 24 Harriett B
Potts 104
CRITCHER, Susanna 81
CRITCHLOW, Margaret 154

CRITES, Ann (Kinkaid) Thurman
104 Elizabeth Lewis 104 Mary
Formash 104
CRITTENDEN, Martha Maria
Robert 58 Sally 52
CRITTENTON, Mary 42
CRITZ, Ann (Kinkaid) Thurman
104 Philip 104
CROCKETT, Mary Hogge 104
Wheaton 104
CROCKWELL, Mary 183
CROFT, Anna Jessee 104
Catharine A 96 Catharine
Sanger 104 Lydia Brower 104
Polly Shotwell 104 Sarah Mil-
ler 104
CROMER, Polly 46
CROMWELL, Hennerts Solmon
105
CRON, Jemima Clemens 105
CRONE, Catharine Shewy 105
Polly Sours 105
CROOK, Anna (---) 95 Elizabeth
G Colier 105 Jane Arena 55
Margaret Lyden 105
CROOKS, Catharine M Hennesy
105 Mary Ann Miller 105
CROPP, Rebecca L 78
CROPPER, Margaret 25
CROPSEY, Sarah (Green) 44
CROSS, Charity (Barnes) 105
Eliza Pitman 105 Elizabeth
136 196 197 Lucy A F 61 Mary
Tinsley 105 Sarah Saunders
105
CROSSER, Catharine 77
CROSSLIN, Elizabeth (---) Hall
105 Susan Daughtry 105
CROSTICK, Martha 27
CROUCH, Basheba Overstreet 105
Charlotte 127 Jane 105 Mar-
garet E 26 Mary Ann Crowder
105 Molly Brooks Temple 105
CROUT, Margaret King 105
CROW, Malinda 31 Mary Deems
106 Nancy Buford Johnson 106
Nancy Hutchinson 105 Sarah
105
CROWDER, Archer 106 Mary Ann
105 Sarah 72 Theopholis 106
Theotholis 106
CROWDIS, Sarah M Taylor 106

CROWER, Theopholis 106
CROWL, Mary A Dillahunt 106
    Sarah 260 Sarah Priest 106
CROWLEY, Mary Burns 106
    Sarah Humphrey 106
CROXTON, Frances G Ware 106
    Mary Clements 106
CRUCY, Polly 14
CRUIDSON, Lucy 24
CRUISE, Hannah Cockram 106
    Mazy Martin 106 Sarah 92
CRUM, Naoma Smith 106
CRUMBAKER, Catharine Koehler
    106
CRUMP, Cintha Ann Rountree 106
    Eliza G Watkins 106 Hammon
    106 James H 106 Jane Powell
    106 Margaret Clark 107 Martha
    Matthews 106 Susan Wynn 106
CRUMPACKER, Elizabeth Hewitt
    107 Elizabeth Royalty 107
    Sarah (Smith) Wolf 107
CRUMPTON, Thomas 94
CRUPPER, Sarah 141
CRUSEN, Louisa 20
CRUTCHFIELD, Susan R Amos
    107
CUBBAGE, Nancy Nichols 107
CULBERSON, Mary Jane (Sparks)
    2
CULLERS, Sarah Keyser 107
CULLY, Elizabeth 107
CULP, Catharine 71 Mary C 60
    Sarah 153
CULPEPER, Nancy 94
CULPS, Mary Ann 148
CULTON, Ann R Johnston 107
CUMBERLEDGE, Alley 133
CUMBO, Ann Bell 107 William
    107
CUMBY, Ann Bell 107
CUMMINGS, Rachel 27 Sally
    Cunningham 107 Sarah Cunnin-
    gham 107
CUMMINS, Lucy Phillips 107
    William L 107
CUNDIFF, Mary 2 Mary R Basye
    107 Pamala Carter 107
CUNNINGHAM, Ariana B 117
    Betsey Hutton 108 Elizabeth
    Via 108 Elizabeth Zolman 108
    Hannah Wilson 108 Jennie

CUNNINGHAM (continued)
    Haines 107 Martha 37 Martha G
    Jones 108 Martha Snodgrass
    108 Mary 108 Mary Hall 107
    108 Mary Jordan 108 Rachel
    108 Rachel Morgan 108
    Rebecca (Bolinger) Kelly 107
    Sally 107 Sarah 107 Sarah May
    108 Sarah Randall 107 Sarah
    Roby 108 Sarah Runion 108
    Sarah Wagner 107
CUPP, Elizabeth (Shaver) Carson
    108 Elizabeth Baker 108
CURD, Martha 108 Susan 108
CURFMAN, Rebecca Carman 108
CURRY, Marbury 109 Margaret
    109 Mary 109 Mary William
    108 Mayberry 109 Polly 139
    Sally 109
CURTIS, Anna A Fox 109 Martha
    L Kirk 109 Nancy Smith 109
    Sarah K Harwood 109 Sydney
    Linsford 109
CURTLEY, Jane 77
CURTS, Elizabeth 118
CUSTARD, Joseph 109 Martha
    Claig 109
CUSTER, Elizabeth 20 Elizabeth
    Trumbo 109
CUSTERD, Joseph 109 Martha
    Claig 109
CUTHRELL, Margaret 109
CUTLIP, Anna Wangburn 109
CUTRIGHT, Elizabeth Westfall
    109 Nancy Westfall 109
CYRUS, Leah Toney 109 Rebecca
    109
DABBS, Susan Coleman 109
DABNEY, Maria Stanfield 109
    Martha B 80 Martha P.Holmes
    110 Nancy Phillips 110 Rachel
    B 109
DADE, Harriet G 183 Magdalin
    173
DAGG, Elizabeth Dutro 110
DAGGETT, Mary A 110
DAGGS, Lovey 155
DAGGY, Sarah McLaughlin 110
DAILEY, Eleanor Carr 110
    Talaifa Honnold 110
DAILY, Rebecca Jane Booth 110
DAINE, Margaret 53

DAINGERFIELD, Sarah Taliaferro 54
DALEY, Elenor 97 John 110 Rebecca Jane Booth 110
DALLAS, Mary A 110
DALRYMPLE, Elizabeth Miller 110
DALTON, Mildred 39
DAME, Elizabeth Oyler 110
DAMERON, Frances C 190
DAMRELL, Elizabeth 110
DAMRON, Sallie Ryan 274
DANCE, Mary Ann Adams 110 Rebecca Simmons 110
DANDRIDGE, Ann O 110
DANFELSER, Barbara Zumbro 110 William 110
DANFIELD, Barbara Zumbro 110
DANGERFIELD, Mary B 29
DANIEL, Cassandra F S Haggett 111 Catherine Glass 111 Eliza M 143 Eliza Smith 111 Elizabeth Kidd 110 Elizabeth Reynolds 111 Elizabeth White 111 Jane 61 Mary M Harris 110 Nancy Carwiles 110 Nancy Newcomb 111 Sarah C Graves 111 Susan O North 110 Susanna 155
DANIELS, Jane S (---) 69
DANNER, Sovina Ryman 111
DANSON, Frances A Tarkelson 111
DARDEN, Dicey Lawrence 111 Elizabeth Whitehead 111 Priscilla (---) Lawrence 111
DARE, Catharine 125
DARELL, Benjamin 131
DARLING, Diana 158
DARNAL, Louisa 111
DARNALL, Catherine 18 Narcissa Coppage 111
DARNEL, Levi 111 Louisa 111
DARNELL, Elizabeth Wright 111
DARRELL, James 124
DARROWS, Elizabeth O 96
DASHIELL, Mary Ann Weston McCobb 111
DASHNER, Sarah 167
DAUGHERTY, Hannah Turkeyhizer 111
DAUGHTRY, Sally 66 Susan 105

DAVENPORT, Ann Eliza Thompson 112 Elizabeth King 112 Ellen Branchet 112 Harriet A Hart 112 Lydia M (---) Doss 112 Nancy 112
DAVIDSON, Caroline Lane 112 Catherine 120 Elizabeth 112 Jane Wooten 112 John 112 Lucy A Walker 112 Margaret 159 172 Nancy 76 Tabitha Witten 112
DAVIES, Harriett Little 115 Lucinda Talliaferro 112 Nancy Franklin 112 Rebecca E P Thompson 112 Samuel C 115
DAVIS, --- 15 Amelia 127 Ann E 165 Ann Joyner 115 Betsey Hill 113 Bridget McAnan 113 Casandria M Leeke 114 Catharine 123 Catharine Maxson 114 Catharine McCahan 115 Catharine McCatharine 115 Catherine 25 Content 112 Cythia 168 Delila Clark 114 Drucilla (---) (Taylor) 31 Edith 56 Eleanor Dean 114 Elisabeth Boles 113 Elizabeth 8 31 92 147 277 Elizabeth Gunnell 115 Elizabeth Harris 114 Fanny 210 Frances T 113 Frances West 113 Hanna Shafer 112 Hannah 80 Harriet 72 Harriett Little 115 Henry L 112 Ingram H 115 Jane 115 159 Jincy D McCauley 113 Julia Ann Wissman 114 Leanner 130 Learma 130 Lida 113 Lucinda Grafton 114 Lucy C (Haynes) 121 Martha Gilliam 114 Martha Graham 113 Martha H Dixon 113 Martha Harris 114 Martha J 87 Martha Michie 114 Mary 114 Mary Hampton 113 Mary Hawley 115 Matilda Fleming 115 Matilda Wamble 115 Mildred 45 Nancy 79 113 115 Nancy Farrell 115 Nancy Franklin 112 Nancy Joyner 115 Nancy L Toon 114 Nancy L Toone 114 Polly Brewer 113 Rachel 30 Rachel Ward 113 Rebecca 182 Rebecca E P

DAVIS (continued)
Thompson 112 Sarah 98 192
195 Sarah (Burton) Wright 115
Sarah B Slater 114 Sarah E
(---) Pankey 114 Sarah E
Hickey 113 Sarah French 114
Sarah Gladden 113 Sarah Hicks
115 Sarah Shearer 115 Sarah
Talbott 113 Sarah Wilkins 113
Susan B Sandridge 114 Susan E
Elder 115 Susan Miller 113
Susanna 176 Susanna Faris 114
Susannah B Sandridge 114
Tabitha 115 Ville Middleton
113
DAVISON, Delila 16
DAWES, Nancy Farrell 115
DAWKINS, Susannah Barnett 115
DAWS, Ingram 115 Nancy Farrell
115
DAWSON, Eliza Ann Bukey 116
Elizabeth (Pitman) 116
Frances 116 Frances L
Woodroff 116 Hannah 136 Mar-
garet Bates 116 Mary Jane
Garrison 116 Nancy Sanger 116
Nat 116 Sarah Jewell 115
DAY, Catherine 10 Dick 116
Emily H 7 Louisa J 89
Lucretia Guthrie 116 Sarah Ann
20 Sarah J 116
DE WITT, --- 19
DEAL, Joice 116
DEALY, Mary Lewis 116
DEAN, Alcy Smith 117 Anna F
Conaway 116 Betsey 171
Charles 117 Eleanor 114
Elizabeth Boston 117 Margaret
116 Mary 117 Mary Ann Hol-
loway 117 Mary Houston 116
Nancy Killingsworth 117 Pattie
Clements 117 Zaney Saunders
116
DEANE, Ann W Askin 117 Ariana
B Cunningham 117 Elizabeth
Boston 117 Polly Fisher 117
DEANER, George 119
DEANS, Elizabeth Hubbard 117
DEARE, Joel 118 Sarah Garnet
118 Susan Mallory 118
DEARING, Anne Jackson 117
Elizabeth Keith 117 Mary T

DEARING (continued)
Harrison 117 Nellie (---)
McGregor 117 Polly Nance 117
DEATHERAGE, Elizabeth 145
DEATLEY, Sarah Tate 117
DEAVERS, Aaron 120 Catherine
Davidson 120 Mary Ann (---)
Robuck 120
DEBO, Catherine 197
DECKARD, Polly Roach 117
DECKER, Harriet 131
DECKHARD, John 117 Polly
Roach 117
DEEDS, Amy 10 Catherine
Broofman 118
DEEM, Margaret Hill 118
DEEMS, Hannah 118 Mary 106
DEEN, Nancy Killingsworth 117
William 117
DEER, Lucy 158 Martha Clarke
118 Sarah Garnet 118 Susan
Mallory 118
DEHART, Elizabeth Howard 118
Thomas 118
DEHORT, Elizabeth Howard 118
DELAPLAINE, Elizabeth Curts
118 Elizabeth Kurtz 118 Emily
Smith 118
DELBRIDGE, Elizabeth Phillips
118 Martha Phillips 118
DELK, Louisa Pleasants 118
Margaret Warren 118
DELLINGER, Mary Rye 118
DELOACH, Elizabeth 165
DELPH, Betsey Racer 118
Catharine Barlow 118 Caty
Barlow 118
DEMARE, Agnes Long 132
DEMASTERS, Mary Ann Coffey
118
DEMORY, Eve 183
DEMOSS, Lydia McDowell 118
DEMPSEY, Louisa 62
DEMPSY, Milly 70
DENBY, Mary DeShon 119 Mary
Rogers 118 Polly Lawrence
118 Rebecca 137
DENEAFRILL, Augustin 119
DENIS, David 122
DENNEY, Neomy Loving 119
DENNIS, Elizabeth 119 Jane 119
DENNY, Margaret Swatz 119 Mary

DENNY (continued)
Jones 119
DENSON, Nancy Ballard 119
Nancy Barrett 119
DENT, Lucy 78 Mahala 119
DENTON, Mary 4 Polly 4 Sarah J
Toler 119
DEPRIEST, Jeminia Ramsey 119
John 119 Martha Wood 119
DEQUASIE, Elizabeth Cary 119
DERENBARGER, Peggy Anderson
119
DERENBERGER, Christena 169
George 119 Peggy Anderson
119 Mary 287
DERRY, Susannah Karn 119
DESHIELDS, Emily C Crewdson
119 Mary Martin 119 Matilda
Wade 119
DESHON, Mary 119
DESPER, Elizabeth England 119
Sallie H 49
DETTIMORE, Mary Elizabeth 173
DEVAUGHN, Celeste 228 Nancy
Coddy 119 Nancy Harper 120
DEVAULT, Mary Steele 120 Sarah
120
DEVEREUX, Mary 13
DEVERS, Catherine Davidson 120
Mary Ann (---) Robuck 120
DEVIN, Margaret West 120
DEVINS, Elizabeth 16
DEVRSE, Aaron 120 Catherine
Davidson 120 Mary Ann (---)
Robuck 120
DEWESE, Easter Poff 120 Nancy
Byrd 120
DIAL, Nancy Rogers 120
DIBRELL, Martha Shrewsbury 120
DICE, Eveline E 120 Margaret
Seldonridge 120
DICK, Barbary Moats 120 Chris-
tina 5 Frederick 120
DICKENSON, Cadwalader Lewis
120 Edmond 121 Hezekiah 120
James 121 Mary 120 Mary
Honaker 121 Nancy Robinson
120 Rebecca W Bryan 120
Tabitha 167
DICKERSON, Frances McGeorge
121 Mary Cock 121 Nancy S
208 Robert 121 Sally

DICKERSON (continued)
Thompson 120 Serena Martin
121 Susannah Hytton 121
DICKEY, Elizabeth S 295
DICKIE, Lucy C (Haynes) Davis
121
DICKINSON, Ann 134 Martha S
121 Mary Honaker 121
DICKSON, --- 21 Anna Burge 122
Archibald 122 James 121 122
Jane 121 Judith 123 Sarah
Swisher 122 Selina White 121
DIDOWICK, Susan 88
DIGGS, Elizabeth Ripley 121 Jane
Pace 121 Lucinda Cash 121
Rachel A Belvin 121 Susan
Treacle 121
DIL, Anne 51
DILL, Hannah Heisler 121 Hannah
K Gorgas 121 Polly 122
DILLAHUNT, Mary A 106
DILLARD, Alcy Guthrie 122 Bet-
sey 122 Emily Twyman 121
Martha 122 Mary Moon 121
Polly 121
DILLE, Jane Magill 122
DILLEY, Jane Magill 122 Moses
122
DILLION, Polly Houseman 122
DILLON, Lucy 12 Mary C 70
Sally Doss 122 Vashti Borton
122
DILMAN, Mary Watkins 122
Polly Dill 122
DILON, Rebecca 63
DIMET, Jacob 122 Sidney Buckey
122
DIMIT, Sidney Buckey 122
DINGLEDINE, Mary Barrinton 122
DINKINS, Martha 187
DITTY, Jansie Fergus 122 Sarah
C (---) Dyer 122
DIVERS, Lydia Plyborne 122
Margaret Weaver 122
DIX, Frances A (---) Zuccarello
122 Martha M Edmundson 122
DIXON, Anna Burge 122 Eliza 123
Hanna G Irvine 122 Hannah 41
Jane 12 123 Judith 123 Mar-
garet Crautz 123 Martha H 113
Martha J 138 Nancy (---) 122
Pamela 123 Sally Hall 122

DIXON (continued)
Sally Miller 123 Sarah Swisher
122 Susan 123
DOBSON, Mary (Hodges)
Barnsgrove 123 Sally Jett 123
DODD, Agnes A Johnson 123
Elizabeth 123 Elizabeth
(Embertemer) Thomas 123 El-
vira A 55 Julia A 66 Letitia 99
Lucy A 123 Mary C 286
DODS, Elizabeth (Embertemer)
Thomas 123 John 123
DODSON, Dicey 81 Hannah A Al-
len 123 Judith Dickson 123
Judith Dixon 123 Martha 123
Nancy 136 Obedience Newbell
123 Sarah S Gill 123 Susan
Morris 123 Telitha (Van
Hoosir) 186
DOGGETT, Eliza 124 Eliza Moon
123 Lucinda 163 Lucinda
Shepard 123 Mary 123 Polly
123
DOLD, Elizabeth M Fadden 124
DOLLY, Annis 44
DONAGHE, Sarah L 31
DONAHOE, Frances T 45
Rebecca Garvin 124
DONALDSON, Ann (Williams)
Faithfull 124 Bailey 124
Catharine P Barron 124
Elizabeth Burch 124 Mary Mil-
ler 124
DONAVAN, Mary 252
DONLEY, Sarah 65
DOOLEY, Elner Ellmore 124
DOORS, William J 124
DORAN, Elizabeth Lowry 124
DORCHESTER, Hannah 69
DORMAN, Barbara Gates 124
DORSETT, Ann A McRea 124
DORSEY, Mary A Shades 124
Nicholas 124
DORSON, John 116 Matilda 3
Nancy Sanger 116
DOSH, Lucy 299
DOSS, Jane 125 Judith Hodges
125 Lydia M (---) 112 Martha
Elam 124 Mary Thomas 125
Sally 122 Sarah Hendley 124
DOSSE, Nancy Thomas 125
DOSSON, John 116 Nancy Sanger

DOSSON (continued)
116
DOTSON, Ingaba (Louther?)
Eustler/Utchler 125 Margaret
(---) Jenkins 125 Mary 125
Nancy 125 Susannah 125
DOUGHERTY, Rachel 125
DOUGHTREY, Margaret 67
DOUGHTY, Elizabeth Gay 125
DOUGLAS, Elizabeth 125 Mary E
264
DOUGLASS, Fanny 125 Mary
Hughes 150 Sarah Smith 125
Sarah White 125
DOVE, Catharine Dare 125
Catharine Fitzwaters 125 Julia
W Payne 125 Margaret 125
Martha Irby 125 Mary Irby 125
Mary Mustain 126 Oney
Sanders 126 Polly Mustain 126
Sarah 1
DOVEL, Christena Long 126
DOWDY, Celia Hopkins 126 Fer-
raby 127 Hannah (Bowles)
Fagg 126 Martha Smith 126
Nancy Elder 126
DOWELL, Frances Collins 126
Nancy A 179 Sarah 37
DOWNER, Maria Woodson 126
DOWNING, Elizabeth 8 Fanny
Sale 126 Sarah Ann 268
DOWNS, Eleanor Archer 126
Femity Wilson 126 Mary 160
DOYLE, Ann G Sproul 126
Elizabeth Haselton 126 Hannay
(Bradford) Smith 127 Leanah
Moses 127 Margaret Bur-
gaydine 127 Mary Lake 126
Mary Teake 126 Peachey Nor-
vell 127
DRAFFIN, Nancy Foster 127
DRAKE, Elizabeth Sinnett 127
Elizabeth T 127 Jerusha
Baugham 127 Kitty 73 Mary
Elizabeth Birdson 127 Mary
Gay 127 Mary Newton 127
Rieves 127
DRAPER, Martha 31 Mary Turner
127 Rebecca 168
DRESSLER, Elizabeth 127
DREW, Lavinia Hart 127
DREWRY, Amelia Davis 127

DREWRY (continued)
Charlotte Crouch 127 Ferraby
Dowdy 127
DRINKARD, Elizabeth A F---
127 Jane E (---) Ellyson 127
Polly 127
DRISGAL, Mary P 36
DRODDY, Sarah Grandee 127
DRUMHELLER, Jane A Suthards
128
DRUMMOND, Catherine Hawkins
128 Elizabeth Starke 128 Mar-
garet (Henderson) 128 Naomi
128 Sally 23
DRURY, Charlotte Crouch 127
Ferraby Dowdy 127 John 127
DRYDEN, Margart Craig 128
DUCK, Nancy B 128
DUDLEY, Elizabeth 128
Elizabeth Joiner 128 Jane T
128 Nancy Rankin 128
DUELL, Salome (---) 148
DUERSON, Nancy B Holladay 128
DUFF, Mahala Farmer (---) 6
DUFFER, Elizabeth P (---) Han-
nah 128 Sicely 128
DUFFEY, Catherine 128
DUFFLER, Nancy M (---) Shaner
128 Rebecca Hawkins 128
DUGGAN, Jane 128
DUGGER, Ann Eliza Clayton 128
DUKE, Elizabeth Mallory 128
Emily 55 Lucinda Shepherd
128 Martha Martin 128 Sarah P
128
DUKES, Ellen (---) 195
DULANEY, Nancy R 100
DULANY, Mary 269
DULIN, Anna Maria (Woodard)
Fisher 129 Frances 129 Pris-
cilla L 129 Rebecca 129 Sally
129
DULTY, Sarah B Scott 129
DULTZ, Michael 129 Sarah B
Scott 129
DUNAVANT, Hezekiah 130 Jane
Bowling 130 Mary Breeden 130
Nancy 129
DUNAVENT, Jane Ellis 129
DUNAWAY, Mary 129
DUNBAR, Nancy Dunston 129
DUNCAN, America Ann Pearson

DUNCAN (continued)
129 Elizabeth 129 Elizabeth B
McCreary 129 Greenberry 129
Hannah 180 Judida 91 Judith
58 Lucy Landrum 129 Mary
Fulton 129 Mary Gilbert 129
Mary Poe 129 Nancy Philips
129 Polly R 55 Sally W Cam-
den 129 Susan P 144 Susan
Ramsey 129
DUNDORE, Nancy Grove 130
DUNFIELD, Leanner Davis 130
Learma Davis 130
DUNHAM, Elizabeth Manor 130
DUNKEL, Elisabeth 32
DUNKIN, Berry 129 Nancy Philips
129 Ruth 230
DUNKLEY, Susan T 94
DUNLAP, Ann Ligget 130 Hanay
130 Rachel McJemeson 130
DUNLAVEY, Mary A 130
DUNLOP, Mary Ann 178
DUNN, Ailcy Johnson 130 Betsey
Jackson 130 Catharine 154
Elizabeth Johnson 130 Mary F
McAlister 130 Nancy 139
Nancy Norcutt 130 Nancy Vice
130 Polly 286 Sarah B 131
Sarah Jane Lippford 130 Susan
Maupin 130 Temperance Pier-
point 130
DUNNAVANT, Jane Bowling 130
Mary Breeden 130 Sarah 92
DUNNINGTON, Alsadana Stibbon
131
DUNSMORE, Jane Erskine 131
Letitia M Love 131
DUNSTON, Nancy 129
DUPREE, Sarah B Dunn 131
DURFEY, Eliza W 46
DURHAM, Mary James Burriss
131 Nancy 63 Rebecca (---)
131
DURRETT, Eliza M (---) Terrell
131 Martha H Polk 131 Mary D
Wood 131
DUTRO, Elizabeth 110
DUTROE, Sarah 203
DUTTON, Betsey R Threadgill
131 Elizabeth R Threadgill 131
Margaret B Ross 131
DUVALL, Polly Godfrey 131

347

ELDER, Eliza A Jones 136 Lidia
Grishaw 136 Martha Johnson
136 Mary Jeffers 84 Nancy 126
Susan E 115
ELDRIDGE, Agnes Lewis 136
Mary S Peebles 136
ELEY, Martha (---) Marshall 136
Polly Moody 136
ELGIN, Elizabeth Cross 136
ELKINS, Lucy 66 Sarah Ann (---)
2
ELLETT, Ann 24
ELLINGTON, Sall T 168
ELLIOT, Anna R 36 Elizabeth
Wigner 136 Nancy Shaw 137
Susan 147
ELLIOTT, Elizabeth 155
Elizabeth W Harness 137 Mar-
garet Fizen 136 Martha Rus-
sell 137 Phebe 202
ELLIS, --- 28 Abigail Hicks 29
Eliza 137 Ellenor 164 Jane 129
Margaret W 137 Maria (---)
Bales 137 Martha Rountree 137
Mary 137 Nancy 1 Nancy Shuf-
field 137 Rebecca Denby 137
Ritter Ann Mason 137 Susan
Meadows 137
ELLISON, Elsey 5 Lucinda 5
Patsey Perdue 137
ELLMORE, Elizabeth Ann Rose
137 Elner 124
ELLYSON, Jane E (---) 127
ELMORE, Elizabeth A 47
Frances 137
EMANUEL, Elizabeth Powers 137
EMBEROON, Elizabeth Perry 138
Judson 138
EMBERTEMER, Elizabeth 123
EMBREY, Dillyla 210 Elizabeth
Brown 137 Judah Perry 137
Kitty 137
EMERSON, Catherine Williams
138 Elizabeth Perry 138
Elizabeth R Beeson 138 Jane
Watson 137
EMRY, Judy 138
ENDAILY, David 138
ENGLAND, Elizabeth 119 James
138 Martha Thacker 138 Polly
138 Sarah Ann 138
ENGLISH, Martha Corbett 138

ENGLISH (continued)
Mary 138 Phebe Wellons 138
ENNIS, Ann Eliza Saunders 138
Jane McKinney 138 Peggy
Brian 138 Sally 138
ENOS, Elizabeth Slater 138 Sarah
A 138
ENROUGHTY, Nathaniel 138
ENSOR, Fanny Wright 138 Louisa
Nelson 138
ENSTMINGER, Martha J Dixon
138 Sarah Knick 138
ENTLER, Mary Rickard 138
ENTSMINGER, Rachel 14
EPERSON, Frances S 48
EPES, Catherine G 180
EPPARD, Samuel 138
EPPERLY, Nancy 139
EPPERSON, Elizabeth Buys 139
John 9 Major 9 Martha 9 Sally
Gray 139 Sidney 9 William 9
EPPS, Frances Easley 139 Mary
P Jordan 139 Nancy Dunn 139
ERAMBERT, Eliza Mann 139
ERSKINE, Amelia D Riggs 139
Jane 131 Mary Alexander 139
ERVIN, Mary 145
ERVINE, Frances 139 Jane E 206
Polly Curry 139
ERWIN, Frances 139 Nancy 139
William 139
ESHON, Catherine Robins 139
ESKEW, Catharine Fletcher 139
Mary Wadkins 139
ESKRIDGE, Ann Hickerson 139
Nancy Bridewell 139
ESSLEY, Louise M 223
ESTERS, Sallie (---) Cox 139
ESTES, Ann Moore 140 Catharine
Hawkins 140 Elizabeth
Chisholm 140 Ephraim 139
Jane Howard 140 Margaret
Jones 140 Martha Farley 140
Martha J Morgan 140 Nannie
W 140 Sallie (---) Cox 139
Susan H Shelton 140 Susanah
Butler 140
ESTILL, Patsey 140
ESTIS, Ann Moore 140 Frances 7
John R 140
ETHERIDGE, Katy (---) 103
ETHERTON, James 133 Nancy M

ETHERTON (continued)
Crawford 133
ETZEL, Dorcas 70
EUBANK, Catharine Norvell 140
Catherine 140 Elizabeth Claxton 140 Elizabeth G Melton
140 Frances Wilkinson 140
Joseph 140 Martha 140 Mary C
140 Mary Gibson 140 Mary
Smothers 140 Nancy 182 Nancy
Grimes 140 Nancy M Smith
140 Thomas 140
EUBANKS, Catherine 140
Elizabeth G Melton 140 Joseph
140
EURIT, Mary Angling 141
EUSTLER, Ingaba (Louther?) 125
EUTSLER, Mary Ann 302
EVANS, Agnes W Thompson 141
Ann Becroft 142 Ann McGowan
142 Catharine Foster 141
Catherine Stewart 142 Delilah
133 Elizabeth 27 141 161 201
Elizabeth Ann 39 Elizabeth
Hester 142 Frances 141 Hasting 141 Jane B Gowan 142
Keziah 63 Margaret Skinner
141 Maria Maxwell 142 Mary
141 Mary Armstrong 141 Mary
Carpenter 141 Mary E 191
Nancy 141 Nancy Rock 142
Norway Blair 141 Peggy 141
Polly 141 Polly Ann Crews 141
Polly Chaffins 141 Sarah Crupper 141 Sarah Skeen 141 Sarah
Walker 141 Susan Hudson 141
EVERLEY, Eliza B Crebs 142
EVERLY, Eliza B Crebs 142
George 133 John H 142 Rhoda
(---) Conaway 142
EVERS, Frances Alcock 142
Polly H Hudson 142
EVERSOLE, Elizabeth Allemong
142
EVILSIZER, Anne Huffnow 142
EWEN, Elizabeth 47
EWING, Ann Eliza Fisher 142
Theresa 142
EYLENBURGH, Mary Roberts 142
EYMAN, Hannah 151
EYRES, John 14 Mary 71 Rachel
14

FACEN, Mary 48
FACKLER, Mary White 142
FADDEN, Elizabeth M 124
FADELEY, Elizabeth 90
FADELY, Sarah Heaton 142
FADLY, Elizabeth Coffman 142
FAGG, Hannah (Bowles) 126
FAINT, Sally Ann 133
FAIR, Edy Olive (Martin) Clark
143 Martha McDaniel 143
FAIRCHILD, Rebecca McSpaden
143
FAITHFULL, Ann (Williams) 124
FALL, Elizabeth Jenkins 143
FALLS, Elizabeth 143 Elizabeth
Jenkin Fall 143
FALWELL, Margaret 143
FAMER, Burwell 204
FANDREE, Frances Nuckols 143
Jane Roundtree 143
FANNON, Abigail Muncy 143
FANT, Lucy E D M Phillips 143
FARGUSON, Newby 161 Prudence
Pudue 161
FARGUSSON, Newby 161
Prudence Pudue 161
FARIS, Christian 147 Eliza Fassett 143 Eliza M Daniel 143
Mason/Mace Childris 143
Nancy Campbell 147 Nancy
Griffin 143 Stephen M 143
Susanna 114
FARISS, Rebecca 143
FARLEY, Maria Pincham 143 144
Maria Winfree 143 Martha 140
Mary Ann 77 Matilda 63
FARMER, Catharine Edwards 144
Edith 144 Edith (---) 204
Elizabeth W McClung 144
Margaret 193 Martha K 75 Martha Willard 144 Mary Page 46
Matilda Allison 144 Nancy
Nunley 144 Nancy Wilson 144
Obedience A 33 Rachel 168
Susan 49
FARNES, George 144 Sarah Webb
144
FARRAR, Mary Minter 144 Nancy
P Johnson 144 Polly 190 Sally
144 Sarah G Shumate 144 Sarah
J Grubbs 144 Susan P Duncan
144 Winney B Smith 144

FARRELL, Julia A Fletcher 147
Nancy 115 Robert 147
FARRENS, Sarah Webb 144
FARRIS, Charles 143 Eliza Fas-
sett 143 Elizabeth Higgins 144
Jordin 143 Kisiah Blanken-
beekler 144 Mary Bishop 144
Nancy 139 Susan McCullen 144
FARROW, Sarah Smith 58
FASSETT, Eliza 143
FAUBER, Catharine 144
FAUCETT, Sarah C 14
FAUDREE, Nancy 83
FAULCONER, Nancy 144 Susan
Oakes 145
FAULIN, Elizabeth 152 Thomas
152
FAULKNER, Anna 104 Elizabeth
H Perry 145 Mary B Averett
145 Mary T 166 Sarah B
Standfield 145
FAUT, Ann S Ficklen 145 Betsy
158 Elizabeth Deatherage 145
FAWCETT, Philadelphia Hol-
loway 145
FAYMAN, Frances Keiffer 145
FEAGANS, Elizabeth 152
FEARS, Nancy Hays 145
FEASTER, Elizabeth Crider 145
FEATHER, Mary Ervin 145
FEATHERLINE, Sarah Bly 145
FEATHERNAGLE, Mary Ramey
145
FEATHERSTON, Ann Wilkinson
145 Elizabeth Jones 145
Joshua 145 Rebecca Adams
145
FEATHERSTUN, Ann Wilkinson
145
FEAZEL, Martha St Clair 145
FEAZELLE, Aaron 145 Martha St
Clair 145
FELICIAMA, Amarylles 313
FELTY, Nancy 146
FENN, Allen 148 Delila Butter-
worth 148 Eliza Jackson 146
Martha F E Scott 148
FENNELL, Eliza H 146 James
146
FENTON, Sally 65
FEREBEE, Sarah Poyner 146
FERGASON, Edmond 146 Lucinda

FERGASON (continued)
Buckner 146
FERGASSON, Edmond 146
Lucinda Buckner 146
FERGESON, Janes Ayres 146
Margaret (---) Tucker 146
Thomas 146
FERGESS, Sarah E 146
FERGUS, Jansie 122 Mary 55
FERGUSON, Amy 146 Ann Nettle
146 Eliza 9 Elizabeth 7 176
Elizabeth Boaz 146 Elizabeth
Davis 147 Elizabeth H Gooch
146 Elizabeth Norris 146 Ellen
C 146 Jane 146 Lucinda Buck-
ner 146 Lucy Jennings 146
Margaret (---) Tucker 146
Margaret Kelly 146 Martha 191
Mary Brodus 147 Mary Robbins
146 Nancy Roberts 146 Susan
201
FERRELL, Julia A Fletcher 147
FERRIS, Archibald A 143 Mace
Childris 143 Mason Childris
143 Nancy Campbell 147
FERRY, Jane Brough 147
FESTOR, Frances 100
FICKES, Maria Brown 147
FICKLEN, Ann S 145
FIELD, Elizabeth Burford 147
Lucy M 13 Nancy 15
FIELDING, Matilda C Gillespie
147 Sarah A Thompson 147
FIELDS, Elizabeth 169 Nancy
(---) 186 Nancy Ann Williams
147 Sarah Wilder 147
FIFE, Sarah J (---) Hopson 147
FIFER, Lydia Fry 147 Rosana 4
FIGGS, Patsy 101
FILBATES, Mary 147
FILCHER, Ann Inde 147
FILSON, Susan Elliot 147
FINCH, Elizabeth 174
FINKS, Fanny Berry 148 Frances
32 Frances B Triplett 148
FINLEY, Sarah Bailey 148
FINN, Delila Butterworth 148
Martha F E Scott 148
FINNALL, Margaret Cox 148
FINNELL, Elizabeth B Thorn 148
Elizabeth Thorn 148 Lucinda
Hoffman 148

351

FINNEY, Elizabeth Chickton
Wood 148 James 148 Margaret
Cox 148 Sarah Fletcher 148
FISER, Hannah 60
FISHER, Amy Hudson 149 Ann
Eliza 142 Anna Maria
(Woodard) 129 Eliza 1
Elizabeth 92 206 Elizabeth
Balsley 148 Emsey 29 Isabella
Lutz 148 Jane Thomas 148
Janetta R 193 Mary Ann Culps
148 Mary G 166 Nancy
(Meadows) Greer 148 Polly 117
Salome (---) (Duell) Abey 148
Sarah Houston 148 Susan (---)
McCraw 148
FITNAM, Ann 32
FITTS, Sarah Randolph 149
Tabitha Hughes 149
FITZER, Nancy Ward 149
FITZGERALD, Stacy 36
FITZHUGH, Ann G 149
FITZPATRICK, Amy 28 Martha
193 Mary Bellar 149 Mary Bel-
lah 149 Mary Jane (Broome)
Babb 149 Polly 149
FITZWATER, Isaac 149 Nancy
Hamrick 149 Sarah Hamrick
149
FITZWATERS, Catharine 125
Sarah Hamrick 149
FIX, Hannah 160
FIZEN, Margaret 136
FIZER, Elizabeth 149
FLACK, Rebecca 8
FLAHERTY, Kitty Cheek 149
FLANAGAN, Peggy Wall 149
Sarah 62
FLANNAGAN, Ann E Hughson
149 Eliza 103 Sarah C Johnson
149
FLEEMAN, Martha Pergeson 149
FLEENOR, Susan --- 149
FLEGER, Elizabeth McCrumb
149
FLEMING, Ann 150 Anthony 150
Indiana B Bowden 150 Martha
M Montague 149 Mary Bohan-
non 150 Mary J Williams 150
Matilda 115 Nancy Hol-
lingsworth 150 Sally Spicer 149
Sarah Foxwell 150

FLESHER, Elizabeth 150 168
FLESHMAN, Eleanor Callahan
150
FLETCHER, Amelia 161 Ann
Inde 147 Catharine 139
Elizabeth (---) Putnam 150
Julia A 147 Mary 150 Nancy
Caynor 150 Peter 147 Sarah 88
148 Susannah 150 Townsan 150
Townsand 150
FLEUHART, Catharine Murphy
151 Nancy Gaylord 151 Wil-
liam 151
FLIFFIN, Nancy 4
FLING, Catharine 90 Maria Biggs
150 Rebecca Fluhart 150 Sarah
Taylor 150
FLIPPEN, Catharine Pell 150
John 150 Maria C 157 Mary
Hughes Douglass 150
FLIPPIN, Catharine Pell 150
Louisa B 15 Lucinda B 195
FLOOD, Ann S Coleman 150
Elizabeth 7 Martha M 7
FLORENCE, Elizabeth (---) 118
Ellen 151
FLOURNOY, Elizabeth 168
FLOWERS, Elizabeth 151
Elizabeth Branch 151 Eveline
Coffey 151 Hannah (Eyman)
Hampson 151 Jane Clark 151
Sarah B Watkins 151
FLOYD, Christiana S Stegall 151
Elizabeth Thompson 151 Sally
31 Susan 196 Susan E 151
FLUART, Catharine Murphy 151
Nancy Gaylord 151 Catharine
Murphy 151 Nancy Gaylord 151
Rebecca 150 William 151
FLUHARTY, Mary 151
FLUSE, Margaret 152 Nicholas
152
FLYTHE, Sally 26
FODGE, Amy 48
FOESE, Caroline Sublete 151
FOGELSONG, Mary Fox 151
FOLAND, Elizabeth Hinkel 151
Volentine 151
FOLEY, Nancy Brown 151 Sallie
20
FOLK, Harriet McKewan 151
FOLKES, Martha (McDowell)

FOLKES (continued)
McKenney 152 Martha R Austin 152
FOLKS, Elijah 151
FOLLEN, Mary Ann Vermillion 152
FOLLIN, Ann 74 Elizabeth 152
FONTAINE, Mary O 152
FOOS, Margaret 152
FORAN, Mary Agner 152
FORBES, Elizabeth 48 Nancy 201 Sally Innes Thornton 152
FORD, Ann Maria Brooks 152 Anna 152 Betsy 96 Catharine 94 Eleanor Warder 152 Elizabeth 96 Elizabeth Feagans 152 Elizabeth S Smith 152 Keziah Witt 152 Margaret Grady 152 Martha Toddy 152 Mary 152 Mary Smith 152 Nancy S 152 Phebe (---) Tedroe 152
FORE, Ann 162 Sallie Richardson 152 Sarah Galloway 153
FOREHAND, Mary Agner 152
FOREMAN, Katy 208
FOREN, Elizabeth Martin 153
FOREST, Nancy 177
FORESTER, Anne Olinger 153
FORMASH, Mary 104
FORON, Elizabeth Martin 153 William 153
FORREST, Parmelia A 153 Susan Holt 153
FORRESTER, Elizabeth 153
FORSEE, 165
FORSYTHE, Hulda Foster 153
FORTNEY, Hannah 153
FORTUNE, Jane McAlexander 153 Martha Hagar 153
FOSSETT, Jesse 145 Philadelphia Holloway 145
FOSTER, Amy Prebble 154 Catharine 141 Catharine B 154 Courtnay C Thornton 154 Eliza S Jones 154 Elizabeth 31 Elizabeth Mitchell 154 Frances E 72 Hulda 153 Jemima Waggoner 153 Lucinda (---) Bradford 153 Lucresia 154 Lucy 4 Lucy Manly 153 Lucy T Rogers 153

FOSTER (continued)
Marandy S 72 Margaret Critchlow 154 Margaret M 102 Martha Bradshaw 153 Martha Hobson 154 Mary 34 Mary Craig 154 Mary Hawley 154 Mary Skaggs 154 Nancy 127 157 Nancy (---) Brown 154 Parcilla Lawson 153 Rachel H Rogers 153 Sarah Culp 153 Sarah McCormick 154 Sarah Young 153 Susan W Adams 154 Zipearius 154 Ziperius 154
FOUCH, Catharine Dunn 154
FOULKES, 166 Julia 190
FOULKS, Martha 100
FOUSHEE, Mary Ann Pendleton 154 Mildred J Thatcher 154
FOUST, Susanna Daniel 155
FOUT, Ann Tate 155 Mary 179
FOUTS, Hetty Spickard 155
FOWLE, Esther Jane 54
FOWLER, Caroline 38 Elizabeth (---) Gill 155 Elizabeth Neal 155 King 155 Lovey Daggs 155 Martha Mathews 155 Mary Lane 155 Rebecca Martin 155
FOWLKES, Anne Jones 155 Elizabeth Elliott 155 Melinda Brumley 155 Sally 206 Verrinia Hill 187
FOWLKS, Anne Jones 155 John 155 Melinda Brumley 155
FOX, Anna A 109 Catharine 155 Catharine Snyder 155 Elizabeth 155 Margaret 69 Maria 40 Martha 155 Martha Moore 155 Mary 151 Phebe 179
FOXWELL, Peggy Coffey 155 Sarah 150
FRANCE, Henry 156 Phebe Taylor 155 Phoebe F Morgan 156
FRANCIS, Abraham 155 Elizabeth (---) 162 Jane R Hall 156 Levinah Boylan 156 Melvina L Simpkins 156 Phebe Taylor 155 Phoebe F Morgan 156 Rebecca Saunders 156 Sallie Raglin 156
FRANK, Elizabeth Bare 156 Priscilla 156 Sarah Pugh 156

FRANKHOUSER, Elizabeth
Moyers 156
FRANKLIN, Elijah 156 Elizabeth
Helmandolar 156 Elizabeth
Hooper 156 Jane C Moses 156
Lucy Lester 156 Martha K
Tucker 156 Mary Ann (---) 78
Mildred 169 Nancy 112 Nancy
Clark 156 Rhoda Ann Thomas
156 Sarah Gowin 156
FRANKS, Sarah 156
FRASER, Elizabeth 204
FRAVEL, Jane A 157 Millie Lock
157 Rebecca 17 Rosa
Gochenour 157
FRAVIL, Jane A 157 John 157
FRAYSER, Maria C Flippen 157
Nancy Edwards 157
FRAZER, Martha L 157
FRAZIER, Eliza Wright 157
Elizabeth 157 Elizabeth Aikin
157 Rebecca Jenkins 157 Sarah
Long 157
FREDERICK, Nancy Pugh 157
FREELAND, Sarah A Noel 157
FREEMAN, Ann Robertson 157
Anna 91 Eleanor 202 Mary C
Parrish 157 Mille 12 Nancy
Foster 157 Sarah Belshur 157
FREEZE, Elvira 157
FRENCH, Diana (Darling) Grubbs
158 Dorcas 234 Elizabeth A
Haydon 158 Levina Bailey 158
Lucy Deer 158 Margaret Long-
ley 158 Mary M 158 Mildred P
Vawter 158 Nancy 189 Sarah
114
FRESHOUR, George 158
FRETWELL, Elizabeth Walters
158 Margaret Mars 158 Sarah J
Barksdale 158
FRIDLEY, Elizabeth 177 Mar-
garet 158
FRIEL, Jane Ann Stewart 158
FRIESIBES, Rachel 180
FRITTER, Bartley 158 Betsy
Faut 158 Dicey 158
FRIZZEL, Rebecca 86
FRY, Adam 158 Catharine
Grandstaff 159 Catherine
Snodgrass 158 Elizabeth A 159
Elizabeth Taylor 159 Emiley B

FRY (continued)
Crider 158 Frances 158 Hannah
Cowgill 158 Kate Taylor 158
Lydia 147 Mary C 159 Polly
159 Rhoda A 159
FRYE, Catharine Grandstaff 159
Emily B Crider 158 Henry 158
John 158 159
FRYER, Mary Miller 159
FUDGE, Susan Barnett 159
FUGATE, Nancy A 159
FUGITT, Ann Jourdan 159
Augusta 159 Clarinda Roberts
159 George Gustavus 159
FULCHER, Betsey 9 Catharine M
12 Delilah 159 Elizabeth 9
Jane Davis 159 Mary 36 Rod-
ham 159 Rowland 159
Saraphena 159
FULK, Elizabeth 18
FULKERSON, Margaret (---)
McCune 159 Margaret David-
son 159 Polly Nicewarder 159
FULKS, Elizabeth Elliott 155
Redford 155
FULLER, Clarissa W 36
Elizabeth Messer 159
Elizabeth Taylor 160 Mary
Hundley 160 Mary J Morrison
160 Mary Swain 159
FULTON, Eliza 35 Elizabeth
McGeorge 160 Jane S Jett 160
Mary 129 Mary Ellen Newman
160 Sarah Stoneburner 160
FULTZ, Nancy Smith 160
FULWIDER, Elizabeth 50 Hannah
Fix 160
FULWILER, Catherine Beaker
160
FUNK, Catherine Rittenour 160
Elizabeth Simpson 160 Mar-
garet 173 Mary Downs 160
Priscilla Houck 160 Sarah Car-
rier 160
FUNKHOUSER, Elizabeth Long
161 Mary 43
FUQUA, Judith 161 Martha 161
Mary 161
FUR, Margaret Tracy 161
FURBUSH, Elizabeth (---)
Walker 161
FURGASON, Edmond 146 Lucinda

FURGASON (continued)
Buckner 146
FURGUSSEN, Elizabeth 85
FURGUSSON, Prudence Pudue
161
FURR, Margaret Tracy 161
FURROW, Amelia (Fletcher)
Brooks 161 Elizabeth Evans
161
FUTRELL, Jason 161 Tem-
perance Vinson 161
FUTRILL, Temperance Vinson
161
FYE, Catharine Baugher 161
GABLE, Christina 164 Elizabeth
66
GADD, Frances 161
GAINER, Fanny (---) Manier 161
Susan Osler 161
GAINES, Elizabeth Jackson 161
Euphama Holliday 161 Harriet
161 Judith (---) White 161
Magdalen Neff 161 Mary Ann
Buchanan 161 Matilda 63
Nancy Jasper 162
GAITHER, Margaret Brumley 162
GALAHER, Sarah 15
GALBREATH, Isabel 28
GALDSTUN, Elizabeth Creel 171
GALESPY, Elizabeth McGlaugh-
lin 169 James 169
GALLADAY, David 173 Magdalin
Dade 173
GALLAGER, Sarah 15
GALLEHER, Martha Leith 162
Sidney S Green 162
GALLEHUGH, Mary Catharine
173
GALLION, Ruth Watson 162
GALLOWAY, Augusta Kracht 162
John 162 Mary Little 162 Sarah
153
GAMBLE, Eliza 64
GAMES, Elizabeth (---) Francis
162 Mercy 162
GAMMON, Elizabeth Harp 162
Lizzie Bailey 162 Mary 50
GANAWAY, Elizabeth Snead 162
Warren 162
GANDER, Elizabeth Grooves 162
GANMAR, Permelia 18
GANNAWAY, Ann Fore 162 Lydia

GANNAWAY (continued)
Lascellas 162 Sally 162
GANNOWAY, Elizabeth Snead
162
GARARD, Elizabeth Pultz 162
Sarah Murphy 162
GARDNER, Amelia H Bowles 163
America R (Elam) Batts 163
Comfort M Rust 163 Elizabeth
Hawkins 163 Elizabeth Page
163 Jane Grady 163 Jane Keel
163 John 302 Lucy T Quisen-
bery 163 Mary Young 163
Nancy 68 Zernah Hall 163
GARELY, Abel 176 Elizabeth
Richards 176
GARETSON, Nancy 164 William
M 164
GARLAND, Mary L Anderson 163
Mary Leckie 163 Sarah J 163
GARNER, Alice J 165 Catharine
44 Elizabeth Howard 163
Elizabeth Read 163 Harriet A
Read 163 Lockey 164 Lucinda
Doggett 163 Malinda 172 Mar-
garet Haga 163 Mary A
(Hagaman) (Lampkin) 196
GARNET, Sarah 118
GARNETT, Elizabeth J 164 Sarah
(---) Baldwin 164
GARR, Martha Chelf 164
GARRARD, Caleb 162 Elizabeth
Pultz 162 Sarah Murphy 162
GARRET, Anna Haley 164 Chris-
tina Gable 164 William 164
GARRETSON, Ellenor Ellis 164
Nancy 164
GARRETT, Anna Haley 164 Eliza
J Watson 164 Fanny Earles
164 Harriet 186 Mary C Ock-
erman 164 Mary D Crawley 164
Sarah Toombs 164
GARRISON, Agnes 233 Ellenor
Ellis 164 French 164 Isabella
McNut 164 Mary Alexander 164
Mary Jane 116 Resa Brashear
164
GARTHRIGHT, Elizabeth 192
GARVIN, Nancy S Lack 164
Rebecca 124
GATES, Ann E Davis 165 Ann O
(---) Mann 165 Barbara 124

GATES (continued)
Dolly D 174 Martha 24 Susannah Simpson 165
GAUDLING, Chloe McDaniel 165 Mary M Nance 165
GAWEN, Alice J Garner 165
GAWN, Alice J Garner 165 William 165
GAY, Catherine (Tazewell) Ambler 165 Elizabeth 125 Elizabeth Deloach 165 Jane 68 Mary 127 Mary Mead 165 Ruth Lot 165
GAYLE, Mary 165
GAYLORD, Nancy 151
GEARHART, Elizabeth Edwards 165 Mary Mills 165
GEE, Andrew 165 Catharine Byers 166 Frances W Harper 165 Mahala A Sturdivant 166 Mary G (Fisher) Willis 166
GEEDING, Elizabeth Teaford 166
GEERHART, Elizabeth Edwards 165 Henry 165 Mary Mills 165
GEISENDOFFER, Barabara Wilke 166 Sabina Keene 166
GENTRY, Mary Ann Willis 166 Mildred 23
GEORGE, Alice B Payne 166 Amanda E 235 Elizabeth Atwood 166 Harriet 166 Jane 210 Jemima 166 Margaret 208 Mary 166 Nancy Eastham 166 Rebecca A Turner 166 Susan W Holeman 166
GERRELL, Mary T Faulkner 166
GHISELIN, Mary B Wells 166
GIBB, Margaret 167
GIBBONS, Rachel 80 Sarah 22
GIBBS, --- 22 Angelina 207 Eleanor Stuart Thornton 167 Harriet Strother 167 Mary 102 Mary G Trueheart 167 Paulina Jones 167 Perlina Jones 167 Sarah Dashner 167
GIBSON, Catharine Bell 167 Elizabeth 190 Elizabeth Leonard 167 Ester 60 Esther 60 Henry 170 Lucinda Hoskins 167 Mary 140 170 Mary F Mayo 167 Mary Johnson 167 Mary W Shackelford 167 Nancy

GIBSON (continued)
188 Nancy Longest 167 Polly 167 Polly Best 167 Sarah 70 Susan Kimbrau 167 Tabitha Dickenson 167 Tempy Perkins 167
GIDEON, Easter (Conklin) (Green) 168 Fannie Jacobs 168 Luann Rowley 168
GIDLEY, Rebecca Draper 168
GIFFORD, Asel 168 Sarah Waldo 168
GILBERT, Elizabeth Hewitt 168 Lucy Sharp 168 Mary 129 Nancy Anderson 168 Rachel Farmer 168 Sarah 104
GILES, Elizabeth Flesher 168 Mary B Abbott 168 Perin 168 Sall T Ellington 168
GILHAM, Cythia Davis 168 Eliza Jackson 168 Elizabeth Buker 168 Mary Wiseman 168
GILKERSON, Delilah 168 James 168 Nancy 168
GILL, Christena Derenberger 169 Elizabeth (---) 155 Elizabeth (---) Tucker 169 Elizabeth Flournoy 168 Elizabeth Young 169 Jane 169 Judith Henry 169 Maiza H 169 Martha Morris 169 Mary L 168 Sarah H 169 Sarah S 123 Stacia 316 Tenagh 169 Tenaugh 169
GILLAM, Elizabeth Fields 169
GILLASPIE, Johathan H 169 Matilda C Breedlove 169 Susan Margaret (---) (Smith) Hughes 169 William 169
GILLASPY, Elizabeth McGlaughlin 169 William 169
GILLELAND, Jane H Haynes 170 Sheperd 170 Shipard 170
GILLEN, Rosanna Kidd 170 William 170
GILLESPIE, Lettie 57 Mahala Reynolds 169 Matilda C 147 Matilda C Breedlove 169 Mildred Franklin 169 Susan Margaret (---) (Smith) Hughes 169
GILLEY, Lucy 62
GILLIAM, Edie 170 Gilche 170

GILLIAM (continued)
Hannah 177 Martha 114 Nancy
40 Rosanna Kidd 170 Sally
Long 169 Sarah (Townsend)
Routt 169 William 170
GILLIAN, Rosanna Kidd 170
GILLILAN, Martha Hill 170
GILLILAND, James 170 Jane H
Haynes 170 Mahaleth Griffin
170 Sallie Colly 170 Shipard
170
GILLISPIE, Elizabeth 170
Marinda (Ransom) Baughan
170
GILLS, M A Hewey 170
GILMORE, Margaret Leach 170
GIPSON, Mary 170
GIRGSBY, Catharine Weekley 182
GISH, Susan 73
GITTINGS, Mary P Williams 170
Sophia C Jackson 170
GIVEN, Catharine Laymaster 170
David 170 Elizabeth 170 Mar-
garet 132
GIVENS, Catharine Laymaster
170 Elizabeth Graham 170
GIVIDEN, Patsey Woodey 170
GLADDEN, Sarah 113
GLADDON, Elizabeth 171
GLADON, Rachel 17
GLADSTUN, Edna Goff 171 Mary
Heflin 171
GLADWELL, Betsey Dean 171
Matilda A Jones 171
GLAIZE, Annie Yeakley 171
GLANVILLE, Frances Hartnett
177 Patrick 177
GLASCOCK, John 171 Nelly
Casey 171
GLASE, Anna Wolf 172
GLASS, Catherine 111 Catherine
Wood 171 Elizabeth Eagle 171
Fannie Martin 171 Johanna 171
Margaret M Cramer 171 Nancy
171 Nancy Humphrey 171
Polina Camlin 171 Rebecca
171 Sally Butler 171 Susan
Wilcox 171
GLASSBURN, Samuel 171
GLASSCOCK, Elizabeth 171 Mary
171 Nelly Casey 171 Win-
nafred 57

GLAZE, Elizabeth 179 Elizabeth
Lynn 171 Rachel (Rearden) 171
GLENN, Mary A Whitehead 172
GLISAN, Eliza Poole 172
GLOVER, Eliza Anderson 172
Mary Ann Parker 172 Sarah 33
Susan 33 Susan Williamson
172
GOAD, Ellenor Cock 172 Mary
Jacobs 172 Nancy 41
GOEN, Nancy 193
GOARD, Nancy 41
GOCHENOUR, Catharine Wol-
gamoth 172 Rosa 157
GODARD, Cynthia Lewis 172
James 172
GODBER, Catharine 94
GODDARD, Cynthia Lewis 172
GODFREY, Mary Williamson 172
Polly 131
GODLOVE, Sarah 82
GODSEY, Elizabeth (---) Graves
172 Margaret Davidson 172
Phebe Hancock 172
GODWIN, Cherry G Kelly 172
Eliza S Bess 172 Jane G 210
Mary Barb 172
GOES, Eunice Kellum 204
Nicholas 204
GOFF, Athaliah 40 Edna 171
Eliza 40 Malinda Garner 172
GOIN, Nancy 193
GOLDEN, Chloe McDaniel 165
Lucy Gooch 173 Mary M Nance
165 Samuel 165
GOLLADAY, Eliza Lowny 173
Magdalin Dade 173 Margaret
Funk 173
GOLLIVER, Lydia Ann 173
GOLLOHORN, Penelope Hagan
173
GOOCH, Elizabeth H 146 Lucy
173
GOOD, Arabella (---) Stevenson
173 Catharine Burnes 173 Eva
Witicks 173 Mary Elizabeth
Dettimore 173 Nancy Sullins
173 Rachael Ordnorff 173
Susan Tanner 173
GOODALL, Margaret Seel 173
Mary Catharine Gallehugh 173
Mourning Marshall 173

GOODE, Benjamin 173 Dorothy
Patterson 173 Judith W 94
Maria 181 Mary Eliza Hayes
173 Sarah P Young 174
GOODEN, Mary 16 Polly 16
GOODIN, Susan Huffman 174
GOODLAND, Elizabeth Finch 174
Thomas 174
GOODLING, Elizabeth Finch 174
GOODMAN, Barbara Nicodemus
174 Mary Barksdale 174 Mary
E Lucas 174 Mary Kinder 174
Philadelphia C 174 Rachel
Wassom 174 Susan Mahan 174
GOODNIGHT, Christian M 174
Jane Mason 174
GOODRICH, Dolly D Gates 174
Ella Huffman 174
GOODSON, America Sandefur 174
GOODWIN, Elizabeth Hickman
174 Frances Jane 175 Janet G
Carmichael 175 Jesse T 175
Jincy Nance 175 Mary 16 Mary
Barb 172 Nancy A Carter 175
Polly 16 Robert 172 Thomas
174
GOODWYN, Jincy Nance 175
GOOLSBY, Abigail Lawhorn 175
Susan 175
GOORLEY, John 175 Mary 175
Susan 175
GOOWIN, Susan Huffman 174
GORDAN, Nancy D Hamlet 175
GORDEN, Susan 98
GORDON, Delia McKinney 175
Elizabeth Harris 175 Frances
G 192 Jane B Triplett 175 Judy
Carter 175 Mary 175 Mary H 26
Mary Jane Pamplin 175
Obedience Sallee 175 Sarah
Knowles 175
GORE, Elizabeth Rountree 175
Frances Cochran 175
GORGAS, Hannah K 121
GORIN, Lucinda 194
GORSUCH, Ann 223 Susanna
Davis 174
GOSNEY, Mary 26
GOSS, Mary Ann 103
GOSSUM, Fannie 61
GOULD, Calysta Bartlett 176 Es-
ther A 12 Lydia 176 Polly

GOULD (continued)
Johnson 176 Rhoda 176
GOURLEY, Catherine Trenary 176
Elizabeth Richards 176 Hannah
Lewis 176
GOWAN, Jane B 142 Judith H At-
kinson 176
GOWEN, Judith H Atkinson 176
William H 176
GOWIN, Anna Amos 176 Eliza-
beth Ferguson 176 Sarah 156
GOWING, Elizabeth Ferguson 176
Samuel 176
GRACE, Adeline M 61
GRADY, Jane 163 Lucy 34 Mar-
garet 152 Sarah Taylor 176
GRAFTON, Lucinda 114
GRAHAM, Amanda E Koontz 177
Elizabeth 170 Elizabeth
Haynes 176 Elizabeth Koontz
177 Elizabeth Reeder 177 Julia
87 Lydia Ann Kimble 177 Mar-
garet 306 Martha 113 Mary Ann
Barbary 177 Mary Bickle 176
Susan 78
GRALEY, Sarah Trail 177
GRANDEE, Sarah 127
GRANDSTAFF, Catharine 159
Elizabeth Clinedinst 177 Mary
Reedy 177
GRANT, Elizabeth 64 Elizabeth
Fridley 177 Hannah Gilliam
177 Lucy M Allen 177 Mara
177 Mary 177 Mary Ann
Swepston 177 Nancy Forest
177 Sarah Bowles 177
GRANVILLE, Fanny 177 Frances
Hartnett 177
GRASS, Sally A Haybarger 177
Sarah A Haybarger 177 Susan
Cotton 178
GRATEHOUSE, Sarah A 99
GRAVELLY, Joseph 178 Polly
Higg 178
GRAVELY, Mary 131 Polly Higg
178
GRAVES, Adelia 178 Christina
Sigler 178 Elizabeth (---) 172
Elizabeth Nalley 178 Emma F
Hobbs 178 Fanny 178 Harriet
Smith 178 Judith Turner 178
Mary A Speeny 178 Sarah C

GRAVES (continued)
111 Sarah H Turner 178
GRAY, Belinda Ward 178 Calva
33 Eliza Jane (---) Hannon
179 Harriett Mason 178 Libby
Burke 178 Mary 178 Mary Ann.
Dunlop 178 Mary M 178 Mary
Smith 60 Nancy A Dowell 179
Phebe Fox 179 Priscilla 210
Ruth 50 Sally 139 Sarah 22
Sarah Moore 178 Susan W 178
GRAYHAM, Elizabeth Reeder 177
Isaac 177 Lydia Ann Kimble
177 Mary Ann Barbary 177
Thomas 177
GRAYLEY, James 177 Sarah
Trail 177
GRAYSON, Mary Fout 179 Rhoda
Merritt 179 Susannah Britt 179
GREANER, Sarah (---) Talbert
179 Temperance Temple 179
GREEAR, Luticia 179
GREEN, Ann Lewis 179 Ann P 21
Ann R Hubball 180 Dolly 179
Easter (Conklin) 168 Elizabeth
25 Elizabeth Glaze 179 Hannah
Duncan 180 Jane 59 Jinsey 179
Kirgan Ann 179 Lucy 83
Mahala 67 Mary Ann Riley 179
Mary C 36 Nancy Ann Parmer
179 Nany 65 Nathan 59 Patsey
E Walden 179 Percilla Hood
179 Rachel Kaylor 179 Sallie
Clark 179 Sally E 65 Sarah
Stone 179 Sidney S 162 Susan
180
GREENLEE, Henry 183
GREENSTREET, Rocksey Tate
180 Susan Bland 180
GREENWOOD, Elizabeth 82 Mary
10
GREER, Nancy (Meadows) 148
Rachel Friesibes 180 Rhoda
180
GREGG, Catherine G Epes 180
Margaret 180
GREGGS, Fanny 54
GREGORY, Anna Stephens 180
Betsey Ann Chatham 180 Dor-
cas Benston 180 Dulcena Berry
180 Elizabeth 180 Frances 213
Jane 76 Margaret 196 Mariah

GREGORY (continued)
Bradner 181 Martha 136 Martha
L Reynolds 180 Mary Ann
Massey Amos 181 Mary D
Long 181 Nancy 181 188 Nancy
Robinson 181 Rachel Campbell
180 Sally M Kean 181 Sarah 50
GRESHAM, Maria Goode 181
Sarah Chatham 181
GREYER, Elizabeth Alford 181
GRICE, Eliza (---) Edwards 181
GRIFFIN, Ann Northington 181
Eliza T Withers 181 Gemima
Neale 181 Jane A Barrett 181
Malinda Wright 181 Nancy 143
Rhoda Ann 48
GRIFFITH, Allay Sheridan 181
Elender 181 Leter 181
Mahaleth 170 Mary 182 Mollie
181 Samuel 182 Sarah
Elizabeth Van Horn 181
GRIFFITS, Mary 182 Samuel 182
Mary 182
GRIGG, Catherine G Epes 180
Peter 180
GRIGGS, Martha Marie Cox 182
GRIGSBY, Redman 182
GRIM, Martha 182 Rebecca Davis
182
GRIMES, Edward 183 Nancy 140
GRIMM, Elizabeth (---) (Reeves)
Sherry 182
GRIMMETT, Peggy Cox 182
GRIMSLEY, Dolly 182
GRINNEL, Sarah 10
GRINSTEAD, Elizabth Clopton
182 Nancy Eubank 182 Nancy
Totty 182
GRISBY, Massa 182
GRISHAW, Lidia 136
GRISWOLD, Calista 59
GROGAN, Mary 15
GROOM, Martha Butler 182
GROOVES, Elizabeth 162
GROSS, Emily Purdy 182 Hetty
Brock 182 Margaret 182
GROVE, Elizabeth 182 Elizabeth
Coffman 182 Eve Demory 183
Jane Young 183 Lawrinda 182
Mary Crockwell 183 Mary Mal-
lory 182 Nancy 130 William
183

GROVES, Betsy Austin 183
  Deborah Russell 183 Sarah 11
  Susan Tapp 183
GROW, Catherine Zimbro 183
GRUBB, Elizabeth Jackson 161
  183 214 215 Leah Virtz 183
  Magdalena Carl 183 Polly
  Saunders 183 Sally Hodges 183
GRUBBS, Diana (Darling) 158
  Jemima 183 Martha Mallory
  183 Sarah J 144
GRUBER, Martha Baughman 183
GRUNDY, Augusta 149
GRYMES, Edmund 183 Edward
  183 Harriet G Dade 183
GUANT, Mary E 99
GUERANT, Elizabeth 7
GUIE, Mathew 184
GUILL, Mary H 183
GUILLIAMS, Rosanna Scott 183
GULICK, Ivy 184
GUMPH, Margaret 38
GUNAWAY, Catharine Routen 162
  Thomas 162
GUNN, Mary S 184 Susanna 48
GUNNAWAY, Catharine Routen
  162
GUNNELL, Catharine (Saylor) Al-
  bert 184 Elizabeth 115
  Elizabeth Lanham 184
  Elizabeth Trunnell 184 Em-
  maline Young 184 Helen M
  Mackall 184 Lucy Ratcliffe
  184
GURDEN, Nancy 2
GUSEMAN, Jane Reed 184
GUSTER, Betsy Junny 184
GUSTIN, Hester 184
GUTHRIDGE, Presley 184
GUTHRIE, Alcy 122 Castilla
  Simpson 184 Lucretia 116
  Mary C Stedman 184 Mary New
  184 Nancy Blackwell 184 Sarah
  Stowe 184
GUY, Margaret 303 Martha 98
  Peggy 303
GWATHMEY, Lucy Ann 184 Lucy
  Ann Able 184
GWINN, Rachel Harshburger 184
HAAS, Sarah 185
HACKER, Elizabeth 190 Margaret
  Keith 185

HACKMAN, Rebecca 210
HACKWORTH, Mary Hologan 185
HADEN, Elizabeth Murphy 185
  Sarah 185
HAFFNER, Susanna 185
HAGA, Margaret 163 Sarah 185
HAGAMAN, Mary A 196
HAGAN, Penelope 173
HAGAR, Martha 153
HAGGETT, Cassandra F S 111
HAGGOMAN, Sarah 226
HAGISH, Julia 185
HAGNE, Mary 134
HAIGH, Elizabeth Carline 185
HAIL, Celia 185 Frances Bourn
  185 Lenora 185 Lewis 185
HAILE, Frances Oliver 185 Lucy
  Creasy 185
HAILEY, Joana 185 Nancy Sisk
  185
HAINES, Jennie 107
HAIR, Abigail 185 Elizabeth 185
  Nancy Lee 185
HAISLIP, Mary T 185
HALBERT, Sally 14
HALE, Jehu 186 Susan 104
  Thomas Lewis 185
HALES, Emily 186
HALEY, Ann Wright 186 Anna
  164 Benjamin 185 Frances H
  Bell 186 Harriet Garrett 186
  Henry 185 Jane 55 Joana 185
  Margaret Young 186 Mary 186
  Nancy Sisk 185
HALL, Ann 187 Annie Simpson
  186 Catharine W Tompkins
  186 Celia 185 Delila Reickman
  186 Elizabeth 187 204
  Elizabeth (---) 105 Elizabeth
  Smith 186 Ester 25 Harriet
  Stringfellow 186 Jane 187 Jane
  R 156 Jane S Paxton 186 Kin-
  chen 186 Lucinda S 186 Lucy
  200 Lucy W 186 Malinda 10
  Martha Perrine 187 Mary 34
  107 108 Mary H 187 Morning
  187 Nancy 186 187 211 Nancy
  (---) Fields 186 Rachel 25
  Rachel C 186 Sallie Scanland
  186 Sally 122 Sarah 213 Sarah
  Bruce 186 Spicy 187 Susan
  (Jarvis) 133 Telitha (Van

HALL (continued)
Hoosir) Dodson 186 Zernah 163
HALLER, Ann Rossman 187
Eliza Sill 187 Hannah Winner
187
HALLEY, Sarah E 187
HAMBLEN, Verrinia Hill Fowlkes
187
HAMBLETON, Robert M 187
HAMBLIN, Sarah E 187 Verrinia
Hill Fowlkes 187 William
Henry 187
HAMILTON, Ann Maria Callis
187 Eliabeth Bough 188
Elizabeth 188 Elizabeth
McCartney 187 Esther 68 Mar-
garet 187 Martha Dinkins 187
Mary 187 Mary Ann Armitage
187 188 Nancy 4 188 Rebecca
Boatwright 187 Sarah E Moore
187 Tilman 188
HAMLET, Elias 188 Nancy D 175
Rebecca 188
HAMLETT, Rebecca 188
HAMLINGTON, Esther 68
HAMLY, Nancy 200
HAMMAN, Anna 188 George 188
Regina 188
HAMMER, Cynthia 188
HAMMILL, Elizabeth 188
HAMMON, Regina 188
HAMMOND, George 188 Regina
188 Sarah 5
HAMMONDS, Lucy Lowery 188
HAMMONTREE, Judith Howell
188
HAMPSON, Hannah (Eyman) 151
HAMPTON, Elenor 205 Mary 113
Pamela 188
HAMRICH, Lettice 84
HAMRICK, Amelia 188 Nancy 149
Nancy Gregory 188 Rhoda C 85
Sarah 149
HAMSLEY, Nancy Rhodes 188
HANCHER, Nancy Ann 188
HANCOCK, Deniza B Anderson
188 Frances Rucker 188 Han-
nah Wooldridge Walthall 188
Mary Burton 188 Nancy 92 188
Nancy D 31 Nancy Gibson 188
Phebe 172
HAND, James 188 Malinda 188

HANDLEY, Dorcas 101
HANEY, Catharine Carter 189
Elizabeth 189
HANGER, Margaret Cook 189
Mary Allen 189 Mary Ann 189
HANKINS, Sally 59 Susan Staples
189
HANKS, Elizabeth 189
HANLON, Margaret Williamson
189 Nancy French 189
HANNA, Ann 189 Margaret Harris
189
HANNAH, Elizabeth P 128
Lucretia Black 189
HANNANSON, William 191
HANNON, Eliza Jane (---) 179
HANNUM, Mary 190 Peter 189
HANSBARGER, Elizabeth 189
Rebecca 189
HANSBOROUGH, Patsey 305
HANSBROUGH, Fanny C Sampson
189
HANSELL, Margaret 189 Nancy
Jamison 189
HANSFORD, Mahala J Adkins 189
HANSON, Margaret Aery 189 Sid-
ney 9
HANUM, Mary 190
HARBERT, Catharine 190 Peter
190
HARBETT, Margaret 254
HARBOUR, Martha Slaughter 190
HARBOUT, Catharine 190
HARDAWAY, Elizabeth Gibson
190 Mary A Berry 190
HARDEN, Frances C Dameron
190
HARDESTY, Martha McMullen
190
HARDIMAN, Beverley 190
HARDING, Elizabeth W 190
Fanny Harper 190 Julia
Foulkes 190 Mary P 67 Polly
Farrar 190 Sally 81 Sarah 81
190
HARDMAN, Elizabeth Hacker 190
Julia Ann Rinehart 190
HARDWAY, Margaret Sharrit 190
HARDWICK, Mary Ann 210
HARDY, Alsey Yeates 190 Ann R
24 Evy Pigg 190
HARE, Catharine Welch 190

HARFORD, Mary 96 Sally Rambo
190
HARGRAVE, Catharine B Parker
191
HARGRAVES, Lucy F 83
HARGROVE, Martha G Mason 191
HARKLESS, Mary L 191
HARL, Susan F Shoemaker 191
HARLAN, Adaline R 191 Frances
Eliza Street 191 Mary E Evans
191
HARLESS, Lucy 191
HARLING, Levi 191 Mary E
Evans 191
HARLOW, Maria 191 Martha Fer-
guson 191 Rosanna Butler 191
Susan H 66
HARMAN, Elizabeth 191 Lucy
Blankenship 191 Nancy K 191
HARMANSON, Margaret C Mapp
191
HARMON, Elizabeth 191 Margaret
191 Nancy 191 Susannah C 191
William 191
HARNED, Mary Ann Morrison 191
HARNESS, Elizabeth W 137
Eunice 192
HARNSBARGER, Sarah 86
HARP, Elizabeth 162
HARPER, Angelina McGelvee 192
Elizabeth Kinsale 192 Fanny
190 Frances McCoull 192
Frances W 165 Jane Maria 73
Lucy 96 Martha A Hester 192
Mary 192 Nancy 120 Nancy
Pettit 192 Rachel W 32 Thursa
101
HARPOLD, Margaret 192
HARRAH, Elizabeth 192
HARRASS, Delilah 131
HARRELL, Lavinia 17
HARRIS, Abbie 192 Ann 193
Cassee Ann 102 Catharine 192
Drusilla 193 Eliza H 53
Elizabeth 14 114 175 193 194
Elizabeth Garthright 192
Elizabeth Newcomb 192
Elizabeth T 193 Frances G
Gordon 192 Jane 11 Jane
Badger 193 Jane S Wilson 192
Jane W 192 Lucinda Clardy
194 Lucy A 192 Margaret 189

HARRIS (continued)
Martha 114 193 Martha
Fitzpatrick 193 Mary 192 193
Mary A 66 Mary Ann Tyler 193
Mary M 110 Mary S 6 Mary W
192 Moses 194 Nancy Goen
193 Nancy Goin 193 Peggy 11
Phebe 287 Rachel 193 Rebecca
192 Sallie 192 Sally 193 Sarah
Davis 192 Sarah Powell 192
Sarah W 11
HARRISON, Ann Coleburn 194
Caroline 194 Elizabeth 100
Elizabeth Mazena 193 Fanny
94 Janetta R Fisher 193
Leonora 193 Lucinda Gorin 194
Malcom 194 Malcomb 194
Margaret Farmer 193 Margaret
L 96 Mary 194 Mary A 194
Mary B 194 Mary E 86 Mary F
193 Mary T 117 Penelope 194
Sally 194 Susan P Helmstatter
193
HARRISS, Lucinda Clardy 194
HARROW, Ellen S Hove 194
HARRY, Caroline 194
HARSHBURGER, Rachel 184
HART, Ann 101 Deborah 42
Elizabeth 194 Harriet A 112
Judith 54 Lavinia 127 Margaret
194 Mildred H 86 Rebecca 194
HARTLESS, Benjamin Sr 191
Mary L 191
HARTMAN, Margaret 40 Sarah 55
Susanna Long 194
HARTNETT, Frances 177
HARTSOF, Frances 49
HARTSOOK, Ann Wooten 194
HARTWELL, Sarah 275
HARVEY, Betsey Ward 194
Elizabeth Harris 194 Ellen
(---) Dukes 195 Judy
Wooldridge 194 Magdalene 23
Martha J 53 Prudence Owen
194 Salley (---) 96 Sarah (---)
96 Sarah Tyler 194
HARWOOD, Sarah K 109 Susan
227
HASELTON, Elizabeth 126
HASLIP, Mary T 185 Robert 185
HASTINGS, Sarah Martin 195
HATCHER, Lucinda B Flippen

362

HATCHER (continued)
195 Lucy Rucken 195 Martha
195 Rebecca 79 Rhoda 232
HATCHET, Tabitha 195
HATCHETT, Amelia 75 Elizabeth
Love 195
HATFIELD, Zerrilda 195
HATTEN, Elizabeth McGinnis
195
HATTON, Elijah 195 Elizabeth
McGinnis 195
HAUGHT, Ann Elizabeth 195
HAUPE, Polly 74
HAUSENFLUCH, Catherine 207
Mary 207
HAUT, Ann Elizabeth 195 Joseph
195
HAVANS, Nancy 195
HAVELY, Elizabeth Crider 195
HAVENS, Sarah Davis 195
HAWKINS, Calley 196 Catharine
140 Catherine 128 Christena
195 Christiana 195 Elizabeth
163 Mary Perry 195 Nancy 195
Rebecca 128 Susanna 195
HAWKS, John 195
HAWLEY, Barton D 115 130
Catharine Cofer 205 Hannah
130 James 205 Lucinda 82
Mary 115 154
HAWLING, Frances Best 196
HAY, Barbary 196 Elizabeth Car-
line 185 George 185
HAYBARGER, Sally A 177 Sarah
A 177
HAYBERGER, Elizabeth 196
HAYDON, Elizabeth A 158
HAYES, Mary Eliza 173 Mary
Vanscoy 196
HAYHURST, Eliza J 196
HAYMOND, Jane Somerville 196
Mary Carpenter 196
HAYNES, Amanda 196 Elizabeth
176 Elizabeth Pulley 196 Jane
H 170 Lucy C 121 Mary A 196
Mary R Converse 196 Sarah
Ann 196 Susan Floyd 196
HAYNIE, Mary A (Hagaman)
(Lampkins) Garner 196 Sarah
196
HAYS, Harriet 196 Jane Surface
196 Nancy 145 Rachel 42

HAYS (continued)
Rachel Strong 196
HAYSE, George 196 Mary
Vanscoy 196
HAYTER, Margaret Gregory 196
HAYTH, Mary 196
HAYWOOD, Ann B 200 Robert S
200
HAYZLETT, Mahala 196
HAZARD, Lucy 94
HAZELGROVE, Elizabeth Cross
196 197 Martha A Archer 197
HAZELL, Nancy 197
HAZELRIGG, Abagail Jemason
197 Abigail Jemason 197
HAZZARD, Elizabeth 197
HEABERLIN, Elizabeth 197
HEADEN, Elizabeth Murphy 185
John 185 Mary 92
HEADLEY, Sarah 52
HEATH, Catharine 197 Eliza
Cureton 197 Mary W 90
HEATHERLY, Jane 321
HEATON, Eliza Cureton 197
Sarah 142
HEAVENER, Catharine 116
HEAVENOR, George Sr 200
HEAVER, E Rod 66
HEAVNER, George Sr 200
HEBB, Ann E Caricow 197
HEDRICK, Catherine Debo 197
Elizabeth Johnson 197
HEFFERTON, Catharine D
Tucker 197
HEFLIN, Margaret 40 Mary 171
Sarah 197
HEISLER, Hannah 121
HEIZER, Elizabeth 197
HELBERT, Sarah 197
HELFIN, Alexander W 197 Sarah
197
HELLRIGLE, Ann Maria Jackson
197
HELMANDOLAR. Elizabeth 156
HELMICH, Sarah 43
HELMICK, Anna Minnis 197 Jane
197 Sarah (Williams)
(Calhoun) Vandevander 197
HELMSTATTER, Susan P 193
HELSLEY, Mary G Helzel 197
HELVESTINE, Nancy Caldwell
198

HELVISTON, Nancy Caldwell 198
HELZEL, Mary G 197
HEMMICK, Catherine 198
HEMPENSTALL, Abraham 198
HENAGE, Catharine Jones 198
HENDERSON, Anna 198 Catherine
198 Elizabeth Clark 198 Jane
198 Margaret 128 Peggy 86
Susan 248
HENDLEY, Mary (Board) 102
Sarah 124
HENDREE, Sarah A Tinsley 198
HENDREN, Sallie 198
HENDRICK, Eliza G Steyer 198
Judith Ann 198 Sally Palmore
198
HENDRIX, Elizabeth 10
HENEEM, Elizabeth 49
HENEHIE, Mary 41
HENING, Eliza Parke Scott 198
HENINGER, Sophia (---) 16
HENLEY, Catharine N Lightfoot
198 Elizabeth 198 Frances 198
Sarah 198
HENLINE, Catharine 99
HENNESY, Catharine M 105
HENRY, Ann Elizabeth 65
Elizabeth Ryno 198 Judith 169
Mary Ambrose 198 Nancy 88
Rachel 199
HENSEY, Mary A 77
HENSHAW, Thirza Ann E 84
HENSLEY, Elizabeth 212 Liddy
199 Lydia 199 Patsey 85 Sarah
Bailey 199 Susan Peters 199
HENSON, Lucy Pulliam 199 Mary
Lewis 199
HENTHORN, Margaret (Hickman)
136
HENTON, Lurenna 199 Mary S
205
HEPLER, Elizabeth Kessler 199
HERBERT, Maria 199 Mary 275
HERNDIN, John 199
HERNDON, Charlotte Brown 199
Elizabeth A 199 Jane West
199 John 199 Lourena Cave
199 Mary 199 Melinda 199
Mildred 199 Sarah 199
HERRING, Lucy 199
HERRON, Abigale 200 Jane Col-
vin 199

HERSHBERGER, Susannah (---)
64
HESKET, Henrietta 200
HESKETT, Henrietta 200 James
200 Nancy 200
HESS, Elizabeth Romake 200 Har-
riet A 9
HESSER, Catherine Venable 200
HESTER, Elizabeth 142 Martha A
192
HEVENER, William 200
HEWEY, M A 170
HEWITT, Elizabeth 107 168
HEYWOOD, Ann B 200
HICKERSON, Ann 139
HICKEY, Ann M 60 Harriet 200
Sarah E 113
HICKLE, Hannah Sigler 200 Mary
99
HICKMAN, Elizabeth 174 200
Lucinda 200 Margaret 136
Nancy 68 Peggy 16
HICKOK, Sally A 200
HICKS, Abigail 29 Ann A Bradford
201 Cary 87 Clarissa 200
Frances 200 Jane McBane 200
Lucy Hall 200 Mary 83 200
Mary Williams 200 Nancy 200
201 Nancy Hamly 200 Rebecca
200 Reuben 201 Sally E 201
Sarah 115 Sarah B Sale 200
HICMAN, Catherine 200
HIDACRE, Christina Mace 201
Frances Woodford 201
HIDECKER, Christina Mace 201
Frances Woodford 201 Jacob
201
HIETT, Elizabeth Ann Waid 201
Nancy Forbes 201 Susan Fer-
guson 201
HIGG, Polly 178
HIGGINBOTHAM, Isabella 201
HIGGINS, Elizabeth 144 Elizabeth
Evans 201 Elizabeth H Pollard
201
HIGH, Frances Shoemaker 201
Mary Ann (Mitchell) Shoe-
maker 201
HIGHTEFFER, John 203 Sarah
Dutroe 203
HILBRANT, John 201 Nancy 201
HILDEBRAND, Susannah 201

HILDRUP, Elizabeth L Powers
202 Robert 201 202
HILL, Betsey 113 Eliza W 103
Elizabeth 202 Elizabeth Pan-
nell 201 Emeline 201 Margaret
118 Maria A 49 Martha 170
Mary 201 202 Nancy M 23
Peggy 34 Permelia 35 Rebecca
Brown 203 Sarah 26 Sarah H
201 Sarah Houston 201 Sarah
Pennell 201 Sophronia M Lake
201 Susan 84 Thaddeus 203
HILLDRUP, Elizabeth L Powers
202
HILLEARY, Eleanor Freeman 202
Elijah 202
HILLHOUSE, Lucy 202 Martha 58
Mary Ann Collings 202
HILLIARD, Betsy Taylor 202
Phebe Elliott 202 Sarah 6
HILLIARY, Eleanor Freeman 202
HILLIS, David 202 Mary Ann
Collings 202
HILLMAN, Charlotte Copenhaver
202 Delilah 83
HILMAN, Squire 202
HINCHEN, Margaret Barley 202
HINCHEY, Sallie 56
HINES, Aurora B 202 Elizabeth 38
Hannah Briles 202 Hester 202
Mary C Thomas 202 Nancy R
202
HINKEL, Elizabeth 151
HINKLE, Charlotte 202 Elizabeth
Arrowood 202
HINKLEY, Sarah A 202
HINSON, Catherine 249 Caty 249
HINTON, Lurenna 199 Mary S 205
Peter 199 Polly 202
HIPES, Catherine 202
HIRSCHMAN, Lucinda 132
HISER, Catharine Showalter 203
Elizabeth 203 Polly 33
HISEY, Abigail 203
HISSOM, Elizabeth 203
HITAFFER, Sarah Dutroe 203
HITCH, Mary Barbee 203
HITE, Lusander 31 Magdaline 203
Mary 135 Matilda 43 Rebecca
203 Sarah 203
HITT, Elizabeth M Vaughan 203
Joanna Murdock Jett 203

HITT (continued)
Joseph 203 Mary Lafferty 203
Polly 203 Rebecca Brown 203
HITTS, Nancy 81
HIVELY, Ann 68 Martha E 203
HIX, Benjamin 200 Catharine
Mullen 203 Clarissa 200 Delila
Lykins 203 Harriet Jenkins 203
Mary 83 Sarah H 203 Sophia
203
HIXSON, Priscilla Woodyard 203
HIZER, Adam 203 Elizabeth 203
George 203 Jemima 203
HOBACK, Cynthia 203
HOBBS, Eliza (---) Taylor 204
Eliza Olinger 204 Elizabeth
Rebecca Hobbs 117
Elizabeth/Betsy 203 Emma F
178 Mary Smith 204 Sarah 21
HOBSON, Adcock 144 Edith 144
Edith (---) Farmer 204 Louisa
W 204 Martha 154 Sallie 25
Sarah E 47
HOCKER, Sarah Darrah 204
HOCKMAN, Elizabeth 133
HODGES, Carolina 204 Elizabeth
Hall 204 Ellen (---) 23 Harriet
204 Judith 125 Lucinda 204
Mary 123 Mary Jane 204 Mary
T 204 Sally 183 Sarah Bomar
204
HODGKIN, Clara Taylor 204
Elizabeth Fraser 204
HOES, Eunice Kellum 204
HOFF, Martha 204
HOFFMAN, Elizabeth 204
Jemima 70 Lucinda 148
HOGAN, Martha 204
HOGANS, Sally 2
HOGELAND, Jane 204
HOGELIN, Israel 204 Jane 204
HOGG, Julia 204 Mary E 204
HOGGE, Mary 104
HOGWOOD, Amelia 204
HOLBROOK, Mary 204 Thomas
W 204
HOLCOMB, Frances B 204 Polly
S (---) 46
HOLCOMBE, Hannah 132
HOLDEN, Sarah 204
HOLDER, Nancy 204 Toliver 204
HOLDERBY, Rebecca Hoskins

HOLDERBY (continued)
204 205 Susan A 204
HOLDING, Anna 25
HOLDREN, Bartholomew 205
Jane 205
HOLDRIGHT, John D 205 Sarah
Chapman 205
HOLDRON, Jane 205
HOLDRYDE, Sarah Chapman 205
HOLEMAN, Susan W 166
HOLESAPPLE, Elizabeth 205
HOLLADAY, Nancy B 128
HOLLAND, Christina 205 Harriet
W 89 Judith R 209 Margaret
205 Polly 205
HOLLEMAN, Nancy 205
HOLLENBACK, Elenor Hampton
205
HOLLER, Lydia 88
HOLLEY, Betsy Ralph 205
Catharine Cofer 205 James 205
John 187 Sarah E 187 Sophia
Smith 205
HOLLIDAY, --- 3 Ann P
McDonough 205 Euphama 161
HOLLINGSWORTH, Nancy 150
Rebecca 3
HOLLINS, Mary 205
HOLLINSWORTH, Elizabeth 205
HOLLOWAY, Eliza 62 Jane 205
Margaret 205 Mary Ann 117
Mary S Hinton/Henton 205
Nancy 85 Philadelphia 145
HOLLY, Betsy Ralph 205
Catharine Cofer 205
HOLMES, Elizabeth B Horton 205
Elizabeth S Ryan 205 Martha P
110 Susan 79
HOLOGAN, Mary 185
HOLSAPPLE, Elizabeth 205
Henry 205
HOLSHOPPLE, Elizabeth 205
Henry 205 Susannah 205
HOLSTEIN, Jane Wilson 206
HOLSTIN, Martha 206
HOLT, Jane 50 Mary 13 Sally
Fowlkes 206 Susan 153 Wil-
moth Bradley 206 Winifred M
206
HOMAN, Mary 62 Rachel 206
HONAKER, Anna 206 Mary 121
HONNOLD, Talaifa 110

HOOD, Nancy 206 Percilla 179
HOOE, Sarah Jane 31 Virginia 206
HOOK, Martha L 84
HOOKE, Elizabeth Fisher 206
HOOPER, Elizabeth 156 Rebecca
79
HOOVER, Barbara 206 Elizabeth
206
HOPKINS, Ann E 206 Celia 126
Dorothy Proctor Choate 206
Elizabeth 207 Fanny Morely
206 Jane E Ervine 206 Mary
206 Mary Ann 207 Nancy 207
Nancy Andrews 206 Patsey
Bailey 206 Polly Mathhews
206 Portia Lee 18 Susan
(Kelles) Ross 206 Tempey
(Ball) 71
HOPPER, Elizabeth B 207 Martha
207
HOPSON, Sarah J (---) 147
HORD, Elizabeth 207
HORN, Ann 207 Margaret 294
Nancy 207
HORNE, Matilda 42
HORNER, Keturah 207
HORNOR, Dolly O 207 Mary A
207
HORTON, Elizabeth 207
Elizabeth B 205
HOSCHAR, Susan 207
HOSKINS, Lucinda 167 Rebecca
204 205
HOSSENFLUCK, Catherine 207
Mary 207
HOST, Angelina 207
HOSTETTER, Nancy 207
HOTTEL, Catharine 207
HOTTINGER, Elizabeth 35
HOUCK, Priscilla 160
HOUGH, Mary 207 Mary S 208
HOUNSHELL, Polly 103
HOUSE, Elizabeth 208 Lucy 208
HOUSEHOLDER, Ann 208
HOUSEMAN, Polly 122
HOUSERIGHT, Malinda 208
HOUSEWORTH, Margaret 67
HOUSTON, Mary 116 Sarah 148
201
HOVE, Ellen S 194
HOWARD, Eliza 208 Elizabeth
118 163 212 Elizabeth D 10

HOWARD (continued)
Jane 140 Mary 208 Mary P 208
Nancy S 208 Sarah 208 Sarah B
208
HOWDERSHELT, Katy 208 Mary
208
HOWELL, Chrissey 208
Elizabeth 208 Judith 188 Julia
208 Margaret 208 Namoie K
208 Nancy 89 Nancy G 15
HOWISON, Jane B 26
HOWLETT, Martha C 132 Mary
134
HUAGINS, Elizabeth A 223
HUBBALL, Ann R 180
HUBBARD, Ann N 51 Elizabeth
117 Lucy 304 Margaret 209
Nancy 209 Pamelia Jane 209
HUDDLESTON, Sarah 80
HUDGENS, Susan 15
HUDGIN, Milly 209
HUDGINGS, Lucy E 209
HUDGINS, Agnes B 209 Anna 209
Frances 209 Mary 209 Sarah
209
HUDLOW, Rachel 47
HUDNALL, Mary 40 Mary A 209
HUDSON, Amy 149 Ann 209 Dicey
209 Elizabeth 17 Grizell 209
Jane 210 Judith R 209 Lavinia
P P 210 Lucretia 209 Malinda
210 Mancy A 48 Mary Ann 210
Mary E 209 Mary H 209 Nancy
210 Nancy E 209 Parmelia 209
Polly H 142 Sarah 209 Sarah G
68 Susan 141
HUFF, Anna 210 Eliza Ann 210
Elizabeth 210 Harriet D 210
Jane G 210 Maria 49 Mary T
210
HUFFMAN, DILLYLA 210
Elizabeth 57 66 210 Ella 174
Jane 210 Parmelia 210 Pris-
cilla 210 Rebecca 210 Susan
174
HUFFNOW, Anne 142
HUGHES, Benete 85 Catharine 9
Delilah 210 Eliza 16 Elizabeth
211 Elizabeth H 6 Fanny 210
Joyce 210 Judith Soy 210
Letecia 211 Martha C 211
Mary 53 211 Mary S 211 Nancy

HUGHES (continued)
211 Polly 211 Susan Margaret
(---) (Smith) 169 Susannah 211
Tabitha 149 Virginia 56
HUGHLETT, Thomas 211
HUGHS, Charity 31 Rhoda 211
HUGHSON, Ann E 149
HULETT, Barbara 1
HULL, Anne M 211
HUMMER, Julia 211 Martha 211
HUMPHREY, Elizabeth 211
Matilda 211 Nancy 58 171
Rutha 211 Sarah 106 Sarah C
211
HUMPHREYS, Eliza 84 Elizabeth
W 211 Margaret 211 Nancy 10
Sarah G 211
HUMPHRIES, Elizabeth 212 Mary
212 Susan 212
HUNDLEY, Elizabeth 132 212
Mary 160 212 Tabitha 212
HUNDON, Ann 62
HUNSBARGER, John 189 Rebecca
189
HUNT, Dianisha 212 Eliza A ----
212 Jane 212 Maria 212 Nancy
212 Sallie J 212 Sally 212
Sarah 212
HUNTER, Frances 212 Margaret
W 212 Mary Ann 76 Nancy 6
Remelia Anna 64
HUNTON, Fannie 212
HURN, Marks 212 Nancy C 212
HURSEY, Margaret E 213
HURST, Elenor 213 Sarah 213
HURT, Ann 213 Dianisha 212
Elizabeth 213 Frances 213
Litha 51 Louisa 213 Rebecca
213
HURTON, Phoebe 22
HUSTON, Margaret G 213
HUTCHERSON, Elizabeth B 213
Polly 213
HUTCHINGS, Mary 213
HUTCHINS, Mary 213 Mindwell
213
HUTCHINSON, Abigail 213 Emily
44 Margaret 213 Martha 213
Mary 213 Nancy 105 Susanna
290
HUTCHISON, Frances M 213
HUTSELL, Margaret 213 Mary

HUTSELL (continued)
Ann 213
HUTSON, Lucy 81 Mary 126 209
HUTTON, Betsey 108 Nancy 213
HUXTER, Mary 2
HYATT, Ann 213 Mary Ann 213
Priscilla 134
HYDE, Rhoda 260
HYTTON, Susannah 121
I'ANSON, Jane T 214
IDEN, Hannah 102
IDLE, Susannah 214
IMBODEN, Isabella 214
INCHMINGER, John 138 Martha J
Dixon 138 Sarah Knick 138
INDE, Ann 147
INGE, Frances M 214
INGLES, Malinda Jane 82
INGRAM, Alice L 214 Margaret
214 Melinda 214 Nancy 214
INGYEARD, Catherine 214
INNES, Robert 214
INSKEEP, Mary A 214
INSLEY, Mary Ann 214
IRBY, Catharine B 7 Martha 125
Mary 125
IRELAND, Sarah 214
IRVIN, Isabella P 214 Jane S 214
IRVINE, Hanna G 122 Selina A C
214
IRVING, Frances A 214 Mary 214
IRWIN, Leanna 214
IRWINE, Selina A C 214
ISAACS, Caroline 214
ISBELL, Celia Ann 214
ISLER, Martha L 214 Sarah 214
IVEY, Elizabeth P 214
IVIE, Elizabeth 214
IVINS, David 141 Polly 141
IVY, Elizabeth P 214
JACKSON, Ann Maria 197 Anne
117 Betsey 130 ELiza 146
Eliza 168 Elizabeth 161 183
214 215 Julia 215 Lucy 215
Martha B 215 Martha R 215
Mary 85 215 Nancy M 215
Rachel 215 Rhoanna 215
Sophia C 170 Temperance 215
JACOBS, 147 Fannie 168 Malinda
215 Mary 172 187 Mary E 51
JAMES, Betsey 215 Catherine T
215 Elizabeth 215 Hannah M

JAMES (continued)
34 Mary 215 Rachel 87
JAMESON, Charlotte 215 Rebecca
215
JAMIESON, Charlotte 215 Maria
C 215
JAMISON, Nancy 189
JANEGAN, Nancy 215
JANNEGAN, Nancy 215
JANNEY, Mary 215
JARNEGAN, Nancy 215
JARRARD, Nancy 17
JARRATT, Sally 215
JARRETT, Elvira E 215
JARVIS, Elizabeth 215 Margaret
215 Mary 215 Sally 215 Susan
133
JASPER, Lucy A G 215 Nancy
162
JEFFERSON, Elizabeth 215
JEFFREIS, Kitty 216
JEFFRIES, Ann 80 Anna M 215
Elizabeth 216 Martha B L 216
Mary Ann 34 Sally 215
JELPH, Fielding 82 Virenda 82
JELT, Elizabeth 216
JEMASON, Abagail 197 Abigail
197
JEMERSON, Mary 52
JENKINS, Charity 216 Elizabeth 2
216 Frances 67 Harriet 203
Jane E 216 Jemima 216 Mar-
garet (---) 125 Martha 216
Rachel 69 199 Rebecca 157
Rosanna 216 Sally 216 Tulip
216
JENNET, Ann 316
JENNIE, Mary 215
JENNIKEN, Nancy 215
JENNINGS, Frances B 216 Lucy
146 Mary 216 Mary C 216
Nancy K 216 Rebecca 216
JENNO, Frances 67
JESSE, Catherine 92 Fanny 216
JESSEE, Anna 104
JETT, Jane S 160 Joanna Mur-
dock 203 Julia M 216 Nancy
216 Sally 123
JEWELL, Elizabeth 22 Sarah 115
JIRVORDAND, Nancy 2
JOHNS, Dianisha 212 Elizabeth L
13 Jane 98

JOHNSON, Agnes A 123 Ailcy 130
Ann 217 Ann M 217 Anna 217
Anna (---) 94 Anne 217 Be-
hethland 217 Catharine 217
Delila 16 Eliza 216 Elizabeth
130 197 216 217 Elizabeth R
217 Fanny 55 Hannah 217 Har-
denia 217 Harriet T (---) 49
Jane E 217 Letitia 216 Liddie
217 Litha (Hurt) 51 Lockey 217
Lucy Ann 217 Lucy H 6 Mar-
garet 217 Martha 68 136 216
Mary 39 66 167 Mary H 217
Mary K 217 Mary T 217
Matilda 86 Mildred A 7 Nancy
3 49 216 217 Nancy Buford 106
Nancy F 217 Nancy L 217
Nancy P 144 Parthenia C 32
Peyton 94 Phebe 216 217
Phoebe 4 Polly 176 Rebecca
77 Sally 216 217 Sarah 259
Sarah Ann 217 Sarah C 149
Sary 216 Susan 26 Susannah
217 Susannah B 217 Zellen 217
JOHNSTON, Ann R 107 Letitia
216 Lucy H 6 Polly 44 Sallie
218 Sally 217 218 Sally Hogan
218 Zellen 217
JOINER, Diza 220 Elizabeth 128
JOLLIFFE, Fanny 218
JONAS, Elizabeth 218
JONES, 180 Amanda G 219 Ann
Jane 219 Anne 155 Catharine
198 Catherine 219 Catherine P
219 Celia 219 Clarkey 299
Delilah 219 Dick 108 Elanor
218 Eliza A 136 Eliza S 154
Elizabeth 145 218 219
Elizabeth C 219 Ellen K 218
Fanny 218 Frances 218
Frances E 219 Francis 50
Hannah 97 219 Harriet W 218
Jane 218 219 Jane Ann 218
Judith B 219 Julia Ann 218
Kitty 219 Luanna M 218
Lucinda 218 Lucy 218 219
Magdaline 203 Malinda 218
Margaret 140 219 Martha 9 219
Martha G 108 Mary 33 119 219
Mary E 218 Mary P 218 Mary S
218 Mary W 219 Matilda A 171
Milly 218 Molsey 219 Nancy

JONES (continued)
52 218 Nancy W 218 Patient
Ann 90 Patsy 219 Paulina 167
Perlina 167 Phebe 218 Polley
E 218 Rachel 94 Rachel P 218
Rebecca 219 Ruth 218 Sally
219 Sarah H 169 Sarah K 218
Susan 82 102 108 218 Susan A
219 Susan L 218 Susanna 87
Virginia 218
JOPLING, Patience 219
JORDAN, Catharine 220 Elender
64 Elizabeth 20 219 220 Julia
208 Margaret 220 Martha E 219
Mary 50 108 220 Mary Ann 219
Mary F 8 Mary P 139 Nancy 17
Paulina 219 220 Polly 220
JORDEN, Catharine 220
JOSEPH, Annis 220 Sarah 83
JOURDAN, Ann 159
JOYNER, Ann 115 Diza 220 Jane
220 Martha 220 Nancy 115
Patsy 220 Salley 135
JOYNES, Maria S 220
JUDD, Elizabeth 76
JUDKINS, Rebecca 220
JULIEN, Sarah 18
JUNNY, Betsy 184
JUSTICE, Sarah 220
KABRICK, Susan 220
KAIN, Hannah 220
KALAR, Jane 220
KALE, David 69 Elizabeth 69
John 69
KANSON, Louisa 20
KARN, Susannah 119
KARNES, Jane 220
KAY, Lucy 220
KAYLOR, Rachel 179
KEAN, Hannah 220 Sally M 181
KEARNES, Mary 221
KECKLEY, Leah 220 Sarah
Elizabeth 52
KEEL, Jane 163
KEELING, Fanny 220 Jane 9 Mar-
tha R 220
KEEMLE, Mary 220
KEEN, Elizabeth J 85
KEENE, Margaret 28 220 Sabina
166
KEENEY, Frances 50
KEESLING, Elizabeth 265

KEETON, Annie 220
KEEZEL, Amanda F 220
KEFFER, Elizabeth 261 Lucy 220
   Mary 21
KEGLEY, Catherine 68 George 68
KEIFFER, Frances 145
KEISTER, Mary C 220
KEITH, Elizabeth 117 Margaret
   185
KELLAM, Eliza 220 Harriet B D
   220
KELLER, Dorothy 220 Elizabeth
   220
KELLES, Susan 206
KELLEY, Mary 220 Nancy 220
   Nancy B 29
KELLUM, Eunice 204
KELLY, Anna 16 Catherine 77
   Cherry G 172 Elizabeth 23
   Margaret 146 Mary R 220
   Nancy 220 Phoebe Ann 4
   Rebecca (Bolinger) 107 Sarah
   P 220 Sophia 100
KEMP, Mary G 220
KEMPER, Matilda 220 221
KENDALL, Elizabeth A 221 Mary
   221 Polly 221 Roxy A 221
KENDRICK, Margaret 221 Nancy
   L 221
KENNEDY, Ruth 221
KENNER, Eliza 221
KENNERLY, Amanda F 221
KENNEY, Sarah 221
KENT, Sallie T 24
KEPPLER, Sarah 61
KERFOOT, Catharine 19
KERLIN, Barbara 221
KERNELL, Elizabeth 221
KERNES, Mary 221
KERNS, Mildy 221 Nancy 70
KERR, James M 74 Sally N 221
KERSEY, Catharine 221 Sally 221
KESLER, Catherine 221 Elizabeth
   221
KESSEL, Sidney 78
KESSLER, Catharine 136
   Elizabeth 26 199 221
KESTERSON, Catherine 221
KETCHUM, Martha 91
KETTERMAN, Mary Ann 221
   Sarah 221
KEY, Elizabeth 221 Harriet B 64

KEY (continued)
   Mary A R 221
KEYES, Jane H 221
KEYSER, Sarah 107
KIAS, Susanna 222
KIDD, Charity 221 Elizabeth 110
   Lucy 221 Rosanna 170
KIDDY, Lucinda 221
KIDWELL, Emeline E 221
KIFFLE, Margaret 268
KIGER, Anna J 221 Lydia 222
   Polly 221 222
KILBY, Sallie L 222 Susan B 222
KILGORE, Isabell 16 Lucy 222
KILGROW, Verressa 222
KILLINGSWORTH, Nancy 117
   Rebecca 222
KILPATRICK, Eliza 22
KIMBLE, Lydia Ann 177
KIMBLER, Nancy 222
KIMBRAU, Susan 167
KIMBROUGH, Nancy 222 Susan
   222
KINCAID, Elizabeth 222 Mary 222
KINCHLOW, Courtney Ann 222
KINDER, Mary 174 222
KING, Ann H 222 Catharine 222
   Catherine 222 Elizabeth 112
   222 Elizabeth Jane 222
   Elizabeth V 222 Linia 222
   Margaret 105 222 Mary 92 222
   Mary T 40 Polly 222 Roan 135
   Sarah 51 222 Verlinda 222
KINGERY, Elizabeth 90
KINGRED, Sarah 222
KINGREE, Sarah 222
KINGREY, Sarah 222
KINGRY, Sarah 222
KINGSBERRY, Mary (---) 24
KININGHAM, Jane 222
KINKAID, Anna 104 Elizabeth 222
   Mary 222
KINKEAD, Henrietta 222
KINNARD, Lavinia 222
KINNEAR, Martha 222 Patty 222
KINNINGHAM, Jane 222
KINSALE, Elizabeth 192
KINSEY, Elizabeth F 47
KIOUS, Susanna 222
KIPPER, Jane 222 223
KIPPS, Mary 222
KIRACOFE, Mary A 223

LARRANCE, Elizabeth 225
LASCELLES, Lydia 162
LASLEY, Susan P 225 Willia C 225
LATHAM, Juliet A 225 Lucy 225
LATHERS, Ann (Ardinger) 78
LATIMER, Elizabeth 225
LAUCK, Catherine 225
LAVANARD, Elizabeth 97
LAVEL, Lucy A 225
LAVELL, Lucy A 225
LAVEN, Frances 225
LAVENDER, Sallie 225
LAVIN, Frances 225
LAVINDER, Mary Ann 225 Sallie 225
LAW, Sally 225 Susan 37
LAWHORN, Abigail 175 Margaret 225
LAWLACE, Elizabeth 225
LAWLER, Nancy A 225
LAWLESS, Elizabeth 225 Polly 225 226 Prudence T 226 Sarah 226
LAWRENCE, Charlotte 226 Dicey 111 Elizabeth 226 Hannah G 226 John O 59 Polly 118 Priscilla (---) 111 Sally 59
LAWSON, Delia 226 Eve 226 Martha 23 Pracilla 153 Rachel 226 Sallie E 24 Winney 65
LAYCOCK, Rebecca A 226
LAYMAN, Barbara 226 Christena 226
LAYMASTER, Catharine 170
LAYNE, Dilecia T 226 Elizabeth 226 Matilda 226 Susanna 226
LAYTON, Sarah 226
LE SUEUR, Martha 228
LEA, Mary 226 Nancy 26
LEACH, Margaret 170 Mary 226 Nancy 226 Sarah 226
LEADBETTER, Jane W 226
LEAK, Sarah 226
LEAL, Sarah B 135
LEANARD, Annie 227
LEAPLY, Louisa 226
LEATH, Mary 48 Nancy 226
LECKIE, Emily S 226 Mary 163
LECKLIGHTER, Ann 226
LEDBETTER, Martha Elizabeth 37

LEE, Ann J 227 Catharine 227 Elizabeth 227 Hannah A 227 Jane R 227 Martha W 59 Mary 227 Mary P 226 Nancy 185 Polly 226 227 Presha 157 Rachael 227 Sally 227 Sarah 226 227 Susan 227
LEEKE, Casandria M 114
LEEPER, Martha 227
LEET, Nancy 78
LEETMAN, Anna 89
LEFTRICH, Jane 227
LEFTRIDGE, Ann 134
LEFTWICH, Ann 134 Chaarlotte C 227 Elizabeth 227 Emelia 9 Jane 227 Margaret 227 Mildred 227 Mildred O 227 Sarah 227
LEFTWICK, Margaret 227 Sally 14 Sarah 14
LEGAN, Nancy 227
LEGG, Hannah C 227 Nancy 227
LEIGH, Damaris 227 Julia 227 Sarah Jane 75
LEITCH, Frances M 227
LEITH, Martha 162
LELAND, Ann N (Hubbard) 51
LEMLEY, Rosanna 227
LEMON, Eleanor 227 Nancy 227
LEMONS, 98
LENEVE, Permelia 227
LENORD, Margaret M 97
LENOX, Sarah 227
LEONARD, Annie 227 Elizabeth 167 227 Levina R 227 Mary H 228 Phebe 228
LESENEY, Anna 18
LESTER, Annie 228 Lucy 156 Sally 228
LETT, Susan 228
LEVANT, Celeste 228
LEWELLEN, Catherine 228
LEWELLIN, Elizabeth H 25
LEWIS, Agnes 136 Ann 228 Cassandra 228 Catherine 228 Cynthia 172 Elizabeth 104 228 Frances 228 Hannah 176 Harriet 228 Jane 228 Joicy 228 Louisa 228 Lucy 215 Mahala 75 Maria Isabella 228 Martha 84 Mary 116 134 199 228 Mary Ann 80 Nancy 228 Polly 228 Susan R 228

LEYCOCK, Rebecca 18
LICHLITER, Catharine 228 Sarah 228
LICKLIGHTER, Ann 226
LIGGET, Ann 130
LIGHT, Hannah 228
LIGHTFOOT, Catharine N 198
LIGON, Jane 229 Sarah 228
LIKENS, Ruth 229
LILLARD, Mary 48 Polly 48
LINCOLN, Catherine 229
LINDAMOOD, Christian 3
LINDEMOOD, Christina 229
LINDSAY, Elizabeth 229 Frances D 229 Nancy 229
LINDSEY, Elizabeth 229 Mary 100 Nancy 229 Tabitha 229
LINDZY, Nancy 229
LINE, Elizabeth 229
LINEBAUGH, Betsy 229 Fanny E 229
LINEWEAVER, Catherine 229
LINGER, Sarah 42
LINK, Barbara 229 Rebecca 229
LINKONS, Margaret 229
LINKUS, Margaret 229
LINN, Martha 29
LINRY, Elizabeth 59
LINSFORD, Sydney 109
LINTON, Jemimah 53 Rachael M 229
LIONS, Mary 38
LIPFORD, Elizabeth 229
LIPP, Frances 229
LIPPFORD, Sarah Jane 130
LIPPS, Barbary 229
LIPSCOMB, Anna M 229 Elizabeth 229 Gabrilla H 43
LIPSCORD, Mildred 21
LIPSTRAP, Margaret 229
LIPTRAP, Margaret 229
LITCHFORD, Sarah 229
LITTEN, Nancy 229
LITTERAL, Elizabeth 229 Sarah 229
LITTLE, Harriet 115 Mary 162 222 230
LITTLEJOHN, Sarah 230
LITTRELL, Frances 230
LIVELY, Ophelia 230
LIVESAY, Leathy 230 Rebecca 230

LLOYD, Agnes 230 Ann 230 Ellen 151 John 151 Ruth 230
LOCK, Martha J 53 Millie 157 Patty 53
LOCKE, Sarah 230
LOCKER, Frances 230
LOCKET, Mary 230
LOCKETT, Sarah 230
LOCKEY, Doss 124
LOCKWOOD, Rachel 45
LOGAN, Elizabeth 21 Rebecca 230
LOHR, Margaret 230 Susan 24
LONDON, Rachel M 230
LONG, Catharine T 3 Christena 126 Eliza A 36 Elizabeth 161 230 Frances 230 Lucy 230 Mary 182 Mary D 181 Mary E 230 Nancy 230 Sally 169 Sarah 157 Susanna 194
LONGACRE, Rebecca 254
LONGDEN, Elizabeth 53
LONGEST, Nancy 167
LONGLEY, Margaret 158
LOSSON, Delia 226
LOT, Ruth 165
LOTT, Martha 230
LOTTS, Eve 230
LOUDENBACK, Joseph 230
LOUGH, Elizabeth 68 Sally 230
LOUTHER, Ingaba 125
LOVE, Caty 230 Cynthiana 230 Elizabeth 195 Letitia M 131 Teliza 230
LOVEL, Martha 19
LOVELESS, Elizabeth 230
LOVELL, Rhoda 230
LOVENS, Reity 81
LOVIN, Maria 230
LOVING, Anna 231 Elizabeth 231 Henrietta 231 Leah 231 Maria 230 Mary 231 Neomy 119
LOW, Easter 231 Elizabeth 231
LOWDER, Ann 231
LOWE, Eliza 231 Isaac 136 Mary 56 Wilsey 231
LOWER, Nancy 7
LOWERY, Lucy 188
LOWHORN, Sarah Jane 231
LOWMAN, Susannah 231
LOWNY, Eliza 173
LOWRY, Elizabeth 124 Margaret

LOWRY (continued)
28 Polly 231 Rebecca 231
LOWTHER, Mary 231 Rachel M
231
LOY, Magdalen 231
LOYD, Harriet A 231 Mary 231
Nancy 231 Sarah 231
LOYER, Elizabeth 27
LUCAS, Elizabeth 231 Mary E
174
LUCK, Elizabeth 231 Ellen Bran-
chet 112
LUCKETT, Louise A 231
LUDWICK, Mary 231
LUFFMIRE, Elizabeth 231
LUKE, Permelia 231 Sophronia
231
LUNDY, Mary 232
LUSBY, Susan 53
LUSTER, Sally 228
LUTER, Sarah 232
LUTES, Mary 232
LUTTRELL, Elizabeth 232
LUTZ, Elizabeth 232 Isabella 148
LYDEN, Margaret 105
LYKINS, Delila 203
LYLE, Jane 232 Sarah Wallace
70
LYNCH, Jane 232 Mary 232
Nancy 232 Sally 232 Sarah 232
LYNN, Elizabeth 171 232 Martha
29
LYON, Elenor H 232 Eliza 232
Jane 232 Rhoda 232
MABERRY, Mary Ann 232
MABRY, Sally 232
MACDANIEL, Ann 232
MACE, Christina 201 Eunice 95
Hannah 232
MACKALL, Helen M 184
MACKINSON, Sarah 16
MACKY, Sally 18
MADDEN, Sally 79
MADDOX, Elizabeth 236 Nancy 7
MADEN, Sarah H 236
MADISON, Elizabeth 236 Nancy T
236
MAGEE, Jackey P 2 Sally 236
MAGGARD, Ellenor 236
MAGILL, Jane 122
MAHAN, Susan 174
MAHANES, Virginia A 236

MAHONEY, Eliza 236
MAIDEN, Julia 236 Sarah H 236
MAJOR, Nancy 236 Virginia J 84
MAJORS, Nancy 39
MALCOM, Sarah 236
MALIN, Harriet 236
MALLET, Elizabeth 69
MALLOR, Mary Jane 236
MALLORY, Elizabeth 128
Elizabeth C 236 Martha 183
Mary 182 Nancy 236 Susan 118
MALONE, Rebecca 236
MANESS, Susannah 236
MANGES, Mary 236
MANIER, Fanny (---) 161
MANIS, Susannah 236
MANKIN, Elizabeth 237 Judith
237
MANLEY, Malinda 237
MANLY, Lucy 153
MANN, Ann O 165 Edith 237
Eliza 139 Frances 237 Jane T
128 Mary 237 Mary W 237
Nancy 237 Susan D 237 Susan-
nah 237
MANNING, Catharine 237
Rebecca 237
MANOR, Elizabeth 130
MANOS, Susannah 236
MANSFIELD, Elizabeth 237 Mary
85 Selina 237
MANSKIN, Nancy 135
MANSPILE, Ursula 237 Ushey
237
MANTON, Adeline 37
MANUEL, Malinda 237
MAPP, Critty 237 Margaret C 191
MARABLE, Elizabeth 237 Fanny
A 237 Fanny H 32 Mary M 57
Rebecca T 237
MARCH, Sarah 237
MARCUM, Alice 264 Mary 237
Rody 237
MARICLE, Sarah 237
MARK, Ellen K 237
MARKER, Elizabeth 64
MARKHAM, Nancy 237
MARKLE, Lucinda 243
MARKS, ---- 212
MARLER, Jane 237
MARNEY, Ann P 237
MARQUESS, Polly 237

MARR, Catherine F 237
MARRIBLE, Elizabeth 40
MARRS, Sarah 237
MARS, Margaret 158
MARSH, Amelia 237 238 Isabella 12
MARSHALL, Elizabeth M 268 Harriett 238 Henrietta 238 Jane 93 Julia 238 Lucy Ann 48 Lucy B 238 Malinda 238 Martha 136 Mary 238 Massy 238 Mourning 173 Sarah Ann 28 Susan 238
MARSTON, Maria A 15
MARTIN, Ann R 77 Camilla 14 Delila 88 Docia 238 Edy Olive 143 Elizabeth 153 238 Elizabeth D 66 Ellen 238 Fannie 171 Frances 238 Frances W 238 Hannah 24 Kissey 238 Lucinda 238 Lucy 238 Maria A 238 Martha 128 Mary 43 119 238 239 Mary Ann 238 Mary F 238 Mazy 106 Milla 44 Nancy 96 98 238 Nancy M 238 Polly 238 Rebecca 155 Rosa 238 Rosey 238 Sarah 68 195 238 239 Serena 121 Sophia 238 Susanna 238 Telitha J 238
MARTZ, Elizabeth 239
MARYE, Jane Hamilton 238
MASLING, Elizabeth 238
MASON, Annie 239 Elizabeth 239 Elizabeth W 239 Fannie 239 Harriett 178 Jane 174 Lucinda 239 Martha G 191 Ritter Ann 137 Sally 239 Sally E 239 Susan 239 Susannah 239
MASSEY, 123 Elizabeth 83 Mary Ann 181
MASSIE, Elizabeth 239 Frances 239 Nancy S 239 Sarah 239
MASTERS, Anna 273
MASTIN, Ann Eliza Caroline 239
MATHAS, Polly 99
MATHENA, Margaret 239
MATHENY, Margaret 239 Mary 239
MATHERLY, Rhoda 239
MATHEWS, Christian 239 Lucy Weston 69 Lydia 45 Margaret Susan 239 Martha 155

MATHIS, Elizabeth 57
MATTHEWS, Christian 239 Martha 106 Polly 206
MAUCK, Rebecca R 3
MAUK, Eva 239
MAUND, Annis 239
MAUPIN, Susan 130
MAUPIND, Rosanna 239
MAURY, Ellen 240 Peggy 239
MAUSSEE, Millie 35
MAUZY, Christina 240
MAXEY, Elizabeth 20 146 Mary W 9
MAXSON, Catharine 114
MAXWELL, Agnes 93 Maria 142 Nancy 240
MAY, Elizabeth (---) 65 John 65 Margaret 240 Mary 240 Mary E 240 Nancy C 240 Sarah 108
MAYBERRY, Patsey W 4
MAYER, Catherine 240
MAYERS, Elizabeth 96
MAYES, Mary 240
MAYFIELD, Frances 60
MAYHUE, Letitia 59
MAYHUGH, Deidamia 240
MAYO, Carline E 240 Catherine 240 Elizabeth D 240 Frances D 240 Mary F 167
MAYS, Cynthia 77 Manerva E 240 Mary 240 Mary M 240 Orphia 70 Polly 240 Sarah 240 Sophia 70
MAYSE, Nancy 79
MAZENA, Elizabeth 193
MCALEXANDER, Jane 153
MCALISTER, Mary F 130 Naba 232 Neba 232
MCALLISTER, Mary 232 Naba 232 Neba 232
MCANAN Bridget 113
MCBANE, Jane 200
MCBRIANT, Mary Ann 134
MCBRIDE, Elizabeth 232
MCCABE, Elizabeth 39 Mary 232
MCCAHAN, Catharine 115
MCCALL, Mary 63
MCCALLISTER, Mary 232 Naba 232 Neba 232
MCCAMMANT, Rebecca 232
MCCAN, Sarah Ann 232
MCCANDISH, Eliza T 250

MCCANN, Margaret 232 Sarah
Ann 232
MCCANNON Catharine 76
MCCARTNEY, Elizabeth 187
MCCARTY, Mary B 232
MCCATHARINE, Catharine 115
MCCAULEY, Agnes 233 Jincy D
113 Julia 233
MCCAULLY, Sarah 1
MCCLAIN, Elizabeth 92 Martha
233 Mary 233 Sarah 233
MCCLALLAN, Mary 94
MCCLANAHAN, Charity 233
Emily Nevil 233 Margaret 233
Sallie 233
MCCLANE, Mary 233
MCCLANEN, Sarah 233
MCCLARY, Ellen 28
MCCLELLAN, 98 Sarah L 287
MCCLELLAND, Margaret Ann
233 Sallie C 23
MCCLUN, Margaret 233
MCCLUNG, Elizabeth W 144 Es-
ther 233 Jane 233 Jenette 79
Margaret 233 Maria 233
MCCLURE, Ruth 233
MCCOBB, Mary Ann Weston 111
MCCOLLUM, Celia 44
MCCOMAS, Nancy 233
MCCOMB, Sallie 233
MCCONNELL, Louisa C 233
Susan B 233
MCCOOK, Mary 233 Polly 233
MCCORD, Sarah 233
MCCORKLE, Susan 233
MCCORMACK, Polly 233
MCCORMICK, Elizabeth 234
Grissell 233 Sarah 154
MCCOULL, Frances 192
MCCOWN, Elizabeth E 234
MOURNING 234
MCCOY, Ann 234 Dorcas 234
Elizabeth J 234 Sally A 234
MCCRAW, Hugh 148 Susan 148
MCCRAY, Druzilla 234 Isabell
234
MCCREARY, Elizabeth B 129
MCCRUMB, Elizabeth 149
MCCUE, Betsey 79 Elizabeth 79
MCCULLEN, Susan 144
MCCULLOCH, Martha 234 Martha
A 234 Mary C 234

MCCULLOCK, Martha A 234
Patsy 234
MCCULLOUGH, Edith 41
Elizabeth 37
MCCULLY, Grace 90
MCCUNE, Margaret (---) 159
MCCUTCHAN, Elizabeth 234
Mary G 134
MCCUTCHEN, Elizabeth 234
Margaret 101 102 Nancy 85
MCDADE, Becky 234 Elizabeth
99 Rebecca 234 Rebeckah 234
MCDANIEL, Chloe 165 Cleopatra
A 39 Martha 143 Polly 234
MCDONALD, Jane 104 Phebe 234
MCDONOUGH, Ann P 205
MCDORMAN, Nancy (---) 6
MCDORMANT, Elizabeth 234
MCDOWELL, Lydia 118 Martha
152
MCELHANEY, Margaret 234
MCELHANY, Miriem 234
MCELROY, Juliet 234
MCELWAIN, Elizabeth 234
MCFADDEN, Sallie 234
MCFALL, Polly 84
MCFARLAND, Nancy 40
MCFARLIN, Sarah 65
MCFEE, Mary 79
MCGEE, Ruth 234
MCGEHEE, Elizabeth 234 Martha
A 234 235
MCGELVEE, Angelina 192
MCGEORGE, Amanda E 235
Elizabeth 160 Frances 121
MCGHEE, Mary M 235 Susan 235
MCGINNIS, Elizabeth 195
MCGLASSEN, Mary 235
MCGLASSON, Mary 235
MCGLAUGHLIN, Elizabeth 169
Nancy 235
MCGOREGHAN, Mary 102
MCGOWAN, Ann 142
MCGRAW, Sarah J 235
MCGREGOR, Nellie (---) 117
MCGRUDER, Mary L 235
MCGUINN, Asenath 235
MCGUIRE, Eliza 235
MCHENRY, Magdaline 235
MCINTIRE, Polly 235
MCINTOSH, Sarah N 235
MCJEMESON, Rachel 130

MCKEE, Jane 6 Margaret K 74
  Sarah 235
MCKENNEY, Martha (---)
  (McDowell) 152 Rebecca A 235
MCKENNIE, Louisa R 235
MCKENZIE, Ann 38 Maria 65
MCKEWAN, Harriet 151
MCKINLEY, Martha 235
MCKINNEY, Delia 175 Jane 138
  Mary 235 Polly 235
MCKNIGHT, Agnes 235 Caltha
  235 Eliza 235 Margaret 235
  Sarah 235
MCLAIN, Martha 233
MCLANE, Sarah 233
MCLAREN, Susan 235
MCLAUGHLAN, Mary 235
MCLAUGHLIN, Mary 235 Sarah
  110
MCMAHON, Mary 235
MCMANAMY, Sophia 83 Mary
  Jane 235 236
MCMANAWAY, Mary 102
MCMANNUS, Sarah 236
MCMORROW, Margaret 236
MCMULLEN, Martha 190
MCMULLIN, May 236
MCNAMARA, Sallie E C 24
MCNEELY, Elizabeth 236
MCNIGHT, Caltha 235
MCNISH, Mary 12
MCNUT, Isabella 164
MCPEAK, Sarah (---) 88
MCPHERSON, Elizabeth 31 Jane
  B 59 Nancy 317
MCQUEEN, Mary 36 Polly 36
MCQUOWN, Elizabeth 27
MCRAE, Mary 54 Mary C 159
MCREA, Ann A 124
MCREYNOLDS, Hannah 236
MCSPADEN, Rebecca 143
MCVAY, Mary 236
MCWILLIAMS, Isabella A 236
  Julia 236
MEACHAM, Mary O 240
MEAD, Ann 240 Mary 165
MEADOR, Mary 240
MEADOWS, Frances 240 Nancy
  148 240 Susan 137
MEALEY, Eliza 240
MEANLY, Ann M 240
MEANS, Huldah S 240

MEARS, Mary Ann 240
MEAUX, Cornelia C 240
MEDDINGS, Susanna 56
MEDLEY, Malinda 240 Nancy C
  240 Rebecca A 19
MEDLIN, Sarah 247
MEDOR, Mildred 101
MEEK, Anna 240 Susan 240
MEEKINS, Catherine 241
MEFFORD, Sarah 59
MEGGINSON, Amanda M 241
MELTON, Elizabeth G 140
  Frances 61
MENCER, Nancy 241
MENIFEE, Ann S 12
MENNICH, Elizabeth 35
MERACLE, Nancy 53
MERCER, Elizabeth 63 241 Sarah
  241
MEREDITH, 114 William A 240
MERRILL, Mercy 240 Priscilla
  10
MERRIMAN, Nancy 241
MERRITT, Nancy 72 Rhoda 179
MERRIWETHER, Sally 8
MESMER, Ann Smith 240
MESSER, Elizabeth 159
MESSICK, Nancy 69
METCALF, Tabitha 241
METHENY, Margaret 239
METTAUER, Mary E 241
MEUX, Eliza 240
MEYERS, Sallie 241
MICHAEL, Catherine 30 241
  Elizabeth 32 241 Marthey 79
  Mary 241 Sarah 241
MICHAELS, Mason 241
MICHIE, Martha 114 Mary A 241
MICK, Mary 241 Ruth 241
MIDCALF, Tabitha 240
MIDDLETON, Elizabeth 241
  Joanna 241 Johanna 241 Mary
  241 Nancy 94 241 Ville 113
MIERS, Sallie 241
MIEURE, Catherine 241
MILBOURN, Mary 241
MILBURN, Mary 241
MILES, --- 76 Delila 241 242
  Hannah 242 Nancy 242
  Rebecca 241 Susan M 242
MILEY, Rebecca 210
MILHORN, Sarah 242

MILLANAX, Mary A 247
MILLER, Amanda J 242 Amy 242
Ann C 242 Anna 242 Catherine
42 Dosha 242 Eliza 124
Elizabeth 54 56 110 242 243
Hannah 242 Harriet J 11 Jane S
242 Julia Ann 242 Malinda 242
Margaret 242 Marthy 86 Mary
124 159 242 276 Mary A 185
Mary Ann 105 Nancy 242
Phoebe 242 Polly 84 242
Rebecca 242 Rhoda R 135
Sally 123 Sarah 88 104 242
Susan 62 113
MILLS, Elizabeth T 243 Ellen
Jane 243 Mary 81 165 Mary S
243 Nancy 242 Patsy 234 Sally
92 Susan 243
MILNER, Anna M 94 Clarissa 243
MILSTEAD, Elizabeth 243 Sally
243
MINITREE, Virginia 87
MINNICK, Elizabeth 243
MINNIS, Anna 197
MINOR, Catherine 243 Lucy A
243 Mary Ann 243
MINSON, Mary E 243
MINTER, Frances W 243 Mary
144 243 Nancy 243
MINTON, Polly 243
MIRACLE, Lucinda 243
MIRAND, William 153
MIRANDA, Martha Hagar Fortune
153
MITCHAM, Mary F 243
MITCHELL, Elizabeth 6 154 243
244 Elizabeth M 243 244
Lucinda 244 Mary Ann 201
Mary C 54 Mary J 243 Nellie
243 Obedience 243 Peggy 244
Polly C 244 Sarah 243 Sarah
Ann 243 Susan 244 Susan A 51
MIX, Mary Ann 244
MOATS, Barbary 120
MODENA, Lucy A E 244
MOFFATT, Phebe 244
MOFFETT, Margaret E H 244
MOHON, Elizabeth 244
MOIER, Dorothy 25
MOLER, Evelina 244
MOLLOHAN, Margaret 90
MONCE, --- 36

MONGAT, Susanna 81
MONROE, Hannah 244 Jane E 244
MONTAGUE, --- 15 Catharine
244 Hannah F 244 Laura L 27
Martha M 149 Mary Ann 244
Sally 244
MONTGOMERY, Martha 4
Rebecca M 244 Sarah 244
Sarah P 244
MOODY, Eliza B 244 Mareekle P
244 Polly 136
MOON, Eliza 123 Lucretia 244
Lydia G 244 Mary 121 Mary E
244 Nancy 244 Sallie 244
MOONEY, Anna 244 Emeline 310
Maria 100
MOOR, Catharine 244 Hannah 244
Nancy 244 Rebecca 245
MOORE, Ann 140 Catharine 244
Catherine 245 Charlotte 22
Eliza A 76 Eliza Ann 245
Elizabeth 13 102 245 Elizabeth
F 245 Fanny E 229 Frances
245 Hannah 245 Jane 82 Letita
S 245 Letitia S 245 Lydia M
245 Marian 245 Martha 155 245
Mary 207 245 Nancy 17 51
Nancy B 245 Rebecca 245
Sarah 100 178 Sarah E 100 187
Sophia 245 Virginia R 245
MOOREFIELD, Sally 245
MOORNEY, Mary 245
MORAN, Sally 245
MORE, Rachel 95
MORECOCK, Mary E 245
MOREFIELD, Elizabeth 245 Sally
245
MORELAND, Martha 245 Mary
245
MORELY, Fanny 206
MOREN, Mary 245
MORGAN, Elizabeth 245 246
Julia A 76 Keturah 207 Martha
J 140 Martha P 245 Mary 245
Phoebe F 156 Rachel 108
Sarah 245
MORING, Emily H 246 Nancy 246
MORMAN, Elizabeth 246
MORMAND, Elizabeth 246
MORMON, Paulina 13
MORRIS, Agness E 246 Eleanor
246 Elizabeth 5 Elizabeth N 29

MORRIS (continued)
Elizabeth W 246 Emily T 246
Louisa 246 Martha 169 Mary B
246 Mary Seward 246 Mildres
246 Phoebe 246 Polley 246
Sarah E 246 Susan 123
MORRISON, Eliza 246 Elizabeth
C 246 Malinda 246 Mary 246
Mary Ann 191 Mary J 160
Roxana 246
MORRISS, Mary Seward 246
MORROW, Ann 213
MORSE, Lois O (---) 53
MORTON, Denicie 246 Elizabeth
246 Lucy H 246 Margaret 246
MOSBY, Susan 4
MOSELEY, Marcia L 41 Martha
246 Mary 246
MOSELY, Harriet 246 Jane M 246
247 Lucy A 246 Nellie 246
MOSER, Christena 247
MOSES, Leanah 127 Mercy 247
MOSS, Elizabeth 247 Jane C 156
Mary 44 247 Susannah 247
MOTHERHEAD, Sarah 84
MOTLEY, Elizabeth 15 Mickey
46
MOTT, Sarah 247
MOULDING, Mary 245
MOUND, Annis 239
MOUNTCASTLE, Mary A 247
MOWLES, Nancy A 247
MOYER, Mary 247 Nancy 247
MOYERS, Elizabeth 156
MOZENEY, Rachel 247
MOZINGO, Nancy 247
MULL, Mary 247
MULLANAX, Mary A 247
MULLEN, Catharine 203
MULLENAX, Anna 247
MULLENIX, Catherine 247
MULLINS, Elizabeth 247 Mary 5
Nancy 22 247 Silvy O 247
MUMFORD, Permelia 48
MUMMEY, Catherine 247
MUMMY, Anne 247
MUNCY, Abigail 143 Elizabeth
247 Mary 247 Susan 247
MUNDAY, Nancy 247 Susan H 247
MUNDEN, Sarah 247
MUNSEY, Mary 247
MURCHIE, Judith A 247

MURDUCK, Louisa 247
MURPHY, Ann 84 Catharine 151
Elizabeth 185 Lucinda 248
Margaret 248 Mary 79 Nancy
248 Nancy (---) 43 Phebe 75
Polly 248 Sarah 162
MURRAY, Amy 28 Jane 248 Jin-
ney 248 Judith 248
MURRER, Mary 248
MURREY, Susan 248
MURRILL, Eliza Ann 248
MURROW, Sally 248
MURRY, Nancy 45
MURTLE, Catherine 248
MUSE, Ann 248 Eliza M 248
Susannah 248
MUSSELMAN, Delila 248
MUSTAIN, Mary 126 Polly 126
MYERS, Catherine 248 Christina
248 Elizabeth 248 Judith 248
Margaret 248 Mary 248 Phebe
217 Ruth 248
MYRICK, Anne Eliza 248 Mary
248
NAFF, Margaret 249
NALLEY, Elizabeth 178
NANCE, Elenor N 248 249 Jincy
175 Mary M 165 Sarah 248
NAOLE, Elizabeth 103
NAPIER, Rhoda 249 Rody 249
Spicey 249
NAPPER, Spicey 249
NASH, Catherine 249 Caty 249
Emily 249 Kesiah 249 Mary
249 Mary F 249
NAYLOR, Anna N 68
NEAL, Eliza 249 Elizabeth 155
Sarah A 249 Usley 249
NEALE, Gemima 181 Virginia C
249
NEAR, Mary Ann 249
NEBLETT, Ann S 249
NEECE, Mary 249
NEELEY, Mary 249
NEELY, Jemimah 249 Judith 249
NEER, Eliza 249
NEFF, Christina 26 Hannah 96
Magdalen 161 Margaret 249
NEIGHBORS, Catharine 249
NEILSON, Mary Archer 249
NELMS, Mildred J 249
NELSON, Frances E 249 Louisa

NELSON (continued)
138 Margaret 249 Martha L 249
Serena A 81
NESBIT, Mary E 59
NESMITH, Elizabeth 249
NESTER, Sarah Ann 249
NETHERLAND, Nancy 249
NETHERY, Elizabeth 250 Sarah
249
NETTLE, Ann 146
NEVIL, Frances 250
NEW, Mary 184
NEWBELL, Obedience 123
NEWBY, Elizabeth 250 Phebe
250 Phebe F 85 Sally 250
NEWCOMB, Elizabeth 192 Jane
75 Nancy 111 Polly 250 Polly
T 250
NEWCOMER, Elizabeth 218
NEWELL, Fanny 250 Martha 258
NEWHOUSE, Rebecca J 250 Sally
59
NEWLAN, Rachel 250
NEWLAND, Margaret 250
NEWLON, Elizabeth 250 Mary 37
Rachel 250
NEWMAN, Ann C 102 Celia 250
Eleanor S 250 Frances M 30
Jane 77 Jeanette J 45 Martha
250 Mary A 250 Mary Ellen
160 Nancy 250 Rebecca J 250
Virenda 82
NEWSAN, Polly S 307
NEWTON, Helen 36 Mary 127
Sarah Ann 250 Sophia 250
NICEWARDER, Polly 159
NICHOLLS, Sacarisa 250
NICHOLS, Lucy 15 Magdalen 250
Nancy 107 Rebecca 250
NICHOLSON, Rebecca J 98
NICKLIN, Mary 250
NICKSON, Mary P 250
NICODEMUS, Barbara 174 Mar-
garet 250
NIGHTEN, Lydia 74
NIMMO, Eliza T 250
NISEWANGER, Lucinda 250
NISLEY, Mary 69
NIXON, Jane 250 Mary A 250
NIXSON, Mary P 250
NOAKES, Sarah 250
NOBB, Mary 67

NOBLE, Harriet D 210 Mary 67
NOEL, Hetta 251 Judith 251 Mar-
tha 251 Sarah A 157
NOELL, Amarilla 103
NOLAN, Lucy A 251
NOLAND, Susannah D 251
NOLIN, Susannah D 251
NORCUTT, Nancy 130
NORMAN, Elizabeth 251 Mildred
F 251
NORRIS, Allie 251 Ann 96
Elizabeth 34 146 Hannah 73
Sarah 5 Susannah 251
NORTH, Mary Ann B 251 Susan O
110
NORTHCRAFT, Ann Hill 251
NORTHCUTT, Mary 251
NORTHINGTON, Ann 181 Mary H
251
NORVELL, Ann M 251 Catharine
140 Elizabeth M 251 Peachey
126
NOTTINGHAM, Elizabeth B 251
Esther S B 251
NOWELL, America 11 Martha
251
NOWLAND, Susan D 251
NOWLIN, Ann T 251
NOWLING, Mary 251
NUCKOLS, Frances 143 Phebe
251
NUGENT, Amanda 251
NUNLEY, Nancy 144
NUNN, Deborah 251
NUNNALLY, Mary H 251 Nancy
251
NUNNERY, Polly 251
NUZUM, Esther 251
O'CONNER, Elizabeth 252
Susanah 252
O'DONOVAN, Mary 252
O'NEAL, Hannah 50 Mary F 43
OAKES, Sallie 251 Sally 251
Susan 145
OAKS, Mary 251 Sallie 251 Sally
251 Susanna 59
OBOYLE, Ellen Maria 80
OCKERMAN, Mary C 164
ODELL, Delilah 252
OGBURN, Mary A 8 Nancy M 252
OGDEN, Elizabeth 252 Joanna E
17 Matilda 252 Sarah 252

OGILVIE, Elizabeth A 252
OGLE, Sarah 252
OHLEAR, Nancy 252
OILER, Elizabeth 101
OKES, Mary 251
OLD, Fannie C 252
OLDHAM, Polly 252
OLDNER, Elizabeth 252
OLEAR, Nancy 252
OLINGER, Anne 153 Eliza 204
    Elizabeth 252
OLIVER, Frances 185 Martha A
    252 Mary 252 Nancy G 252
    Rebecca 62 Susan 83
OLNS, Nancy 98
OMOHUNDRO, Mary D 252
ORDNORFF, Rachael 173
ORISON, Catherine 10 John 10
ORNBAUM, Elizabeth 4
ORNDORFF, Christena 252 Mary
    Catharine 52 Rebecca 52
ORR, Ann E 252 Nancy W 252
    Sarah 252
ORRISON, Elizabeth Ann 252
ORT, Eveline 78
OSBORN, Elizabeth 252 Rebecca
    252 Sarah 252
OSBORNE, Martha 252
OSBURN, Sarah 252
OSKINS, Mary (---) 61
OSLER, Susan 161
OSLIN, Frances 252
OTEY, Frances A 61 Hannah 50
    Rebecca 252 253
OTT, Elizabeth 69 Mary 253
OUTTEN, Nancy 253
OVERBEY, Harriet 253 Nancy 38
OVERBY, Ann 273 Harriet 253
OVERFIELD, Deborah 253
OVERHOLTER, Rebecca 253
OVERHOLTS, Barbara 253
    Rebecca 253
OVERHOLTZER, Rebecca 253
OVERHOTS, Barbara 253
OVERSHINER, Barbara 253
OVERSTREET, Basheba 105
OWEN, Elizabeth 253 Frances
    253 Lucy 208 Maria B 253
    Mary E (Tatum) 42 Nancy L
    253 Prudence 194 Rebecca 253
    Sallie 253 Sarah E R 253 Tem-
    perance 1

OWENS, Adaline 78 Amelia 13
    Hannah 13 Judith 253 Mary 253
    Sarah 26 Susan 253
OYLER, Elizabeth 110
PACE, Dorothy 135 Jane 121 Par-
    thenia 253
PACKET, 155
PADGETT, Sarah 253
PADGIT, Margaret 253
PAGE, Christina 254 Elizabeth
    163 Hannah 254 Lucy A 254
    Mary 257 Mary W 253 Sarah E
    254
PAGET, Eliza 254
PAINE, Mary 254 Sarah 4
PAINTER, Catherine 257
    Elizabeth 254 Nancy 254
PALMER, Cornelia H 88 Eliza N
    63 Elizabeth 254 Evelina 9
    Hannah 254 Lucy B 27 Mar-
    garet 254 Mary M 254 Polly
    254 Sarah E 254
PALMORE, Sally 198
PAMPLIN, Mary Jane 175
PANCOAST, --- 37
PANGLE, Ann 254 Rebecca 254
PANKEY, Sarah E (---) 114
PANNELL, Elizabeth 201
PARE, Elizabeth 254
PARHAM, Mary F 254
PARISH, Catharine A 132 Sarah
    254
PARK, Nancy Ann 254
PARKER, Ann E 255 Annie G 255
    Careen F H 255 Catharine B
    191 Christian 254 Clarissa 254
    Eliza 254 Elizabeth 73 255
    Elizabeth F 76 Hardenia L 254
    Harriett 255 John 255 Louisa B
    254 Mary 255 Mary Ann 172
    Permelia 254 Rebecca 254
    Susannah 255 Tamasa 254
PARKS, Elizabeth 79 Sally 30 50
PARMER, Nancy Ann 179
PARR, Almeda 255
PARRELL, Isabella 257
PARRISH, Elizabeth 255
    Elizabeth A 255 Elizabeth S
    255 Jane H 255 Louisa 255
    Mary A 255 Mary C 157
PARROTT, Sophia Ann 9
PARSELL, Drewsillar 255

PARSLEY, Mary 3
PARSONS, Catharine 26 Frances
255 Mary 26 255 Mary Ann 67
Sarah 255 Sarah M 255
PARTLOW, Maria E 78
PASCUE, Charles 23
PATE, Eliza A 255 Elizabeth 255
Sally 255
PATES, Elizabeth 255
PATRAM, Barbara 255 Elizabeth
255 Lucy 255
PATRICK, Mary 255
PATTERSON, Cynthia 256
Dorothy 173 Elizabeth 256
Jane 256 Lally O 256 Lucinda
256 Nancy 256
PATTON, Ann 256 Elizabeth S
256 Maria 256 Mary Ann 207
Phebe S 256 Sally 256
PATYON, Peachy E 64
PAUL, Jane 256
PAULETT, Sarah 256
PAULEY, Margaret 256
PAWLEY, Margaret 256
PAXTON, Jane S 186 Lucy S 256
PAYNE, Alice B 166 Ann 256
Catharine M 256 Cesy 256
Delila 100 Eliza J 256 Frances
G 256 Jane 256 Julia W 125
Lucy 20 Margaret E 256 Mar-
tha A 256 Mary C 256 Matilda
87 Nancy 256 Patsey 256 Polly
256 Rosa 256 Susan 256 Susan
A 256
PAYNTER, Catherine 257
PEACHER, Lucy A 257
PEACOCK, Nancy 28
PEAD, Cena 257
PEAK, Obediance 257
PEAL, Martha 257
PEALE, Margaret M 257
PEARCE, Mary 257
PEARCY, Joanna 257
PEARMAN, Sarah 257
PEARRILL, Isabella 257
PEARSON, America Ann 129 Ann
257 Ann (Follin) 74 Catherine
257 Nancy 19 Rachel 257
Tabitha W 51
PEATROSS, Eliza Ann 257
PECK, Martha 253 Sarah 257
PEDIGO, Amy T 257

PEEBLES, Ann P 7 Mary 257
Mary S 136 Mary W 257
PEEDE, Cena 257
PEEK, Mary 257
PEERY, Jane 257
PEGRAM, Ciscelia F 257 Mary
Ann F 86
PELL, Catharine 150 Rebecca
257
PEMBERTON, Margaret W 257
PENCE, Elizabeth 101 Harriet
258 Patsey 257
PENDLETON, Anna 210 Louisa
258 Mary 39 258 Mary Ann 154
Mildred 258 Sophia 78
PENINGER, Martha 258
PENINGTON, Celia 99
PENN, Lucinda 258
PENNELL, Sarah 201
PENNINGTON, Anna 210 Sallie
96
PENNS, Caty 102
PENTECOST, Obedience 258
PEPPER, Martha 258
PERDUE, Harriet 258 Jane 13
Patsey 137
PERGESON, Martha 149
PERIAN, Elizabeth A 258
PERKINS, Eliza A 258 Elizabeth
208 Elizabeth C 258 Frances
258 Lucy 258 Margaret 258
Martha 258 Martha P 35 Nancy
258 Rosie M 258 Susan C 24
Tempy 167
PERKINSON, Elizabeth 301 Mary
B 37
PERKS, Mary Ann 258
PERMAN, Susanna 65
PERMAR, Elizabeth 254
PERRILL, Christina 258 Isabella
257 258
PERRIN, Cyrene 258 Elizabeth A
258
PERRINE, Martha 187
PERRY, Catherine 258 Elizabeth
138 207 258 Elizabeth H 145
Jane 257 Judah 137 Lydia 91
Mariah 258 Mary 195 Nancy A
258
PERRYM, Cyrene 258
PERSINGER, Barbary 258
Elizabeth 258

PETERFISH, Catherine 80
PETERS, Catharine 258 Christina 21 George 119 Peggy Anderson 119 Rachel 258 259 Susan 199 258
PETERSON, Susan 1
PETTET, Fanny S 259
PETTETT, Elizabeth 259
PETTIGREW, Ann 21
PETTIS, Mahala 89
PETTIT, Elizabeth A 259 Fanny S 259 Nancy 192 Sophia A 8
PETTY, Lucinda 259 Lucy 259 Mary Ann 259
PETTYPOOL, Lavinia 261
PEUE, Sarah 259
PEYTON, Eliza 259 Elizabeth 259 Helen 259 Sarah 259
PHARIS, Nancy 139
PHEFFLEY, Katie 43
PHELPS, Dixy 259 Eliza A F 259 Elizabeth 259
PHILIPS, Jane 89 Nancy 129
PHILIPY, Barbara 97
PHILLIPS, Elizabeth 36 118 259 Frances 259 Jane 61 Lucinda (---) 63 Lucy 63 107 Lucy E D M 143 Martha 118 Mary 30 Nancy 110 Nancy B 259 Polly 259 Sarah 259 Susan 259
PHILPOTT, Julia 75
PHILPOTTS, Mary A S 259
PHIPPS, Catherine 259 Mary 259
PHIPS, Catherine 259 Mary 259
PICKEL, Margaret 259
PICKERING, Mary 100
PICKETT, Jane 259 Mary 12 William 12
PIERCE, Frances W 260 Sarah 260
PIERCY, Elizabeth 260
PIERMAN, Polly 260
PIERPOINT, Isabel 260 Temperance 130
PIGG, Evy 190 Polly 213
PIKE, Martha 260
PILCHER, Athaline 19 Averilla 260 Canzada 225 Lucy E 260
PILLON, Martha 260
PILLOW, Agnes 319 Mary 260
PINCHAM, Maria 143 144
PINCHBECK, 165

PINES, Elizabeth 29
PINNELL, Martha A 260
PINNER, Nancy 67
PIPPIN, Elizabeth 260
PITCHFORD, Mary 260
PITMAN, Catherine 260 Eliza 105 Elizabeth 116 Leah 133
PITT, Nancy 260
PITTS, Elizabeth 260 Mary C 260 Nancy B 260
PITZER, Nancy 260
PLATT, Rhoda 260
PLEASANTS, Eliza 260 Kesiah 260 Louisa 118 Maria 7 Nancy 260 Zipporah 260
PLEMMONS, Louisa 93
PLOTNER, Sarah 260
PLOTT, Mary 260 Polly 260
PLUMMER, Martha 30
PLYBORNE, Lydia 122
POAGE, Polly E A 260
POAGUE, Polly E A 260
POE, Lucinda 5 Mary 129
POFF, Easter 120
POINDEXTER, Anne L 135 Frances A 261 Lucy T 261 Mary L 261
POLING, Mary 261
POLK, Martha H 131
POLLARD, Arthur H 206 Elizabeth H 201 Elizabeth M 261 Mary A B 261 Philadelphia 261
POLLOCK, Cecily 261 Elizabeth 261
POLLY, Nancy 81
POMEROY, Elizabeth 261 Mary 261
POND, Mary D 42
POOL, Alice 261 Elizabeth P 261 Judith 249 Lavinia 261 Patty 261
POOLE, Eliza 172
POOLUM, Betsy G 263
POOR, Eliza 54
POPE, Elizabeth 18
PORTER, Anna 261 Elizabeth 261 Emily T 90 Hannah K 261 Helena A 261 Maria E 261 Mary 245
PORTERFIELD, Julia A 261
POSELL, Martha A 42

POSEY, Nancy 99
POSTLAW, Clarissa 99
POSTLETHWAIT, Lydia 261
POSTON, Hope 282
POTTER, Cassander 261
POTTS, Eleanor 90 Harriett B 104
POULSON, Mary Ann 57
POUND, Fannie L 80
POWELL, Ann 262 Catharine 262
Charity Ann 262 Dorcas Ann
262 Elizabeth 262 Frances 27
Jane 106 Lucy 6 Margaret M
261 Mary 261 Matilda 262
Rachel 262 Rebecca 95 Sarah
192 Sarah A 261
POWERS, Elizabeth 137 262
Elizabeth L 202 Fanny 262
Lorena 262 Lorena M 262
Prudence 41 Rhoda 262 Selah
262 Sina 262
POYNER, Elizabeth 262 Sarah
146
POYNOR, Elizabeth 262
PRATER, Phebe 262
PRATT, Martha 262
PREBBLE, Amy 154 Martha W
262
PRENTIS, Catharine 262
PRESTON, Frances 262
PREWETT, Nancy 262
PRICE, Betsey 104 Cynthia 262
Elizabeth 75 213 262 Elizabeth
B 213 Fanny 11 Hannah 33
Martha 262 Mary 262 Mary
Mead 262 Nancy D 73 Sarah
262
PRICHARD, Arabell 263
PRICHETT, Mary 52
PRIDDY, Scitty 263
PRIDE, Amelia 262
PRIEST, Ann N 263 Sarah 106
PRINCE, Elizabeth 263 Martha 29
PRITCHETT, Margaret A 93
Sarah H 263 Susan 207
PROCTOR, Frances 263
PROFFITT, Jane S 263
PROPHET, Dorothea 263
PROPST, Esther 263
PRUDEN, Henry 59 Sarah 59
PRUETT, Rebecca 263
PRUNER, Henry 59 Sarah 59
PRUNTY, Tabitha 263

PRYOR, Jane B 263 Louisa Jane
263 Lucie J 263
PUCKETT, Frances W 263 Mary
263 Perlina 263 Susannah 263
PUDUE, Prudence 161
PUFFENBERGER, Ellen 263
PUFFENBURGER, Ellen 263
PUGH, Ann S 263 Catharine 263
Lane 88 Martha 263 Mary 209
263 Nancy 157 263 Polly 73
Sarah 156
PULLEN, Charlotte 263 Leanna
M 65 Margaret 263
PULLER, Mary A 263 Mary Ann
263
PULLEY, Elizabeth 196
PULLIAM, Betsy G 263 Lucy 199
Lucy S 263 Mary H 263 Nancy
263 Nancy R 263
PULLIN, --- 97 Charlotte 263
Lucy A 99
PULTZ, Elizabeth 162
PUMMILL, Margaret 264
PUMPHREY, Elizabeth 264
PURCELL, Martha 264
PURDAM, Sarah 264
PURDOM, Sarah 264
PURDY, Emily 182
PURSELL, Martha 264
PURYEAR, Mary 62 264
PUSEY, Mary Ann 19 Susannah 48
PUSSELL, Mary E 264
PUTNAM, Elizabeth (---) 150
PYRTLE, Millie 264
QUALES, Elizabeth 97
QUARLES, Edmund 14 Elizabeth
264 Martha 264 Mary E 264
QUICK, Jane 264 Nancy 264
QUICKLE, Mary 264
QUICKSALL, Sally 58
QUISENBERRY, Lucy E 53 Mary
264
QUISENBERY, Elizabeth 264
Lucy T 163
RACER, Betsey 118
RADEBAUGH, Isabella 271
RADER, Barbara 264 Catharine
264 Catherine 283 Martha 264
Nancy 264 Permelia 264
RADFORD, Ellender 264 SARAH
F 264
RAGAN, Alice 264 Mary 303

384

385

RICHARDS (continued)
Sally 48
RICHARDSON, Ann 54 268
Catherine 268 Elizabeth 268
Elizabeth M 268 Jane G 268
Judith 72 Louisa 268 Martha
Ann 268 Mary Ann 268 Nancy
268 Sallie 152 Sarah 268 Sarah
Ann 268 Susannah 89
RICHERSON, Sally 165
RICHIE, Mary E 9
RICHMAN, Rebecca 268
RICHMOND, Rebecca 268
RICKARD, Mary 138 268
RICKETS, Delany 133
RICKETTS, Mary 268
RICKHART, Mary 268
RICKMAN, Elizabeth 268
RIDDELL, Anna 268
RIDDICK, Mary 268
RIDDLE, Margaret 268 Ruth 268
RIDENOUR, Mary M 268
RIDGEWAY, Mary A 268 Sophia
268
RIDGWAY, Mary 268
RIDOUT, Eliza D 268 Elizabeth A
268
RIFE, Elizabeth 268 Mildred 268
Nancy 268
RIFFE, Catharine 84 Nancy 268
Sally 268
RIFFLE, Margaret 268 Susannah
B 268
RIGGAN, --- 16
RIGGIN, Elizabeth M 73
RIGGS, Amelia D 139 Elizabeth
268 Matilda 268 Nancy 291
Sarah 268
RIGHTSTINE, Ann 286 Nancy 286
RIGSBY, Nancy 269
RILEY, Catharine 90 Mary Ann
179
RINE, Hester Ann 269
RINEHART, Julia Ann 190 Mary
269 Rosanna 269
RINER, Catherine 269
RINGER, Nancy 269
RION, Margaret 269
RIORDAN, Sarah D 269
RIPLEY, Elizabeth 121 Elizabeth
Murray 269
RIPPETEO, Nancy 19

RIPPETOE, Susan W 269
RISSLER, Margery 269
RITCHIE, Christina 21
RITTENOUR, Catherine 160
RIVERS, Sallie Ann 269
RIVES, Sarah Ann 269
ROACH, Delilah 269 Elizabeth 79
269 Maria A W 269 Mariah 17
Polly 117 Pracilla 269 Sophia
269
ROADCAP, Elizabeth 269
ROADES, Jane Margaret 267
ROANE, Mary M 269
ROARK, Lockey 269
ROBB, Maria 269
ROBBINS, Jemima 131 Mary 146
Mary E B 269
ROBERSON, Fannie F 269 Mary
A 269
ROBERTS, Ann 269 270 Ann M
270 Anna 270 Clarinda 159
Elizabeth 269 Elizabeth S 99
Frances Elizabeth 20 Jane 33
Judith C 270 Mary 142 269 270
Mary B 279 Nancy 146 Sarah
208 Sophronia 59
ROBERTSON, Ann 157 270 Ann D
270 Eleanor 270 Eliza M 270
Eliza S 270 Elizabeth 270
Elizabeth C 270 Elizabeth M
270 Elizabeth W 65 Frances L
270 Martha E 270 Martha M
270 Mary B 270 Miriam 270
Mourning 20 Nancy R F 270
Sally 270 Tabitha A 20
ROBINETT, Elizabeth 270 Selah
270
ROBINS, Catherine 139 Elizabeth
25 Mary F 270
ROBINSON, Clara 270 Cynthia 93
Elizabeth 270 271 Elizabeth M
270 Jane 44 Lucinda 63 Lucy
Beverly 134 Mary 271 Mary A
207 270 Mary M 270 Maxa A
271 Nancy 120 181 Nancy C
212 Polly 271 Rachel 83
Rebecca J M 271 Sarah 270
271 Sarah Ann 271 Sarah S 270
ROBISON, Mary 271
ROBUCK, James 120 Mary Ann
(---) 120
ROBY, Sarah 108

ROCK, Nancy 142 Sallie 271
RODEBAUGH, Isabella 271
RODEFFER, Rebecca 271
RODGERS, Elizabeth 271 Jane
  271 Mary 271 Susan 271
ROE, Frances 271
ROGERS, Eleanor 271 Harriet P
  271 Jane 93 271 Lucy 271
  Lucy G 271 Lucy T 153 Mar-
  garet 271 Martha 5 Mary 118
  271 Mary P 271 Milly 271
  Nancy 120 Phoebe 271 Rachel
  H 153
ROGOR, Hannah 91
ROLAND, Catherine 207 Mary 271
ROLER, Priscilla 91
ROLETH, Eliza 265
ROLLINS, Sophiah 271
ROLLS, Elizabeth 52 Mary
  Catharine 271
ROLSTON, Maria 272
ROMAKE, Elizabeth 200
ROMINE, Asona 94 Nancy A 265
ROOF, Margaret 272
ROOKER, Elizabeth 272
ROOKWOOD, Mary 272
ROOT, Margaret 272
ROPER, Mildred A 34
RORER, Frances 272
ROSAR, Margaret 272
ROSE, Elizabeth Ann 137 James
  131 Jane 272 Lavinia 68 Mar-
  garet E 272 Rebecca (---)
  Durham 131 Sarah 135
ROSEBROUGH, Rebecca 272
ROSER, Esther 272 Margaret 272
ROSIER, Esther 272
ROSS, Elizabeth 272 Ellen 24 El-
  lender 24 Frances H 272 Mar-
  garet B 131 Susan (Kelles) 206
ROSSER, Christine E 272
  Elizabeth 272 Sally M 12 Sarah
  M 12
ROSSMAN, Ann 187
ROTTENBERRY, Elizabeth 272
  Jane 272
ROUNDTREE, Jane 143
ROUNTREE, Cintha Ann 106
  Elizabeth 175 Martha 137
ROUSH, Catharine 272 Judam 272
ROUTEN, Catharine 162
ROUTON, Lucy W 272

ROUTT, Sarah (Townsend) 169
ROW, Anna 272 Fannie 272
ROWAN, Fannie P 272 Margaret
  74
ROWE, Elizabeth 272 Matilda 35
ROWLAND, Elender 273 Eliza
  Jane 272 273 Nancy 273 Ruthie
  69 Winnie M 272
ROWLETT, Mary 273
ROWLEY, Luann 168
ROWLINSON, Sarah 103
ROY, Martha 273 Sarah 54
ROYALL, Mary E 273 Pamela W
  273 Susan J 273
ROYALTY, Elizabeth 107
RUBLE, Anna 273 Maryan 273
  Nancy 273 Sarah 273
RUCKEN, Lucy 195
RUCKER, Fanny 273 Frances 188
  Margaret 273 Mary 273 Mary J
  273 Milly 273 Nancy 60
  Tabitha 273
RUDDELL, Ingabo B 3
RUDDLE, Ingabo B 3
RUDY, Sarah 273
RUFFIN, Ann 273
RUFFNER, Ann 273
RULEY, Sally 273
RUMBERG, Mary 273
RUNION, Sarah 108
RUPART, Rebecca 273
RUPERT, Rebecca 273
RUSH, Hannah 27 Martha 34
  Nancy 273 Susan 273
RUSMISEL, Martha 273 Sally 273
RUSS, Peggy 29
RUSSELL, Ann 273 Cecelia Ann
  89 Celia 274 Deborah 183 Dor-
  cas 273 Eliza A 274 Elizabeth
  15 274 J Louisa 274 Margaret
  44 274 Martha 137 Mary 274
  Nancy (Pinner) 67 Nellie M
  274 Rebecca W 5 Sarah 274
RUST, Comfort M 163 Sarah W
  (---) 101
RUTHERFORD, Eliza 11 Polly
  274
RUTLEDGE, Jane 74
RUTTER, Chloe 274
RYAN, Delilah 274 Elizabeth 274
  Elizabeth S 205 Margaret 267
  Millinder 274 Nancy 274

RYANT, Barbara A 274
RYBURN, Ann 70
RYE, Elizabeth 274 Mary 118
RYHN, Barbara A 274
RYMAN, Sarah 274 Sovina 111
RYNO, Elizabeth 198
SADDLER, Ann 274
SADLER, America H 274
    Catharine 21 Wilmoth 274
SAGESER, Cassandra (---) 8
ST CLAIR, Jane 274 Martha 145
    Mary 274 Sarah 274
ST JOHN, Dicy 274
SALAMON, Dicey 274
SALE, Fanny 126 Jane 274 Polly
    T 274 Sarah B 200
SALING, Mary (Foster) 34
SALISBURY, Keziah 274
SALLE, Julia 274 Julia B 274
SALLEE, Obedience 175
SALMON, Dicey 274 Eliza J 274
    Evelina P 274 Nancy R 131
SAMFORD, Susan A E 274
SAMPLE, Mary 275
SAMPSON, Agnes Poore 275 Ann
    Keyes 275 Fanny C 189 Martha
    213
SAMS, Barbara 275 Nancy 275
SAMUEL, Mary 90 Polly 90
SAMUELS, Margaret 275 Patsey
    14
SANDEFUR, America 174
SANDERS, Lana 275 Margaret 275
    Melviny S 275 Oney 126 Sally
    275 Sarah 275
SANDERSON, Elizabeth R 275
SANDIDGE, Belinda 275
    Catharine 275 Mary 275 Nancy
    44
SANDIFER, Martha 39
SANDRIDGE, Susan B 114 Susan-
    nah B 114
SANDS, Elizabeth 275 Mary 275
    Sarah 275
SANDY, Anne 275 Rebecca 275
SANFORD, Ann J 52 Elizabeth 51
    Fanny F 29 Mary Jane 275
SANGER, Catharine 104 Nancy
    116
SANTEE, Nancy H 6
SARGENT, Elizabeth 275 Pal-
    myra 275

SARVER, Frances 275
SATCHELL, Mary G 275
SAUNDERS, Ann Eliza 138 Ann M
    275 Catherine 275 Dorothy 84
    Elizabeth 276 Elizabeth C 275
    276 Joanna 276 Mary 275 Polly
    183 Rebecca 156 Sally D 276
    Sarah 105 276 Sarah Ann 276
    Sarah F 276 Zaney 116
SAVAGE, Ann 276 Catherine 213
    Elizabeth 276 Nancy 276 Polly
    276
SAXTON, Betsy 93
SAYLOR, Catharine 184
SCALES, Elizabeth 210 Martha T
    95
SCANLAND, Sallie 186
SCARBOROUGH, Margaret G 276
SCARFF, Mary B 276
SCATTERDAY, Ann M 276
SCHAFFER, Susan 276
SCHAPPART, Mary 276
SCHOENDECKER, Sally 280
SCHOOLS, Nancy 276
SCHROCK, Sarah 276
SCHWARTZ, George 34
SCOTES, Martha 276
SCOTT, Annie 276 Catharine 276
    Eliza Parke 198 Elizabeth 276
    Elizabeth M 276 Judith 46
    Judy 46 Juliet 276 June 54
    Martha F E 148 Mary 71 261
    277 Nancy 98 Polly 276
    Rebecca B 9 Rosanna 183 Ruth
    276 Sarah B 129 Sarah E 276
SCOUT, Eliza 81
SCRUGGS, Frances 277 Lucy 276
    Nancy 277 Pollie 76
SCUTT, Martha 5
SCYOC, Nancy 276
SEABORN, Polly 276
SEABURN, Mary 277
SEAL, Susanah 276
SEARES, Mary 276
SEARGENT, Nancy 276
SEARS, Mary 276 Nancy 15
SEAY, Elizabeth 277 Jane 277
    Lucy 277 Lucy B 277 Mary W
    78 Sally A 277 Sarah 277 Susan
    277
SEBASTIAN, Elizabeth 277
SEBRELL, Margaret 277 Sarah

SEBRELL (continued)
277
SECRIST, Mary 277
SEE, Florence 277 Nancy 277
SEEF, Susan 57
SEEL, Margaret 173
SEESE, Catharine 277
SEIBERT, Elizabeth 277 Mary
277
SELBY, Hannah 277
SELDEN, Mary E 277
SELDONRIDGE, Margaret 120
SELF, Nancy 277
SELLARS, Elizabeth 277
SELLERS, Delila 277
SELOCK, Elizabeth 93
SENNETT, Elizabeth 278
SENSENEY, Leah 7
SETTERS, Elizabeth 278
SETTLE, Ann 278 Nancy 278
Polly 278
SEVERNS, Catharine 278
SEWALL, Sarah 278
SEWARD, Tabitha 50
SEXTON, Rebecca 23
SEYMORE, Eliza 278
SEYMOUR, Eliza 278 Margaret
278
SEYOC, Nancy 276
SHACKELFORD, Ann 278
Courtney Ann 278 Lydia 278
Mary W 167 Nancy 278
Rebecca 103 Ann 75 Frances
278
SHACKLEFORT, Mary C 34
SHADE, Mary 278
SHADES, Mary A 124
SHAFER, Hanna 112 Mary 278
Mary A 278 Mary M 278
SHAFFER, Margaret 278 Mary
278 Polly 278
SHAMBAUGH, Nancy 278
SHANDS, Sarah C 278
SHANER, Nancy M (---) 128
SHANK, Ann Mary 278 Margaret
278
SHANNON, Elizabeth 13 Margaret
278 Mary 278
SHARKEY, Mary 280
SHARP, Evaline 278 Frances W
33 Hannah 69 Lucy 168
SHARRIT, Margaret 190

SHARRITTS, Elizabeth 279
SHAULL, Mary 279
SHAVER, Barbara 279 Cynthia
Ann 32 Elizabeth 108 Isabella
279 Josina 279 Mary 278 Mary
M 278 Polly 278 Susan 276
SHAW, Catherine 279 Edith 279
Jane 279 Judy 279 Nancy 137
SHAWL, Mary 279
SHAY, Phebe A 279
SHEARER, Rebecca 40 Sarah 115
SHEETS, Elizabeth 279 Mary 279
Susan 279
SHEETZ, Mary 279
SHELBERN, Mary J 279
SHELL, Elizabeth 279 Margaret
279 Mary B 279
SHELOR, Anna 279
SHELTON, Amy 280 Anna 279
280 Eleasure P 279 Frances S
279 Frances S (---) 1 Jane A
279 Jane B 279 Jane R 85
Lucinda 279 Lucy 279 Mary
233 Mary C 7 Mary Susan 280
Matilda 279 Nancy 279 280
Polly 233 Susan H 140 Susanna
279 280
SHEPARD, Juliet 6 Lucinda 123
Phebe 54
SHEPHARD, Nancy 16
SHEPHERD, Lucinda 128 Malinda
44 Martha G 280 Mildred 24
Sarah 280 Susan E 280
SHEPPARD, Harriet I 57 Martha
Ann 95
SHERIDAN, Allay 181
SHERLEY, Eliza Ellett Shirley
280
SHERMAN, Jesse 280
SHERRY, Elizabeth (---)
(Reeves) 182
SHERWOOD, Anna 90
SHEWY, Catharine 105
SHIELD, Cornelia A 280
SHIELDS, Delila 280 Jane 280
SHIFFETT, Mary T (---) 6
SHIFFIELD, Lucy O 280
SHIFFLET, Mildred 280
SHIFFLETT, Charlotte 280 Lucy
280 Mary 280
SHIFLET, Eliza 280
SHIFLETT, Elizabeth 280 Joice

SHIFLETT (continued)
280 Pollie 280
SHIP, Mary Jane 280
SHIPE, Elizabeth 280
SHIPMAN, Jane 280 Lydia 23
SHIPP, Nancy 89
SHIRK, Rebecca 280
SHIRKEY, Mary 280
SHIVERDECKER, Sally 280
SHOEMAKER, Eve 280 Frances
201 Mary Ann (Mitchell) 201
Nancy 280 Susan F 191
SHOER, Susan 280 281
SHORE, Susan 280 281
SHORES, Martha C 281
SHORT, Eliza 281 Jemina 281
Ruthia 281
SHOTWELL, Polly 104 Sarah 281
Sedam 281
SHOWALTER, Agnes 281
Catharine 203 Lydia 281
SHRADER, Christina 281 Nancy
29
SHRECK, Catharine 281
SHREWSBURY, Martha 120
SHRIGLEY, Penelope 74
SHROCK, Sarah 276
SHUEY, Elizabeth 281
SHUFFIELD, Nancy 137
SHUFFLEBARGER, Vina 281
SHUGART, Harriet 86
SHULL, Margaret 281
SHULTZ, Rachel 281
SHUMAKER, Sarah 281
SHUMATE, Peggy T 281 Sarah G
144
SHUTTERS, Mary 8
SIBERT, Margaret 281
SIBOLD, Lydia 281
SICKELS, Hannah 281
SIDEBOTTOM, Elizabeth 281
SIDELS, Catherine 281
SIGFOOSE, Sarah (Simmons) 69
SIGLER, Christina 178 Hannah
200
SILCOTT, Agnes 281
SILL, Eliza 187
SILLINGS, Nancy 281
SILMAN, Nancy 281
SIMKINS, Rhoda 18
SIMMONS, Ann 281 Barbara 224
Elizabeth D 32 Katie 281 Mar-

SIMMONS (continued)
tha 281 Rebecca 110 281 Ruth
281 Sarah 69 Susannah 133
Theresa Ann 281
SIMMS, Caroline 281 282 Eleanor
70 Martha A 282 Sarah L 282
SIMPKINS, Delilah 282 Melvina L
156
SIMPSON, Ann 282 Annie 186
Belama 282 Castilla 184
Elizabeth 160 282 Henrietta
282 Hope 282 Patience 282
Susannah 164
SIMS, Harriet S 282 Mary 31 Sarah
282
SINES, Amanda A 282
SINFLETON, Joicy K 282
SINGER, Jane F 282
SINGLETON, Lavinia B 282
Lucinda 282 Maria 282 Mar-
sena 282 Mary 282
SINKLER, Mary 274
SINKS, Mary 282
SINNETT, Elizabeth 127
SINOR, Nancy 282
SIPE, Catharine 282
SIRK, Mary Ann 282
SISEMORE, Anna 282
SISK, Nancy 185
SISSON, Nancy E 282 Sarah A E
282
SIZEMORE, Margaret 282 Sarah
Jane 282
SIZER, Elizabeth 282
SKAGGS, Mary 154
SKEEN, Sarah 141
SKIDMORE, Elizabeth 282 Mary
32
SKINKER, Sarah S G 88
SKINNER, Elizabeth 282 Ellen 5
Margaret 141 Winifred 167
SKIPTON, Margaret 62
SLACK, Maria 283 Siggarina 283
SLADE, Sarah M 100
SLAGLE, Mary 283
SLATER, Elizabeth 138 Frances
283 Roda 29 Sarah B 114
SLATES, Rebecca 283
SLAUGHTER, Martha 190
SLEDD, Elizabeth P 25
SLOAN, Catharine 283
SLOAT, Rebecca 283

SLONE, Elizabeth 283
SLUSHER, Rosanna 227
SLUSS, Catherine 68
SLUSSER, Mary 283
SMALLMAN, Nancy 283
SMALLWOOD, Delilah 283
SMALS, Catherine 283
SMALTS, Catherine 283
SMART, Sarah A 78 Susan 86
SMAW, Ann W 283
SMELL, Hannah 283
SMILEY, Barbara 283
SMITH, --- 21 Agnes M 285 Alcy
   117 Amy 284 Ann 284 Ann M
   283 Anna 284 Barbara 285 Cary
   Ann 285 Catharine 284 285
   Catharine (---) 93 Catharine K
   284 Charlotte 12 Delilah 285
   Dorothea 285 Eleanor 285
   Eliza 111 Eliza M 283
   Elizabeth 14 38 186 265 283
   284 285 Elizabeth A 284
   Elizabeth A (Elmore) 47
   Elizabeth K 284 Elizabeth R
   284 Elizabeth S 152 284 El-
   mina 284 Emily 118 Evelena B
   80 Frances 285 Frances A 11
   Frances E 63 Geneva Ann M
   284 Hannay (Bradford) 127 Har-
   riet 178 James 127 Jane 284
   285 Joicy R 285 Julia A 284
   Julia Ann 143 Letitia 28
   Louisa 285 Lucinda 284 Lucy
   284 285 Marandy S (Foster) 72
   Martha 126 283 284 285 Martha
   A 285 Martha W 283 Mary 60
   152 204 212 284 Mary G 284
   Mary Magdaline 69 Mary P 285
   Mary R 89 Mary R V 284
   Melissa 284 Mildred W 283
   Nancy 109 160 283 Nancy H
   285 Nancy M 140 Naoma 106
   Nellie 284 Patsy Ann 285
   Polly 46 283 285 Rachel 83
   285 Rebecca K 284 Rhoda 283
   Sallie G 283 Sally 284 Sarah 6
   11 58 107 125 284 Sarah S 284
   Sinah 285 Sophia 205 Susan 5
   Susan Margaret (---) 169
   Susannah 285 Viola 285 Win-
   ney B 144
SMITHERS, Nancy 285

SMITHEY, Martha 285
SMITHSON, Amanda M F 38 El-
   vira 285 286
SMITHY, Sallie 286
SMOCK, --- 19 Sarah H 286
SMOOT, Catherine 98 Priscilla
   102
SMOTHERS, Mary 140
SMYTHE, Mary C 286
SNARR, Magdalena 286
SNEAD, Elizabeth 162 Elizabeth
   M 286 Polly 24 286 Sally 87
   Susan 286
SNEED, Lucy 286 Mary Jane 286
   Rachel 286
SNELLING, Elizabeth 286 Sarah
   286
SNELSON, Jemima 286
SNIDER, Abigail 286 Harriet 286
   Hester 286 Mary 286
SNODDY, Virlinda 286
SNODGRASS, Catherine 158 Mar-
   tha 108 Mary 286 Nancy 286
SNODY, Virlinda 286
SNOW, Polly 286
SNYDER, Abigail 286 Ann 286
   Catharine 155 Elizabeth 286
   Frances S 286 Henrietta 286
   Hester 286 Margaret 143 Nancy
   286 Rebecca 40 Sarah 286
SOLMON, Hennerts 105
SOLOMON, Dicey 274
SOMERVILLE, Ellen J 44 Jane
   196 Margaret 286
SONDERS, Mary W 42
SORRELL, Cassandra 287 Eliza
   287
SOTLER, Polly 53
SOURS, Polly 105 Sarah 287
SOUTHALL, Martha 287 Phebe
   287 Polly 287
SOUTHARD, Mary 287
SOUTHERLAND, Clementine 287
SOWDER, Martha 287
SOWERS, Mary A 287
SPADER, Mary 18
SPAIN, Lucy 287 Mary 287
SPANGLER, Margaret 69 Sarah
   287
SPARKES, --- 45
SPARKS, Mary Jane 2 Sarah L
   287

SPARROW, Nancy 287
SPEAKER, Experience 287
SPEAKES, Sarah Ann 287
SPEARS, Anna 287
SPEED, Susan M 287
SPEELMAN, Eva 287 Evan 287
SPEENY, Mary A 178
SPEER, Rebecca 287
SPENCER, Ann E 287 Catharine
  35 Delila 287 Elcy 99 Emma
  287 Jane M 72 Martha A 287
  288 Mary 287 May 21 Nancy
  287 Sarah 287 Virginia 287
SPICER, Frances 72 Sally 149
SPICKARD, Hetty 155
SPIERS, Martha 288 Polly W 288
SPIGLE, Mary ---- 207
SPILLER, --- 19 Louisa 288
SPILLMAN, Eve 90
SPILMAN, Cynthia D 11 Mary 288
SPINDLE, Mary 288
SPIRES, Polly W 288
SPOONER, M W 288
SPOTTS, Mary A 288
SPRADLIN, Nancy 83
SPRAGINS, Eliza A 288 Rebecca
  F L 21
SPRAHER, Experience 287
SPRATLEY, Johanna 288
SPRAYER, Experience 287
SPRING, Elizabeth 288 Mary 288
  Patience 133
SPRINGER, Nancy 62
SPROUL, Ann G 126
SPROUSE, Patsey 288 Polly 288
  Rachel 288
SPURLING, Malinda 73
SQUIRE, Nancy 71
SQUIRES, Catharine 288
  Elizabeth 288
STACY, Nancy 74
STAFFORD, Jane 288 Lydia 288
  Margaret 288 Polly 288
STALNAKER, Isabel 288 Sarah
  288
STAMPER, Martha J 288
STANDFIELD, Sarah B 145
STANDFORTH, Mary 11
STANDOFF, Nancy 207 Patsy
  Ann 11
STANFIELD, Maria 109 Martha E
  95

STANLEY, Elizabeth 288 Martha
  55 Tabitha 288
STAPLES, Louisa 288 Mary S 51
  Susan 189
STARCHER, Charity 288
STARGEL, Sarah 71
STARK, Frances S 45
STARKE, Elizabeth 128 Susan L
  288 289
STARKEY, Mary 289 Nancy G 289
  Sabina 289
STARR, Sarah N 289
STAYLEY, Isabella 289
STEADMAN, Margaret 289
STEDMAN, Mary C 184
STEED, Catharine C 22
STEEL, Mary 101 289 Nancy 289
STEELE, Ann W 289 Elizabeth
  81 289 Leah 289 Mary 120
  Sarah 66
STEENBERGER, Caroline 35
STEFFY, Mary 289
STEGALL, Christiana S 151
STEGER, Frances E 289 Sarah J
  289
STELL, Sarah 290
STEMPLE, Margaret 47
STEP, Polly 289
STEPHENS, Anna 180 Chloe Ann
  289 Eliza 9 Harriet 289 Mar-
  garet 17 Martha (---) 100 Mary
  289 Mary A 289 Phebe 289
  Sally 289 Theodosia W 289
STEPHENSON, Courteney Ann
  289 Elizabeth 289 Louisa G
  289 Mary 289 Nancy 289
STEPP, Polly 289
STERLING, Ellen 289
STEVENS, Catherine 289
  Elizabeth 29 290 Nancy 290
  Sally 289
STEVENSON, Arabella (---) 173
  Cynthia 69
STEWART, Catherine 142 Eliza
  72 Elizabeth 133 Isabel 290
  Jane 17 Jane Ann 158 Lucy 91
  Margaret 73 Sally 32 Susan M
  290 Susanna 290
STEYER, Eliza G 198
STIBBON, Alsadana 131
STICKELMAN, Nancy 290
STICKLEY, Rebecca 290

STIFF, Chaney 290
STIFFLE, Sarah 86
STIGLEMAN, Susan 290
STILL, Elizabeth 290 Sally 290
 Sarah 290
STILLWELL, Nancy 40
STINNETT, Elizabeth 290 Nancy
 76
STINSON, Julia A 290 Mazy Ann
 290
STIVERS, Elizabeth B 290
STOCKDALE, Catharine 290 Sally
 290
STOCKEY, Margaret C 292
STOKES, Barbary 290
STONE, Annie 101 Eliza Jane 290
 Elizabeth 85 Joana 101 Mary A
 290 Matilda 290 Permelia 87
 Phebe H 290 Sarah 179 Sarah A
 291 Susan 290 Susannah 290
STONEBURNER, Sarah 160 291
STONER, Eva 100
STOOP, Polly 289
STOOTS, Sally 291
STORY, Mary 291
STOTTS, Ruth 291
STOUT, Elizabeth O 15 Kizziah
 291 Lucy W 291
STOVER, Susannah 64
STOWE, Sarah 184
STRANGE, Mary B 291 Sally 291
 Sarah 291
STRATON, Harriet 291
STRATTON, Margaret (Stridlen)
 92
STREAM, Susannah 291
STREET, Catherine F 17 Frances
 Eliza 191 Malinda 291 Polly
 291
STRICKER, Ann 47
STRICKLAND, Catherine 291
STRICKLING, Catherine 291
STRICLING, Catherine 291
STRIDER, Eliza Jane 291
STRIDLEN, Margaret 92
STRINGFELLOW, Harriet 186
STROB, Elizabeth 94
STROBIA, Ann Maria 291
STROLE, Elizabeth 94 Evy 291
STRONG, Elizabeth 291 Rachel
 196
STROSNIDER, Rachel 291
STROTHER, Elizabeth 291 Har-
 riet 167 Mildred 61 Nancy 291
STROTS, Phebe 19
STROUP, Elizabeth 291
STROUSE, Ann 291
STROYER, Rachael 6
STRUBLING, Mary 103
STRUTTON, Elizabeth 291
STUART, Elizabeth L 291 Lucy
 M 291 Maria H 291
STUBBLEFIELD, Mary 292
 Nancy 291
STUCKEY, Margaret C 292 Nancy
 292
STUFFLEBEAM, Jane 16
STULL, Rebecca G 292
STUMP, Elizabeth 27
STURDIVANT, Mahala A 166
STURM, Susan 292
STUTLER, Rebecca 292
SUBLETE, Caroline 151
SUBLETT, Judith 39 Mary 292
 Nancy 292
SUDDARTH, Elizabeth 292
SUDSBURY, Frances 292
SUGGS, Elizabeth 97
SULIVAN, Emenetia 28
SULLINS, Nancy 173
SULLIVAN, Elizabeth A 292
 Frances 292 Jane 292 Lucy
 292 Margaret 64 Mary M 292
 Susan 292
SULLIVANT, Cordelia 292
SUMMERS, Elizabeth 292 Mar-
 garet 292 Phebe Ann 292
SUMNER, Catharine 292 Lucinda
 292 Lucy 292 Mary A 292
SURFACE, Jane 196
SUSONG, Nancy 100
SUTHARD, Elizabeth H 292
SUTHARDS, Jane A 128
SUTHERLIN, Susan L 104
SUTPHIN, Mary 292 Sarah 292
SUTTENFIELD, Cynthia 292
SUTTLE, Lucy 292 Mary 61
SUTTON, Mary 273 Mary Jane
 292
SWAIN, Emily 41 Mary 159
SWALLOM, Phoebe 292
SWAN, Nancy 293
SWANN, Martha B 293 Mary 39
SWANSON, Mary 293

SWART, Elizabeth 293
SWARTZ, Mary 293
SWATZ, Margaret 119
SWEENEY, Elizabeth 293
SWEENY, Mary Ann 41
SWEPSTON, Mary Ann 177
SWIFT, Eliza A 293 Mary Selena 5
SWIGER, Cassa 293
SWINDLER, Lucy 293
SWINK, Margaret 293 Rachael M 293 Sarah 293
SWISHER, Catharine 293 Margaret 293 Rebecca 293 Sarah 122
SWITZER, Rebecca 293
SWOPE, Mary 77
SWORD, Margaret 293
SYDNOR, Mary Ann 293
SYKES, Amy 71 Elizabeth Ann 51 Lucinda 12
SYLOR, Sarah 293
SYMPSON, Decy 293
SYRES, Leah Toney 109 Rebecca 109 William 109
TABB, Martha T 293
TABOR, Mary 293
TACKETT, Irena 293
TAFFLINGER, Polly 32
TALBERT, Nancy ----- 209 Sarah (---) 179
TALBOTT, Barbara 86 Permelia 293 Sarah 113
TALIAFERRO, 75 Eliza 293 Rebecca Seymour 293
TALLEY, Elizabeth 293 Holly 293 Nancy 293 Sarah D 293 Stacey 293
TALLIAFERRO, Lucinda 112
TALLMAN, Jane G 10
TALMAN, Sarah 293
TANKERSLEY, Cynthia 293 294
TANNER, America 294 Eunice 294 Judith 294 Lucy 294 Margaret 294 Susan 173
TANSVILLE, Sally 76
TAPP, Susan 183
TARGGRET, Nancy 294
TARKELSON, Frances A 111
TARMAN, Mary 294
TARR, Eliza 294
TARRANT, Elizabeth 294

TARTT, Nancy 30
TATE, Ann 155 303 Catherine 221 Lucy 294 Margaret 294 Mary 294 Minnie 294 Nancy 294 Rocksey 180 Sarah 117
TATSAPAUGH, Margaret 294
TATUM, Annie Jane 21 Mary Ann 294 Mary E 42
TAULBEE, Elizabeth 294
TAYLOR, Betsy 202 Catharine 67 Clara 204 Delila 241 242 Dicy A 36 Dosha 294 Drucilla (---) 31 Eliza (---) 204 Eliza Ann 294 Elizabeth 94 159 160 294 295 Elizabeth B 294 Elizabeth C 295 Elizabeth P 295 Elizabeth S 295 Emily 295 Fanny 294 Harriet B 295 Hennie P 294 Jane 294 Kate 158 Kerziah 295 Louisa B 294 Lucretia 60 Lucy M 6 Lucy P 295 Martha 294 295 Mary 295 Mary Ann 295 Mary E 295 Mary S 77 Nancy 13 19 294 295 Peggy 40 Permelia 294 Phebe 155 Polly 25 295 Sallie A 84 Sally McC 295 Sarah 150 176 295 Sarah M 106 Sofa 294 Susannah Glenn 295 T U 27 Tabetha 294
TAZEWELL, Catherine 165
TEAFORD, Elizabeth 166 Sophia Catharine 295
TEAGNIER, Leah 47
TEAKE, Mary 126
TEANEY, Eve 295
TEDROE, Phebe (---) 152
TEMPLE, Molly Brooks 105 Temperance 179
TEMPLEMAN, Elizabeth S 135
TEMPLETON, Sarah 295
TENNIS, Mary 295
TERRELL, Eliza M (---) 131 Elizabeth E 296 Frances C 295 Mary Ann 296 Mary J 295 Nancy 24
TERRILL, Sidner 25
TERRY, Bethena 296 Elizabaeth 296 Elizabeth W 296 Jane 296 Margaret 296 Sarah 296
THACKER, Abigail 296 Martha 138 Mary 296 Polly 296 Sarah

THACKER (continued)
296 Sarah G 296
THACKSTON, Martha H 296 Mary
S 296
THARP, Elizabeth 296 Nancy 296
THARPE, Susanna 296
THATCHER, Mildred J 154
Rachel 296 Vilinda 296
THAXTON, Malinda L 296
THOM, Tamsy Jane 298
THOMAS, Abigail 8 Amanda J
297 Ann 297 Biddy 297
Catharine 296 Catharine S 297
Catherine E 296 Elizabeth 123
297 Elizabeth M 296 Fanny 1
Fanny C 297 Frances 1 296
Jane 76 148 297 Jemima 296
297 John 123 Judiah 297 Lottie
296 Lucy 296 Lucy (---) 33
Mahala 297 Margaret E 297
Margaret Helen 296 Margaret
M 297 Maria 296 Mary 125 212
Mary A 297 Mary Ann S 297
Mary C 202 Matilda 297 Nancy
125 297 Polly 297 Rachel 297
Rebecca 297 Rebecca J 297
Rhoda Ann 156 Sarah 296 297
Sirena C 297 Sophia 134 297
Susan 296 297
THOMPSON, Agnes W 141
Amelia C 76 Ann 298 Ann D
298 Ann Eliza 112 Avis O 298
Catharine 297 Cynthia 297 298
Cynthia Ann 297 Elizabeth 151
298 Fannie 297 Jane 298
Lucretia 297 Lucy 297 Mahala
298 Margaret 298 Martha H 57
Mary 298 300 Mary A Blanton
100 Mary W 298 Mr 100 Nancy
298 Polly 97 Rachel Amanda
298 Rebecca 91 Rebecca E P
112 Sally 120 Sarah A 147
THORN, Elizabeth 148 Elizabeth
B 148
THORNBERRY, Frances 298
THORNELL, Jeanette C 298
THORNHILL, Agnes 298 Jeanette
C 298 Martha 298 Polly 298
Rachel 298
THORNIBY, Mary 298 Polly 298
THORNILEY, Mary 298 Polly 298
THORNLEY, Mary 298 Polly 298

THORNTON, Caroline H 298
Courtney C 154 Eleanor Stuart
167 Elizabeth 298 Harriet E 95
Margaret 133 Nancy 298 Sally
Innes 152
THREADGILL, Betsey R 131
Elizabeth R 131
THRUMAN, Ann (Kinkaid) 104
THUMOND, Judith T 27
THURMAN, Margaret 20 Susannah
47
THURMOND, Letitia 298
THURSTON, Polly 298 Ruth
Nancy 298
TIBBS, Nancy Jane 299
TICE, Cynthia 299
TIES, Cynthia 299
TILL, Libby 299
TILLETT, Elizabeth 299 Martha
G 299 Pleasanat 299
TILMAN, Sarah 61 Teresa 299
TIMBERLAKE, Frances 64
TIMMS, Hannah 299 Nancy 299
TINDER, Emily 299
TINGLE, Barbara 299
TINKER, Mary A 299
TINSEFLEY, Nancy 63
TINSLEY, Mary 105 Parmelia 299
Sarah A 198 Scynthia 299
TIPTON, Rebecca 299
TISDALE, Maria D 299
TITCOMB, Abigail 299
TITMARSH, Nancy 299
TOBRIDGE, Lucinda 132
TODD, Polly 91
TODDY, Martha 152
TOLER, Abigail 300 Ann Atkin-
son 299 Ann Maria 57 Sarah J
119
TOLLEY, Elizabeth 299 Mary 299
TOLLY, Nancy 207
TOLTY, Frances 300
TOMBLIN, Ann 299
TOMBLINSON, Elizabeth 299
TOMBLISON, Catherine 299
TOMERSON, Caroline M 299
TOMLIN, Elizabeth 299
TOMLINSON, Margaret 299
TOMPKINS, Catharine W 186
TONEY, Clarkey 299 Leah 109
TOOMBS, Dicey 209 Sarah 164
TOOMIRE, Sarah 299

TOOMS, Elizabeth 20
TOON, Nancy L 114
TOONE, Nancy L 114
TOOTHMAN, Betsy 299
TOPPING, Ann 62 Nancy 62
TOSH, Lucy 299
TOTTY, Dorothy 300 Frances 300 Nancy 182
TOWELL, Cynthia S 300
TOWLER, Abigail 300 Sally L 300 Sarah 300
TOWNER, Harriet C 300
TOWNES, Sarah 300
TOWNLEY, Mary Jane 300
TOWNSEND, Jane 300 Mary 300 Sarah 169
TRACY, Margaret 161
TRAIL, Sarah 177
TRAINUM, Sarah 300
TRANBARGER, Christena 300
TRANBOYER, Christena 300
TRAVIS, Mary A 300
TRAYLOR, Martha A 300 Sophia 300
TREACLE, Susan 121
TREDWAY, Mary M 211
TRENARY, Catherine 176
TRENT, Mary 300 Nancy 37 Sarah 300
TREVEY, Rebecca 300
TREZVANT, Martha D 300
TRIAL, Elizabeth 300
TRIBBLE, Margaret 300
TRIBLE, Mary Ann 300
TRICE, Frances L 11
TRIMBLE, Dorcas 52
TRIMMER, Elizabeth 300
TRINKLE, Sarah 300
TRIPETT, Elizabeth 301
TRIPLETT, Eliza Ann 300 Elizabeth R 300 Frances B 148 Jane B 175 Rachel G 300 Sarah 88 Susan 300
TROOP, Sarah 23
TROTT, Nancy 301
TROUT, Ann E 301 Sarah 301
TRUE, Nancy 301
TRUEHEART, Mary G 167
TRUEMAN, Elizabeth 301
TRUMAN, Elizabeth 301 Nancy 301
TRUMBO, Elizabeth 109

TRUMP, Mary 29
TRUNNELL, Elizabeth 184
TUCK, Jane 301 Mary 301 Nancy 301
TUCKER, Catharine D 197 Elizabeth 301 Elizabeth 169 Emily 301 Frances 301 Louisa R 301 Lucy 301 Luvina 301 Margaret 146 Martha K 156 Mary 41 Nancy 301 Permela W 301 Polly 301 Sallie 301 Sally 301 Sally O 301 William 169
TUDOR, Charlotte 301
TUNE, Jinnie 301
TUNING, Lucy 83 Nancy 83 Walter 83
TURBEE, Margaret 41
TURKEYHIZER, Hannah 111
TURLEY, Sarah J 45
TURLINGTON, Elizabeth 301
TURNER, Adelphi 302 Agnes C 301 Almira 302 Ann 302 Catharine A 301 Elizabeth L 301 302 Frances J 302 Jane 83 Jemima 302 Judith 178 Lucretia 302 Lucy 83 Margaret 3 Martha 302 Mary 127 Mary A 301 Mary Ann 302 Mary Frances 302 Matilda 302 Mr 100 Nancy 302 Nancy G 302 Polly T 301 Rachel P 302 Rebecca A 166 Sarah 18 Sarah H 178 Sarah M Slade Council 100 Soreno 32 Whitha 3
TURPIN, Lucy F 302 Mary M 302 Selena 42
TUTT, Ann M 302
TWYMAN, Emily 121 Mary Walker 104
TYE, Henrietta 302
TYLER, Julia 302 Louisa V 302 Mary Ann 193 Mary K 302 Sarah 194
TYNES, Judith M 302
TYREE, Charlotte 302 Martha E 302
UNDERHILL, Nancy B 302
UNDERWOOD, Hannah 302 Margaret 302
UPDEGRAFF, Catharine 302
UPDEGRAFFE, Catharine 302
UPTON, Sarah 49

URLSON, 192
UTCHLER, Ingaba (Louther?) 125
UTLEY, Catherine 225 Rhoda 302
Sally 39
UTSLER, Mary Ann 302
UTZ, Rosanna 302
UTZLER, Mary Ann 302
VADEN, Ann Eugenia 302 303
Lavicy F 4 Susan 303
VAIDEN, Caroline 303 Elizabeth
P 303
VALERY, Ann 303
VAN CAMP, Margaret 303
VAN HOOSIER, Telitha 186
VAN HORN, Sarah Elizabeth 181
VANCE, Chloe 303 Mary 56 Polly
56
VANDEGRIFT, Barbara 303
VANDERBURG, Eliza C 85
VANDERENDER, Barbara 45
VANDERVORT, Mary 303
VANDEVANDER, Sarah
(Williams) (Calhoun) 197
Susan 303
VANHOOK, Nancy E 209
VANHORN, Nancy 303
VANMETER, Damaris 303 Han-
nah 303
VANNOY, Mary 303
VANPELT, Arthela 303 Mary 303
VANSCOY, Mary 196
VANSCYOC, Jerusha 303
VANSICKLES, Sarah 3
VANZANT, Margaret 303 Peggy
303
VARDEN, Susan 303
VARNER, Martha 18
VARNUM, Rebecca 303
VASS, Mary R 303
VASSER, Mary 303
VAUGHAN, Elizabeth M 203 Jane
303 304 Lucinda 303 Lucy 303
Mary 304 Mary B 2 Mason J
304 Nancy 303 Narcissa G 303
304 Ruth 303 Sallie 304
VAUGHN, Eliza 123 Lydia 304
Nancy 304 Sarah 98
VAUGHT, Martha 304
VAWTER, Malinda 210 Mildred P
158
VEACH, Charlotte 304
VEATCH, Charlotte 304

VENABLE, Catherine 200
VERMILLION, Carroll 74
Elizabeth 304 Mary Ann 152
Obedience 304
VERMILYE, Hannah 33
VERNON, Nancy E 304
VEST, Martha 87 Patsy 87
VIA, Elizabeth 108
VICE, Nancy 130
VICK, Mary 304
VINCENT, Rebecca 304 Susan
304
VINSON, Prudence Ann 10 Tem-
perance 161
VINT, Delilah 304
VIRTS, Elizabeth 304
VIRTZ, Leah 183
VOSS, Jane Campbell 5
VOWLES, Susan 26
WADDEL, Catherine 304
WADDELL, Nancy Larkin 84
WADDLE, Lucy 304
WADDY, Sophia A 304
WADE, Aoma 304 Dulceana 304
Easter 304 Louisa 304 Mary 21
Matilda 119 Nancy A 304 Pris-
cilla 10 Sallie 12 Sally 19
Sarah A 304 Susan 14
WADKINS, Mary 139
WAGGENER, Mary 304
WAGGONER, Elizabeth 304 305
Jemima 153 Magdalene 104
WAGNER, Sarah 107
WAGONER, Margaret W 38 Mary
W 38
WAID, Elizabeth Ann 201
WALDEN, Elizabeth 305 Jemima
96 Patsey E 179 Sarah A
(Enos) 138 Virginia F 305
WALDO, Sarah 168
WALDROP, Charlotte H 305
WALE, Patsey 305
WALKER, Ann 305 Anna 305
Anne 305 Catherine 305 Char-
lotte C 305 Elizabeth 305
Elizabeth (---) 161 Fanny 305
Frances 87 305 Harriet 305
Lucy A 112 Margaret Ann 14
Martha S 305 Minty 305 Nancy
305 Sarah 141 305 Sarah L 305
Sina 305 Susan J 305 Susannah
305

WALKUP, Margaret 305
WALL, Martha 12 Nancy 99
Peggy 149 Tabitha T 305
WALLACE, Adelia J 306 Ann C
306 Catharine 306 Effie 58
Elizabeth 306 Elizabeth W 306
Frances 101 Letta 305 Mary A
39 Sarah 70
WALLAR, Margaret 306 Sarah
306
WALLER, Elizabeth 306 Julia W
306 Maria 306 Mariah 306
Nancy 306 Nancy L 89 Sarah
306
WALLTON, Hannah 306
WALTERS, Elizabeth 158 306
Fanny 218 Frances 218 Jane 5
Mary ---- 208
WALTHALL, Elizabeth 306 Han-
nah Wooldridge 188 Sarah 306
Sarah A 306
WALTON, Demarius 306 Hannah
306 Luaney P 306 Luraney
306 Lutitia 306 Martha M 306
Mary F 306 Nancy 306 Nancy
H 306 Rhody T 306 Susan 306
WAMBLE, Matilda 115
WAMSLEY, Susannah 306
WANGBURN, Anna 109
WANSTURFF, Catharine 306
WARBERTON, Catharine G 306
WARD, Belinda 178 Betsey 194
Catharine C 44 Ellen 307 Mar-
garet 53 Martha C 307 Mary
307 Nancy 149 Rachel 113
Susan 306 307 Zippora 307
WARDER, Eleanor 152
WARE, Frances G 106 Jane G
307
WARFORD, Rebecca 307
WARING, Ellen H 54
WARNER, Mary Ann 133
WARREN, Elizabeth B 307 Mar-
garet 118 Sarah 307
WARRICK, Mary 307
WARRINER, Elizabeth 307
WARSHAM, Henry 204
WARWICK, Polly C 307
WASHINGTON, Fannie 212 Han-
nah F 307 Louisa W 307
WASSOM, Rachel 174

WATERFIELD, Elizabeth
Amanda 307
WATERS, Catherine T 307 Judy
W 307
WATKINS, Ann W 132 Eliza 307
Eliza G 106 Elizabeth 87
Elizabeth W 307 Jane 307 308
Judith 307 Lucinda G 70 Lucy
A C 307 Margaret 307 Mary
122 Mildred S 307 Narcissa P
(---) 12 Patsey 307 Polly 91
103 Rebecca 307 Sally 307
Sally Davis 307 Sarah B 151
WATLINGTON, Elizabeth R 308
Martha S 308
WATSON, Anne 308 Eliza J 164
Jane 137 Martha 308 Mary Ann
308 Nancy 308 Permelia P 308
Ruth 162 308 Sarah 308 Sarah
D 96
WATTS, Catharine 308 Mary 308
Nancy 308
WAUGH, --- 60 Editha Ann 308
Polly 308
WAUGHOP, Harriet 308 Mary Ann
134
WAULISS, Nancy 308
WAYNE, Judith 308
WEAN, Sarah 308
WEANNING, Sarah 308
WEATHERFORD, Latisha 136
Lette 136
WEAVER, Catharine 45 Elizabeth
308 Hannah 308 Katharine 308
Margaret 47 122 Mary 308
Nancy 308 Susan 308
WEBB, Anna 131 Catharine 308
309 Frances F 309 Hannah 309
Margaret 309 Margaret S 309
Mary 260 308 309 Nancy 308
Nancy A 309 Rebecca 309
Rebecca R 308 309 Sarah 19
144 309 Temperance 309
WEBBER, Catharine C 309 Eliza
C 309
WEBSTER, Catherine 309 Mar-
garet 309 Margaret H 309 Mary
309 Nancy B 135 Rachel 309
Tabitha 28
WEDDLE, Lucy 304
WEEDON, Harriet 93
WEEKLEY, Catharine 182

WEEKS, Lucy 309 Rebecca 22
    Sina 309
WEIR, Louisa 309
WEISIGER, Catherine 309
WEITSEL, Betsey 309
WELCH, Aria 309 Catharine 190
    Mary 309
WELLARD, Elizabeth 309
WELLER, Elizabeth (---) 31
WELLMAN, Julia Ann 309
WELLONS, Eliza 309 Phebe 138
WELLS, Amy 15 Elizabeth 214
    309 Martha 310 Mary B 166
    Mary R 309 Nancy 207 Susan V
    309
WELSH, Nancy 310
WENT, Jane 11
WERSHAM, Elizabeth 132
WERTENBAKER, Louisiana 310
WERTS, Elizabeth 304
WESCOAT, Mary A 310
WEST, Annie 310 Emeline 310
    Frances 113 Jane 199 310
    Lucy 12 Margaret 120 Mary 20
    Mary A 310 Penelope 77 Polly
    20 Sarah R 310
WESTFALL, Elizabeth 109 310
    Nancy 109
WESTMORELAND, Lucinda 134
    Mary D 310
WETHERHOLT, Magdalena 78
WETHERHOLTZ, Elizabeth 310
WETSEL, Mary 310
WETZEL, Mary 310
WHALAN, Maria 59
WHALEY, Sarah 310
WHARTON, Lucy 310 Nancy 91
WHEAT, Malinda U 57
WHEATS, Mary 310
WHEELER, Ann 82 Anna 310
    Malinda 17 Sarah 310 Unity 43
    Verity 43
WHETZEL, Mary 310
WHIDBEE, Susan 310
WHISSON, Elizabeth 310
WHISTON, Elizabeth 310
WHITAKER, Alica 311 Camilla
    310
WHITE, Agnes C 132 Clary 311
    Eliza R 311 Elizabeth 111 311
    Harriet 311 Jane 69 Judith 161
    Lucinda 311 Lucy 311 Mar-

WHITE (continued)
    garet 311 Martha J 311 Mary
    142 228 Mary T 132 Mildred 67
    Nancy 4 102 Polly 311
    Rebecca 311 Sarah 125 311
    Selina 21 121 Susan C 311
    Temperance 311 Tildy 13
WHITEHEAD, Elizabeth 111
    Mary A 172 Nancy W 311
WHITEHORN, Elizabeth 311
WHITELAW, Mary 311
WHITELY, Elizabeth 311
WHITEMAN, Rebecca S 311
WHITESIDES, Sarah 301
WHITEZEL, Betsey 309
WHITFIELD, Martha A 5 Nancy
    311
WHITLOCK, Hannah 311 Mar-
    garet T 9
WHITLOW, Polly 311
WHITMORE, Elizabeth 311
    Rachel 311
WHITTAKER, Camilla 310
WHITTEN, Elizabeth 68 Jane P
    311
WHITTINGTON, Frances J 4
WHITWORTH, Tabitha 7
WHORLEY, Huldah W 311 Mary
    318
WIATT, Ellenor 311 Susan 320
WIBLIN, Deborah 311
WIDENER, Patience 312
WIDGEON, Mary 23
WIGGINTON, Margaret 312
WIGNER, Elizabeth 136
WILBOURN, Ann E 312 Sarah M
    312 Sarah W 311
WILBUN, Sarah M 312
WILCHER, Rachel 312
WILCOX, Hannah H 312 Susan
    171
WILDER, Sarah 147
WILDMAN, Jane D 312 Sarah E
    312
WILES, Adaline 312 Frances 312
WILEY, Catherine 312 Rebecca
    312 Sarah 312 Sinah 312
WILHELM, Hannah 312 Martha
    312 Ruhanna 312
WILHITE, Polly 312
WILHOITE, Katy 312
WILKE, Annie 71 Barbara 166

WILKERSON, Mary R 312 Polly
312 Susanna 86
WILKEY, Elizabeth 312
WILKINS, Catharine 312 Dinah
312 Judith S 312 Nancy 312
Sarah 113 Susan R 312
WILKINSON, Amarylles 313 Ann
145 Emeline H 312 Frances
140 Martha J 313 Rachel 312
313 Susan W 313
WILL, Elizabeth 313
WILLARD, Martha 144
WILLCHER, Rachel 312
WILLET, Mary 313
WILLEY, Anna 313
WILLIAMS, Ann 124 313
Catherine 138 Christiana P 313
Eliza 313 Elizabeth 227 313
314 Elizabeth M 313 Elizabeth
T 313 Esther 314 Eve 313
Fanny 313 Judith 313 314
Juliet 314 Lucinda 48 313 Mar-
tha 313 Martha A 313 Martha C
313 314 Mary 30 41 45 56 108
200 313 Mary A 313 Mary A
(Wallace) 39 Mary B 313 Mary
J 150 314 Mary P 170 Milly 21
Nancy Ann 147 Patsy 313
Priscilla 313 Rebecca 30 52 98
313 Rhoda 313 Sarah 41 197
313 Sarah G 313 Sarah H 57
Temperance 101
WILLIAMSON, Barbary 314
Caroline 314 Elmira 314 Eliza
A 212 Hannah 314 Jane R 314
Margaret 189 Mary 172 Mary H
314 Rhoda 314 Susan 172
WILLIS, Elzira 314 Jane 314
Malinda 314 Mary Ann 2 166
Mary G (Fisher) 166 Matilda
314 Nancy 22 Nancy A 314
Rhoda 314 Sallie 92
WILLOUGHBY, Jane 7 Susan 314
WILLS, Elizabeth T 314 Julia A
314 Mary 314 Rebecca M 314
WILSHER, Nancy 314
WILSON, Amelia 315 Ann R 315
Anna 314 315 Anne H 315
Catharine 315 Catharine R 315
Christina 92 Clarissa 315
Demaris 64 Eliza 132 Eliza T
60 Elizabeth 229 314 315 316

WILSON (continued)
Elizabeth (---) 97 Elizabeth A
315 Emaline B 315 Emily 314
Femity 126 Frances 315 Han-
nah 26 108 Jane 85 206 Jane S
192 Lea (Bollinger) 99 Louisa
315 Lucy D 315 Lydia 315
Malinda 18 Martha A 315 Mar-
tha C 307 Mary 314 315 Mary
A 315 Mary Ann 2 Mary B 315
Mary K 25 Mary M 67 Nancy
144 Orpha 17 Parthena 96
Polly M 315 Rebecca 315
Sarah 314 316 Sarah Ann 315
Sarah M 315 Stacia 316 Stacy
315 Susan 315 Susannah 315
WILY, Mary 316
WIMBISH, Judith A 74
WIMER, Elizabeth Ann 316
WINCE, Christine 98 Polly 316
WINDLE, Sarah T 316
WINE, Elizabeth 316 Lucy Ann
66 Margaret 316
WINFIELD, Nancy 316
WINFREE, Elizabeth 316 Louisa
316 Lucy 316 Maria 143 Mary
A 316
WINGFIELD, Dolly 43 Dorothy 43
Eliza 316 Lucy G 33 Mary H
97
WINGO, Cena Jane 70 Elizabeth
C 65 Mason 29 Sency Jane 70
WININGS, Margaret 320
WINN, Ann 316 Eliza 316
Elizabeth 316 Nancy 316 Sarah
316
WINNER, Hannah 187
WINSTON, Elizabeth H 86 Jane D
316
WINTER, Martha 316
WINTZ, Polly 316
WIRE, Catharine E 316
WIRT, Margaret 318
WISE, Betsy 229 Catherine 32
Elizabeth 316 Harriet A 316
Nancy 55
WISEMAN, Mary 168 Sally 318
WISMAN, Anna 316
WISSMAN, Julia Ann 114
WITCHER, Gilley 316
WITHERS, Eliza T 181 Sarah 316
317

WITICKS, Eva 173
WITT, Frances 317 Keziah 152
 Martha W 317 Nancy 317 Vily
 317
WITTEN, Tabitha 112
WOLF, Anna 172 Catharine 317
 Drusilla 317 Elizabeth 317
 Elizabeth L 317 Sarah (Smith)
 107
WOLFE, Celia A 317 Clara 317
WOLGAMOTH, Catharine 172
WOLTZ, Margaret 317
WOMACK, Elizabeth 38 Jane A E
 317 Martha J 317 Sarah C 317
WOOD, Amanda J 317 Ann E 317
 Catherine 171 Demartha 70
 Dianah 36 Elizabeth 63 102
 317 Elizabeth Chickton 148
 Janetta 317 Juliet 52 Lucinda
 317 Lucy A 317 Margaret 317
 Margaret S 317 Martha 119 317
 Mary 238 Mary Ann 64 Mary D
 131 Mary H 317 Mary Jane 317
 Mary K 217 May E 317 Nancy
 317 Patsey M 317 Rachel 288
 Sallie 192 Sarah 317 Sarah A
 317 Sophia 317 Susan 317
WOODALL, Elizabeth 317 Sally
 317
WOODARD, Anna Maria 129
 Nancy 317
WOODEY, Patsey 170
WOODFIN, Martha E 317 318
WOODFORD, Frances 201
WOODROFF, Frances L 116
WOODS, Catharine 318 Elizabeth
 318 Hannah 318 Janetta 12
 Maria 318 Nancy 89 Susan G
 24
WOODSAM, Nancy R 318
WOODSON, Ann F 42 Maria 126
 Mary Ann 265 Nancy 318
 Nancy R 318 Sarah M 318
WOODWARD, Nancy 317 Sarah
 318
WOODY, Mary Ann 318
WOODYARD, Priscilla 203 Sally
 318
WOOFTER, Mercy 56
WOOLDRIDGE, Elizabeth 3
 Elizabeth R 318 Judy 194
WOOLFORD, Elizabeth 27

WOOLTON, Mary W 318
WOOTEN, Ann 194 Jane 112
WOOTTEN, Mary W 318
WOOTTON, Mary W 318 Sallie C
 318
WORLEY, Frances 318 Mary 318
WORNAL, Mary J 318
WORRELL, Martha 318 Sarah 318
WORSHAM, Emeline 318
 Lucretia 318
WORSTELL, Ann 318
WORSTER, Nancy 318
WORT, Margaret 318
WORTMAN, Sarah J 318
WRAY, Agnes 319 Aphia 318
 Lucy 318 Mary 318 Mary G 319
 Nancy 319 Nancy Ann 318
WREN, Elizabeth 54 Mary Ann
 319 Mary M 319
WRENN, Ester 319
WRIGHT, Ann 186 Ann Jane 320
 Barbara G 319 Catharine W
 320 Caty M P 319 Charity 319
 Charlotte 320 Charlotte C 319
 Christiana 319 Eliza 157
 Elizabeth 111 319 320 Ellen
 319 Ellinder 319 Fanny 138
 Frances 319 Hannah C 319
 Jane 319 Judith 319 Leah 320
 Mahala (---) 63 Malinda 181
 Margaret 90 Martha 319 Mary
 319 Mary A F 320 Mary Ann
 320 Mary Ann H 35 Mary B 319
 Mary S 211 Morning 319 Nancy
 319 Nancy A 319 Rhoda 320
 Ruhanna 319 Sarah 319 320
 Sarah (Burton) 115 Sarah Ann
 319 Sidney 38 Tabitha 319
 Terissa 319
WYANT, Nancy T 320
WYATT, Harriet 88 Jane 320
 Mary 320 Mary A 320 Mary L
 320 Sarah 37 Susan 320 Susana
 320
WYLIE, Rhoda 320
WYNANS, Margaret 320
WYNE, Jane 320
WYNN, Jane 320 Louisa 33 Mary
 320 Susan 106 320
WYSONG, Lucie S 320
YAGER, Ann 320 Christina W 320
 Elizabeth 11 Julia 38

YANCEY, Harriet 320
YANCY, Elizabeth I M 20 Sarah
    W 320
YARBOROUGH, Citivia 320 Lucy
    A 320
YATES, Catharine 14 320
    Elizabeth 320 Frances 320
    Hester 320 Nancy W 218
    Peggy 320 Rachel (---) 60
YEAGER, Catharine 272
YEAKLEY, Annie 171
YEAMAN, Betsy 99
YEATES, Alsey 190
YEATMAN, Mary 320 321
YEATTS, Frances 321
YEOMANS, Mary 321
YERBY, Harriet 321
YOAKUM, Margaret 321
YOE, Elizabeth 23
YOKOM, Elizabeth 321
YONAS, Mary 321
YOST, Elizabeth 321
YOUILL, Margaret 93
YOUNG, Ann C 321 Elizabeth 169
    321 Emmaline 184 Jane 183
    Margaret 186 Mary 13 163 321
    Nancy 321 Sarah 153 Sarah P
    174 Sophia 321 Susannah 321
YOUNGER, Nancy 72
YOWELL, Simphronica 321
ZACHARY, Martha 321
ZAHN, Sally 46
ZIMBRO, Catherine 183
ZIMMERLIE, Margaret 42
ZIMMERLY, Margaret 42
ZIMMERS, Mary Ellen 321
ZINK, Mary 282
ZINN, Jane 321
ZIRKLE, Margaret 272 Matilda
    (---) 18
ZOLLMAN, Polly 321
ZOLMAN, Elizabeth 108
ZUCCARELLO, Frances A 122
ZUMBRO, Barbara 110